T0213631

Lecture Notes in Computer Science 10255

Commenced Publication in 1973
Founding and Former Series Editors:
Gerhard Goos, Juris Hartmanis, and Jan van Leeuwen

More information about this series at http://www.springer.com/series/7412

Luís A. Alexandre · José Salvador Sánchez
João M.F. Rodrigues (Eds.)

Pattern Recognition and Image Analysis

8th Iberian Conference, IbPRIA 2017
Faro, Portugal, June 20–23, 2017
Proceedings

 Springer

Editors
Luís A. Alexandre (iD)
Universidade da Beira Interior
Covilhã
Portugal

João M.F. Rodrigues (iD)
University of the Algarve
Faro
Portugal

José Salvador Sánchez (iD)
University Jaume I
Castellón
Spain

ISSN 0302-9743   ISSN 1611-3349   (electronic)
Lecture Notes in Computer Science
ISBN 978-3-319-58837-7   ISBN 978-3-319-58838-4   (eBook)
DOI 10.1007/978-3-319-58838-4

Library of Congress Control Number: 2017940387

LNCS Sublibrary: SL6 – Image Processing, Computer Vision, Pattern Recognition, and Graphics

Printed on acid-free paper

This Springer imprint is published by Springer Nature
The registered company is Springer International Publishing AG
The registered company address is: Gewerbestrasse 11, 6330 Cham, Switzerland

Preface

It is our pleasure to present the proceedings of the 8th Iberian Conference on Pattern Recognition and Image Analysis, IbPRIA 2017. The conference was held in Faro, Portugal, following in the footsteps of previous successful meetings in Andraxt (2003), Estoril (2005), Girona (2007), Póvoa de Varzim (2009), Las Palmas de Gran Canaria (2011), Madeira (2013), and Santiago de Compostela (2015).

IbPRIA is an international conference co-organized every two years by the Portuguese APRP (Associação Portuguesa de Reconhecimento de Padrões) and Spanish AERFAI (Asociación Española de Reconocimiento de Formas y Análisis de Imágenes), chapters of the IAPR (International Association for Pattern Recognition). IbPRIA is a single-track conference consisting of high-quality, previously unpublished papers, presented either orally or as a poster, intended to act as a forum for research groups, engineers, and practitioners to present recent results, algorithmic improvements, and promising future directions in pattern recognition and image analysis.

This year's IbPRIA was held during June 20–23, 2017, in Faro, Portugal, and was hosted by the University of the Algarve, with the support of CINTAL (Centro de Investigação Tecnológica do Algarve). There was a very positive response to the call for papers for IbPRIA 2017. We received 86 full papers from 34 countries and 60 were accepted (36 as oral and 24 as poster) for presentation at the conference, where each paper was reviewed by at least three reviewers.

The essential actors of any conference are the authors who submit their scientific contributions. They are the ones responsible for the high quality of the scientific program of IbPRIA 2017. The reviewers, members of the Program Committee, and all the others also played a key role with their dedicated and thorough work.

IbPRIA 2017 had an excellent group of invited speakers: Marcello Pelillo (Ca' Foscari University), Ivan Laptev (Inria Paris), and Gavin Brown (University of Manchester). We are grateful to these leading experts for their inspiring participation in IbPRIA 2017.

The success of the conference was also due to the precious collaboration of the co-chairs and the members of the local Organizing Committee.

We wish to express our gratitude to all of the aforementioned participants who enabled the success of this year's edition of IbPRIA.

Finally, we look forward to meeting you again at the next edition of IbPRIA, in Spain in 2019.

June 2017

Luís A. Alexandre
José Salvador Sánchez
João M.F. Rodrigues

Organization

IbPRIA is an international conference co-organized by the Spanish AERFAI and Portuguese APRP chapters of the IAPR International Association for Pattern Recognition.

Executive Committee

General Co-chair APRP

Luís A. Alexandre   Universidade da Beira Interior, Portugal

General Co-chair AERFAI

José Salvador Sánchez   Universitat Jaume I, Castellón, Spain

Local Chair

João M.F. Rodrigues   University of the Algarve, Portugal

Local Committee

Roberto Lam	University of the Algarve, Portugal
Pedro J.S. Cardoso	University of the Algarve, Portugal
Jânio Monteiro	University of the Algarve, Portugal

Invited Speakers

Marcello Pelillo	Ca' Foscari University of Venice, Italy
Ivan Laptev	Inria Paris, France
Gavin Brown	University of Manchester, UK

Program Committee

Adrian G. Bors	University of York, UK
Ajay Kumar	The Hong Kong Polytechnic University, Hong Kong, SAR China
Alessia Saggese	University of Salerno, Italy
Ana Fred	Technical University of Lisbon, Portugal
Ana Maria Mendonça	University of Porto, Portugal
Anders Hast	Uppsala University, Sweden
António Cunha	University of Trás-os-Montes e Alto Douro, Portugal
António J.R. Neves	University of Aveiro, Portugal
Antonio Pertusa	University of Alicante, Spain

Antonio J. Rodríguez-Sánchez	University of Innsbruck, Austria
Armando Pinto	University of Aveiro, Portugal
Arsénio Reis	University of Trás-os-Montes e Alto Douro, Portugal
Bernardete Ribeiro	University of Coimbra, Portugal
Catarina Silva	Polytechnic Institute of Leiria, Portugal
Constantine Kotropoulos	University of Thessaloniki, Greece
Carlos Orrite	University of Zaragoza, Spain
Costantino Grana	Università degli studi di Modena e Reggio Emilia, Italy
Enrique Vidal	Universidad Politécnica de Valencia, Spain
Ethem Alpaydin	Bogazici University, Turkey
Fernando Monteiro	Polytechnic Institute of Bragança, Portugal
Filiberto Pla	Universitat Jaume I, Spain
Francisco Casacuberta	Universidad Politécnica de Valencia, Spain
Francisco Herrera	University of Granada, Spain
Gilson A. Giraldi	National Laboratory for Scientific Computing, Brazil
Giorgio Giacinto	Università degli Studi di Cagliari, Italy
Hans du Buf	University of the Algarve, Portugal
Henning Müller	University of Applied Sciences Western Switzerland, Switzerland
Hermann Ney	RWTH Aachen, Germany
Hugo Proença	Universidade da Beira Interior, Portugal
Jaime S. Cardoso	University of Porto, Portugal
Jerzy Stefanowski	Poznan University of Technology, Poland
João M. Sanches	Universidade Tecnica de Lisboa, Portugal
Jordi Vitrià	Universitat de Barcelona, Spain
Jorge S. Marques	Universidade Tecnica de Lisboa, Portugal
Jose Luis Alba	Universidad de Vigo, Spain
José Silva	Academia Militar, Portugal
Julian Fierrez	Universidad Autónoma de Madrid, Spain
Manuel J. Marin-Jimenez	University of Córdoba, Spain
Manuel Montes y Gómez	INAOEP, Mexico
Marcello Pelillo	University of Venice, Italy
Maria Vanrell i Martorell	University Autònoma de Barcelona, Spain
Margarita Kotti	Imperial College London, UK
Mark J. Embrechts	Rensselaer Polytechnic Institute, NY USA
Max Viergever	University of Utrecht, The Netherlands
Nicolaie Popescu-Bodorin	University of South-East Europe Lumina, Romania
Nicolas Perez de la Blanca	Universidad de Granada, Spain
Nicu Sebe	University of Trento, Italy
Paolo Rosso	Universidad Politécnica de Valencia, Spain
Petra Perner	University Federal do Rio de Janeiro, Brazil
Petia Radeva	Universitat de Barcelona, Spain
Ricardo Marroquim	Institute of Computer Vision and Applied Computer Sciences, Germany
Ricardo Torres	University of Campinas, Brazil

Roberto Alejo   Tecnológico de Estudios Superiores de Jocotitlán,
                              México
Roberto Paredes   Universidad Politécnica de Valencias, Spain
Sergio Velastin   Universidad Carlos III, Spain
Vicente García Jiménez   Universidad Autónoma de Ciudad Juárez, Mexico
Vitor Filipe   University of Trás-os-Montes e Alto Douro, Portugal
Xiaoyi Jiang   University of Münster, Germany

Tutorial Chairs

Armando J. Pinho   University of Aveiro, Portugal
Xose M. Pardo   University of Santiago de Compostela, Spain

Sponsoring Institutions

CRESC ALGARVE 2020, Portugal 2020 and FEEI
SPIC - Creative Solutions
EVA Hotel

Contents

Computer Vision

Image and Signal Processing

Medical Image

Applications

Poster Sessions

Pattern Recognition and Machine Learning

Computer Vision

Image and Signal Processing

Pattern Recognition and Machine Learning

Ordinal Class Imbalance with Ranking

Ricardo Cruz[1]([✉]), Kelwin Fernandes[1,2], Joaquim F. Pinto Costa[3],
María Pérez Ortiz[4], and Jaime S. Cardoso[1,2]

[1] INESC TEC, Porto, Portugal
{rpcruz,kafc,jaime.cardoso}@inesctec.pt
[2] Faculty of Engineering, University of Porto, Porto, Portugal
[3] Faculty of Sciences, University of Porto, Porto, Portugal
jpcosta@fc.up.pt
[4] Universidad Loyola Andalucía, Córdoba, Spain
mariaperez@uloyola.es

Abstract. Classification datasets, which feature a skewed class distribution, are said to be class imbalance. Traditional methods favor the larger classes. We propose pairwise ranking as a method for imbalance classification so that learning compares pairs of observations from each class, and therefore both contribute equally to the decision boundary. In previous work, we suggested treating the binary classification as a ranking problem, followed by a threshold mapping to convert back the ranking score to the original classes. In this work, the method is extended to multi-class ordinal classification, and a new mapping threshold is proposed. Results are compared with traditional and ordinal SVMs, and ranking obtains competitive results.

Keywords: Ordinal classification · Class imbalance · Ranking · SVM

1 Introduction

Class imbalance is pervasive in real world applications of data classification and has been the focus of much research. Data is said to be class imbalance when the distribution of the categorical variable we want to predict is not uniform. Many times dramatically so; this is the case in such fields as medicine where more people are cleared as negative in screening than are accused positives by such tests. In such cases, a naive application of learning algorithms will produce impractical models that have very good overall accuracy at the expense of the minority class.

Several approaches have been proposed for tackling this problem, which usually involve:

1. *Pre-processing:* changing class priors by undersampling the majority class and/or creating new synthetic examples of the minority class [1,2], or even changing class priors by re-assigning the class labels themselves (e.g. Meta-Cost [3]);

© Springer International Publishing AG 2017
L.A. Alexandre et al. (Eds.): IbPRIA 2017, LNCS 10255, pp. 3–12, 2017.
DOI: 10.1007/978-3-319-58838-4_1

2. *Training with costs* instead of maximizing accuracy; the estimation algorithm maximizes weighted accuracy, so that the cost of misclassifying an observation is inversely proportional to the frequency of its class;
3. *Post-processing* by tweaking the decision boundary by such measures as changing a threshold after which one class is selected, sometimes with the aid of a ROC curve [4];
4. *Ensembles* by which each model within the ensemble is trained with balanced subsets of the data, coupled with the previous preprocessing techniques [5].

In previous work, we have suggested a fifth approach: pairwise scoring ranking [6]. Instead of learning from each observation in isolation, this model class builds the decision boundary by training using pairs of observations of opposite classes.

2 Method

In previous work [6], we have suggested the application of several pairwise scoring rankers to binary class imbalance problems.

In ranking, an observation $\mathbf{x}_i$ is compared with another observation $\mathbf{x}_j$, and we are interested in predicting whether $\mathbf{x}_i \succ \mathbf{x}_j$, meaning $\mathbf{x}_i$ is "preferred" to $\mathbf{x}_j$. Three big umbrellas of rankers exist: pointwise, pairwise and listwise. Here, we focus on pairwise and, in particular, scoring pairwise rankers, where each observation $\mathbf{x}_i$ is compared against all others $\mathbf{x}_j$, and if $\mathbf{x}_i \succ \mathbf{x}_j$, then we learn a scoring function s so that if $\mathbf{x}_i \succ \mathbf{x}_j$ then $s(\mathbf{x}_i) > s(\mathbf{x}_j)$, with $s \colon X \to \mathbb{R}$.

In this study, we will focus on a methodology initially proposed as Rank-SVM [7]. Consider two classes, $\mathcal{C}_1$ and $\mathcal{C}_2$, with a set $\mathcal{S}_1$ of N_1 examples from $\mathcal{C}_1$ and a set $\mathcal{S}_2$ with N_2 examples from $\mathcal{C}_2$. Construct all $N_1 \times N_2$ pairs $\mathbf{x}_{ij} = \mathbf{x}_i - \mathbf{x}_j$ with $\mathbf{x}_i \in \mathcal{S}_1$ and $\mathbf{x}_j \in \mathcal{S}_2$. Solve the binary classification problem using an ordinary SVM estimator (without the bias term) in the set of the differences

$$\{(\mathbf{x}_{ij}, +1), (-\mathbf{x}_{ij}, -1) \mid \mathbf{x}_{ij} = \mathbf{x}_i - \mathbf{x}_j\},$$

where $+1$ and -1 are the labels of the samples $\mathbf{x}_{ij}$ and $-\mathbf{x}_{ij}$, respectively.

The decision rule $\mathbf{w} \cdot (\mathbf{x}_i - \mathbf{x}_j) > 0$ can be transformed into a scoring function since $\mathbf{w} \cdot (\mathbf{x}_i - \mathbf{x}_j) > 0 \equiv \mathbf{w} \cdot \mathbf{x}_i > \mathbf{w} \cdot \mathbf{x}_j \equiv s(\mathbf{x}_i) > s(\mathbf{x}_j)$.

This ensuing score needs then to be transformed back to classes. For the binary case, we suggested in [6] choosing a threshold T that maximizes a class imbalance-appropriate objective function, f. Using the training data, we have $s_i = f(\mathbf{x}_i)$ which we sort, and use each midpoint $s_i' = \frac{s_i + s_{i+1}}{2}$ as possible candidate for threshold T, so that $T = \arg\max_{s_i'} f(s_i')$.

This mapping between pairwise ranking scores and classes only works for two classes. A multi-class threshold selection will be suggested in Sect. 2.3, which takes advantage of classes being ordinal for maximum efficiency.

2.1   Ordinal Classification

The ordinal data classification problem has already been addressed using pairs in the space of differences by Herbrich et al. [8].

Let $\mathcal{C}_1 \prec \mathcal{C}_2 \prec \cdots \prec \mathcal{C}_K$ be the K classes involved. Let $\mathcal{S}_k = \{\mathbf{x}_n^{(k)}\}$ be the set of N_k samples from $\mathcal{C}_k$, with $N = \sum_{k=1}^{K} N_k$. Construct the differences $\mathbf{x}_{mn}^{(k\ell)} = \mathbf{x}_m^{(k)} - \mathbf{x}_n^{(\ell)}$ with $\mathcal{C}_k \prec \mathcal{C}_\ell$. Like in the binary setting, solve the binary classification problem in the set of the differences $\{(\mathbf{x}_{mn}^{(k\ell)}, +1), (-\mathbf{x}_{mn}^{(k\ell)}, -1)\}$, where $+1$ and -1 are the labels of the samples $\mathbf{x}_{mn}^{(k\ell)}$ and $-\mathbf{x}_{mn}^{(k\ell)}$, respectively.

An issue with this approach arises when one of the classes is strongly mis-represented when compared with the others. The data from each class $\mathcal{C}_k$ is involved in $2N_k(N - N_k)$ points in the set of the differences. If $2N_k \ll 2N_\ell$ then also $N_k(N - N_k) \ll N_\ell(N - N_\ell)$. For instance, if $N_1{=}10$ and $N_2{=}N_3{=}100$, then the data from $\mathcal{C}_1$ is contributing with 4,000 elements in the new space, while the data from $\mathcal{C}_2$ or $\mathcal{C}_3$ is contributing with 22,000. So, the new learning problem will be dominated by the samples from $\mathcal{C}_2$ and $\mathcal{C}_3$ and it is likely that $\mathcal{C}_1$ will be poorly estimated.

We address this issue in the next section, with our proposal for imbalance ordinal data classification.

2.2   Ranking for Ordinal Class Imbalance

Consider all K-tuples $(\mathbf{x}^{(1)}, \mathbf{x}^{(2)}, \ldots, \mathbf{x}^{(K)})$, with $\mathbf{x}^{(k)} \in \mathcal{S}_k$. There are $\prod_{k=1}^{K} N_k$ of such K-tuples. Generate all pairwise differences between ordered elements in the K-tuple: $\mathbf{x}^{(k)} - \mathbf{x}^{(\ell)}$. There are $K(K-1)$ pairs built from a K-tuple. Like before, learn a binary classifier from the $\frac{K(K-1)}{2} \prod_{k=1}^{K} N_k$ pairs positively labeled, and the corresponding symmetric differences negatively labeled.

Note that in this case, each class is present in exactly the same number of elements in the new space: $(K-1) \prod_{k=1}^{K} N_k$ times. The imbalance binary case presented initially is a special case of this formulation, obtained by setting $K = 2$.

However, this approach is repeating some of the pairs multiple times. In fact, a pairwise difference constructed with elements from classes $\mathcal{C}_\ell$ and $\mathcal{C}_m$ is repeated $\prod_{k=1}^{K} N_k/(N_\ell N_m)$ times. This approach can be seen to be equivalent to the Herbrich method [7] with the additional re-weighting by $\prod_{k=1}^{K} N_k/(N_\ell N_m)$ of each element in the space of the differences.

See Fig. 1 for a sketch of the suggested pipeline.

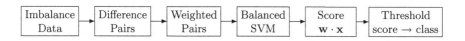

Fig. 1. Balanced ranking training.

2.3 Threshold for Ordinal Classes

After building the decision boundary from the difference pairs, the resulting continuous score from the pairwise scoring ranker needs then to be transformed back to discrete ordinal classes.

Based on the training data, we obtain a score s_i for each observation $\mathbf{x}_i$, ordered by class y_i. Here again, there is an imbalance problem given the class distribution.

Testing a metric against all possible threshold combinations would be infeasible; it would run in factorial time, since there are C^N_{K-1} combinations. With $N = 500$ and $K = 2$, testing all thresholds was more than 35 times slower than the following proposal, with the same results.

It is possible to take advantage of two things; (a) the score produced by the ranker grows with the class order, given that classes are ordinal, and (b) if the error metric is a linear function, and therefore each misclassification contributes to the metric additively, then the threshold selection can be divided into subproblems.

We here propose threshold strategy by defining recursively the threshold path of minimum error. Let s_i be the ordered score of the i-th observation and k_i be the true class, we search the threshold increasingly by invoking the function f with initial parameters $(s_0, k_0, 1)$.

$$f(s_i, k_i, \hat{k}) = \begin{cases} 0 & \text{when } i = N \\ \varepsilon_{k_i\hat{k}} + f(s_{i+1}, k_{i+1}, \hat{k}) & \text{when } \hat{k} = K \\ \min\left\{\varepsilon_{k_i\hat{k}} + f(s_{i+1}, k_{i+1}, \hat{k}), f(s_i, k_i, \hat{k}+1)\right\} & \text{otherwise} \end{cases}$$

where $\varepsilon = \left[\varepsilon_{k\hat{k}}\right]$ is a cost matrix. Informally, f tests whether, at any given time, it is less costly to continue assuming observation i to be of class $\hat{k}$ or if it less costly to make a threshold and start assuming observations are now $\hat{k}+1$. Notice observations are ordered by the score and classes are ordinal.

The threshold itself can then be inferred by transversing the $\hat{k}+1$ breaking points (second term of min) which result in the minimum error.

Several strategies can be used for the cost matrix. For instance:

- **Homogeneous:** $\varepsilon_{k\hat{k}} = \left\{1 \text{ if } k \neq \hat{k} \text{ and } 0 \text{ otherwise} \mid \forall k, \hat{k}\right\}$
- **Absolute costs:** $\varepsilon_{k\hat{k}} = \left\{|k - \hat{k}| \mid \forall k, \hat{k}\right\}$
- **Inverse class frequency:** $\varepsilon_{k\hat{k}} = \left\{\frac{N}{KN_k+1} \text{ if } k \neq \hat{k} \text{ and } 0 \text{ otherwise} \mid \forall k, \hat{k}\right\}$.

By using dynamic programming's memoization, the function can be computed in $\mathcal{O}(KN)$ in worst case scenarios; for instance, when all classes belong to the last class, $k_i = K, \forall i$. This efficiency is based on the fact that classes are ordinal, and comes at the expense of flexibility of the error function f. Error needs to be defined using a constant cost matrix because it is computed additively. Therefore, maximizing metrics from binary problems such as F_1 or g-mean (geometric mean) is not possible.

3 Experiments

The imbalance ranking method proposed, based on [6,7], is contrasted against state-of-the-art methods: One-vs-Rest SVM, One-vs-Rest SVM with a inverse class frequency cost matrix, SVOR [9], and oSVM [10]. SVOR encompasses SVORIM and SVOREM which differ on how the constraints are defined. The idea is to find $k-1$ parallel discriminant hyperplanes in order to properly separate the data into ordered classes by modelling ranks as intervals [9].

Each model is cross-validated by grid-search with $C \in \{0.001, 0.01, 0.1, 1, 10, 100\}$ using k-fold with $k = 3$. Final scores are obtained by 30-fold validation, using the same folds from [2].

Both linear and RBF kernels are tested. The proposed model with linear kernel is implemented by ourselves, while the RBF kernel version uses SVM^{rank} by Thorsten Joachims[1]. His version has been modified to allow setting weights for each pair of differences. All implementations from our work including the dataset folds are made publicly available[2]. Python and scikit-learn were used.

3.1 Evaluation Metrics

Typically, in binary imbalance problems, special balanced metrics are used. The most popular are F_1 and G-mean.

F_1 is defined as $F_1 = \frac{2\,\text{TP}}{2\,\text{TP}+\text{FP}+\text{FN}}$, where TP, FP and FN are true positives, false positives, and false negatives, respectively. While, G-mean is the geometric average between sensitivity and specificity, G-mean $= \sqrt{\frac{TP}{TP+FN}\left(1 - \frac{FP}{FP+TN}\right)}$.

However, these metrics are only well-established for binary settings. Typically, Mean Absolute Error (MAE) is used for ordinal classification,

$$\text{MAE} = \frac{1}{N} \sum_i |k_i - \hat{k}_i|.$$

But this metric suffers from two problems. First, it treats an ordinal variable as a cardinal variable. Second, the metric is sensible to the per-class distribution of the magnitude of the errors, and is therefore not suitable for class imbalance. Like Pérez-Ortiz et al. [2], since the datasets are imbalance, we will contrast our imbalance ranking approach against conventional methods by using the Maximum Mean Absolute Error (MMAE) metric proposed by [11]. MMAE is defined as

$$\text{MMAE} = \max\{\text{MAE}_k \mid k = 1, \ldots, K\}.$$

3.2 Data

Datasets from [2] were used for the experiments (see Table 1). Here, the Imbalance Ratio (IR) metric represents IR $= \frac{\min_k N_k}{\max_k N_k}$, i.e. the ratio between the number of elements of the minority class to that of the majority class. IR $\in [0, 1]$,

---

[1] https://www.cs.cornell.edu/people/tj/svm_light/svm_rank.html.
[2] http://vcmi.inescporto.pt/reproducible_research/ibpria2017/OrdinalImbalance/.

Table 1. Datasets used in the experiments.

Dataset	N	#vars	K	IR
abalone5	4177	10	5	0.002
abalone10	4177	10	10	0.002
balance-scale	625	4	3	0.170
car	1728	21	4	0.054
ERA	1000	4	9	0.099
ERA1vs23456vs7vs8vs9	1000	4	5	0.023
ESL	488	4	9	0.015
ESL12vs3vs456vs7vs89	488	4	5	0.040
LEV	1000	4	5	0.067
newthyroid	215	5	3	0.200
stock10	950	9	10	0.131
SWD	1000	10	4	0.080
toy	300	2	5	0.356
triazines5	186	60	5	0.081
triazines10	186	60	10	0.040

ranging from very imbalance to balanced, respectively. This provides a sense of the imbalance in each dataset. Tables are ordered alphabetically.

3.3   Models

Results contrasting our proposal to different approaches are displayed in Tables 2 and 3 for SVM with linear and RBF kernels, respectively. Three tables are presented for each kernel for the metrics discussed above: MAE, MMAE, and ranking correlation using Kendall's Tau-b. This correlation metric refers to the correlation between the different classes predicted and the true classes. The metric is undefined when in one fold all predictions are the same (tied).

The SVM models tested are:

– **Rank Abs:** proposed ranking method with threshold based on absolute costs;
– **Rank Inv:** proposed ranking method with threshold based on inverse frequency costs;
– **OvR SVM:** ordinary One-vs-Rest SVM;
– **OvR SVM/w:** One-vs-Rest SVM with balanced weights;
– **SVOREX** and **SVORIM** [9];
– **oSVM** [10].

The average of these metrics for each dataset is exhibited for the 30-fold validation. The best scores are presented in bold. Also in bold are scores which are statistically identical to the best score, using a paired difference Student's t-test with a 95% confidence level.

Table 2. Results for linear SVMs.

Dataset	Rank Abs	Rank Inv	OvR SVM	OvR SVM/w	SVOREX	SVORIM	oSVM
abalone5	**0.24**	2.90	**0.24**	0.28	0.31	0.31	0.41
abalone10	**0.54**	6.32	0.58	0.71	0.62	0.64	1.24
balance-scale	0.12	0.12	0.20	0.19	**0.11**	**0.11**	0.55
car	**0.09**	0.10	0.12	**0.09**	0.14	0.12	1.46
ERA	**1.22**	4.69	1.33	1.88	**1.21**	**1.22**	1.38
ERA1vs23456vs7vs8vs9	**0.25**	0.85	0.29	0.28	0.29	0.29	1.28
ESL	**0.32**	0.34	0.56	0.61	0.32	**0.31**	**0.31**
ESL12vs3vs456vs7vs89	**0.17**	0.25	0.32	0.22	0.17	0.17	0.21
LEV	**0.41**	0.59	0.47	0.56	0.43	0.43	0.51
newthyroid	**0.04**	**0.04**	**0.04**	**0.03**	**0.04**	**0.04**	0.18
stock10	0.64	2.64	**0.42**	0.42	0.68	0.63	1.03
SWD	**0.45**	0.81	0.46	0.56	**0.44**	0.45	0.47
toy	**0.84**	1.14	1.02	1.01	1.13	0.95	1.10
triazines5	0.70	1.04	0.69	**0.67**	**0.67**	**0.67**	0.70
triazines10	1.40	2.09	**1.33**	1.51	**1.37**	1.39	1.49
Average	0.49	1.59	0.54	0.60	0.53	0.52	0.82
Deviation	0.39	1.79	0.39	0.50	0.40	0.39	0.46
Winner	73%	6%	26%	20%	40%	33%	6%

a) MAE metric

Dataset	Rank Abs	Rank Inv	OvR SVM	OvR SVM/w	SVOREX	SVORIM	oSVM
abalone5	1.95	3.93	2.28	**1.12**	3.00	3.00	**1.07**
abalone10	4.27	8.68	5.13	5.70	5.48	5.22	**3.02**
balance-scale	0.21	0.19	1.00	0.96	**0.17**	**0.14**	1.05
car	0.47	0.36	0.77	**0.29**	1.36	1.01	1.91
ERA	2.08	7.21	2.61	2.47	2.21	2.37	**1.96**
ERA1vs23456vs7vs8vs9	**1.25**	**1.10**	2.73	1.99	3.00	3.00	1.76
ESL	1.05	**0.96**	2.37	1.24	1.19	1.17	**0.91**
ESL12vs3vs456vs7vs89	0.72	**0.48**	1.87	0.70	0.78	0.77	1.05
LEV	1.33	**0.91**	1.37	1.08	1.25	1.22	1.34
newthyroid	0.14	**0.09**	0.16	0.13	0.14	0.14	1.00
stock10	1.02	4.27	1.03	**0.85**	1.30	1.05	1.80
SWD	1.01	1.21	1.12	**0.77**	1.05	1.06	1.19
toy	**1.79**	1.88	1.92	**1.57**	3.00	2.00	1.96
triazines5	**2.77**	**2.55**	2.99	2.94	3.00	3.00	2.91
triazines10	**6.14**	**5.85**	6.58	**6.35**	7.00	6.83	6.40
Average	1.75	2.65	2.26	1.88	2.26	2.13	1.95
Deviation	1.56	2.65	1.63	1.79	1.85	1.81	1.35
Winner	26%	46%	0%	40%	6%	6%	26%

b) MMAE metric

Dataset	Rank Abs	Rank Inv	OvR SVM	OvR SVM/w	SVOREX	SVORIM	oSVM
abalone5	0.54	–	0.51	**0.59**	–	–	0.47
abalone10	**0.61**	–	0.56	0.47	0.51	0.50	0.59
balance-scale	0.89	0.89	0.82	0.82	**0.90**	**0.90**	0.82
car	**0.89**	**0.89**	0.85	**0.88**	0.86	0.87	0.00
ERA	0.47	–	0.44	0.43	**0.48**	**0.48**	0.46
ERA1vs23456vs7vs8vs9	**0.46**	0.41	–	–	–	–	0.34
ESL	**0.87**	**0.87**	0.75	0.80	0.86	**0.86**	**0.87**
ESL12vs3vs456vs7vs89	**0.78**	0.74	0.30	0.72	0.74	0.75	0.74
LEV	**0.65**	**0.64**	0.59	0.61	0.64	0.63	0.61
newthyroid	**0.93**	**0.94**	**0.93**	**0.94**	**0.93**	**0.93**	0.70
stock10	0.83	0.58	**0.89**	**0.89**	0.81	0.82	0.81
SWD	**0.54**	0.47	0.53	0.51	**0.54**	0.52	0.53
toy	**0.30**	0.21	–	–	–	–	0.12
triazines5	0.21	**0.22**	–	–	–	–	0.16
triazines10	**0.35**	0.32	–	–	–	–	0.27
Average	0.62	0.60	0.65	0.70	0.73	0.73	0.50
Deviation	0.23	0.26	0.20	0.18	0.16	0.17	0.26
Winner	80%	33%	13%	26%	26%	26%	6%

c) Kendall's Tau-b metric

Table 3. Results for SVMs with RBF kernel.

Dataset	Rank Unif	Rank Inv	OvR SVM	OvR SVM/w	SVOREX	SVORIM
abalone5	**0.24**	2.90	0.27	0.39	0.31	0.31
abalone10	**0.55**	6.33	0.61	2.68	0.66	0.69
balance-scale	0.12	0.11	0.14	0.18	0.11	**0.05**
car	**0.09**	0.10	0.12	0.21	0.41	0.41
ERA	**1.27**	4.71	1.33	1.70	1.44	1.32
ERA1vs23456vs7vs8vs9	**0.26**	1.02	**0.26**	0.31	0.27	0.27
ESL	0.32	0.33	0.33	0.38	0.32	**0.30**
ESL12vs3vs456vs7vs89	**0.16**	0.27	**0.17**	0.30	0.21	0.18
LEV	0.42	0.61	**0.41**	0.52	**0.41**	0.42
newthyroid	0.04	**0.03**	0.25	0.23	0.16	0.16
stock10	0.68	2.71	0.18	**0.17**	0.27	0.26
SWD	0.45	0.78	0.45	0.56	**0.44**	0.46
toy	1.00	1.14	0.91	**0.66**	1.08	0.95
triazines5	0.69	1.05	**0.67**	1.18	0.67	0.67
triazines10	**1.38**	1.89	**1.37**	2.45	1.37	1.37
Average	0.51	1.60	0.50	0.79	0.54	0.52
Deviation	0.41	1.79	0.40	0.80	0.41	0.39
Winner	46%	6%	33%	13%	13%	13%

a) MAE metric

Dataset	Rank Unif	Rank Inv	OvR SVM	OvR SVM/w	SVOREX	SVORIM
abalone5	**1.95**	3.96	3.00	2.89	3.00	3.00
abalone10	**4.47**	8.76	5.80	**4.63**	5.80	5.80
balance-scale	0.24	0.16	1.00	0.24	1.00	**0.13**
car	0.52	0.36	1.13	**0.27**	3.00	3.00
ERA	**2.14**	7.27	**2.16**	2.68	2.65	2.45
ERA1vs23456vs7vs8vs9	1.45	1.29	1.65	**1.01**	1.94	1.91
ESL	1.16	**0.95**	1.46	1.17	1.53	1.26
ESL12vs3vs456vs7vs89	0.67	**0.49**	0.75	0.50	1.21	0.92
LEV	1.31	**0.92**	1.25	**0.92**	1.35	1.35
newthyroid	0.16	**0.08**	1.00	0.97	0.64	0.64
stock10	1.31	4.35	0.66	**0.45**	1.14	1.11
SWD	0.97	1.17	1.08	**0.69**	1.08	1.13
toy	1.83	1.86	1.83	**1.15**	2.80	2.00
triazines5	2.77	**2.52**	3.00	2.82	3.00	3.00
triazines10	6.47	**5.95**	7.00	**5.66**	7.00	7.00
Average	1.83	2.67	2.18	1.74	2.48	2.31
Deviation	1.63	2.68	1.81	1.60	1.75	1.83
Winner	20%	40%	6%	60%	0%	6%

b) MMAE metric

Dataset	Rank Unif	Rank Inv	OvR SVM	OvR SVM/w	SVOREX	SVORIM
abalone5	**0.53**	–	0.42	–	–	–
abalone10	**0.61**	–	0.51	–	0.46	0.43
balance-scale	0.89	0.90	0.88	0.85	0.90	**0.95**
car	**0.89**	**0.89**	**0.89**	0.77	–	–
ERA	**0.47**	–	0.40	–	0.42	0.43
ERA1vs23456vs7vs8vs9	0.40	0.40	0.37	**0.45**	0.28	0.28
ESL	**0.87**	**0.87**	0.85	0.85	0.86	**0.87**
ESL12vs3vs456vs7vs89	**0.79**	0.73	0.75	0.71	0.66	0.73
LEV	**0.65**	0.64	**0.65**	0.63	0.64	0.64
newthyroid	0.92	**0.94**	–	0.48	0.67	0.67
stock10	0.82	0.58	0.95	**0.95**	0.93	0.93
SWD	**0.54**	0.49	**0.54**	**0.54**	**0.54**	0.51
toy	0.20	0.22	–	**0.56**	–	–
triazines5	**0.25**	0.23	–	–	–	–
triazines10	**0.37**	0.33	–	–	–	–
Average	0.61	0.60	0.66	0.68	0.64	0.64
Deviation	0.24	0.26	0.21	0.16	0.21	0.22
Winner	66%	33%	20%	26%	6%	13%

c) Kendall's Tau-b metric

4   Results

Ranking performs competitively for ordinal classification (Tables 2 and 3). From the thresholds cost strategies tested (Sect. 2.3), absolute costs seem the most stable, considering deviation, albeit many times outperformed by inverse frequency costs. The volatility from inverse frequency costs might be caused by undue weights in classes of very rare elements.

One-vs-Rest SVM is also competitive, possibly due to the extra flexibility offered by decision boundaries not being parallel, even if such decision boundaries do not make sense in an ordinal context [12].

Considering the question of how much of the gain from using a scoring pairwise ranking steams from the post-processing thresholding step, we also measured Kendall's Tau correlation before applying the threshold. Using the same paired difference Student's t-test, the threshold step statistically improved correlation in 89% of cases for absolute costs and 44% for inverse frequency costs. But the gain is very small, only decreasing average error by a magnitude of 0.06 for absolute costs.

5   Conclusion

Four main strategies are traditionally used in improving imbalance datasets metrics: pre-processing, using cost matrices, post-processing and ensembles, and often combinations of these. In a previous work, we have suggested ranking as an unexplored alternative to imbalance problems [6], in particular pairwise scoring ranking. Pairwise ranking models use an underlying estimator training in the space of difference pairs, therefore a necessarily balanced dataset in the binary case.

In this work, we expand from binary classification to multiclass ordinal classification, by applying weights to the pairs in the space of differences. A new threshold technique is also suggested for the multiclass ordinal context. Again, the empirical results suggest that ranking is a promising approach, sorely lacking in the literature.

Working in the space of pairs of differences does greatly increase the time complexity of the problem. As future work, it would be of interest to ascertain how much of the gain is from a kind of regularization that could be applied directly to the original SVM formulation.

Acknowledgment. This work was funded by the Project "NanoSTIMA: Macro-to-Nano Human Sensing: Towards Integrated Multimodal Health Monitoring and Analytics/NORTE-01-0145-FEDER-000016" financed by the North Portugal Regional Operational Programme (NORTE 2020), under the PORTUGAL 2020 Partnership Agreement, and through the European Regional Development Fund (ERDF), and also by Fundação para a Ciência e a Tecnologia (FCT) within PhD grant numbers SFRH/BD/122248/2016 and SFRH/BD/93012/2013.

References

1. Chawla, N.V., Bowyer, K.W., Hall, L.O., Philip Kegelmeyer, W.: SMOTE: synthetic minority over-sampling technique. J. Artif. Intell. Res. **16**, 321–357 (2002)
2. Pérez-Ortiz, M., Gutiérrez, P.A., Hervás-Martínez, C., Yao, X.: Graph-based approaches for over-sampling in the context of ordinal regression. IEEE Trans. Knowl. Data Eng. **27**(5), 1233–1245 (2015)
3. Domingos, P.: MetaCost: a general method for making classifiers cost-sensitive. In: Proceedings of the Fifth ACM SIGKDD International Conference on Knowledge Discovery and Data Mining, vol. 55, pp. 155–164 (1999)
4. Hanley, J.A., McNeil, B.J.: The meaning and use of the area under a receiver operating characteristic (roc) curve. Radiology **143**(1), 29–36 (1982)
5. Liu, X.-Y., Jianxin, W., Zhou, Z.-H.: Exploratory undersampling for class imbalance learning. IEEE Trans. Syst. Man Cybern. **39**(2), 539–550 (2009)
6. Cruz, R., Fernandes, K., Cardoso, J.S., Pinto Costa, J.F.: Tackling class imbalance with ranking. In: International Joint Conference on Neural Networks (IJCNN). IEEE (2016)
7. Herbrich, R., Graepel, T., Obermayer, K.: Support vector learning for ordinal regression a risk formulation for ordinal regression. In: Proceedings of the Ninth International Conference on Artificial Neural Networks, pp. 97–102 (1999)
8. Herbrich, R., Graepel, T., Obermayer, K.: Support vector learning for ordinal regression. In: Ninth International Conference on Artificial Neural Networks, ICANN 1999 (Conf. Publ. No. 470), vol. 1, pp. 97–102. IET (1999)
9. Chu, W., Keerthi, S.S.: New approaches to support vector ordinal regression. In: Proceedings of the 22nd International Conference on Machine Learning, pp. 145–152. ACM (2005)
10. Cardoso, J.S., Costa, J.F.: Learning to classify ordinal data: the data replication method. J. Mach. Learn. Res. **8**, 1393–1429 (2007)
11. Cruz-Ramírez, M., Hervás-Martínez, C., Sánchez-Monedero, J., Gutiérrez, P.A.: Metrics to guide a multi-objective evolutionary algorithm for ordinal classification. Neurocomputing **135**, 21–31 (2014)
12. Pinto, J.F., Costa, R.S., Cardoso, J.S.: An all-at-once unimodal SVM approach for ordinal classification. In: 2010 Ninth International Conference on Machine Learning and Applications (ICMLA), pp. 59–64. IEEE (2010)

Performance Metrics for Model Fusion in Twitter Data Drifts

Joana Costa[1,2(✉)], Catarina Silva[1,2], Mário Antunes[1,3],
and Bernardete Ribeiro[2]

[1] School of Technology and Management,
Polytechnic Institute of Leiria, Leiria, Portugal
{joana.costa,catarina,mario.antunes}@ipleiria.pt
[2] Department of Informatics Engineering,
Center for Informatics and Systems of the University of Coimbra (CISUC),
Coimbra, Portugal
{joanamc,catarina,bribeiro}@dei.uc.pt
[3] Center for Research in Advanced Computing Systems, INESC-TEC,
University of Porto, Porto, Portugal
mantunes@dcc.fc.up.pt

Abstract. Ensemble approaches have revealed remarkable abilities to tackle different learning challenges, namely in dynamic scenarios with concept drift, e.g. in social networks, as Twitter. Several efforts have been engaged in defining strategies to combine the models that constitute an ensemble. In this work, we investigate the effect of using different metrics for combining ensembles' models, specifically performance-based metrics. We propose five performance combining metrics, having in mind that we may take advantage of diversity in classifiers, as their individual performance takes a leading role in defining their contribution to the ensemble. Experimental results on a Twitter dataset, artificially timestamped, suggest that using performance metrics to combine the models that constitute an ensemble can introduce relevant improvements in the overall ensemble performance.

Keywords: Ensembles · Twitter · Dynamic environments

1 Introduction

Nowadays most learning problems demand dynamic models, which can adapt to new circumstances as they emerge. Paradigmatic to this setting are social networks scenarios, as Twitter, where new information appears all the time. Different approaches have been pursued with such goals, like ensemble systems for classification problems, presented and discussed in this work.

Ensembles of classifiers integrate multiple classifiers to classify each example with the aim of improving classification performance. There are many approaches for ensemble of classifiers, such as boosting [1], bagging [2], or random forests [3],

© Springer International Publishing AG 2017
L.A. Alexandre et al. (Eds.): IbPRIA 2017, LNCS 10255, pp. 13–21, 2017.
DOI: 10.1007/978-3-319-58838-4_2

but their original form is usually applied in static environments. However, ensembles are specially adequate to tackle dynamic evolving settings, given their modular nature, and different studies and approaches have been pursued [4,5].

In this work, we investigate the effect of using different metrics for combining ensembles' classifiers, specifically performance-based metrics. We propose a framework where the diversity in classifiers is explored using their individual performance as driver for the definition of their weight in the ensemble. The approach is then embedded with the importance that weight asymmetry performance metrics has in boosting the model fusion overall success. Five performance evaluation metrics are then proposed.

The rest of the paper is organized as follows. In Sect. 2 we introduce background concepts and state of the art on model fusion and social networks, focusing on Twitter approaches. In Sect. 3 we introduce our approach for model fusion using different metrics to evaluate their individual performance in order to define their contribution to the ensemble. In Sect. 4 we present the experimental setup with the construction of the benchmark dataset and the evaluation metrics. In Sect. 5 we present and analyse the results obtained by comparing the metrics for combining models in an ensemble and, finally, conclusions and future work.

2 Background

2.1 Ensembles

Ensembles are cutting-edge solutions to many different learning challenges. Different researchers have been studying ensembles and their applications in various fields [4,6–8].

Classifier committees or ensembles are based on the idea that, given a task that requires expert knowledge, k experts (baseline classifiers) may perform better than one, if their individual judgements are appropriately combined. A classifier committee is then characterized by (i) a choice of k classifiers, and (ii) a choice of a combination function, sometimes denominated a *voting algorithm*. The classifiers should be as independent as possible to guarantee a large number of inductions on the data. By using different classifiers to exploit diverse patterns of errors to make the ensemble better than just the sum (or average) of the parts, we may obtain a gain from synergies between the ensemble classifiers.

Ensembles are used in different setting like novelty detection [9], and though the simplest combination function is just a majority voting mechanism with an odd number of baseline classifiers, different fusion mechanisms have been proposed, namely: average, minimum, maximum, median, majority vote, and oracle [10].

In [11,12] two approaches of incremental learning of concept drift in non-stationary environments are presented. The authors describe ensemble-based approaches of classifiers for incrementally learning from new data drawn from a distribution that changes in time and generates a new classifier using each additional dataset that becomes available from the changing environment.

2.2 Social Networks: Twitter Case Study

Social networks are paradigmatic examples of dynamic environments. Specifically, Twitter is such a case where drift phenomena commonly occur in a text-base scenario. Twitter is a micro-blogging service where users post text messages up to 140 characters, also known as tweets. Twitter is also responsible for the popularization of the concept of hashtag, a single word started by the symbol "#" that is used to classify the message content and to improve search capabilities. hashtags can also be used as a classification label. If we can classify a tweet based on a set of hashtags, we are able to suggest an hashtag for a new given tweet, bringing a wider audience into discussion [13], spreading an idea [14], get affiliated with a community [15], or bringing together other Internet resources [16].

This case study aims to classify Twitter messages. A Twitter classification problem can be described as a multi-class problem that can be cast as a time series of tweets. It consists of a continuous sequence of instances, in this case, Twitter messages, represented as $\mathcal{X} = \{x_1, \ldots, x_t\}$, where x_1 is the first occurring instance and x_t the latest. Each instance occurs at a time, not necessarily in equally spaced time intervals, and is characterized by a set of features, usually words, $\mathcal{W} = \{w_1, w_2, \ldots, w_{|\mathcal{W}|}\}$. Consequently, instance x_i is denoted as the feature vector $\{w_{i1}, w_{i2}, \ldots, w_{i|W|}\}$.

We have used a classification strategy previously introduced in [17]. Assuming x_i is a labelled instance it is represented as the pair (x_i, y_i), being $y_i \in \mathcal{Y} = \{y_1, y_2, \ldots, y_{|\mathcal{Y}|}\}$ the class label for instance x_i, or the hashtag that labels the Twitter message x_i.

3 Proposed Approach

Figure 1 depicts the ensemble model that underpins the proposed framework of metrics for combining ensembles. The model can be divided in three parts, from top to bottom: (i) models' construction; (ii) learning process; (iii) models' combination.

The construction of the models is carried out by defining time-windows and learning models for each time-window. Different scenarios can be constructed, i.e., the exact examples that are considered in each time-window depend on the specific approach. The simplest approach is to consider just the timestamp of the example, but more elaborate approaches may consider the relevance of the example or the effort for it to be learned [18].

The learning process focuses on the definition of the k baseline classifiers. Notice that in dynamic environments, the ensemble must adapt to deal with changes usually dependent of hidden contexts. One of the major challenges in dynamic environments is the amount of data, specially when dealing with streams. It is sometimes infeasible to store all the previously seen data, but it may carry substantial information for future use. Hence, not all previously constructed models are kept in the ensemble and, in the learning process the

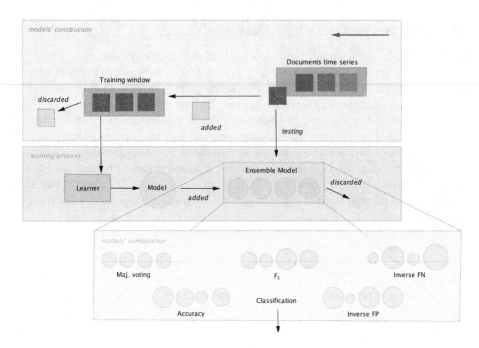

Fig. 1. Proposed ensemble model ($k = 4$) with combining metrics

decision of which ones should be kept (or added) and which ones should be discarded takes place [19, 20].

The framework proposed in the paper uses a combination of models with different performance metrics. The underpinning idea behind the deployed framework is to test and evaluate different strategies to combine baseline models into an ensemble. By doing this we aim to increase the classification performance, as we may tackle the problem of not being able to store all the previously unseen examples.

To evaluate a binary classification task, TP, FP, TN and FN values are obtained and then a set of performance metrics can be defined: error rate ($\frac{FN+FP}{TP+TN+FP+FN}$), accuracy ($\frac{TP+TN}{TP+TN+FP+FN}$), recall ($R = \frac{TP}{TP+FN}$), and precision ($P = \frac{TP}{TP+FP}$), as well as combined measures, such as, $F_1 = \frac{2 \times P \times R}{P+R}$ [21]. As can be gleaned from Fig. 1, the proposed metrics are: majority voting, accuracy, inverse FP ($\frac{1}{FP}$), inverse FN ($\frac{1}{FN}$), and F_1.

Considering the proposed approach and the fact that we are working with a time series in a "one-against-all" strategy, we will have a classifier for each batch of the time series that is composed by $|Y|$ binary classifiers, being $|Y|$ the collection of possible labels. To perceive the performance of the classification for each drift pattern, we will consider all the binary classifiers that were created in all the time series batches. To evaluate the performance obtained across time, we will average the obtained results. Two conventional methods are widely used, specially in multi-label scenarios, namely macro-averaging and micro-averaging.

Macro-averaged performance scores are obtained by computing the scores for each learning model in each batch of the time series and then averaging these scores to obtain the global means. Differently, micro-averaged performance scores are computed by summing all the previously introduces contingency matrix values (a, b, c and d), and then use the sum of these values to compute a single micro-averaged performance score that represents the global score.

The metrics we are proposing are based on the performance of each model whenever a new example arrives. As a consequence, if a model is unable to correctly classify examples in a given moment, its performance metrics will decrease, or even be null, excluding the contribution of the model to the ensemble in the subsequent moments. However, if in another moment, the model regains the ability to correctly classify the example, the increase of its performance will allow it to contribute again. This is particularly important in dynamic environments where concepts can appear and reappear.

4   Experimental Setup

The Twitter dataset we have defined to evaluate and validate our strategy was carried out by defining 10 different hashtags that represent different drifts, based on the assumption that they would denote mutually exclusive concepts.

The Twitter API (https://dev.Twitter.com/) was then used to request public tweets containing the defined hashtags. The requests were submitted between 28 December 2014 and 21 January 2015 and tweets were only considered if the user language was defined as English. We have requested more than 75.000 tweets with the given hashtags. The hashtag was then removed from the tweet and was exclusively used as the document label. The tweets were then labelled for classification purposes, and were used by their appearing order in the public feed. Our final dataset comprises 34.240 tweets.

Table 1. Mapping between type of drift and hashtag.

Drift	Hashtag
Sudden #1	#syrisa
Gradual #1	#isis
Incremental #1	#android
Reoccurring	#realmadrid
Normal #2	#sex
Sudden #2	#airasia
Gradual #2	#bieber
Incremental #2	#ferrari
Normal #1	#jobs
Normal #3	#nfl

Table 1 presents the hashtags and the corresponding type of drift represented by each one. This correspondence was arbitrary and does not correspond to any real occurrence in a real Twitter scenario, since as stated above, no information is known about the occurrence of drifts in Twitter. The final dataset was constructed using DOTS (Drift Oriented Tool System), a free drift oriented framework we have developed to dynamically create datasets with drift [22]. It can be freely downloaded at http://dotspt.sourceforge.net/. The evaluation of our approach was done by the previously described dataset and using Support Vector Machines (SVM) [23].

5 Experimental Results

In this section we evaluate the performance obtained with the Twitter data set using the approach described in Sect. 3. Besides a majority voting strategy, five performance metrics were used to combine the ensemble model: accuracy, F_1 measure, the inverse of false positives and the inverse of false negatives. The majority voting strategy is used as baseline, as all models contribute equally to the final decision of the ensemble, despite their previous performance.

Table 2 summarises the performance results obtained by classifying the dataset, considering the micro-averaged F_1 measure.

Table 2. Micro-averaged F_1 for different combining metrics

Drift	Performance metrics for model fusion				
	Maj. voting	Accuracy	F_1	Inverse FP	Inverse FN
Sudden #1	74.80%	79.67%	87.95%	89.12%	89.15%
Sudden #2	87.80%	89.12%	92.76%	93.20%	93.17%
Gradual #1	52.55%	54.82%	65.72%	68.27%	68.27%
Gradual #2	62.21%	65.20%	76.83%	78.93%	78.93%
Incremental #1	88.58%	88.89%	89.50%	91.68%	91.80%
Incremental #2	77.21%	77.31%	78.08%	80.31%	80.13%
Reoccurring	35.33%	36.75%	59.76%	63.95%	64.53%
Normal #1	70.89%	70.95%	71.26%	73.01%	73.01%
Normal #2	90.49%	90.51%	90.55%	90.81%	90.90%
Normal #3	81.52%	81.63%	81.97%	82.10%	82.08%
Micro-averaged F_1	**78.27%**	79.39%	82.99%	84.36%	**84.39%**

Analysing the table we can observe that using different metrics to combine the ensemble can lead to different performance results, considering the Twitter classification problem. Globally we can achieve a 6% increase in the F_1 measure, when comparing the use of a majority voting strategy with a performance based strategy like inverse FN.

It is particularly important to note that this performance increase is observed in all different types of drifts, despite their nature. We have also observed that the obtained results where achieved because the number of false negatives was reduced when using metrics based on the performance. Though this might be problem dependent, it is also relevant to pinpoint.

Table 3 summarises the performance results obtained by classifying the dataset, considering the micro-averaged Recall measure. Recall is highly dependent on the true positives, and the increased show us that using different metrics can reduce false negatives and consequently increase the true positives. The reduction of false negatives is, consequently, responsible for the increase of the F_1 results presented in Table 2, as precision is not significantly affected when using different combining strategies.

Table 3. Micro-averaged Recall for different combining metrics

Drift	Performance metrics for model fusion				
	Maj. voting	Accuracy	F_1	Inverse FP	Inverse FN
Sudden #1	59.78%	66.25%	78.53%	80.48%	80.52%
Sudden #2	78.36%	80.50%	86.61%	87.42%	87.39%
Gradual #1	35.67%	37.79%	49.00%	51.92%	51.92%
Gradual #2	45.54%	48.79%	62.67%	65.54%	65.54%
Incremental #1	79.87%	80.40%	81.40%	85.01%	85.24%
Incremental #2	63.67%	63.79%	64.83%	67.92%	67.68%
Reoccurring	21.47%	22.53%	42.67%	47.13%	47.73%
Normal #1	54.95%	55.03%	55.39%	57.53%	57.54%
Normal #2	82.93%	82.97%	83.03%	83.56%	83.68%
Normal #3	68.91%	69.07%	69.56%	69.80%	69.77%
Micro-averaged recall	**64.55%**	66.08%	71.18%	73.25%	**73.29%**

6   Conclusions

In this paper we evaluate the use of performance metrics to combine models that constitute an ensemble in a Twitter classification problem. The main idea is to boost the classification performance of the ensemble model by combining its models based on their previous performance, and thus giving more weight to the contribution of a best performer model when compared to a less performer one.

We have used a Twitter case study to evaluate our approach. Since it is not known which types of drift occur in the context of social networks, and particularly in Twitter, we have also simulated different types of drift in a dataset generated artificially with real tweets to evaluate and validate our strategy.

The results revealed the usefulness of our strategy, as using different performance-based metrics led to the improve by 6%. This result was obtained considering the micro-averaged F_1, when comparing to the baseline approach, a majority voting strategy, where all models contribute equally to the final decision of the ensemble, despite their previous performance.

We may also to conclude that results obtained and the improvement observed are independent from the drift pattern the class represents, and thus can be applied in different dynamic scenarios. A more suited metric can better weight the best performer models and thus increase the ensemble overall performance, as less performer models can cease their contribution. Future work will include more complex performance metrics. More efforts are needed to understand if longevity can also be included in the contribution of a model in the ensemble and if a pruning strategy is worth applying.

Acknowledgment. It is also financed by national funding via the Foundation for Science and Technology and by the European Regional Development Fund (FEDER), through the COMPETE 2020 - Operational Program for Competitiveness and Internationalization (POCI).

References

1. Freund, Y., Schapire, R.E.: A decision-theoretic generalization of on-line learning and an application to boosting. J. Comput. Syst. Sci. **55**(1), 119–139 (1997)
2. Breiman, L.: Bagging predictors. Mach. Learn. **24**(2), 123–140 (1996)
3. Breiman, L.: Random forests. Mach. Learn. **45**(1), 5–32 (2001)
4. Bagul, R.D., Phulpagar, B.D.: Survey on approaches, problems and applications of ensemble of classifiers. Int. J. Emerg. Trends Technol. Comput. Sci. **5**(1), 28–30 (2016)
5. Ditzler, G., Polikar, R.: Incremental learning of concept drift from streaming imbalanced data. IEEE Trans. Knowl. Data Eng. **25**(10), 2283–2301 (2013)
6. Tabassum, N., Ahmed, T.: A theoretical study on classifier ensemble methods and its applications. In: 3rd International Conference on Computing for Sustainable Global Development, pp. 67–78 (2016)
7. Ren, Y., Zhang, L., Suganthan, P.N.: Ensemble classification and regression - recent developments, applications and future directions. IEEE Comput. Intell. Mag. **1**(1), 41–43 (2016)
8. Ponti Jr., M.P.: Combining classifiers: from the creation of ensembles to the decision fusion. In: 24th Conference on Graphics, Patterns and Images, pp. 1–10 (2011)
9. Faria, E., de Carvalho, A., Gonçalves, I., Gama, J.: Novelty detection in data streams. Artif. Intell. Rev. **45**(2), 235–269 (2016)
10. Kuncheva, L.: A theoretical study on six classifier fusion strategies. IEEE Trans. Pattern Anal. Mach. Intell. **24**(2), 281–286 (2002)
11. Elwell, R., Polikar, R.: Incremental learning of concept drift in nonstationary environments. IEEE Trans. Neural Netw. **22**, 1517–1531 (2011)
12. Karnick, M., Muhlbaier, M.D., Polikar, R.: Incremental learning in non-stationary environments with concept drift using a multiple classifier based approach. In: International Conference on Pattern Recognition, pp. 1–4 (2008)
13. Johnson, S.: How Twitter will change the way we live. Time Mag. **173**, 23–32 (2009)

14. Tsur, O., Rappoport, A.: What's in a hashtag?: content based prediction of the spread of ideas in microblogging communities. In: Proceedings of the 5th International Conference on Web Search and Data Mining, pp. 643–652 (2012)

15. Yang, L., Sun, T., Zhang, M., Mei, Q.: We know what @you #tag: does the dual role affect hashtag adoption? In: Proceedings of the 21st International Conference on World Wide Web, pp. 261–270 (2012)

16. Chang, H.-C.: A new perspective on Twitter hashtag use: diffusion of innovation theory. In: Proceedings of the 73rd Annual Meeting on Navigating Streams in an Information Ecosystem, pp. 85:1–85:4 (2010)

17. Costa, J., Silva, C., Antunes, M., Ribeiro, B.: Defining semantic meta-hashtags for Twitter classification. In: Tomassini, M., Antonioni, A., Daolio, F., Buesser, P. (eds.) ICANNGA 2013. LNCS, vol. 7824, pp. 226–235. Springer, Heidelberg (2013). doi:10.1007/978-3-642-37213-1_24

18. Costa, J., Silva, C., Antunes, M., Ribeiro, B.: Choice of best samples for building ensembles in dynamic environments. In: Jayne, C., Iliadis, L. (eds.) EANN 2016. CCIS, vol. 629, pp. 35–47. Springer, Cham (2016). doi:10.1007/978-3-319-44188-7_3

19. Costa, J., Silva, C., Antunes, M., Ribeiro, B.: The impact of longstanding messages in micro-blogging classification. In: International Joint Conference on Neural Networks (IJCNN), pp. 1–8 (2015)

20. Costa, J., Silva, C., Antunes, M., Ribeiro, B.: Concept drift awareness in Twitter streams. In: Proceedings of the 13th International Conference on Machine Learning and Applications, pp. 294–299 (2014)

21. Sokolova, M., Lapalme, G.: A systematic analysis of performance measures for classification tasks. Inf. Process. Manage. **45**(4), 427–437 (2009)

22. Costa, J., Silva, C., Antunes, M., Ribeiro, B.: DOTS: drift oriented tool system. In: Arik, S., Huang, T., Lai, W.K., Liu, Q. (eds.) ICONIP 2015. LNCS, vol. 9492, pp. 615–623. Springer, Cham (2015). doi:10.1007/978-3-319-26561-2_72

23. Vapnik, V.: The Nature of Statistical Learning Theory. Springer, New York (1999)

Online Learning of Attributed Bi-Automata for Dialogue Management in Spoken Dialogue Systems

Manex Serras[1], María Inés Torres[2(✉)], and Arantza Del Pozo[1]

[1] Vicomtech-IK4 HSLT Department, Donostia, Spain
{mserras,adelpozo}@vicomtech.org
[2] Speech Interactive Research Group, Universidad del País Vasco,
UPV/EHU, Leioa, Spain
manes.torres@ehu.es
http://www.vicomtech.org
http://www.ehu.es/en/web/speech-interactive/about-us

Abstract. Online learning of dialogue managers is a desirable but often costly property to obtain. Probabilistic Finite State Bi-Automata (PFSBA) have shown to provide a flexible and adaptive framework to achieve this goal. In this paper, an Attributed PFSBA (A-PSFBA) is implemented and experimentally compared with previous non-attributed PFSBA proposals. Then, a simple yet effective online learning algorithm that adapts the probabilistic structure of the Bi-Automata on the run is presented and evaluated. To this end, the User Model is also represented by an A-PFSBA and the impact of different user behaviors is tested. The proposed approaches are evaluated on the Let's Go corpus, showing significant improvements on the dialogue success rates reported in previous works.

Keywords: Spoken Dialogue Systems · Online learning · Attributed Bi-Automata · Dialogue management

1 Introduction

Spoken Dialogue Systems (SDS) enable people to interact with computers, using spoken language in a natural way [1]. A key task that every SDS has to carry out is controlling the logic structure of the interaction, usually done by the Dialogue Manager (DM). Several approaches have been proposed to model the DM statistically: Bayesian networks [3], Stochastic Finite-State models [4,10], Partially Observable Markov Decision Processes [8] and Deep Learning approaches which are capable of building end-to-end dialogue systems [5,18,19].

In this work, we deal with the Interactive Pattern Recognition (IPR) framework [13] that has also been proposed to represent SDS [11]; this formulation needs to estimate the joint probability distribution over the set of semantic units provided by the SU and the set of actions to be provided by the DM. In [10], such joint probability distribution was modeled by stochastic regular *bi-languages*. These languages had also been successfully proposed to deal with

© Springer International Publishing AG 2017
L.A. Alexandre et al. (Eds.): IbPRIA 2017, LNCS 10255, pp. 22–31, 2017.
DOI: 10.1007/978-3-319-58838-4_3

Machine Translation [12]. To this end, a Probabilistic Finite State Bi-Automata (PFSBA) was defined in [10]. Because dialog management also requires keeping the values of all relevant internal variables that can be updated after each user turn, an attributed model that allows dealing with task attribute values was also proposed. So far, only the PFSBA has been experimentally validated in [11], thus, the potential of the A-PFSBA remains unexplored. On the other hand, a turn-by-turn online learning procedure was proposed in [6] aimed at adapting the PFSBA's structure and parameters at each new interaction with an user. Although the capability and flexibility of the PFSBA to learn new edges and nodes was demonstrated, there was no dialogue success rate improvement.

The first goal of this paper is to validate the A-PFSBA framework showing that attributes can contribute to a significant increase of the dialogue success rate. The second goal is to propose a novel online learning algorithm capable of improving the dialogue success rate by learning on a dialogue basis, exploiting a criterion similar to the reward functions used in reinforcement learning [15]. Because the learning procedure requires a user model to interact with the DM, an additional contribution is the proposal of a User Model that exploits the prior probabilities modeled under the A-PFSBA framework. The proposed approaches have been evaluated through various dialog generation tasks over the Let's Go corpus [7], allowing direct comparison with previous works and resulting in significant dialogue task success rate improvements.

The paper is structured as follows: Sect. 2 explains spoken dialogue interaction as an IPR framework and describes the PFSBA and A-PFSBA formulations, detailing how the Dialogue Manager and the User can be modeled. The proposed online dialogue learning procedure is then described in Sect. 3. Section 4 presents the evaluation experiments carried out and their results. Finally, the main conclusions are summarized in Sect. 5, where future guidelines are set.

2   Attributed Probabilistic Finite State Bi-Automata as Dialogue Manager

This section describes spoken dialogue interaction in terms of the Interactive Pattern Recognition (IPR) framework and how Probabilistic Finite State Bi-Automata can be used to model these interactions. At the end, the definition of a Dialog Manager and a User Model over the structure of the Attributed PFSBA is presented.

2.1   Interactive Pattern Recognition Framework

Human-machine interaction can be seen as a pattern recognition process, where both interact under an unknown distribution of states in order to complete some objectives. Within the IPR framework, the user provides feedback signals f. As a response, the system will provide an hypothesis or system action a to disambiguate the user's intention through the dialogue.

Ignoring the user feedback except for the last interaction and assuming a classical minimum-error criterion, the Bayes decision rule is simplified to maximize the posterior $P(a_t \mid q_{t-1}, f_{t-1})$ where a_t is the system action at current turn, f_{t-1} is the last user feedback and q_{t-1} the previous state. The interpretation of the decoding d of the user feedback $f \in F$ cannot be considered a deterministic process due to Automatic Speech Recognition (ASR) errors. Thus, the space of decoded feedback is the input to the SDS from the user, usually achieved by filtering the ASR output through some Spoken Language Understanding module. Then, the best hypothesis or system action $\hat{a}$ can be obtained as follows [11]:

$$\hat{a}_t = \arg \max_a P(a \mid q_{t-1}, f_{t-1}) = \arg \max_a \sum_d P(a, d \mid q_{t-1}, f_{t-1})$$

As considering every possibility for the joint probability of the action and the decoding is computationally expensive, a sub-optimal approach can be performed:

$$\hat{d}_{t-1} = \arg \max_d P(f_{t-1} \mid d)P(d \mid q_{t-1})$$

$$\hat{a}_t \approx \arg \max_a P(a \mid \hat{d}_{t-1}, q_{t-1})$$

Similarly, the user feedback f_t depends on the previous state q_{t-1} and system action, through an unknown distribution $P(f_t|q_{t-1}, a_{t-1})$. In this case, as the feedback produced by the system is known, there is no noisy channel that corrupts the signal f_t and no decoding procedure is needed.

2.2   Probabilistic Finite State Bi-Automata

Probabilistic Finite State Bi-Automata are suitable to model both probabilities: $P(a_t| q_{t-1}, f_{t-1})$ and $P(f_t| q_{t-1}, a_{t-1})$. Their goal is to maximize the probability of model M to generate a given sample of dialogues Z, being $\mathbf{z}$ the dialogues that compose sample Z.

$$\hat{M} = \arg \max_M P_M(Z) = \arg \max_M \prod_{z \in Z} P_M(\mathbf{z})$$

As the model learns its structure by maximizing the likelihood to fit the samples, it can also generate dialogue samples, as done by end-to-end neural networks [20].

The PSFBA model can then be defined as $\hat{M} = (\Sigma, \Delta, \Gamma, \delta q_0, P_f, P)$ where

- Σ is the alphabet of user's decoded feedbacks, $d \in \Sigma$.
- Δ is the alphabet of system actions, $a \in \Delta$.
- Γ is an extended alphabet $\Gamma \subseteq (\Sigma^{\geq m} \times \Delta^{\geq n})$ that contains the combinations of user's decoded feedbacks and system actions.
- $Q = Q_S \cup Q_U$ is the set of states labeled by bi-strings: $(\tilde{d}_i : \tilde{a}_i) \in \Gamma$.
- $\delta \subseteq Q \times \Gamma \times Q$ is the union of two sets of transitions $\delta = \delta_S \cup \delta_U$ as follows:
  - $\delta_S \subseteq Q_S \times \Gamma \times Q_U$ is a set of system transitions of the form $(q, (\epsilon : \tilde{a}_i), q')$ where $q \in Q_S$, $q' \in Q_U$ and $(\epsilon : \tilde{a}_i) \in \Gamma$.

- $\delta_U \subseteq Q_U \times \Gamma \times Q_S$ is a set of user transitions of the form $(q, (\tilde{d}_i : \epsilon), q')$
  where $q \in Q_U$, $q' \in Q_S$ and $(\tilde{d}_i : \epsilon) \in \Gamma$.
- $q_0 \in Q_S$ is the unique initial state: $(\epsilon : \epsilon)$ where ϵ is the empty symbol.
- $P_f : Q \to [0, 1]$ is the final-state probability distribution.
- $P : \delta \to [0, 1]$ defines the transition probability distributions $P(q, b, q') \equiv$
  $P(q', b \mid q)$ $\forall b \in \Gamma$ and $q, q' \in Q$ such that:

$$P_f(q) + \sum_{b \in \Gamma, q' \in Q} P(q, b, q') = 1 \ \forall q \in Q$$

where transition (q, b, q') is completely defined by the initial state q and the transition state b. Thus, $\forall q \in Q$, $\forall b \in \Gamma$, $|\{q' : \{(q, b, q')\}| \leq 1$.

Taking advantage of the structural flexibility provided by the PFSBA formulation presented above, dialogue attributes can be easily incorporated to represent the transcendent variables of the dialogue as discrete values that are kept from one dialogue turn to another (e.g. specified bus number, current departure place etc.) through the inclusion of an additional alphabet Ω, which includes the discrete valued dialogue attributes seen in the sample set Z. As a result, the elements of the state alphabet Q are enhanced to $[(\tilde{d}_i : \tilde{a}_i), \tilde{\omega}_i] \in \Gamma \times \Omega$.

2.3 Dealing with Unseen Situations

Field-deployed SDS have to deal with unseen situations, so each time the user gives feedback that leads to a state $q' \notin Q$ the system state q has to be approximated using a smoothing strategy [11] as shown in Fig. 1:

$$q = \begin{cases} q', & \text{if } q' \in Q \\ \min_{q \in Q} G(q', q), & \text{otherwise} \end{cases} \tag{1}$$

where G is some function that defines the distance between the nodes. This smoothing procedure ensures that the DM can estimate unseen states. The Distance Function (G) used in the paper is defined as follows:

$$G(q, q') = \text{dist}((\tilde{d}_q : \tilde{a}_q), (\tilde{d}_{q'} : \tilde{a}_{q'})) + \lambda(|\tilde{\omega}_q \cap \tilde{\omega}_{q'}| - |\tilde{\omega}_q \cup \tilde{\omega}_{q'}|)$$

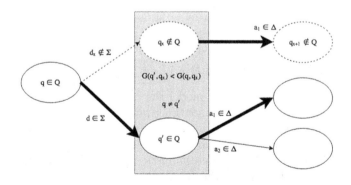

Fig. 1. Creation of candidate states and transitions through smoothing

where $dist$ corresponds to the Levenshtein distance and λ is a parameter which penalizes the distance by the amount of attributes that both states differ.

Figure 1 shows how candidate states and transitions are created through the smoothing procedure. Unknown nodes such as $q_x \notin Q$ are generated through the user decoded feedback d_x and the most similar node q' is used to determine the system action $a_1 \in \Delta$. In this process, two new states q_x and q_{x+1} are estimated.

2.4   Modeling the Dialogue Manager

Given the A-PFSBA model $\hat{M}$, a DM can be defined as a function whose goal is to return the best system action given an user feedback decoding and the state at the current turn under a policy Π_{DM} and a smoothing strategy with a distance function G:

$$DM_\Pi : Q \times \Sigma \rightarrow \Delta \times Q$$

$$\Pi_{DM}(q_t, d_t, \hat{M}, G) \rightarrow a_{t+1},\ q_{t+1}$$

where the policy Π_{DM} can be any function that decides which action to perform. The policy used for the DM in the experimental section of the paper is the Maximum Probability (MP); in which the system action to be done is the one that maximizes $P(a_t \mid f_{t-1},\ q_{t-1})$. This is equivalent to choosing the edge of the current state with the highest transition probability at each system turn:

$$\tilde{a}_t = arg\ max_{a_{t-1,j} \in \Delta(q_{t-1})}\ P(q_{t-1}, (\ \epsilon : a_{t-1,\ j}), q'_j)$$

2.5   Modeling the User

As data gathering and evaluation is very expensive, the most common approach to train and evaluate stochastic dialogue managers is to model a simulated user from the available data. These User Models UM interact with the DM generating synthetic dialogues, for evaluation purposes [16,17].

Since the A-PFSBA paradigm is a generative model, it captures user behavior over the intercourse of the dialogue. Thus, an structure similar to that of the Dialog Manager can be used to design an User Model, whose goal is to return some user feedback given a system hypothesis and the current state under a certain policy Π_{UM}:

$$UM_\Pi : Q \times \Delta \rightarrow F \times Q$$

$$\Pi_{UM}(q_t, a_t, \hat{U}, G) \rightarrow f_{t+1},\ q_{t+1}$$

where $\hat{U}$ is the A-PFSBA used to model the user dialogue samples and G is the distance function used in the smoothing procedure for the UM. The main advantage is that its implementation is straightforward, as the same methodology can be applied both for the DM and the UM. It is important to note that the UM's policy Π_{UM} has to be non-deterministic, in order to achieve the highest possible variance while keeping the sensibility induced to the UM using the priors defined by the bi-automaton. In order to do so, the policy employed in the current implementation is an α-weighted Random Sampling (RS), in which the action to perform is sampled from the distribution of the hypotheses seen in the current state. These priors are modified using an $\alpha \in [0, 1]$ structural constraint parameter. Being $\delta_{i,j}$ the transition probability from the state q_i to q_j it can be re-scored by α as follows:

$$\alpha(\delta_{i,j}) = \frac{\delta_{i,j}^{\alpha}}{\sum_k \delta_{i,k}^{\alpha}}$$

So, the higher α, the more constrained the user variability under the priors modeled by $\hat{U}$. Note that using $\alpha = 0$ is the same as randomly picking a possible user feedback available from the current state q_t.

3   Online Learning

The ability to adapt and learn from unseen situations on the run is a powerful property of the PFSBA formulation. [6] showed that it is flexible enough to adapt to unseen situations using smoothing techniques and controlled structural learning. The learning process was done turn-by-turn and so, there was no quality check of the learned content and every new state and transition, both good and bad, were learned. The online learning algorithm presented in this section fixes this problem, learning only useful dialogues when they are finished through the exploitation of a quality metric QM that discriminates whether a dialogue is valid or not, in a way similar to the reward function used in reinforcement learning.

Being z' the A-PFSBA structure that models an unseen dialogue sample generated by some user and the DM with dialogue model $\hat{M} = (\Sigma, \Delta, \Gamma, \Omega, \delta, q_0, P_f, P)$, the online learning method consists on merging the new states and transitions estimated during the smoothing procedure employed to deal with unseen situations by the A-PFSBA framework in z', as described in Sect. 2.3, with the dialogue model $\hat{M}$ only if the quality metric QM decides that z' is a valid dialogue. Thus, for generated unseen dialogues rendered valid by QM, the new states $q_x \notin Q$ and the corresponding set of new transitions $\delta[q_x]$ shown in Fig. 1 are learned by the DM dialogue model $\hat{M}$, so they no longer need to be estimated by the smoothing procedure. The update pseudo-algorithm is defined as follows:

4   Setup and Experiments

This section describes the experiments made on the Let's Go Corpus [7] to test the presented approaches. The main goal is to show the improvements obtained by the inclusion of attributes in the PFSBA implementation, the proposed online learning procedure and to evaluate the impact of the User Model in the learning process.

Algorithm 1. Online Learning

1: **procedure** A-PFSBA UPDATE
2:      $\hat{M} \leftarrow DM$'s A-PFSBA model
3:      $z' \leftarrow$ Unseen Dialogue's A-PFSBA model
4:      **if** $QM(z')$ is True **then**
5:          **for** $q_z \in Q_{z'}$ **do:**
6:              $\hat{M} \leftarrow merge(\hat{M}, q_z, \delta[q_z])$
7:              $\hat{M} \leftarrow update\_edge\_count(\hat{M})$
8:      **return** $\hat{M}$

4.1 Corpus Description

The Let's Go SDS developed by Carnegie Mellon University (CMU) exploits the Olympus architecture using RavenClaw [2] as DM to provide schedule and route information about the city of Pittsburgh bus service to the general public. The corpus linked to such SDS was collected from real user interactions during 2005, so events like unexpected dialogue closing, spontaneous talking, sudden noise etc. are observed. Some of the corpus statistics are shown in Table 1. In the corpus, every feedback decoding is done with the CMU Phoenix Parser [14], so each user state Q_U and system state Q_S is represented by a string. The attributes are discrete values related to bus schedule information. Table 2 shows some dialogue formatting examples. The corpus was split in half to model two A-PFSBA, $\hat{M}$ to be used as the DM and $\hat{U}$ as the UM.

Table 1. Main features of the Let's Go Corpus

Let's Go Corpus statistics					
Dialogues	1840	System turns	28141	System dialogue acts	49
Attributes	14	User turns	28071	User dialogue acts	138

4.2 Impact of the Attributes and the User Model

The inclusion of attributes changes the structural behavior of the PFSBA. To evaluate this change, a total of 25 000 dialogues have been generated between the DM and the UM, using both the PFSBA and A-PFSBA formulations under the same DM/UM policy and dialogue partitions as in [6]. The employed evaluation metrics are the Task Completion (TC) rate and the Average Dialogue Length (ADL). The task is rendered complete when the DM does a coherent query to the database and retrieves the information asked by the user. Note that this metric is more constrained than the one used in previous works [6] due to the inclusion of attributes. These metrics have also been calculated for the Let's Go SDS, that uses an agenda based DM.

Table 3 shows that the inclusion of attributes increases the number of unique nodes and edges in the graph. Also, it is clear that this structural complexity is

Table 2. Let's Go dialogue formatting example

$q = [(\tilde{d}_i : \tilde{a}_i), \tilde{\omega}_i]$	System actions and user Feedbacks
$q_0 = [(\epsilon : \epsilon), \epsilon] \in Q_S$	S: Welcome to the CMU Let's Go bus information system. To get help... $\tilde{a_1}$ = inform_welcome,inform_get_help,request_query_departure_place
$q_1 = [(\tilde{a_1} : \epsilon), \epsilon] \in Q_U$	U: I'm leaving from CMU. $\tilde{d_1}$ = inform_departure_place, PlaceInformation_registered_stop $\tilde{\omega_0}$ = {}
$q_2 = [(\tilde{a_1} : \tilde{d_1}), \tilde{\omega_0}] \in Q_S$	S: Departing from <query.departureplace CMU>. Did I get that right? $\tilde{a_2}$ = Explicit_confirm, request_query_departure_place $\tilde{\omega_0}$ = {}
$q_3 = [(\tilde{a_2} : \tilde{d_1}), \tilde{\omega_0}] \in Q_U$	U: Yes. $\tilde{d_2}$ = Generic_yes $\tilde{\omega_1}$ = {< $query.departure.place$ >}

needed to create a more sensible representation of the dialogues, as the TC rate increases from 20% to 31, 5%.

Results also show the impact of the UM, as better performance is achieved when the UM behavior is constrained with the priors seen in the data. A rough 31% is achieved when the α parameter is set to 0 and the UM chooses its actions from the action set at random. However, when $\alpha = 1$ the TC metric goes up to 60, 02%. Because the frequent actions seen in the data are more likely to appear, this constraint results in a more sensible UM and manages to improve the RavenClaw baseline.

4.3   Online Learning Procedure

As described before, the online learning procedure is done in a dialogue basis, merging those unseen dialogues that are rendered valid by a quality metric QM in the DM model $\hat{M}$. In order to test the performance of the algorithm, 400000 dialogues were generated using the RS $\alpha = 1$ policy for both UM and DM and using the TC metric as QM. Note that the UM's Bi-Automata $\hat{U}$ never learns during this process. Results in Table 3 show that the proposed algorithm is capable of changing the shape and structure of the A-PFSBA model on the run, adapting its internal parameters to increase the dialogue task completion rate from 60, 02% to 69, 39%.

In addition, the evolution of the TC mean over the amount of generated dialogues and the impact of the α constraint of the UM have also been analysed. For such purpose, the TC mean was evaluated after each run of 100 generated

Table 3. Attribute and Online Learning (OL) impact on $PFSBA$.

	Nodes-DM	Edges-DM	Nodes-UM	Edges-UM	TC (%)	ADL (%)
CMU RavenClaw	—	—	—	—	54.0	32.33 ± 1.2
PFSBA $\alpha = 0$	4030	7781	4044	7652	20.08 ± 0.51	29.23 ± 0.28
A-PFSBA $\alpha = 0$	11005	14737	11058	14988	31.58 ± 1.54	31.39 ± 0.722
A-PFSBA $\alpha = 1$	11005	14737	11058	14988	$\mathbf{60.02 \pm 1.36}$	30.98 ± 0.94
A-PFSBA OL $\alpha = 1$	14700	21952	11058	14988	$\mathbf{69.39 \pm 1.34}$	31.46 ± 0.69

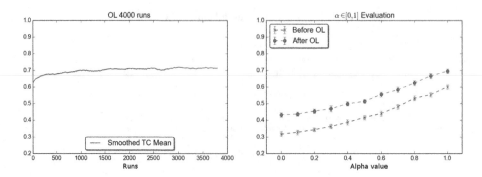

Fig. 2. Online learning impact on task completion

dialogues. The left graph of Fig. 2 depicts the TC smoothed mean over the 4000 runs. The right graph shows the mean TC score for differently constrained UM ($\alpha \in [0, 1]$) before and after the online learning process. Results demonstrate how the learning strategy converges quite rapidly after around 40 000 dialogues and that the procedure is valid for User Models with different structural constraints, where a 8–10% TC rate improvement is achieved in average.

5   Conclusions and Future Work

Throughout this paper various improvements have been proposed to previous implementations of the PFSBA. First of all, the inclusion of discrete dialogue attributes has been tested. As a consequence, the Task Completion rate has significantly increased making the generated dialogues more coherent. In addition, the inclusion of a quality metric to discriminate between successful and failed dialogues for online learning purposes has demonstrated to be a cheap-yet-effective way of controlling the learning process, as the overall improvement on the dialogue strategy is also significant. Finally, the inclusion of prior probability distributions in the User Model has shown to very significantly improve it's sensibility, demonstrating its capability to capture the user's behavior and creating a simple model to test Dialogue Managers.

Despite the promising results, the A-PFSBA is a recently proposed framework that still requires thorough experimentation and testing. As future work, we plan to explore more complex policies for the Dialog Manager, additional online learning procedures and other User Modeling techniques. The implementation of the A-PFSBA in other dialogue databases is also intended, as it is the development of an end-to-end Spoken Dialogue System.

References

1. Gorin, A.L., Riccardi, G., Wright, J.H.: How may i help you? Speech Commun. **23**(1–2), 113–127 (1997)
2. Bohus, D., Rudnicky, A.I.: The RavenClaw dialog management framework: architecture and systems. Comput. Speech Lang. **23**, 332–361 (2009)

3. Thomson, B., Yu, K., Keizer, S., Gasic, M., Jurcicek, F., Mairesse, F., Young, S.: Bayesian dialogue system for the let's go spoken dialogue challenge. In: Spoken Language Technology Workshop (SLT), pp. 460–465. IEEE (2010)

4. Hurtado, L.F., Planells, J., Segarra, E., Sanchis, E., Griol, D.: A stochastic finite-state transducer approach to spoken dialog management. In: INTERSPEECH, pp. 3002–3005 (2010)

5. Vinyals, O., Le, Q.: A Neural Conversational Model. abs/1506.05869 CoRR (2015)

6. Orozko, O.R., Torres, M.I.: Online learning of stochastic bi-automaton to model dialogues. In: Paredes, R., Cardoso, J.S., Pardo, X.M. (eds.) IbPRIA 2015. LNCS, vol. 9117, pp. 441–451. Springer, Cham (2015). doi:10.1007/978-3-319-19390-8_50

7. Raux, A., Langner, B., Bohus, D., Black, A.W., Eskenazi, M.: Let's go public! Taking a spoken dialog system to the real world. In: Proceedings of Interspeech (2005)

8. Young, S., Gasic, M., Thomson, B., Williams, D.J.: POMDP-based statistical spoken dialog systems: a review. Proc. IEEE **101**(5), 1160–1179 (2013)

9. Jurcicek, F., Thomson, B., Young, S.: Reinforcement learning for parameter estimation in statistical spoken dialogue systems. Comput. Speech Lang. **26**(3), 168–192 (2012)

10. Torres, M.I.: Stochastic bi-languages to model dialogs. In: Finite State Methods and Natural Language Processing, p. 9 (2013)

11. Torres, M.I., Benedí, J.M., Justo, R., Ghigi, F.: Modeling spoken dialog systems under the interactive pattern recognition framework. In: Gimel'farb, G., et al. (eds.) SSPR&SPR 2012. LNCS, vol. 7626, pp. 519–528. Springer, Heidelberg (2012)

12. Torres, M.I., Casacuberta, F.: Stochastic k-TSS bi-languages for machine translation. In: Proceedings of the 9th International Workshop on Finite State Models for Natural Language Processing (FSMNLP), pp. 98–106. Association for Computational Linguistics, Blois (2011)

13. Toselli, A.H., Vidal, E., Casacuberta, F. (eds.): Multimodal Interactive Pattern Recognition and Applications. Springer, Heidelberg (2011)

14. Ward, W., Issar, S.: The CMU ATIS system. In: Proceedings of ARPA Workshop on Spoken Language Technology, pp. 249–251 (1995)

15. Sutton, R.S., Barto, A.G.: Reinforcement Learning: An Introduction, vol. 1, No. 1. MIT press, Cambridge (1998)

16. Schatzmann, J., Young, S.: The hidden agenda user simulation model. IEEE Trans. Audio Speech Lang. Process. **17**(4), 733–747 (2009)

17. Schatzmann, J., Georgila, K., Young, S.: Quantitative evaluation of user simulation techniques for spoken dialogue systems. In: Proceedings of 6th SIGDIAL, pp. 45–54 (2005)

18. Williams, J.D., Zweig, G.: End-to-end LSTM-based dialog control optimized with supervised and reinforcement learning. CoRR abs/1606.01269 (2016)

19. Zhao, T., Eskenazi, M.: Towards end-to-end learning for dialog state tracking and management using deep reinforcement learning. In: Proceedings of 17th Annual Meeting of the Special Interest Group on Discourse and Dialogue, pp. 1–10 (2016)

20. Serban, I.V., et al.: Building end-to-end dialogue systems using generative hierarchical neural network. In: Proceedings of 30th conference of AAAI (2016)

Log-Linear Weight Optimization Using Discriminative Ridge Regression Method in Statistical Machine Translation

Mara Chinea-Rios[1(✉)], Germán Sanchis-Trilles[2], and Francisco Casacuberta[1]

[1] Pattern Recognition and Human Language Technology Research Center,
Universitat Politècnica de València, 46022 Valencia, Spain
{machirio, fcn}@prhlt.upv.es
[2] Sciling, Valencia, Spain
gsanchis@sciling.es

Abstract. We present a simple and reliable method for estimating the log-linear weights of a state-of-the-art machine translation system, which takes advantage of the method known as discriminative ridge regression (DRR). Since inappropriate weight estimations lead to a wide variability of translation quality results, reaching a reliable estimate for such weights is critical for machine translation research. For this reason, a variety of methods have been proposed to reach reasonable estimates. In this paper, we present an algorithmic description and empirical results proving that DRR, as applied in a pseudo-batch scenario, is able to provide comparable translation quality when compared to state-of-the-art estimation methods (i.e., MERT [1] and MIRA [2]). Moreover, the empirical results reported are coherent across different corpora and language pairs.

Keywords: Statistical Machine Translation · Log-linear model · Discriminative Ridge Regression

1 Introduction

One important breakthrough in Statistical Machine Translation (SMT) was provided by the use of log-linear models for modelling the translation process [3,4]. The log-linear models are defined as follow: given a source sentence $\mathbf{f} = f_1, \ldots, f_j, \ldots, f_J$ which is to be translated into a target sentence $\mathbf{e} = e_1, \ldots, e_i, \ldots, e_I$.

$$\hat{\mathbf{e}} = \operatorname*{argmax}_{\mathbf{e}} Pr(\mathbf{e} \mid \mathbf{f}) = \operatorname*{argmax}_{\mathbf{e}} \sum_{m=1}^{M} \lambda_m h_m(\mathbf{f}, \mathbf{e}) = \operatorname*{argmax}_{\mathbf{e}} \boldsymbol{\lambda} \cdot \mathbf{h}(\mathbf{f}, \mathbf{e}) \quad (1)$$

In this framework, we have a set of M features function $h_m(\mathbf{f}, \mathbf{e}), m = 1, \cdots, M$. For each function, there exists a weight parameter $\boldsymbol{\lambda}_m, m = 1, \cdots, M$. Common feature functions $h_m(\mathbf{f}, \mathbf{e})$ include different translation models (TM), but also distortion models or even the target language model (LM). Typically, $h(\cdot, \cdot)$ and $\boldsymbol{\lambda} = [\lambda_1, \ldots, \lambda_M]$ are estimated by means of training and development sets, respectively.

© Springer International Publishing AG 2017
L.A. Alexandre et al. (Eds.): IbPRIA 2017, LNCS 10255, pp. 32–41, 2017.
DOI: 10.1007/978-3-319-58838-4_4

The use of log-linear models implied an important break-through in SMT, allowing for a significant increase in the quality of the translations produced. The problem then arises of how to optimize the weights $\boldsymbol{\lambda}$, in other words how to find a set of weights which will offer the best translation quality. In this work, we used the Discriminative Ridge Regression [5] technique for estimating the weights of such log-linear models according to a development data set.

The main contributions of this paper are:

- We present an algorithmic description of Discriminative Ridge Regression in a batch setting, as applied to estimating the log-linear weights of a state-of-the-art.
- We evaluate empirically the DRR algorithm proposed in two different domains and with two different language pairs.
- We provide a thorough comparison with state-of-the-art $\boldsymbol{\lambda}$ estimation methods, such as Minimum Error Rate Training (MERT) [1], and batch Margin Infused Relaxed Algorithm (MIRA) [6].

The rest of this paper is structured as follows. In Sect. 2, we perform a brief review of current approaches to log-linear weight estimation in SMT. In Sect. 3, we describe the algorithmic approach for applying DDR in a batch scenario for estimating $\boldsymbol{\lambda}$. In Sect. 4, the experimental design and empirical results are detailed. Conclusions and future work are explained in Sect. 5

2   Related Work

Once the bilingual phrases have been extracted from a sentence aligned bilingual corpus, the features $\mathbf{h}$ can already be computed. However, at this point it is still necessary to obtain an appropriate value for the scaling factors $\boldsymbol{\lambda}$. The process of obtaining such a vector is often called *tuning*. To this end, numerous methods have been proposed.

The most popular approach for adjusting the scaling factors is the one proposed in [1], commonly referred to as Minimum Error Rate Training (MERT). This algorithm implements a coordinate-wise global optimisation and consists on two basic steps. However, such algorithm has an important drawback. Namely, it requires a considerable amount of time to translate the development set several times, and in addition it has been shown to be quite unstable whenever the amount of adaptation data is small [7].

Various alternatives to MERT have been proposed, motivated primarily by scalability considerations. One popular alternative is the use of margin infused MIRA [2,6] which is a perception-like online tuning algorithm with passive-aggressive updates. Tellingly, in the entire proceedings of ACL 2015[1], only one paper describing a statistical MT system cited the use of MIRA for tuning [8], while the others used MERT.

Alternatively, [9] proposed to view the problem as a ranking problem (PRO), where each step of the tuning procedure consists in deciding whether a given

---

[1] www.aclweb.org/anthology/P/P15/.

translation hypothesis should be ranked lower or higher within the set of possible hypotheses that are provided by the search procedure.

3   Discriminative Rigde Regression for SMT

In this section, the Discriminative Ridge Regression method is for estimating λ is reviewed. DRR was proposed by [5], uses the concept of ridge regression technique to develop a discriminative algorithm for estimating λ online, i.e., as new adaptation samples are introduced into the system. The key idea is to find a configuration of the weight vectors using all the hypotheses within a given N-best list, so that good hypothesis are rewarded, and bad hypothesis are penalised, trying to narrow the correlation between the score function σ, and the quality criterion used. Since DRR was proposed for an online computer-assisted translation scenario, it requires an N-best list of hypotheses for each one of the sentences that are evaluated by the professional translator post-editing the system's output. Algorithm 1 shows the procedure. Here, $A = \{\mathbf{f}1, \ldots, \mathbf{f}_s, \ldots, \mathbf{f}_S\}$ is a bilingual development corpus, S is the number of sentences in A and $s \in S$, and I is the maximum number of epochs desired.

Data: Development corpus A
Result: λ
Initialize: λ^0;
forall *desired number of iterations I* **do**
    forall *number sentences in dev-corpus $S = |A|$* **do**
        optimization: compute gradient vector $\check{\lambda}_i^s$;
        estimation: $\lambda_i^s = (1 - \alpha)\lambda_i^{s-1} + \alpha\check{\lambda}_i^s$;
    end
end
    selection: output vector λ_I^S

Algorithm 1: Pseudo-code for DRR estimating λ as described in Sect. 3

During the **optimization** step, we obtain the gradient vector $\check{\lambda}$ for each one of the development sentences a_s. Within DRR, this optimisation is performed by computing the solution to an overdetermined system, described in detail in next section, so that changes in the scoring function σ are correlated to changes in the objective function (potentially BLEU).

3.1   Sentence-Based Optimisation in DRR

As exposed in the previous section, DRR obtains λ based on obtaining the best log-gradient vector for each one of the sentences of a development corpus. In order to compute the new log-linear weight vector λ^s, the previously learned λ^{s-1} needs to be combined with an appropriate update step $\check{\lambda}^s$. The aim is to compute an appropriate update term λ^s that best fits the translation search space (approximated as an n-best list) of the development sentence pair observed at s. This is often done as a linear combination [10], where $\boldsymbol{\lambda}^s = (1-\alpha)\boldsymbol{\lambda}^{s-1}+\alpha\check{\boldsymbol{\lambda}}^s$ for a certain learning learning rate α. Let n-best$(\mathbf{f})$ be such a list computed by our models for sentence $\mathbf{f}$. To obtain $\check{\boldsymbol{\lambda}}^s$, we define an $N \times M$ matrix $H_{\mathbf{f}}$ that contains the feature functions $\mathbf{h}$ of every hypothesis, where M is the number of features in Eq. 1, and N is the size of n-best$(\mathbf{f})$.

$$H_{\mathbf{f}} = [\mathbf{h}(\mathbf{f}, \mathbf{e}_1), \ldots, \mathbf{h}(\mathbf{f}, \mathbf{e}_N)]' \tag{2}$$

Additionally, let $H_{\mathbf{f}}^*$ be a matrix such that

$$H_{\mathbf{f}}^* = [\mathbf{h}(\mathbf{f}, \mathbf{e}^*), \ldots, \mathbf{h}(\mathbf{f}, \mathbf{e}^*)] \tag{3}$$

where all rows are identical and equal to the feature vector of the best hypothesis $\mathbf{e}^*$ within the n-best list. Then, $R_{\mathbf{f}}$ is defined as: $R_{\mathbf{f}} = H_{\mathbf{f}}^* - H_{\mathbf{f}}$.

The key idea is to find a vector $\check{\boldsymbol{\lambda}}$ such that differences in scores are reflected as differences in the quality of the hypotheses. That is $R_{\mathbf{f}} \cdot \check{\boldsymbol{\lambda}} \propto \mathbf{l}_{\mathbf{f}}$ where $\mathbf{l}_{\mathbf{f}}$ is a column vector of N rows such that:

$$\mathbf{l}_{\mathbf{f}} = [l(\mathbf{e}_1), ..., l(\mathbf{e}_n), ..., l(\mathbf{e}_N)]', \forall \mathbf{e} \in \text{nbest}(\mathbf{f}) \tag{4}$$

The objective is to find $\check{\boldsymbol{\lambda}}^s$ such that:

$$\check{\boldsymbol{\lambda}}^s = \underset{\lambda}{\text{argmin}} |\mathbf{R}_{\mathbf{f}} \cdot \boldsymbol{\lambda} - \mathbf{l}_{\mathbf{f}}| = \underset{\lambda}{\text{argmin}} ||\mathbf{R}_{\mathbf{f}} \cdot \boldsymbol{\lambda} - \mathbf{l}_{\mathbf{f}}||^2 \tag{5}$$

where $|| \cdot ||^2$ is the Euclidean norm. Although 5 is equivalent (i.e., the $\check{\boldsymbol{\lambda}}^s$ that minimizes the first one also minimizes the second one), Eq. 5 allows for a direct implementation thanks to the ridge regression. $\check{\boldsymbol{\lambda}}^s$ can be computed as the solution to the overdetermined system $R_{\mathbf{f}} \cdot \check{\boldsymbol{\lambda}}^s = \mathbf{l}_{\mathbf{f}}$, which is given by

$$\check{\boldsymbol{\lambda}}^s = (\mathbf{R}_{\mathbf{f}}' \cdot \mathbf{R}_{\mathbf{f}} + \beta \mathbf{I})^{-1} \cdot \mathbf{l}_{\mathbf{f}} \tag{6}$$

where a small β is used as a regularization term to stabilize $R_{\mathbf{x}}' \cdot R_{\mathbf{x}}$ and to ensure that it is invertible.

$$H_{\mathbf{f}_s} \leftarrow [\mathbf{h}(\mathbf{f}_s, \mathbf{e}_{s,1}), \ldots, \mathbf{h}(\mathbf{f}_s, \mathbf{e}_{s,N})]', \forall \mathbf{e}_{s,i} \in \text{nbest}(\mathbf{f}_s)$$

Algorithm 2 shows the pseudo-code for obtain $\check{\boldsymbol{\lambda}}^s$. In this work, we apply the original DRR approach proposed by [5] to a batch scenario, so that the method proposed is effectively able to compete with state-of-the-art $\boldsymbol{\lambda}$ estimation approaches. In this case, DRR obtains an estimation of $\boldsymbol{\lambda}$ by previously adjusting the $\boldsymbol{\lambda}$ vector to each one of the sentences in a development corpus, i.e., the optimal $\boldsymbol{\lambda}$ is computed after performing a complete epoch on the development set.

for *each of the sentences* $\mathbf{f}_s$ *in* A **do**

$\quad H_{\mathbf{f}_s} \leftarrow [\mathbf{h}(\mathbf{f}_s, \mathbf{e}_{s,1}), \dots, \mathbf{h}(\mathbf{f}_s, \mathbf{e}_{s,N})]'$, $\forall \mathbf{e}_{s,i} \epsilon$ nbest($\mathbf{f_s}$) ;

$\quad H^*_{\mathbf{f}_s} \leftarrow [\mathbf{h}(\mathbf{f}_s, \mathbf{e}^*_s), \dots, \mathbf{h}(\mathbf{f}_s, \mathbf{e}^*_s)]'$;

$\quad R_{\mathbf{f}_s} \leftarrow H_{\mathbf{f}^*_s} - H_{\mathbf{f}_s}$;

$\quad \check{\boldsymbol{\lambda}}_s \leftarrow (\mathbf{R}'_{\mathbf{f}_s} \cdot \mathbf{R}_{\mathbf{f}_s} + \beta \mathbf{I})^{-1} \cdot \mathbf{l}_{\mathbf{f}_s}$;

$\quad \boldsymbol{\lambda}^s \leftarrow (1 - \alpha) \boldsymbol{\lambda}^{s-1} + \alpha \check{\boldsymbol{\lambda}}^s$

end

Algorithm 2: Pseudo-code for computing the vector $\boldsymbol{\lambda}^s$ as described in Sect. 3.1

4   Experiments

In this section, we describe the experimental framework employed. Then, we show a comparative by our strategy with two optimization methods (MERT and MIRA).

4.1   Experimental Setup

All experiments were carried out using the SMT toolkit Moses [11]. The LM used was a 5-gram, with modified Kneser-Ney smoothing [12], built with the SRILM toolkit [13]. The phrase table was obtained with GIZA++ [3].

Translation quality was assessed by means of the BLEU [14]. BLEU measures n-gram precision with a penalty for sentences that are too short. However, it must be noted that BLEU is not well defined at the sentence level, since it implements a geometrical average of n-gram counts which is zero whenever there is no common 4-gram between reference and hypothesis, even if the reference has only three words. In our experiments, we used the *smoothed* BLEU approximation in [15] to calculate sentence-level BLEU. Note that the original work by [5] applied DRR to optimise TER scores [16], ignoring the problem of BLEU not being well defined at the sentence level. In this work we favour the use of BLEU because of its wider acceptance in the SMT community.

For each corpus, we trained baseline systems with which to compare the systems. This baseline was obtained by training the SMT system without tuning process obtaining the `baseline-emea` and `baseline-nc`. Since optimization methods require a random initialisation of $\boldsymbol{\lambda}$ that often lead to different local optima being reached, every point in each plot of this paper constitutes the average of 10 repetitions with 95% confidence intervals, with the purpose of providing robustness to the results.

DRR has different parameters that affect the experimental result, the most critical one being α. We conducted experiments with different α. Another meta-parameter is the regularization term β, which was fixed to 0.02 according to the work in [5]. The initial weight λ^0 used by our method was obtained using Moses random method.

4.2   Corpora

The experiments conducted in this paper were carried out on two different corpora (EMEA and NewComentary). The EMEA[2] corpus [17] contains documents from the European Medicines Agency. The News Commentary[3] (NC) corpus [18] is composed of translations of news articles. We focused on the English-French (Fr-En) and German-English (De-En) language pairs. Table 1 shows the main figures of the corpora.

4.3   Comparison Between DRR and MERT and MIRA

We compare our method with MERT and MIRA. We study the effect of increasing the number of development samples made available to the system. Figures 1

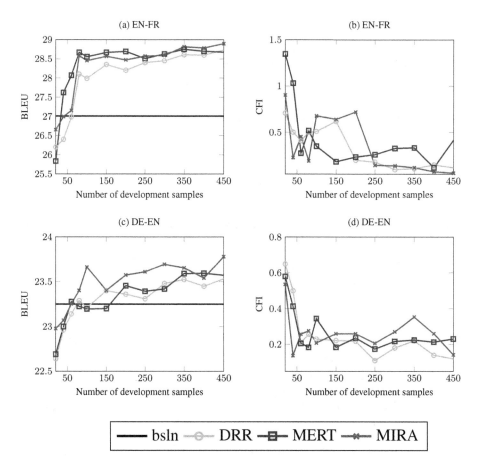

Fig. 1. Performance comparison across the corpus EMEA with different language pairs analysed. The two plots on the left display BLEU, while two plots on the right display the confidence intervals.

[2] www.opus.lingfil.uu.se/EMEA.php.

[3] www.statmt.org/wmt13.

Table 1. Main figures of the corpora. Train is the training set, Dev is development set, and Test is the test data. M denotes millions of elements and k thousands of elements, $|S|$ for number of sentences, $|W|$ for number of words and $|V|$ for vocabulary size.

Corpus	$|S|$	$|W|$	$|V|$	Corpus	$|S|$	$|W|$	$|V|$
EMEA-Train	1.0M	12.1M	98.1k	NC-Train	120k	2.4M	27.6k
		14.1M	112k			2.8M	33.7k
EMEA-Test	1000	21.4k	1.8k	NC-Test	3000	56k	4.8k
		26.9k	1.9k			61k	5.0k
EMEA-Dev	501	9850	979	NC-Dev	1600	43k	3.9k
		11.6k	1.0k			47k	4.1k

Table 2. Summary of the best result obtained for each corpus and language.

Corpus	Strategy	EN-FR BLEU	DE-EN BLEU
EMEA	MERT	28.7 ± 0.3	23.5 ± 0.2
	MIRA	28.9 ± 0.2	23.7 ± 0.1
	DRR	28.8 ± 0.2	23.6 ± 0.1
NC	MERT	18.4 ± 0.2	19.3 ± 0.2
	MIRA	18.6 ± 0.2	19.3 ± 0.1
	DRR	18.5 ± 0.1	19.2 ± 0.1

and 2 show the effect of adding sentences to development corpus and confidence intervals. These results show the quality translations in BLEU terms of each test corpus (EMEA-Test and NC-Test). Confidence intervals are displayed in different plots, instead of using error bars, because otherwise the translation quality plots would present vertical lines across the complete plot, rendering it unreadable. We only show results for the best learning rate α for clarity and the best configuration obtain to MERT and MIRA. Figure 1 shows the principal result obtained using the EMEA corpus.

- Results obtained with our DRR method are similar than the ones obtained with MIRA and MERT. Behavior DRR results is increase when the amount of development corpus larger.
- Confidence interval sizes are shown in Figs. 1b and d. Our DRR technique have a behaviour more stable that the MERT and MIRA that that shown more instability.

Figure 2 shows the principal result obtained using the NC corpus.

- Increase the number of adaptation sample all the method obtain similar results, buy we can see MERT and MIRA are only to able to yield improvements when provided with at least 500 (MERT) and 200 (MIRA) development sample displaying a very chaotic behaviour until these point.

– Confidence interval sizes are shown in Figs. 2b and d. MERT and MIRA yields large confidence intervals (as large as 3 BLEU points for less than 100 samples), turning a bit more stable from that point on, where the size of the confidence interval converges slowly to 0.5 BLEU point. In contrast, our DRR technique yields small confidence intervals, about 1 BLEU point in the worst case. This is worth emphasising, since estimating Λ by means of MERT or MIRA when very few development data is available may improve the final translation quality, but may also degrade it to a much larger extent. In contrast, our DRR technique shows stable and reliable improvements from the very beginning.

Table 2 shows the best results in terms of BLEU achieved by the three methods, i.e., DRR, MERT and MIRA. As shown, our method is able to yield competitive

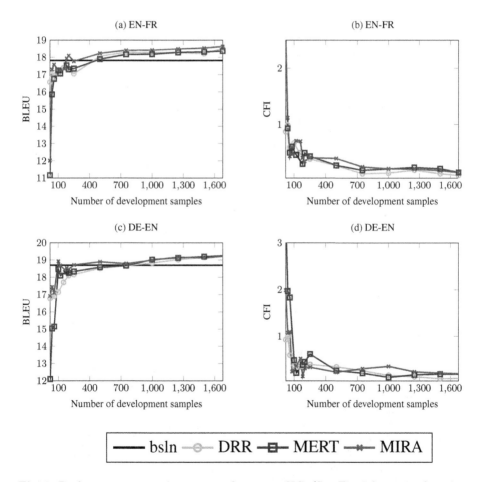

Fig. 2. Performance comparison across the corpus NC. (See Fig. 1 for an explanation of the figures.)

results in all scenarios considered. We understand that is important, since it proves the competitiveness of our proposal in this task, with respect to the other techniques state-of-the-art.

5 Conclusion and Future Work

We have proposed a simple technique for log-linear weight optimization an SMT system based in discriminative ridge regression method that is on par with the leading techniques, exhibits reliable behaviour and is remarkably easy to implement and use. We have demonstrated, via an empirical experiments, that our DRR method obtain comparable result than MERT and MIRA. In future work, we will carry out new experiments with large amounts of corpus, and languages diversity.

Acknowledgement. The research leading to these results has received funding from the Generalitat Valenciana under grant PROMETEOII/2014/030 and the FPI (2014) grant by Universitat Politècnica de València.

References

1. Och, F.J.: Minimum error rate training in statistical machine translation. In: Proceedings of ACL, pp. 160–167 (2003)
2. Crammer, K., Dekel, O., Keshet, J., Shalev-Shwartz, S., Singer, Y.: Online passive-aggressive algorithms. J. Mach. Learn. Res. **7**, 551–585 (2006)
3. Och, F.J., Ney, H.: A systematic comparison of various statistical alignmentbreak models. Comput. Linguist. **29**, 19–51 (2003)
4. Koehn, P.: Statistical Machine Translation. Cambridge University Press, Cambridge (2010)
5. Martínez-Gómez, P., Sanchis-Trilles, G., Casacuberta, F.: Online adaptation strategies for statistical machine translation in post-editing scenarios. Pattern Recogn. **45**(9), 3193–3203 (2012)
6. Cherry, C., Foster, G.: Batch tuning strategies for statistical machine translation. In: Proceedings of NAACL, pp. 427–436 (2012)
7. Sanchis-Trilles, G., Casacuberta, F.: Log-linear weight optimisation via Bayesian adaptation in statistical machine translation. In: Proceedings of ACL, pp. 1077–1085 (2010)
8. Marie, B., Max, A.: Multi-pass decoding with complex feature guidance for statistical machine translation. In: Proceedings of ACL, pp. 554–559 (2015)
9. Hopkins, M., May, J.: Tuning as ranking. In: Proceedings of EMNLP, pp. 1352–1362 (2011)
10. Stauffer, C., Grimson, W.E.L.: Learning patterns of activity using real-time tracking. Pattern Anal. Mach. Intell. **22**(8), 747–757 (2000)
11. Koehn, P., Hoang, H., Birch, A., Callison-Burch, C., Federico, M., Bertoldi, N., Cowan, B., Shen, W., Moran, C., Zens, R., Dyer, C., Bojar, O., Constantin, A., Herbst, E.: Moses: open source toolkit for statistical machine translation. In: Proceedings of ACL, pp. 177–180 (2007)
12. Kneser, R., Ney, H.: Improved backing-off for m-gram language modeling. In: Proceedings of ICASSP, pp. 181–184 (1995)

13. Stolcke, A.: Srilm-an extensible language modeling toolkit. In: Proceedings of ICSLP, pp. 901–904 (2002)
14. Papineni, K., Roukos, S., Ward, T., Zhu, W.-J.: BLEU: a method for automatic evaluation of machine translation. In: Proceedings of ACL, pp. 311–318 (2002)
15. Chen, B., Cherry, C.: A systematic comparison of smoothing techniques for sentence-level BLEU. In: Proceedings of WMT, pp. 362–367 (2014)
16. Snover, M., Dorr, B.J., Schwartz, R., Micciulla, L., Makhoul, J.: A study of translation edit rate with targeted human annotation. In: Proceedings of AMTA, pp. 223–231 (2006)
17. Tiedemann, J.: News from opus-a collection of multilingual parallel corpora with tools and interfaces. In: Proceedings of RANLP, pp. 237–248 (2009)
18. Tiedemann, J.: Parallel data, tools and interfaces in opus. In: Proceedings of LREC, pp. 2214–2218 (2012)

Deep Convolutional Neural Networks and Maximum-Likelihood Principle in Approximate Nearest Neighbor Search

Andrey V. Savchenko[✉]

Laboratory of Algorithms and Technologies for Network Analysis,
National Research University Higher School of Economics,
Nizhny Novgorod, Russia
avsavchenko@hse.ru

Abstract. Deep convolutional neural networks are widely used to extract high-dimensional features in various image recognition tasks. If the count of classes is relatively large, performance of the classifier for such features can be insufficient to be implemented in real-time applications, e.g., in video-based recognition. In this paper we propose the novel approximate nearest neighbor algorithm, which sequentially chooses the next instance from the database, which corresponds to the maximal likelihood (joint density) of distances to previously checked instances. The Gaussian approximation of the distribution of dissimilarity measure is used to estimate this likelihood. Experimental study results in face identification with LFW and YTF datasets are presented. It is shown that the proposed algorithm is much faster than an exhaustive search and several known approximate nearest neighbor methods.

Keywords: Statistical pattern recognition · Approximate nearest neighbor · Image recognition · Deep learning · Convolutional neural networks

1 Introduction

In image recognition task it is required to assign an observed image X to one of $C > 1$ classes. The classes are specified by the training set of $R \geq C$ instances X_r, $r \in \{1, \ldots, R\}$. At first, each image should be described with a feature vector. Nowadays feature extraction is typically implemented with the deep convolutional neural network (CNN) [1, 2]. The CNN is trained with an external large dataset, e.g., ImageNet or Casia WebFaces [2, 3]. The outputs of the CNN's last layer for the input image X and each r-th reference image are used as the D-dimensional feature vectors $\mathbf{x}$ and $\mathbf{x}_r$, respectively. After that, conventional machine learning techniques, e.g., support vector machines (SVM) are applied for these features to recognize image X.

It is known that the count of images for each class is too low to train a complex classifier in many practical tasks. In this small-sample-size case ($R \approx C$) an appropriate dissimilarity measure $\rho(\mathbf{x}, \mathbf{x}_r)$, e.g. Euclidean distance, is chosen, and the nearest neighbor (NN) methods can be applied [4]. The run-time complexity of the NN classifier is as follows: $O(D \cdot R)$. As the dimension size D is usually rather high (256…4096), this method cannot be implemented in real-time, if the count of different classes C

© Springer International Publishing AG 2017
L.A. Alexandre et al. (Eds.): IbPRIA 2017, LNCS 10255, pp. 42–49, 2017.
DOI: 10.1007/978-3-319-58838-4_5

(and, hence, the training set size R) is large [1]. To speed-up the recognition procedure, one can apply an appropriate approximate NN algorithm [5, 6], e.g., randomized k-d tree [7], variants of Locality-Sensitive Hashing [8], permutation-based methods [1, 9], etc. In the paper [10] we have recently proposed the maximum-likelihood approximate NN (ML-ANN) method. It is characterized by superior performance in image recognition with conventional HOG features, when the training set contains thousands of classes, i.e., the database is not very large. The ML-ANN method can be used only in statistical image recognition, i.e., with the NN rule and probabilistic dissimilarity measure (Kullback-Leibler divergence, Jensen-Shannon divergence, chi-squared distance, etc.). Thus, it is important to explore the possibilities of the ML-ANN applied with the widely used distances between CNN features.

The rest of the paper is organized as follows. In Sect. 2 we propose a modification of the ML-ANN method, which can be applied with a wide class of dissimilarity measures and high-dimensional features extracted by deep CNN. In Sect. 3 experimental results are presented in face recognition with Labeled Faces in the Wild (LFW) and YouTube Faces (YTF) datasets. Finally, concluding comments are discussed in Sect. 4.

2 Proposed Algorithm

To speed up the recognition procedure, we convert the NN criterion to a simplified form of range query [10]:

$$W_v : \rho(\mathbf{x}, \mathbf{x}_v) < \rho_0. \tag{1}$$

In fact, this formula defines the termination condition of the approximate NN method. Instead of looking for the closest instance with the brute force, we search for the first reference image with rather small distance to the observed image.

If the false-accept rate (FAR) β is fixed, then the threshold ρ_0 can be evaluated as a β-quantile of the distances between images from distinct classes [4]. This procedure requires quadratic run-time complexity to estimate the distances between all reference images. Hence, we will use the standard technique for approximate NN in medium-sized databases [9, 10]. Namely, $P \ll R$ instances (pivots) $\{X_{r_1}, \ldots, X_{r_P}\}$ are chosen. The pivots are typically incrementally selected [9] by using, e.g., the following farthest-first traversal procedure [10]. The first pivot X_{r_1} is chosen randomly. The distances between this pivot and all other reference images are computed, and the most distant instance is selected as the second pivot. The procedure is repeated so that every pivot is the farthest reference instance to all previous pivots:

$$r_{i+1} = \operatorname*{argmax}_{r \in \{1,\ldots,R\} - \{r_1,\ldots,r_i\}} \sum_{j=1}^{i} \rho(\mathbf{x}_r, \mathbf{x}_{r_j}), i \in \{1, \ldots, P-1\}, \tag{2}$$

Next, the distances between these pivots and all reference images $\rho_{r,p} = \rho(\mathbf{x}_r, \mathbf{x}_{r_p})$, $p \in \{1, \ldots, P\}$, $r \in \{1, \ldots, R\}$ are computed. Finally, threshold in (1) is estimated as β-quantile of the sequence $\{\rho_{r,p}\}$.

At first stage of the pivot-based approximate NN methods [1, 9] the distances between input image $\mathbf{x}$ and all P pivots are computed. If one of them satisfies the condition (1), the search is terminated, and the label of the corresponding pivot is returned as an approximate solution. Otherwise, it is necessary to choose the sequence (order) of other instances, which should be matched with the observed image. If the image recognition is considered as a testing of statistical hypothesis W_r, $r \in \{1, \ldots, R\}$ about distribution of feature vector $\mathbf{x}$, we can use the idea of our ML-ANN method and look for the instance, which maximizes the likelihood of previously computed distances:

$$\max_{v \in \{1, \ldots, R\} - \{r_1, \ldots, r_P\}} \prod_{p=1}^{P} f\left(\rho\left(\mathbf{x}, \mathbf{x}_{r_p}\right) \middle| W_v\right), \tag{3}$$

where $f\left(\rho\left(\mathbf{x}, \mathbf{x}_{r_p}\right) \middle| W_v\right)$ is the conditional distribution of the distance between p-th pivot and the input image given the correct nearest instance is $\mathbf{x}_v$.

In the previous paper [10] we used the maximum likelihood criterion to estimate the images similarities. Hence, we could apply the non-central chi-squared distribution of this distance to estimate the conditional distributions in (2). On the contrary, in this paper we use more common dissimilarity measures $\rho(\mathbf{x}, \mathbf{x}_r)$, which can be computed as a sum of identical distances between corresponding features. As the dimensionality D of features is high, it is possible to approximate the probability density of $\rho(\mathbf{x}, \mathbf{x}_r)$ with the Gaussian distribution [11, 12]. Namely, we use a simple assumption that the conditional distribution of the distance $f\left(\rho\left(\mathbf{x}, \mathbf{x}_{r_p}\right) \middle| W_v\right)$ given hypothesis W_v is normal with the mean $\rho_{v,p}$ and unknown variance σ^2. It was empirically demonstrated that the variation of the distances between high dimensional vectors is approximately equal [12]. Hence, for simplicity, we will further assume that the variance does not depend on the correct nearest neighbor. In this case, the conditional distribution in (3) is estimated as follows:

$$f\left(\rho\left(\mathbf{x}, \mathbf{x}_{r_p}\right) \middle| W_v\right) = \frac{1}{\sqrt{2\pi\sigma^2}} \exp\left[-\left(\rho\left(\mathbf{x}, \mathbf{x}_{r_p}\right) - \rho_{v,p}\right)^2 / \sigma^2\right]. \tag{4}$$

It is easy to demonstrate by simple substitution of this equation to criterion (3), that the latter is equivalent to minimizing the following expression:

$$\varphi_{\Sigma;v} = \sum_{p=1}^{P} \left(\rho\left(\mathbf{x}, \mathbf{x}_{r_p}\right) - \rho_{v,p}\right)^2, \tag{5}$$

The proposed algorithm is summarized in Table 1. The memory complexity of this algorithm is linear: $O(PR)$. The run-time complexity is determined by the maximal count $E_{\max}$ of instances to check. If the distance calculation complexity is proportional to the features dimensionality, then the worst-case computation complexity of our algorithm is defined by $O(R\log(E_{max} - P) + E_{max} \cdot D)$. However, in general situations the performance should be much higher due to the primarily exploration of the most probable instances (3). The next section experimentally supports this statement.

Table 1. Proposed approximate NN algorithm for high-dimensional deep CNN features

---

Data: an observed image X, reference database of features $\{\mathbf{x}_r\}$

Output: identifier v^* of the reference image, which is either the nearest neighbor of X, or satisfies the condition (1), or the count of distance computations exceeds E_{max}

1.   Extract features $\mathbf{x}$ of observed image from the output of one of the last layers of CNN

2.   Assign $v^* := r_1$, $k := P+1$

3.   For each pivot $p \in \{1,...,P\}$

    3.1.   Compute the distance $\rho\left(\mathbf{x}, \mathbf{x}_{r_p}\right)$

    3.2.   If $\rho\left(\mathbf{x}, \mathbf{x}_{r_p}\right) < \rho\left(\mathbf{x}, \mathbf{x}_{v^*}\right)$, then

        3.2.1.   Assign $v^* := r_p$.

4.   For each $v \in \{1,...,R\} - \{r_1,...,r_p\}$ repeat

    4.1.   Assign $\varphi_{\Sigma;v} := 0$

    4.2.   For each $p \in \{1,...,P\}$ repeat

        4.2.1.   Assign $\varphi_{\Sigma;v} := \varphi_{\Sigma;v} + \left(\rho\left(\mathbf{x}, \mathbf{x}_{r_p}\right) - \rho_{v,p}\right)^2$

5.   Partial sort the array $\{\varphi_{\Sigma;v}\}$ in ascending order and extract $E_{max} - P$ smallest elements. Obtain the identifiers of the corresponding reference instances $\{r_i\}, i \in \{P+1,...,R\}$ so that $\varphi_{\Sigma;r_i} \leq \varphi_{\Sigma;r_j}$ for all $i \leq j$.

6.   While $\rho\left(\mathbf{x}, \mathbf{x}_{v^*}\right) \geq \rho_0$ AND $k < E_{max}$, repeat

    6.1.   If $\rho\left(\mathbf{x}, \mathbf{x}_{r_k}\right) < \rho\left(\mathbf{x}, \mathbf{x}_{v^*}\right)$, then

        6.1.1.   Assign $v^* := r_k$.

    6.2.   Assign $k := k+1$

7.   Return the v^*-th image as an approximate NN

---

3   Experimental Results

Our experimental study is focused on unconstrained face identification with the medium-sized database [13]. The Caffe framework is applied to extract image features. We used two CNN models, namely, the well-known VGG-13 Network [2], and the Lightened CNN [3]. The VGGNet is trained from scratch using over 2.5 million images of celebrities collected from the web and extracts $D = 4096$ non-negative features from 224×224 RGB image. We fine-tuned the Lightened CNN-B [3] with the Casia Web-Face dataset, which allowed increasing the face identification accuracy by 1.5 – 2.5% for LFW and PubFig 83 datasets when compared with the original Lightened CNN [3]. The resulted CNN[1] extracts $D = 256$ features from 128×128 grayscale image. The outputs of the CNNs were L_2 normalized to form the final feature vectors, which are matched using Euclidean distance. The features in the VGGNet are positive, hence we also perform L_1 normalization to treat them as the probability distributions and match them using the chi-squared distance.

The proposed algorithm (Table 1) is compared with the OpenCV's version of the traditional linear SVM, exhaustive search of the nearest reference image, original pivot-based ML-ANN [10], and the known approximate NN methods, namely, randomized kd-tree [7] with 4 trees from FLANN library [5] and the pivot-based ordering permutations (Projection incremental sort) method [9] from NMSLIB (Non-Metric Space Library) [6]. We estimated the 1-error rate $\bar{\alpha}$ (%) and the average time $\bar{t}$ (ms.) to recognize one image on a MacBook Pro 2015 laptop (2.2 GHz Intel Core i7, 16 Gb RAM) and g++ 4.2 compiler and optimization by speed. The source code is freely available[2] in order to make it easy to replicate all our experiments.

The parameters of all methods were tuned using an extra PubFig 83 dataset. To obtain threshold $\rho_0(1)$, FAR $\beta = 1\%$. The count of pivots P in our method and in the ordering permutations is set to 1.5% of the size R of the training set.

In the first experiment we take $C = 1680$ persons from the LFW dataset with two or more photos. The resulted dataset contains 9034 facial photos of these persons. The following cross-validation procedure is used. At first, the whole dataset is 50/50 randomly split into the training and test sets so that at least one photo of each person is put in both sets. If the count of photos of a person is odd, then the training set will contain 1 more photo of this person, than the testing set. As a result, the training set size R is equal to 4857, and the test set contains other 4177 images. Then we estimated the performance of identification of all images form the test set. Finally, we computed the mean and the standard deviation of the error rate and recognition time for this experiment repeated 10 times (see Table 2).

Here, firstly, the traditional one-vs-all implementation of SVM is not suitable for recognition with many classes and low count of images per class. Secondly, the usage of conventional approximate NN methods can cause the dramatic improvements (in 2 – 14 times) of recognition performance, especially for very high-dimensional features from the VGGNet. However, randomized k-d tree is not so fast as other methods for the

---

[1] https://github.com/HSE-asavchenko/HSE_FaceRec/tree/master/src/caffe_models.

[2] https://github.com/HSE-asavchenko/HSE_FaceRec/tree/master/src/recognition_testing.

Table 2. Face identification results, LFW dataset

	VGGNet				Lightened CNN	
	Euclidean distance		Chi-squared distance		Euclidean distance	
	$\bar{\alpha}$ [%]	$\bar{t}$ [ms]	$\bar{\alpha}$ [%]	$\bar{t}$ [ms]	$\bar{\alpha}$ [%]	$\bar{t}$ [ms]
SVM	49.6 ± 1.2	3356.2 ± 5.2	–	–	28.9 ± 1.1	214.3 ± 2.7
NN, brute force	10.7 ± 0.3	19.49 ± 0.02	10.2 ± 0.3	54.50 ± 0.02	9.6 ± 0.2	1.25 ± 0.01
Randomized k-d tree [7]	11.0 ± 0.3	3.23 ± 0.03	10.6 ± 0.3	7.77 ± 0.05	9.9 ± 0.3	0.48 ± 0.04
Ordering permutations [9]	10.9 ± 0.3	1.79 ± 0.11	10.6 ± 0.4	3.79 ± 0.15	9.9 ± 0.4	0.63 ± 0.03
ML-ANN [10]	10.9 ± 0.4	1.65 ± 0.16	10.6 ± 0.3	1.78 ± 0.17	10.5 ± 0.4	0.81 ± 0.03
Proposed algorithm	10.9 ± 0.3	1.04 ± 0.13	10.5 ± 0.4	1.52 ± 0.14	9.9 ± 0.4	0.35 ± 0.02

chi-squared distance. This experimental observation emphasizes the need of k-d trees for a dissimilarity measure, which satisfies the triangle inequality property. Thirdly, the lightened CNN is more preferable in this particular task due to the lower error rate and run-time complexity when compared to the VGGNet. Fourthly, the maximal likelihood search in the ML-ANN provides the best performance among the known methods for high-dimensional data (VGGNet), but its implementation in the pivot ML-ANN [10] includes quite costly additional computations. Hence, it is the worst choice for Euclidean distance and 256 features from the Lightened CNN [3]. However, the proposed algorithm (Table 1) is extremely efficient. It is 3.5 – 35-times faster, than the brute force. Moreover, its performance is 1.6 – 2.3-times higher, than the original ML-ANN for Euclidean distances. At the same time, both methods have comparable speed for the chi-squared distance. It is not surprisingly, because the ML-ANN was specially developed for dissimilarity measures, which are used to match probability densities. However, our algorithm is slightly faster even in this case due to the very simple extra computations of expression (5). Thus, the proposed algorithm is the most reasonable choice to speed-up the image recognition for high-dimensional deep CNN features.

In the next experiment we deal with the still-to-still video-based face identification from YTF dataset. As practically all persons from this database appear in the LFW, we decided to solve the most challenging task. Namely, we choose all photos and videos of $C = 1589$ classes as the intersection of people from LFW and YTF. The training set contains all $R = 4732$ photos of these persons taken from LFW dataset. The test set consists of all their 122756 video frames from YTF. The error rates for such setup are presented in Table 3. To compare performance of the approximate NN algorithms, we launched this experiment 10 times. The mean and standard deviation of the recognition time are also shown in this table.

These results are very similar to the results of the first experiment (Table 2). An exhaustive search of the NN instance is the most accurate, but very inefficient recognition method. For example, the proposed algorithm makes it possible to speed up the video recognition in 3 – 12 times. Moreover, our procedure is in most cases the fastest way to find rather accurate solution. For example, its performance is 1.5 – 3-times

Table 3. Video-based face identification results, YTF dataset

	VGGNet				Lightened CNN	
	Euclidean distance		Chi-squared distance		Euclidean distance	
	$\bar{\alpha}$ [%]	$\bar{t}$ [ms]	$\bar{\alpha}$ [%]	$\bar{t}$ [ms]	$\bar{\alpha}$ [%]	$\bar{t}$ [ms]
SVM	87.1	2615.7 ± 4.7	–	–	82.5	201.5 ± 4.5
Brute force	59.6	18.47 ± 0.02	59.4	56.1 ± 0.02	53.1	1.26 ± 0.01
Randomized k-d tree	59.9	4.36 ± 0.03	60.7	47.01 ± 0.11	53.5	0.47 ± 0.02
Ordering permutations	59.7	3.26 ± 0.03	59.8	12.98 ± 0.31	53.5	0.52 ± 0.01
ML-ANN	59.7	2.22 ± 0.02	59.4	8.56 ± 0.26	53.6	0.65 ± 0.02
Proposed algorithm	59.7	1.43 ± 0.03	59.4	8.95 ± 0.28	53.6	0.39 ± 0.01

better for VGGNet features and Euclidean distance. However, in this experiment the ML-ANN based on the properties of distances between probabilistic distributions [10] is slightly faster, than our algorithm for the chi-squared distance.

4   Conclusion

In this paper we proposed the novel approximate NN algorithm (Table 1) for high-dimensional features from the outputs of the deep CNNs based on statistical approach (3). We used the pivot selection techniques (2) to efficiently implement this procedure with the linear memory space complexity. The proposed algorithm is an optimal (maximum likelihood) greedy method in terms of the count of distance cal-culations for the normally distributed dissimilarity measures, e.g., the sum of identical distances between corresponding features. The experimental results have clearly demonstrated the potential of our approach in real-time face identification for either traditional VGGNet [2] or our implementation of the Lightened CNN [3].

The main direction for further research of the proposed algorithm is its applications with more accurate approximation of the distance probability distributions, e.g., the usage of different variances in (4), or the usage of the more appropriate Weibull distribution [11]. As our approach was evaluated with two rather small datasets, it is necessary to analyze effects using other, much larger datasets (Casia Web-Face, MS-Celeb-1 M, etc.). It is also important to explore the sensitivity of the proposed algorithm to the choice of its parameters, namely the count of pivots P and the distance threshold (1). Finally, it is necessary to use our approach with just released (C) variant of the Lightened CNN trained on MS-Celeb-1 M database.

Acknowledgements. The work is supported by Russian Federation President grant no. МД-306.2017.9 and Laboratory of Algorithms and Technologies for Network Analysis, Natio-nalResearch University Higher School of Economics. The research in Sect. 2 was supported by RSF (Russian Science Foundation) project No. 14-41-00039.

References

1. Amato, G., Falchi, F., Gennaro, C., Vadicamo, L.: Deep permutations: deep convolutional neural networks and permutation-based indexing. In: Amsaleg, L., Houle, M.E., Schubert, E. (eds.) SISAP 2016. LNCS, vol. 9939, pp. 93–106. Springer, Cham (2016). doi:10.1007/978-3-319-46759-7_7

2. Parkhi, O.M., Vedaldi, A., Zisserman, A.: Deep face recognition. In: Proceedings of the British Machine Vision, pp. 6–17 (2015)

3. Wu, X., He, R., Sun, Z.: A lightened CNN for deep face representation. arXiv preprint arXiv:1511.02683 (2015)

4. Savchenko, A.V.: Search Techniques in Intelligent Classification Systems. Springer International Publishing, Heidelberg (2016)

5. Muja, M., Lowe, D.G.: Scalable nearest neighbor algorithms for high dimensional data. IEEE Trans. Pattern Anal. Mach. Intell. **36**(11), 2227–2240 (2014)

6. Boytsov, L., Naidan, B.: Engineering efficient and effective non-metric space library. In: Brisaboa, N., Pedreira, O., Zezula, P. (eds.) SISAP 2013. LNCS, vol. 8199, pp. 280–293. Springer, Heidelberg (2013). doi:10.1007/978-3-642-41062-8_28

7. Silpa-Anan, C., Hartley, R.: Optimised KD-trees for fast image descriptor matching. In: IEEE International Conference on Computer Vision and Pattern Recognition (CVPR), pp. 1–8 (2008)

8. He, J., Kumar, S., Chang, S.: On the difficulty of nearest neighbor search. In: 29th International Conference on Machine Learning (ICML-2012), pp. 1127–1134 (2012)

9. Gonzalez, E.C., Figueroa, K., Navarro, G.: Effective proximity retrieval by ordering permutations. IEEE Trans. PAMI **30**(9), 1647–1658 (2008)

10. Savchenko, A.V.: Maximum-likelihood approximate nearest neighbor method in real-time image recognition. Pattern Recogn. **61**, 459–469 (2017)

11. Burghouts, G., Smeulders, A., Geusebroek, J.-M.: The distribution family of similarity distances. In: Advances in Neural Information Processing Systems, pp. 201–208 (2008)

12. P'kalska, E., Duin, R.P.: Classifiers for dissimilarity-based pattern recognition. In: Proceedings of the 15th IEEE International Conference on Pattern Recognition (ICPR), pp. 12–16 (2000)

13. Savchenko, A.V.: Clustering and maximum likelihood search for efficient statistical classification with medium-sized databases. Optim. Lett. **11**(2), 329–341 (2017)

BMOG: Boosted Gaussian Mixture Model with Controlled Complexity

Isabel Martins[1,2]([⊠]), Pedro Carvalho[2,3], Luís Corte-Real[3,4],
and José Luis Alba-Castro[1]

[1] University of Vigo, Vigo, Spain
[2] School of Engineering, Polytechnic Institute of Porto, Porto, Portugal
`mis@isep.ipp.pt`
[3] INESC TEC, Porto, Portugal
[4] Faculty of Engineering, University of Porto, Porto, Portugal

Abstract. Developing robust and universal methods for unsupervised segmentation of moving objects in video sequences has proved to be a hard and challenging task. The best solutions are, in general, computationally heavy preventing their use in real-time applications. This research addresses this problem by proposing a robust and computationally efficient method, BMOG, that significantly boosts the performance of the widely used MOG2 method. The complexity of BMOG is kept low, proving its suitability for real-time applications. The proposed solution explores a novel classification mechanism that combines color space discrimination capabilities with hysteresis and a dynamic learning rate for background model update.

Keywords: GMM · MOG · Background Subtraction · Change detection

1 Introduction

Unsupervised segmentation of moving objects in video sequences, based on background subtraction (BS), is a fundamental step in many computer vision applications. However, there is no universal solution that successfully deals with all the many challenges presented, including poor lighting conditions, sudden illumination changes and parasitic background motion. Comprehensive reviews of BS approaches have been presented [1,2]. Recent research has shown that BS methods appear to be complementary in nature [3], driving to a more complex, and time consuming, solution in general.

Gaussian Mixture Model (GMM), or Mixture of Gaussians (MoG), has been well explored and it is probably the most popular strategy to model the background. It is a parametric model capable of handling several modes in a pixel value [4]. It can deal with slow lighting changes, periodical motion in the cluttered background, slow moving objects, long-term scene changes, and camera noise. It is widely used due to its computational efficiency and good performance in a large number of applications. These traits inspired improvements and extensions, such as [5,6], many at the cost of increased computational load.

© Springer International Publishing AG 2017
L.A. Alexandre et al. (Eds.): IbPRIA 2017, LNCS 10255, pp. 50–57, 2017.
DOI: 10.1007/978-3-319-58838-4_6

This paper proposes a robust and computationally efficient method to address the problem of BS. It is based on an adaptive GMM background model proposed by Zivkovic [5], commonly known as MOG2, which achieves increased performance in multi-modal backgrounds without penalizing computational performance, a critical issue in real time applications. This efficiency makes it a common choice in real-world applications, despite the emergence of other methods with better performance. Our method, named "Boosted MOG" (BMOG), explores the characteristics of the color spaces and further adapts the algorithm using simple but efficient rules to boost the performance of MOG2. An exhaustive set of experiments was performed on public datasets. Results show that BMOG consistently outperforms MOG2, and that it approaches top ranking, but much more complex, algorithms. Its controlled complexity makes it a good choice for real-time applications.

2   Selection of Color Space

RGB is the most common color space used in BS. However, color spaces such as YUV, YCbCr and CIE L*a*b*, that separate the luminance component, have proven to be advantageous in image processing applications [7,8]. CIE L*a*b* is a perceptual color space, where the non-linear relationships for the L*, a*, and b* components are intended to mimic the Human Visual System features. The advantages of using other color spaces than RGB in BS have been pointed out in terms of increased robustness to noise and shadows [9].

We performed a Receiver Operating Characteristic (ROC) and Area Under the Curve (AUC) analysis to assess the discrimination capability of different color spaces based on the color distance between the input and the background model pixel generated by MOG2, applied to a set of samples obtained from frames with moving objects, extracted from different videos from the CDnet 2014 Dataset [10], with the corresponding ground truth classification. The distance used was the squared Mahalanobis distance. This study showed the superior discrimination capability, for the task of BS, of alternative color spaces, particularly CIE L*a*b* (AUC 0.8) compared to RGB (AUC 0.52). Moreover, this analysis revealed that the distance of each of the color components has a discrimination capability similar to the color distance (AUC for independent channels R, G, B: 0.527, 0.527, 0.526, and L*, a*, b*: 0.742, 0.716, 0.777, respectively). These results led us to conclude that not only the adoption of the CIE L*a*b* color space could yield a significant improvement in the classification accuracy but also to define a new decision rule where the distance of each of the color components could be used as an independent classifier followed by the fusion of the independent decisions. The combination of these independent classifiers revealed, experimentally, better results than just one classifier based on the color distance.

3   Background Model

The background model adopted is based on MOG2 [5]. We extended it to deal with the characteristics of color spaces with separate channels for luminance and chrominance. The proposed BMOG algorithm performs consistently better using L*a*b*, YUV or YCbCr color spaces than using RGB; from these three, the best results were achieved with L*a*b*. Separating luminance from chrominance allows to set meaningful variance thresholds for each channel. Apart from having different discrimination capabilities, large luminance variance threshold with smaller chrominance variance thresholds can also accommodate shadows without changing the state of the pixel. In our proposal, each channel component of L*a*b* is analyzed independently, and their decisions combined with the AND rule (that provided better results than a decision based on majority voting).

3.1   Pixel Classification with Hysteresis

For each Gaussian in the mixture, if the distance between one color component of the incoming pixel $x = \{x_L, x_a, x_b\}$ and the mean of the Gaussian component is above a pre-defined threshold, the overall match is rejected. Therefore, the decision rule for a sample being classified as belonging to the background (BG) becomes

$$(x_L - \mu_L)^2 < (T_L \pm d_{th})\sigma_L^2 \ \wedge \ (x_a - \mu_a)^2 < (T_a \pm d_{th})\sigma_a^2 \ \wedge \ (x_b - \mu_b)^2 < (T_b \pm d_{th})\sigma_b^2 \ (1)$$

where μ_L, μ_a, μ_b are the Gaussian means, σ_L, σ_a, σ_b are the Gaussian variances and T_L, T_a, T_b are the independent thresholds. As the probability of a pixel changing classification from the previous frame to the current frame is much lower than the probability of a pixel maintaining the same classification, a hysteresis mechanism has been implemented to prevent noisy pixels, whose color distance is very close to the decision threshold, from incorrectly changing the classification. Therefore, the threshold values in (1) depend on the classification of the same pixel in the previous frame. If the pixel was previously classified as FG, the threshold values for that pixel are decreased by d_{th} in order to make the change to BG more difficult; if the pixel was previously classified as BG, the threshold values are increased by d_{th} in order to hinder the change to FG.

3.2   Dynamic Learning Rate

The background model is updated by using the recursive equations of MOG2, described in [5], modified by embedding a conditional mechanism at the pixel level. The learning rate α is adapted independently for each pixel and depends on the change of classification decision, as shown in Fig. 1. In this context, a change from FG to BG is sub-classified as uncovered background (UBG) and is, therefore, treated differently from other BG samples. This approach is followed in order to avoid phantom images, by promoting a quick adaptation when the background is uncovered. Thus, if the pixel is classified as UBG a faster learning rate α_{UBG} is applied. This learning rate is then decreased for each successive frame by a fixed step size d_{α} until it reaches the dynamic BG learning rate. On the other hand, if the change is from BG to FG a slow learning rate α_{FG} is applied, in order to prevent foreground objects to be quickly absorbed by the background model, while assuring that pixels misclassified as FG in consecutive frames are not completely ignored.

As a MOG2 feature, dynamic areas of the scene are modeled using more gaussians than static areas. Hence, so that the learning rate is better adapted to the characteristics of the scene background, the dynamic BG learning rate is made dependent on the number of gaussians in the mixture M ($M^*\alpha_{BG}$). This ensures that the model adaptation is faster for dynamic areas and slower for static ones.

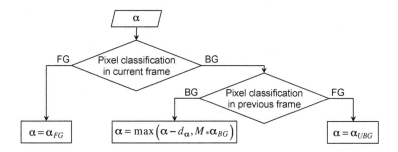

Fig. 1. Conditional learning rate update at the pixel level.

3.3 Embedded Post-processing

As we use the current BG/FG segmentation mask to make decisions when processing the next frame, the post-processing step is embedded in our algorithm to increase the success of decisions. The binary segmentation mask is filtered with an $N \times N$ median filter followed by filling of closed contours.

4 Experimental Setup

The experiments were conducted on the complete set of videos of the CDnet 2014 Dataset [10], consisting of 53 videos representative of a wide variety of challenges, grouped in 11 categories: Bad Weather (BW), Baseline (BL), Camera Jitter (CJ), Dynamic Background (DB), Intermittent Object Motion (IOM), Low Frame Rate (LFR), Night Videos (NV), Pan-Tilt-Zoom (PTZ), Shadows (SW), Thermal (TH) and Turbulence (TB). Evaluation was performed using the ground truth (GT) segmentation provided along with the videos. Pixels in the mask may have one of 5 labels: *Moving*, corresponding to foreground pixels; *Static*, corresponding to background pixels; *Shadow* corresponding to moving shadows; $Non - ROI$ corresponding to regions outside the ROI; $Unknown$ corresponding to pixels whose status is unclear.

These experiments involved the generation of all masks for our method, BMOG and, in a second step, the comparison with the results:

– for MOG2 [5],
– for a recent MoG based method RMoG [6], which claims to be computationally very efficient,
– and for a top-ranked state-of-the-art method, SuBSENSE [11],

using the results reported in the CDnet site [10] for all the methods. In the context of this comparison, the authors considered to be relevant to assess performance as a balance between complexity and segmentation quality. To this end, the OpenCV implementation of MOG2 was used as a reference. SuBSENSE was selected as representative of a state-of-the-art method whose algorithm implementation code is made available by the authors [12]. This allowed the comparison of the processing time running the algorithms in exactly the same conditions.

Only one set of parameters was used for all the videos. We set $T_a = T_b = 12$, $T_L = 35$, $d_{th} = 5$, $\alpha_{FG} = 0.0005$, $\alpha_{BG} = 0.001$, $\alpha_{UBG} = 0.01$ and $d_\alpha = 0.005$. The post-processing filter dimension $N \times N$ was set to 11×11. The maximum number of Gaussians allowed in the GMM was set to 5. These default values were determined empirically and worked well for many different scenarios as demonstrated by the results obtained with videos that incorporate a wide range of challenges.

The F-measure was used as an indicator of performance since, as reported in [3], it correlates more strongly with the rankings produced by evaluation algorithms. The processing time was used as a measure of complexity (it does not include image I/O operations). In real time applications, this feature can be critical. All algorithms were run in exactly the same conditions, using an Intel Core i7 2 GHz processor with 16 GB 1333 MHz DDR3 and OS X Yosemite 10.10.5. Our code has no low-level optimization.

5   Results and Discussion

The exhaustive set of experiments performed allowed us to assess the performance of BMOG. Figure 2 shows the average F-measure for each video category, and across all categories for the overall set of videos, as reported in CDnet site [10], for MOG2 algorithm (GMM|Zivkovic in CDnet), the proposed BMOG method, RMoG, and SuBSENSE. It is clear that BMOG consistently outperforms MOG2, approaching SuBSENSE. RMoG slightly outperforms BMOG only for IOM and PTZ scenarios. For most categories, BMOG approaches SuBSENSE, but with a much faster solution. Mind that the best state-of-the-art methods, like SuBSENSE, are complex algorithms combining different approaches.

It must be highlighted that for 18 of the 53 videos (approximately 34%), belonging to 9 different categories, BMOG outperforms SuBSENSE. Only in two categories, PTZ and TH, BMOG does not perform better than SuBSENSE in any of the videos.

The charts in Fig. 3 show that the proposed method, BMOG, achieves an excellent compromise in performance versus complexity when compared to MOG2 and SuBSENSE.

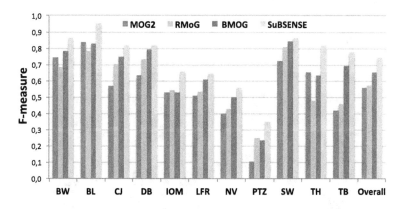

Fig. 2. Average F-measure for each category and across all categories.

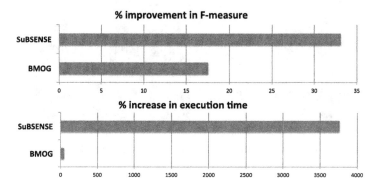

Fig. 3. Comparison of improvement in performance and increase in complexity for BMOG and a top-ranked method (reference: $0 = $ MOG2).

A comparative example of foreground masks obtained with BMOG, MOG2, RMoG and SuBSENSE is illustrated in Fig. 4. This picture shows the original frame (Input), the ground truth (GT), and the segmentation masks for BMOG, MOG2, RMoG and SuBSENSE, with the pixels that are not labeled *Static* (BG) or *Moving* (FG) marked in gray. From left to right it pictures: frame 1138 of video highway (BL); frame 1389 of video bridgeEntry (NV); frame 3190 of video copyMachine (SW); and frame 2412 of video overpass (DB). These masks are all available at the CDnet site [10].

Results demonstrate that the proposed method, BMOG, achieves a good performance in a wide range of scenarios, both for indoor or outdoor scenes either in daytime or nighttime. Even in very difficult scenarios such as nighttime videos, one of the most difficult categories in the CDnet dataset [3], consisting of traffic scenes captured at night. In these videos, the main challenge is to deal with low-visibility of vehicles and their very strong headlights that cause halos and reflections on the street. BMOG shows very interesting results, outperforming SuBSENSE in 4 of the 6 nighttime videos.

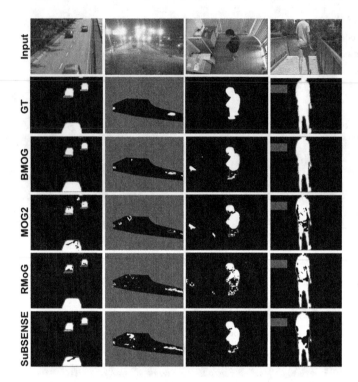

Fig. 4. Example of foreground masks for BMOG, MOG2, RMoG and SuBSENSE.

6   Conclusion

This paper proposes a computationally efficient boosted GMM method, BMOG, for the unsupervised segmentation of moving objects in video sequences that proves to be more robust than a widely used approach (MOG2) and more recent proposals like RMoG. The choice of the color space, the decision criteria and a classification mechanism with hysteresis along with a dynamic learning rate for the background model update, proved to boost the overall detection accuracy while keeping complexity low, making it a good choice for real-time applications. It must be highlighted that, for each method, all the experiments in all the testing scenarios were run with the same set of parameters.

Remark. The authors are willing to share the code if requested by e-mail and, in the meantime, the code will be prepared to be submitted to OpenCV as a candidate for inclusion in future updates of the library.

Acknowledgments. This work has received financial support from the Xunta de Galicia (Agrupación Estratéxica Consolidada de Galicia accreditation 2016-2019) and the European Union (European Regional Development Fund - ERDF) and research contract GRC2014/024 (Modalidade: Grupos de Referencia Competitiva 2014) and project "TEC4Growth - Pervasive Intelligence, Enhancers and Proofs of Concept with Industrial Impact/NORTE-01-0145-FEDER-000020", financed by the North Portugal Regional Operational Programme (NORTE 2020), under the PORTUGAL 2020 Partnership Agreement, and through the European Regional Development Fund (ERDF).

References

1. Bouwmans, T.: Traditional and recent approaches in background modeling for foreground detection: an overview. Comput. Sci. Review **11**, 31–66 (2014)
2. Sobral, A., Vacavant, A.: A comprehensive review of background subtraction algorithms evaluated with synthetic and real videos. Comput. Vis. Image Underst. **122**, 4–21 (2014)
3. Wang, Y., Jodoin, P.-M., Porikli, F., Konrad, J., Benezeth, Y., Ishwar, P.: CDnet 2014: an expanded change detection benchmark dataset. In: Proceedings of IEEE Workshop on Change Detection (CDW-2014) at CVPRW-2014, pp. 393–400 (2014)
4. Stauffer, C., Grimson, E.: Adaptive background mixture models for real-time tracking. In: Proceedings of IEEE International Computer Society Conference on Computer Vision and Pattern Recognition, vol. 2, pp. 246–252 (1999)
5. Zivkovic, Z., van der Heijden, F.: Efficient adaptive density estimation per image pixel for the task of background subtraction. Pattern Recogn. Lett. **27**(7), 773–780 (2006)
6. Varadarajan, S., Miller, P., Zhou, H.: Region-based mixture of Gaussians modelling for foreground detection in dynamic scenes. Pattern Recogn. **8**(11), 3488–3503 (2015)
7. Lissner, I., Urban, P.: Toward a unified color space for perception-based image processing. IEEE Trans. Image Process. **21**(3), 115–1168 (2012)
8. Balcilar, M., Amasyali, M.F., Sonmez, A.C.: Moving object detection using Lab2000HL color space with spatial and temporal smoothing. Appl. Math. Inf. Sci. **8**(4), 1755–1766 (2014)
9. Cucchiara, R., Grana, C., Piccardi, M., Prati, A.: Detecting moving objects, ghosts, and shadows in video streams. IEEE Trans. Pattern Anal. Mach. Intell. **25**(10), 1337–1342 (2003)
10. ChangeDetection.NET. http://www.changedetection.net. Accessed Nov 2016
11. St-Charles, P.-L., Bilodeau, G.-A., Bergevin, R.: SuBSENSE : a universal change detection method with local adaptive sensitivity. IEEE Trans. Image Process. **24**(1), 359–373 (2015)
12. SuBSENSE. https://bitbucket.org/pierre_luc_st_charles/subsense. Accessed May 2016

Measuring the Quality of Annotations for a Subjective Crowdsourcing Task

Raquel Justo[(⊠)], M. Inés Torres, and José M. Alcaide

Universidad del País Vasco UPV/EHU, Sarriena s/n, 48940 Leioa, Spain
`raquel.justo@ehu.es`

Abstract. In this work an algorithm devoted to the detection of low quality annotations is proposed. It is mainly focused on subjective annotation tasks carried out by means of crowdsourcing platforms. In this kind of task, where a good response is not necessarily prefixed, several measures should be considered in order to pick the different behaviours of annotators associated to bad quality results: time, inter-annotator agreement and repeated patterns in responses. The proposed algorithm considers all these measures and provide a set of workers whose annotations should be removed. The experiments carried out, over a sarcasm annotation task, show that once the low quality annotations were removed and acquired again a better labeled set was achieved.

Keywords: Supervised learning · Annotation · Crowdsourcing · Subjective language

1 Introduction

Within the Pattern Recognition framework supervised learning methods make use of great amounts of annotated data in order to build robust models. However, the annotation process is a challenging task that usually requires a lot of effort, time and/or money. Traditionally, expert annotators, trained for the specific task, were involved in this process. But finding this kind of annotators is difficult and the whole process results expensive and tedious. Moreover, there are subjective tasks, such as emotion or sentiment analysis, for which the training of the annotators is not desirable and it is more interesting to pick up the diversity of people's opinion as a reflection of reality. In the last years, crowdsourcing have emerged as an alternative and more efficient method to carry out annotations and it has been used in different areas related to information retrieval, speech recognition, natural language processing, etc. Amazon's Mechanical Turk[1] or CrowdFlower[2] are good examples of crowdsourcing platforms that have been extensively used for completing annotation tasks. Within this framework task requesters can reach a large number of freelance employees to solve the annotation of microtasks. Dividing the work in microtasks makes possible to have

---

[1] www.mturk.com.
[2] www.crowdflower.com.

© Springer International Publishing AG 2017
L.A. Alexandre et al. (Eds.): IbPRIA 2017, LNCS 10255, pp. 58–68, 2017.
DOI: 10.1007/978-3-319-58838-4_7

an annotation task completed by a wide variety of different annotators, in cases where the diversity means a plus.

In this work, we dealt with a very subjective task focused on the identification of text excerpts as sarcastic or not sarcastic. Since the sarcasm cannot be unambiguously defined and often depends on diverse factors like the perception of the reader, the cultural environment, etc. [8,20], the diversity of people's opinion is very valuable in this case. That is, we wanted to use what people understand as sarcasm more than what the dictionary says. Thus, the most appropriate way of carrying out the annotation process is to use crowdsourcing.

Although crowdsourcing is now widely accepted and represents the basis for data collection and resource annotation or validation, the quality of the provided results are still in question. In fact, measuring the reliability of data is not straightforward and there are different works dealing with it [9,13–15, 17,21]. According to [10] there are several dysfunctional worker types, *Incapable workers* that do not fulfil the needed requirements. *Malicious workers* that try to invalidate experiments by submitting wrong answers on purpose and *Distracted workers* that do not pay full attention to the task. All of these workers provide poor quality results. The origin of this behaviour can be diverse but the incentives associated to the completion of microtasks can explain it to some extent.

The most common way of detecting unreliable workers is to introduce gold-standard work units alongside normal work units. They consist of very simple questions with a known answer that have to be well answered by annotators not to be rejected. Although it is an effective mechanism for some tasks it is not applicable in all the cases (tasks with open questions, etc.). Additionally, malicious workers can find innovative ways to circumvent gold-standard work units such as learning the answers to test questions and then reusing those answers under different accounts [22]. Moreover, in subjective tasks, the gold-standard does not seem to be an effective mechanism since the selection of questions without ambiguous cases is subjective itself. Let us note that our annotation task is drastically different from an audio transcription task, or a medical cancer diagnosis, where there is a real transcription or a biopsy result that can be objectively assumed as a ground truth.

In fact, if we focus on those subjective tasks, there are additional problems related to the data quality not gathered in the aforementioned cases. In our specific task, for instance, we have detected workers whose perception is highly different from the rest of annotators. It does not compulsorily mean that they are *Incapable workers*, *Malicious workers*, or *Distracted workers*, the problem seems to be more related to a misunderstanding of what sarcasm means that might be due to a different cultural background. In these cases, although gold-standard could help, additional information is needed to evaluate the reliability of data.

In a similar task, where irony and sarcasm were annotated using crowdsourcing [11], majority voting was used along with the quality control algorithm designed specifically for quality management on Amazon Mechanical Turk [15]. However, a high multiplicity is needed to use majority voting as a good quality control measure and this has associated a high cost. On the other hand, the algorithm described in [15] was based on the inter-annotator agreement. It was inspired in [7] which proposed an expectation maximisation algorithm that iterates until convergence. However, the agreement information among annotators on its own might fail to detect malicious workers that uses bots and can learn the estimated distribution of the provided answers. Moreover, the proposed algorithm was based on the error rate estimation of workers, thus, a pool of data, that should be big enough to achieve good estimations, is needed to start working.

Up to our knowledge, it does not exist a reliable way of measuring the quality of data for highly subjective annotation tasks. Moreover, even when considering measures related to inter-annotator agreement there is a great confusion and the selected measures are not well motivated. The main contribution of this work is (1) to select one of the most general inter-annotator agreement coefficient and use its difference to provide a score for each annotator (2) to define a new agreement coefficient that is capable of picking a different kind of information and (3) to propose an algorithm that can detect low quality annotations, due to different behaviors, in a subjective task where ambiguity is very significant. It can be applied in any time during the annotation process and takes into consideration the main issues related to all kind of annotators that provide bad quality results.

This paper is organized as follows, Sect. 2 provides a definition of the annotations task and Sect. 3 describes the measures and the methodology employed to detect unreliable workers. In Sect. 4 a description of the experiments carried out is provided and finally, the conclusions and future work are detailed in Sect. 5.

2   Definition of the Task and the Annotation Procedure

The aim of this work is to detect bad quality results in a subjective crowdsourcing annotation task. To this end Spanish SOFOCO corpus, which draws on the website Menéame[3], was considered. Menéame is a social news aggregation site, modeled after Digg. Registered users can submit content in the form of stories: links to news published on other web sites accompanied by a short comment. Besides, they can post their own comments on each story, resulting in a comment thread. The term "comment" is the word used in Menéame for the different interactions of the users. However, from now on we will refer to those "comments" with the term "post". A procedure for finding, retrieving and processing stories and posts related to some specific controversial categories *Terrorism, Independence of Catalonia, Abortion, Gay Marriage* and *Creationism* was carried out.

Once the selected set of posts was retrieved from the Menéme website we wanted to had the posts labeled as *sarcastic* or *not-sarcastic* to develop an automatic sarcasm detection system. We used a custom crowdsourcing platform, CrowdScience[4] [16] to carry out the annotation task. The motivations of choosing this option are (1) Amazon's Mechanical Turk is not available in European

---

[3] www.meneame.net.

[4] Available for the scientific community under specific constraints. http://cz.efaber. net.

Countries only in USA. (2) In other available platforms like Crowdflower only around 19% of contributors who speaks Spanish are from Spain. Let us note that in the proposed task it is very important to have as much annotators from Spain as possible, because the differences with regard to american Spanish are very noticeable and (3) We wanted to have a controlled set of annotators at first to drive a pilot annotation task.

The platform shows the registered user a post and asks him to *Indicate whether a sarcastic tone is present in the post* and the annotator has to respond *yes* or *no*. In order to take some control of the annotators involved in the task, they have to make a registration at the website to start annotating. When the worker wanted to receive any incentive, identifying information (complete name and identity card number) was needed. Additionally, they had to indicate whether they had some skills related to the specific task, like linguistic knowledge or fluency in Spanish language, etc. Depending on the skills they indicated, the annotators were able to access different active tasks. However, as we could see looking at randoms examples, this was not enough to avoid bad quality annotations. Thus, a methodology was designed to detect annotations that should be removed and acquired again.

3   Measuring the Annotations Quality

In this section an algorithm that takes into account different measures employed to evaluate the quality of annotations is proposed.

3.1   Measures Related to the Time Employed in the Annotation

The time employed in carrying out annotations might provide information about the quality of them. It may initially seem that shorter average annotation times are indicators of bad quality annotators. However, after a bit deeper analysis, it can be concluded that average annotation times are very dependent on the skills of the annotators. Thus, there are very fast annotators, may be people used to the annotation procedure, or people that are able to read and understand very fast, that carry out high quality annotations. But there also slower annotators, that need more time, and also provide annotations with a high agreement percentage. Therefore, the time related measures were only used to detect very extreme behaviours associated to programmed bots or similar fraudulent annotators. In this work two measures were collected for each user:

Maximum period of time working continuously (without a stop interval above a threshold). It is assumed that a real annotator cannot work, for instance, more than 6 h without pauses longer than 10'. Detecting such kind of behaviors would indicate an automatic way annotating, i.e. a bot.

Average annotation time and the corresponding standard deviation. The items to be annotated in the proposed tasks are very different between each others (in terms of length, annotation difficulty, etc.) and they usually require very different annotation times even for the same annotator. Thus, very low standard deviations would indicate that the annotator is using the same annotation time for all the items, which is considered a suspicious behavior.

3.2 Measures Related to the Interannotator Agreement

According to [1,18], researchers who wish to use hand-coded data, that is, data in which items are labeled with categories, need to show that such data are reliable. Data are reliable if coders agree on the categories assigned to units to an extent determined by the purposes of the study. Different coefficients which measure agreement have been discussed in the literature, such us percentage agreement, χ^2, κ-like measures, etc. The simplest measure of agreement between two coders is the percentage of agreement or observed agreement in Eq. (1).

$$A_o = \frac{1}{n_I} \sum_{i \in I} agr_i \tag{1}$$

where n_I is the number of labeled items, or posts in this case, in set I and agr_i is defined as follows:

$$agr_i = \begin{cases} 1 \text{ if the two coders assign i to the same category} \\ 0 \text{ if the two coders assign i to different categories} \end{cases} \tag{2}$$

Although observed agreement is considered in the computation of all the measures of agreement presented in the literature [1], since some agreement is due to chance, it does not yield values that can be compared across studies. Thus, the observed agreement has to be adjusted for chance agreement like in S [2], π [23] or κ [5] coefficients as shown in Eq. (3), where A_e represents how much agreement is expected by chance. Expected agreement is the probability of two coders c_1 and c_2 agreeing on any class and is obtained according to Eq. (4), where T is the set of all items that the two coders have classified.

$$S, \pi, \kappa = \frac{A_o - A_e}{1 - A_e} \tag{3}$$

$$A_e = \sum_{t \in T} P(t|c_1) \cdot P(t|c_2) \tag{4}$$

The difference between S, π, and κ lies in the assumptions leading to the calculation of $P(t|c_i)$. S is based on the assumption that if coders were operating by chance alone, we would get a uniform distribution: that is, for any two coders c_m and c_n and any two categories k_j, k_l, $P(t_j|c_m) = P(t_l|c_n)$. π assumes that if coders were operating by chance alone, we would get the same distribution for each coder: for any two coders c_m, c_n and any category k, $P(t|c_m) = P(t|c_n)$. Finally, κ considers that if coders were operating by chance alone, we would get a separate distribution for each coder.

Generalizations of π and κ coefficients, *Fleiss' Multi-π* [12] and *Multi-κ* [6], were proposed for the cases in which more than two coders were involved in the classification of an item. However, a serious limitation of the aforementioned coefficients is that all disagreements are treated equally, although it is not relevant for this specific task it would be a disadvantage in similar subjective tasks like annotation of nastiness, disgust, etc., where annotators should provide a number in a scale. Thus, in this work we will focus on the more general and versatile Krippendorff's α [18] that is appropriate for use with multiple coders, different magnitudes of disagreement, and missing values, and is based on assumptions similar to those of π; and weighted kappa κ_w [4] (defined only for two coders). It provides a measure of the overall agreement found in the task that can be compared to other studies. It is given by Eq. (5), where D_o^α and D_e^α are the observed and expected disagreements respectively.

For the specific task proposed in this work where nominal data (Sarc Yes (1)/Sarc No(0)) and more than two annotators were involved the specific way of computing this coefficient is given by Eq. (5) according to [19].

$$\alpha = 1 - \frac{D_o^\alpha}{D_e^\alpha} = \frac{(n-1)\sum_c o_{cc} - \sum_c n_c(n_c - 1)}{n(n-1) - \sum_c n_c(n_c - 1)} \tag{5}$$

where $o_{ck} = \sum_u \frac{\text{Number of c-k pairs in reliability matrix}}{m_u - 1}$, m_u is the number of values of the item u in the reliability matrix (in our case m_u is always 5), $n_c = \sum_k o_{ck}$ and $n = \sum_c n_c$. For further details see [1].

The terms in (5) are computed considering a reliability $p \cdot q$ matrix, where p is the number of annotators and q the number of items that would be labeled. Since in this work we wanted to detect low quality annotations, which is to say low quality annotators, we propose to measure the variations of Krippendorff's α when an annotator k was removed from the set as follows: $\Delta\alpha_k = \frac{\alpha - \alpha_k}{n_k}$ where n_k is the number of annotations carried out by annotator k. Given that Krippendorff's α is an agreement measure, a negative $\Delta\alpha_k$ means that when removing the k annotator a better agreement is obtained. The lower the $\Delta\alpha_k$ value the higher the disagreement introduced by the k annotator.

$\Delta\alpha_k$ is measured to evaluate an specific annotator's influence. However, other items and agreement percentages included in the overall task influence the obtained results. Thus, in this work we define a new coefficient, β_k, defined as an observed agreement of an annotator and the rest of annotators that labeled the same items. In this coefficient only the items classified by an specific k annotator are involved.

Let K be a set of annotators and J a set of items (posts in this case) labeled by the different annotators $k \in K$. Thus, K_j will represent the set of annotators that labeled a specific item $j \in J$ and J_k will represent the set of items labeled by an specific annotator $k \in K$. β_k is defined as shown in Eq. (6):

$$\beta_k = \frac{1}{|J_k|} \sum_{j \in J_k} \sum_{m \in K_j - k} \frac{c_{mk}}{|K_j| - 1} \tag{6}$$

where $|J_k|$ is the number of posts labeled by the annotator k, $|K_j|$ is the number of different annotations given to the j item and c_{mk} is defined as follows:

$$c_{mk} = \begin{cases} 1 \text{ if } m \text{ and } k \text{ coders assign j to the same category} \\ 0 \text{ if } m \text{ and } k \text{ coders assign j to different categories} \end{cases} \qquad (7)$$

3.3 Measures Related to the Given Responses

It is also very valuable to detect when an annotator is providing random answers to the proposed questions, or always the same response. When binary questions are proposed (with a yes/no response for instance) it is even easier to say always "yes", or always "no". Thus, measures that detect such kind of response patterns would also be useful to detect fraudulent annotators. Moreover, the ratio of a kind of response, depending on the nature of the task, might indicate a low quality in annotations.

In the proposed task, where annotators are asked about the presence of a sarcastic tone, the *percentage of sarcastic responses* was measured for each annotator. In this specific case, since the sarcasm is less frequent that the absence of it, a high percentage of sarcastic responses would indicate a fraudulent annotator, an annotator that do not make the annotations carefully, an annotator that did not properly understand the task, etc.

3.4 Algorithm for the Detecion of Low Quality Data

Once the different measures presented in previous sections were collected for each annotator we proceed as shown in Algorithm 1 to select the annotators and the corresponding annotations that should be removed. The annotators in the resulting set have to be considered fraudulent, so their annotations are not reliable enough and should be removed and picked up again.

4   Experiments and Results

Using the platform described in Sect. 2, 13.717 annotations were carried out by 207 annotators fluent in European Spanish. Each post was labeled by 5 different annotators. The inter-annotator agreement was measured in terms of Kripendorff's α to evaluate the reliability of the task and a value of 0.24 was achieved. Although this is a low value, it is similar to the one obtained with IAC (0.22) [24], its counterpart corpus in English, in which SOFOCO is inspired. Furthermore, similar values were also achieved when considering different tasks for emotionally annotating synthesised speech [3] where subjectivity is also present.

However, a manual analysis of the annotations reveals that there were bad quality annotations that would lead to a poor training set for the sarcasm detection system. Thus, the quality measures and the methodology described in Sect. 3 were employed to detect annotators that should be removed.

Considering that annotators that wanted to obtain incentives for their work had to label at least 50 posts, $M = 50$ was selected to build the first set of

---

Algorithm 1. Detection of low quality data

Input: K_M: A set of annotators that carried out at least a minimum number of annotations (M).
The annotators that made very few annotations were not considered to be influential enough.
N : selected threshold for the number of worst elements in a set. T_{min} : Minimum required
stop interval for continuous work. TP_{max} : Maximum time working continuously without stops
longer than T_{min}. SD_{min} : Minimum standard deviation time for the different annotations of
a worker.

Output: K_R: A subset of annotators from K_M whose annotations are not reliable.
```
 1: K₁, K₂, K₃ = ∅
 2: K_{M_{Sorted_α}} ← Sort K_M in terms of descendent Δα_k values.
 3: while |K₁| <= N do           ▷ K₁: set of the N annotators with the highest Δα_k values.
 4:     K₁ ← k ∈ K_{M_{Sorted_α}}
 5: K_{M_{Sorted_β}} ← Sort K_M in terms of ascendent β_k values.
 6: while |K₂| <= N do           ▷ K₂: set of the N annotators with the lowest β_k values.
 7:     K₂ ← k ∈ K_{M_{Sorted_β}}
 8: K_{M_{Sorted%sarc}} ← Sort K_M in terms of descendent percentage of sarcastic responses.
 9: while |K₃| <= N do           ▷ K₃: set of the N annotators with the highest % sarc. resp.
10:     K₃ ← k ∈ K_{M_{Sorted%sarc}}
11: K_R = {K₁ ∩ K₂ ∩ K₃}
12: for all k ∈ K_M do
13:     Compute TP_{max}(t_k) ▷ Compute maximum period of time working continuously without a
            minimum stop T_{min}.
14:     if TP_{max}(t_k) < TP_{max} then
15:         K_R ← k
16: for all k ∈ K_M do
17:     Compute SD(t_k)               ▷ Compute the time standard deviation of annotator k.
18:     if SD(t_k) < SD_{min} then
19:         K_R ← k
```

---

annotators. The achieved set was comprised by 116 annotators. Then, $N = 20$ was selected to build the different sets with the highest percentage of sarcastic responses and worse $\Delta\alpha_k$ and β_k values. Besides, annotators with a maximum period of 6 h of continuous work without stops longer than $10'$ were included in the suspicious set ($TP_{max} = 6$ h, $T_{min} = 10'$) along with those with standard deviation from average time lower than $10''$ ($SD_{min} = 10''$). Finally, there were 5 annotators in the resulting suspicious user set (see Stage 1 column in Table 1).

Focusing on agreement coefficients, all the annotators shown in Stage 1 have significantly lower β_k values than the highest β_k value achieved by the best annotator that was 0.802 and also than the average β_k achieved with all 116 annotators that is 0.566. In fact, the β_k-s shown in the Table are the 5 worst values among the 116 annotators. Moreover, all the annotators have also negative values of $\Delta\alpha_k$, as expected, meaning that Kripendorff's α value increased when those annotators were removed. Besides, $\Delta\alpha_k$ values of 296, 288, 282 and 40 annotators are the worst values among the 116 annotators that were considered and the value of 279 annotator is among the 10 worst ones. This means that although the information gathered in both β_k and $\Delta\alpha_k$ is related to inter-annotator agreement, it is not exactly the same and can be complementary. Additionally, the percentage of sarcastic responses for all the annotators in the Table is very high, note 91% achieved by 282 that is the annotator with the highest percentage of sarcastic responses in the set. The percentage of the sarcastic responses given in Table 1 are among the 11 highest values in the set and all of them are significantly higher than the average value (42.77%). Regarding maximum working

Table 1. Values of the different parameters (number of posts, β_k, $\Delta\alpha_k$, ratio of sarcastic responses, maximum working time without stops loner than $10'$, average time and standard deviation) for the annotators of the K_R set given by the proposed algorithm in the first annotation stage. Additionally, values for the parameters obtained in a second annotation stage are also given.

	Stage 1					Stage 2	
	Ann. ID					Ann. ID	
	282	40	296	288	279	308	325
No. posts	500	50	150	303	497	67	65
β_k	**0.311**	0.373	0.377	0.430	0.439	0.522	0.523
$\Delta\alpha_k$	−0.211	−0.127	**−0.215**	−0.122	−0.076	−0.077	−0.114
Resp. sarc. ratio (%)	**91.0**	78.0	65.3	74.6	82.5	59.7	67.7
Max. work. time (sec.)	3964	2013	1752	2825	**4669**	1254	777
t_avg. (sec.)	33.42	27.20	**8.42**	37.07	17.03	35.14	12.55
t_dev. (sec.)	51.20	39.45	**2.90**	42.88	20.88	61.01	14.65

times, the highest one is 4669 meaning that the annotator has been continuously working around 1.3 h without stops higher than $10'$. According to our judgement it is not a suspicious working time and it seems that there are not automatic bots carrying out the annotations in our set. In the same way, the average times and the corresponding standard deviation do not indicate suspicious behaviours, except when regarding 296 annotator, which standard deviation is below $10''$.

Finally, the annotations carried out by the annotators given in Stage 1 were removed and a new annotation stage was carried out to get the labels again. When incorporating the new annotations, a higher Kripendorff's α is obtained (it changed from 0.22407 to 0.23193). Applying the same criterion described above a new set of suspicious annotators was achieved with the quality measures gathered in Stage 2 column of Table 1. All the quality measures in this set are better than those in the previous column. The values of β_k and $\Delta\alpha_k$ are much higher in this case and the percentage of sarcastic responses much lower. The same happens with the values associated to annotation times and there are not standard deviations under $10''$. Thus, we keep the annotations in the new set as the correct ones to build the training sets for the sarcasm detection system.

5   Conclusions

This work is devoted to the design of an algorithm capable of detect low quality annotations in a very subjective crowdsourcing task. It considers different measures to take into account different behaviours of workers that provide poor performing annotations: measures related to time, inter-annotator agreement and repeated patterns in responses. Regarding inter-annotator agreement measures a deep study of the most appropriate existing coefficients was carried out and the increment of one of them was employed. Besides, a new coefficient was proposed to obtain complementary information. An extended comparison of the two coefficients would be carried out in future work. The experimental results show that the algorithm performs well in the proposed task and we propose to use it in other subjective tasks, like the annotation of nasty or disgusting posts.

References

1. Artstein, R., Poesio, M.: Inter-coder agreement for computational linguistics. Comput. Linguist. **34**(4), 555–596 (2008)
2. Bennet, E.M., Alpert, R., Goldstein, A.C.: Communications through limited response questioning. Public Opin. Q. **18**, 303–308 (1954)
3. Buchholz, S., Latorre, J., Yanagisawa, K.: Crowdsourced Assessment of Speech Synthesis. Wiley, Chichester (2013)
4. Cohen, J.: Weighted kappa: nominal scale agreement provision for scaled disagreement or partial credit. Psychol. Bull. **70**(4), 213–220 (1968)
5. Cohen, J.: A coefficient of agreement for nominal scales. Educ. Psychol. Meas. **20**(1), 37–46 (1960)
6. Davies, M., Fleiss, J.L.: Measuring agreement for multinomial data. Biometrics **38**(4), 1047–1051 (1982)
7. Dawid, A.P., Skene, A.M.: Maximum likelihood estimation of observer error-rates using the em algorithm. Appl. Stat. **28**(1), 20–28 (1979)
8. Dress, M.L., Kreuz, R.J., Link, K.E., Caucci, G.M.: Regional variation in the use of sarcasm. J. Lang. Soc. Psychol. **27**(1), 71–85 (2008)
9. Eickhoff, C., de Vries, A.P.: How crowdsourcable is your task? In: Workshop on Crowdsourcing for Search and Data Mining (CSDM), Hong Kong, China (2011)
10. Eickhoff, C., de Vries, A.P.: Increasing cheat robustness of crowdsourcing tasks. Inf. Retrieval **16**(2), 121–137 (2013)
11. Filatova, E.: Irony and sarcasm: corpus generation and analysis using crowdsourcing. In: Proceedings of LREC 2012, Istanbul, Turkey, pp. 392–398, 23–25 May 2012
12. Fleiss, J., et al.: Measuring nominal scale agreement among many raters. Psychol. Bull. **76**(5), 378–382 (1971)
13. Gadiraju, U., Kawase, R., Dietze, S., Demartini, G.: Understanding malicious behavior in crowdsourcing platforms: the case of online surveys. In: Proceedings of the ACM CHI 2015, Seoul, Republic of Korea, pp. 1631–1640 (2015)
14. Gennaro, R., Gentry, C., Parno, B.: Non-interactive verifiable computing: outsourcing computation to untrusted workers. In: Rabin, T. (ed.) CRYPTO 2010. LNCS, vol. 6223, pp. 465–482. Springer, Heidelberg (2010). doi:10.1007/978-3-642-14623-7_25
15. Ipeirotis, P.G., Provost, F., Wang, J.: Quality management on Amazon mechanical turk. In: Proceedings of the ACM SIGKDD, pp. 64–67. New York, USA (2010)
16. Justo, R., Alcaide, J.M., Torres, M.I.: Crowdscience: crowdsourcing for research and development. In: Proceedings of IberSpeech 2016, Portugal, pp. 403–410 (2016)
17. Kou, Z., Stanton, D., Peng, F., Beaufays, F., Strohman, T.: Fix it where it fails: pronunciation learning by mining error corrections from speech logs. In: Proceedings of ICASSP 2015, South Brisbane, Australia, pp. 4619–4623, 19–24 April 2015
18. Krippendorff, K.: Content Analysis: An Introduction to its Methodology. Sage, Thousand Oaks (2004)

19. Krippendorff, K.: Computing Krippendorff's Alpha Reliability. Technical report, University of Pennsylvania, Annenberg School for Communication, June 2007
20. Nunberg, G.: The Way we Talk Now: Commentaries on Language and Culture from NPR's "Fresh Air". Houghton Mifflin, Boston (2001)
21. Rodrigues, F., Pereira, F.C., Ribeiro, B.: Learning from multiple annotators: distinguishing good from random labelers. Pattern Recogn. Lett. **34**(12), 1428–1436 (2013)
22. Rothwell, S., Elshenawy, A., Carter, S., Iraga, D., Romani, F., Kennewick, M., Kennewick, B.: Controlling quality and handling fraud in large scale crowdsourcing speech data collections. In: Proceedings of Interspeech 2015, Dresden, Germany, pp. 2784–2788. ISCA, 6–10 September 2015
23. Scott, W.A.: Reliability of content analysis: the case of nominal scale coding. Public Opin. Q. **19**(3), 321–325 (1955)
24. Swanson, R., Lukin, S.M., Eisenberg, L., Corcoran, T., Walker, M.A.: Getting reliable annotations for sarcasm in online dialogues. In: Proceedings of LREC 2014, Reykjavik, Iceland, pp. 4250–4257, 26–31 May 2014

Pre-trained Convolutional Networks and Generative Statistical Models: A Comparative Study in Large Datasets

John Michael[(✉)] and Luís F. Teixeira

INESC TEC, FEUP - MIEEC, Porto, Portugal
Michael.Galveira@gmail.com, luisft@fe.up.pt

Abstract. This study explored the viability of out-the-box, pre-trained ConvNet models as a tool to generate features for large-scale classification tasks. A juxtaposition with generative methods for vocabulary generation was drawn. Both methods were chosen in an attempt to integrate other datasets (transfer learning) and unlabelled data, respectively. Both methods were used together, studying the viability of a ConvNet model to estimate category labels of unlabelled images. All experiments pertaining to this study were carried out over a two-class set, later expanded into a 5-category dataset. The pre-trained models used were obtained from the Caffe Model Zoo.

The study showed that the pre-trained model achieved best results for the binary dataset, with an accuracy of 0.945. However, for the 5-class dataset, generative vocabularies outperformed the ConvNet (0.91 vs. 0.861). Furthermore, when replacing labelled images with unlabelled ones during training, acceptable accuracy scores were obtained (as high as 0.903). Additionally, it was observed that linear kernels perform particularly well when utilized with generative models. This was especially relevant when compared to ConvNets, which require days of training even when utilizing multiple GPUs for computations.

Keywords: Computational geometry · Graph theory · Hamilton cycles

1 Introduction

Image classification is a central problem of Computer Vision and Machine Learning. One of the greatest obstacles faced when handling large volumes of images and video is tied to the fact that, more often than not, the visual data is unlabelled. Whilst unlabelled data is readily available and easy to extract, labelled data is scarce and quite costly to obtain. It's therefore important to find reliable methods which minimize the need for labelled data. A similar argument could be drawn towards using labelled data from categories or applications which are sufficiently similar to the desired one, a form of transfer learning. This can be done indirectly by utilizing pre-trained models as estimators for the class of images from the target dataset. Exploring these various options can help understand

© Springer International Publishing AG 2017
L.A. Alexandre et al. (Eds.): IbPRIA 2017, LNCS 10255, pp. 69–75, 2017.
DOI: 10.1007/978-3-319-58838-4_8

how to overcome the scarcity of labelled data. The pre-trained ConvNets used to carry out this study (trained on the full Imagenet dataset) follow a slightly modified AlexNet architecture [2] and an architecture based on the one proposed for the ZFNet ConvNet [1]. The models were obtained from the Caffe Model Zoo page. A SPM+SVM classification scheme [5] was used to study the performance of methods for generation of a visual vocabulary, namely Sparse Coding (SC, [4]), Latent Dirichilet Alocation (LDA, [7]), probabilistic Latent Semantic Analysis (pLSA, [3]) and Ficher's Vectors (these built on top of a GMM model instead, as seen in [6]). These generative methods can be seen as a form of feature reduction and description, and are interesting due to being fairly orthogonal to lower-level feature manipulation (in analogy to what's achieve in preprocessing steps for ConvNets). In an attempt to bring both approaches together, the ConvNet was also utilized together with these generative methods to explore the viability of utilizing these pre-trained models to estimate the class of unlabelled images.

2   Methodology

All methods were tested on two distinct datasets: an initial dataset with 5 thousand images of the dog and cat categories, varied in resolution, background and race (obtained from Kaggle competitions), which was then supplemented with three additional categories, whale, fish and galaxy (obtained from other Kaggle competitions and the Imagenet dataset). These classes were picked for their very high variability between each individual image (especially true for the cat and dog classes), their similar backgrounds (fish and whale classes frequently have marine backgrounds with predominant shades of blue, in an attempt to understand if the classifiers learn interesting features from the class and not the backgrounds themselves) and due to their uniqueness and sheer oddity (the galaxy class being highly regular and featuring a low amount of colour information, as well as low resolution). The datasets for each class were randomly split between test and training sets for each trial. Features were initially obtained from images utilizing both PCA-SIFT (64 components) and colour information in the form of a Bag-of-Colours (BoC) descriptor with 32-bins. Lastly, as previously explained, an attempt to enhance their performance through assistance of the pre-trained ConvNet was studied, by altering the typical SVM cost function:

$$\gamma := \min_{\tilde{\gamma},w} \|w^2\| - C \sum_{i=1}^{n} \epsilon_i$$

Subject to: $\quad\quad\quad\quad\quad\quad\quad\quad$ (1)

$$\epsilon_i > 1$$

$$y_i(w^T x_i) \geq 1 - \epsilon_i$$

So that the scalar term C becomes a diagonal matrix, where each non-zero entry $c_{(i,i)}$ represents the weight of the ith sample, estimated by class score assigned by the ConvNet. In the training scheme, the sample scores were fixed to $0.5 \times \alpha \times c_{CONV,i} \times \lambda$, where α represents the accuracy score of the pre-trained ConvNet on all the available training labelled data and $c_{CONV,i}$ the class score attributed to unlabelled image i by the ConvNet. This weighting reflects both an estimation of the confidence in the ConvNet's tentative performance (through the parameter α) and an estimation of the tentative classification of the image through $c_{CONV,i}$. After class scores were generated for all unlabelled data, each image was assigned a tentative label through $\max(c_{cat,i}, c_{dog,i}, ...)$, where $c_{cat,i}, c_{dog,i}, ...$ are the normalized scores for the various categories (such as "cat" or "dog"). Values for the average score and maximum score for each class, $c_{max,j}, c_{avg,j}; j = cat, dog, ...$, were also were computed. These were used to discard images which were exceptionally noisy or in which the ConvNet struggled to attribute a class with some certainty. In practice, unlabelled images are drawn if their score is greater than $c_{avg,i}$ (and therefore not necessarily the highest scoring images for either class in the list). If there aren't enough images scoring over $c_{avg,i}$, images with lower scores are drawn until enough unlabelled samples are obtained. Furthermore, the parameter λ is a SVM empirical parameter, optimized through model cross-validation. This parameter controls the penalty of misclassifying a data point to maximize the margin for the remaining points.

Generated Topic Vectors. The LDA/pLSA models are generated utilizing labelled images from both categories and unlabelled images without distinction. The interpretation of the labelled corpus of either category is tied to the overall dataset- that is, the topical vectors generated for an image of a certain category depends upon the corpus of images utilized when creating the LDA/pLSA model (and thus, its topic representation varies with the corpus of other categories and the unlabelled corpus used to create the model in the first place). Once the model is obtained, one can now generate a topic representation for each image belonging to each category. These topic vectors can be used to generate an overall frequency representation for topics belonging to each category. If this is done for each class, it can subsequently be normalized to obtained a new, category-specific multinomial model that represents each individual probability $p(z_i|C_j)$, with z_i the ith topic and C_j the jth category. In order to keep some form of sparsity-constraint, mirroring what the original LDA/pLSA formulation aims to achieve (it's desirable that topics are associated with a small portion of the most salient words, as to represent the variance between different classes correctly), the median number of topics represented in each category, $\hat{z}_j$, is also computed. After computing the new multinomial model, uniformly drawn random numbers can be used to create new, "fictitious" topic vectors. This is useful when supplementing classes for which the amount of data is smaller, and was tested upon as an alternative to oversampling (as it involves some variance when creating new samples). It also bypasses a number of feature detection, extraction and reduction steps, saving some computational resources. A topic is added to this new vector if the random number, r, is such that $r \geq p(z_i|C_j)$ with $0 \geq r \geq 1$. If the number of topics for this vector is greater than $1.5\hat{z}_j$, topics with smaller probabilities (smaller $p(z_i|C_j)$ factors) are set to zero until the sparsity constraint is verified. While this method has the advantage of promoting more salient topics, it also has the adverse effect of being much more prone to overfitting, so the number of generated topic vectors has to be kept conservatively small. The factor of 1.5 utilized in the sparsity constraint is purely empirical and was set after some brief experimentation with other factors in the 1–2 range.

2.1   Cross-Validation Scheme and Testing

A stratified 4-fold cross validation scheme was used for all the experiments. The final model is obtained by aggregating the results of all the folds through model averaging. Testing each model for performance was done on 12500 images on both the binary and the 5-category datasets. In both cases, the number of images belonging to each category was the same, allowing for isotropic priors which simplify calculations without any meaningful loss of generality. Training and testing was carried out on an Intel i7 4720 processor and 16 GB RAM for the majority of the methods. The exception was training and testing with the pre-trained ConvNet, which required two Nvidia GTX970 GPUs to yield results in a timely manner (training took roughly two days on this hardware).

3   Results

A summary of the main results achieved during the course of this study is presented in Table 1. The classical SPM+SVM approached applied to a visual vocabulary obtained through the Sparse Coding or Latent Semantic Analysis used one thousand labelled images for training. The hybrid ConvNet+generative approach used 500 labelled and 500 unlabelled images. Furthermore, optimization regarding the generative methods used for visual vocabulary generation is present in Fig. 1, where the effect of overfitting and underfitting can be observed, as expected.

As is customary, ConvNets remain unparalleled in terms of performance for similar image categories. Furthermore, if sufficient computational resources and labelled examples are available, they'll always outperform any other of the presented methods. However, when labelled data is limited, simpler SPM formulations paired up with generative methods offer a viable and computationally

Table 1. Summary table of the best accuracy in each dataset (results presented- SC for the binary case, pLSA for the 5-category case)

Method	Dataset	
	Bin	5-class
SPM+SVM	0.82696	0.8848
Pre-trained ConvNet	0.945	0.861
Both methods	0.80928	0.87648

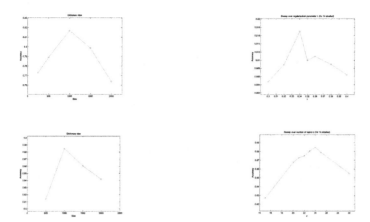

Fig. 1. Example images of the 5-category dataset. From top to bottom, a pair of images with the galaxy, cat, dog, fish and whale labels are presented, respectively

Table 2. SPM+pLSA confusion matrix for training with 1000 labelled examples for the 5-category dataset, accuracy of 0.8848

Labelled	Predicted				
	Cat	Dog	Fish	Whale	Galaxy
Cat	2013	429	-	-	-
Dog	440	2004	-	-	-
Fish	-	-	2249	201	-
Whale	-	-	144	2309	-
Galaxy	-	-	-	-	2481

Table 3. SPM+pLSA confusion matrix for training with 500 labelled and 500 unlabelled examples for the 5-category dataset, accuracy of 0.87648

Labelled	Predicted				
	Cat	Dog	Fish	Whale	Galaxy
Cat	1998	466	-	-	-
Dog	473	2000	-	-	-
Fish	-	-	2231	202	-
Whale	-	-	189	2261	-
Galaxy	-	-	-	-	2466

lighter solution. These can be used ether in alternative to pre-trained ConvNet models or in conjunction with these, in an ensemble that utilizes the strong points of either approach. One thing to note is that the regularity of classes (that is, how similar elements of each class are) is correlated with accuracy in methods which use SVMs. This can be seen by observing the confusion matrices Tables 2 and 3, noting that the galaxy, fish and whale category have higher regularity. This is an obvious result, as variance within the same class results in more features being captured in each individual image and also in the possibility of some of those features being similar to those present in other classes (as is the case for the cat and dog categories). If a class is very regular, it's also very easily predicted as some very salient, distinct features can be found across all elements of such a class. Considerations about the nature of dataset, the idiosyncrasies of the classification task and limiting factors related to computational resources and time available can weight in favor of some methods and detriment of others. A trade-of was ultimately shown to be present when choosing which method better fits a specific problem.

4 Conclusion

Despite the limitations on available computational resources and the modest time frame in which the study was carried, it was shown that the features extracted by the pre-trained ConvNet model were useful for image classification tasks, yielding comparable accuracy to more traditional methods. Furthermore, when used in conjunction with more typical generative methods for visual vocabulary generation, these allowed to replace labelled data with unlabelled data through the class estimation scheme described without incurring a significant accuracy loss. The results validate the hypothesis that pre-trained ConvNet models can be quite useful in providing an earlier estimation of the class to which an unlabelled image belongs, for posterior use in other models. Furthermore, it was shown that, through some empirical tuning of various weight parameters, the class scores generated by these pre-trained models can offer a satisfactory estimation of the confidence for the tentative labelling provided by the ConvNet. Through the various experiments in both datasets, the performance of multiple SPM models with generative methods creating a visual vocabulary on a dataset with a mixture of labelled and unlabelled data was either kept at a competitive accuracy level. Particularly, the pLSA formulation showed slight performance increases in the labelled and unlabelled mixed sets (of slight over 1%) compared to utilizing only the ConvNet, whilst displaying only very minimal accuracy losses (less than 2% in all cases) compared to the usage of solely labelled data for training. The study showed the benefit of allying the statistical formulation from generative models, which captures richer information in smaller, sparser feature vectors, with out-the-box ConvNet models trained in large, generic datasets. Further, this yielded a decrease in the training time, due to a shorter vocabulary creation step. The fictitious topic vectors created from the multinomial model built on top of the LDA/pLSA models were also validated as another tool to combat insufficient data for some categories, if used with care.

In the future, studying other ways to further integrate these generative methods with ConvNets or explore more elaborate schemes for utilizing the class scores from pre-trained networks might yield even better results.

References

1. Jia, Y., Shelhamer, E., Donahue, J., Karayev, S., Long, J., Girshick, R., Guadarrama, S., Darrell, T.: Caffe: Convolutional Architecture for Fast Feature Embedding (2014)
2. Krizhevsky, A., Sutskever, I., Hinton, G.E.: ImageNet classification with deep convolutional neural networks. Adv. Neural Inf. Process. Syst. **25**(2), 1–9 (2012)
3. Bosch, A., Zisserman, A., Munoz, X.: Scene classification using a hybrid generative/discriminative approach. IEEE Trans. Pattern Anal. Mach. Intell. **30**, 712–727 (2008)
4. Yang, J., Yu, K., Gong, Y., Huang, T.: Linear spatial pyramid matching using sparse coding for image classification. In: CVPR 2009 (2009)
5. Lazebnik, S., Schmid, C., Ponce, J.: Beyond bags of features: spatial pyramid matching for recognizing natural scene categories. In: Proceedings of the IEEE Computer Society Conference on Computer Vision and Pattern Recognition, vol. 2, pp. 2169–2178 (2006)
6. Sanchez, J., Perronnin, F., Mensink, T.: Image classification with the fisher vector: theory and practice. In: CVPR 2013 (2013)
7. Lee, C., Chiang, K.: Latent semantic analysis for classifying scene images. In: Proceedings of the International MultiConference of Engineers and Computer Scientists, vol. 2, pp. 17–20 (2010)

Simple and Effective Multi-word Query Spotting in Handwritten Text Images

Ernesto Noya-García, Alejandro H. Toselli[(✉)], and Enrique Vidal

PRHLT Research Centre, Universitat Politècnica de València,
Camino de Vera, s/n, 46022 Valencia, Spain
{noya,ahector,evidal}@prhlt.upv.es

Abstract. Keyword spotting techniques are becoming cost-effective solutions for information retrieval in handwritten documents. We explore the extension of the single-word, line-level probabilistic indexing approach described in [1,2] to allow page-level Boolean combinations of several single-keyword queries. We propose heuristic rules to combine the single-word relevance probabilities into probabilistically consistent confidence scores of the multi-word boolean combinations. As a preliminary study, this paper focuses on evaluating the search performance of word-pair queries involving just one *OR* or *AND* Boolean operation. Empirical results of this study support the proposed approach and clearly show its effectiveness.

1 Introduction

In recent years, large collections of historical handwritten documents are being scanned into digital images, in order to make them available through web sites of libraries and archives all over the world. Despite this, the wealth of information conveyed by the text captured in these digitizations remains largely inaccessible, as the vast majority of these text images are not transcribed. Moreover, it is also well known that transcribing such documents by paleography experts is usually very expensive. Consequently, to exploit and make profit of such mass-digitization efforts, affordable information retrieval methods are required which allow the users to accurately and efficiently search for textual contents in large image collections. Actually, this is one of the goals of the *tranScriptorium*[1] project [3], where probabilistic indexing methods based on *segmentation-free line-oriented Keyword spotting* (KWS) are being developed [1,2]. These methods rely on handwritten text recognition (HTR) models such as optical *Hidden Markov Models* (HMMs) and *N*-gram language models. Using these models, probabilistic word indices are built, assuming the finest search unit is the line

---

This work was partially supported by the Generalitat Valenciana under the Prometeo/2009/014 project grant ALMAMATER, and through the EU projects: HIMANIS (JPICH programme, Spanish grant Ref. PCIN-2015-068) and READ (Horizon-2020 programme, grant Ref. 674943).

[1] http://www.transcriptorium.eu.

L.A. Alexandre et al. (Eds.): IbPRIA 2017, LNCS 10255, pp. 76–84, 2017.
DOI: 10.1007/978-3-319-58838-4_9

image; that is, whole line images are analyzed to determine the degree of confidence that each given keyword appears in the image.

However, for searching in large collections involving millions of page images, line-level indexing can be less than adequate. The storage space required for the fine-grained line-level indices might become prohibitive and, on the other hand, a coarser, page-level search can be more than enough in most applications.

In this work, we (rather straightforwardly) extend the line-level indexing approach described in [1,2] to build word indices at page-level. In addition, we explore the feasibility of Boolean combination of single-word queries by introducing heuristic, albeit probabilistically consistent confidence score combination rules. To avoid large computational costs entailed by experimentation with many-word queries, in this preliminary study, we report empirical results of page-level *AND* and *OR* boolean queries involving only two keywords.

2   Single-Word Probabilistic Indexing

The indexing approach proposed in this work follows the KWS ideas originally presented in [1]. A probabilistic word index is built at the page level. Let a page image, $\mathbf{x}$, be represented by their text line images: $\mathbf{x}_1, \ldots, \mathbf{x}_L$, where L is the total number of lines in the page. In turn, let each text line, $\mathbf{x}_l$, be represented by a feature vector sequence: $\mathbf{x}_l = x_{l1}, x_{l2}, \ldots, x_{lJ_l}$, where J_l is the length of $\mathbf{x}_l$. For each query word v and each page image $\mathbf{x}$, a score $S(\mathbf{x}, v)$ is obtained which measures how likely is the event "keyword v is written in $\mathbf{x}$", or re-phrased as "page image $\mathbf{x}$ is relevant for keyword v". This score is computed as:

$$S(\mathbf{x}, v) \stackrel{\text{def}}{=} \max_{\substack{1 \leq l \leq L \\ 1 \leq j \leq J_l}} P(v \mid \mathbf{x}, l, j) \tag{1}$$

where $P(v \mid \mathbf{x}, l, j)$, called *line-level frame word posterior*, is the probability that the word v is present in the page image $\mathbf{x}$ at line l and frame position j.

As shown in [1], for a given lexicon or vocabulary, V, this posterior can be accurately computed for each word in $v \in V$ and line image $\mathbf{x}_l$ using the same kind of optical, lexical and language statistical models as those used in HTR. In most previous works, N-grams and Hidden Markov Models (HMM) have been used for language and character optical modeling, respectively. These models are trained from moderate amounts of training images accompanied by the corresponding transcripts using well known statistical estimation techniques [4]. The lexicon, V, on the other hand, is also obtained from the training transcripts and possibly expanded with additional words obtained from other relevant texts, if they are available. Using these models, $P(v \mid \mathbf{x}, l, j)$ is computed for each l through an extension of the conventional process used to decode $\mathbf{x}_l$ [1].

Since $P(v \mid \mathbf{x}, l, j)$ is a well-defined discrete probability mass function, the score $S(\mathbf{x}, v)$ given in Eq. (1) can be properly used to define the following Bernoulli distribution:

$$P(\mathcal{R} \mid \mathbf{x}, v) \stackrel{\text{def}}{=} \begin{cases} S(\mathbf{x}, v) & \mathcal{R} = 1 \\ 1 - S(\mathbf{x}, v) & \mathcal{R} = 0 \end{cases} \tag{2}$$

where the random variable $\mathcal{R}$ represents the event "page image $\mathbf{x}$ is relevant for keyword v". In order to explicitly assume this probabilistic meaning of $S(\mathbf{x}, v)$, from now on we will refer to it as $P(\mathcal{R} = 1 \mid \mathbf{x}, v)$, or simply $P(\mathcal{R} \mid \mathbf{x}, v)$.

It is worth pointing out that $P(v \mid \mathbf{x}, i, j)$ and thereby $P(\mathcal{R} \mid \mathbf{x}, v)$, can be easily computed during an off-line indexing phase for each page image and for all v in V (or for all v for which $P(\mathcal{R} \mid \mathbf{x}, v)$ is not negligible). This avoids having to carry out heavy computations during user's query lookup and permits extremely fast query processing.

3   Multi-keyword Spotting

To simplify notation, in this section $P(\mathcal{R} \mid \mathbf{x}, v)$ will be just denoted as $P(\mathcal{R}_v \mid \mathbf{x})$. Moreover, we restrict the discussion to a fixed page image $\mathbf{x}$, so it can be dropped from the formulation. This way, $P(\mathcal{R} \mid \mathbf{x}, v)$ becomes just $P(\mathcal{R}_v)$.

We are interested in queries that are boolean combinations of several keywords, $v_1, ..., v_M$, using the three basic boolean operators: OR, AND and NOT, respectively denoted as "$\vee$", "$\wedge$" and "$\neg$". The relevance of $\mathbf{x}$ for an m-fold AND query is then written as $\mathcal{R}_{v_1} \wedge \mathcal{R}_{v_2} \cdots \wedge \mathcal{R}_{v_M}$, or just $\mathcal{R}_1 \wedge \mathcal{R}_2 \cdots \wedge \mathcal{R}_M$, for the sake of further simplifying notation. Similarly, the event for an OR query is denoted as $\mathcal{R}_1 \vee \mathcal{R}_2 \cdots \vee \mathcal{R}_M$.

Computing the probability of events associated with arbitrarily complex combinations of these boolean operators can become very complex and, moreover, even for the simplest cases, the probabilities of conditional dependencies (which can hardly be ignored) are needed. Therefore, in this paper we propose convenient, efficiently computable approximations and we assess their suitability for multi-keyword KWS through empirical tests presented in Sects. 4 and 5. These approximations are:

$$P(\mathcal{R}_1 \wedge \mathcal{R}_2 \cdots \wedge \mathcal{R}_M) \approx \min(P(\mathcal{R}_1), P(\mathcal{R}_2), \ldots, P(\mathcal{R}_M)) \qquad (3)$$

$$P(\mathcal{R}_1 \vee \mathcal{R}_2 \cdots \vee \mathcal{R}_M) \approx \max(P(R_1), P(\mathcal{R}_2), \ldots, P(\mathcal{R}_M)) \qquad (4)$$

In addition, the relevance probability of the NOT operator applied to a Boolean query combination, $\mathcal{B}$, is computed as:

$$P(\neg \mathcal{B}) = 1 - P(\mathcal{B}) \qquad (5)$$

Using these equations, the (approximate) relevance probability of any arbitrary boolean combination of single-keyword queries can be easily and very efficiently computed. For example, to search for image regions containing both the words "cat" and "dog" but none of the words "mouse" or "rabbit" the relevance probability will be computed as:

$$P(\mathcal{R}_1 \wedge \mathcal{R}_2 \wedge \neg(\mathcal{R}_3 \vee \mathcal{R}_4)) \approx$$

$$\min(P(\mathcal{R}_1), P(\mathcal{R}2), (1 - \max(P(\mathcal{R}_3), P(\mathcal{R}_4))))$$

where the events $\mathcal{R}_1, \mathcal{R}_2, \mathcal{R}_3$ and $\mathcal{R}_4$ correspond to the keywords "cat", "dog", "mouse" and "rabbit", respectively.

4   Experimental Setup

To assess the effectiveness of the proposed multi-word query spotting approach, several experiments were carried out. The dataset, the evaluation measures and the experimental setup are presented next.

4.1   Dataset

The whole set contains more than 80 000 images of manuscripts written by the renowned English philosopher and reformer Jeremy Bentham (1748-1832) and his secretarial staff [5]. From the Bentham data currently available, only a small (and relatively simple) set of 433 page images is used in this work. It is exactly the same dataset used in the ICFHR-2014 HTRtS contest [6]. These pages contain nearly 110 000 running words and a vocabulary of more than 9 500 different words. The last column in Table 1-left summarizes the basic statistics of these pages.[2]

Table 1. Basic statistics of the Bentham dataset used in the ICFHR-2014 HTRtS contest [6] (left) and of the single and word-pair query sets for *AND* and *OR* Boolean operations (right).

Number of:	Training	Valid.	Test
Pages	350	50	33
Lines	9 198	1 415	860
Run. words	86 075	12 962	7 868
Lexicon	8 658	2 709	1 946
Run. OOV	-	857	417
OOV Lex.	-	681	377
Char set size	86	86	86
Run. Chars	442 336	67 400	40 938

	Operat.	Total	Pertin.
	Single	3 293	674
Qrys	*OR*	5 420 278	1 992 007
	AND	5 420 278	11 784
	Single	108 669	836
Qry Events	*OR*	178 869 174	2 739 674
	AND	178 869 174	12 438

The dataset was divided into three subsets for training, validation and test, respectively encompassing 350, 50 and 33 images. Since it was not possible to accurately identify the writers in all cases, the pages were shuffled before distributing them over these three subsets. This means that some writers can appear both in the training and in the test sets. Table 1-left contains details of these partitions. The rows "Running words" and "Running OOV" show the total number of words and Out-Of-Vocabulary (OOV) words, respectively. The OOV words in the Validation column are words that do not appear in the training set, while those in the Test column are words that do not appear neither in the training nor in the validation sets. The row "OOV Lexicon" shows the number of *different* OOV words.

---

[2] Note that these statistics were obtained without any kind of tokenization; that is, each non-blank sequence of characters is assumed to be a "word".

For each page image, text line regions were automatically obtained and manually revised. Note that many of these images are short lines; for example, 9.5% of the line images contain just one word. It should be emphasized that word N-gram language models are of little help to capture context in this kind of lines.

4.2   Query Selection

As commented in Sect. 1, this preliminary study explores queries encompassing only two words, combined using the two Boolean operators *AND* and *OR*. The query selection procedure for both single and word-pair queries consisted in choosing all the words from a subset of the *training* vocabulary. This subset is composed of 3 293 words whose frequency of occurrence in the training partition ranges from 2 to 10. In this way, we avoid including most *stop words* (generally with word frequencies greater than 10) and also words that are unlikely to appear in the test partition (these words are called *"non-pertinent"* below). In page-level KWS experiments, rather than the number of queries, it is more informative to consider the total number of *query events*; that is, the number of pairs composed of an image and a query. A query event is *pertinent* if the page image is relevant for the query (i.e., the query is actually written in the image). Table 1-right shows basic information about the query sets used.

According to Table 1-right, from the large amount of query events, only a few are actually *pertinent*, even though most of the test page images are relevant to at least one of the selected queries.

Note that, by selecting the queries in this way, there may be many queries involving words which are not actually written in any of the test page images. We say that these queries are *non-pertinent*. Clearly, spotting *non-pertinent* queries is also challenging, since the system may erroneously find other similar queries, thereby leading to important precision degradation. Overall, the selected queries constitute rather challenging sets.

4.3   KWS Evaluation Measures

To assess KWS effectiveness, we employed the standard *recall* and *interpolated precision* measures, which are functions of a threshold used to decide whether a relevance probability $P(\mathcal{R} \mid \mathbf{x}, v)$ (see Eq. (2)) is high enough to assume that a word v is in the page $\mathbf{x}$. Interpolated precision is widely used to avoid cases in which plain precision can be ill-defined [7]. Moreover, the popular scalar measure called *average precision* (AP) [8,9] and the so-called *R-precision* (RP) are also used. The AP is defined as the area under the Recall-Precision curve. On the other hand, the most simple RP measure is defined as the precision (or recall) for some not null threshold such that *recall* is equal to *interpolated precision*. In addition, the maximum value of the *harmonic mean* of precision and recall, called F_1-*measure*, is used also to assess the overall behavior of a search and retrieval system.

4.4   System Setup

In order to build the page-level index, transcribed line images of the training partition were used to train both the morphological, lexical and language models.

86 left-to-right character HMMs were trained from the line images, represented as 24-dimensional feature vector sequences computed according to [10]. HMM training consisted in 20 iterations of the Embedded Baum Welch algorithm [4,11], followed by 10 iterations of Lattice Based Extended Baum-Welch Discriminative Training, as described in [12]. Likewise, for better lexicon and language model training, an improved text tokenization was applied which rules white-space among words, punctuation marks and digits (see [13]). A 2-gram word language model was trained using the Kneser-Ney back-off smoothing technique [14]. Meta-parameters associated with 2-gram and HMM training (*grammar scale factor, word insertion penalty, number of states* per HMM and *number of gaussians* per state) were tuned using the validation partition. See [13] for more details about these settings.

Finally, using the previously trained models, page-level posterior probabilities of single-word queries, $P(\mathcal{R} \mid \mathbf{x}, v)$, were obtained as in Eq. (2) (see Sect. 2), as well as the corresponding probabilities for *AND* and *OR* word-pair queries, according to Eqs. (3 and 4).

5   Results and Discussion

Recall – Precision (R-P) curves and corresponding overall KWS performance in terms of *average-precision, R-precision* and maximum F_1-*measure* were obtained for the tree different query sets defined in Sect. 4.2 (see Fig. 1).

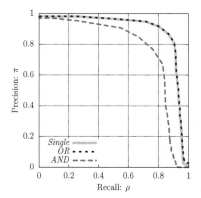

Operat.	AP	RP	F_1^*
Single	0.894	0.867	0.871
OR	0.897	0.868	0.872
AND	0.775	0.765	0.772

Fig. 1. Left: KWS *Recall-Precision* curve (with interpolated precision) for *Single* (one-word) and for word-pair *AND* and *OR* queries. Right: Average Precision (**AP**), R-Precision (**RP**) and maximum F_1-measure (**F_1^***) for the three query sets considered.

From the R-P curves and the reported AP, RP and **F_1^*** figures, we can observe that *Single* and word-pair *OR* queries achieve very similar, good performance, being the latter slightly better than the former. This is as expected, since it is obviously more likely to find one of the words of a word pair in a page that each of them individually.

On the other hand, the search performance of word-pair *AND* queries, is significantly worse than both that of *OR* combinations and single words. We have to note here that for *AND* combinations, the proportion of *pertinent* queries is much smaller than those for *OR* combinations and single words (see Table 1-right). In fact, we measured the performance considering only the 11 784 *pertinent* queries, and the AP increased to 0.931 (also RP and $\mathbf{F}_1^*$ went up to 0.913 and 0.929 respectively). This means that most of the degradation for *AND* queries is due to false positives produced when trying to spot non-pertinent word-pairs. Clearly, when trying to find a word-pair which does not actually exist in any of the test images, a perfect system should not produce any spot, unless the confidence threshold is set to 0. So precision performance may degrade in these cases if false positives are obtained for non-negligibly high confidence thresholds.

Despite this relative degradation of *AND* queries, we should point out that the performance achieved in all the cases is very good, as compared with similar performance figures reported in most recent works on KWS. The high degree of usability of these results can be checked through real tests using the public demonstration system described in the following section.

6   Demonstration System

In order to provide a user-friendly interface that allows for public testing of this approach, a demonstrator[3] was implemented. Figure 2 show search results corresponding to the query "`easy Jail`" at the book and the page levels, respectively.

Fig. 2. KWS GUI showing search query results at page (left) and at line (right) levels.

---

[3] http://transcriptorium.eu/demots/kws/index.php.

7 Remarks, Conclusion and Future Work

Following the live-level, single-keyword, probabilistic KWS approach introduced in [1,2], in this paper we have presented simple but probabilistically consistent approximations to deal with boolean combinations of single-word KWS queries at the page level. We have also presented a preliminary study to evaluate the search performance of multi-keyword spotting based on these approximations.

Both single-query and word-pair *OR* query results are excellent, while a significant (albeit natural) degradation is observed for word-pair *AND* queries.

In future works we plan to extend the empirical study by studying the performance achieved for queries entailing more than 2 keywords and more complex Boolean expressions, including a variety of combinations of *OR*, *AND* and *NOT* operations. Additionally, it is indeed of interest to study how the word occurrence frequencies in the training data can affect the search performance of multi-word queries.

References

1. Toselli, A.H., Vidal, E., Romero, V., Frinken, V.: HMM word-graph based keyword spotting in handwritten document images. Int. J. Inf. Sci. **370**, 497–518 (2015)
2. Toselli, A.H., Vidal, E., Romero, V., Frinken, V.: Word-graph based keyword spotting and indexing of handwritten document images. Technical report, Universitat Politècnica de València (2013)
3. Sánchez, J., Mühlberger, G., Gatos, B., Schofield, P., Depuydt, K., Davis, R., Vidal, E., de Does, J.: tranScriptorium: an European project on handwritten text recognition. In: DocEng, pp. 227–228 (2013)
4. Jelinek, F.: Statistical Methods for Speech Recognition. MIT Press, Cambridge (1998)
5. Causer, T., Wallace, V.: Building a volunteer community: results and findings from Transcribe Bentham. Digit. Humanit. Q. **6**(2) (2012)
6. Sanchez, J.A., Romero, V., Toselli, A., Vidal, E.: ICFHR2014 Competition on Handwritten Text Recognition on Transcriptorium Datasets (HTRtS). In: 2014 14th International Conference on Frontiers in Handwriting Recognition (ICFHR), pp. 785–790, September 2014
7. Manning, C.D., Raghavan, P., Schutze, H.: Introduction to Information Retrieval. Cambridge University Press, New York (2008)
8. Zhu, M.: Recall, Precision and Average Precision. Working Paper 2004–09 Department of Statistics & Actuarial Science, University of Waterloo, 26 August 2004
9. Robertson, S.: A new interpretation of average precision. In: Proceedings of the International ACM SIGIR Conference on Research and Development in Information Retrieval (SIGIR 2008), pp. 689–690. ACM, New York (2008)
10. Kozielski, M., Forster, J., Ney, H.: Moment-based image normalization for handwritten text recognition. In: Proceedings of the 2012 International Conference on Frontiers in Handwriting Recognition, ICFHR 2012, pp. 256–261. IEEE Computer Society, Washington, DC (2012)
11. Young, S., Odell, J., Ollason, D., Valtchev, V., Woodland, P.: The HTK Book: Hidden Markov Models Toolkit V2.1. Cambridge Research Laboratory Ltd. (1997)

12. Young, S., Evermann, G., Gales, M., Hain, T., Kershaw, D.: The HTK Book: Hidden Markov Models Toolkit V3.4. Microsoft Corporation & Cambridge Research Laboratory Ltd., March 2009
13. Toselli, A., Vidal, E.: Handwritten text recognition results on the Bentham collection with improved classical N-gram-HMM methods. In: 3rd International Workshop on Historical Document Imaging and Processing (HIP 2015), pp. 15–22, August 2015
14. Kneser, R., Ney, H.: Improved backing-off for N-gram language modeling. In: International Conference on Acoustics, Speech and Signal Processing (ICASSP 1995), vol. 1, Los Alamitos, CA, USA, pp. 181–184. IEEE Computer Society (1995)

Computer Vision

Recognizing Activities of Daily Living from Egocentric Images

Alejandro Cartas[1](✉), Juan Marín[1], Petia Radeva[1,2], and Mariella Dimiccoli[1,2]

[1] MAIA Department, University of Barcelona, 08007 Barcelona, Spain
alejandro.cartas@ub.edu, jmarinve7@alumnes.ub.edu
[2] Computer Vision Center, Cerdanyola del Vallès, 08193 Barcelona, Spain

Abstract. Recognizing Activities of Daily Living (ADLs) has a large number of health applications, such as characterize lifestyle for habit improvement, nursing and rehabilitation services. Wearable cameras can daily gather large amounts of image data that provide rich visual information about ADLs than using other wearable sensors. In this paper, we explore the classification of ADLs from images captured by low temporal resolution wearable camera (2 fpm) by using a Convolutional Neural Networks (CNN) approach. We show that the classification accuracy of a CNN largely improves when its output is combined, through a random decision forest, with contextual information from a fully connected layer. The proposed method was tested on a subset of the NTCIR-12 egocentric dataset, consisting of 18,674 images and achieved an overall accuracy of 86% activity recognition on 21 classes.

Keywords: Egocentric vision · Lifelogging · Activity recognition · Convolutional neural networks

1 Introduction

The Activities of Daily Living (ADLs) include, but are not limited to the activities that an independent person performs on daily basis for living at home or in a community [8]. The monitoring of these activities on elderly people could prevent health problems [8,11]. Recently, egocentric (first-person) cameras have been used to monitor ADLs, because they can provide richer contextual information than using only traditional sensors [9]. These lifelogging devices can generate large volumes of data in matter of days. For instance, a wearable camera such as the Narrative Clip can take more than 2,800 pictures per day from an egocentric (first-person) point of view. To extract information about the behavior of a user, these data needs to be classified in an orderly and timely fashion.

Over the last five years, egocentric activity recognition has been an active area of research. Fathi et al. [2] presented a probabilistic model that classifies activities from short egocentric videos. Their approach models an activity into

---

A. Cartas and J. Marín—Equally contributed.

L.A. Alexandre et al. (Eds.): IbPRIA 2017, LNCS 10255, pp. 87–95, 2017.
DOI: 10.1007/978-3-319-58838-4_10

a set of different actions, and each action is modeled per frame as a spatio-temporal relationship between the hands and the objects involved on it. They further extend their work [3] by another probabilistic generative model that incorporates the gaze features and that models an action as a sequence of frames. Pirsiavash and Ramanan [10] introduced a dataset of 18 egocentric actions of daily activities performed by 20 persons in unscripted videos. Furthermore, they presented a temporal pyramid to encode spatio-temporal features along with detected active objects knowledge. These temporal pyramids are the input of support vector machines trained for action recognition. More recently, Ma et al. [7] proposed a twin stream Convolutional Neural Network (CNN) architecture for activity recognition from videos. One of the streams is used for recognizing the appearance of an object based on a hand segmentation and a region of interest. The other stream recognizes the action using an optical flow sequence. In order to recognize activities, both streams are join and the last layers are finetuned.

Activity classification from egocentric photo streams is even more difficult problem than from video, since they provide less contextual action information. Castro et al. [1] introduced a lifelogging dataset composed of 40,103 egocentric images from one subject taken during a 6 months period. The images from this dataset were annotated in 19 different activity categories. In this dataset, the activities performed by the user tend to be routinary and in the same environment. In other words, the activities are almost performed daily at the same time and involved the same objects. Consequently, time and global image features such as color convey useful information for describing activities. To exploit both characteristics, the authors introduced the Late Fusion Ensemble (LTE) method that combines, through a random decision forest, the classification probabilities of a CNN with time and global features, namely color histogram, from the input image. The shortcoming of this approach is that it cannot be generalized to multiple users, since the network need to learn contextual information for each new user. For instance, two distinct persons might have different daily routines, depending on their job, age, etc.

In this work, we make a step forward on activity recognition from egocentric images by generalizing the task of activity recognition to multiple users. Our approach combines the outputs of different layers of a CNN and use them as the input of a random decision forest. We tested our method on a subset of the NTCIR-12 egocentric dataset [4], consisting of 18,674 pictures acquired by three users and annotated with 21 activity labels. Some examples of labeled images with their corresponding category are shown in Fig. 1. Our approach is similar to the LTE introduced in [1], in the sense that it uses a random forest to combine the output of a CNN with contextual information. However, there are several differences that should be highlighted. First, the problem itself we face is different: instead of classifying the activities of a single user, we classify the activities of three different users from a dataset having less than half the number of images of the one used in [1]. Hence, our task is more challenging because we must deal with an increased intra-class variability with a much smaller number of images. In addition, since the pictures from the dataset were taken by users with

Fig. 1. Examples of annotated images with their corresponding activity label.

different lifestyles, our method cannot take advantage of their time information and color histogram. To face these problems, instead of using time and color as contextual information, we use the output of a fully connected layer of the CNN.

The rest of the paper is organized as follows: in Sect. 2 we provide an overview of our approach. In Sect. 3, we introduce the dataset used in the experiments and we briefly describe the annotation tool we created for labeling. We detail the methodology we followed for conducting our experiments and the different combinations of networks and layers we used in Sect. 4. The results we obtained are discussed in Sect. 5. Finally, in Sect. 6, we present our conclusion and final remarks.

2   Activity Classification

Our activity classification method is an ensemble composed of a CNN and a random forest. Specifically, our approach joins the output vectors from two layers of a CNN, i.e. the fully connected and the softmax layers, and gives them as input to a random forest. The training of the ensemble is a two-step process. First, a CNN is finetuned and then a random forest is trained over its output vectors.

The objective of our experiments was to show how the classification performance of the CNN improves by using contextual information. In these experiments, we used two networks as the base of our ensembles, namely the AlexNet [6] and GoogLeNet [12]. Both neural networks were finetuned on a subset of images from the NTCIR-12 dataset [4] annotated for activity classification.

3   Dataset

In our experiments, we used a subset of images from the NTCIR-12 dataset [4] that consists of 89,593 egocentric pictures belonging to three persons. Each user

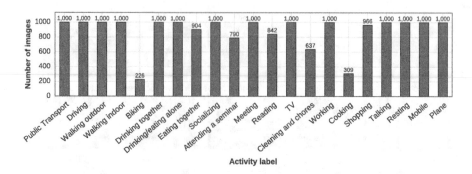

Fig. 2. Our dataset summary.

worn a first-person camera in a period of almost a month, totaling 79 days. This camera passively took two pictures per minute.

The dataset we used in this work, consists of a subset of 18,674 images from the NTCIR-12 dataset. These pictures correspond to all users and have different dates and times. We used 21 activity categories to label them using our annotation tool, which is briefly detailed in the next subsection. Although our subset of annotated images is imbalanced, less than the half of categories have less instances than the rest. Some examples of annotated activities and the distribution of the number of images by category are shown in Figs. 1 and 2, respectively. The dataset was split in 13,991 training images, 1,857 validation images, and 2,796 testing images. This split maintained the same proportion of examples per category and was used in all our experiments.

Annotation Tool. We created a web-based annotation tool specifically target for labeling large amounts of images. The following design guidelines were considered:

- *Easy interaction.* Browsing and annotating large number of images can be done in an intuitive way. Additionally, descriptive tags can be individually added to a specific picture.
- *Speed and performance.* The tool can handle several connected users at the same time and present their large collection of pictures.
- *Privacy and security.* Personal pictures of a user are maintained private.

4 Methodology

The main objective of the experiments was to determine if contextual information can improve the activity classification accuracy of a CNN by ensembling the CNN with a random forest. Additionally, we tried to find out the ensemble with the best combination of layers for performance improvement. For training and testing purposes we used the dataset split described in the last section. Since the dataset was imbalanced, we assessed the performance of the ensembles by not only using the accuracy, but also macro metrics for precision, recall, and F1-score. The next subsection presents all the proposed ensemble configurations with their respective training procedure.

4.1   Ensemble Configurations

In order to train our ensembles, we first fine-tuned AlexNet and GoogLeNet on our dataset. Both models were fine-tuned using the Caffe framework [5] with the same number of iterations (approx. 10 epochs) and the following settings:

– **AlexNet**. It was trained using stochastic gradient descent for 2,180 iterations with a batch size of 64 images, a learning rate $\alpha = 3 \times 10^{-5}$, and a momentum $\mu = 0.9$.
– **GoogLeNet**. It was trained for 4,370 iterations with a batch size of 32 images, a learning rate $\alpha = 3.7 \times 10^{-5}$, and a momentum $\mu = 0.9$.

After fine-tuning our baseline networks, we train several ensembles of random forests combining different final output layers of the CNNs. The following combinations were used in our experiments:

– **AlexNet+RF on Prob**. This configuration was trained using a random forest of 500 trees on the softmax probability layer.
– **GoogLeNet+RF on Prob**. This configuration was trained using a random forest of 500 trees on the softmax probability layer.
– **AlexNet+RF on FC6**. We trained a random forest of 500 trees on only the first fully connected layer (FC6), containing a vector of 4,096 elements.
– **AlexNet+RF on FC6+Prob**. A random forest of 500 trees was trained on the FC6 and the softmax layers of AlexNet, thus summing a vector of 4,117 elements.
– **GoogLeNet+RF on Pool5/7 × 7+Prob**. This configuration was trained using a random forest of 500 trees on the pool5/7 × 7 fully connected layer and the softmax probability layer, thus having a vector of 1,045 features.

5   Results

Our experiments show that the ensemble of CNN plus a random forest improves the performance for both baseline CNN. Table 1 shows the classification performance on the baseline CNN and on different ensembles. The baseline CNN have a similar performance. After using the random forest on the output the softmax layer, the accuracy improved around 4%. Specifically, the recall of some categories with fewer learning instances improved significantly, such as *Cooking*, and *Cleaning and Choring*. Additionally, high overlapping classes such as *Drinking/Eating alone* and *Eating together* also improved their accuracy. The improvement over the overlapping classes can also be seen the confusion matrices

Table 1. Comparison of the ensembles of CNN+Random forest on different combinations of layers. Upper table shows the recall per class and the lower table shows the performance metrics.

Activity	AlexNet	AlexNet+RF on FC6	AlexNet+RF on Prob	AlexNet+RF on FC6+Prob	GoogLeNet	GoogLeNet+RF on Prob	GoogLeNet+RF on pool5/7x7+prob
Public Transport	82.17	**87.60**	86.05	86.82	79.07	80.62	84.50
Driving	100.00	100.00	100.00	100.00	100.00	100.00	100.00
Walking outdoor	84.52	86.31	**88.10**	86.31	83.93	85.12	**88.10**
Walking indoor	61.88	68.75	65.00	**71.88**	60.00	63.75	68.75
Biking	**81.58**	73.68	78.95	73.68	68.42	71.05	76.32
Drinking together	84.09	**90.91**	82.58	87.88	76.52	80.30	87.88
Drinking/eating alone	70.89	**84.81**	74.05	80.38	60.13	70.25	75.95
Eating together	76.56	**86.72**	80.47	82.81	75.78	82.03	85.16
Socializing	65.31	**89.80**	77.55	83.67	63.95	72.11	79.59
Attending a seminar	89.92	**93.28**	89.08	**93.28**	82.35	86.55	89.08
Meeting	78.01	85.82	80.14	85.11	73.76	82.98	**87.94**
Reading	69.40	84.33	77.61	82.09	85.82	83.58	**86.57**
TV	88.74	95.36	92.72	94.04	94.70	96.03	**98.01**
Cleaning and chores	44.74	61.40	56.14	71.93	51.75	67.54	**77.19**
Working	89.24	**95.57**	91.14	**95.57**	90.51	91.77	94.94
Cooking	31.11	46.67	**48.89**	42.22	24.44	37.78	44.44
Shopping	73.88	**85.07**	76.12	81.34	76.87	76.87	78.36
Talking	70.47	82.55	77.85	81.88	71.81	78.52	**83.89**
Resting	98.70	**99.35**	98.70	**99.35**	97.40	98.70	**99.35**
Mobile	79.19	85.91	85.23	**88.59**	79.87	84.56	86.58
Plane	90.91	93.01	91.61	90.91	93.71	94.41	**96.50**
Accuracy	78.51	**86.58**	82.36	85.79	78.11	82.22	86.04
Macro precision	78.46	**87.29**	81.57	86.83	77.17	81.55	86.20
Macro recall	76.73	**84.61**	80.86	83.80	75.75	80.22	84.24
Macro F1-score	77.09	**85.45**	81.11	84.68	76.06	80.64	84.84

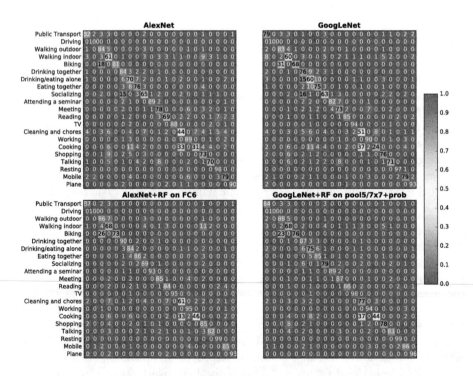

Fig. 3. Normalized confusion matrices of the best combination of layers for each baseline convolutional neural network. This figure is best seen in color. (Color figure online)

Drinking/eating alone   Meeting   Reading

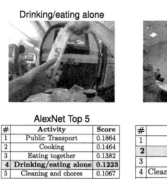  

AlexNet Top 5

#	Activity	Score
1	Public Transport	0.1864
2	Cooking	0.1464
3	Eating together	0.1382
4	**Drinking/eating alone**	**0.1223**
5	Cleaning and chores	0.1067

GoogLeNet Top 5

#	Activity	Score
1	Plane	0.2004
2	Public Transport	0.1943
3	Cleaning and chores	0.1450
4	Cooking	0.0925
5	**Drinking/eating alone**	**0.0748**

AlexNet Top 5

#	Activity	Score
1	Talking	0.2034
2	**Meeting**	**0.1701**
3	Cooking	0.1090
4	Cleaning and chores	0.0903
5	Shopping	0.0878

GoogLeNet Top 5

#	Activity	Score
1	**Eating together**	**0.3065**
2	Talking	0.1215
3	Socializing	0.1062
4	Cleaning and chores	0.08126
5	Meeting	0.0664

AlexNet Top 5

#	Activity	Score
1	**Drinking/eating alone**	**0.5002**
2	Cleaning and chores	0.1511748880
3	Eating together	0.1263086796
4	Shopping	0.0589886233
5	Drinking together	0.0251834411

GoogLeNet Top 5

#	Activity	Score
1	**Cleaning and chores**	**0.4259**
2	Eating together	0.1145323068
3	Drinking/eating alone	0.1137253270
4	Drinking together	0.0841688886
5	Reading	0.06203

Fig. 4. Classification activity examples. On top of each image is shown its true activity label and on bottom its top 5 predictions by AlexNet and GoogLeNet. Additionally, the result of the ensembles *AlexNet+RF on FC6* and *GoogLeNet+RF on Pool5/7 × 7+prob* is highlighted on color in its corresponding table. The green and red colors means true positive and false positive classification, respectively. (Color figure online)

shown in Fig. 3. This means that the random forest improved the classification of images belonging to categories that score similar probabilities. Moreover, the only decrease on accuracy is presented on the class *Biking*. Since its accuracy on the baseline CNN is very high (81.68%) considering the small number of learning instances (226), we believe this decrease is a consequence of the random forest trying to balance the prediction error among classes.

The results of adding contextual information from fully connected layers show a better performance on classification. Table 1 shows that the best ensembles were the *AlexNet+RF on FC6* and *GoogLeNet+RF on Pool5/7 × 7+prob*. Furthermore, these ensembles improved the baseline accuracy by 8.07% and 7.93% for AlexNet and GoogLeNet, respectively. Although the performance metrics improved decreasingly with respect to the ensembles that only used the softmax layer, the extra features removed the overfitting problem on the *Walking outdoor* category. Some classification examples are shown in Fig. 4.

6 Conclusion

We presented an egocentric activity classifier ensemble method, which combines different layers of a CNN through a random forest. Specifically, the random forest takes as input a vector containing the output of the softmax probability layer and a fully connected layer encoding global image features. We tested several ensembles based on AlexNet and GoogLeNet, achieving a 8% performance improvement on our dataset. The proposed method has been tested on a subset of the NTCIR-12 egocentric dataset consisting of 18,674 images that we labeled with 21 different activity labels. Although we obtained 86% accuracy on a quite difficult task, we believe that there is still room for improvement. Indeed, the proposed approach operates at image-level, without taking into account the temporal coherence of photo-streams. Future work will investigate how to take temporal coherence into account.

Acknowledgments. A.C. was supported by a doctoral fellowship from the Mexican Council of Science and Technology (CONACYT) (grant-no. 366596). This work was partially founded by TIN2015-66951-C2, SGR 1219, CERCA, *ICREA Academia'2014* and 20141510 (Marató TV3). The funders had no role in the study design, data collection, analysis, and preparation of the manuscript. M.D. is grateful to the NVIDIA donation program for its support with GPU card.

References

1. Castro, D., Hickson, S., Bettadapura, V., Thomaz, E., Abowd, G., Christensen, H., Essa, I.: Predicting daily activities from egocentric images using deep learning. In: Proceedings of the 2015 ACM International Symposium on Wearable Computers, pp. 75–82. ACM (2015)

2. Fathi, A., Farhadi, A., Rehg, J.M.: Understanding egocentric activities. In: 2011 International Conference on Computer Vision, pp. 407–414. IEEE (2011)

3. Fathi, A., Li, Y., Rehg, J.M.: Learning to recognize daily actions using gaze. In: Fitzgibbon, A., Lazebnik, S., Perona, P., Sato, Y., Schmid, C. (eds.) ECCV 2012. LNCS, vol. 7572, pp. 314–327. Springer, Heidelberg (2012). doi:10.1007/978-3-642-33718-5_23

4. Gurrin, C., Joho, H., Hopfgartner, F., Zhou, L., Albatal, R.: Overview of NTCIR-12 lifelog task. In: NTCIR-12, National Institute of Informatics (NII)

5. Jia, Y., Shelhamer, E., Donahue, J., Karayev, S., Long, J., Girshick, R., Guadarrama, S., Darrell, T.: Caffe: convolutional architecture for fast feature embedding (2014). arXiv preprint arXiv:1408.5093

6. Krizhevsky, A., Sutskever, I., Hinton, G.E.: Imagenet classification with deep convolutional neural networks. In: Pereira, F., Burges, C.J.C., Bottou, L., Weinberger, K.Q. (eds.) Advances in Neural Information Processing Systems, vol. 25, pp. 1097–1105. Curran Associates Inc. (2012)

7. Ma, M., Fan, H., Kitani, K.M.: Going deeper into first-person activity recognition. In: The IEEE Conference on Computer Vision and Pattern Recognition (CVPR), June 2016

8. Martin-Lesende, I., Vrotsou, K., Vergara, I., Bueno, A., Diez, A., et al.: Design and validation of the vida questionnaire, for assessing instrumental activities of daily living in elderly people. J Gerontol. Geriat. Res. **4**(214), 2 (2015)

9. Nguyen, T.-H.-C., Nebel, J.-C., Florez-Revuelta, F.: Recognition of activities of daily living with egocentric vision: a review. Sensors (Basel), **16**(1), 72 (2016). sensors-16-00072[PII]

10. Pirsiavash, H., Ramanan, D.: Detecting activities of daily living in first-person camera views. In: 2012 IEEE Conference on Computer Vision and Pattern Recognition (CVPR), pp. 2847–2854. IEEE (2012)

11. Schüssler-Fiorenza Rose, S.M., Stineman, M.G., Pan, Q., Bogner, H., Kurichi, J.E., Streim, J.E.: Potentially avoidable hospitalizations among people at different activity of daily living limitation stages. Health Serv. Res. **52**(1), 132–155 (2016)
12. Szegedy, C., Liu, W., Jia, Y., Sermanet, P., Reed, S., Anguelov, D., Erhan, D., Vanhoucke, V., Rabinovich, A.: Going deeper with convolutions. In: Computer Vision and Pattern Recognition (CVPR) (2015)

Strategies of Dictionary Usages for Sparse Representations for Pedestrian Classification

Carlos Serra-Toro, Ángel Hernández-Górriz, and V. Javier Traver[✉]

Institute of New Imaging Technologies (INIT),
Universitat Jaume I, Castellón de la Plana, Spain
vtraver@uji.es

Abstract. Sparse representations and methodologies are currently receiving much interest due to their benefits in image processing and classification tasks. Despite the progress achieved over the last years, there are still many open issues, in particular for applications such as object detection which have been much less addressed from the sparse-representation point of view. This work explores several strategies for dictionary usages and study their relative computational and discriminative values in the binary problem of pedestrian classification. Specifically, we explore whether both class-specific dictionaries are really required, or just any of them can be successfully used and, in case that both dictionaries are required, which is the better way to compute the sparse representation from them. Results reveal that different strategies offer different computational-classification trade-offs, and while dual-dictionary strategies may offer slightly better performance than single-dictionary strategies, one of the most interesting findings is that just one class (even the negative, non-pedestrian class) suffices to train a dictionary to be able to discriminate pedestrian from background images.

Keywords: Sparse coding · Dictionary learning · Pedestrian classification

1 Introduction

Sparse representations have received increasing interest in the last few years. These methodologies seek to represent a signal as a linear combination of a (reduced) number of atoms (code-words) of a dictionary, either predefined or learned from data. In the context of computer vision, these representations were initially applied to "reconstruction" problems, such as image denoising [6], or inpainting [7], with very competitive results. However, they have also been more recently applied, with reported benefits, in classification tasks such as face recognition [3,16], object and pedestrian detection [9,12] or action recognition [1,19].

Work partially supported by Spanish Ministry of Economy (TIN2013-46522-P) and Generalitat Valenciana (PROMETEOII/2014/062).

L.A. Alexandre et al. (Eds.): IbPRIA 2017, LNCS 10255, pp. 96–103, 2017.
DOI: 10.1007/978-3-319-58838-4_11

Despite the progress made on sparse and redundant representations and dictionary learning algorithms [10,15,17], there are still many theoretical and practical open issues, which makes this a hot topic today. As an illustrative example, a current debate exists on whether image classification in general or face recognition in particular are appropriate problems for sparse representations, or simpler approaches suffice, with different views and results being reported [3,13,14,18].

In this paper we focus on some practical aspects of dictionary usage for pedestrian classification. The problem of pedestrian classification/detection has received significantly less attention than face recognition with sparse representations. However, being a binary problem ("pedestrian" vs "non-pedestrian" classes), it has its own particularities worth addressing. For instance, in face verification, many possible classes (person identities) are considered and sparsity can be favourably related to more (non-zero) sparse coefficients being concentrated on the part of the representation corresponding to a single class (out of many others). This situation is somehow different with only two classes. Additionally, pedestrian classification can be seen as a one-class problem, where one class is well-defined (pedestrian), but the other one (non-pedestrian) is very broad and not so well-defined (there are a huge number of possible images of many things that do not look like pedestrians). The choice of the dictionary has an impact on the semantics of the data that is captured [17], and this may affect the classification performance. Therefore, it is relevant to study the effect on the computational and classification performances of learning and using different dictionaries. Since there are two classes, one choice is to learn two different class-specific dictionaries, but it is also possible to just learn a single dictionary, for the pedestrian (positive) class, for the non-pedestrian (negative) class or for both classes. In turn, there are several choices when generating the sparse representation of a new image given one or two of these dictionaries. Since it is not straightforward to decide in advance which option is best, in this work we experimentally evaluate these different approaches.

Although in most cases in image processing the atoms of the dictionary are taken or learned from the raw image data, our signal is the well-known HOG (Histogram Of Gradients) descriptor [2]. The use of this higher-level signal makes sense in classification tasks, in contrast to low-level reconstruction-like image processing tasks. It is also customary to divide an input image into a grid for computational or discriminatory purposes, with either all cells in the grid contributing to a single dictionary or having one dictionary per cell. However, we use the full HOG descriptor as an atom, without considering parts.

2 Methodology

We consider dictionaries $\mathbf{D} \in \mathbb{R}^{n \times k}$, i.e. with k atoms (code-words) each of dimension n. For convenience, we will refer to the "size" of the dictionary as its number of atoms, k. A signal $\mathbf{x} \in \mathbb{R}^n$ is represented by the sparse representation $\boldsymbol{\alpha} \in \mathbb{R}^k$ found from a given (fixed or learned) dictionary $\mathbf{D}$. In a reconstruction-like task, the signal $\mathbf{x}$ could be (approximately) recovered by $\tilde{\mathbf{x}} = \mathbf{D}\boldsymbol{\alpha}$, whereas in a classification task, the sparse representation $\boldsymbol{\alpha}$ can be used as the feature vector, which is the approach we take in this work. In the following paragraphs, we describe the design decisions regarding the formulation used to learn the dictionaries, how the different sparse representations proposed are computed, and how they are used for classification.

Several optimization models are possible to learn the dictionary $\mathbf{D}$ and the sparse representation coefficients $\boldsymbol{A} = [\boldsymbol{\alpha}_1, \ldots, \boldsymbol{\alpha}_m] \in \mathbb{R}^{k \times m}$ from m training instances $\mathbf{X} = [\mathbf{x}_1, \ldots, \mathbf{x}_m] \in \mathbb{R}^{n \times m}$. One choice is to minimize the L_1 norm of the coefficients $\boldsymbol{\alpha}$ while guaranteeing a reconstruction error lower than an upper bound ϵ, as used in [16]. Alternatively, one can seek to minimize the reconstruction error for a given sparsity constraint λ (i.e. the maximum number of non-zero entries allowed), $\min_{\mathbf{D}, \boldsymbol{A}} \|\mathbf{X} - \mathbf{D}\boldsymbol{A}\|_2^2$ s.t. $\|\boldsymbol{\alpha}_i\|_0 \leq \lambda$, $\forall i \in \{1, \ldots, m\}$, which is the approach taken in [12], and the one used here because setting the sparsity constraint λ can be relatively more intuitive than setting the allowed reconstruction error ϵ, since λ is a natural number with known bounds given $\mathbf{D}$, and it is more user-meaningful.

Typically, in face recognition and other multi-class problems, several dictionaries are learnt, one per class, which are afterwards concatenated into a larger dictionary. However, in a binary problem like pedestrian classification, we wonder whether both dictionaries are required or just any one of them can successfully be used, or how is the better way to combine them. Therefore, the following strategies are explored (Table 1):

Table 1. Dictionary learning and usage strategies studied

Strategy name	Training data for dict. learning	Dictionary/-ies notation	Sparse representation notation
S^+	Positive instances	$\mathbf{D}^+$	$\boldsymbol{\alpha}^+$
S^-	Negative instances	$\mathbf{D}^-$	$\boldsymbol{\alpha}^-$
S^*	All instances together	$\mathbf{D}^*$	$\boldsymbol{\alpha}^*$
$S^\pm$	All instances, per class	$[\mathbf{D}^+, \mathbf{D}^-]$	$\boldsymbol{\alpha}^\pm$
S^{+-}	All instances, per class	$\{\mathbf{D}^+, \mathbf{D}^-\}$	$\boldsymbol{\alpha}^{+-} = [\boldsymbol{\alpha}^+, \boldsymbol{\alpha}^-]$

Single-dictionary Strategies. A single dictionary is learnt, but three possibilities (S^+, S^-, S^*) are considered depending on which data is used for learning, either the positive instances (i.e. those from the positive class), the negative instances, or all of them, respectively.

Dual-dictionary Strategies. Here, the two class-specific dictionaries are learnt separately and then either concatenated into a larger one $[\mathbf{D}^+, \mathbf{D}^-] \in \mathbb{R}^{n \times 2k}$, or considered separately from the set $\{\mathbf{D}^+, \mathbf{D}^-\}$. The sparse representations are respectively obtained from the concatenated dictionary (strategy $S^\pm$), or by concatenating the representations $\boldsymbol{\alpha}^+$ and $\boldsymbol{\alpha}^-$ separately built from $\mathbf{D}^+$ and $\mathbf{D}^-$

(strategy S^{+-}). In other words, in $S^{\pm}$ it is the dictionaries that are concatenated and yield a single sparse representation $\boldsymbol{\alpha}^{\pm}$ for a given instance $\mathbf{x}$, whereas in S^{+-} it is the coefficients $\boldsymbol{\alpha}^+$ and $\boldsymbol{\alpha}^-$ that are concatenated, resulting in $\boldsymbol{\alpha}^{+-} = [\boldsymbol{\alpha}^+, \boldsymbol{\alpha}^-]$, also for each instance.

The sparse representations have k components in the single-dictionary strategies, and $2k$ for the dual-dictionary strategies.

The goal is then to study the relative merits of these five sparse representations, three $(\boldsymbol{\alpha}^+, \boldsymbol{\alpha}^-, \boldsymbol{\alpha}^*)$, with single dictionaries, and two $(\boldsymbol{\alpha}^{\pm}, \boldsymbol{\alpha}^{+-})$ with dual dictionaries, and how they behave in computational and discriminative terms.

As in common practice, learnt dictionaries are (atom-wise) L_2-normalized, and (HOG) instances are subtracted the average of the training instances, both before dictionary learning and afterwards, when computing their sparse representation. In S^+, S^- and S^{+-}, it is the average of the instances of corresponding class that is subtracted, while in S^*, it is the global average (without distinction of classes). In $S^{\pm}$, the three possibilities (i.e. subtracting the global mean, the positive-class mean, and the negative-class mean) were tried.

Classification. One interesting aspect of sparse representations is that they can very directly and quite efficiently be used for classification. Thus, simple decision functions have been proposed such as choosing the class whose corresponding dictionary induces representations with either minimum reconstruction error [16], or the maximum sum of coefficients [1]. Although interesting, these functions have two limitations: they are heuristic in nature, and are not (directly) applicable to single-dictionary cases. Therefore, we used a general-purpose classifier that can be computationally costlier, but it does not have these limitations.

3   Experiments

The experiments were performed over the INRIA Person Dataset [2]. We took the training set of 2416 already-cropped pedestrian images as positive windows, and the 1218 human-absent scenes of 240×320 pixels were randomly cropped 5 times thus yielding 6090 negative windows in total. The test set consists of 1132 positive windows and 453 negative scenes, which we randomly cropped 3 times to obtain an almost balanced test set with 1359 negative instances.

Each image in our dataset was described by HOG [2]. An efficient implementation [4,5] and recommended optimal parameters [2] were used.

We tested with the values $k \in \{20, 50, 100, 200, 400, 800, 1600\}$ and $\lambda \in \{1, 2, 5, 10, 20, 40, 60, 80\}$. Notice that the size of the dictionary is k for the single-dictionary strategies, but it is $2k$ for the dual-dictionary strategy $S^{\pm}$. In S^{+-}, two dictionaries are separately involved, each of size k.

We used a linear Support Vector Machine (SVM) to classify the sparse representation obtained. For validation, we randomly split the original training set $\mathcal{T}$ into two disjoint halves, each one maintaining the original proportion of positive and negative examples. We repeated this split three times, thus obtaining the halves $\mathcal{T}_t^i$ and $\mathcal{T}_v^i$ for training and validation, respectively, with $i \in \{1, 2, 3\}$.

We then used each $\mathcal{T}_t^i$ to obtain its corresponding dictionary/-ies, which in turn was/were used to obtain the sparse representations of both the training and validation subsets.

We then used those three pairs of sets to choose the optimal value for the penalty parameter C required by SVM by using a coarse-to-fine grid search in which $C = 2^j$, with $j \in \{-14, -12, \ldots, 6\}$, was explored first to determine the optimal j^* from which the final C was obtained after exploring $C = 2^{j^*}$, $j \in \{j^* - 1.8, j^* - 1.6, \ldots, j^* + 1.8\}$. For the final training, the dictionary/-ies was/were learned using the corresponding classes of the complete training set $\mathcal{T}$, then the sparse representation of all these instances were computed and fed to an SVM which was trained with the optimal C found during validation. In both validation and final testing, the F-Measure was used as the performance measure, because of the unbalanced nature of the dataset used.

In the particular case of $S^\pm$, we only report the results obtained when subtracting the global mean and the negative mean (i.e. only considering the negative examples), since the results obtained when considering the positive mean were very similar to those obtained with the latter.

The efficient LIBLINEAR SVM implementation [8] and the open-source SPAMS 2.3 (SPArse Modeling Software) [10,11] were used. In SPAMS, the number of iterations was set to $n_{\text{iters}} = 150$. The Python-interface functions used were `spams.trainDL()` (with parameters `mode = 3`, and `lambda1 = ` λ) for dictionary learning, and `spams.omp()` (with parameter `lambda = ` λ) for computing the sparse representation of a given signal using a learned dictionary.

3.1   Results

For all strategies, the higher the sparsity constraint λ, the better the results (Fig. 1). While poor performance is obtained with the smallest values ($\lambda \in \{1, 2, 5\}$), results quickly become competent for higher values, observing a convergence at $\lambda \approx 60$. This strong dependency on λ suggests that many coefficients are required to represent the signal, which can be understood due to the large variety in the input signal (even the positive class has large intra-class variance due to the many possible human poses, clothing, etc.). It can be observed that which average is used to subtract the instances in strategy $S^\pm$ makes a difference.

As for the dictionary size (k), it has little impact for a given λ, but performance tends to decrease slightly with larger λ, or behave erratically with smaller λ. Therefore, the sparsity constraint is much more important than the dictionary size in classification and, in general, once $\lambda \geq 60$, $k \approx 100$ atoms suffice.

Since the HOG descriptor has $n = 4608$ dimensions, the redundancy factor, k/n (i.e. atoms over signal dimensionality), of the studied dictionaries sizes is significantly less than 1. However, the trend of the plots do not suggest that complete ($k/n \approx 1$) or overcomplete ($k/n > 1$) dictionaries would help. In fact, one possible reason for the observed decaying performance with bigger dictionaries (most noticeable under $S^\pm$, S^{+-}, and S^+) is not having enough training data. More atoms available means more "degrees of freedom" that call for more training data. This hypothesis is supported by the fact that strategies

S^- and S^* are significantly less sensitive to the dictionary size (Fig. 1(b, c)), since they are learnt from more training data (more negative instances are available for learning $\mathbf{D}^-$ than positive instances are for $\mathbf{D}^+$; and the total number of instances used when learning $\mathbf{D}^*$ is also bigger). The effect of the training size might also be compounded by the need of bigger sparsity constraint λ or more iterations n_{iters} in dictionary learning. To verify this, we tested some bigger values of λ and n_{iters} for the particular case of $k = 800$ under S^+, and results

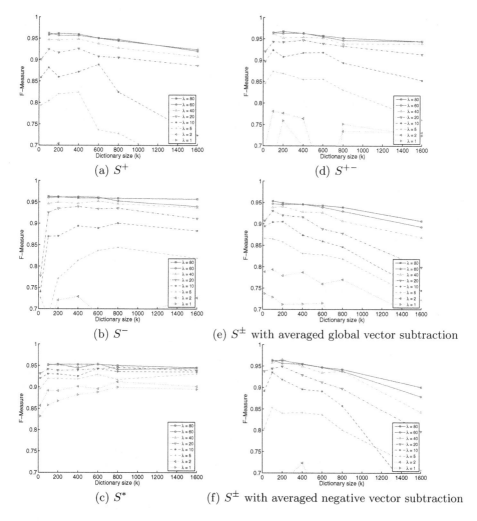

Fig. 1. Classification performance for each studied strategy varying the dictionary size (k) and the sparsity constraint (λ). Left (a, b, c): single-dictionary strategies, Right (d, e, f): dual-dictionary strategies. Notice that results for two versions of $S^\pm$ are reported (e, f). Since $S^\pm$ uses two concatenated dictionaries, its effective size is $2k$. (Plots better seen in color and by zooming in their digital version) (Color figure online)

(not shown here) suggested that performance can increase slightly with bigger values of λ or n_{iters}, or both, although it seems to converge for $n_{\text{iters}} \geq 300$.

Since the best performances for the different strategies are similar, several strategies are possible with different computational-classification trade-offs and practical implications. In this regard, it is noticeable that learning a single dictionary may suffice, and it is particularly interesting that the sparse representations derived from the dictionary learned *only* from the *negative* class (strategy S^-) turns out to be discriminative, *without* learning from the class of interest at dictionary-learning stage. Unlike the other strategies, S^* (Fig. 1) achieves a competent performance with a sparsity constraint as small as 1 or 2. In absolute terms, the best result is obtained with strategy S^{+-} whose performance peaks at $k = 200$ and $\lambda = 80$, but it is closely followed by alternative strategies, with S^- behaving more consistently across dictionary sizes k, although the reason for this might be due to the higher number of negative instances used for learning dictionary $\mathbf{D}^-$. For the smaller $\lambda \in \{10, 20\}$, the strategy S^* generally outperforms the others, in particular for larger dictionaries.

Computationally, although S^* is a single-dictionary strategy, it can be expected to use more training data since the examples of both classes are required. Learning a dictionary took in the order of minutes. For instance, with $k = 100$ and $\lambda = 60$, it took less than 3 min to learn a positive dictionary $\mathbf{D}^+$, and less than 6 min to learn a negative dictionary $\mathbf{D}^-$. Computing the sparse representation once the dictionary/-ies is/are learned would take approximately the same in the single-dictionary strategies because their dictionaries are all the same size. For the dual-dictionary strategies, it would take more time since a bigger dictionary (in $S^\pm$) or two dictionaries (in S^{+-}) are involved. As a final recommendation, S^{+-} or S^- seem the overall better strategies in terms of classification performance. If computational-classification tradeoffs are considered, some strategies may turn to be more suitable than others.

Finally, although this work does not aim at outperforming strategies not using sparse representations, we compared these results with a classical HOG on the same dataset, classifier, and validation protocol, and obtained F-Measure = 0.968, which is similar to the best of any performance results we get (corresponding to F-Measure = 0.967, obtained for S^{+-} with $k = 200$ and $\lambda = 80$). Therefore, sparse representations are competitive with the-state-of-the-art results, with feature vectors of reduced dimensionality. However, better models or approaches might be required for a more remarkable performance.

4   Conclusions

The five different strategies for dictionary learning and usage for pedestrian classification explored in this work differ in which data is used for dictionary learning (the positive instances, the negative ones, or both), and how the dictionaries are used to compute the sparse representations. In all cases, the sparse representations are used for classification.

Results reveal that learning a single dictionary provides similar classification performance over learning two dictionaries, the latter offering just a marginal benefit. Interestingly, results are competitive even when the dictionary is learnt *only* from the negative class (non-pedestrian). This has important practical implications when it comes to computational-classification trade-offs. It has also been observed that the sparsity constraint used in dictionary learning may have a bigger impact on classification performance than the size of the dictionary.

References

1. Castrodad, A., Sapiro, G.: Sparse modeling of human actions from motion imagery. Int. J. Comput. Vis. (IJCV) **100**(1), 1–15 (2012)
2. Dalal, N., Triggs, B.: Histograms of oriented gradients for human detection. In: CVPR (2005)
3. Deng, W., Hu, J., Guo, J.: In defense of sparsity based face recognition. In: CVPR (2013)
4. Dollár, P.: Piotr's image and video matlab toolbox (PMT). http://vision.ucsd.edu/~pdollar/toolbox/doc/index.html
5. Dollár, P., Belongie, S., Perona, P.: The fastest pedestrian detector in the west. In: BMVC (2010)
6. Elad, M., Aharon, M.: Image denoising via learned dictionaries and sparse representation. In: CVPR (2006)
7. Fadili, M.-J., Starck, J.-L., Murtagh, F.: Inpainting and zooming using sparse. Comput. J. **52**, 64–79 (2009)
8. Fan, R.-E., et al.: LIBLINEAR: a library for large linear classification. J. Mach. Learn. Res. **9**, 1871–1874 (2008)
9. Liu, Y., Lasang, P., Siegel, M., Sun, Q.: Multi-sparse descriptor: a scale invariant feature for pedestrian detection. Neurocomputing **184**, 55–65 (2016)
10. Mairal, J., Bach, F., Ponce, J., Sapiro, G.: Online dictionary learning for sparse coding. In: ICML (2009)
11. Mairal, J., et al.: SPArse Modeling Software (SPAMS). http://spams-devel.gforge.inria.fr
12. Ren, X., Ramanan, D.: Histograms of sparse codes for object detection. In: CVPR (2013)
13. Rigamonti, R., Brown, M., Lepetit, V.: Are sparse representations really relevant for image classification? In: CVPR (2011)
14. Shi, Q., Eriksson, A., van den Hengel, A., Shen, C.: Is face recognition really a compressive sensing problem? In: CVPR, (2011)
15. Tošić, I., Frossard, P.: Dictionary learning. IEEE Sig. Process. Mag. **28**(2), 27–38 (2011)
16. Wright, J., et al.: Robust face recognition via sparse representation. PAMI **31**(2), 210–227 (2009)
17. Wright, J., et al.: Sparse representation for computer vision and pattern recognition. Proc. IEEE **98**(6), 1031–1044 (2010)
18. Wright, J., Ganesh, A., Yang, A.Y., Zhou, Z., Ma, Y.: Sparsity and robustness in face recognition (2011). CoRR abs/1111.1014
19. Zheng, J., Jiang, Z., Chellappa, R.: Cross-view action recognition via transferable dictionary learning. IEEE Trans. Image Process. **25**(6), 2542–2556 (2016)

What Do Datasets Say About Saliency Models?

Xosé M. Pardo[(⊠)] and Xosé R. Fdez-Vidal

Centro Singular de Investigación en Tecnoloxías da Información (CiTIUS),
Universidade de Santiago de Compostela, 15782 Santiago de Compostela, Spain
{xose.pardo,xose.vidal}@usc.es

Abstract. Given the amount and variety of saliency models, the knowledge of their pros and cons, the applications they are more suitable for, or which are the more challenging scenes for each of them, would be very useful for the progress in the field. This assessment can be done based on the link between algorithms and public datasets. In one hand, performance scores of algorithms can be used to cluster video samples according to the pattern of difficulties they pose to models. In the other hand, cluster labels can be combined with video annotations to select discriminant attributes for each cluster. In this work we seek this link and try to describe each cluster of videos in a few words.

Keywords: Visual attention · Video saliency · Feature selection

1 Introduction

In the past few decades, a large number of computational models of visual saliency has been proposed, and their use has been extended in applications such as image and video compression [2], multi sensory 3D saliency [3], object and action recognition [4], video surveillance [5], etc. The wide diversity of models makes comparison and evaluation of progress in the field particularly difficult. Although different taxonomies have been created, they do not seem useful for discovering strengths and weaknesses of the models in predicting human attentional behavior. It is not always clear in what specific aspects some models are better than others, and besides we do not know what combination of simple or complex features, or specific contexts of application, are more challenging.

The assessment of any computational model always establish a link between algorithms and datasets. Performance scores can be used to characterize datasets, but also to characterize algorithms according to their scores on specific type of scenes.

Ocular movements are measurable manifestations of visual attention. From discrete fixations recorded by an eye tracker for a set of humans, a continuous human saliency map can be computed and then objectively compared to saliency maps obtained by computational models. Researchers have reached a broad consensus on using this methodology to assess static saliency models and to identify pending challenges [6–8].

© Springer International Publishing AG 2017
L.A. Alexandre et al. (Eds.): IbPRIA 2017, LNCS 10255, pp. 104–113, 2017.
DOI: 10.1007/978-3-319-58838-4_12

As Bruce et al. [7] stated, the absolute magnitude of values in a saliency map might be considered less important than relative values, and, similarly the contrast of saliency maps should have little impact on observed fixations, therefore the relative performance of models should be considered more important than absolute values in any appraisal of model performances. ROC metric gives scores which are insensitive to the absolute numeric values or contrast of saliency maps, therefore it is a good candidate to compare model performances across different data sets.

Recently a number of comprehensive benchmark studies have been presented, with the goal of assessing the performance of saliency models under varying conditions. In [7] authors presented a high-level examination of challenges in computational modeling of visual saliency, including careful assessment of different metrics for performance of visual saliency models, and identification of remaining difficulties in assessing model performance. They also considered the importance of a number of issues relevant to all saliency models including scale-space, the impact of border effects, and spatial or central bias. They also identified important obstacles that remain in visual saliency modeling, for instance: (1) task-related observations may contribute to observed behavior even for cases where no specific task definition is provided, (2) although there is some evidences of the influence of complex features in visual saliency, it is no clear whether their impact can be explained from simple basic features or not, or (3) to which extent these complex features should be included in saliency models, taking into account the intricate interplay between attention and recognition.

In another paper [9], a new method of explicit judgment was proposed for performance evaluation as alternative to fixation data, in order to correct the effects of spatial bias in fixation data, and thus facilitating the improvement of saliency models.

Among the difficulties in comparing visual attention models and driving their improvement that Bylinskii et al. [8] have identified, is the lack of benchmarking datasets. Saliency benchmark datasets are few, have a moderate size, and they do not capture the space of complex behaviors that are attributable to visual attention. A good benchmark dataset should offer multiple tasks on which performance can be reported to discover in which aspects each model is more predictive than others.

In this paper we propose a methodology to find the link between relative performance of saliency models and videos of public datasets annotated with visual attributes. This is, to the best of our knowledge, the first attempt to look for this connection.

2   Datasets, Models and Relative Performance

We have selected a set of saliency models to characterize groups of videos across different datasets that pose different patterns of difficulty to models. These videos were manually annotated with a set of visual attributes. We performed video-clustering using model scores as features and eventually we tried to establish the links between models performance and video annotations.

We have used the following publicly available datasets: sport videos of *Actions in the Eye (AE) Dataset* [10], *Abnormal Surveillance Crowd Moving Noise (ASCMN) dataset* [11], *DIEM Project* [12], *GazeCom (GC) Dataset* [13], *CRCNS Datasets* [14], and *CITIUS Dataset* [15]. That makes a total of $N_v = 448$ videos and 362,228 frames.

2.1   Selection of Computational Saliency Models

To select a set of static and dynamic saliency models, we departed from the set of dynamic models considered for the experimental comparison in [15]: GBVSm [16], ICL-D [17], SUNDAy [18], SURP [19], PQFT [2], SEOD [20], ESA-D [21], DCOF [22], MSM-SM [23], PNSP-CS [24], OBDL-MRF [26], MVE+SRN [25] and two variants of ITTI model [1]: CIOFM and CIORFM. We have also used the following static models: AIM [27], DCTS [28], SR [29], DCTQ [30], TORR [31], RARE12 [32], SIM [33], SPAMS-S [34] and SPAMS-C [35].

The models were selected based on two criteria: (1) they are representative of the diversity of the state-of-the-art and they are either dynamic models or static ones that provide results comparable to those obtained with dynamic models, and (2) author's code is publicly available.

We also considered a benchmarking model *H-50* which calculates the saliency map of each frame from the 50% of the total number of fixations of all the subjects in the experiment, for the sake of normalization.

Owing to the dynamic nature of videos, the number of fixations on individual frames is usually low. Therefore, it is advisable to use robust measures to cope with data-poor situations. In this work we use a shuffling AUC measurement (s-AUC) adapted to videos as described in [15].

The correlation among saliency models is assessed from their scores on videos from the aforementioned public datasets of videos with annotated human fixations. First, in order to normalize s-AUC values, they are divided by the s-AUC scores of the H-50 model. Second, a hierarchical clustering was performed and we chose one representative of each cluster. In order to visualize the clustering, we did a Principal Component Analysis to identified the 3 dimensions with greater variance. Figure 1 shows the spatial layout of de models after clustering. Finally, the $N_m = 8$ selected models were: AWS-D, ICL-D, CIORFM, PNSP-CS, OBDL-MRF, PQFT, ESA-D and DCOF.

2.2   Measures of Relative Performance

The relative performance of a set of algorithms on a given video can be depicted by their ranking based on the statistical significance of the performance differences observed from all pairwise comparisons [36]. The rank ordering is statistically significant if the confidence intervals $[ci^l, ci^h]$-computed as explained in [15], are not overlapped.

For each pair of saliency models, M_a, M_b, if M_a is significantly better than M_b, then the relative performance of M_a is increased with one point, if there

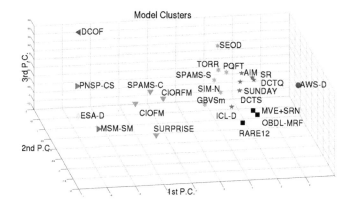

Fig. 1. Spatial layout of saliency models projected in the 3 dimensions of maximal variance. Different color and markers identify the members of the eight clusters. (Color figure online)

is no difference each one gets half a point. The relative performance of each model is computed by adding the values of all pairwise comparison. Relative performance, RP, is a $N_v \times N_m$ whose elements are normalized to be in [0,1] by dividing by $N_m - 1$. In the case of no significant differences every model would get a 0.5 score.

We used 448 videos from 6 public datasets and the relative performance of 8 computational saliency models on them to discover similarities among videos. This way, we get a 448×8 RP matrix, where $RP(i, j)$ represents the relative performance of saliency model i (M_i), on video j. This matrix represents explicitly the relationship among videos of public available datasets and state-of-the-art dynamic saliency models.

3   Our Approach

To tackle the problem of identifying patterns of videos which pose a similar level of difficulties to the saliency algorithms, we propose to use an unsupervised data mining method that partitions the input space into different homogeneous clusters such that the samples within same cluster are as similar as possible, while the objects belonging to different clusters are as dissimilar as possible.

This method allows us to identify clusters of annotated visual saliency videos with similar features and to quantify the degree of diversity of videos across public available datasets.

3.1   Video Clustering

An agglomerative hierarchical clustering, using the Ward's method, was used to select the number of clusters and to provide an initialization to the final k-means clustering. Based on the fact that intra-cluster similarity is nondecreasing and inter-cluster error sum is non increasing as the agglomerative clustering proceeds, we use the minimization of the *Clustering Balance*, ξ, as the criterion to find the optimal clustering configuration [37]:

$$\xi = \alpha \sum_{j=1}^{k} \|\mathbf{r\bar{p}}^k - \mathbf{r\bar{p}}\|^2 + (1 - \alpha) \sum_{j=1}^{k} \sum_{i=1}^{n_j} \|\mathbf{rp}_i^j - \mathbf{r\bar{p}}^j\|^2, \qquad (1)$$

where $\mathbf{rp}_i^j$ is the row of the RP corresponding to the video i in cluster j, $\mathbf{r\bar{p}}^j$ is the centroid of the cluster j, α weights the inter cluster sum of the square Euclidean distance between each cluster center and the global centroid $\mathbf{r\bar{p}}$, $(1-\alpha)$ weights the within cluster sum of the square Euclidean distances between each sample and its cluster centroid, and k is the number of clusters. By searching the compromising point between intra-cluster and inter-cluster error sums, it is possible to detect the optimal clustering configuration for any hierarchical clustering algorithms [37]. From the minimum clustering balance the desired number of clusters can be estimated from the best configuration. We use this clustering as the initialization of a final k-means clustering, which assigns to each cluster a label in the set $\mathcal{L}$ of cluster labels.

3.2   Gaining Further Insights

How could a pattern of videos on which we expect some algorithms to perform well/average/bad be described? Could we identify gaps that need to be filled in public available datasets? To answer theses questions, and others, we need to have a visual description of videos because results of clustering are often difficult to interpret. We tried to get a description of each cluster in terms of the distributions of the values of the annotated video attributes within it. Selected attributes for each cluster will serve as basic descriptors of each pattern.

We have considered a vector template of annotated attributes $\mathbf{\check{v}a} \in \mathbb{R}^{N_a}$, that includes the following: camera movement (static or different dynamic types) and position (ground, bird-eye, underwater), scene lighting (hight or low, hard or soft), type of shots (close, medium, large, x-large), shot size, presence of text, presence of humans (person, people or crowd) and animals, type of interactions, type of scene (indoor, urban, natural or synthetic), etc. Video annotations were manually created by filling a template with the list of attributes, where 1 indicates the presence of the attribute and the absence is scored as zero. Given the low ratio between the number of videos in the experiment and the number of visual features, making a well-generalizing feature selection is impossible, but we can get some knowledge about the completeness of the datasets an detect their lack individually and as a whole, and identify patterns of challenges that actual datasets pose to state-of-the-art saliency models.

Selection of Annotated Attributes. First of all we have to identify those attributes that are irrelevant to describe the video clusters. Irrelevancy can be due to the fact that very few samples include some features, they are very common or they are not independent. A screening of redundant or irrelevant visual attributes was done based on Mutual Information, $\text{MI}(\check{v}a(i), \mathcal{L})$, between each annotated visual attribute $\check{v}a(i)$ and cluster labels. According to them a chosen number of features having the highest values can be selected. In this step only the k features with null values of MI were discarded, $\check{\mathbf{v}}\mathbf{a} \in \mathbb{R}^{N_a} \to \mathbf{v}\mathbf{a} \in \mathbb{R}^{N_a - k}$. In a second step, the least absolute shrinkage and selection operator (Lasso) was applied to select a subset of the annotated attributes that are able to predict output class labels provided by the previous clustering [38]. This way a connection among RP of saliency methods and video annotations was found.

We addressed the case of binary classification and applied the one vs. all strategy to the multi-class scenario. Given the set of N_v videos, each of them described as a vector $\mathbf{v}\mathbf{a}_j$ of $N_a - k$ attributes with values in $[0, 1]$, let V be the $N_v \times (N_a - k)$ matrix of video samples, and $\mathbf{t}$ the vector of size N_v with values in $[0,1]$ (1 for videos of one-class c and 0 for the remainder all-classes in $\mathcal{L}$). The goal of supervised feature selection is to find m_c components ($m_c < N_a - k$) of the input vector $\mathbf{v}\mathbf{a}$ that are responsible for predicting output $\mathbf{t}$, for each one (c) vs. all classification problem. The Lasso optimization problem is given as:

$$\arg\min_{\mathbf{w}} \frac{1}{2}\|\mathbf{V}\mathbf{w} - \mathbf{t}\|_2^2 + \lambda\|\mathbf{w}\|_1 \tag{2}$$

where $\mathbf{w} = [w_1, \ldots, w_{(N_a - k)}]$ is a column regression coefficients vector, w_k denotes the regression coefficient for the k-th feature, $\|\|_1$ and $\|\|_2$ are the l1- and l2-norms, and $\lambda > 0$ is the regularization parameter. The $\|\|_1$ regularizer in Lasso tends to produce sparse solutions, which are more easily interpreted.

Using the one-vs-rest strategy, a different subset of attributes, m_c, which best discriminates video cluster c from others, is assigned to each $c \in \mathcal{L}$. Besides, we can determine which selected attributes are more or less frequent in a cluster than in all the others ($\mathbb{E}(\text{va}(j)|t_j = 1) \geq \mathbb{E}(\text{va}(j)|t_j = 0)$), to get a textual description of each video cluster.

4   Results

In this section we show the results of video clustering and description. Clustering was performed in two steps. First we did a hierarchical clustering to determine the number of clusters and provide an initialization to the k-means clustering. From the clustering balance measure for a number of configurations, we found that the best configuration corresponded to 8 clusters.

Second, the output of the hierarchical clustering was fed into a k-means clustering. Figure 2 shows the average RP of the models for the eight clusters provided by k-means. These clusters correspond to different RP patterns: cluster 4 gives the most homogeneous RP and the lowest maximum RP score; cluster 8 presents the minimum performance of AWS model and the maximum score of the DCOF model; clusters 2 and 6 show a similar pattern of scores for all methods but DCOF; cluster 7 provides the best results for PQTF model;

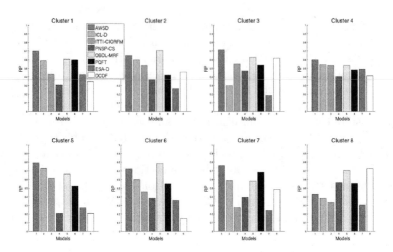

Fig. 2. Video clusters versus the average relative performances of the models.

and the highest RP score is for the AWSD model in cluster 5. The samples on cluster 8 are short videos captured mainly with static cameras of three different types: (1) bird-eye of crowds in x-long shots, (2) long shots of people interacting mainly in simple natural environments, and (3) close shots of talking heads.

After the clustering we sought the link among video clusters and video annotations. This was done in two steps. First, irrelevant attributes were discarded after performing a MI analysis. This analysis was done considering the vector template with the visual attributes for each video and the cluster labels obtained after the k-means clustering.

After discarding irrelevant attributes, a supervised Laso based feature selection was applied to find the subsets of input annotated visual attributes that are able to predict the class labels provided by the clustering driven by relative performance features. The connection among relative performance of saliency methods and the description of videos provided by manual annotations (RP $\leftrightarrow$ V) was done by conducting eight one-vs-rest binary classifications.

As the visual attributes take binary values, the frequency of each selected attribute in each cluster can be computed and compared to the frequency in the rest of clusters. The sign of the difference between each pair of frequencies allows to split the predictor attributes between mostly present and mostly absent in each cluster, which helps to build a textual description of each cluster. Figure 3 shows in black and white the selected features for describing each cluster. Black bars represent the attributes that are more frequent in each cluster than in others, and white bars indicates the opposite condition.

After performing the selection of annotated attributes for the description of the eight video clusters in Fig. 2 we found, for example, that: cluster 6 have a good proportion of videos captured with cameras following a horizontal translation/rotation, also with eye-bird and or long and x-long views, in natural scenarios and with few people and interactions, and in this cluster de DCOF model

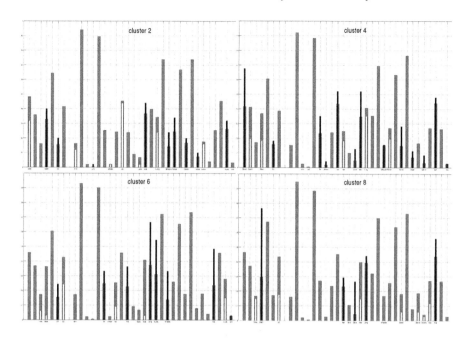

Fig. 3. Bar diagrams of annotated attributes for 4 clusters versus the rest. Black (White) bars represent the frequency of selected attributes that are more (less) frequent in a given cluster than in the rest. Gray bars in each diagram represent the average frequency of each attribute in the rest of clusters.

reaches the lowest performance; or that cluster 8 includes videos captured by static cameras, with close shots and interactions among animated beings (people and/or animals), with a good proportion of natural environments, but no synthetic ones, and with no many frames per shot, and it is with this pattern of videos where AWS-D model gets its worst results, while DCOF gets its best ones. However, cluster 4 is more difficult to describe because it includes several videos with pieces of very different scenes and therefore their descriptions are very complex. In general the number of frames between cuts is short, the views are mainly close and medium, and crowds, urban scenes and vertical displacements of cameras are more common here than in other clusters.

5 Conclusions

In this paper, we address the problem of automatically discovering the main challenges that general dynamic scenes pose to saliency models, described by a set of visual attributes. Videos are clustered forming different patterns of difficulties and described by means of a selected group of attributes which are relevant because they are more frequent in a cluster than in others or because they are rare in a given cluster. To the best of our knowledge, this is the first attempt to shed light in this issue, however a wider collection of annotated videos without the mixture of so different scenes could provide cleaner descriptions and conclusions.

Acknowledgements. This work has received financial support from the Consellería de Cultura, Educación e Ordenación Universitaria (accreditation 2016–2019, ED431G/08) and the European Regional Development Fund (ERDF).

References

1. Itti, L., Koch, C., Niebur, E.: A model of saliency-based visual attention for rapid scene analysis. IEEE Trans. Pattern Anal. Mach. Intell. **20**(11), 1254–1259 (1998)
2. Guo, C., Zhang, L.: A novel multiresolution spatiotemporal saliency setection model and its applications in image and video compression. IEEE Trans. Image Process. **19**(1), 185–198 (2010)
3. Lanillos, P., Ferreira, J.F., Dias, J.: Multisensory 3D saliency for artificial attention systems. In: REACTS Workshop, CAIP 2015, pp. 1–6 (2015)
4. Seo, H.J., Milanfar, P.: Action recognition from one example. IEEE Trans. Pattern Anal. Mach. Intell. **33**(5), 867–882 (2011)
5. Mehmood, I., Sajjad, M., Ejaz, W., Baik, S.W.: Saliency-directed prioritization of visual data in wireless surveillance networks. Inf. Fusion **24**, 16–30 (2015)
6. Borji, A., Sihite, D.N., Itti, L.: Quantitative analysis of human-model agreement in visual saliency modeling: a comparative study. IEEE Trans. Image Process. **22**(1), 55–69 (2013)
7. Bruce, N., Wloka, C., Frosst, N., Rahman, S., Tsotsos, J.K.: On computational modeling of visual saliency: examining what's right, and what's left. Visi. Res. Part B **116**, 95–112 (2015)
8. Bylinskii, Z., DeGennaro, E.M., Rajalingham, R., Ruda, H., Zhang, J., Tsotsos, J.K.: Towards the quantitative evaluation of visual attention models. Vision Res. Part B **116**, 258–268 (2015)
9. Rahman, S., Bruce, N.: Visual saliency prediction and evaluation across different perceptual tasks. PloS One **10**(9), e0138053 (2015)
10. Mathe, S., Sminchisescu, C.: Dynamic eye movement datasets and learnt saliency models for visual action recognition. In: Fitzgibbon, A., Lazebnik, S., Perona, P., Sato, Y., Schmid, C. (eds.) ECCV 2012. LNCS, pp. 842–856. Springer, Heidelberg (2012). doi:10.1007/978-3-642-33709-3_60
11. Riche, N., Mancas, M., Culibrk, D., Crnojevic, V., Gosselin, B., Dutoit, T.: Dynamic saliency models and human attention: a comparative study on videos. In: Lee, K.M., Matsushita, Y., Rehg, J.M., Hu, Z. (eds.) ACCV 2012. LNCS, vol. 7726, pp. 586–598. Springer, Heidelberg (2013). doi:10.1007/978-3-642-37431-9_45
12. Henderson, J.M., Ferreira, F.: Scene Perception for Psycholinguists. The Interface of Language, Vision, and Action: Eye Movements and the Visual World, pp. 1–58. Psychology Press, New York (2004)
13. Dorr, M., Martinetz, T., Gegenfurtner, K.R., Barth, E.: Variability of eye movements when viewing dynamic natural scenes. J. Vis. **10**(10), 28 (2010)
14. Itti, L., Carmi, R.: Eye-tracking data from human volunteers watching complex video stimuli (2009)
15. Leborán, V., Garcia-Diaz, A., Fdez-Vidal, X.R., Pardo, X.M.: Dynamic whitening saliency. IEEE Trans. Pattern Anal. Mach. Intell. **39**(5), 893–903 (2017)
16. Harel, J., Koch, C., Perona, P.: Graph-Based Visual Saliency. Advances in Neural Information Processing Systems, pp. 545–552. MIT Press, Cambridge (2007)
17. Xiaodi, H., Zhang, L.: Dynamic visual attention: searching for coding length increments. In: NIPS, pp. 681–688. Curran Associates Inc. (2008)

18. Zhang, L., Tong, M.H., Garrison, W.: SUNDAy: saliency using natural statistics for dynamic analysis of scenes. In: CogSci 2009 (2009)
19. Itti, L., Baldi, P.F.: Bayesian surprise attracts human attention. Vis. Res. **49**(10), 1295–1306 (2009)
20. Seo, H.J., Milanfar, P.: Training-free, generic object detection using locally adaptive regression kernels. IEEE Trans. Pattern Anal. Mach. Intell. **32**(9), 1688–1704 (2010)
21. Rahtu, E., Kannala, J., Salo, M., Heikkilä, J.: Segmenting salient objects from images and videos. In: Daniilidis, K., Maragos, P., Paragios, N. (eds.) ECCV 2010. LNCS, vol. 6315, pp. 366–379. Springer, Heidelberg (2010). doi:10.1007/978-3-642-15555-0_27
22. Zhong, S.-H., Liu, Y., Ren, F., Zhang, J., Ren, T.: Video saliency detection via dynamic consistent spatio-temporal attention modelling. In: AAAI, Technical Track, pp. 1063–1069 (2013)
23. Muthuswamy, K., Rajan, D.: Salient motion detection in compressed domain. IEEE Sig. Process. Lett. **20**(10), 996–999 (2013)
24. Fang, Y., Lin, W., Chen, Z., Tsai, C.-H., Lin, C.-W.: A video saliency detection model in compressed domain. IEEE Trans. Circuits Syst. Video Technol. **24**(1), 27–38 (2014)
25. Khatoonabadi, S.H., Bajić, I.V., Shan, Y.: Compressed-domain correlates of human fixations in dynamic scenes. Multim. Tools Appl. **74**(22), 10057–10075 (2015)
26. Khatoonabadi, S.H., Vasconcelos, N., Bajić, I.V., Shan, Y.: How many bits does it take for a stimulus to be salient? In: CVPR 2015, pp. 5501–5510 (2015)
27. Bruce, N., Tsotsos, J.K.: Saliency, attention, and visual search: an information theoretic approach. J. Vis. **9**(3), 1–24 (2009)
28. Hou, X., Harel, J., Koch, C.: Image signature: highlighting sparse salient regions. IEEE Trans. Pattern Anal. Mach. Intell. **34**(1), 194–201 (2012)
29. Hou, X., Zhang, L.: Saliency detection: a spectral residual approach. In: CVPR 2007, pp. 1–8 (2007)
30. Schauerte, B., Stiefelhagen, R.: Predicting human gaze using quaternion DCT image signature saliency and face detection. In: WACV 2012 (2012)
31. Torralba, A., Oliva, A., Castelhano, M.S., Henderson, J.M.: Contextual guidance of eye movements and attention in real-world scenes: the role of global features in object search. Psychol. Rev. **113**(4), 766–786 (2006)
32. Riche, N., Mancas, M., Gosselin, B., Dutoit, T.: RARE: a new bottom-up saliency model. In: ICIP 2012 (2012)
33. Murray, N., Vanrell, M., Otazu, X., Parraga, C.A.: Saliency estimation using a non-parametric low-level vision model. In: CVPR 2011, pp. 433–440 (2011)
34. Li, Y., Zhou, Y., Xu, L., Yang, X., Yang, J.: Incremental sparse saliency detection. In: ICIP 2009, pp. 3093–3096 (2009)
35. Li, Y., Zhou, Y., Yan, J., Niu, Z., Yang, J.: Visual saliency based on conditional entropy. In: ACCV 2009, pp. 246–257 (2010)
36. Kalousis, A., Gama, J., Hilario, M.: On data and algorithms: understanding inductive performance. Mach. Learn. **54**(3), 275–312 (2004)
37. Jung, Y., Park, H., Du, D.-Z., Drake, B.L.: A decision criterion for the optimal number of clusters in hierarchical clustering. J. Global Optim. **25**(1), 91–111 (2003)
38. Tibshirani, R.: Regression shrinkage and selection via the lasso. J. R. Stat. Soc. Ser. B **58**(1), 267–288 (1996)

Combining Defocus and Photoconsistency for Depth Map Estimation in 3D Integral Imaging

H. Espinos-Morato[1,3(✉)], P. Latorre-Carmona[1], J. Martinez Sotoca[1],
F. Pla[1], and B. Javidi[2]

[1] Institute of New Imaging Technologies - INIT, University Jaume I Castellon,
12071 Castellon de la Plana, Spain
hespinos@uji.es

[2] Department of Electrical and Computer Engineering, University of Connecticut,
Storrs, CT 06269-4157, USA

[3] Mathematical Modelling and Numeric Simulation Group,
Catholic University of Valencia, 46001 Valencia, Spain
http://www.init.uji.es

Abstract. This paper presents the application of a depth estimation method for scenes acquired using a Synthetic Aperture Integral Imaging (SAII) technique. SAII is an autostereoscopic technique consisting of an array of cameras that acquires images from different perspectives. The depth estimation method combines a defocus and a correspondence measure. This approach obtains consistent results and shows noticeable improvement in the depth estimation as compared to a minimum variance minimisation strategy, also tested in our scenes. Further improvements are obtained for both methods when they are fed into a regularisation approach that takes into account the depth in the spatial neighbourhood of a pixel.

Keywords: Integral imaging · Depth map · Regularisation · Defocus · Minimum variance

1 Introduction

Three-dimensional (3D) optical image sensing and visualisation technologies are currently applied in areas like medical sciences, entertainment devices or robotics [8–10]. One of the most promising 3D approach is based on Integral Imaging (hereafter II), in which an autostereoscopic imaging method is used to gather together 3D information and visualize it in 3D space, either optically or computationally [1]. II operates under incoherent or ambient light. This is a big advantage as compared to other sensing techniques (i.e. holography, Ladar), which require an active illumination system [2]. II can also provide the three dimensional profile and range of the objects in the scene [5].

3D sensing with an II architecture has specific benefits for specific applications such as segmentation of objects from heavy background, and imaging

© Springer International Publishing AG 2017
L.A. Alexandre et al. (Eds.): IbPRIA 2017, LNCS 10255, pp. 114–121, 2017.
DOI: 10.1007/978-3-319-58838-4_13

through obscuration and scattering medium (see e.g. [3,4] for details). With the important and recent advances in optical and display devices and detectors, II has been significantly boosted, applying in a wide variety of fields [10,11]. Currently, II is considered as a promising technology for 3D acquisition and visualisation. Authors in [5] propose a methodology for estimating the depth of objects in a scene employing a minimum variance approach (hereafter MinVar method). The minimum variance approach has two limitations (i) the accuracy of depth estimation is very sensitive to the nature of the object surfaces (it does not work for non Lambertian surfaces), and (ii) this methodology is primarily noisy at the boundaries of the image objects [13].

In order to cope with these restrictions, we apply two approaches proposed in [12] for light field displays, consisting of the definition of a defocusing strategy, and a regularisation approach to deal with spatial information surrounding a pixel. The methodology shown in [12] assumes that there is a very small disparity between images. In our case, the distance between cameras is such that the disparity among elemental images is an order of mangnitude bigger than in [12]. This makes that some of the assumptions and strategies that they apply are not applicable in our case. Thus, we consider a simplified version of their strategy.

The paper is organised in the following sections. Section 2 provides a brief overview of II acquisition and visualisation technology. The methods used in this paper for depth estimation are shown in Sect. 3. Section 4 shows the different results applied on a series of simulated synthetic aperture integral imaging scenes and conclusions are given in Sect. 5.

2   Overview of Integral Imaging

Acquisition and visualisation of 3D objects using II can be divided in two different stages, called pickup and reconstruction. In the pickup stage, multiple 2D images (referred to as elemental images) are captured through a camera array. This acquisition strategy is called Synthetic Aperture Integral Imaging (SAII) [7] (Fig. 1 left). Computational reconstruction of the 3D image can be achieved using a computer synthesized virtual pinhole array for inverse mapping of each elemental image into the object space, which are computationally overlapped afterwards (Fig. 1 right). In particular, the superposition of properly shifted elemental images provides the 3D reconstructed images $R(x, y, z)$ as follows [6]:

$$R(x, y, z) = \frac{1}{O(x, y)} \sum_{k=0}^{K-1} \sum_{l=0}^{L-1} E_{kl}\left[x', y'\right] \tag{1}$$

where $x' = x - k\frac{N_x \cdot p}{c_x \cdot M(z)}$, $y' = y - l\frac{N_y \cdot p}{c_y \cdot M(z)}$, p is the pitch of the cameras, x and y are the indexes of the pixel, $N_x \times N_y$ is the total number of pixels for each elemental image, $R(x, y, z)$ represents the reconstructed 3D image at depth z, $M(z)$ is the magnification factor $\left(M = \frac{z}{f}\right)$, f is the focal lenght, $c_x \times c_y$ is the physical size of the camera sensor, E_{kl} represents the intensity of the kth

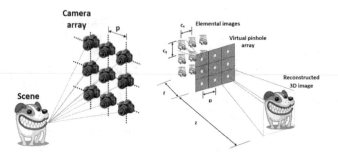

Fig. 1. Left figure shows the acquisition strategy using a camera array. Right figure shows 3D scene reconstruction by back projecting the elemental images through virtual pinholes. Each elemental image is back-projected through its own viewpoint and the superposition of the ray cones projected from the elemental images reconstructs the 3D scene.

row ($0 \leq k < K$) and lth column ($0 \leq l < L$) elemental image, $O(x, y)$ is the overlapping number matrix, i.e., it is a number indicating the number of cameras in the camera array that contribute to that (x, y) reconstruction position.

3   Depth Estimation Approaches

3.1   Depth Estimation Using Variance Minimisation

The minimum variance criterion was chosen as the reference method for estimating objects in a scene [5]. Let us assume light distribution described as $\Gamma(\theta, \phi)$ for a certain point of coordinates (x, y, z) in 3D space, where (θ, ϕ) is the intensity direction. The variance associated to Γ can be defined as:

$$V(x, y, z) = \frac{\sum_{c=1}^{3} \sum_{k=0}^{K-1} \sum_{l=0}^{L-1} \left[\Gamma(\theta_{kl}, \phi_{kl}, \lambda_c), -\overline{\Gamma}(\theta, \phi, \lambda_c) \right]^2_{(x,y,z)}}{3} \quad (2)$$

where $\overline{\Gamma}$ is the mean light distribution over all image sensors. This approach selects those z values from a range, $z \in [Z_{min} \ldots Z_{max}]$, where the variance among these voxels is minimum (if all the cameras see the same part of the 3D scene, the corresponding variance should reach a minimum). This can be expressed as $\widehat{z}(x, y) = \arg \min_{z \in Z} V(x, y, z)$.

3.2   Combining Defocus and Correspondence for Depth Estimation

This section describes the application of a simplified version of a method to infer depth based on a defocusing criteria proposed in [12] for light-field displays, in our case for integral imaging. The method estimates the depth of a scene combining a defocus and a correspondence measure. The defocus measure allows to obtain an optimal contrast on a certain region of the image, but occlusions and lighting changes may easily affect the accuracy of the measurement. The patch size may also affect the measure sensitivity because the defocus measure may exceed the patch size. Correspondence measurement allows to estimate depth using photoconsistency and has been widely used in stereo problems. In these cases, a statistical measure is usually applied to resolve matching ambiguities.

In light fields, the disparities between elemental images are usually of very few pixels [12]. In II applied in this work, the disparity among images is an order of magnitude higher. In our approach, the first term (correspondence term) defines an initial cost function equal to the square root of the variance $V(x, y, z)$ as per Eq. 2. The second term (defocus term) acts locally and involves the reconstructed image (at each depth plane) defined as $R(x, y, z)$ in the Eq. 1, on the one hand, and the image acquired by the central camera in the array, on the other hand:

$$L(x, y, z) = \frac{1}{N} \sum_{p_i \in W} D_{cost}(p_i) G_s \left(\left| \left| \left(I_c(p_i) - I_c(x, y) \right) \right| \right| \right)$$

$$+ \sum_{p_i \in W} H_{foc}(p_i) G_s \left(\left| \left| \left(I_c(p_i) - I_c(x, y) \right) \right| \right| \right) \tag{3}$$

D_{cost} is a square root of the variance where for each coordinate $p_i = (x_i, y_i, z_i)$ with a specific depth $z = z_i$, we have $D_{cost}(p_i) = \sqrt{V(p_i)}$. $H_{foc}(p_i)$ is defined as $H_{foc}(p_i) = \left| \left| \left(R(p_i) - I_c(p_i) \right) \right| \right|$, where R is the reconstructed image at a specific depth z. I_c is the image of the central camera (in the camera array) and therefore $H_{foc}(x)$ compares the reconstruction to a certain depth with the scene. $L(x, y, z)$ is the cost function that should be minimised, (x, y) are the coordinates of the current pixel to be filtered, p_i is the different p-coordinates of a window W centered in (x, y), and G_s is a gaussian function that smooths image colour or grey scale differences and with a normalisation term N defined as $N = \sum_{p_i \in W} G_s \left(\left| \left| \left(I_c(p_i) - I_c(x, y) \right) \right| \right| \right)$. Finally, the optimal depth is determined as $\hat{z}(x, y) = \arg \min_{z \in Z} (D_{cost} + H_{foc})$.

3.3   Depth Regularisation

Given an initial depth map obtained by the Min-Var method or the method explained in Sect. 3.2, the following functional proposed in [12] can be applied

$$F = \sum_p E_1 \left(p, d(p) \right) + \lambda \sum_{p,q} E_2 \left(p, q, d(p), d(q) \right) \tag{4}$$

where d is the depth value, and p, and q are neighboring pixels, λ is a regularisation factor. E_1 term is related with the final labeled depths of z obtained in the initial depth map. We adopt a nomenclature similar to that in [12]. The regularisation term E_2 is defined as:

$$E_2 \left(p, q, d(p), d(q) \right) = \frac{exp \left[\frac{-[d(p) - d(q)]^2}{2\sigma^2} \right]}{\left| \nabla \left(I_c(p) \right) - \nabla \left(I_c(q) \right) \right|} \tag{5}$$

where $\nabla(I_c)$ is the gradient of the central camera image. The minimisation is solved using a standard graph cut algorithm [14].

4 Results

A series of synthetic scenes (shown in Fig. 2) were created using Autodesk 3DS Max 2015. Three of them are indoor spaces (Bathroom, Toysroom and Livingroom). The fourth is the foreground image of a statue. In the first three there are many objects of different sizes and shapes whose purpose is the assessment of the proposed algorithms performance. For all the images used, the depth map ground truth is available using Autodesk 3DS Max in terms of graphical units. We use the following equivalence $1GU \equiv 1\,mm$ for indoor scenes and $1GU \equiv 1\,mm$ for the statue. Table 1 shows the acquisition configuration parameters used, where p is the pitch of cameras, (c_x, c_y) are the physical size of camera sensor, the array of cameras is the number of cameras that formed the rack of cameras and $(Z_{min} : Z_{step} : Z_{max})$ indicate the depth range, where Z_{step} is the step size. In all images a focal lenght ($f = 50\,mm$) is applied. Figure 3 shows the results obtained by the different methods on the four synthetic images. The first row shows the ground truth of each scene. The second row shows the results obtained by the Min-Var method without regularisation.

The third row shows the Min-Var results with the regularisation strategy shown in Eqs. 4 and 5. The fourth and fifth rows shows the method in Eq. 3 without and with the regularisation strategy applied, respectively. The Root Mean Squared Error (RMSE), defined as $RMSE = \sqrt{\frac{1}{rc}\sum_{(i,j)}[G(i,j) - Z(i,j)]^2}$ was

Fig. 2. Synthetic images used in the work. From left to right: Bathroom, Toysroom, Livingroom and Statue scenes.

Table 1. Experimental SAII acquisition parameters

Image name	Array cameras	Depth range ($Z_{min} : Z_{step} : Z_{max}$)	(c_x, c_y)	p
Statue	7×7	90:1:341	(36,36)	5
Bathroom	7×7	220:10:830	(36,36)	5
Toysroom	7×7	220:10:750	(36,36)	5
Livingroom	7×7	370:10:900	(36,36)	5

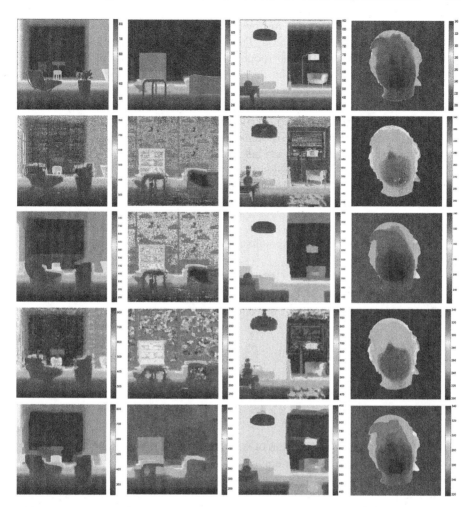

Fig. 3. From left to right rows, Bathroom, Toysroom, Livingroom and Statue scenes. From top to bottom columns, ground-truth depth map, depth map result obtained by Min-Var without regularisation, depth map result obtained by Min-Var with regularisation, depth map result obtained by Defocusing without regularisation and depth map result obtained by Defocusing with regularisation.

used to assess the depth map estimation quality. In this expression, r and c are the number of rows and columns in each image, G is the ground truth map and Z is the estimated depth map for a pixel at position (i,j). Table 2 shows the depth estimation errors obtained using Min-Var and Defocusing methods without and with regularisation (abbreviated in the Table 2 as "reg"). As it can seen, the method shown in Sect. 3.2 gives better results and the regularisation substantially reduces the $RMSE$. However, there is a windowing effect that makes the visual results to appear of a worse visual quality. For instance, the Defocusing method greatly improves the result in the window part of the *Livingroom* scene. In addition, in the *Toysroom* scene better results can be seen in the bed foot board and in the room wallpaper. None of them however, are able to resolve the problem of the mirror in the *Bathroom* scene. This fact is probably due to the fact that it is a very polished surface or in this case reflective surface. The pixels around object boundaries in the Min-Var method present a higher number of artifacts in relation to the depth estimation made with the Defocusing method. Better RMSE values are obtained when the regularisation is applied, partly because there are large and homogeneous areas in the scene, which reduce the error. Nevertheless the regularisation also produces windowing effects. Therefore the results of the defocusing strategy, without regularisation, could be considered as visually more acceptable.

Table 2. Quantitative RMSE results (in centimeters) on synthetic images.

Image name	Min-Var	Min-Var reg	Defocus	Defocus reg
Bathroom	84.45	60.04	65.58	53.77
Livingroom	87.59	48.94	72.15	42.88
Toysroom	116.82	95.31	71.66	31.85
Statue	1.71	1.62	1.71	1.61

5 Conclusions

This paper presents the application of two depth estimation (Min-Var and Defocusing based) strategies and a regularisation post-processing on four synthetic scenes simulated using synthetic aperture integral imaging acquisition and visualisation approach. Results show that the application of a Defocusing approach gives better visual results in terms of depth image generation. The use of a regulariser, in all cases, improves the RMSE values. However, this regularisation produces windowing effects, which make the quality of the visual results worse. The methods applied in this paper do not take occlusions into account, and therefore an important part of the errors may come from this effect. A functional dealing with this problem is part of the future research to be made.

Acknowledgments. This work was supported by the Spanish Ministry of Economy and Competitiveness (MINECO) under the projects SEOSAT (ESP2013-48458-C4-3-P) and MTM2013-48371-C2-2-P, by the Generalitat Valenciana through the project PROMETEO-II-2014-062, and by the University Jaume I through the project UJI-P11B2014-09. B. Javidi would like to acknowledge support under NSF/IIS-1422179.

References

1. Arimoto, H., Javidi, B.: Integral three-dimensional imaging with digital reconstruction. Opt. Lett. **26**, 157–159 (2001)
2. Benton, S.A., Bove, V.M.: Holographic Imaging. Wiley-Interscience, New York (2008)
3. Cho, M., Javidi, B.: Three-dimensional visualization of objects in turbid water using integral imaging. J. Disp. Technol. **6**(10), 544–547 (2010)
4. Cho, M., Mahalanobis, A., Javidi, B.: 3D passive photon counting automatic target recognition using advanced correlation filters. Opt. Lett. **36**(6), 861–863 (2011)
5. DaneshPanah, M., Javidi, B.: Profilometry and optical slicing by passive three-dimensional imaging. Opt. Lett. **34**(7), 1105–1107 (2009)
6. Hong, S.H., Jang, J.S., Javidi, B.: Three-dimensional volumetric object reconstruction using computational integral imaging. Opt. Express **3**(3), 483–491 (2004)
7. Jang, J.S., Javidi, B.: Three-dimensional synthetic aperture integral imaging. Opt. Lett. **27**, 1144–1146 (2002)
8. Javidi, B., Shen, X., Markman, A., Latorre-Carmona, P., Martnez-Uso, A., Sotoca, J.M., Pla, F., Martinez-Corral, M., Saavedra, G., Huang, Y.P., Stern, A.: Multidimensional optical sensing and imaging systems (MOSIS): from macro to micro scales. Proc. IEEE **105** (2017, to appear)
9. Sinha, S., Steedly, D., Szeliski, R., Agrawala, M., Pollefeys, M.: Interactive 3D architectural modeling from unordered photo collections. ACM Trans. Graph. **27**, 1–10 (2008)
10. Son, J.Y., Son, W.H., Kim, S.K., Lee, K.H., Javidi, B.: Three-dimensional imaging for creating real-world-like environments. Proc. IEEE **101**(1), 190–205 (2013)
11. Stern, A., Javidi, B.: Three-dimensional image sensing, visualization and processing using integral imaging. Proc. IEEE **94**, 591–607 (2006)
12. Wang, T.-C., Efros, A.A., Ramamoorthi, R.: Depth estimation with occlusion modeling using light-field cameras. IEEE Trans. Pattern Anal. Mach. Intell. **38**(11), 2170–2181 (2016)
13. Xiao, X., Javidi, B., Dey, D.K.: Bayesian estimation of depth information in three-dimensional integral imaging. In: Three-Dimensional Imaging, Visualization, and Display (SPIE) Conference Series, vol. 9177, pp. 911714-1–911714-8 (2014)
14. Boykov, Y., Veksler, O., Zabih, R.: Fast approximate energy minimization via graph cuts. IEEE Trans. Pattern Anal. Mach. Intell. **23**(11), 1222–1239 (2001)

Multi-channel Convolutional Neural Network Ensemble for Pedestrian Detection

David Ribeiro[1(✉)], Gustavo Carneiro[2], Jacinto C. Nascimento[1], and Alexandre Bernardino[1]

[1] Instituto de Sistemas e Robótica, Instituto Superior Técnico, Lisboa, Portugal
david.ribeiro@ist.utl.pt, {jan,alex}@isr.ist.utl.pt
[2] Australian Centre for Visual Technologies, The University of Adelaide, Adelaide, Australia
carneiro.gustavo@gmail.com

Abstract. In this paper, we propose an ensemble classification approach to the Pedestrian Detection (PD) problem, resorting to distinct input channels and Convolutional Neural Networks (CNN). This methodology comprises two stages: (i) the proposals extraction, and (ii) the ensemble classification. In order to obtain the proposals, we apply several detectors specifically developed for the PD task. Afterwards, these proposals are converted into different input channels (e.g. gradient magnitude, LUV or RGB), and classified by each CNN. Finally, several ensemble methods are used to combine the output probabilities of each CNN model. By correctly selecting the best combination strategy, we achieve improvements, comparatively to the single CNN models predictions.

Keywords: Pedestrian Detection · Convolutional Neural Networks · Inputs channels · Ensemble classification

1 Introduction

Driver assistance systems, autonomous vehicles, robots that interact with humans, and surveillance systems, all of them need to robustly and accurately detect people in order to perform their task correctly. Therefore, Pedestrian Detection (PD) emerges as a relevant and demanding problem, which already has more than ten years of study. The main factors that increase the difficulty of this task are: the illumination settings, the pedestrian's articulations and pose variations, the different types of clothes and accessories, and the occlusions.

As a result of this research, various image channels and feature representations [1] have been proposed (surveys are presented in [2,3]). Although the handcrafted features based detectors were popular in the past, the current state-of-the-art detectors rely on Deep Learning architectures, namely Convolutional

This work was partially supported by FCT[UID/EEA/50009/2013], and by the FCT project AHACMUP-ERI/HCI/0046/2013.

© Springer International Publishing AG 2017
L.A. Alexandre et al. (Eds.): IbPRIA 2017, LNCS 10255, pp. 122–130, 2017.
DOI: 10.1007/978-3-319-58838-4_14

Neural Networks (CNN). Some of these later models, result from the adaptation and extension of object detection frameworks, such as R-CNN [4], Fast R-CNN [5], and Faster R-CNN [6].

Regarding the CNN inputs, the most recent approaches use the RGB images (for example, [7,8]), but other color spaces (e.g. LUV) and representations (e.g. HOG) have been explored in other recent works [9].

In this paper, we propose an improvement to the pipeline of the R-CNN, and to the PD works of [9,10]. Two stages can be identified in these methods: (1) the proposal's extraction from the original image, and (2) the CNN post-processing. In our methodology (depicted in Fig. 1), we maintain the first stage, by obtaining proposals with conventional and already developed pedestrian detectors, based on handcrafted features. Then, we introduce improvements in the second stage, by using an ensemble of CNN classifiers, instead of a single CNN model. Each CNN is trained with a different input channel, generated from the original RGB proposals (e.g. LUV or gradient magnitude), and applied to the test proposals. Then, the outputs of each of the input channel's CNN models are combined. We observe gains, when comparing the combination's performance with the one from each individual input channel CNN model.

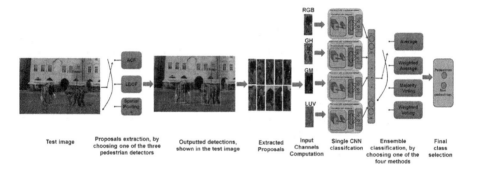

Fig. 1. Pipeline of our method's overall architecture.

2   Proposed Method

As mentioned in Sect. 1, our methodology (shown in Fig. 1) consists of the following two stages: (1) proposals extraction, and (2) multi-channel CNN ensemble classification.

In the first stage, we apply conventional PD detectors to the images, in order to obtain proposals, i.e. regions of interest that might contain pedestrians. More specifically, we resort to the Aggregated Channel Features (ACF) [11], the Locally Decorrelated Channel Features (LDCF) [12] and the Spatial Pooling + (SP+) [13,14] detectors. This stage performs the multi-scale sliding window task and Non-Maximal-Suppression, which reduces the computational demands imposed to the CNNs, used in the next stage.

In the second stage, we convert the proposals, originally in RGB, to distinct input channels, namely: gradient magnitude, normalized sum of gradient histograms for six orientations[1] and LUV. Each CNN is trained with a different input channel, and applied to the test proposals. Afterwards, the probabilities (of a certain proposal containing a pedestrian), resulting from each of the input channel's CNN models, are combined. This combination is performed according to four different ensemble methodologies [16]: (*i*) averaging, (*ii*) weighted averaging, (*iii*) majority voting, and (*iv*) weighted voting.

2.1 Datasets and Proposals Extraction

To reduce the computational demands required by the CNN, we generate proposals with conventional pedestrian detectors, which do not use Deep learning architectures. These detectors are applied to a pedestrian dataset, represented by: $\widetilde{\mathcal{D}} = \{(\widetilde{\mathbf{x}}, \mathcal{B}^{gt})_i\}_{i=1}^{|\widetilde{\mathcal{D}}|}$, with $\widetilde{\mathbf{x}} \in \mathbb{R}^{\tilde{H} \times \tilde{W} \times \tilde{D}}$ denoting the input RGB images (height, width and depth, respectively), and $\mathcal{B}^{gt} = \{\widetilde{\mathbf{b}}_k\}_{k=1}^{|\mathcal{B}^{gt}|}$ denoting the set of ground truth bounding boxes containing the pedestrians, with $\widetilde{\mathbf{b}}_k = [x_k, y_k, w_k, h_k] \in \mathbb{R}^4$ corresponding to the top-left point and width and height, respectively.

The set of detections provided by the detectors mentioned above, are denoted by $\mathcal{O} = \{(\widetilde{\mathbf{x}}(\mathcal{B}^{dt}), \mathcal{S})_i\}_{i=1}^{|\mathcal{O}|}$, where $\mathcal{B}^{dt} = \{\mathbf{b}_k\}_{k=1}^{|\mathcal{B}^{dt}|}$ are the bounding boxes corresponding to the detections, $\widetilde{\mathbf{x}}(\mathcal{B}^{dt})_i$ constitutes the proposals for image $\widetilde{\mathbf{x}}_i$, i.e. represents the regions of the image $\widetilde{\mathbf{x}}_i$ delimited by the bounding boxes in $\mathcal{B}_i^{dt}$, having $\mathcal{S}_i = \{s_k\}_{k=1}^{|\mathcal{B}^{dt}|}$, with $s_k \in \mathbb{R}$ as the corresponding scores, expressing the confidence in the existence of a pedestrian.

From the output of the detectors, we build a new dataset, where the CNNs are used. We denote this dataset by: $\mathcal{D} = \{(\mathbf{x}, \mathbf{y})_i\}_{i=1}^{|\mathcal{D}|}$, where $\mathbf{x}_i = \widetilde{\mathbf{x}}(\mathcal{B}^{dt})_i \in \mathbb{R}^{H \times W \times D}$ represents the proposals, and $\mathbf{y}_i \in \mathcal{Y} = \{0, 1\}^C$ denotes the classes for the proposal $\mathbf{x}_i$: non-pedestrian (label zero) and pedestrian (label one), in our case the number of classes is $C = 2$.

2.2 Input Channels

In order to generate several inputs for the CNNs ensemble, we compute three input channels from the original RGB proposals. In total there are four input channels (as illustrated in Fig. 2), denoted by: $\mathbf{x}_t \in \mathbb{R}^{H \times W \times D}$, for $t \in T = \{$RGB,GH,GM,LUV$\}$, which correspond to RGB, normalized sum of gradient histograms for six orientations, gradient magnitude (computed from each channel in RGB) and LUV [1]. Since, originally, the normalized sum of gradient histograms for six orientations only has one channel in the third dimension, we replicate this channel to obtain the remaining depth dimensions.

---

[1] The six orientations are obtained in equally spaced intervals in the range $[0, \pi[$, see details in [15].

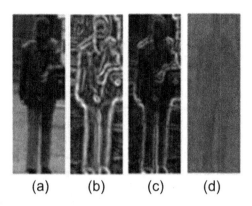

(a)   (b)   (c)   (d)

Fig. 2. Depiction of the input channels applied in each CNN model: (a) RGB, (b) normalized sum of gradient histograms for six orientations, (c) gradient magnitude, and (d) LUV.

2.3   Convolutional Neural Networks

Convolutional Neural Networks (CNNs) are architectures based on the composition of multiple layers, i.e. the output at layer l is obtained from the input at layer $l-1$ and from the parameters at layer l, according to: $\mathbf{x}^l = f^l(\mathbf{x}^{l-1}, \theta^l)$, where $\theta^l = [\mathbf{w}^l, \mathbf{b}^l]$ denotes the weights and biases (respectively) for the l-th layer out of the total L layers [17].

The initial input at layer $l = 0$, is an image with three channels (height, width and depth, e.g. RGB), i.e. $\mathbf{x}_0 \in \mathbb{R}^{H_0 \times W_0 \times D_0}$, with $D_0 = 3$.

The main operations assumed by these networks at a certain layer l, are represented by the function f^l, and can be of several types: (i) convolutional (followed by an activation function), (ii) pooling, (iii) fully connected (a particular instance of the convolutional one) and (iv) multinomial logistic regression [18].

Therefore, the CNN model $f(.)$ maps each image $\mathbf{x} = \mathbf{x}_0$ to classification probabilities for each class: $p_c = softmax(\mathbf{x}^{L-1}, \theta^L) \in [0, 1]$, where $c = \{0, 1\}$ denotes the non-pedestrian and pedestrian classes (respectively), and the last function is a softmax, defined by: $softmax(\mathbf{x}_c^{L-1}) = \frac{\exp^{\mathbf{x}_c^{L-1}}}{\sum_j \exp^{\mathbf{x}_j^{L-1}}}$, where $c = \{0, \ldots, C-1\}$ denotes the classes (in our case, $C = 2$).

The convolution is defined by:

$$\mathbf{x}^l_{m',n',d'} = \sum_{mnd} \mathbf{w}^l_{m,n,d,d'} \cdot \mathbf{x}^{l-1}_{m+m',n+n',d} + \mathbf{b}^l_{d'}, \tag{1}$$

where m, n, d, index the image height, width and depth, respectively, and d' is the number of filters (see [17]). The convolution is followed by the Rectified Linear Unit (ReLU) activation function [18] defined by $a(\mathbf{x}^l_{m',n',d'}) = max(0, \mathbf{x}^l_{m',n',d'})$ (see [17]). The max pooling is defined by $\mathbf{x}^l_{m,n,d} = max(\mathbf{x}^{l-1}_{m',n',d})$ (see [17]), with $m', n' \in \mathcal{I}(m, n)$, where $\mathcal{I}(m, n)$ are the input locations.

2.4   CNN Architecture

Regarding the choice of the CNN architecture and initialization, we have considered the work of [19]. The authors mention the advantages of transfer learning, i.e. using a model pre-trained with an auxiliary dataset, and re-training (i.e. fine-tuning) it with the target dataset, instead of randomly initializing the network.

Consequently, we adopt the configuration D of the VGG Very Deep 16 CNN model [20], which was subject to pre-training with the Imagenet dataset [21] (which contains generic objects). Then, we adapt this architecture to the PD task, by introducing the following changes. First, the original input size is downscaled from $224 \times 224 \times 3$ to $64 \times 64 \times 3$, in order to ease the computational expense associated with the CNN. As a result, we adjust the fully connected layers to this modification, by randomly initializing and resizing them. To obtain the probability of the non-pedestrian and pedestrian classes, the softmax was adjusted to this new number of outputs. Afterwards, we re-train (i.e. fine-tune) this model with the pedestrian dataset, as described in Sect. 2.1.

The main pre-processing steps required to use the CNN are: the mean subtraction (computed from the training images) and the resize to the defined CNN input dimensions.

2.5   Ensemble Classification

The ensemble is composed of four single CNN models, trained with each of the four input channels, described in Sect. 2.2. Each CNN model constitutes an individual learner $f_t(\mathbf{x}_t)$, $t \in T =$ {RGB,GH,GM,LUV}), where $\mathbf{x}_t$ corresponds to the proposal for the t-th input channel, and $f_t(.)$ denotes the t-th CNN model. As mentioned in Sect. 2.3, each of these CNNs provides a classification score (i.e., a probability) for each class, denoted by $p_t^c = f_t^c(\mathbf{x}_t) \in [0,1]$, where $c = 0$ represents the non-pedestrian class, and $c = 1$ represents the pedestrian class.

To combine the probabilities of the four CNN models, we consider a set G that contains all possible probabilities combinations[2].

For the i-th probability configuration, denoted as $G^i \in G$, four different ensemble methods are used, that is: (i) averaging, (ii) weighted averaging, (iii) majority voting, and (iv) weighted voting [16].

For the average computation, we consider the probabilities p_t^c, and for the voting computation, we transform the probabilities in votes v_t^c, according to: $v_t^c = 0$, if $p_t^c < 0.5$, and $v_t^c = 1$, if $p_t^c \geq 0.5$.

For the simple and weighted average, for the class c, we consider the following expression:

$$P^c = \sum_{t \in G^i} w_t \cdot f_t^c(\mathbf{x}_t) = \sum_{t \in G^i} w_t \cdot p_t^c, \tag{2}$$

where $\sum_{t \in G^i} w_t = 1$. In the simple average case, we have $w_t = \dfrac{1}{|G^i|}$, and in the weighted average case, we use the CNN model's log average miss rate metric [2]

---

[2] Considering four input channel's CNN models, the cardinality of G is $|G| = 15$.

to build the weights, i.e. $w_t = \dfrac{(1/\mathrm{MR}_t)}{\sum_{t \in G^i}(1/\mathrm{MR}_t)}$, where MR_t denotes the log average miss rate for the input channel's CNN model t.

For the majority voting, the class c is selected, if the number of votes for that class is greater than half the total number of votes. If there is a tie, the pedestrian class ($c = 1$) is selected. The weighted voting is similar to the majority voting, but the votes v_t^c are weighted by w_t, similarly to the weighted average case.

To find which combination of the probabilities (resulting from different CNN models, associated with distinct input channels) achieves the best performance, we try all the possible combination's subsets $G^i \subset G$. Then, for $c = 1$, if $P^c \geq 0.5$, or if c has the most votes, we consider that the proposal $\mathbf{x}$ contains a pedestrian, and, consequently, remains unchanged (including the score provided by the detector). Otherwise, the proposal is regarded as a negative, i.e. not enclosing a pedestrian, and is discarded. In fact, we use this final probability to reduce the number of false positives provided by the detector in the first stage, and, therefore, improve the accuracy of the method.

3   Experiments

We perform experiments in the Caltech [2] and INRIA [22] pedestrian datasets, using three detectors for the proposals extraction, namely: LDCF, ACF (ACF-Caltech+ for Caltech as in [12,15], and mentioned as ACF+) and SP+. All the combination methods described in Sect. 2.5 are used, for all the possible input channels probabilities combination sets. We adopt the log average miss rate as the performance metric, as described in [2]. We use the following toolboxes: for the CNN [17], for the performance assessment, ACF and LDCF [15], and for SP+, the code provided at[3]. The CNN train settings are: ten epochs with a batch size of 100, a learning rate of 0.001 and a momentum of 0.9.

3.1   Caltech Dataset

In order to build the dataset to train the CNN (as described in Sect. 2.1), we extract positive proposals (i.e. containing pedestrians) using the ground truth annotations from the Caltech dataset with third frame sampling (for further details, see [2]). Afterwards, we augment this set by horizontally flipping each of the proposals. In total, we obtain 32752 positive train proposals.

The negative proposals (i.e. not containing pedestrians) result from applying a non-completely trained version of the LDCF detector to the Caltech dataset with thirtieth frame sampling (for additional information, see [2]). A maximum of five negative proposals are extracted in each image, and the Intersection over Union with the ground truth is restricted to be less than 0.1. By not training this specific LDCF detector with the same amount of data as in [15], we are able to obtain more negative proposals, which correspond to false positive detections (i.e. detector errors). In total, we obtain 17420 negative train proposals.

---

[3] https://github.com/chhshen/pedestrian-detection.

Finally, the positive and negative proposals collected previously (50172, in total), are split into train (90% of the total amount, i.e. 45155) and validation (10% of the total amount, i.e. 5017) sets.

We assess the performance in the Caltech test set according to the reasonable setting, i.e. the pedestrians must have 50 pixels of height or more, and the occlusion must be partial or inexistent (additional details can be found in [2]).

3.2 INRIA Dataset

For the construction of the CNN training set, we resort to the ground truth annotations of the INRIA positive images, in order to obtain positive proposals (i.e. containing pedestrians). Subsequently, this set is expanded by using horizontal flipping. Then, the overall set is further augmented by applying random deformations. In total, we extract 4948 positive proposals.

The negative proposals (i.e. not containing pedestrians) are acquired with a non-completely trained version of the LDCF detector (similarly to the Caltech case), by establishing that only a maximum of 18 negative proposals could be obtained from each of the INRIA negative images. In total, we extract 12552 negative proposals.

Finally, the acquired positive and negative proposals (17500, in total) are split into train (90% of the total amount, i.e. 15751) and validation (10% of the total amount, i.e. 1749) sets.

3.3 Results

Table 1 presents an overview of the results for the INRIA and Caltech datasets by using the proposals extracted with various detectors (column "Proposals"), adding the CNN classification for different input channels (columns from "RGB" to "LUV") and finally, selecting the best combination of the probabilities for these input channels (the column "Inputs" contains the input channels used for the method in the column "Method", to achieve the performance in the column "Comb.").

From Table 1, it can be seen that adding the CNN classification generally improves the baseline detector performance. Although there are some exceptions where the CNN performance is worst than the baseline, we can see that,

Table 1. Log average miss rate % of the detector's proposals, the proposals with CNN classification for distinct input channels, and the best combination of probabilities for several input channels, evaluated using the INRIA and Caltech datasets.

Dataset	Detector	Proposals	RGB	GH	GM	LUV	Comb.	Inputs	Method
INRIA	ACF	16.83	15.24	15.84	16.52	15.55	15.03	{RGB,LUV}	Weighted average
	LDCF	13.89	12.43	14.75	13.53	13.29	12.15	{RGB,GM}	Weighted average
Caltech	ACF+	29.54	23.23	28.93	28.19	25.09	22.55	{RGB,LUV}	Weighted average
	LDCF	25.19	21.49	27.19	26.14	22.42	21.10	{RGB,GH,LUV}	Weighted average
	SP+	21.48	16.85	22.94	21.48	19.00	16.60	{RGB,LUV}	Simple average

by correctly choosing the best combination strategy, the proposed ensemble classification is always able to boost the results, reaching the top classification score. This means that the proposed method is effective in the exploration of synergies among individual learners.

4   Discussion and Conclusions

A novel approach to the PD problem, based on ensemble classification with several input channel's CNN models, is proposed. Comparatively to the individual CNN models performance, we achieve gains by combining the classification results of various CNNs, where each one of them was trained with different input channels (namely, RGB, normalized sum of the gradient histograms, gradient magnitude, and LUV). We show that synergies can be found resorting to ensemble methods, and our approach is easily extensible to more channels and features of different types. As further work, the weights used during the combination could be learned jointly by all CNN models during training, or the CNN features of the top layers could be extracted to train a classification model.

References

1. Dollar, P., Tu, Z., Perona, P., Belongie, S.: Integral channel features. In: BMVC (2009)
2. Dollár, P., Wojek, C., Schiele, B., Perona, P.: Pedestrian detection: an evaluation of the state of the art. IEEE Trans. Pattern Anal. Mach. Intell. **34**(4), 743–761 (2012)
3. Benenson, R., Omran, M., Hosang, J., Schiele, B.: Ten years of pedestrian detection, what have we learned? In: Agapito, L., Bronstein, M.M., Rother, C. (eds.) ECCV 2014. LNCS, vol. 8926, pp. 613–627. Springer, Cham (2015). doi:10.1007/978-3-319-16181-5_47
4. Girshick, R., Donahue, J., Darrell, T., Malik, J.: Rich feature hierarchies for accurate object detection and semantic segmentation. In: Proceedings of the IEEE Conference on Computer Vision and Pattern Recognition (CVPR) (2014)
5. Girshick, R.: Fast R-CNN. In: Proceedings of the International Conference on Computer Vision (ICCV) (2015)
6. Ren, S., He, K., Girshick, R., Sun, J.: Faster R-CNN: towards real-time object detection with region proposal networks. In: Neural Information Processing Systems (NIPS) (2015)
7. Cai, Z., Fan, Q., Feris, R.S., Vasconcelos, N.: A unified multi-scale deep convolutional neural network for fast object detection. In: Leibe, B., Matas, J., Sebe, N., Welling, M. (eds.) ECCV 2016. LNCS, vol. 9908, pp. 354–370. Springer, Cham (2016). doi:10.1007/978-3-319-46493-0_22
8. Zhang, L., Lin, L., Liang, X., He, K.: Is faster R-CNN doing well for pedestrian detection? In: Leibe, B., Matas, J., Sebe, N., Welling, M. (eds.) ECCV 2016. LNCS, vol. 9906, pp. 443–457. Springer, Cham (2016). doi:10.1007/978-3-319-46475-6_28
9. Hosang, J., Omran, M., Benenson, R., Schiele, B.: Taking a deeper look at pedestrians. In: Proceedings of the IEEE Conference on Computer Vision and Pattern Recognition (CVPR), pp. 4073–4082 (2015)

10. Ribeiro, D., Nascimento, J.C., Bernardino, A., Carneiro, G.: Improving the performance of pedestrian detectors using convolutional learning. Pattern Recogn. **61**, 641–649 (2017)
11. Dollár, P., Appel, R., Belongie, S., Perona, P.: Fast feature pyramids for object detection. IEEE Trans. Pattern Anal. Mach. Intell. **36**(8), 1532–1545 (2014)
12. Nam, W., Dollár, P., Han, J.H.: Local decorrelation for improved pedestrian detection. In: NIPS (2014)
13. Paisitkriangkrai, S., Shen, C., Hengel, A.: Strengthening the effectiveness of pedestrian detection with spatially pooled features. In: Fleet, D., Pajdla, T., Schiele, B., Tuytelaars, T. (eds.) ECCV 2014. LNCS, vol. 8692, pp. 546–561. Springer, Cham (2014). doi:10.1007/978-3-319-10593-2_36
14. Paisitkriangkrai, S., Shen, C., van den Hengel, A.: Pedestrian detection with spatially pooled features and structured ensemble learning. IEEE Trans. Pattern Anal. Mach. Intell. **38**(6), 1243–1257 (2016)
15. Dollár, P.: Piotr's Computer Vision Matlab Toolbox (PMT). http://vision.ucsd.edu/pdollar/toolbox/doc/index.html
16. Zhou, Z.H.: Ensemble Methods: Foundations and Algorithms. CRC Press, Boca Raton (2012)
17. Vedaldi, A., Lenc, K.: MatConvNet - convolutional neural networks for MATLAB. In: Proceeding of the ACM International Conference on Multimedia (2015)
18. Krizhevsky, A., Sutskever, I., Hinton, G.E.: Imagenet classification with deep convolutional neural networks. In: NIPS (2012)
19. Yosinski, J., Clune, J., Bengio, Y., Lipson, H.: How transferable are features in deep neural networks? In: NIPS, pp. 3320–3328 (2014)
20. Simonyan, K., Zisserman, A.: Very deep convolutional networks for large-scale image recognition. In: ICLR (2015)
21. Russakovsky, O., Deng, J., Su, H., Krause, J., Satheesh, S., Ma, S., Huang, Z., Karpathy, A., Khosla, A., Bernstein, M., Berg, A.C., Fei-Fei, L.: ImageNet large scale visual recognition challenge. Int. J. Comput. Vis. (IJCV) **115**(3), 211–252 (2015)
22. Dalal, N., Triggs, B.: Histograms of oriented gradients for human detection. In: CVPR (2005)

Human Pose Estimation by a Series of Residual Auto-Encoders

M. Farrajota[(✉)], João M.F. Rodrigues [ID], and J.M.H. du Buf

Vision Laboratory, LARSyS, University of the Algarve, 8005-139 Faro, Portugal
{mafarrajota,jrodrig,dubuf}@ualg.pt

Abstract. Pose estimation is the task of predicting the pose of an object in an image or in a sequence of images. Here, we focus on articulated human pose estimation in scenes with a single person. We employ a series of residual auto-encoders to produce multiple predictions which are then combined to provide a heatmap prediction of body joints. In this network topology, features are processed across all scales which captures the various spatial relationships associated with the body. Repeated bottom-up and top-down processing with intermediate supervision for each auto-encoder network is applied. We propose some improvements to this type of regression-based networks to further increase performance, namely: (a) increase the number of parameters of the auto-encoder networks in the pipeline, (b) use stronger regularization along with heavy data augmentation, (c) use sub-pixel precision for more precise joint localization, and (d) combine all auto-encoders output heatmaps into a single prediction, which further increases body joint prediction accuracy. We demonstrate state-of-the-art results on the popular FLIC and LSP datasets.

Keywords: Human pose · ConvNet · Neural networks · Auto-encoders

1 Introduction

Human pose estimation has substantially progressed on many popular benchmarks [1,2], including single person pose estimation [3–8]. For a pose estimation system to be effective it must be robust to deformation and occlusion, and be invariant to changes in appearance due to factors like clothing and lighting, and yet be sufficiently accurate on rare and novel poses. Early work on pose estimation tackled these difficulties by using robust image features and sophisticated structured prediction [4]. Deep learning methods [3] have replaced the conventional pipeline with the use of convolutional neural networks (ConvNets) which constitute the main driver behind the huge leap in performance of many computer vision tasks. Pose estimation systems [5–8] adopted ConvNets as their main building block, often replacing hand-crafted features and graphical models.

In this paper we employ a regression-based ConvNet, adding improvements for single-person pose estimation methods based on 2D heatmaps of body joints with intermediate supervision. Similar to Newell et al. [8], we use stacks of

© Springer International Publishing AG 2017
L.A. Alexandre et al. (Eds.): IbPRIA 2017, LNCS 10255, pp. 131–139, 2017.
DOI: 10.1007/978-3-319-58838-4_15

deep residual auto-encoder networks connected end-to-end and trained jointly in a pipeline which iteratively refines the final prediction of the model. This topology allows for repeated bottom-up and top-down inferences across scales, which in conjunction with the use of intermediate supervision yields performance improvements. Furthermore, by combining all predictions from the auto-encoder networks in the pipeline with a weighted sum, we further increase the overall accuracy.

The main contributions of this paper are (a) the increase of the number of parameters of the auto-encoder networks in the pipeline, (b) the use of stronger regularization along with heavy data augmentation in order to increase the robustness of the network, (c) sub-pixel precision for more precise body joint localization, and (d) the combination of multiple predictions obtained from the network's auto-encoders at all stages into a single weighted heatmap prediction. The last step provides additional accuracy at negligible cost. We demonstrate state-of-the-art results on standard benchmarks, i.e., the FLIC [4] and LSP [9] datasets.

2   Related Work

Early approaches to articulated pose estimation were pictorial structure models [10] in which spatial relations between parts of the body are expressed as a tree-structured graphical model with kinematic priors that link connected limbs. Other approaches like hierarchical models [11] represent the relationships between parts at different scales and sizes in a hierarchical tree structure. Non-tree models [12] refine predictions by introducing loops to augment the tree structure with additional edges that capture occlusion, symmetry and long-range relationships. In contrast, methods based on a sequential prediction framework [13] learn an implicit spatial model with complex interactions between variables by directly training an inference procedure.

Recently, there has been an increased interest in ConvNets [5,14,15] models, which can be categorized as detection-based [5,6,14–16] or regression-based [17,18]. Detection-based methods rely on ConvNets as part detectors that are later combined with graphical models [6,15], which require hand-designed energy functions or heuristic initialization of spatial probability priors to remove outliers on the regressed confidence maps. Some of these methods also employ a dedicated network for precision refinement [5,14]. The method by Bulat et al. [19] uses a cascade-based ConvNet for a two-step detection, followed by a regression approach that is related to both detection-based [5,14] and regression-based methods [18]. Recent development of regression-based methods has been the replacement of the standard L2 loss between body parts prediction and ground truth locations, by a confidence map regression in which an L2 loss is defined between predicted and ground truth confidence maps, encoded as 2D Gaussian blobs which are centered at the part locations [15].

Very recently, residual learning [20] has been applied to articulated pose estimation [8,16]. Insafutdinov et al. [16] used residual learning for part detection, whereas Newell et al. [8] applied stacked hourglass networks. The latter extended residual learning to fully convolutional [21] and deconvolutional [8] networks, allowing for a more sophisticated top-down processing. Here, we further explore residual learning and stacked auto-encoders as in [8]. We use auto-encoders with progressively more features in layers as the spatial receptive field increases, heavy data augmentation with stronger regularization in order to increase the model's generalization to novel poses, and exploit the predictive capabilities of the stacked network's pipeline by combining all inference heatmaps of body parts from all stages (i.e. from all auto-encoder outputs) to compose the final prediction. This final step takes advantage of the ability of the network to provide multiple predictions with increasingly higher fidelity of body part locations at each stage of the pipeline. Hence, more information can be used when producing the final prediction, thus increasing the overall accuracy.

3   Person Pose Estimation

The articulated pose estimation scheme works as follows: (i) the model takes as input an image with a centered person and outputs a heatmap of all body joints; then (ii) the final prediction of the network consists of extracting the maximally activated locations of the heatmap for any given joint. In the following section we will describe the network's architecture.

3.1   Model Architecture

The architecture (Fig. 1, top row) is based on a deep ConvNet composed of multiple auto-encoders stacked together end-to-end, feeding the output of each into the next. This provides the network with a mechanism for repeated bottom-up and top-down inference, producing a refinement of the initial estimate and features across the stacks. We also use intermediate supervision to refine the heatmaps produced at each stage of the network. By doing so, the problem of vanishing gradients is addressed by replenishing them at each stage of the network during training. This results in faster convergence and ultimately in better heatmap predictions. Also, after the model is trained, we combine all responses from all auto-encoders in the network to form an ensemble of predictions to produce the final heatmap. This is achieved by combining all output heatmaps and feeding them into a sequence of two 1×1 convolutional layers, which maps a weighted sum of all heatmap predictions into a single one.

An ensemble of several networks is often used to improve the overall performance of a method. We also take advantage of the multiple predictions that the networks provide. In addition, the final accuracy of the model is increased most without additional cost, since we can train one network once and employ this multiple times. Although the predictions are similar, their combination still improves the final score.

The auto-encoder networks used are composed of a sequence of residual blocks [20] followed by max pooling and up-sampling layers to produce a heatmap. Their architecture is similar to the hourglass networks as used in [8], where consecutive residual blocks and max-pooling layers process and reduce the feature map to a low resolution (a minimum of 4×4 pixels), and then up-sampling (bilinear interpolation) layers with bicubic interpolation and shortcut connections to previous layers before max-pooling, restoring the feature map resolution to a size of 64×64 pixels. A series of 1×1 convolutions reduce the feature dimensionality to match the number of body joints to be detected when producing the output heatmap.

The differences between our auto-encoders and Newell's hourglass networks [8] are the following: (1) we use increasingly wider residual blocks (more features) as the feature map's resolution is decreased, and (2) an auto-encoder's output heatmap is composed by a combination of the current output produced by the network with the previous auto-encoder's output through a 1×1 convolution. First, by increasing the auto-encoders total number of parameters we effectively increased the overall network's prediction capability at the cost of a larger footprint in memory and a moderate increase in processing time. Second, by combining the current prediction of an auto-encoder with the previous one in the pipeline, we further increase the network's overall performance with a negligible increase in training time. Our empirical tests showed that this combination provides a boost in accuracy with a small cost associated with the training time. These modifications significantly improve the overall accuracy of the network, justifying the increase in memory usage and processing time.

We apply residual bottleneck blocks [20] throughout the network. These blocks are composed of a sequence of convolutions with a maximum filter size of 3×3 with bottlenecking, combined with a shortcut connection (for more information see [20]). This scheme helps to reduce the total memory usage and processing time of the network, while maintaining strong feature representations.

4   Implementation, Tests and Results

In the following sections we provide implementation and optimization details of the model and show benchmark results on two popular pose estimation datasets.

4.1   Implementation Details

We used RGB images with 256×256 pixels as input for the network (Fig. 1, top row; see Sect. 3.1). To have normalized input samples, we centered the cropping region around the persons and only applied zero padding and resizing. This is different depending on the dataset used; see Sect. 4.2. In case of FLIC [4], samples were cropped by centering along the center of the torso bounding box annotation. In case of LSP [9], we used the person-centric annotations to obtain the center coordinates of the person by determining the minimum and maximum coordinate limits of all body joint annotations, and then computed the center coordinate. In case of MPII [1], annotations of the center of the person and size were used for cropping and scaling. During training, we applied data augmentation by image

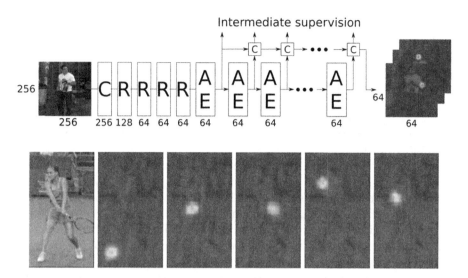

Fig. 1. Top: Network architecture, where C represents a 7×7 convolution, R a residual block [20], AE an auto-encoder network, c a 1×1 convolution, and 256, 128 and 64 indicate the resolution (in pixels) of a layer/block in a stage of the pipeline. Bottom: examples of results.

rotation $[-40°, 40°]$, scaling $[0.7, 1.3]$, horizontal flipping with 50% chance, and color transformations by varying the image brightness, contrast and saturation by up to 40%.

The model architecture is composed of a stack of eight auto-encoders with residual blocks, and two 1×1 convolutional layers as a final regression network for combining all the outputs of the auto-encoders in the stack. This setup was selected due to memory limitations of the hardware, since a bigger model would not fit in memory. The model starts with a convolutional layer with a 7×7 kernel and stride 2, followed by a residual block, a max-pooling layer, and 3 more residual blocks in order to reduce the resolution from 256 to 64 pixels. Then, 3 additional residual blocks precede the first auto-encoder network of the eight auto-encoders connected end-to-end in the network. Finally, the model is completed with a concatenation layer to join all output heatmaps of the auto-encoders, followed by two 1×1 convolutional layers, one with 512 feature maps and the other with the number of body joints needed for a specific dataset (these layers are trained separately after the model has been fully trained). All auto-encoder's residual blocks have filters with sizes between 256 and 768, where residual blocks with higher resolution (bigger feature maps) have a size of 256. Residual blocks with feature sizes of increasingly smaller resolutions increase by 96 filters, ending with residual blocks with 640 filters at the lowest resolution.

The networks were trained on two NVIDIA GeForce GTX TITAN Black GPUs with 6 GB of memory each, using Torch7 [22] and optimization using Adam [23] for 50 epochs with a learning rate of $2.5 \cdot 10^{-4}$, $\alpha = 0.99$ and $\epsilon = 10^{-8}$. Then the learning rate was reduced two times, to 10^{-4} for 15 epochs and to $5 \cdot 10^{-5}$ for another 10 epochs. After the network was trained, we trained the ensemble layers again using Adam as the optimizer for an additional 15 epochs with a learning rate of 10^{-3}, $\alpha = 0.99$ and $\epsilon = 10^{-8}$, reducing the learning rate two additional times to 10^{-4} for 5 epochs and to $5 \cdot 10^{-5}$ for 5 more epochs. All network weights were randomly initialized with a uniform distribution. We used mini-batches of 4 randomly sampled persons centered in the input image, batch normalization [24], randomized rectified linear unit [25] non-linearities and spatial dropout with 20% probability prior to all convolutions with filter sizes of 1×1 and 3×3, with the exception of bottlenecking convolutions in the residual block.

During back-propagation we used intermediate supervision [15], where an L2 loss is applied for comparing the predicted heatmaps of all auto-encoders outputs to a ground-truth heatmap. Heatmaps consisted of 2D Gaussians centered on the joint locations with a standard deviation of 1 pixel. Additionally, when predicting a body joint's coordinates, we refined the position localization by fitting a 1D parabola over the neighborhood of the peak's (x, y) coordinates by 1 pixel on the x and y axis separately, obtaining sub-pixel precision before resizing the coordinates to the original scale.

4.2   Datasets and Quantitative Analysis

The proposed method was trained and evaluated on two popular datasets for single person pose prediction: Leeds Sports Pose (LSP) [9] and Frames Labeled In Cinema (FLIC) [4]. These datasets were applied under the same conditions as detailed in Sect. 4.1. Evaluation was done using the standard Percentage of Correct Keypoints (PCK) metric [26], which reports the percentage of detections that fall within a normalized distance (we use 0.2 times the torso size) of the ground truth joint positions.

We first evaluated our method on the LSP dataset [9], which consists of 10.000 images for training and 1.000 images for testing. We also used the MPII dataset [1] to augment the number of training samples as the other methods used for comparison in Table 1 did. We applied the person-centric (PC) annotations. Our

Table 1. Performance comparison on the LSP dataset (eval. protocol PCK@0.2).

Methods	Head	Shoulder	Elbow	Wrist	Hip	Knee	Ankle	Total
Belagiannis et al. [27]	95.2	89.0	81.5	77.0	83.7	87.0	82.8	85.2
Lifshitz et al. [28]	96.8	89.0	82.7	79.1	90.9	86.0	82.5	86.7
Pishchulin et al. [14]	97.0	91.0	83.8	78.1	91.0	86.7	82.0	87.1
Insafutdinov et al. [16]	97.4	92.7	87.5	84.4	91.5	89.9	87.2	90.1
Wei et al. [18]	**97.8**	92.5	87.0	83.9	91.5	90.8	89.9	90.5
Bulat et al. [19]	97.2	92.1	88.1	85.2	**92.2**	91.4	88.7	90.7
Ours	97.7	**93.0**	**88.9**	**85.5**	91.5	**92.0**	**92.1**	**91.5**

Table 2. Performance comparison on the FLIC dataset (eval. protocol PCK@0.2).

Methods	Elbow	Wrist	Total
Sapp et al. [4]	72.5	54.5	63.5
Chen et al. [6]	89.8	86.8	88.3
Wei et al. [7]	92.5	90.0	91,3
Newel et al. [8]	98.0	95.5	96.8
Ours	**98.3**	**96.0**	**97.2**

model achieved top results on almost all body joints with an average PCK@0.2 of 91.5%. We also evaluated our method on the FLIC dataset, which consists of 3.987 images for training and 1.016 for testing. We report accuracy using the metric introduced by Sapp et al. [4] for the elbow and wrist joints. Our method also shows state-of-the-art results, reaching 98.3% PCK@0.2 accuracy on the elbow and 96.0% on the wrist joints.

Tables 1 and 2 show in detail our results ("Ours") compared with other state-of-the-art methods for human pose estimation on the LSP and FLIC datasets.

5 Conclusions

We presented a method for articulated human pose estimation using a series of residual auto-encoders. The proposed method employs a regression-based ConvNet composed of a series of deep residual auto-encoders connected end-to-end and trained jointly. The resulting model is then used as an ensemble of models by combining the responses of all individual auto-encoders along the pipeline, in order to convey the final prediction output. Heavy data augmentation and strong regularization were used because the network is a stack of auto-encoders with more parameters than previous state-of-the-art models [8].

We achieved top-performing results on the LSP dataset, with an average PCK of 91.5% for several body joints. On the FLIC dataset we achieved state-of-the-art results with a PCK@0.2 of 98.3% for elbows and 96.0% for wirst joints.

In future work we will extend the model for the detection of joints and poses of multiple persons in a scene.

Acknowledgments. This work was supported by the FCT project LARSyS (UID/EEA/50009/2013) and FCT PhD grant to author MF (SFRH/BD/79812/2011).

References

1. Andriluka, M., Pishchulin, L., Gehler, P., Schiele, B.: 2D human pose estimation: new benchmark and state of the art analysis. In: CVPR, pp. 3686–3693. IEEE (2014)
2. Ess, A., Leibe, B., Schindler, K., Van Gool, L.: A mobile vision system for robust multi-person tracking. In: CVPR, pp. 1–8 (2008)

3. Pishchulin, L., Andriluka, M., Gehler, P., Schiele, B.: Strong appearance and expressive spatial models for human pose estimation. In: ICCV, pp. 3487–3494 (2013)
4. Sapp, B., Taskar, B.: MODEC: multimodal decomposable models for human pose estimation. In: CVPR, vol. 13, p. 3 (2013)
5. Tompson, J., Goroshin, R., Jain, A., LeCun, Y., Bregler, C.: Efficient object localization using convolutional networks. In: CVPR, pp. 648–656 (2015)
6. Chen, X., Yuille, A.L.: Articulated pose estimation by a graphical model with image dependent pairwise relations. In: NIPS, pp. 1736–1744 (2014)
7. Wei, S.-E., Ramakrishna, V., Kanade, T., Sheikh, Y.: Convolutional pose machines. arXiv:1602.00134 (2016)
8. Newell, A., Yang, K., Deng, J.: Stacked hourglass networks for human pose estimation. arXiv:1603.06937 (2016)
9. Johnson, S., Everingham, M.: Learning effective human pose estimation from inaccurate annotation. In: IEEE Proceedings of CVPR (2011)
10. Pishchulin, L., Andriluka, M., Gehler, P., Schiele, B.: Poselet conditioned pictorial structures. In IEEE Proceedings of CVPR, pp. 588–595 (2013)
11. Sun, M., Savarese, S.: Articulated part-based model for joint object detection and pose estimation. In: ICCV, pp. 723–730. IEEE (2011)
12. Dantone, M., Gall, J., Leistner, C., Van Gool, L.: Human pose estimation using body parts dependent joint regressors. In: IEEE Proceedings of CVPR, pp. 3041–3048 (2013)
13. Ramakrishna, V., Munoz, D., Hebert, M., Andrew Bagnell, J., Sheikh, Y.: Pose machines: articulated pose estimation via inference machines. In: Fleet, D., Pajdla, T., Schiele, B., Tuytelaars, T. (eds.) ECCV 2014. LNCS, vol. 8690, pp. 33–47. Springer, Cham (2014). doi:10.1007/978-3-319-10605-2_3
14. Pishchulin, L., Insafutdinov, E., Tang, S., Andres, B., Andriluka, M., Gehler, P., Schiele, B.: Deepcut: joint subset partition and labeling for multi person pose estimation. arXiv:1511.06645 (2015)
15. Tompson, J.J., Jain, A., LeCun, Y., Bregler, C.: Joint training of a convolutional network and a graphical model for human pose estimation. In: NIPS, pp. 1799–1807 (2014)
16. Insafutdinov, E., Pishchulin, L., Andres, B., Andriluka, M., Schiele, B.: Deepercut: a deeper, stronger, and faster multi-person pose estimation model. arXiv:1605.03170 (2016)
17. Toshev, A., Szegedy, C.: Deeppose: human pose estimation via deep neural networks. In: IEEE Proceedings of CVPR, pp. 1653–1660 (2014)
18. Wei, S., Ramakrishna, V., Kanade, T., Sheikh, Y.: Convolutional pose machines. arXiv:1602.00134 (2016)
19. Bulat, A., Tzimiropoulos, G.: Human pose estimation via convolutional part heatmap regression. In: Leibe, B., Matas, J., Sebe, N., Welling, M. (eds.) ECCV 2016. LNCS, vol. 9911, pp. 717–732. Springer, Cham (2016). doi:10.1007/978-3-319-46478-7_44
20. He, K., Zhang, X., Ren, S., Sun, J.: Deep residual learning for image recognition. arXiv:1512.03385 (2015)
21. Long, J., Shelhamer, E., Darrell, T.: Fully convolutional networks for semantic segmentation. In: IEEE Proceedings of CVPR, pp. 3431–3440 (2015)
22. Collobert, R., Kavukcuoglu, K., Farabet, C.: Torch7: a matlab-like environment for machine learning. In: BigLearn, NIPS Workshop, no. EPFL-CONF-192376 (2011)
23. Kingma, D., Ba, J.: Adam: a method for stochastic optimization. arXiv:1412.6980 (2014)

24. Ioffe, S., Szegedy, C.: Batch normalization: accelerating deep network training by reducing internal covariate shift. arXiv:1502.03167 (2015)
25. Xu, B., Wang, N., Chen, T., Li, M.: Empirical evaluation of rectified activations in convolutional network. arXiv:1505.00853 (2015)
26. Johnson, S., Everingham, M.: Clustered pose and nonlinear appearance models for human pose estimation. In: BMVC, vol. 2, p. 5 (2010)
27. Belagiannis, V., Zisserman, A.: Recurrent human pose estimation. arXiv:1605.02914 (2016)
28. Lifshitz, I., Fetaya, E., Ullman, S.: Human pose estimation using deep consensus voting. arXiv:1603.08212 (2016)

Context-Aware Distance for Anomalous Human Trajectories Detection

Ignacio San Román[✉], Isaac Martín de Diego, Cristina Conde,
and Enrique Cabello

Universidad Rey Juan Carlos, C/Tulipán s/n, 28933 Móstoles, Madrid, Spain
ignacio.sanroman@urjc.es
http://frav.es

Abstract. In this paper, a novel methodology for the representation and distance measurement of trajectories is introduced in order to perform outliers detection tasks. First, a features extraction procedure based on the linear segmentation of trajectories is presented. Next, a configurable context-aware distance is defined. Our representation and distance are significant in that they weigh the relative importance of several relevant features of the trajectories. A clustering method is applied based on the distances matrix and the outliers detection task is performed in any of the clusters. The results of the experiments show the good performance of the method when applied in two different real data sets.

Keywords: Context-aware distance · Anomaly trajectory · Outliers detection

1 Introduction

Many different types of video surveillance systems have been recently developed (see, for instance, [1,2]). A video surveillance system is a combination of hardware and software components that are used to capture and analyze video. The primary aim of these systems is to monitor the behaviour of objects or individuals. Often, human trajectories are extracted in order to check for suspicious or abnormal behaviours. In the last years, several representations of trajectories, time series and sequential data have been proposed (for example, Wavelets [3], Symbolic Mappings [4], or Piecewise Linear Representation [5]). However, most of these representations are not associated with a configurable distance between trajectories. In addition, regarding trajectory anomaly detection, it is necessary to define what is considered abnormal behaviour, because this could differ from one data set to another. For example, an anomaly in an airport (a place where people usually wander) is very different from an anomaly in a street (where people usually go straight). The point is that usual representations do not represent this kind of features, making it impossible to use it for a context-aware solution.

Although a number of outlier detection algorithms have been presented in the literature, trajectory outlier detection has not been paid much attention (Fig. 1).

© Springer International Publishing AG 2017
L.A. Alexandre et al. (Eds.): IbPRIA 2017, LNCS 10255, pp. 140–148, 2017.
DOI: 10.1007/978-3-319-58838-4_16

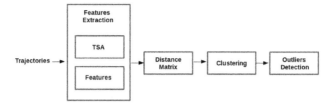

Fig. 1. Method for trajectories outlier detection based on a context-aware distance.

In [6] a method to detect outlying line segments for trajectory outliers is presented, specially designed to discover outlying subtrajectories from a trajectory database. In [7] trajectories are represented by several easily calculable features and a distance-based algorithm is used to detect outliers. In this work we present a novel trajectory representation as well as a configurable distance for context-aware outliers detection. We will compare this new distance with other classical methods in the literature in two different data sets.

The rest of the paper is organized as follows. Section 2 presents the proposed methodology step by step. These steps are the feature extraction, the definition of the configurable distance, an unsupervised learning method and finally, the outliers detection. The experiments to evaluate the performance of the method are in Sect. 3. Conclusions and a brief discussion about the method and results are presented in Sect. 4.

2   Method

A complete methodology to detect anomalous human trajectories is presented. Given a trajectory extracted from a videosurveillance system, the aim is to detect whether the trajectory is normal or could be considered as anomalous. To perform this task, the proposed method has four main stages. The first step is the feature extraction. Firstly, a linear segmentation algorithm based on the time-honored idea of looking for feature points where extreme changes on the trajectory occurs is used. The output of this algorithm is a set of subtrajectories that best represent the global behaviour of the original trajectory. Next, each subtrajectory is represented as a vector of features. Details will be presented in the following Section. The second step is to define and to compute a proper context-aware based distance between trajectories. Once the complete distance matrix has been calculated, a divisive partition clustering is applied. Thus, groups of homogeneous trajectories are detected. Finally a 1-Nearest Neighbour method is proposed to define what an outlier is in any of the obtained clusters.

2.1   Features Extraction

In this Section, an algorithm for converting a trajectory of points into a features vector is presented. These features will be informative and intuitive to interpret. First, the global trajectory is splitted into representative sections (or subtrajectories). Next, each subtrajectory is represented as a tuple of features.

Trend Segmentation Algorithm. The proposed methodology begins with the simplification of the trajectories to some subtrajectories supported by keypoints. The main purpose of this process is to reduce the noise and to get a simple and easy to manage representation of the information. In order to achieve this aim, we will use the Trend Segmentation Algorithm (TSA) [9]. TSA is an iterative algorithm that starts by fitting a regression line to the complete trajectory. Next, the coefficient of determination is calculated to evaluate the goodness-of-fit of the regression method. On the one hand, if the coefficient of determination is greater than a stablished threshold, the regression line is accepted as a proper representation of the trajectory. On the other hand, if the coefficient of determination is lower than the threshold, the regression line is rejected as a proper representation of the trajectory, and as a consequence, the trajectory is splitted into two sets. The algorithm iterates until all the splitted sets achieved a proper coefficient of determination. The result is a simplified trajectory whose points are the keypoints (splitting points), and the subtrajectories are segments defined by these points.

Features. The TSA trajectory representation defines a trajectory t_i as a set of m_i subtrajectories. In our approach, the representation of each subtrajectory is a tuple with three features (θ, ρ, n), where n is the number of original points in the subtrajectory, and θ and ρ are the polar coordinates of the subtrajectory. Figure 2 shows an interpretation of these features. Let $y = \beta_0 + \beta_1 x$ be the regression line that fits the points in a subtrajectory. The parameter θ is the angle between the x axis and the line from the origin $(0,0)$ to the closest point of the regression line:

$$\theta = \arctan(-1/\beta_1).\tag{1}$$

The parameter ρ stands for the Euclidean distance from the origin $(0,0)$ to the closest point of the regression line, and it is calculated as follows:

$$\rho = x\cos\theta + (\beta_0 + \beta_1 x)\sin\theta.\tag{2}$$

Thus, each i-trajectory t_i is represented as a vector of m_i tuples $\{(\theta_k, \rho_k, n_k)\}_{k=1}^{m_i}$, one tuple for each subtrajectory in the trajectory.

2.2 Configurable Distance

Let two subtrajectories t_a and t_b represented as two vectors of tuples (θ_a, ρ_a, n_a) and (θ_b, ρ_b, n_b), respectively. In order to measure the relationship between the subtrajectories t_a and t_b, the proposed Context-aware Distance (CaD) is defined as follows:

$$CaD(t_a, t_b) = [(\omega_\theta * \sin(\theta_{ab}))^2 + (\omega_\rho * \rho_{ab} * \cos(\theta_{ab}))^2 + (\omega_n * n_{ab})^2]^{1/2},\tag{3}$$

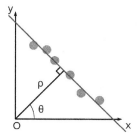

Fig. 2. Example of polar coordinates for a regression line (red line) fitted over a 7-points subtrajectory. (Color figure online)

where: $\theta_{ab} = |\theta_a - \theta_b|$, $\rho_{ab} = |\rho_a - \rho_b|$, $n_{ab} = |n_a - n_b|/max(n_a, n_b)$, and $\omega_\theta + \omega_\rho + \omega_n = 1$. Notice that ω_θ, ω_ρ and ω_n are the weights used to configure the distance and are fixed base on applications. The parameter ω_θ represents the relative importance of the angle between the regression lines of the subtrajectories. For instance, if $\omega_\theta = 1$ and the two trajectories are parallel, then CaD equals 0. The parameter ω_ρ represents the relative importance of the distance between the regression lines. For instance, if $\omega_\rho = 1$ and the two trajectories are parallel, then CaD equals the Euclidean distance between the two trajectories. The parameter ω_n represents the relative importance of the distance between the number of points in each subtrajectory. This term appears to control the amount of time that the individual has been following the subtrajectory.

Finally, given the CaD distances between each pair of subtrajectories in two trajectories t_i and t_j, to calculate the distance between the trajectories, the well-known Dynamic Time Warping technique is used [10].

2.3   Unsupervised Learning

Once the matrix of distances between trajectories is obtained, a hierarchical divisive partition clustering algorithm is performed. The algorithm is intended to find homogenous groups of trajectories. A classical "top down" approach is proposed: all the trajectories are in one unique cluster, and splits are performed recursively as the method moves down the hierarchy. To split the trajectories data set a "partition around medoids" (PAM) clustering algorithm is applied [11]. The PAM algorithm recursively divides the set of trajectories using $k = 2$ as number of groups. A measure of split improvement is needed to determine whether the split is adequate or not. In this work, to evaluate the split improvement we propose to use the difference between the silhouettes in the original cluster and the silhouettes in the splitted clusters (those generated after division). The silhouette is a measure of how similar a trajectory is to the trajectories in its own cluster compared to other clusters. On the one hand, if the maximum silhouette in the splitted clusters is greater than the silhouette in the original cluster, then the split is considered adequate. Otherwise the split is not neccessary, since a cohexed (homogeneous) cluster has been detected.

2.4   Outliers Detection

After the unsupervised learning, the trajectories have been grouped into homogeneous clusters. In order to detect outliers, it is necessary to define what an outlier is. This task strongly depends on the problem under consideration. In this particular case, we are interested in the detection of anomalous human trajectories. We define an anomalous trajectory as a trajectory with a very high CaD distance to its nearest trajectory in its corresponding cluster. To determine a threshold for that distance to be considered as outlier, the $90th$ percentile of the distances in the distances matrix has been used. Notice that if a greater value were used, the number of trajectories labeled as outliers would decrease. Conversely, if a lower value will be used, the number of trajectories labeled as outliers would increase.

3   Experiments

The proposed outliers detection methodology has been tested in two different Data Bases: the INVISUM and the BARD data sets. To test the relative performance of our method, it has been compared with a classical Euclidean DTW approximation and with the method proposed by Knorr in [7]. In addition, we will evaluate the CaD method when it was trained using the same value for its parameters: $\omega_\theta = \omega_\rho = \omega_n = 1/3$. We will call this approach $CaD_{1/3}$. In the DTW approach, no simplification neither transformation of the original trajectory is performed. Next, the Euclidean distance point-to-point is considered to feed the DTW method.

In order to compare the performance of the methods, the average of the outlier detection errors and standard deviations have been calculated over 10 runs of each technique. That is, each data set has been randomly partitioned 10 times in a training (70% of the sample) and a testing set (30% of the sample), and a run of the experiment has been done over each partition.

3.1   INVISUM Data Base

INVISUM (Intelligent VideoSurveillance System) is a project funded by the Spanish Ministry of Economy and Competitivity focused on the development of an advanced and complete security system [8]. The goal of the project is the development of an intelligent video surveillance system that addresses the limitations of scalability and flexibility of current video surveillance systems incorporating new compression techniques, pattern detection, decision support, and advanced architectures to maximize the efficiency of the system. To validate the performance of the INVISUM system, we have performed experiments using an indoor scenario at the campus of the University Rey Juan Carlos in Mostoles, Spain. The image covers most of the main hall of a classroom building. The hall is mainly used to move from one classroom to other and to enter the building. For the purposes of this paper, the trajectories obtained from a RGB camera were considered.

Table 1. Outliers trajectories detection in the INVISUM database. The average NPV percentages and standard deviation values of 10 runs.

Method	NPV
CaD	75.8 ± 12.7
Euclidean DTW	63.4 ± 19.5
Knorr	16.0 ± 5.20
$CaD_{1/3}$	22.8 ± 12.2

Given a sequence of images, all the human trajectories are extracted. We use the background subtraction method based on Gaussian Mixture of Models (GMM) for object detection. After background subtraction, a bag-of-soft-biometric features is extracted from each detected object. These features are related to the RGB color space, grayscale statistics and histograms, geometry, HSV color space, co-occurrence matrix and Local Binary Patterns [12]. The Kalman filter algorithm is used for trajectory prediction. Thus, a total of 182 trajectories were obtained, 127 were used to train the method, and 55 were used for testing tasks in 10 different runs of the experiment. Given the problem under consideration, the most important feature is considered to be the angle between trajectories. The less important features, associated with the lowest weight in CaD, are given to the Euclidean distance between trajectories and the number of points. Thus, the CaD parameters are fixed to $(\omega_\theta, \omega_\rho, \omega_n) = (0.8, 0.1, 0.1)$. Since no label information is provided, to evaluate the relative performance of the methods, the detected outliers were evaluated by two different human experts. Those experts validate whether the detected trajectories are, in fact, outliers (from a human point of view), or not. Thus, it is possible to calculate the Negative Predictive Value (NPV) as the proportion of detected outliers that are true outliers.

Table 1 presents the outliers detection results achieved for the INVISUM data set. The proposed methodology (CaD) outperforms alternative methods. More than 75% of the trajectories detected as outliers using CaD were, in fact, be labeled as outliers for the experts. In 7 of the 10 runs, CaD method improves the best alternative method. The results for the Knorr method are similar to those achieved for the $CaD_{1/3}$ method. These two methods grant the same importance to any of the considered metrics. Given the results, it does not appear to be a proper approach for the INVISUM data set. It is further obvious that when the weights in CaD are suitably chosen, based on the problem context, a significative improvement is obtained. Figure 3 shows an image representation of the trajectories detected as outliers in one of the runs for the CaD and the DTW methods.

3.2   BARD Data Set

The BARD data set is a set of videos used for human behavior analysis and recognition [13,14]. The data set currently contains several video sequences. The captures are taken place outdoors, under an uncontrolled scenario. In this case, the trajectories are available in the literature. Although these trajectories are

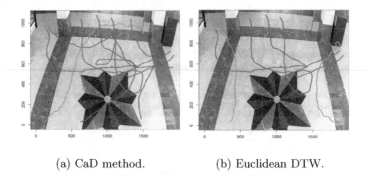

(a) CaD method.   (b) Euclidean DTW.

Fig. 3. INVISUM database. Detected outliers. The red trajectories are confirmed as outliers by experts. The green trajectories are not confirmed. (Color figure online)

Table 2. Outliers trajectories detection in the BARD dataBase. The average NPV and specificity percentages and standard deviation values of 10 runs.

Method	NPV	Specificity
CaD	99.4 ± 1.98	78.6 ± 14.0
Euclidean DTW	96.2 ± 4.46	98.1 ± 3.02
Knorr	60.1 ± 20.4	65.5 ± 12.3
$CaD_{1/3}$	95.8 ± 4.70	75.2 ± 12.2

labeled (as normal/anomalous), we have not used the label information until the evaluation of the proposed outlier detection algorithms. A total of 608 trajectories were considered, 426 were used to train the method, and 182 were used for testing tasks in 10 different runs of the experiment. Since no prior information about the problem was considered, similar values for the CaD parameters were used: $(\omega_\theta, \omega_\rho, \omega_n) = (0.4, 0.3, 0.3)$. Since label information is presented, it is possible to consider two kinds of errors. As in the INVISUM data set, the NPV is considered to evaluate the capability of each method to detect true outliers. In addition, it is posisble to calculate the Specificity: the proportion of true outliers detected as outliers. Table 2 presents the outliers detection results achieved for the BARD data set. The proposed methodology with the CaD distance outperforms the alternative methods. The CaD method obtained the best NPV results (99.4%), that is, it has a high capability to detect true outlier trajectories. Similar results were obtained for the DTW method. The Knorr method shows the worst performance overall. In 9 of the 10 runs, the CaD method improves or ties the best alternative method.

4   Conclusions

The main contribution of this paper is a novelty methodology for the detection of outlier trajectories. First, a segmentation algorithm for the proper representation of the trajectory information has been described. Next, representative features based on the polar coordinates of the trajectory have been built. A context-aware distance has been proposed based on these features. One of the main advantage of our distance is that it can be characterized based on the problem. Thus, it could be used in diverse situations based on the outlier definition. The proposed distance can be configured to give more importance to the expected cause of the anomaly: the angle, the distance to normal trajectories or the amount of time associated. Thus, the user can employ prior information about the problem in order to define the best distance to deal with outliers detection tasks. Then, the distances matrix is used to train a clustering algorithm in order to split the trajectories data set into homogeneous groups. Finally, following a 1-NN method it is possible to detect outliers in each group.

The proposed methodology has been applied in two real data sets, the well-known BARD data set and the INVISUM data set (first presented in this paper). The results of the experiments have demonstrated the utility of our representation and the proposed context-aware distance providing useful information to develop the outliers detection tasks. Overall, the results have been promising and the proposed methodology can serve as the foundation for further improvements. Future research directions include methods for the automatic parameter selection in the context-aware distance based on specific problem characteristics.

Acknowledgments. This work is supported by the Ministerio de Economía y Competitividad from Spain INVISUM (RTC-2014-2346-8). This work has been part of the ABC4EU project and has received funding from the European Unions Seventh Framework Programme for research, technological development and demonstration under grant agreement No 312797.

References

1. Zhang, T., Chowdhery, A., Bahl, P.V., Jamieson, K., Banerjee, S.: The design and implementation of a wireless video surveillance system. In: Proceedings of the 21st Annual International Conference on Mobile Computing and Networking, pp. 426–438. ACM (2015)
2. Rho, S., Rahayu, W., Nguyen, U.T.: Intelligent video surveillance in crowded scenes. Inf. Fusion **24**, 1–2 (2015)
3. Chan, K., Fu, W.: Efficient time series matching by wavelets. In: Proceedings of the 15th IEEE International Conference on Data Engineering (1999)
4. Lin, J., Keogh, E., Lonardi, S., Chiu, B.: A symbolic representation of time series, with implications for streaming algorithms. In: Proceedings of the 8th ACM SIGMOD Workshop on Research Issues in Data Mining and Knowledge Discovery DMKD 2003, pp. 2–11 (2003)
5. Keogh, E., Pazzani, M.: An enhanced representation of time series which allows fast and accurate classification, clustering and relevance feedback. In: KDD, pp. 239–243 (1998)
6. Lee, J.-G., Han, J., Li, X.: Trajectory outlier detection: a partition-and-detect framework. In: ICDE, pp. 140–149 (2008)
7. Knorr, E.M., Ng, R.T., Tucakov, V.: Distance-based outliers: algorithms and applications. VLDB J. **8**(3), 237–253 (2000)

8. INVISUM (2014). http://www.invisum.es
9. Siordia, O.S., de Diego, I.M., Conde, C., Cabello, E.: Section-wise similarities for clustering and outlier detection of subjective sequential data. In: Pelillo, M., Hancock, E.R. (eds.) SIMBAD 2011. LNCS, vol. 7005, pp. 61–76. Springer, Heidelberg (2011). doi:10.1007/978-3-642-24471-1_5
10. Meinard, M.: Dynamic Time Warping, Information Retrieval for Music and Motion. Springer, Heidelberg (2007)
11. Kaufman, L., Rousseeuw, P.J.: Finding Groups in Data: An Introduction to Cluster. Wiley, New York (1990)
12. Moctezuma, D., Conde, C., Martín de Diego, I., Cabello, E.: Soft-biometrics evaluation for people re-identification in uncontrolled multi-camera environments. EURASIP J. Image Video Process. 1–20 (2015)
13. Cancela, B., Ortega, M., Penedo, M.G., Novo, J., Barreira, N.: On the use of a minimal path approach for target trajectory analysis. Pattern Recogn. **46**(7), 2015–2027 (2013)
14. Cancela, B., Ortega, M., Penedo, M.G.: Multiple human tracking system for unpredictable trajectories. Mach. Vis. Appl. **25**(2), 511–527 (2014)

A Historical Document Handwriting Transcription End-to-end System

Verónica Romero[(✉)], Vicente Bosch, Celio Hernández, Enrique Vidal,
and Joan Andreu Sánchez

PRHLT Research Center,
Universitat Politècnica de València, Valencia, Spain
{vromero,vbosch,ceherto,evidal,jandreu}@prhlt.upv.es

Abstract. To provide access to the contents of the document collections that are being digitized, transcription is required. Unfortunately manual transcription is generally too expensive and, in most cases, current automatic techniques fail to provide the required level of accuracy. An alternative that can speed up and lower the cost of this process is the use of computer assisted, interactive techniques. These techniques work at line-level thus the transcription task assumes that the page images have been correctly decomposed into the relevant text line images. In this paper we present an end-to-end system that takes as input a page image and provides a fully correct transcript with the help of user interaction. The system automatically performs the text block and text line detection to be fed into the interactive computer assisted transcription. Experiments carried out show that the expected amount of user effort needed to produce perfect transcripts, can be reduced by using the proposed end-to-end system.

Keywords: Handwritten text recognition · Text line segmentation · Computer assisted transcription · Historical documents

1 Introduction

An increasing number of organizations are carrying out the digitization of large amounts of historical handwritten documents. However, for these raw digital images to be really useful, they need to be *transcribed* in order to provide new ways of indexing and querying the image collections. However, fully manual transcription requires highly qualified experts, making it a time-consuming and expensive process. Clearly, when the amount of text images to be processed is large, this is not a feasible solution. On the other hand, fully automatic transcription based on state-of-the-art Handwriting Text Recognition (HTR) methods is cheaper but often fails to provide the required level of transcription accuracy.

An alternative that can speed up and lower the cost of the process, while guaranteeing fully correct transcriptions, is the use of recently developed computer assisted, interactive HTR approaches such as CATTI (Computer Assisted Transcription of Text Images) [9]. For a given *text line image* to be transcribed an iterative interactive process is performed between a CATTI system and the user,

© Springer International Publishing AG 2017
L.A. Alexandre et al. (Eds.): IbPRIA 2017, LNCS 10255, pp. 149–157, 2017.
DOI: 10.1007/978-3-319-58838-4_17

the system yields successively improved transcription hypotheses in response to the simple user corrective feedback.

For the successful use of CATTI in practice an accurate detection of the text lines of each page image is required. In the case of *historical handwritten* text images, line detection and extraction is in itself a difficult task. In these cases, advanced line detection techniques such as that proposed in [2] can be used.

The traditional HTR (and/or CATTI) workflow thoroughly decomposes the page image transcription task into two separated tasks: (a) image preprocessing and text block and line detection and extraction and (b) transcription of each extracted line image. This decomposition is very convenient for experimental purposes as each task can be tackled independently, but it is inappropriate for practical text image transcription tasks. In fact, real scenarios demand a system that accepts a full page image as input and provide full transcripts of all the text elements as output.

In this paper we present an end-to-end system that takes as input a page image and provides a fully correct transcript with the help of user interaction. This system have been assessed through experiments on a relatively small historical Spanish document, with encouraging results.

2   System Overview

As previously said, the system we are presenting takes as input a handwritten page image to be transcribed and returns its best transcription hypothesis. Then, the transcription errors can be interactively corrected in an assisted scenario. The system is composed of the following modules: (i) document image preprocessing [10]; (ii) layout analysis; (iii) line image recognition [10] (iv) and finally, a computer assisted transcription module [9].

2.1   Preprocessing

Each page image is preprocessed in order to reduce the noise, recover handwritten strokes damaged due to page degradation and correcting basic geometry distortions (see Fig. 1(b)). First, each image is converted to grey scale and the text is enhanced [11]. Then, a bi-dimensional median filter [5] is applied to the grey scale image to remove background and reduce the noise. At this step the global text image skew angle is also determined and corrected [3,8].

2.2   Layout Analysis

The layout analysis is performed in a two step top-down process.

Text Block Detection. To detect the different text blocks of each page an automatic localization of text areas is performed by means of horizontal and vertical line detection methods based on the use of enhanced profiles. The block information obtained is used in order to further preprocess the pages and eliminate all issues outside the text blocks (Fig. 1(c)). Finally, the text lines are detected on the cleaned images.

Text Line Detection and Segmentation. The text line analysis and detection (TLAD) approach is based on HMMs and finite state or N-gram vertical layout models [1,2]. It follows the same successful statistical framework which is firmly established for automatic speech and handwritten text recognition. In this context, each page must be represented as a feature vector sequence which conveys information about the vertical page layout; namely, information about where text-lines may appear along the vertical page dimension and of which kind these lines (or other non-textual objects) are. These features consist of horizontal projection profiles computed in several vertical slabs of the page [1,2].

We formulate the TLAD as the problem of finding the most likely line label sequence hypothesis, $\hat{\mathbf{h}}$, for a given handwritten page image, represented as a sequence of feature vectors $\mathbf{o}$. In addition to adequately labelling each horizontal region, we are also interested in actually determining their corresponding *vertical position* inside the page. Let $\mathbf{b}$ be the sequence of *boundary marks*, that define the different lines found in the page (see Fig. 1(d)). Following the same discussion presented in [1], from the decoding process we can obtain both the best label sequence, $\hat{\mathbf{h}}$, and the best segmentation, $\hat{\mathbf{b}}$:

$$(\hat{\mathbf{b}}, \hat{\mathbf{h}}) \approx \arg\max_{\mathbf{b},\mathbf{h}} P(\mathbf{h})\, P(\mathbf{o}_{b_0}^{b_1} \mid h_1) \ldots P(\mathbf{o}_{b_{n-1}}^{b_n} \mid h_n) \qquad (1)$$

where $P(\mathbf{o} \mid \mathbf{h})$ is a *vertical line shape model* and $P(\mathbf{h})$ is a *vertical layout model* (VLM). $P(\mathbf{o} \mid \mathbf{h})$ is approximated by HMMs, while $P(\mathbf{h})$ is modelled by a finite-state model representing a-priory restrictions of how the different types of horizontal regions (called "line labels") are concatenated to form a text page. In our approach only three horizontal region are considered; namely BlankSpace (BS), Normal (base)Line (NL) and InterLine (IL). Accordingly, a very simple finite-state VLM is used which allows for any concatenation of pairs NL-IL, surrounded by BS regions.

Finally, for each detected baseline, an extraction polygon can be easily calculated (see Fig. 1(e)) by taking some pixels above and below the base-line as per the documents script.

2.3 Handwritten Text Recognition

Recognition can be formulated as the problem of finding the most likely word sequence, $\hat{\mathbf{w}} = (\hat{w}_1\, \hat{w}_2 \ldots \hat{w}_l)$, for a given handwritten sentence image represented by a feature vector sequence $\mathbf{x} = (\mathbf{x}_1\, \mathbf{x}_2 \ldots \mathbf{x}_n)$ [7]:

$$\hat{\mathbf{w}} = \arg\max_{\mathbf{w}} P(\mathbf{w} \mid \mathbf{x}) \approx \arg\max_{\mathbf{w}} P(\mathbf{x} \mid \mathbf{w})P(\mathbf{w}) \qquad (2)$$

where $\mathbf{w}$ ranges over all possible sequences of words. $P(\mathbf{w} \mid \mathbf{x})$ is typically approximated by concatenated character HMMs [4]. On the other hand, $P(\mathbf{w})$ represents probabilistic syntactic knowledge and is approximated by an n-gram language model [4].

The search of Eq. (2) is carried out by using the Viterbi optimization algorithm [4]. In addition to the optimal solution, $\hat{\mathbf{w}}$, a huge set of best solutions

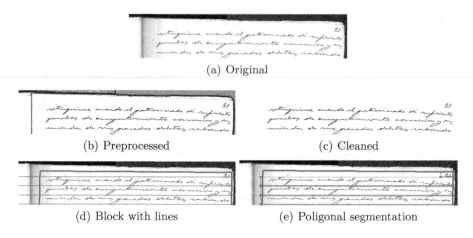

(a) Original

(b) Preprocessed   (c) Cleaned

(d) Block with lines   (e) Poligonal segmentation

Fig. 1. Figure shows the process that a sample page section undergoes through out the document layout process.

can be obtained as a by-product in the form of a word graph (WG). WGs will be used in the interactive HTR.

2.4   Computer Assisted Transcription of Text Images

The last step of our system consists in assisting the human in the obtention of the perfect transcription as per the CATTI scenario [9].

In the CATTI approach, the process starts when the HTR system proposes a full transcription $\hat{s}$ of a feature vector sequence $\mathbf{x}$, extracted from a handwritten text line image. Then, the human transcriptor validates the longest prefix of the transcription which is error-free and introduces some amendments to correct the erroneous text that follows the validated prefix, producing a new prefix (p). Next, the HTR system takes into account the new prefix to suggest a suitable continuation (i.e., a new $\hat{s}$), thereby starting a new cycle. This process is repeated until a correct, full transcription t of $\mathbf{x}$ is accepted by the user.

In the CATTI framework, in addition to the given feature sequence, $\mathbf{x}$, a prefix p of the transcription is also available and the HTR module is asked to complete this prefix by searching for a most likely suffix $\hat{s}$ as:

$$\hat{s} = \arg \max_{s} P(s \mid \mathbf{x}, p) = \arg \max_{s} P(\mathbf{x} \mid p, s) \cdot Pr(s \mid p) \qquad (3)$$

$P(s \mid \mathbf{x}, p)$ is modelled by HMM morphological words models [4] and $Pr(s \mid p)$ is modelled by an n-gram language model conditioned by p [9]. Using word-graph to implement these techniques, very efficient linear cost search is achieved.

3   The RSEAPV Database

The "Real Sociedad Económica de Amigos del País de Valencia" (RSEAPV) is a partnership that was established in 1776. It was a reference center for discussion and treatment of the most important and cutting-edge issues of that moment.

The RSEAPV posseses an archive composed of more than 8,000 documents that has been digitalized and made available to the public.[1] In this paper we have chosen a document of this collection to test our end-to-end system on it. The selected document was written by a single writer in Spanish in 1905 and it is composed of 170 pages.

To carry out layout, HTR and CATTI experiments we used a small set of the first 42 pages of the document. This set was annotated with two different types of annotations. First, a layout analysis of each page was manually done to indicate text blocks and lines, resulting in a dataset of 651 lines. Second, the dataset was transcribed line by line by an expert paleographer. The column "Total" of the Table 1 summarizes the basic statistics of the dataset text transcriptions.

Table 1. Basic statistics of RSEAPV dataset.

Number of:	Total	Train	Test	Cross-Val
Pages	42	22	20	5.25
Lines	651	303	348	81.4
Running words	4,573	2,150	2,439	572
Lexicon size	1,497	838	936	299.6
Out-of-vocabulary words	–	–	813	143

Two different partitions were defined in this RSEAPV dataset to carry out the experiments. The *train-test* partition was composed of two consecutive blocks. The first one, composed of the first 22 pages, was used to train the statistical models. The second one, composed by the remaining 20 pages, was used to test the system. The columns "Train" and "Test" of Table 1 summarizes the basic statistics of the two blocks.

Given the difficulty of this partition and in order to assess how increasing the number of training data affects to the quality of the automatic transcription, a second partition was defined. In this partition the 42 pages were divided into 8 blocks to carry out *cross-validation* experiments.

4   Experimental Framework

4.1   System Setup

Experiments were carried out to test the different steps of the end-to-end system.

---

[1] https://riunet.upv.es/handle/10251/18484.

With respect to the text line segmentation, the same feature extraction and HMM meta parameters determined in previous works [2] were adopted here. The VLM used was fixed on the base of prior knowledge of the general structure of the pages. In the text line segmentation experiments the *Train-Test* partition was used. The train block was used to train the vertical line shape HMMs using the Baum-Welch training algorithm [4].

For the HTR system, experiments with the two defined partitions were carried out. The training line images were used to train corresponding character HMMs for the HTR system, using also the standard embedded Baum-Welch training algorithm. Standard values, that have been proven to work well in previous experiments, were chosen [9].

In addition, two experimental condition were considered in each experiment: *Open* and *Closed Vocabulary* (OV and CV). In the OV setting, only the words seen in the training transcriptions were included in the recognition lexicon. In CV, all the words which appear in the test set but were not seen in the training transcriptions were added to the lexicon. In both cases a 2-gram with Kneser-Ney back-off smoothing [6] was estimated only from the training transcriptions. Finally, for each recognized test line image a WG was obtained [9].

4.2   Assessment Measures

Line Segmentation Evaluation Measures. In order to assess the quality of the line segmentation approach, two kinds of measures were adopted: *line error rate* (LER) and *Alignment Accuracy Rate* (AAR). LER is calculated as the number of incorrectly detected lines divided by the total number of actual lines. On the other hand, the AAR is a more quantitative measure which evaluates the geometrical accuracy of the detected horizontal baseline coordinates with respect to the corresponding (correct) reference marks. The AAR is computed in two steps: first, for each page, we find the best alignment between the system-proposed horizontal baseline positions and the corresponding references. In a second step we compute the final AAR as the ratio (in %) between the average error (computed in the first step) and the average text line height (also in pixels) for the whole corpus.

Handwritten Text Recognition Measures. The quality of the transcriptions given by the system with any kind of user interaction is assessed by the well know *Word Error Rate* (WER) and *Character Error Rate* (CER). They are defined as the minimum number of words/characters that need to be substituted, deleted or inserted to convert the text produced by the system into the reference transcripts, divided by the total number of words/characters in these transcripts.

Computer Assisted Transcription Measures. To asses CATTI effectiveness we use the *word stroke ratio* (WSR). It is defined as the number of required word level user interaction steps necessary to achieve the reference transcripts, divided by the total number of reference words. The WSR gives an estimate of the (simulated) human effort needed to produce correct transcripts using CATTI.

The definitions of WSR and WER make these measures directly comparable. The relative difference between them provides a good estimate of the reduction in human effort that can be achieved by using CATTI with respect to using conventional HTR system followed by human post-editing (EFR).

5   Empirical Results

Line Segmentation Results: Table 2 shows the results obtained in the text line segmentation process. We obtained a LER of 2.6%, which means that, for every 100 lines less than 3 caused issues to the line detection system. Furthermore we provide the AAR measure that indicates the geometrical accuracy of the detected horizontal baseline coordinates with respect to the corresponding ground-truth baselines, in average the detected lines are close to the actual baseline reference.

Table 2. LER and AAR results of the text line segmentation process.

LER (%)	AAR (%)	
	Average	Standard deviation
2.6	11	30

An important aspect to remark in these experiments is the really few number of pages required to obtain good results. Only 22 pages were necessary to obtain a detection accuracy above the 2.6% mark without having to perform specific parameter tuning for the corpus.

HTR Results: Table 3 shows the results obtained in the HTR step. The first row (Aut. TLD) shows the recognition result of the lines automatically segmented in the previous step. The high WER obtained is mainly due to the few samples (only 22 pages) used to train both the HMM and the LM. Note that more than 33% of the words in the test set are OOV words, and these OOV words are sure errors in the recognition step. Note that the CV experiment is a very optimistic evaluation, but allows us to study the influence of the availability of a lexicon for the given task: it gives a lower bound for the error rate that could be obtained by the availability of a better lexicon. In the Automatic TLD experiment the WER could be reduced by more than 15 points.

In order to test how much errors are due to the automatic line segmentation, we have carried out the same experiment (train with only 22 pages and test with the remaining 20) using the perfect lines marked in the GT (row GT TLD). Only 5 points are lost using the automatic detected lines. Considering that verifying by a human expert and correcting the automatic detected line errors is a very tedious and slow task, this 5% of WER is an affordable cost.

Finally, we carried out some experiments increasing the number of pages used for training the models. Given that only 42 pages are available with annotated GT, we performed a cross-validation experiment with the 8 folds previously described. We carried out eight rounds, with each partition used once as test (5 pages) and the remaining 35 pages belonging to the other 7 folds used as the training data. The average results obtained can be seen in the last row (Cross-Val) of Table 3. We can see that increasing the number of training pages only in 15, the obtained WER is reduced by more than 20%. Finally, using a better lexicon, a WER around 36% can be obtained.

Table 3. WER and CER for the two scenarios considered (OV and CV) using both partitions Train-Test (Tr-Ts rows) and Cross-Validation (Cross-Val row).

		CV		OV	
		WER	CER	WER	CER
Tr-Ts	Aut. TLD	55.6	30.3	70.7	43.0
	GT TLD	45.3	25.2	65.8	39.1
Cross-Val	GT TLD	35.9	16.4	55.7	29.6

CATTI Results: With respect to the experiments carried out to assess the performance of the CATTI system, they were performed using the WGs generated only with the OV cross-validation experiment. The estimated human effort (WSR) obtained was 45.8%, and the estimated effort reduction (EFR) computed as the relative difference between WER and WSR is 18.1%.

According to these results, to produce 100 words of a correct transcription, a CATTI user should only have to type 46 words; the remaining 54 would be automatically predicted by the system. On the other hand, if interactive transcription is compared with post-edition approach: for every 100 word errors corrected in post-edition approach the CATTI user would interactively correct only 72. The remaining 18 words would be automatically corrected by CATTI.

6   Conclusions and Future Work

In this paper, we have presented an end-to-end system that takes as input an handwritten text line image and returns the corresponding transcription. The system is based on state-of-the-art preprocessing, layout analysis and handwritten text recognition techniques. We have studied the capability of this system when applied to historical handwritten documents. The obtained results are quite encouraging. In addition, the use of assisted technologies show that the expected amount of user effort can be reduced.

Acknowledgment. This work has been partially supported through the European Union's H2020 grant READ (Recognition and Enrichment of Archival Documents) (Ref: 674943), the MINECO/FEDER-UE project TIN2015-70924-C2-1-R, and the HIMANIS EU project, JPICH programme, (Spanish grant Ref. PCIN-2015-068).

References

1. Bosch, V., Toselli, A.H., Vidal, E.: Statistical text line analysis in handwritten documents. In: Proceedings ICFHR, pp. 201–206 (2012)
2. Bosch, V., Toselli, A.H., Vidal, E.: Semiautomatic text baseline detection in large historical handwritten documents. In: ICFHR, pp. 690–695, September 2014
3. Pastor, M., Toselli, A., Vidal, E.: Projection profile based algorithm for slant removal. In: Campilho, A., Kamel, M. (eds.) ICIAR 2004. LNCS, vol. 3212, pp. 183–190. Springer, Heidelberg (2004). doi:10.1007/978-3-540-30126-4_23
4. Jelinek, F.: Statistical Methods for Speech Recognition. MIT Press, Cambridge (1998)
5. Kavallieratou, E., Stamatatos, E.: Improving the quality of degraded document images. In: DIAL 2006, pp. 340–349, April 2006
6. Kneser, R., Ney, H.: Improved backing-off for N-gram language modeling. In: ICASSP 1995, Los Alamitos, CA, USA, vol. 1, pp. 181–184 (1995)
7. Kozielski, M., Forster, J., Ney, H.: Moment-based image normalization for handwritten text recognition. In: Proceedings of the ICFHR, pp. 256–261 (2012)
8. Rezaei, S.B., Sarrafzadeh, A., Shanbehzadeh, J.: Skew detection of scanned document images. In: IMECS, Hong Kong, vol. 1, March 2013
9. Romero, V., Toselli, A.H., Vidal, E.: Multimodal Interactive Handwritten Text Transcription. MPAI. World Scientific Publishing, River Edge (2012)
10. Toselli, A.H., et al.: Integrated handwriting recognition and interpretation using finite-state models. IJPRAI **18**(4), 519–539 (2004)
11. Villegas, M., Toselli, A.H.: Bleed-through removal by learning a discriminative color channel. In: ICFHR, pp. 47–52, September 2014

Image and Signal Processing

Interactive Layout Detection

Lorenzo Quirós[✉], Carlos-D. Martínez-Hinarejos, Alejandro H. Toselli,
and Enrique Vidal

Pattern Recognition and Human Language Technologies Research Center,
Universitat Politècnica de València,
Camino de Vera, s/n, 46022 Valencia, Spain
loquidia@prhlt.upv.es

Abstract. The amounts of ancient documents transcribed by means
of Handwritten Text Recognition (HTR) technology have been rising
dramatically over the last years. Consequently, the development and
enhancement of HTR methods and algorithms have become an important issue in the field, with significant contributions in performance for
documents with segmented layout. However, Layout Analysis remains
a bottleneck in the development and generalization of HTR technology.
In this work a new Interactive-Probabilistic method to obtain document
layout is presented. This new method incorporates the user feedback in
the Layout Analysis process, in order to provide not just a very accurate
layout, but an interactive framework in which user feedback is used to
help the system to fix any error.

Keywords: Layout analysis · Page segmentation · Interactive Pattern
Recognition · Conditional Random Field · Handwritten Text Recognition

1 Introduction

Handwritten Text Recognition can be defined as the problem of finding the most
likely word sequence, for a given handwritten sequence image [10]. Under this
definition the presence of an input image is needed, but this image should contain
only a handwritten sequence. This is only one "line" of handwritten text which
is processed at once. However, since the main goal of HTR systems is to translate
not just a single line, but the complete page or even the complete book, a previous
system is needed in order to extract those lines from the whole page and, in an
upper level, to extract the different zones of the page (paragraph, marginal notes,
illustrations, page number, etc.). Consequently, this is a very important stage
of the HTR process. For example, if we develop a system to recognize text in
an image but we provide an illustration without text, the results of that system
are expected to be erroneous or, in the best case, the system would be able to
ignore that kind of inputs. In addition, knowledge on the type of zone is very
useful to provide some context to the text in the zone (since each zone can be
semantically different), and each zone can be processed differently.

Document Layout analysis (DLA) is the process of identifying and categorizing the regions of interest in an image of document. Commonly this process is

© Springer International Publishing AG 2017
L.A. Alexandre et al. (Eds.): IbPRIA 2017, LNCS 10255, pp. 161–168, 2017.
DOI: 10.1007/978-3-319-58838-4_18

divided into two sub problems [3]: detection and labeling of the different zones in the image (body, illustrations, marginalia) is called geometric layout analysis, and the classification of those zones into their logical role (title, caption, footnote, etc.) is called the logical layout analysis. Several methods have been developed for DLA [2,6,14], most of them based on Computer Vision techniques like binarization, skew correction, or Connected Components labeling, among others. All of these methods are designed as user-free systems. As a consequence, any error in the system result must be fixed from scratch by the user.

In this work, an Interactive-Probabilistic approach for image layout analysis is proposed, with the aim of providing not just a very accurate layout, but an interactive framework in which user feedback is used to fix any error. Conditional Random Fields (CRF) models [12] have been combined with a prior-probability model and Interactive Pattern Recognition [13] to build the new method.

The paper is organised as follows. First, in Sect. 2 the proposed method is explained. Then performance evaluation metrics and corpora used in the experiments are described in Subsects. 3.2 and 3.1, respectively. The experiments and models are described in Subsect. 3.3, while results are reported and discussed in Subsect. 3.4. Finally, conclusions are presented in Sect. 4, where potential threads for future work are suggested.

2   Interactive Layout Analysis

Document Layout analysis is the process of identifying and categorizing the regions of interest in an image of a document. As an input we have an image $\mathcal{X} = \{x_{1,1}, x_{1,2}, \ldots, x_{n,m}\}$, which is associated with a rectangular grid G of size $n \times m$. Each image site s is associated to a cell in the grid defined by its coordinates over G and denoted $G_{ij}, 1 \leq i \leq n, 1 \leq j \leq m$, because we do not necessarily use all pixels in the image. The site set is denoted $S = \{s_1, s_2, \ldots, s_D\} 1 \leq D \leq n \times m$.

Let be $L = \{l_1, l_2, \ldots, l_\ell\}$ the set of all the possible zones in a layout. Under this definition, L is an unconstrained set and any combination of zones is allowed (for instance, paragraph, marginalia, illustrations, lines, words, etc.).

On the other hand, each image is associated to some K-zones layout defined as $h^* = \{h_1, h_2, \ldots, h_K\}, h_k \in L, 1 \leq k \leq K$; henceforth, h^* is called the layout ground-truth of that specific image. Each site s_d belongs to a single zone into the layout, i.e., $s_d \Rightarrow h_k; h_k \in h^*, s_d \in S$.

We assume that each layout zone is a rectangle defined by its coordinates over G as $h_k = (\mathbf{u}_k, \mathbf{b}_k), 1 \leq k \leq K$, where $\mathbf{u}_k$ is the upper-left corner, and $\mathbf{b}_k$ is the bottom-right one. Figure 1 shows an example of this kind of layout zones.

Let define a *structured hypotheses space* [8,13] $\mathcal{H} = \{h^1, h^2, \ldots, h^T\}$ over the site set S, where $h^t = \{h_1, h_2, \ldots, h_K\}, h_k \in L, 1 \leq k \leq K, 1 \leq t \leq T$. We want the hypothesis $\hat{h}$ which provides the best layout for the site set. Under *minimal error criterion*, a best hypothesis is shown to be the one which maximizes the posterior probability [4]. However, in many cases it is difficult to directly estimate this posterior probability and it is better to apply the Bayes rule [13]:

Fig. 1. Layout zones example. Red = Paragraph, Green = marginalia, Blue = catch-word. (Color figure online)

$$\hat{h} = \operatorname*{argmax}_{h \in \mathcal{H}} \frac{P(S|h)P(h)}{P(S)} = \operatorname*{argmax}_{h \in \mathcal{H}} P(h)P(S|h) \qquad (1)$$

where the term $P(S)$ has been dropped since it does not depend on the maximization variable, h. $P(S|h)$ is the probability of a site set S given the layout hypothesis h, and $P(h)$ is its prior probability.

Prior probability $P(h)$ can be modeled by a Gaussian Mixture Model, which is a Gaussian mixture for each corner of each layout zone, where each corner is assumed to be independent of the others but constrained to $\mathbf{u}_k > \mathbf{b}_k \forall k \in h$ (element-wise), by computational reasons.

$$P(h) \approx \prod_{k=1}^{K} P(\mathbf{u}_k)P(\mathbf{b}_k) \qquad (2)$$

The likelihood $P(S|h)$ can be approached through a simple naïve Bayes decomposition, under spatial independence assumption, as follows:

$$P(S|h) = \prod_{d=1}^{D} P(s_d|h) \qquad (3)$$

where each $P(s_d|h)$ can be modeled by some classifier (e.g., by K-NN, CRFs, RBMs+linear regression function, etc.). Now, Eq. (1) can be re-written as:

$$\hat{h} \approx \operatorname*{argmax}_{h \in \mathcal{H}} \prod_{k=1}^{K} P(\mathbf{u}_k)P(\mathbf{b}_k) \prod_{d=1}^{|D_k|} P(s_d|(\mathbf{u}_k, \mathbf{b}_k)) \qquad (4)$$

where D_k is the sub-set of sites inside the layout zone k.

Interactive Pattern Recognition (IPR) framework [13] aims to improve the classical paradigm results by taking into account user feedback. A basic instance of IPR consists of the inclusion of the user feedback (f) and the history made from previous interaction steps (h') into the classical Pattern Recognition approach (i.e. Eq. (1)). Taking feedback and history into Eq. (4), an interactive version of the system is defined as:

$$\hat{h} \approx \underset{h \in \mathcal{H}}{\operatorname{argmax}} \prod_{k=1}^{K} P(\mathbf{u}_k|h',f)P(\mathbf{b}_k|h',f) \prod_{d=1}^{|D_k|} P(s_d|(\mathbf{u}_k,\mathbf{b}_k),h',f) \qquad (5)$$

As a result, the new system must be designed to compute Eq. (4) as a first hypothesis, and then Eq. (5) will be computed on each iteration[1] until the presented hypothesis satisfies the user. Both Eqs. (4) and (5), are computed by means of exhaustive search on this work, other methods should be taken into account for future improvements.

3   Experiments and Results

3.1   Corpus

The manuscript chosen for the present work is the first tome of a seven volume manuscript entitled "Historia de las Plantas" (PLANTAS for short), a XVII century handwritten botanical specimen book compiled by Bernardo Cienfuegos, one of the most outstanding Spanish botanists in the XVII century. The first volume has 1 035 pages, containing about 20,000 handwritten text lines. This corpus is already digitized at 300ppi in 24 bit RGB color, available as JPG images along with their respective ground-truth layout in PAGE XML format [9] compiled by PRHLT group [1] using seven categories, namely: catch-word, heading, marginalia, page-number, paragraph, signature-mark, and float (illustrations); see Fig. 1 for reference.

Since experiments on this paper are conducted on the detection of the main paragraph, only a sub-set of 122 pages was considered, excluding pages that contain indexes, reference tables, and illustrations. 22 of these pages were selected for training the model, and the remaining 100 for test.

Preprocessing of the images consisted of a conversion to color intensity and a image size reduction to fit feature extraction constraints. Feature selection was applied for selecting the CRF model features. For each site $s_d \in S$ we extracted color intensity of the site color and its neighbors, and the site position. Neighbors are defined from a ($w \times w$) window, centered on the site s_d. Depending on w, the number of features could be very high; thus, in order to reduce the size of the attributes vector, we apply PCA over it in order to reduce data dimensionality. Finally, CRF features are only 11, 5 directly related to color of site and neighbors, 4 bigram features, and 2 more related to site position.

---

[1] To avoid numerical problems, calculations are implemented in the logarithm form.

3.2   Evaluation Measures

Two different evaluation measures are employed:

- Pixel-wise performance: is computed by means of the well known performance (P), recall (R) and F1-score
- Goal-Oriented Success Rate (GoSR) [11]: aims at evaluating how much of the information contained in the ground-truth is also contained in the system result (only foreground pixels are taken into account).

3.3   Models

The posterior distribution probability described in Eq. (3) is modeled by a CRF model, estimated by using the `CRFSuite` tool [7]. After training, marginal probability of each class is extracted using the `tag` option, giving $P(s_d|h_0)$ and $P(s_d|h_1)$, were h_0 and h_1 means background and paragraph, respectively. In Fig. 2(a) we can see an example of the marginal probabilities obtained from the CRF model.

The prior-probability model (Eq. (2)) of corner location of the zones in the image can be estimated by a multi-variable GMM. Thus, corners in the ground-truth (h^*) are used to estimate a GMM model over each corner. Since only the main paragraph is taken into account, upper-left corner of the zone ($\mathbf{u}_k$) is modeled by a Gaussian mixture of two components, whereas bottom-right corner ($\mathbf{b}_k$) is modeled by three components (bottom-right corner varies much more than upper-left corner, then is more difficult to be modeled); in both of them a diagonal covariance matrix is used, in order to keep mixture axis parallel to image axis. GMMs estimation using the EM algorithm was done with a Python library called `scikit-learn`. In Fig. 2(b), log-probability of main paragraph corners is drawn for all possible $\mathbf{u}_k$ and $\mathbf{b}_k$ (k equal paragraph in this case) in an image.

User interaction was limited to a deterministic mouse clicking[2] and employed the following rules:

1. Left-click over the image: mouse pointer coordinates are a correct corner of some zone in h^*.
2. Right-click over the image: layout is correct (i.e. "OK signal").

User feedback is taken as f in Eq. (5). Feedback under this context means a constrain under the search space $\mathcal{H}$, i.e., rule (1) limits the search space to only those hypotheses where the selected coordinates in the image are part of h; then, that coordinate will be considered as "anchored". History constrains the search space to only those zone corners in the hypothesis which are not "anchored" by the user in previous iterations.

---

[2] Notice that, under deterministic feedback, the signal can be used directly in the system without any decoding [13].

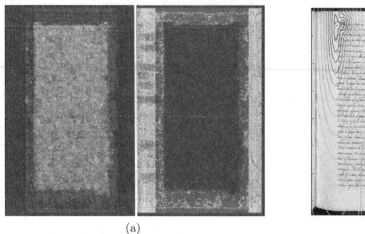 

(a)   (b)

Fig. 2. (a) Marginal probability maps extracted from CRF model results. Left image is the map for background and right one is the map for paragraph zone. Dark red means high, and blue/yellow means low. (b) Gaussian Mixture Models over main paragraph corners. (Color figure online)

3.4   Results

Experiments have been conducted over the selected corpus to obtain the model parameters, such as features to train CRF models, window size of those features, and training algorithm, among others.

For CRF, different experiments in order to determine the best combination of parameters (image scale factor Z, window size W, grid size G) were performed. Minimum Log-Likelihood, at training stage, were obtained with $Z = 0.3$, $W = 33$, and $G = 3$. In these conditions, the CRF model achieved an average pixel-wise performance of precision (90.81%), recall (95.08%), and F1 (92.82%).

In order to obtain a baseline of layout analysis performance using CRF, a connected components labeling (CCL) approach was taken [5]. Thus, all adjacent sites classified as "paragraph" by the CRF model are grouped; then, we search for the minimum rectangle where all sites of the same group fits; and finally, based on user experience, only the biggest rectangle is selected.

This baseline was first improved by using the prior probability approach, including the GMM estimation of main block corners described in Subsect. 3.3, instead of the CCL algorithm. Finally, the interactive approach was performed by using the mouse click as feedback.

Results of the different approaches in terms of GoSR can be seen in Table 1, ordered as were described previously.

As it can be seen, the effect of including the prior probability estimation provides a benefit in the layout detection, which is even higher when user interaction is taken into account. In this last case, the cost of interaction must be considered, but in our experiment only 52 clicks (for a total of 100 pages) were needed, which seems a reasonable amount of effort for the produced benefit. Also, hypothesis reviewed by the user can be considered as ground-truth to update the probabilistic model.

Table 1. GoSR average values (the higher the better) for the test corpus by using different approaches.

SR	CCL	GMM-prior	Interactive
GoSR	0.9656	0.9752	0.9945^a

^{a}100% was not reached because in some cases two o more blocks cannot be divided by a single line.

4   Conclusions and Future Work

In this work, a new method for Layout Analysis for ancient documents is presented. It was also shown that the method works, at least, to extract the main paragraph of the page, which is commonly where most of the information remains. Results show that the inclusion of the prior-probability in the model improves the baseline use of CCL without any heuristics, and that the interactive approach provides even a greater improvement with a reduced number of feedback interactions. Apart from that, the proposed method does not need a binarization step, which makes it independent of one of the most difficult steps in current image processing systems.

As future work, it is previewed to study the use of the technique with more than a single zone, the improvement of the CRF features, the inclusion of non-deterministic feedback, the use of a Gradient Descent search for corner estimation, and the use of different and more complex corpora.

Acknowledgements. First author has been partially supported by MICITT of Costa Rica through the PINN program (PEM-002-15-2). Moreover this work has been also partially supported by the Generalitat Valenciana under the Prometeo/2009/014 project grant ALMAMATER, by MINECO/ FEDER under project TIN2015-70924-C2-1-R (CoMUN-HaT), and through the EU projects: HIMANIS (JPICH programme, Spanish grant Ref. PCIN-2015-068) and READ (Horizon-2020 programme, grant Ref. 674943).

References

1. Bosch, V., Bordes-Cabrera, I., Muñoz, P.C., Hernández-Tornero, C., Leiva, L.A., Pastor, M., Romero, V., Toselli, A.H., Vidal, E.: Computer-assisted transcription of a historical botanical specimen book: organization and process overview categories and subject descriptors. In: Proceedings of the First International Conference on Digital Access to Textual Cultural Heritage, Madrid, Spain, pp. 125–130 (2014)

2. Bukhari, S.S., Breuel, T.M., Asi, A., El-Sana, J.: Layout analysis for Arabic histor-ical document images using machine learning. In: Proceedings of the 2012 ICFHR, pp. 639–644. (2012). http://dx.doi.org/10.1109/ICFHR.2012.227

3. Cattoni, R., Coianiz, T., Messelodi, S., Modena, C.M.: Geometric layout analysis techniques for document image understanding: a review. Technical report, ITC-irst (1998)

4. Duda, R.O., Hart, P.E., Stork, D.G.: Pattern Classification, 2nd edn. Wiley-Interscience, Hoboken (2000)

5. Gonzalez, R.C., Woods, R.E.: Digital Image Processing, 3rd edn. Prentice Hall, Englewood Cliffs (2008)

6. Lazzara, G., Geraud, T., Levillain, R.: Planting, growing, and pruning trees: con-nected filters applied to document image analysis. In: 2014 11th IAPR International Workshop on Document Analysis Systems, pp. 36–40 (2014)

7. Okazaki, N.: CRFsuite: a fast implementation of conditional random fields (CRFs) (2007). http://www.chokkan.org/software/crfsuite/

8. Parker, C., Altun, Y., Tadepalli, P.: Guest editorial: special issue on structured prediction. Mach. Learn. **77**(2–3), 161–164 (2009)

9. Pletschacher, S., Antonacopoulos, A.: The PAGE (Page Analysis and Ground-truth Elements) format framework. In: Proceedings - International Conference on Pattern Recognition, pp. 257–260 (2010)

10. Romero, V., Serrano, N., Toselli, A.H., Sanchez, J.A., Vidal, E.: Handwritten text recognition for historical documents. In: Proceedings of the Workshop on Language Technologies for Digital Humanities and Cultural Heritage, Hissar, Bulgaria, pp. 90–96, September 2011

11. Stamatopoulos, N., Louloudis, G., Gatos, B.: Goal-oriented performance evaluation methodology for page segmentation techniques. In: 13th International Confrence on Document Analysis and Recognition - ICDAR 2015, pp. 281–285 (2015)

12. Sutton, C., McCallum, A.: An introduction to conditional random fields. Found. Trends Mach. Learn. **4**(4), 267–373 (2012)

13. Toselli, A.H., Vidal, E., Casacuberta, F.: Multimodal Interactive Pattern Recog-nition and Applications. Springer, Heidelberg (2011)

14. Vil'kin, A.M., Safonov, I.V., Egorova, M.A.: Algorithm for segmentation of doc-uments based on texture features. Pattern Recogn. Image Anal. **23**(1), 153–159 (2013)

Impact of the Acquisition Time on ECG Compression-Based Biometric Identification Systems

João M. Carvalho[1(✉)], Susana Brás[1], Jacqueline Ferreira[2,3],
Sandra C. Soares[2,4,5], and Armando J. Pinho[1]

[1] Department of Electronics Telecommunications and Informatics, IEETA,
University of Aveiro, Aveiro, Portugal
{joao.carvalho,susana.bras,ap}@ua.pt
[2] Department of Education and Psychology, University of Aveiro, Aveiro, Portugal
{jacquelineferreira,sandra.soares}@ua.pt
[3] Faculty of Medicine, IBILI, University of Coimbra, Coimbra, Portugal
[4] CINTESIS-UA, University of Aveiro, Aveiro, Portugal
[5] Department of Clinical Neurosciences, Karolinska Institute, Stockholm, Sweden

Abstract. The ECG signal conveys desirable characteristics for biometric identification (universality, uniqueness, measurability, acceptability and circumvention avoidance). However, based on the current literature review, there are no results that evaluate the number of heartbeats needed for personal identification. This information is undoubtedly useful when building a biometric identification system – any system should ask participants to provide data for identification, using the smallest time interval that is possible, for practical reasons. In this paper, we aim at exploring this topic using a measure of similarity based on the Kolmogorov Complexity, called the Normalized Relative Compression (NRC). To attain the goal, we built finite-context models to represent each individual – a compression-based approach that has been shown successful for several other pattern recognition applications like image similarity, DNA sequences or authorship attribution.

Keywords: Kolmogorov Complexity · Biometric identification · Finite-context models · Similarity metrics · Compression algorithms · ECG

1 Introduction

1.1 Motivation

Data compression models have been used to address several data mining and machine learning problems, usually by means of a formalization in terms of the information content of a string or of the information distance between strings [3–6]. This approach relies on solid foundations of the concept of algorithmic entropy and, because of its non-computability, approximations provided by data compression algorithms [7].

© Springer International Publishing AG 2017
L.A. Alexandre et al. (Eds.): IbPRIA 2017, LNCS 10255, pp. 169–176, 2017.
DOI: 10.1007/978-3-319-58838-4_19

The ECG is a well-known and studied biomedical signal. To understand pathological characteristics, in clinical practice, it is usual to try to reduce the inter-variability that characterizes the signal. This inter-variability is precisely the source of richness that renders the ECG an interesting signal for biometric applications. Recent work, using Ziv-Merhav cross parsing algorithm [8,9], as well as finite-context models (FCM) [10], has shown that compression-based approaches are suitable to ECG biometric identification. Nonetheless, a good acceptability when identifying a person for biometry should be fulfilled in as short time as possible. For that, we need to evaluate the minimal number of heartbeats that is needed to be collected, which has not yet been explored in the literature.

1.2   Database Used

The database used in our experiments, and in previous works, was collected *in house* [10], where 25 participants were exposed to different external stimuli – *disgust, fear* and *neutral*. Data were collected on three different days (once per week), at the University of Aveiro, using a different stimulus per day.

The data signals were collected during 25 min on each day, giving a total of around 75 min of ECG signal per participant. Before being exposed to the stimuli, during the first 4 min of each data acquisition, the participants watched a movie with a beach sunset and an acoustic guitar soundtrack, and were instructed to try to relax as much as possible.

The ECG was sampled at 1000 Hz, using the MP100 system and the software AcqKnowledge (Biopac Systems, Inc.). During the preparation phase, the adhesive disposable Ag/AgCL-electrodes were fixed in the right hand, as well as in the right and left foot. We are aware that such an intrusive set-up is not desirable for a real biometric identification system. However, for testing purposes, it seems appropriate, as this approach is more reliable – produces less noise.

1.3   Compression-Based Measures

Compression-based distances are tightly related to the Kolmogorov notion of complexity, also known as algorithmic entropy. Let x denote a binary string of finite length. Its **Kolmogorov complexity**, $K(x)$, is the length of the shortest binary program x^* that computes x in a universal Turing machine and halts. Therefore, $K(x) = |x^*|$, the length of x^*, represents the minimum number of bits from which x can be computationally retrieved [11].

The **Information Distance** (ID) and its normalized version, the **Normalized Information Distance** (NID), were proposed by Bennett *et al.* almost two decades ago [12] and are defined in terms of the Kolmogorov complexity of the strings involved, as well as the complexity of one when the other is provided.

However, since the Kolmogorov Complexity of a string is not computable, an approximation (upper bound) for it can be used by means of a compressor. Let $C(x)$ be the number of bits used by a compressor to represent the string x. We will use a measure based on the notion of *relative compression* [4], denoted by $C(x||y)$, which represents the compression of x relatively to y. This measure obeys the following rules:

- $C(x||y) \approx 0$ iff string x can be built efficiently from y;
- $C(x||y) \approx |x|$ iff $K(x|y) \approx K(x)$.

Based on this rules, the **Normalized Relative Compression** (NRC) of string x given string y is defined as

$$\text{NRC}(x, y) = \frac{C(x||y)}{|x|}, \tag{1}$$

where $|x|$ denotes the length of x.

2 Method

In ECG biometric identification, the signal should be processed, in order to extract the useful information for similarity evaluation. The workflow for biometric identification is represented in Fig. 1. Each block will be explained through this section.

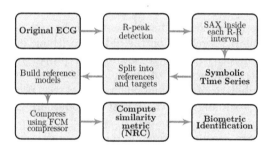

Fig. 1. Overview of the biometric identification method used in this work.

2.1 R-peak Detection

The development of a robust automatic *R-peak* detector is essential, but it is still a challenging task, due to irregular heart rates, various amplitude levels and *QRS* morphologies, as well as all kinds of noise and artifacts [13].

We have decided to use a *partially fiducial* method for segmenting the ECG signal and, since this was not the major focus of the work, we used a preexisting implementation to detect *R-peaks*, based on [13]. This method detects the *R-peak* by calculating the average point between the Q and S peaks (from the *QRS complex*) – this may not give the real local maximum of the *R-peak*, but it produces a very close point. Some evaluations were done using *R-peak* detection performed by humans, in order to validate this step.

The process used for detecting the *QRS* complexes is somewhat similar to the one described in [13]. It uses bandpass filtering and differentiation operations, aiming to enhance the *QRS* complexes and to reduce out-of-band noise. A nonlinear transformation is used to obtain a positive-valued feature signal, which includes large candidate peaks corresponding to the *QRS* complex regions.

2.2   Quantization

We consider that the signal is already discrete in the time domain, i.e., that it is already sampled. However, we perform re-sampling using the previously detected R-peaks (Fig. 1).

The design of the *quantizer* has a significant impact on the amount of compression obtained and loss incurred in a lossy compression scheme. We have used the widely known Symbolic Aggregate ApproXimation [14], SAX, in order to quantize the ECG values into a discrete alphabet.

There is a fundamental trade-off to take into account while performing the choice of the *alphabet size*: the quality produced versus the amount of data necessary to represent the sequence [15]. From experiments, we found that using an alphabet size of 6 and 200 symbols per each R-R segment (per heartbeat) produced good results for biometric identification. However, this result does not guarantee that the same will hold true for a different dataset or application.

2.3   Compressing Using Finite-Context Models

Finite-context modeling (FCM) has been used in several areas, such as in text and image. Recent work has shown that these models have the ability to measure similarity (or dissimilarity), relying on the data algorithmic entropy [2,16,17].

A finite-context model complies to the Markov property, i.e., it estimates the probability of the next symbol of the information source using the $k > 0$ immediate past symbols (order-k context) to select the probability distribution [18]. Therefore, assuming that the k past outcomes are given by $x^n_{n-k+1} = x_{n-k+1} \cdots x_n$, the probability estimates, $P(x_{n+1}|x^n_{n-k+1})$ are calculated using symbol counts that are accumulated while the information source is processed, with

$$P(s|x^n_{n-k+1}) = \frac{v(s|x^n_{n-k+1}) + \alpha}{v(x^n_{n-k+1}) + \alpha|\mathcal{A}|}, \qquad (2)$$

where $\mathcal{A} = \{s_1, s_2, \ldots s_{|\mathcal{A}|}\}$ is the alphabet that describes the objects of interest, $v(s|x^n_{n-k+1})$ represents the number of times that, in the past, symbol $s \in \mathcal{A}$ was found having x^n_{n-k+1} as the conditioning context and where

$$v(x^n_{n-k+1}) = \sum_{a \in \mathcal{A}} v(a|x^n_{n-k+1}) \qquad (3)$$

denotes the total number of events that has occurred within context x^n_{n-k+1}. The parameter α allows balancing between a maximum likelihood estimator and a uniform distribution. Notice that when the total number of events, n, is large (2) behaves as a maximum likelihood estimator [18].

After processing the first n symbols of x, the total number of bits generated by an order-k FCM is given by

$$-\sum_{i=1}^{n} \log_2 P(x_i|x^{i-1}_{i-k}), \qquad (4)$$

where $P(x_i|x_{i-k}^{i-1}) = \frac{1}{|\mathcal{A}|}, i = \{1, \ldots, k\}$, or, in other words, we assume that the first k symbols follow a uniform distribution.

3   Experimental Results

Parameter free data mining methods are reported in the literature as efficient in classification and extraction of information. Since there is no pre-assumption about the premises, it allows true exploratory data mining. The use of FCM based compressors are examples of such methods. These methods correctly deal with some of the problems reported in the literature for ECG biometric processing, such as: variability, noise, and others.

In the models design, the algorithm takes some time (around one second). However, in testing, they are characterized by being fast. After the model is built, we found that a regular computer can run hundreds of similarity evaluations per second, using just one processor[1]. In other words, when a small ECG signal is collected, we can obtain the similarity measures to hundreds of models (one model per participant, in the case of biometric identification) that are previously built in our database and loaded into RAM. Another important factor is that this process is easily parallelizable, which means that this computation can scale as much as we want.

Since memory usage was not a concern for these preliminary tests, we computed all possible context depths k from 1 up to 40. Theoretically speaking, the number of possible contexts found by an FCM of $k = 40$, with an alphabet size of 6, would be 6^{40} (higher than 10^{31}). However, using hash tables, we do not need to compute all those combinations. In fact, from all the contexts that we computed, no model used more than 10^5 different contexts – different participants have a tendency to produce, statistically speaking, very different contexts, which is in fact what we exploit in order to distinguish amongst them.

As mentioned in [19], there is an intra-variability for each participant from one day to another, which makes the biometric identification more challenging. The tests (a) Day 1, (b) Day 2 and (c) Day 3 contained no information of the ECG being tested when building the models for each participant. Test (d) was performed using the baselines from all days (the first 350 heartbeats) and then by running the biometric identification tests using different segments from all days.

Given that the goal of this work was to measure the minimal number of heartbeats in which it was possible to identify subjects, even in situations where they are under the effect of fear or disgust, we tried different setups: using from just one heartbeat for biometric identification, up to twenty heartbeats, in order to see the differences obtained in accuracy. In Fig. 2, it is possible to see very significant gains in performance from using one heartbeat to using ten heartbeats, for all possible contexts $k = \{1, \ldots, 40\}$.

---

[1] All the experiments were done using Python 3.5 on an Intel(R) Core(TM) i7-6700 CPU @ 3.40 GHz, with 32 GB of RAM.

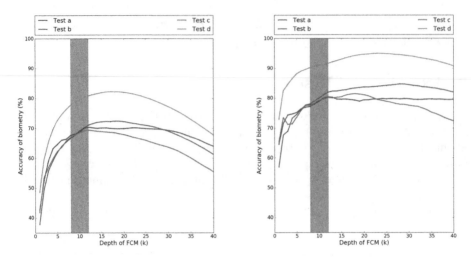

Fig. 2. Comparison of accuracies obtained using test segments with (**left**) 1 heartbeat and (**right**) 10 heartbeats, for all possible contexts $k = \{1, \ldots, 40\}$. The area in red represents what we consider the best choices for k, taking into account the complexity of the models produced. (Color figure online)

However, in order to have a more accurate way of choosing the "ideal" number of heartbeats to collect for testing, we show a plot with the maximum performance obtained for each of the tests ran in Fig. 3. It is possible to see that

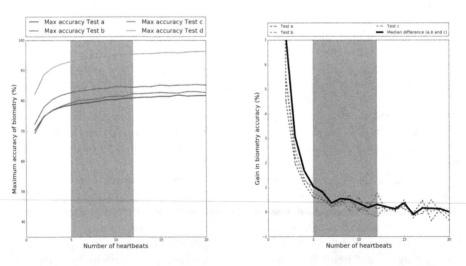

Fig. 3. (**left**) Best accuracy obtained using all individual contexts tested ($k = \{1, \ldots, 40\}$) for each number of heartbeats as target (from 1 to 20). (**right**) Difference in gain of accuracy when adding more heartbeats for the testing segments. (Color figure online)

the performance does not improve significantly when using more than a certain number of heartbeats for testing (area marked in red). In fact, the only test which accuracy does continue to increase is test (**d**), which is the only one that includes the baseline for all the days – even the one we are testing, which does not simulate a real world biometric identification.

4   Conclusions and Future Work

Our results showed that it is possible to identify participants accurately around 75–80% of the time with only 5 to 12 heartbeats, at least for the database used. Even though the result is lower than what would be desirable for a real system, each of the experiments was performed using only one context depth ($k = \{1, \ldots, 40\}$). Previous works regarding similarities have shown empirically that collaborative models of FCMs [2–4] produce better approximations to the Kolmogorov Complexity (better compression ratios) and, therefore, better similarity metrics. We plan on improving the current results by using a similar approach in the near future.

Besides that, future work includes developing a compressor based on FCMs that is specific for quantized time-series. The idea is to use the fact that there is a periodical repetition, which is not currently being taken into account. This compressor will then be tested for biometric identification using the ECG.

Acknowledgments. This work was partially supported by national funds through the FCT - Foundation for Science and Technology, and by European funds through FEDER, under the COMPETE 2020 and Portugal 2020 programs, in the context of the projects UID/CEC/00127/2013 and PTDC/EEI-SII/6608/2014. S. Brás acknowledges the Postdoc Grant from FCT, ref. SFRH/BPD/92342/2013.

References

1. Karimian, N., Wortman, P.A., Tehranipoor, F.: Evolving authentication design considerations for the internet of biometric things (IoBT). In: Proceedings of Eleventh IEEE/ACM/IFIP International Conference Hardware/Software Codesign System Synthesis - CODES 2016, New York, USA, pp. 1–10. ACM Press, New York (2016)
2. Pinho, A., Ferreira, P.: Image similarity using the normalized compression distance based on finite context models. In: 18th IEEE International Conference Image Process (2011)
3. Pratas, D., Pinho, A.J.: A conditional compression distance that unveils insights of the genomic evolution. In: 2014 Data Compression Conference, p. 421. IEEE, March 2014
4. Pinho, A.J., Pratas, D., Ferreira, P.: Authorship attribution using compression distances. In: Data Compression Conference (2016)
5. Pinho, A., Ferreira, P.: Finding unknown repeated patterns in images. In: 19th European Signal Processing Conference (EUSIPCO 2011) (2011)
6. Coutinho, D.P., Figueiredo, M.A.T.: Text classification using compression-based dissimilarity measures. Int. J. Pattern Recogn. Artif. Intell. **29**(05) (2015)

7. Li, M., Chen, X., Li, X.: The similarity metric. IEEE Trans. Inf. Theor. **50**(12), 3250–3264 (2004)
8. Coutinho, D.P., Silva, H., Gamboa, H., Fred, A., Figueiredo, M.: Novel fiducial and non-fiducial approaches to electrocardiogram-based biometric systems. IET Biometrics **2**(2), 64–75 (2013)
9. Coutinho, D., Fred, A., Figueiredo, M.: One-lead ECG-based personal identification using Ziv-Merhav cross parsing. In: 20th International Conference on Pattern Recognit. (ICPR), pp. 3858–3861(2010)
10. Brás, S., Pinho, A.J.: ECG biometric identification: a compression based approach. In: 2015 37th Annual International Conference on IEEE Engineering in Medicine and Biology Society, pp. 5838–5841, August 2015
11. Li, M., Vitányi, P.: An Introduction to Kolmogorov Complexity and Its Applications, 3rd edn. Springer, Heidelberg (1997)
12. Bennett, C., Gács, P., Li, M.: Information distance. IEEE Trans. Inf. Theor. **44**(4), 1407–1423 (1998)
13. Kathirvel, P., Sabarimalai Manikandan, M., Prasanna, S.R.M., Soman, K.P.: An efficient R-peak detection based on new nonlinear transformation and first-order Gaussian differentiator. Cardiovasc. Eng. Technol. **2**(4), 408–425 (2011)
14. Lin, J., Keogh, E., Lonardi, S., Chiu, B.: A symbolic representation of time series, with implications for streaming algorithms. In: DMKD 2003 Proceedings of 8th ACM SIGMOD Workshop on Research Issues in Data Mining and Knowledge Discovery, pp. 2–11(2003)
15. Gonzalez, R.C., Woods, R.E.: Sampling and Quantization. Digital Image Processing. Prentice Hall PTR, Englewood Cliffs (2007)
16. Garcia, S., Rodrigues, J., Santos, S., Pratas, D., Afreixo, V., Bastos, C., Ferreira, P., Pinho, A.: A genomic distance for assembly comparison based on compressed maximal exact matches. IEEE/ACM Trans. Comput. Biol. Bioinform. **10**(3), 793–798 (2013)
17. Pratas, D., Pinho, A.J., Garcia, S.P.: Computation of the normalized compression distance of DNA sequences using a mixture of finite-context models. In: Bioinformatics, pp. 308–311(2012)
18. Brás, S., Ferreira, J., Soares, S.C., Pinho, A.J.: Biometric and emotion identification: an ECG compression based method (2016, submitted)
19. Agrafioti, F., Hatzinakos, D., Anderson, A.K.: ECG pattern analysis for emotion detection. IEEE Trans. Affect. Comput. **3**(1), 102–115 (2012)

Z-Images

Vincent Vigneron[1](✉), Tahir Q. Syed[3], Leonardo T. Duarte[2], Elmar Lang[5], Sadaf I. Behlim[3], and Ana-Maria Tomé[4]

[1] IBISC-lab EA-4526, Université d'Evry val d'Essonne, Évry, France
vincent.vigneron@ibisc.univ-evry.fr
[2] Laboratory of Signal Processing for Communications FCA/UNICAMP,
Limeira, Brazil
leonardo.duarte@fca.unicamp.br
[3] Department of Computer Science,
National University of Computer and Emerging Sciences, Karachi 75030, Pakistan
{tahir.syed,sadaf.iqbal}@nu.edu.pk
[4] Departamento de Electronica, Telecomunicacoes e Informática,
Universidade de Aveiro, Aveiro, Portugal
ana@ua.pt
[5] Computational Intelligence and Machine Learning Group,
Universität Regensburg, Regensburg, Germany
Elmar.Lang@biologie.uni-regensburg.de

Abstract. Local patterns and other patch based features have been an integral part of various computer vision applications as they encode local structural and statistical information. In this paper, we propose an image coding technique that utilizes Zeckendorf representation of pixel intensities and basic mathematical operators such as intersection, set difference, maximum, summation etc. for summarization of image regions. The algorithm produces a *Z-coded* image that tells about the homogeneity or the contrast in image regions with all codes in a range of 0 to 255.

Keywords: Image descriptor · Generative model · Zeckendorf theorem · LBP

1 Introduction

Summarizing local image content is considered a fundamental step in all classical computer vision tasks such as object detection and recognition [3,8], texture analysis [11], motion analysis [2,11], image restoration and reconstruction [6] etc. This step usually involves extraction of low level features such as finding

V. Vigneron—This research was supported by the program *Cátedras Franco-Brasileiras no Estado de São Paulo*, an initiative of the French consulate and the state of São Paulo (Brazil). We thank our colleagues Prof. João M.T. Romano, Dr. Kenji Nose and Dr. Michele Costa, who provided insights that greatly assisted this work.

© Springer International Publishing AG 2017
L.A. Alexandre et al. (Eds.): IbPRIA 2017, LNCS 10255, pp. 177–184, 2017.
DOI: 10.1007/978-3-319-58838-4_20

out where the edges are, detecting interest points and their region of inter-
ests by applying local neighborhood operations. Since imaging data are noisy,
locally-correlated and usually with too many data points per 'unit' of useful
information, these *intermediate representations* lead to an understanding of the
scene in an image without the noisy and meaningless influence of very many pixels that carry little inferable information. These representations usually encode
either structural information that is extraction of texture as a set of repeated
primitive textons or statistical information that how different pixel intensities
are distributed in a local neighborhood.

The amount of information extracted from different regions of an image usually depends on the size of the neighborhood, the reading order of the neighbors
and the mathematical function that is used to extract the relationship between
two neighboring pixels. Most of the descriptors that encode local structures i.e.
Local Binary Patterns (LBP) [4] and its variants [5] such as Census Transform
(CT) [9] etc. depend on the *reading order* as they compute the feature value as
the weighted sum of neighboring pixels $\{g_p | p = 0, \ldots, P-1\}$ w.r.t. their order
in the neighborhood.

There exists many variants of LBP (see [5, Chap. 2, p. 26] for a summary of
the variants) because basic LBP has many problems that need to be addressed.
For instance, LBP and CT both generates $8 - bit$ string for a 3×3 neighborhood
by computing the Heaviside function $t(\cdot)$ of the difference between neighboring
pixels and the central pixel *i.e.* $(g_i - g_c)$ which is shown in Fig. 1. The only
difference between these two descriptors is the reading order of neighboring pixels
and the sign of the difference which results in 2 different bit patterns. Given the
$8 - bit$ string, the LBP and CT code is calculated as:

$$L_{P,R}(\mathbf{r}_c) = \sum_{p=0}^{P-1} 2^p \cdot t(g_p - g_c), \text{ with } t(x) = \begin{cases} 1 & \text{if } x \geq 0 \\ 0 & \text{otherwise.} \end{cases}, \qquad (1)$$

where P is the number of pixels in the neighborhood considering the distance R
between central pixel and its neighbors.

Local Binary Pattern (LBP) is considered a computationally efficient structural descriptor and its applications have evolved into almost all fields of computer vision, because of its robustness to monotonic gray-scale changes, illumination invariance and its computational simplicity. Invariance w.r.t. any monotonic

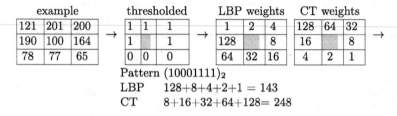

Pattern $(10001111)_2$
LBP $128+8+4+2+1 = 143$
CT $8+16+32+64+128 = 248$

Fig. 1. Neighbors of center pixel g_c participating in LBP or CT code generation in the
case of a 3×3 neighborhood ($P = 8$ and $R = 1$).

transformation of the gray scale is achieved by considering in Eq. (1) the signs of the differences $t(g_i - g_c), i = 0, \ldots, P - 1$. But the *independence* of g_c and $\{|g_0 - g_c|, \ldots, |g_{P-1} - g_c|\}$ is not warranted in practice. Moreover, under certain circumstances the LBP misses the local structure as it does not consider the central pixel. The binary data produced by them are sensitive to noise mostly in uniform regions of an image.

To reduce this noise sensitivity, a 3-level operator has been proposed by Tan and Trigg [7] which describes a pixel relationship with its neighbor by a ternary code *i.e.* $\{-1, 0, 1\}$ rather than a binary code. The size of this code is reduced by splitting it into two LBP codes (Positive and Negative) which results into two $8 - bit$ strings thus needing 16 bit space for representation.

This paper discusses an encoding scheme that is *independent* of the size of neighborhood and the reading order of neighboring pixels in Sect. 2. An algorithm is also proposed for generating Z-codes of an image in Sect. 3, which could be utilized in contour detection, image segmentation and adaptive image quantization. In Sect. 4 we discuss the results and compare its characteristics with the classic LBP.

2   Zeckendorf Encoding

The LBP operator generates an integer value in the range of 0 to 255. We propose to represent each pixel intensity N as an ordered collection of positive integers whose sum is N.

2.1   Zeckendorf's Theorem

The Zeckendorf's theorem [10] states that every positive integer N can be represented uniquely as the sum of distinct Fibonacci numbers such that the sum *does not include any two non-consecutive Fibonacci numbers.*

Theorem 1 (Zeckendorf's theorem). *Every positive integer can be expressed as a sum of distinct Fibonacci numbers. If N is any positive integer, there exist positive integers $n_i \geq 2$, with $n_{i+1} \geq n_i + 1$, such that $N = \sum_{i=0}^{k} F_{n_i}$, where F_j is the $j-th$ Fibonacci number.*

The famous Fibonacci sequence $< 1, 1, 2, 3, 5, 8, \ldots >$ is a sequence of numbers, $x(n)$, that satisfies the difference equation

$$x(n) = x(n - 1) + x(n - 2) \quad \text{for} \quad n \geq 0 \tag{2}$$

that is $x(n)$ is the sum of the 2 previous values with initial conditions $x(0) = x(1) = 1$.

Proof. For any positive integer n, there is always a positive integer m such that $x(m) \leq n \leq x(m + 1)$. If $n \neq x(m)$,

$$0 < n - x(m) < x(m + 1) - x(m) = x(m - 1). \tag{3}$$

Since $n - x(m)$ is positive, there exists a positive integer p such that

$$x(p) \leq n - x(m) < x(p+1). \tag{4}$$

Now $x(p) \leq n - x(m) < x(m-1)$ implies $p \leq m - 2$, i.e. $x(p)$ and $x(m)$ are not consecutive Fibonacci numbers. If $n - x(m) \neq x(p)$, there exists a positive integer $q \leq p - 2$ such that

$$x(q) \leq n - x(m) - x(p) < x(q+1) \tag{5}$$

and the process continues. Ultimately, we must reach the point where the partial sum equals a Fibonacci number – say $x(t)$ – and thereby obtain the desired representation

$$n = x(m) + x(p) + x(q) + \ldots + x(t). \tag{6}$$

2.2   Z-Representation

An 8-bit gray scale image has the intensity values in the range of [0,255]. The distinct Fibonacci numbers below 255 are $\{1, 2, 3, 5, 8, 13, 21, 34, 55, 89, 144, 233\}$. Each pixel intensity of an image can be represented as a sum of distinct non-consecutive Fibonacci numbers. For instance the only Zeckendorf representation of pixel value 255 is $(233, 21, 1)_{\text{Zck}}$. Since there are 12 different possibilities to represent any 8-bit intensity value, therefore each number is represented using 12 bits no consecutive bits are ON i.e. 1 because of non-consecutive Fibonacci numbers constraint. Table 1 shows some Zeckendorf representations and their bit patterns.

Table 1. Zeckendorf's representation of some numbers.

N	Partition	Bit pattern	N	Partition	Bit pattern
1	1	1 0 0 0 0 0 0 0 0 0 0 0	50	34 + 13 + 3	0 0 1 0 0 1 0 1 0 0 0 0
2	2	0 1 0 0 0 0 0 0 0 0 0 0	51	34 + 13 + 3 + 1	1 0 1 0 0 1 0 1 0 0 0 0
3	3	0 0 1 0 0 0 0 0 0 0 0 0	131	89 + 34 + 8	0 0 0 0 1 0 0 1 0 1 0 0
4	3 + 1	1 0 1 0 0 0 0 0 0 0 0 0	132	89 + 34 + 8 + 1	1 0 0 0 1 0 0 1 0 1 0 0
5	5	0 0 0 1 0 0 0 0 0 0 0 0	154	144 + 8 + 2	0 1 0 0 1 0 0 0 0 0 1 0
6	5 + 1	1 0 0 1 0 0 0 0 0 0 0 0	159	144 + 13 + 2	0 1 0 0 0 1 0 0 0 0 1 0
7	5 + 2	0 1 0 1 0 0 0 0 0 0 0 0	174	144 + 21 + 8 + 1	1 0 0 0 1 0 1 0 0 0 1 0
8	8	0 0 0 0 1 0 0 0 0 0 0 0	190	143 + 34 + 8 + 3	0 0 1 0 1 0 0 1 0 0 1 0
9	8 + 1	1 0 0 0 1 0 0 0 0 0 0 0	222	144 + 55 + 21 + 2	0 1 0 0 0 0 1 0 1 0 1 0
10	8 + 2	0 1 0 0 1 0 0 0 0 0 0 0	254	233 + 21	0 0 0 0 0 0 1 0 0 0 0 1

3   Proposed Algorithm for Z-Coding

Based on the proposed partition property of integers, we design an algorithm that encodes pixel relationship with its local neighborhood of dimension $m \times n$ by an integer value ranging from 0 to 255 we named $Z - code$. We apply different basic mathematical functions and operators *i.e.* minimum, maximum, summation and some set operators i.e. intersection, set difference etc. The sequence in which operations and functions are applied results in images that could be directly used in computer vision pipeline for object *detection* and *recognition*.

Example 1 (Z-coding). Consider a pixel, of intensity 183, surrounded by the following gray-levels $\{210, 106, 231, 233, 79, 142, 209, 188\}$.

The Zeckendorf decomposition for the neighboring pixel is respectively $\{144 + 55 + 8 + 3, 89 + 13 + 3 + 1, 144 + 55 + 21 + 8 + 3, 233, 55 + 21 + 3, 89 + 34 + 13 + 5 + 1, 144 + 55 + 8 + 2, 144 + 34 + 8 + 2\}$ and for the central pixel is $\{144, 34, 5\}$. Applying the Algorithm 1, we find when considering the first neighboring pixel $\{144, 34, 5\} \cap \{144, 55, 8, 3\} = \{144\}$ Since dummy $\neq \emptyset$ therefore $s(1)$ will be equal to 144. Similarly for the second pixel $\{144, 34, 5\} \cap \{89, 13, 3, 1\} = \emptyset$. Since dummy $= \emptyset$ therefore the $s(2)$ will be equal to J_0 which is 183. After the vector s is populated with the values

---

Algorithm 1. Algorithmic principle behind the image Z-coding

Require: Image I of size $J \times K$: texel of size O; N is number of pixels arround center
      pixel J_0
Ensure: Z-coded image Z of size $J \times K$ of input image I
1: Initialization $Z \leftarrow \emptyset$; $j = 2, k = 2$
2: **for** $j = 2$ to $J - 1$ **do**
3:     **for** $k = 2$ to $K - 1$ **do**
4:        $J_0 = I(j, k)$; $\triangleright$ central pixel of the texel
5:        $texel \leftarrow$ Intensity Values of N neighbouring pixels arround J_0
6:        $\mathbf{s} \leftarrow \mathbf{0}$
7:        $\mathcal{S}^0 \leftarrow$ **zeckendorf** (J_0)
8:        **for** $i = 1$ to N **do**
9:           $\mathcal{S} \leftarrow$ **zeckendorf** $(texel(i))$;
10:          dummy $\leftarrow \mathcal{S}^0$ op $\mathcal{S}$ $\triangleright$ op is intersection or set difference operator
11:          **if** (dummy $= \emptyset$)) **then**
12:             $s(i) \leftarrow J_0$ $\triangleright$ J_0 for quantization and 0 for contours
13:          **else**
14:             $s(i) \leftarrow \max(\text{dummy})$ $\triangleright$ *max* for quantization and *sum* for contours
15:          **end if**
16:        **end for**
17:        $Z(j, k) \leftarrow \max(\mathbf{s})$
18:     **end for**
19: **end for**return Z
20: **Function zeckendorf** (x)
21: Decomposes an integer x as a sequence of Fibonacci numbers
22: **EndFunction**

---

s = 144, 183, 144, 183, 183, 34, 144, 144, the maximum value is computed of this set which is treated as the Z-code for the given pixel i.e. 183 in this example.

4   Results and Discussion

The algorithm proposed in Sect. 2.1 results in two different kinds of images based on the initial operator which is applied i.e. either set difference or intersection. The *intersection* operator find the similarity among the pixel and its neighborhood Zeckendorf representation and place a value which is common among them thus results in an image that is quantized in terms of their representation as shown in Table 2 2nd row. The set *difference operator* extracts *ultrametric* contours of an image resulting in image segmentation [1] shown in 3rd and 4rth row of Table 2.

Compared to other local descriptors (see Sect. 1), the Z-coding

Table 2. Z-coded images using Zeckendorff representation – 1st row shows original images, 2nd row shows quantized images obtained by applying intersection operator, 3rd row contains ultrametric contours obtained by applying set-difference operator and last row shows complemented results of 3rd row

- can be extended to any neighborhood size or geometry – this is because in Table 1, the Z-value is computed from a set of differences of stack values (set difference operation). This stack contains the grayscale values of the pixels. It is arbitrarily extendable. In addition, 2^p weighting or any binary coding is disregarded,
- is *invariant* to any shift in grayscale as there is no ranking in the set of differences of grayscale values nor in the weights,
- is *order-invariant* (same argument as above)
- does not consider the central pixel effect as the central pixel value does not enter in the set difference operation but since the pick values in a finite and bounded set of integers, the algorithm guarantee that the z-value $z_i \in \{0, \ldots, 255\}$,
- is *nonlinear* because the set difference operation is nonlinear,
- follows an integer generating scheme as the stacked values are provided by the recurrence Eq. (2),
- is less sensitive to any noise influence as the Z-coding acts as a *quantizer*. The quantization error is considered an additive noise source, and it is assumed to be uniformly distributed over the range of values of the quantization error Δ,[1]
- comes with a *performance criterion*. The criterion to maximize is, for each pixel (i, j) of the image, the sum $S_{ij} = \sum_p (\frac{g_{\sigma(p)}}{g_{\sigma(p+1)}} - \frac{2}{1+\sqrt{5}})^2$ over the neighboring pixels ranked in increasing order.

5   Conclusion

In this paper we describe a new image coding algorithm *Z-coding* based on integer generating function and Zeckendorf theorem of integer decomposition. This image coding method is invariant to shift and rotation, could be extended to any neighborhood size and is independent of the reading order of neighboring pixels. It summarizes an image either by identifying the homogeneity in various irregular regions of image or by extracting soft contours using local contrast quantification which could be utilized in computer vision pipeline.

References

1. Arbelaez, P.: Boundary extraction in natural images using ultrametric contour maps. In: IEEE Conference on Computer Vision and Pattern Recognition, CVPR Workshops 2006, New York, NY, USA, 17–22 June 2006, p. 182 (2006)
2. Delicato, L.S., Serrano-Pedraza, I., Suero, M., Derrington, A.M.: Two-dimensional pattern motion analysis uses local features. Vis. Res. **62**, 84–92 (2012)
3. Heikkilä, M., Pietikäinen, M.: A texture-based method for modeling the background and detecting moving objects. Pattern Anal. Mach. Intell. **28**(4), 657–662 (2006)

---

[1] This assumption is generally valid for a small number of values and the noise power (variance) is $\frac{\Delta^2}{P-1}$, where $P - 1$ is the number of surrounding pixels.

4. Ojala, T., Pietikäinen, M., Harwood, D.: A comparative study of texture measures with classification based on feature distributions. Pattern Recogn. **29**, 51–59 (1996)
5. Pietikinen, M., Hadid, A., Zhao, G., Ahonen, T.: Computer Vision Using Local Binary Patterns. Computer Imaging and Vision, vol. 40. Springer, London (2011)
6. Syed, T.Q., Behlim, S.I., Merchant, A.K., Thomas, A., Khan, F.M.: Leveraging mutual information in local descriptions: from local binary patterns to the image. In: Murino, V., Puppo, E. (eds.) ICIAP 2015. LNCS, vol. 9280, pp. 239–251. Springer, Cham (2015). doi:10.1007/978-3-319-23234-8˙23
7. Tan, X., Triggs, B.: Enhanced local texture feature sets for face recognition under difficult lighting conditions. In: Zhou, S.K., Zhao, W., Tang, X., Gong, S. (eds.) AMFG 2007. LNCS, vol. 4778, pp. 168–182. Springer, Heidelberg (2007). doi:10.1007/978-3-540-75690-3˙13
8. Uijlings, J.R.R., van de Sande, K.E.A., Gevers, T., Smeulders, A.W.M.: Selective search for object recognition. Int. J. Comput. Vis. **104**(2), 154–171 (2013)
9. Zabih, R., Woodfill, J.: Non-parametric local transforms for computing visual correspondence. In: Eklundh, J.-O. (ed.) ECCV 1994. LNCS, vol. 801, pp. 151–158. Springer, Heidelberg (1994). doi:10.1007/BFb0028345
10. Zeckendorf, E.: Représentation des nombres naturels par une somme de nombres de fibonacci ou de nombres de lucas. Bull. Soc. Roy. Sci. Liege **41**, 179–182 (1972)
11. Zhao, G., Pietikainen, M.: Dynamic texture recognition using local binary patterns with an application to facial expressions. IEEE Trans. Pattern Anal. Mach. Intell. **29**(6), 915–928 (2007)

Oversegmentation Methods: A New Evaluation

Bérengère Mathieu[1]([⊠]), Alain Crouzil[1], and Jean Baptiste Puel[2]

[1] UPS, IRIT, Université de Toulouse, Toulouse, France
{berengere.mathieu,alain.crouzil}@irit.fr
[2] ENFA, IRIT, Université de Toulouse, Toulouse, France
jean-baptiste.puel@irit.fr

Abstract. Using superpixels instead of pixels has become a popular pre-processing step in computer vision. Currently, about fifteen oversegmentation methods have been proposed. The last evaluation, realized by Stutz *et al.* in 2015, concludes that the five more competitive algorithms achieve similar results. By introducing HSID, a new dataset, we point out unexpected difficulties encountered by state-of-the-art oversegmentation methods.

Keywords: Superpixel · Segmentation · Comparative study

1 Introduction

The idea and definition of superpixel is given for the first time by Ren *et al.*, in [12]. The two authors describe a segmentation method including an *oversegmentation* pre-processing grouping pixels into small homogeneous and regular regions called *superpixels*. By using them instead of pixels, they significantly reduce the complexity of their algorithm. Subsequently, superpixels have been integrated with success to a lot of methods, [4,20]. Currently, oversegmentation is an active research field, with steady publication of new methods [1,2,8].

Previous Work. Made in 2012 by Achanta *et al.*, the first review of oversegmentation methods [1] compare six algorithms: Normalized Cut (NC) [12], Felzenszwalb algorithm (FZ) [3], Quick Shift (QS) [17], TurboPixels (TP) [6], Veksler method (VK) [18] and the Simple Linear Iterative Clustering method (SLIC) [1]. Tests were carried out using 100 images of Berkeley Segmentation Dataset [9] (BSD[1]). For each method Achanta *et al.* [1] analyze the complexity, the execution time and the quality of the produced oversegmentation results. They use two metrics: the undersegmentation error rate (UE) and the boundary recall measure (BR). Both of them compare the oversegmentation result S to a ground-truth G. The UE score takes into account for each object G_i in G the set of superpixels required to cover it and counts the number of pixels

---

The work of Bérengère Mathieu was partially supported by ANR-11-LABX-0040-CIMI within the program ANR-11-IDEX-0002-02.

[1] https://www2.eecs.berkeley.edu/Research/Projects/CS/vision/bsds/.

leaking: $UE(S,G) = \frac{1}{N}\sum_{G_i \in G}\sum_{S_j \cap G_i \neq \emptyset} min(|S_j \cap G_i|, |S_j - G_i|)$ where N is the pixel number and $|E|$ denotes the cardinality of the set E. The result is a rate between 0 and 1, 0 denoting an error-free oversegmentation result. The BR score checks if whether boundary pixels around objects in G match with boundary pixels in S. We indicate by B_G the set of boundary pixels in G and B_S the set of boundary pixels in S. If we assume that there is no doubt about the fact that a pixel belongs or not to a boundary, the quality of an oversegmentation can be evaluated by calculating the rate of boundary pixels in G corresponding to boundary pixels in S: $BR(S,G) = \frac{|B_S \cap B_G|}{|B_G|}$.

In fact, even for a human, it is sometimes difficult to know whether a pixel belongs or not to a boundary. Achanta $et\ al.$ allow a distance τ_{br} of 2 pixels between pixels in B_G and in B_S. The BR score is in the range $[0, 1]$, 1 meaning that all boundaries in G match with boundaries in S. In 2015, Stutz made a second evaluation [14]. Their first contribution is to include seven supplementary oversegmentation methods: Entropy Rate Superpixels (ERS) [7], Superpixels via Pseudo-Boolean Optimization (SPBO) [21], Contour Relaxed Superpixels (CRS) [2], Superpixels Extracted via Energy-Driven Sampling (SEEDS) [16], Topology Preserved Superpixels (TPS) [15], Depth-Adaptive Superpixels (DAS) [19] and Voxel Cloud Connectivity Segmentation (VCCS) [11]. They also use as additional dataset, 400 images of New York University [13], NYU[2]. As the dimensions of the two datasets photographs are not identical (481×321 pixels for BSD, 640×480 pixels for NYU), Stutz $et\ al.$ modify the threshold τ_{br}, allowing matching between boundary pixels $0.0075 \times diag$ away, where $diag$ is the image diagonal length. In Achanta $et\ al.$ review [1], FZ and SLIC methods achieve the best scores. Stutz $et\ al.$ evaluation [14] corroborates this result and shows that QS, CRS and ERS algorithms achieve performances similar to those of FZ and SLIC. On the BSD images, best scores are achieved with oversegmentation containing approximately 1000 superpixels. For FZ, SLIC, QS, ERS and CRS methods, UE is lower than or equal to 0.04 and BR is greater than or equal to 0.99. On NYU dataset, with about 1500 superpixels, UE is lower than or equal to 0.09 and BR is greater than or equal to 0.99. For these two datasets, execution times are about one second on a computer with a 3.4 GHz Intel Core i7 processor and 16 Go RAM.

Contributions. In Stutz $et\ al.$ [14], evaluation the BR results achieved by the five best oversegmentation methods are so close to the maximal score, that it seems difficult to suggest a new method allowing a significant improvement. However, one can ask whether the two used datasets are sufficient for an exhaustive evaluation. The BSD and NYU images cover a wide panel of situations, containing both outdoor (BSD) and indoor (NYU) images with weak local contrast, important noise and lighting problems. However, images of the two datasets have similar sizes (some thousand of pixels) and small size in comparison to images taken with common cameras. Hence, our first contribution is a Heterogeneous Size Image Dataset (HSID), mainly containing big size images

---

[2] http://cs.nyu.edu.

(millions of pixels). HSID allows to check that algorithms do not suffer from a bias related to image dimensions and to better evaluate their scaling up. As HSID contains images with heterogeneous sizes, we need to transform BR into a fuzzy boundary adherence measure, FBR, which is the second contribution of this article. Moreover, we show that UE is not suitable for HSID. The demonstration leading us to this conclusion allows to better understand the behavior of UE and should be valuable for other works. The major contribution of this paper is a careful analysis of the result of the five best oversegmentation methods (FZ, QS, SLIC, ER and CRS) and of a recently proposed algorithm, Waterpixel (WP) [8]. Unlike previous evaluations, we show that, applied on HSID, each method encounters specific difficulties. The remainder of the article is organized as follows: in Sect. 2 we indicate properties of a suitable oversegmentation algorith and we describe the algorithms that we will compare. In Sect. 3 we describe HSID and we discuss about UE and BR measures. In Sect. 4 we analyze the evaluation results. We conclude with a discussion about perspectives of this work.

2   State-of-the-Art Methods

The review of works using superpixels [4,5,10,20,22,23] shows that a good oversegmentation method must satisfy five properties: **validity** (an oversegmentation must be an image partition into connected components) **boundary adherence** (superpixels must not overlap different objects of the image) **conciseness** (an oversegmentation must give as few superpixels as possible) **simplicity** (the number of neighbors of each superpixel must be as small as possible, to avoid a complex adjacency graph) **efficiency** (an oversegmentation algorithm must have an execution time as low as possible). Simplicity and efficiency properties ensure that the time spent to oversegment the image and the time necessary to take superpixel neighborhood into account, will not be longer than the time saved by the usage of superpixels instead of pixels. Because boundary adherence is much more difficult to satisfy with large superpixels, this property is generally in contradiction with conciseness. We call *adaptivity*, the ability of an algorithm find the best compromise between these two properties, by reducing the number of superpixels in wide homogeneous regions.

According to Stutz *et al.* review [14] five methods outperform other algorithms: FZ [3], QS [17], ERS [7], SLIC [1] and CRS [2]. The FZ [3] and ERS [7] algorithms use a graph-based representation of the image $G < V, E >$, with V the set of elements to be grouped (*i.e.* the pixels) and E, the set of edges linking pairs of neighboring elements. Each edge is weighted using a dissimilarity measure. FZ uses a predicate checking that the dissimilarity between elements along the boundary of two components is greater than the dissimilarity between neighboring elements within each of the two components, to produce a partition of G in K connected components corresponding to superpixels. ERS is a greedy algorithm selecting a subset $A \subset E$ and removing these edges. The result is a partition of G, which maximizes an entropy rate. The QS method [17] is a modification of the medoid-shift algorithm to efficiently find modes of a Parzen density estimate P. Color and location of each pixel are used as feature vectors that are clustered by linking each vector to its nearest neighbor which increases P. The SLIC method [1] is an adaptation of the k-means algorithm. Starting from an image oversegmentation into a regular grid, the average color and location features of each superpixel are computed. Then, each pixel is re-assigned to the most similar superpixel and the average features of superpixels are recomputed. Finally a post-processing step reassigns disjoints pixel sets to nearby superpixels, to ensure an image partition into connected components. The CRS algorithm [2] finds a partition S into superpixels, which has a high likelihood of having generated the observed image. Starting from an initial segmentation into rectangular superpixels, CRS maximizes the probability function by reallocating some boundary pixels to another superpixel. In our evaluation, we add to these five state-of-the-art methods, WP, a watershed transformation based algorithm using a spatially regularized gradient, which has been recently suggested by Machairas *et al.* [8].

3   New Oversegmentation Evaluation Benchmark

We provide a new oversegmentation evaluation dataset, including 100 images from Wikimedia Common[3]. Photographs have been selected to cover a wide variety of difficulties, including blur, noise, shadow, weak contrast and objects with similar colors. For each image, a hand drawn ground truth is provided. First, objects to extract are identified. Then a segmentation is designed by locating and fitting each region corresponding to a same object with a same color. Finally, boundaries of regions are automatically extracted allowing to visually check and remove some mistakes in the previous step. The images, ground truth and a file giving image licenses are available online[4].

Need for a Cautious Use of Undersegmentation Error. In reviews [1,14] UE was one of the two measures used to check boundary adherence of superpixels. However, our investigation shows that this measure must be used with cautions, in particular for dataset like HSID containing images of highly varying complexities. Figure 1 shows an oversegmentation into regular squared superpixels of two kind of images: a portrait-like in Fig. 1a with a unique big object on foreground and a panoramic-like in Fig. 1b, with multiple small objects on foreground. The foreground areas in the two images are the equal and a visual analysis show that superpixels similarly fail to match object boundaries. However, the UE score equals to 0.09 in the first case (Fig. 1a) and to 0.23 in the second case (Fig. 1b). This difference is explained by the fact that in Fig. 1a, superpixels wholly included within the objects boundaries are more numerous than in Fig. 1b (105 against 68). These superpixels do not carry information about boundary adherence and yet are taken into account by UE score, decreasing it. Hence the average UE score for these two images is not relevant to measure

---

[3] https://commons.wikimedia.org/wiki/Accueil.
[4] http://image.ensfea.fr/hsid/.

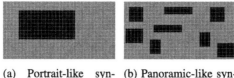

(a) Portrait-like syn- (b) Panoramic-like synthetic image.   thetic image.

Fig. 1. Background is in gray, foreground in black and superpixel boundaries in white.

boundary adherence. We encountered the same problem with HSID images and chose not to use UE.

Fuzzy Boundary Recall Measure. The metric BR measures the capacity for a method to give superpixels whose boundaries match with ground truth boundaries. To take into account the uncertainty about boundary location in hand-drawn ground truth, previous approaches use a static threshold. They accept matching between boundary pixels at a distance of $0.0075 \times diag$ pixels, where $diag$ is the image diagonal length. On big images of HSID (several millions of pixels) this distance (more than 30 pixels) is clearly too large. Rather than choosing another static threshold, we suggest to amend standard BR formula using fuzzy-set theory to introduce some tolerance error near the border pixels. Let G be a partition of the image into L connected components corresponding to objects $(G_1, \cdots, G_L)$ and S an oversegmentation into K superpixels $(S_1, \cdots, S_K)$, with $L << K$. A pixel p_i in S is on a boundary if $\exists p_j$ such as $p_j \in \text{nei}(p_x) \wedge (p_i \in R_n^S \Rightarrow p_j \notin R_n^S)$ where nei is a function giving for each pixel the set of its neighbors. Likewise, p_i is a boundary pixel in G, if $\exists p_j$ such as $p_j \in \text{nei}(p_x) \wedge (p_i \in R_n^G \Rightarrow p_j \notin R_n^G)$. Let B_G be the set of boundary pixels in G and B_S the set of boundary pixels in S. The rate of boundary pixels in G matching with boundary pixels in S is given by the classic BR measure. From B_G we define the fuzzy set $B_{G\cap S}^*$ with the membership function

$$f_{G\cap S}(p_i) = \exp(-\frac{d(p_i - p_{i'})^2}{2\sigma^2})$$ where $d(p_i - p_j)$ is the distance between p_i and p_j locations and $p_{i'} = \underset{p_j \in B_S}{\arg\min}(d(p_i - p_j))$. The function $f_{G\cap S}$ returns a value in the range $[0, 1]$, a value of 1 meaning a perfect coincidence between an element in B_G and an element in B_S. Finally, we propose the fuzzy boundary recall measure $FBR(S, G) = \frac{1}{|B_G|} \sum_{p \in B_G} f_{G\cap S}(p)$.

4 Experimental Results

We evaluate the ability of the algorithms FZ [3], QS [17], SLIC [1], ERS [7], CRS [2] and WP [8] to satisfy the properties defined in Sect. 2, using the implementations provided by their authors. By design all the tested algorithms satisfy the validity property. The boundary adherence of the superpixels is evaluated using FBR score, the simplicity by computing the average number of neighbors by superpixel (Nei), the conciseness by giving the average number of superpixels by image (K) and the efficiency by measuring the execution time (T), on a desktop computer with a 2.6 GHz Intel Core i7 processor and 16 Go of RAM. We focus this evaluation on two distinct aspects: the adaptivity and the scale up of the algorithm. To measure adaptivity, we analyze the evolution of mean and standard variation for both FBR and K scores. The fact that HSID contains a majority of big images allows us to check the ability to scale up of each method, by comparing the scores achieved on HSID with the results obtained in previous evaluations. Table 1 gives the mean and the standard deviation achieved by the six algorithms for all these measures. We made 8 tests where methods are configured to respectively produce about 500 (test 1), 700 (test 2), 900 (test 3), 1100 (test 4), 1300 (test 5), 1500 (test 6), 1700 (test 7) and 1900 (test 8) superpixels. Because the execution time strongly depends on the image size, the standard deviation for this measure is high, often similar to the mean. Even if these two measures must be analyzed with caution, they are sufficient to compare the ability of algorithms to scale up. Visual results for the complete dataset and values for each method parameters are available online[5].

Table 1. Quantitative results of the evaluated algorithms.

Test	K	Nei	T	FBR
1	539±94	6±0.11	12±12	0.52±0.17
2	756±135	6±0.12	11±11	0.54±0.17
3	974±184	6±0.12	11±11	0.55±0.16
4	1185±236	6±0.13	10±11	0.57±0.16
5	1390±285	6±0.14	10±10	0.57±0.16
6	1596±338	6±0.15	10±11	0.59±0.16
7	1801±391	6±0.16	10±10	0.59±0.15
8	1998±446	6±0.17	10±10	0.60±0.15

(a) FZ, parameters of [10].

Test	K	Nei	T	FBR
1	478±456	6±0.43	215±213	0.42±0.13
2	662±625	6±0.36	171±168	0.45±0.13
3	859±808	6±0.36	141±140	0.48±0.13
4	1174±1095	6±0.37	116±113	0.51±0.13
5	1443±1341	6±0.37	102±100	0.52±0.13
6	1676±1556	6±0.39	97±95	0.53±0.13
7	2583±2383	6±0.45	79±77	0.57±0.12
8	10030±9129	6±0.72	53±52	0.66±0.1

(b) QS, parameters of [14].

Test	K	Nei	T	FBR
1	474±28	6±0.08	3±3	0.51±0.14
2	663±37	6±0.1	3±3	0.53±0.13
3	860±42	6±0.12	3±3	0.55±0.13
4	1053±54	6±0.12	3±3	0.56±0.13
5	1253±63	6±0.14	3±3	0.56±0.13
6	1446±68	6±0.15	3±3	0.57±0.13
7	1648±79	6±0.14	3±3	0.58±0.13
8	1854±101	6±0.18	3±3	0.59±0.13

(c) SLIC, parameters of [1].

Test	K	Nei	T	FBR
1	500±0	6±0.19	32±34	0.54±0.16
2	700±0	6±0.18	32±35	0.56±0.16
3	900±0	6±0.18	31±33	0.57±0.15
4	1100±0	6±0.17	31±33	0.58±0.15
5	1300±0	6±0.18	31±33	0.59±0.15
6	1500±0	6±0.18	36±39	0.60±0.15
7	1700±0	6±0.18	36±39	0.61±0.15
8	1900±0	6±0.19	36±38	0.61±0.15

(d) ERS, parameters of [14].

Test	K	Nei	T	FBR
1	530±12	6±0.13	16±11	0.21±0.17
2	743±21	6±0.15	17±11	0.23±0.19
3	959±34	6±0.15	19±12	0.28±0.19
4	1167±47	6±0.16	19±12	0.3±0.2
5	1381±41	6±0.14	20±13	0.32±0.21
6	1601±63	6±0.16	21±12	0.34±0.21
7	1797±87	6±0.17	22±13	0.35±0.21
8	2025±92	6±0.16	23±13	0.37±0.22

(e) CRS, parameters of [2].

Test	K	Nei	T	FBR
1	613±11	6±0.09	24±42	0.43±0.17
2	858±20	6±0.07	25±43	0.45±0.17
3	1104±29	6±0.08	26±45	0.46±0.17
4	1346±44	6±0.08	26±46	0.47±0.18
5	1587±38	6±0.07	27±47	0.49±0.17
6	1840±60	6±0.07	27±49	0.50±0.17
7	2069±84	6±0.08	28±50	0.51±0.17
8	2320±77	6±0.08	29±51	0.51±0.17

(f) WP, parameters of [8].

Initially designed as a segmentation method, **FZ** [3] cannot be used with the parameters suggested by its authors. We first use the parameters learned by Stutz *et al.* [14]. But a visual analyze of the produced results shows that they have been over-fitted for BSD and NYU datasets and are not suitable for HSID, where they produce segmentation-like results. A second attempt with the parameters learned by Mathieu *et al.* [10] gives much better results and allows a fair comparison with the rest of the state-of-the-art methods. The analysis of superpixel numbers and FBR scores shows that FZ has a good adaptability. When its parameters are set to produce a lot of superpixels ($K > 1500$), both mean of FBR

---

[5] http://image.ensfea.fr/hsid/.

and standard deviation of K increase, showing that images, that are correctly oversegmented when setting FZ to produce less superpixels (for example 500), are always partitioned in a small number of superpixels. Boundary adherence is satisfactory with FBR scores better than those of SLIC and slightly worse than those of ERS. The only drawback of FZ is its execution time. With a FBR score significantly lower than FZ, SLIC and ERS algorithms, and the longer execution times of all the evaluated methods, **QS** is the first case of algorithm failing to oversegment HSID. A visual analysis of the produced superpixels shows that QS has strong difficulties with images where some boundaries are slightly blurred. Moreover, QS parameters are related to the image size. Thus, the large standard deviation of K is not the consequence of a good adaptivity, but the result of these size-dependent parameters, reducing the superpixel number when dealing with a small image. Evaluation on HSID including images with several millions of pixels, allow to highlight the huge advantage of the linear complexity of **SLIC**, which has an execution times from 3 to 71 times faster than the other algorithms. This main strength is offset by the FBR results, SLIC requiring more superpixels to achieve performance similar to ERS or FZ algorithms. Moreover, the standard deviation for K is low, revealing that, even if configuring SLIC to produce more superpixels reduces boundary adherence errors, this improvement suffers from an oversegmentation of simple (with a few objects) images in much more superpixels than necessary. In other terms, SLIC is not adaptive. **ERS** is the method achieving the best compromise between conciseness and boundary adherence. Unfortunately this result come with the second highest execution time after QS. The second drawback of ERS is its complete lack of adaptability, with a standard deviation of superpixel numbers equals to 0, meaning that the superpixel numbers is fixed by the user, without any possibility for the method to adapt it to the image complexity. Thus, to reduce errors in images with a lot of tiny details, photographs with large homogeneous areas are oversegmented into numerous small superpixels. Conversely, even if with 1900 superpixels, thin elements of some images are not correctly segmented. The algorithm **CRS** is the second case of algorithm failing to oversegment HSID. Even with more than 2000 superpixels, it achieves poor FBR scores, lower than 0.5. This result is easily explained by the study of CRS algorithm. Even with numerous superpixels, the initial partition in regular rectangles, corresponds to a significant error on HSID biggest images. Consequently, the convergence to a more relevant solution by only moving boundary pixels is very slow. In addition, statistical distributions of color inside superpixels are often so wrong that the algorithm remains stuck in local optimum far away from a correct oversegmentation. For example, when multiplying the number of iteration by 100, no visible improvement is shown, but the execution time raises over 2000 s. **WP** method is the last case of method achieving good results on BSD and failing to have similar performance on HSID. While evaluation of Machairas *et al.* [8] shows that WP and SLIC have similar boundary adherence, with execution time lower for WP, FBR results and computational times are, in our evaluation of WP, far away from those of SLIC.

In addition, WP is the only algorithm unable to oversegment the totality of HSID, failing for *img-012*, *img-066* and *img-072*.

5   Conclusion and Perspectives

Evaluation of QS [17], CRS [2] and WP [8] shows that even if these algorithms achieve good results on BSD and NYU datasets, they fail to correctly oversegment HSID images. Moreover, none of the remaining algorithms (FZ, SLIC and ERS) reaches a satisfactory compromise between boundary adherence, conciseness and efficiency. Thus, the proposed dataset HSID shows that is room for improvement and new propositions in oversegmention research area. We are currently working on a method based on a region merging approach. Our goal is to obtain a new algorithm able of adapting to the image content, reaching a compromise between conciseness and boundary adherence, while keeping short execution time. Regarding HSID, even if this dataset is sufficient to make interesting conclusion the state-of-the-art oversegmentation methods, we think that enlarge it with some supplementary images and the associated ground truth should be valuable. We hope that a collaborative effort, will be made. Finally, we invite all researchers working on a new oversegmentation method to not only evaluate their algorithms using previous benchmarks but also to show that they are competitive when dealing with HSID.

References

1. Achanta, A., Shaji, A., Smith, K., Lucchi, A., Fua, P., Susstrunk, S.: Slic superpixels compared to state-of-the-art superpixel methods. IEEE Trans. Pattern Anal. Mach. Intell. **34**(11), 2274–2282 (2012)
2. Conrad, C., Mertz, M., Mester, R.: Contour-relaxed superpixels. In: Heyden, A., Kahl, F., Olsson, C., Oskarsson, M., Tai, X.-C. (eds.) EMMCVPR 2013. LNCS, vol. 8081, pp. 280–293. Springer, Heidelberg (2013). doi:10.1007/978-3-642-40395-8_21
3. Felzenszwalb, P.F., Huttenlocher, D.P.: Efficient graph-based image segmentation. Int. J. Comput. Vis. **59**(2), 167–181 (2004)
4. Gould, S., Rodgers, J., Cohen, D., Elidan, G., Koller, D.: Multi-class segmentation with relative location prior. Int. J. Comput. Vis. **80**(3), 300–316 (2008)
5. Irie, K., Tomono, M.: Road recognition from a single image using prior information. In: IEEE/RSJ International Conference on Intelligent Robots and Systems, pp. 1938–1945 (2013)
6. Levinshtein, A., Stere, A., Kutulakos, K.N., Fleet, D.J., Dickinson, S.J., Siddiqi, K.: Turbopixels: fast superpixels using geometric flows. IEEE Trans. Pattern Anal. Mach. Intell. **31**(12), 2290–2297 (2009)
7. Liu, M.Y., Tuzel, O., Ramalingam, S., Chellappa, R.: Entropy rate superpixel segmentation. In: IEEE Conference on Computer Vision and Pattern Recognition (2011)
8. Machairas, V., Faessel, M., Cárdenas-Peña, D., Chabardes, T., Walter, T., Decenciére, E.: Waterpixels. IEEE Trans. Image Process. **24**(11), 3707–3716 (2015)

 9. Martin, D., Fowlkes, C., Tal, D., Malik, J.: A database of human segmented natural images and its application to evaluating segmentation algorithms and measuring ecological statistics. In: 8th International Conference on Computer Vision, vol. 2, pp. 416–423 (2001)
10. Mathieu, B., Crouzil, A., Puel, J.B.: Segmentation interactive pour l'annotation de photographies de paysages (2016)
11. Papon, J., Abramov, A., Schoeler, M., Worgotter, F.: Voxel cloud connectivity segmentation-supervoxels for point clouds, pp. 2027–2034 (2013)
12. Ren, X., Malik, J.: Learning a classification model for segmentation. In: Ninth IEEE International Conference on Computer Vision, vol. 1, pp. 10–17 (2003)
13. Silberman, N., Hoiem, D., Pushmeet, K., Fergus, R.: Indoor segmentation and support inference from RGBD images, pp. 746–760 (2012)
14. Stutz, D.: Superpixel segmentation: an evaluation. In: German Conference on Pattern Recognition, pp. 555–562 (2015)
15. Tang, D., Fu, H., Cao, X.: Topology preserved regular superpixel. In: IEEE International Conference on Multimedia and Expo, pp. 765–768 (2012)
16. Bergh, M., Boix, X., Roig, G., Capitani, B., Gool, L.: SEEDS: superpixels extracted via energy-driven sampling. In: Fitzgibbon, A., Lazebnik, S., Perona, P., Sato, Y., Schmid, C. (eds.) ECCV 2012. LNCS, vol. 7578, pp. 13–26. Springer, Heidelberg (2012). doi:10.1007/978-3-642-33786-4_2
17. Vedaldi, A., Soatto, S.: Quick shift and kernel methods for mode seeking. In: Forsyth, D., Torr, P., Zisserman, A. (eds.) ECCV 2008. LNCS, vol. 5305, pp. 705–718. Springer, Heidelberg (2008). doi:10.1007/978-3-540-88693-8_52
18. Veksler, O., Boykov, Y., Mehrani, P.: Superpixels and supervoxels in an energy optimization framework. In: Daniilidis, K., Maragos, P., Paragios, N. (eds.) ECCV 2010. LNCS, vol. 6315, pp. 211–224. Springer, Heidelberg (2010). doi:10.1007/978-3-642-15555-0_16
19. Weikersdorfer, D., Gossow, D., Beetz, M.: Depth-adaptive superpixels. In: 21st International Conference on Pattern Recognition, pp. 2087–2090 (2012)
20. Zhang, L., Yang, Y., Wang, M., Hong, R., Nie, L., Li, X.: Detecting densely distributed graph patterns for fine-grained image categorization. IEEE Trans. Image Process. **25**(2), 553–565 (2016)
21. Zhang, Y., Hartley, R., Mashford, J., Burn, S.: Superpixels via pseudo-boolean optimization. In: CIEEE International Conference on Computer Vision, pp. 1387–1394 (2011)
22. Zhou, C., Liu, C.: Interactive image segmentation based on region merging using hierarchical match mechanism. In: International Conference on Computer Science & Service System, pp. 1781–1784 (2012)
23. Zitnick, C.L., Kang, S.B.: Stereo for image-based rendering using image oversegmentation. Int. J. Comput. Vis. **75**(1), 49–65 (2007)

ASARI: A New Adaptive Oversegmentation Method

Bérengère Mathieu[1]([⊠]), Alain Crouzil[1], and Jean Baptiste Puel[2]

[1] Université de Toulouse, UPS, IRIT, Toulouse, France
{berengere.mathieu,alain.crouzil}@irit.fr
[2] Université de Toulouse, ENFA, IRIT, Toulouse, France
jean-baptiste.puel@irit.fr

Abstract. Using superpixels instead of pixels has become a popular pre-processing step in computer vision. However, there are few adaptive methods able to automatically find the best comprise between boundary adherence and superpixel number. Moreover, no algorithm producing color and texture homogeneous superpixels keeps competitive execution time. In this article we suggest a new graph-based region merging method, called Adaptive Superpixel Algorithm with Rich Information (ASARI) to solve these two difficulties. We will show that ASARI achieves results similar to the state-of-the-art methods on the existing benchmarks and outperforms these methods when dealing with big images.

Keywords: Graph-based oversegmentation · Superpixels · Local Ternary Patterns

1 Introduction

The idea and definition of superpixel is given for the first time by Ren *et al.*, in [9]. The two authors describe a segmentation method including an *oversegmentation* pre-processing grouping pixels into small homogeneous and regular regions called *superpixels*. Currently, oversegmentation is an active research field, with steady publication of new methods [1, 2, 6]. Some examples of oversegmentation results are given in Fig. 1. A good oversegmentation method must satisfy five properties: **validity** (an oversegmentation must be an image partition into connected components), **boundary adherence** (superpixels must not overlap different objects of the image), **conciseness** (an oversegmentation must give as few superpixels as possible), **simplicity** (the number of neighbors of each superpixel must be as small as possible, to avoid a complex adjacency graph), **efficiency** (an oversegmentation algorithm must have an execution time as low as possible). We call **adaptivity**, the fact that an algorithm is able to find the

The work of Bérengère Mathieu was partially supported by ANR-11-LABX-0040-CIMI within the program ANR-11-IDEX-0002-02.

best compromise between these two properties, reducing the number of super-pixels in wide homogeneous regions and increasing it to segment correctly thin details.

Oversegmentation algorithms may be region-based [1,5], when clustering pixels, or boundary-based [2,3], when focusing on edge evidence. The review of Stutz [12] shows that five methods achieve similar results and outperform other algorithms: the Felzenszwalb *et al.* algorithm (FZ) [3], Quick Shift (QS) [14], Entropy Rate Superpixels (ERS) [5], Simple Linear Iterative Clustering (SLIC) [1] and Contour Relaxed Superpixel [2]. The FZ [3] and ERS [5] algorithms use a graph-based representation of the image $G < V, E >$, where V is the set of elements to be grouped (*i.e. the pixels*) and E, the set of edges linking pairs of neighboring elements. Each edge is weighted using a dissimilarity measure. FZ uses a predicate checking that the dissimilarity between elements along the boundary of two components is greater than the dissimilarity between neighboring elements within each of the two components, to produce a partition of G into K connected components corresponding to superpixels. ERS is a greedy algorithm selecting a subset $A \subset E$ and removing these edges. The result is a partition of G, which maximizes an entropy rate. The QS method [14] is a modification of the medoid-shift algorithm to efficiently find modes of a Parzen density estimate P. Color and location of each pixel are used as feature vectors that are clustered by linking each vector to its nearest neighbor which increases P. The SLIC method [1] is an adaptation of the k-means algorithm. Starting from an image oversegmentation into a regular grid, the average color and location features of each superpixel are computed. Then, each pixel is re-assigned to the most similar superpixel and the average features of superpixels are re-computed. The CRS algorithm [2] finds a partition S into superpixels, which has a high likelihood of having generated the observed image. Starting from an initial segmentation into rectangular superpixels, CRS maximizes the probability function by reallocating some boundary pixels to another superpixel. In our evaluation, we add to these five state-of-the-art methods, WP, a watershed transformation based algorithm recently suggested by Machairas *et al.* [6].

The main contribution of this article is a graph-based oversegmentation method (Sect. 2), called Adaptive Superpixel Algorithm with Rich Information (ASARI). As its name suggest, ASARI is able to adjust the size and the number of superpixels to fit the image complexity, partitioning uniform objects (like the sky) in a few large superpixels and producing a lot of thin superpixels to match with small details. In addition, ASARI groups pixels using both color and texture information, without dramatically increasing the computation time. The only oversegmentation algorithm using texture has been proposed by Ren *et al.* in [9]. Unfortunately, its high execution time discouraged its usage in practical applications. Using Stutz benchmark [12], we show in Sect. 3 that ASARI is competitive with the state-of-the-art methods. However, the benefit of this new algorithm is more significant on a new dataset, that we recently made available: Heterogeneous Size Image Dataset (HSID). Contrary to other oversegmentation evaluation datasets, HSID contains photographs having extremely different sizes (from some thousand to several millions of pixels) and a majority of big images. This leads us to an interesting application of ASARI, as a preprocessing step in the Superpixel Classification based Interactive Segmentation (SCIS) method [8].

2   ASARI: A Region Merging Algorithm

ASARI is a region-merging algorithm, following the approach of Salembier *et al.* [10], which is still the base of successful works in image analysis [4,15]. Let $G_0 =< V_0, E_0 >$ be a graph related to an image I, where V_0 is the set of vertices and E_O the set of edges connecting them. Each vertex v_i corresponds to a pixel or a small group of pixels and there is an edge (v_i, v_j) between each pair of neighboring pixels or regions. A region merging algorithm with G_0 as input, produces a graph $G_K =< V_K, E_K >$, where V_K is a partition of V_0 into connected components and E_K is a subset of E_0. More concretely, some vertices of G_0 are merged and edges linking them are removed. Salembier *et al.* [10] show that such an algorithm can be defined by a merging order (the order in which the edges are processed), a merging criterion (how to decide if an edge must be removed) and a region model (how to represent the union of two vertices).

Merging order - Merging order in the case of an oversegmentation algorithm must ensure that visually similar regions will be merged, while maintaining regions with reasonably similar areas. We associate to each vertex v_i a variable Δ_i referring to the number of times v_i has been previously selected. At the beginning of each iteration, the algorithm selects the vertex with the smallest Δ_i (when several vertices have the same Δ_i value, one is arbitrary chosen). ASARI merging order keeps among the set of edges linking v_i to its neighbors, the one maximizing a similarity measure f_{sim}. Whether v_i and its most similar neighbor are merged or not[1], Δ_i is incremented.

Similarity measure - When designing ASARI, one of our objectives was to propose a similarity measure using both color and texture features and keeping reasonable execution times (a few seconds on a desktop computer, for images of size 3000×4000). So, we chose the Local Ternary Patterns (LTP) [13] largely for their rapidity. The LTP of a pixel p is a pair of identifiers, (LTP_N, LTP_P), corresponding to gray level variations of its 8-neighborhood. Let $T = \{g_0, \cdots, g_7\}$ be the set the gray levels of the 8 neighbors of p. The identifiers are given by:

$$LTP_N(p) = \sum_{n=0}^{7} 2^n \delta(p - g_n) \text{ and } LTP_P(p) = \sum_{n=0}^{7} 2^n \delta(g_n - p) \qquad (1)$$

where δ is a threshold function, returning 1 if its input is greater than a threshold ω_{LTP}, 0 otherwise. In the binary representation of LTP_N and LTP_P, digits equal to 0 correspond to neighbors with gray levels similar to the center gray level. So, pixels with a pair of LTP identifiers equals to $(0,0)$, have a neighborhood with similar gray levels. The ratio between the number of this kind of pixels

---

[1] The decision to merge or not v_i and its most similar neighbor is related to the merging criterion.

and the total number of pixels in a region gives the probability for the region to be textured or not. If this probability is lower than a threshold ω_{tex}, the region is textured. We assume that a similarity measure must give a low value when comparing a textured region to an untextured region. Let $f_c(i,j)$ be a color-based similarity measure between regions v_i and v_j, $f_t(i,j)$ be a texture-based similarity measure, and h be a binary function, returning 1 for a textured region, 0 otherwise. The similarity function is the following:

$$f_{sim}(i,j) = \begin{cases} f_c(i,j) \text{ if } h(i) + h(j) = 2 \\ \dfrac{f_t(i,j) + f_c(i,j)}{2} \text{ if } h(i) + h(j) = 0 \\ 0 \text{ otherwise.} \end{cases} \tag{2}$$

Let c_i be a vector containing the normalized average color of v_i:

$$f_c(i,j) = \exp(-\frac{1}{N_c}||c_i - c_j||^2) \tag{3}$$

where N_c is the length of c_i. Let t_i be the concatenation of the normalized histograms of LTP_N and of LTP_P, for the region v_i. We have:

$$f_t(i,j) = \exp(-\frac{1}{N_t}\sum \frac{(t_i^k - t_j^k)^2}{t_i^k + t_j^k}) \tag{4}$$

where N_t is the number of strictly positive bins in t_i or t_j and the superscript k denotes the k-th element of the vector. Notice that f_t is derived from the χ^2 measure. Distinguishing between textured and untextured regions reduces the execution time of ASARI, the computation time for f_c being significantly lower than for f_t.

Merging criterion - A merging criterion $g(i,j)$ must ensure both visual consistency and regularity of the region and can be expressed by the following boolean function:

$$g(i,j) = g_{sim}(i,j) \wedge g_{reg}(i,j) \tag{5}$$

where g_{sim} checks that similarity between the two regions is greater than a threshold ω_{sim} and g_{reg} verifies that the new region size is not disproportionate to the size of the other regions, using a threshold ω_{reg}. So we have:

$$g_{sim}(i,j) = f_{sim}(i,j) > \omega_{sim} \text{ and } g_{reg}(i,j) = (\phi(i)+\phi(j)) < \frac{\omega_{reg}}{M}\sum_{n=0}^{M}\phi(n) \tag{6}$$

where $\phi(i)$ is the number of pixels belonging to v_i and M the number of regions. The adaptive nature of ASARI results from g_{sim} function, which stops merging in image parts containing small distinct details. The function g_{reg} prevents a segmentation-like behavior and ensures that superpixel sizes remain much smaller than object areas. ASARI stops when any edge cannot be removed any more or when all vertices have been selected 10 times[2].

---

[2] Our experiments show that this number of iterations is sufficient to provide good results.

Initialization - To produce V_0, we use the SLIC algorithm [1], which has the two benefits of drastically reducing the number of initial regions and simplifying the use of the texture similarity measure, which requires at least one hundred of pixels to give a significant histogram. The drawback of this approach is to introduce two more parameters, ω_{min} and ω_{comp}, which must be designed to produce very small regions. Parameter ω_{min} gives an average region size and parameter ω_{comp} is the SLIC compactness parameter [1].

Parametrization - ASARI has 6 parameters: ω_{LTP}, ω_{tex}, ω_{sim}, ω_{reg}, ω_{min} and ω_{comp}. As these parameters impact different aspects of ASARI, sometime related to contradictory properties (like conciseness and boundary adherence), it is not simple to learn them at once. We processed in three steps, first with parameters linked to untextured region detection (ω_{LTP}, ω_{tex}), then setting SLIC parameters (ω_{min}, ω_{comp}) and finally focusing on thresholds for the merging criterion (ω_{sim}, ω_{reg}). Parameters $\omega_{LTP} = 19$ and $\omega_{tex} = 0.8$ have been learned by solving an intermediary classification problem of small patches extracted both of Wikimedia Common[3] images and Brodatz texture images[4], and then, classified into textured or untextured patches. The value of $\omega_{comp} = 10$ has been set following previous evaluation of SLIC [1]. The parameter ω_{min} is the only one which must be set by the user. In all of our tests we use a value of $0.00015 \times N$, with N the number of pixels in the image. The value of $\omega_{reg} = 4$ is related to an assumption about region growing: in an ideal case, at each step, 4 regions will be merged, to maintain a grid structure. The value of parameter $\omega_{sim} = 0.05$ has been learned on Berkeley dataset, and chosen to allow a satisfactory compromise between conciseness and boundary adherence properties. Experimental results of Sect. 3 show that these parameters allow ASARI to achieve competitive results and that they do not require to be re-learned anymore when dealing with other datasets.

3   Experimental Results

We evaluated ASARI using both Stutz experimental design [12] and a new benchmark, Heterogeneous Size Image Dataset (HSID) that we proposed recently[5]. Contrary to Stutz datasets, *i.e.* the 100 images of the Berkeley Segmentation Dataset[6] (BSD) [7] and the 400 images of the New York University[7] (NYU) [11] which only contains small images of thousand pixels, HSID is made up of 100 Wikimedia Common photographs, with a majority having several millions of pixels. In addition, variations of image size are significantly more important in HSID than in BSD or NYU.

In Stutz review [12], boundary adherence of evaluated methods is analyzed using two measures: the Undersegmentation Error (UE) and the Boundary Recall

---

[3] https://commons.wikimedia.org/wiki/Main_Page.

[4] http://www.ux.uis.no/~tranden/.

[5] http://image.ensfea.fr/hsid/.

[6] https://www2.eecs.berkeley.edu/Research/Projects/CS/vision/bsds/.

[7] http://cs.nyu.edu.

(BR). Let G be a ground truth segmentation for an image I, S be an overseg-mentation of I, B_G be the set of boundary pixels in G, B_S be the set of boundary pixels in S and N be the number of pixels. The undersegmentation error gets for each object G_i in G the set of superpixels required to cover it and counts the number of pixels leaking of G_i. The boundary recall checks whether boundaries of superpixels contain boundaries in G:

$$UE(S,G) = \frac{1}{N} \sum_{G_i \in G} \sum_{S_j \cap G_i \neq \emptyset} min(|S_j \cap G_i|, |S_j - G_i|) \text{ and } BR(S,G) = \frac{|B_S \cap B_G|}{|B_G|} \quad (7)$$

In fact, even for a human, it is sometimes difficult to know exactly whether a pixel belongs or not to a boundary, Stutz allows a distance of $0.0075 \times diag$ (where $diag$ is the image diagonal length) pixels between boundary points in G and in S.

Unfortunately these two measures are not suitable to evaluate boundary adherence on HSID. To put it in a nutshell, the average score of UE is not significant due to the important variations in foreground areas in HSID images and the Stutz threshold is not suitable for big images. So, we suggest a modi-fication of BR using fuzzy set theory. From B_G we define the fuzzy set $B^*_{G \cap S}$ with membership function $f_{G \cap S}(p_i) = \exp(-\frac{d(p_i - p_i')^2}{2\sigma^2})$ where $d(p_i - p_j)$ is the distance between p_i and p_j locations, and $p_i' = \arg\min_{p_j \in B_S}(d(p_i - p_j))$. The function $f_{G \cap S}$ returns a value in the range $[0, 1]$, a value of 1 meaning a perfect coinci-dence between an element in B_G and an element in B_S. Finally, we propose the fuzzy boundary recall measure $FBR(S,G) = \frac{1}{|B_G|} \sum_{p \in B_G} f_{G \cap S}(p)$.

Comparison to the state-of-the-art methods - By design, ASARI satisfy validity property, the only requirement is that vertices in G_0 are con-nected components. Then, because only adjacent regions are merged, the result-ing superpixels are always a partition of I into connected components. The average number of neighbors by superpixel equals to 6 on BSD, NYU and HSID dataset, that is similar to all state-of-the-art oversegmentation methods.

Table 1 compares the results of ASARI to those achieved by the methods QS [14], FZ [3], SLIC [1], ERS [5] and CRS [2], in Stutz review [12]. On BSD, UE and BR scores of ASARI are similar to those of the state-of-art methods,

Table 1. Comparison between ASARI and the state-of-the-art oversegmentations methods reviewed by Stutz [12]. K is the average number of superpixels and T the execution time in seconds.

Methods	UE	BR	K	T
ASARI	0.04	0.99	899	1.38
QS	0.03	1	≈ 1000	1.24
FZ	0.03	0.99	≈ 1000	0.059
ERS	0.04	0.99	≈ 1000	1.11
SLIC	0.04	0.99	≈ 1000	0.09
CRS	0.04	1	≈ 1000	0.9

(a) Scores achieve on BSD.

Methods	UE	BR	K	T
ASARI	0.1	0.99	899	2.89
CRS	0.09	1	≈ 1897	1.19
ERS	0.08	0.99	≈ 1500	2.21
SLIC	0.09	0.99	≈ 1500	0.17
FZ	0.07	0.99	≈ 1500	0.1
QS	0.07	0.99	≈ 1500	1.24

(b) Scores achieve on NYU.

Methods	FBR	K	T
ASARI	0.61	1528	6
WP parameters of [6]	0.51	1587	27
CRS parameters of [2]	0.34	1601	21
ERS parameters of [12]	0.60	1500	36
SLIC parameters of [1]	0.58	1648	3
FZ parameters of [8]	0.59	1596	10
QS parameters of [12]	0.53	1676	97

(c) Scores achieve on HSID.

(a) Image 42049 of BSD: $K = 472$; $UE = 0.03$; $FBR = 0.99$. (b) Image 00001315 of NYU: $K = 905$; $UE = 0.07$; $BR = 1$. (c) Image : img-010 of HSID: $K = 1445$; $FBR = 0.66$. (d) Image : img-025 of HSID: $K = 928$; $FBR = 0.61$.

Fig. 1. Results achieved by ASARI on BSD, NYU and HSID.

with a lower average number of superpixels (about 100 superpixels below). The adaptive nature of ASARI allows it to increase the conciseness of the produced oversegmentation, with some images partitioned into about 500 superpixels. An example is given in Fig. 1a. On NYU, UE of ASARI is slightly less good but BR is similar. The average number of superpixels is more important (about 300 superpixels above). Figure 1b shows that, despite these difficulties, ASARI keeps its ability to adapt. Table 1c shows that ASARI is the method providing the best compromise between boundary adherence and compactness properties on the HSID dataset. The gap is significant with WP (+10% on FBR, for a similar number of superpixels), CRS (+17% with 100 superpixels fewer), SLIC (+2% with 100 superpixels fewer) and QS(+10% with 200 superpixels fewer). The differences with FZ (+2% with a similar number of superpixels) and ERS (+1% with a similar number of superpixels) are less important, but execution times of ASARI are better (near to 2 times faster than FZ and more than 6 times faster than ERS). Figure 1c and d show some examples of ASARI results. In Fig. 1d, the use of texture information allows a clear separation between the foreground and the background, which have similar colors.

Practical application - Interactive segmentation is a semi-automatic segmentation process. The user chooses some pixels (named seeds) and indicates for each of them the element to which it belongs. Features of desired regions are deduced by analyzing these seeds. Usually, adding or removing some seeds can improve the produced result, allowing the user to get any desired segmentation results. Suggested in 2016, Superpixel Classification-based Interactive Segmentation (SCIS) [8] creates a segmentation of the image by learning features of superpixels labeled by the user and classifying the remaining superpixels. The image is first oversegmented using FZ, then the average color and the center of mass location of each superpixel are computed. The learning and classification steps are made using a Support Vector Machine (SVM). Currently, despite its promising result, SCIS is not suitable to segment a dataset like HSID. The oversegmentation step using FZ produces a lot of small superpixels, often misclassified by the SVM. The resulting segmentation is noisy and correcting these errors by adding seeds is tedious. An example of this problem

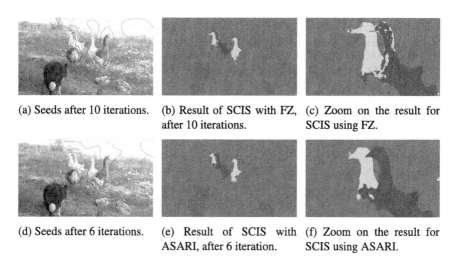

(a) Seeds after 10 iterations.   (b) Result of SCIS with FZ, after 10 iterations.   (c) Zoom on the result for SCIS using FZ.

(d) Seeds after 6 iterations.   (e) Result of SCIS with ASARI, after 6 iteration.   (f) Zoom on the result for SCIS using ASARI.

Fig. 2. SCIS with FZ and ASARI: a comparison.

is shown in Fig. 2. As shown in this figure, ASARI, by producing more larger superpixels, considerably reduces this noise. In addition, ASARI is faster than FZ.

4   Conclusion

The main contribution of this paper is the description and the evaluation of a new oversegmentation algorithm, ASARI, which is suitable for datasets with important variations on image sizes and image complexities. The adaptive nature of ASARI and the fact that ASARI creates color and texture homogeneous superpixels while keeping reasonable execution times, allow it to outperform the state-of-the-art methods in such dataset. On other dataset, ASARI obtains results greater or equal to the state-of-the-art methods. The trade-off between boundary adherence, conciseness and efficiency achieved by ASARI offers interesting perspectives. We show a example of ASARI application as a preprocessing step of SCIS method. An implementation of ASARI is available online[8].

References

1. Achanta, A., Shaji, A., Smith, K., Lucchi, A., Fua, P., Susstrunk, S.: SLIC superpixels compared to state-of-the-art superpixel methods. IEEE Trans. Pattern Anal. Mach. Intell. **34**(11), 2274–2282 (2012)
2. Conrad, C., Mertz, M., Mester, R.: Contour-relaxed superpixels. In: Heyden, A., Kahl, F., Olsson, C., Oskarsson, M., Tai, X.-C. (eds.) EMMCVPR 2013. LNCS, vol. 8081, pp. 280–293. Springer, Heidelberg (2013). doi:10.1007/978-3-642-40395-8_21

---

[8] http://image.ensfea.fr/asari/.

3. Felzenszwalb, P.F., Huttenlocher, D.P.: Efficient graph-based image segmentation. Int. J. Comput. Vis. **59**(2), 167–181 (2004)

4. Li, M., Stein, A., Bijker, W., Zhan, Q.: Region-based urban road extraction from VHR satellite images using binary partition tree. Int. J. Appl. Earth Obs. Geoinformation **44**, 217–225 (2016)

5. Liu, M.Y., Tuzel, O., Ramalingam, S., Chellappa, R.: Entropy rate superpixel segmentation. In: IEEE Conference on Computer Vision and Pattern Recognition, pp. 2097–2104 (2011)

6. Machairas, V., Faessel, M., Cárdenas-Peña, D., Chabardes, T., Walter, T., Decencière, E.: Waterpixels. IEEE Trans. Image Process. **24**(11), 3707–3716 (2015)

7. Martin, D., Fowlkes, C., Tal, D., Malik, J.: A database of human segmented natural images and its application to evaluating segmentation algorithms and measuring ecological statistics. In: 8th International Conference on Computer Vision, vol. 2, pp. 416–423 (2001)

8. Mathieu, B., Crouzil, A., Puel, J.B.: Segmentation interactive pour l'annotation de photographies de paysages. Reconnaissance des Formes et l'Intelligence Artificielle (2016). (in French)

9. Ren, X., Malik, J.: Learning a classification model for segmentation. In: IEEE International Conference on Computer Vision, Proceedings, vol. 1, pp. 10–17 (2003)

10. Salembier, P., Garrido, L.: Binary partition tree as an efficient representation for image processing, segmentation, and information retrieval. IEEE Trans. Image Process. **9**(4), 561–576 (2000)

11. Silberman, N., Hoiem, D., Pushmeet, K., Fergus, R.: Indoor segmentation and support inference from RGBD images. pp. 746–760 (2012)

12. Stutz, D.: Superpixel segmentation: an evaluation. In: Gall, J., Gehler, P., Leibe, B. (eds.) GCPR 2015. LNCS, vol. 9358, pp. 555–562. Springer, Cham (2015). doi:10.1007/978-3-319-24947-6_46

13. Tang, D., Fu, H., Cao, X.: Topology preserved regular superpixel. In: IEEE International Conference on Multimedia and Expo, pp. 765–768 (2012)

14. Vedaldi, A., Soatto, S.: Quick shift and kernel methods for mode seeking. In: Forsyth, D., Torr, P., Zisserman, A. (eds.) ECCV 2008. LNCS, vol. 5305, pp. 705–718. Springer, Heidelberg (2008). doi:10.1007/978-3-540-88693-8_52

15. Xu, Y., Géraud, T., Najman, L.: Connected filtering on tree-based shape-spaces. IEEE Trans. Pattern Anal. Mach. Intell. **38**(6), 1126–1140 (2016)

A New Normalized Supervised Edge Detection Evaluation

Hasan Abdulrahman$^{(\boxtimes)}$, Baptiste Magnier, and Philippe Montesinos

Ecole des Mines d'Alès, Parc scientifique Georges Besse, 30000 Nîmes, France
hasan.abdulrahman@mines-ales.fr

Abstract. In digital images, edges characterize object boundaries, then their detection remains a crucial stage in numerous applications. To achieve this task, many edge detectors have been designed, producing different results, with different qualities. Evaluating the response obtained by these detectors has become a crucial task. In this paper, several referenced-based boundary detection evaluations are detailed, pointing their advantages and disadvantages through concrete examples of edge images. Then, a new supervised edge map quality measure is proposed, comparing a ground truth contour image, the candidate contour image and their associated spacial nearness. Compared to other boundary detection assessments, this new method has the advantage to be normalized and remains a more reliable edge map quality measure.

Keywords: Edge detection · Distance measure · Supervised evaluation

1 Importance of a New Error Measure

In image processing tasks, edge detection remains a key point in many applications. Boundaries include the most important structures of the image, and an efficient boundary detection method should create a contour image containing edges at their correct locations with a minimal of misclassified pixels. Different algorithms have been developed in the past, but few of them give an objective performance comparison. The evaluation process should produce a result that correlates with the perceived quality of the edge image, which is relied on human judgment. In other words, a reliable edge map should characterize all the relevant structures of an image. On the other hand, a minimum of spurious pixels or holes (oversights) must be created by the edge detector at the same time. Therefore, an efficient evaluation can be used to assess and improve an algorithm, or to optimize edge detector parameters [1].

The measurement process can be classified into either an unsupervised or a supervised evaluation criteria. The first class of methods exploits only the input contour image and gives a score of coherence that qualifies the result given by the algorithm [1]. The second one computes a dissimilarity measure between a segmentation result and a ground truth obtained from synthetic data or an expert judgment (i.e. manual segmentation) [2–4]. This work focusses on comparisons of supervised assessment of edge detection evaluations. Furthermore,

© Springer International Publishing AG 2017
L.A. Alexandre et al. (Eds.): IbPRIA 2017, LNCS 10255, pp. 203–213, 2017.
DOI: 10.1007/978-3-319-58838-4_23

a new supervised edge map quality measure based on the distances of misplaced pixels is presented and compared to the others, using synthetic and real images.

2   Supervised Image Contour Evaluations

As introduced above, a supervised evaluation process estimates scores between a ground truth and a candidate edge map. In image processing, the Structural Similarity Index ($SSIM$) corresponds to an image quality evaluation, which estimates the visual impact of gray scale shifts in an image [5]. Otherwise, contours (binary images) could be evaluated counting the number of erroneous pixels, but also throughout spatial distances of misplaced or oversights contours.

2.1   Error Measures Involving Only the Confusion Matrix

Let G_t be the reference contour map corresponding to ground truth and D_c the detected contour map of an image I. Comparing pixel per pixel G_t and D_c, common positive or negative presence of points is the first criterion to be assessed. A basic evaluation is compounded of statistics issued of a confusion matrix. To that effect, G_t and D_c are combined. Afterward, denoting $|\cdot|$ the cardinality of a set, all points are partitioned into four sets:

- True Positive points (TPs), common points of G_t and D_c: $TP = |D_c \cap G_t|$,
- False Positive points (FPs), spurious detected edges of D_c: $FP = |D_c \cap \neg G_t|$,
- False Negative points (FNs), missing boundary points of D_c: $FN = |\neg D_c \cap G_t|$,
- True Negative points (TNs), common non-edge points: $TN = |\neg D_c \cap \neg G_t|$.

In one hand, let us consider boundary detection of images, FPs appear in the presence of noise, texture or other contours influencing the filter used by the edge detection operator. In the other hand, FNs represent holes in a contour of D_c. Finally, a wrong threshold of the segmentation could generate both FPs and FNs. Computing only FPs and FNs enables a segmentation assessment [6,7], and a reliable edge detection should minimize the following indicators [3]:

$$\begin{cases} \text{Over-detection error}\ :\ Over(G_t, D_c) &= \frac{FP}{|I|+|G_t|}, \\ \text{Under-detection error}\ :\ Under(G_t, D_c) &= \frac{FN}{|G_t|}, \\ \text{Localization-error}\quad :\quad Loc(G_t, D_c) &= \frac{FP+FN}{|I|}. \end{cases}$$

Additionally, the $Performance\ measure$ P_m^* presented in Table 1 considers directly at the same time the three entities TP, FP and FN to assess an a binary image. The obtained score reflects the percentage of statistical errors.

Another way to display evaluations are Receiver Operating Characteristic (ROC) [8] curves or Precision-Recall (PR) [9], involving $True\ Positive\ Rates$ ($TPR = \frac{TP}{TP+FN}$) and $False\ Positive\ Rates$ ($FPR = \frac{FP}{FP+TN}$). Derived from TPR and FPR, the three measures Φ, χ^2 and F_α (see Table 1) are frequently used in edge detection assessment.

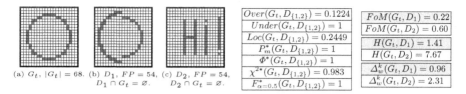

$Over(G_t, D_{\{1,2\}}) = 0.1224$	$FoM(G_t, D_1) = 0.22$
$Under(G_t, D_{\{1,2\}}) = 1$	$FoM(G_t, D_2) = 0.60$
$Loc(G_t, D_{\{1,2\}}) = 0.2449$	$H(G_t, D_1) = 1.41$
$P_m^*(G_t, D_{\{1,2\}}) = 1$	$H(G_t, D_2) = 7.67$
$\Phi^*(G_t, D_{\{1,2\}}) = 1$	$\Delta_w^k(G_t, D_1) = 0.96$
$\chi^{2*}(G_t, D_{\{1,2\}}) = 0.983$	$\Delta_w^k(G_t, D_2) = 2.31$
$F_{\alpha=0.5}(G_t, D_{\{1,2\}}) = 1$	

(a) G_t, $|G_t| = 68$. (b) D_1, $FP = 54$, (c) D_2, $FP = 54$, $D_1 \cap G_t = \varnothing$. $D_2 \cap G_t = \varnothing$.

Fig. 1. Evaluations issued of a confusion matrix can be the same for different D_c. For the two candidate edge images, number of FPs and number of FNs are the same.

P_m^*, Φ, χ^2 and F_α measures are normalized and decrease with the quality of the detection; a score equal to 0 qualifies a perfect segmentation. These measures evaluate the comparison of two edge images, pixel per pixel, tending to penalize severely a misplaced contour (even weak). So they do not indicate significant variations of the desired contour shapes through an evaluation (as illustrated in Fig. 1). As this penalization tends to be too severe, some evaluations issued from the confusion matrix recommend a spatial tolerance, particularly for assimilation of TPs [8,9]. This inclusion could be carried by a distance threshold or a dilation of D_c and/or G_t. A such strategy of assimilation leads to counting several near contours as parallel stripes to the desired boundary. Tolerating a distance from the true contour and integrating several TPs for one detected contour are opposite to the principle of unicity in edge detection expressed by the 3rd Canny criteria: an optimal edge detector must produce a single response for one contour [10]. Finally, to perform an edge evaluation, the assessment should penalize a misplaced edge point proportionally to the distance to its true location.

2.2 Assessment Involving Distances of Misplaced Pixels

Existing Quality Measures Involving Distances. A reference-based edge map quality measure requires that a displaced edge expects to be penalized in function not only of the FPs and/or FNs but also in function of the distance to the position they should be located at. Table 1 reviews the most relevant existing measures. The common feature between these evaluators corresponds to the error distance $d_{G_t}(p)$ or $d_{D_c}(p)$. Indeed, for a pixel $p \in D_c$, $d_{G_t}(p)$ represents

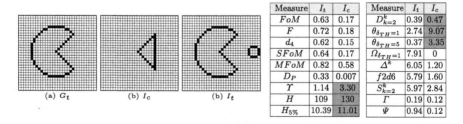

Measure	I_t	I_c	Measure	I_t	I_c
FoM	0.63	0.17	$D_{k=2}^k$	0.39	0.47
F	0.72	0.18	$\theta_{\delta_{TH}=1}$	2.74	9.07
d_4	0.62	0.15	$\theta_{\delta_{TH}=5}$	0.37	3.35
$SFoM$	0.64	0.17	$\Omega_{\delta_{TH}=1}$	7.91	0
$MFoM$	0.82	0.58	Δ^k	6.05	1.20
D_P	0.33	0.007	$f2d6$	5.79	1.60
Υ	1.14	3.30	$S_{k=2}^k$	5.97	2.84
H	109	130	Γ	0.19	0.12
$H_{5\%}$	10.39	11.01	Ψ	0.94	0.12

(a) G_t (b) I_c (b) I_t

Fig. 2. The scores of the over-segmentation evaluations are higher for I_t whereas I_t is more closer visually to G_t than I_c.

Table 1. List of error measures, $k = 1$ or $k = 2$ are the most common values.

Error measure name	Formulation	Parameters
Performance measure [11]	$P_m^*(G_t, D_c) = 1 - \dfrac{TP}{TP + FP + FN}$	None
Complemented Φ measure [12]	$\Phi^*(G_t, D_c) = 1 - \dfrac{TPR \cdot TN}{TN + FP}$	None
Complemented χ^2 measure [13]	$\chi^{2*}(G_t, D_c) = 1 - \dfrac{TPR - TP - FP}{1 - TP - FP} \cdot \dfrac{TP + FP + FPR}{TP + FP}$	None
Complemented F_α measure [9]	$F_\alpha^*(G_t, D_c) = 1 - \dfrac{PREC \cdot TPR}{\alpha \cdot TPR + (1-\alpha) \cdot PREC}$, with $PREC = \frac{TP}{TP + FP}$	$\alpha \in]0; 1]$
Pratt's FoM [14]	$FoM(G_t, D_c) = 1 - \dfrac{1}{\max(|G_t|, |D_c|)} \cdot \sum_{p \in D_c} \dfrac{1}{1 + \kappa \cdot d_{G_t}^2(p)}$	$\kappa \in]0; 1]$
FoM revisited [15]	$F(G_t, D_c) = 1 - \dfrac{1}{|G_t| + \beta \cdot FP} \cdot \sum_{p \in G_t} \dfrac{1}{1 + \kappa \cdot d_{D_c}^2(p)}$	$\kappa \in]0; 1]$ and $\beta \in \mathbb{R}^+$
Combination of FoM and statistics [16]	$d_4(G_t, D_c) = $ $\frac{1}{2} \cdot \sqrt{\dfrac{(TP - \max(|G_t|, |D_c|))^2 + FN^2 + FP^2}{(\max(|G_t|, |D_c|))^2}} + FoM(G_t, D_c)$	$\kappa \in]0; 1]$ and $\beta \in \mathbb{R}^+$
Yasnoff measure [17]	$\Upsilon(G_t, D_c) = \dfrac{100}{|I|} \cdot \sqrt{\sum_{p \in D_c} d_{G_t}^2(p)}$	None
Hausdorff distance [18]	$H(G_t, D_c) = \max(\max_{p \in D_c}(d_{G_t}(p)), \max_{p \in G_t}(d_{D_c}(p)))$	None
Maximum distance [2]	$f_2 d_6(G_t, D_c) = \max(\dfrac{1}{|D_c|} \cdot \sum_{p \in D_c} d_{G_t}(p), \dfrac{1}{|G_t|} \cdot \sum_{p \in G_t} d_{D_c}(p))$	None
Distance to G_t [4,19]	$D^k(G_t, D_c) = \dfrac{1}{|D_c|} \cdot \sqrt[k]{\sum_{p \in D_c} d_{G_t}^k(p)}$, $k = 1$ for [19]	$k \in \mathbb{R}^+$
Oversegmentation [20,21]	$\Theta(G_t, D_c) = \dfrac{1}{FP} \cdot \sum_{p \in D_c} (\dfrac{d_{G_t}(p)}{\delta_{TH}})^k$, $k = \delta_{TH} = 1$ for [20]	for [21]: $k \in \mathbb{R}^+$ and $\delta_{TH} \in \mathbb{R}_*^+$
Undersegmentation [20,21]	$\Omega(G_t, D_c) = \dfrac{1}{FN} \cdot \sum_{p \in G_t} (\dfrac{d_{D_c}(p)}{\delta_{TH}})^k$, $k = \delta_{TH} = 1$ for [20]	for [21]: $k \in \mathbb{R}^+$ and $\delta_{TH} \in \mathbb{R}_*^+$
Symmetric distance [2,4]	$S^k(G_t, D_c) = \sqrt[k]{\dfrac{\sum_{p \in D_c} d_{G_t}^k(p)) + \sum_{p \in G_t} d_{D_c}^k(p)}{|D_c \cup G_t|}}$, $k = 1$ for [2]	$k \in \mathbb{R}^+$
Baddeley's Delta Metric [22]	$\Delta^k(G_t, D_c) = \sqrt[k]{\dfrac{1}{|I|} \cdot \sum_{p \in I} |w(d_{G_t}(p)) - w(d_{D_c}(p))|^k}$	$k \in \mathbb{R}^+$ and a convex function $w : \mathbb{R} \mapsto \mathbb{R}$
Edge map quality measure [23]	$D_p(G_t, D_c) = \dfrac{1/2}{|I| - |G_t|} \cdot \sum_{p \in D_c} (1 - \dfrac{1}{1 + \alpha \cdot d_{G_t}^2(p)}) + \dfrac{1/2}{|G_t|} \cdot$ $\sum_{p \in G_t} (1 - \dfrac{1}{1 + \alpha \cdot d_{G_t \cap D_c}^2(p)})$	$\alpha \in]0; 1]$
Magnier et al. measure [24]	$\Gamma(G_t, D_c) = \dfrac{FP + FN}{|G_t|^2} \sqrt{\sum_{p \in D_c} d_{G_t}^2(p)}$	None

the minimal distance between p and G_t, whereas if $p \in G_t$, $d_{D_c}(p)$ corresponds to the minimal distance between p and D_c. This distance refers to the Euclidean distance, even though some authors involve others, see [4]. Thus, a measure computing an error distance only in function of d_{G_t} estimates the divergence of FPs, which corresponds to an over-segmentation (cases Υ, D^k, Θ, FoM and Γ). On the contrary, the sole use of a distance d_{D_c} enables an estimation of the FNs divergence, representing an under-segmentation, as Ω distance measure. A measure widely computed in matching techniques is represented by the Hausdorff distance H which estimates the mismatch of two sets of points [18]. This max-min distance could be strongly deviated by only one pixel which can be positioned sufficiently far from the pattern (illustrated in Fig. 2); so the measured distance becomes that between the pattern and the (erroneous) point, disturbing in that case the score of H. To improve H such that it becomes less sensitive to outliers, an idea is to compute H with a proportion of the maximum distances (for example 5% of the values [18]); let us note $H_{n\%}$ this measurement for $n\%$ of values ($n \in \mathbb{R}_*^+$). One of the most popular descriptor corresponds to Figure of Merit (FoM). This distance measure ranges from 0 to 1, where 0 corresponds to a perfect segmentation [14], but computes only distances of the FPs [22]. Thus, some improvements have been developed as F and d_4. Furthermore, as concluded in [3], a complete and optimum edge detection evaluation measure should combine assessments of both over- and under-segmentation, as in S^k, Δ_w^k and D_p. As an example, inspired by $f_2 d_6$ [2], another way is to consider the combination of both $FoM\,(G_t, D_c)$ and $FoM\,(D_c, G_t)$, as the two following formulas:

$$\text{Symmetric } FoM : SFoM\,(G_t, D_c) = \frac{1}{2} \cdot FoM\,(G_t, D_c) + \frac{1}{2} \cdot FoM\,(D_c, G_t) \quad (1)$$

$$\text{Maximum } FoM : MFoM\,(G_t, D_c) = \max\,(FoM\,(G_t, D_c), FoM\,(D_c, G_t)). \quad (2)$$

Finally, $SFoM$ and $MFoM$ take into account both distances of FNs (i.e. d_{D_c}) and FPs (i.e. d_{G_t}), so they can compute a global evaluation of a contour image.

Another way to compute a global measure is presented in [23] with the normalized edge map quality measure D_p. In fact, this distance measure seems similar to $SFoM$ with different coefficients. However, both the left and the right terms are composed of a $\frac{1}{2}$ coefficient, so in the presence of only a pure under- or over-segmentation, the score of D_p does not attain over $\frac{1}{2}$.

A New Edge Detection Assessment Measure. In [24] is developed a normalized measure of the edge detection assessment, denoted Γ. This function represents an over-segmentation measure which depends also of FN and FP. As this measure is not sufficiently efficient concerning FNs because it does not consider d_{D_c} for false negative points (see Fig. 7). Thus, inspired by S^k, the new measure Ψ holds different coefficients changing the behavior of the measure:

$$\Psi(G_t, D_c) = \frac{FP + FN}{|G_t|^2} \cdot \sqrt{\sum_{p \in G_t} d_{D_c}^2\,(p) + \sum_{p \in D_c} d_{G_t}^2\,(p)} \quad (3)$$

Compared to Γ, Ψ improves the measurement by combining both d_{G_t} and d_{D_c} (illustrated in Fig. 7). Authors of Γ have studied the influence of the coefficient in different concrete cases [24]. They concluded that such a formulation must take into consideration all observable cases and theoretically observable. In fact, a performing measure has to take into account all the following input parameters $|G_t|$, FN and FP whereas the image dimensions should not be considered. Thus, the parameter $\frac{FP+FN}{|G_t|^2}$ seems a good compromise and has been introduced to the new formula of assessment Ψ.

2.3 Normalization of the Edge Detection Evaluation

In order to compare each boundary detection assessments, all measures must be normalized, but also indicate the same information: an error measure close to 1 means a poor segmentation whereas a value close to 0 indicates a good segmentation. Thereby, the values of FoM, F, d_4 and D_p belongs to $[0, 1]$. However, concerning other distance measures of Table 1, a normalization is required. Introduced in [24], a formula called Key Performance Indicator (KPI) gives value close to 1 for a poor segmentation; alternatively, a KPI value close to 0 translates a good segmentation:

$$KPI_u : [0; \infty[\mapsto [0; 1[$$
$$u \to 1 - \frac{1}{1 + u^h}. \tag{4}$$

where the parameter u represents a distance error and h a constant ($h \in \mathbb{R}_*^+$).

An undeniable parameter of KPI formula is the power of the denominator term called h. Inasmuch as KPI depends on its value, it evolves more or less quickly around 0.5 and embodies a range of observable cases. The advice to choose values between 1 and 2 can be easily checked. Otherwise, the more KPI evolution will be abrupt, the less the transition between 0.5 and 1 will be marked. As a compromise, fixing the power at the *golden ratio* $\phi \simeq 1.6180339887$, the measurement becomes not too strong in the presence a small measure score, but increases to 1 for a high score of the distance measure, see [24].

3   Experimental Results

Experiments realized in this part aim to be the most accomplished, thus the more close and realistic of the reality. In respect of these directives, in a first time, considering a synthetic edge model (i.e. ground truth) the edge detection evaluation measures are subject to the following studies: addition of false positive points close to the true contour, addition of false negative points (under-segmentation), addition of false positive points (over-segmentation), addition of both false negatives and false positive points, translation of the boundary. Thus, 24 measures and the new proposed method are tested and compared together. The KPI in Eq. 4 is computed for the non-normalized algorithms in Table 1.

The first experiment is to create an over-segmentation at a maximal distance of 5 pixels, as illustrated in Fig. 3 (100% of over-segmentation represents a dilatation of the vertical line with a structural element of size 1×6, corresponding of a total saturation of the contour, see Fig. 3(d)). Curves presented here show that F_α, d_4, F, $MFoM$, H, $H_{5\%}$, Δ_k, D^k, $f_2 d_6$, and S^k are very sensitive to FPs, whereas $SSIM$, D_p, Φ and D^k (which is not homogeneous) do not penalize enough D_c. Ω remains constant at 0 because it corresponds to an under-segmentation measure. Moreover, Υ and FoM are not too abrupt, even though they stagnate, like D^k, $SFoM$, $f_2 d_6$, and S^k. Finally, Γ and Ψ are not too abrupt and penalize strongly D_c in the presence of many FPs.

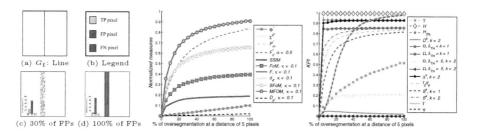

Fig. 3. Measures scores in function of the over-segmentation in the contour area.

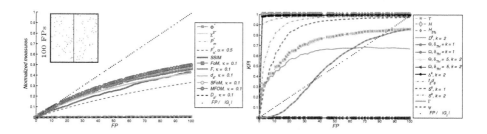

Fig. 4. Evolution of the dissimilarity measures in function of the FPs addition.

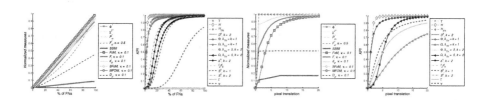

Fig. 5. Measure scores in function of the FNs addition and the edge translation.

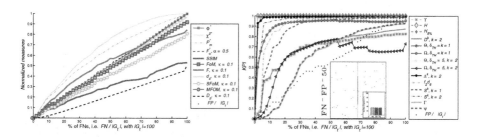

Fig. 6. Dissimilarity measure scores in function of addition of both the FNs and FPs.

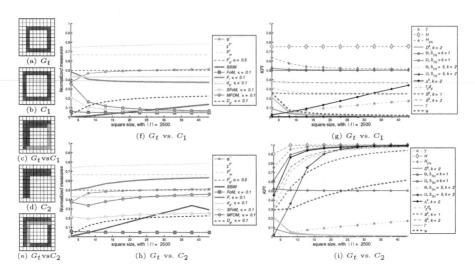

Fig. 7. Dissimilarity measure scores in function of the size of the original square.

The second test is to add random undesirable pixels to G_t until 100 FPs, as represented in Fig. 4 top left. Globally, the curves in Fig. 4 illustrates that the measures using KPI behave like the previous experiment; only Γ and Ψ are not too sensitive to FPs. The normalized evaluation measures increase correctly, but seem stagnant, excepted Φ and D_p which stay close to 0.

Concerning the addition of FNs, Fig. 5 (left) illustrates that H, $H_{5\%}$ and $\Omega_{\delta_{TH}=1}$ are very sensitive to the presence of FNs. Also, D_p attains only the score of $\frac{1}{2}$. The over-segmentation methods Υ, D^k, Ω and Γ remain constant at 0. On the other hand, the score of the KPI of Ψ attains 0.5 for 50% of FNs. Afterward, contrary to the addition of FPs or FNs, error measures without distance measures obtains a score of 1 after one pixel of translation and the score of D_p stays constant at $\frac{1}{2}$ (Fig. 5 (right)). Only FoM, $SFoM$, $MFoM$, the KPI of $\Omega_{\delta_{TH}=5}$, the KPI of Γ and the KPI of Ψ behave correctly.

Concerning the line, the last experiment corresponds to an addition of both FPs and FNs. Thus, Fig. 6 shows that the normalized measures, excepted D_p and $SSIM$ behave correctly. Concerning other measures, the KPI scores of $\Omega_{\delta_{TH}=5}$, Γ and Ψ are not too abrupt for few number or errors and penalize strongly D_c in the presence of many FPs and FNs (but $\Omega_{\delta_{TH}=5}$ is not homogeneous). For example, Fig. 6 (bottom right) illustrates the line where both 50% of the pixels are missing and 50 FPs are added, corresponding to 33% of TPs. In this precise case, the KPI score of new measure Ψ is close to 0.7, thus, reflecting the reality.

Another experiment in Fig. 7, two different shapes are compared to a square (G_t), illustrating the importance to consider both d_{D_c} and d_{G_t}. Furthermore, all the shapes are growing at the same time, keeping the same percentage of FPs and FNs with G_t. The more G_t grows, the more C_1 is visually closer to G_t whereas FNs deviate strongly in the case of C_2. Despite these tow different evolutions, statistical measures, FoM, F, d_4, D_p, Υ and Γ obtain close the same measurements for C_1 and C_2. On the contrary, the KPI of Ψ grows around 0.5 for C_2, whereas it converges towards 0 for C_1, since C_1 becomes visually closer to G_t with the enlargement (note that $MFoM$ behaves identically).

To conclude experimental evaluations, Fig. 8 reports different assessments for five edge detection methods on a real image: Sobel, Canny [10], Steerable Filters of order 1 (SF_1) [25], Steerable Filters of order 5 (SF_5) [26] and Half Gaussian Kernels (HK) [6]. Even though the problem of hand-made ground truth on real images is discussed by some researchers [27], only the comparison of D_c with a G_t is studied here. Compared to G_t (Fig. 8 (a)), the well known Sobel edge detector generates more FPs than the other three methods while SF_5 and HK are less sensitive to noise or texture. Furthermore, HK captures easier straight contours and corners closest to their true positions [6]. So, the measurements in tables of

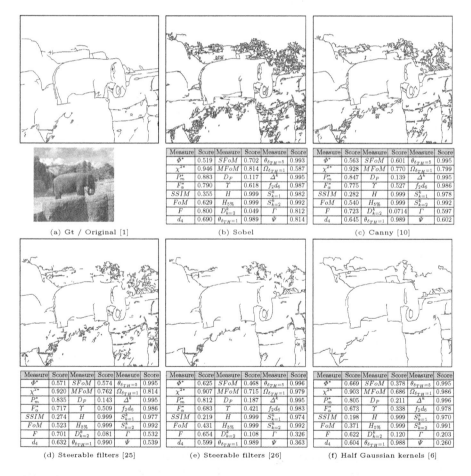

(a) Gt / Original [1]

(b) Sobel

Measure	Score	Measure	Score	Measure	Score
Φ^*	0.519	$SFoM$	0.702	$\theta_{\delta_{TH}=5}$	0.993
χ^{2*}	0.946	$MFoM$	0.814	$\Omega_{\delta_{TH}=1}$	0.587
P^*_m	0.883	D_P	0.117	Δ^k	0.995
F^*_a	0.790	Υ	0.618	$f_2 d_6$	0.987
$SSIM$	0.355	H	0.999	$S^k_{k=1}$	0.982
FoM	0.629	$H_{5\%}$	0.999	$S^k_{k=2}$	0.992
F	0.800	$D^k_{h=2}$	0.049	Γ	0.812
d_4	0.690	$\theta_{\delta_{TH}=1}$	0.989	Ψ	0.814

(c) Canny [10]

Measure	Score	Measure	Score	Measure	Score
Φ^*	0.563	$SFoM$	0.601	$\theta_{\delta_{TH}=5}$	0.995
χ^{2*}	0.928	$MFoM$	0.770	$\Omega_{\delta_{TH}=1}$	0.799
P^*_m	0.847	D_P	0.139	Δ^k	0.995
F^*_a	0.775	Υ	0.527	$f_2 d_6$	0.986
$SSIM$	0.282	H	0.999	$S^k_{k=1}$	0.978
FoM	0.540	$H_{5\%}$	0.999	$S^k_{k=2}$	0.992
F	0.723	$D^k_{k=2}$	0.0714	Γ	0.597
d_4	0.645	$\theta_{\delta_{TH}=1}$	0.989	Ψ	0.602

(d) Steerable filters [25]

Measure	Score	Measure	Score	Measure	Score
Φ^*	0.571	$SFoM$	0.574	$\theta_{\delta_{TH}=5}$	0.995
χ^{2*}	0.920	$MFoM$	0.762	$\Omega_{\delta_{TH}=1}$	0.814
P^*_m	0.835	D_P	0.143	Δ^k	0.995
F^*_a	0.717	Υ	0.509	$f_2 d_6$	0.986
$SSIM$	0.274	H	0.999	$S^k_{k=1}$	0.977
FoM	0.523	$H_{5\%}$	0.999	$S^k_{k=2}$	0.992
F	0.701	$D^k_{k=2}$	0.081	Γ	0.532
d_4	0.632	$\theta_{\delta_{TH}=1}$	0.990	Ψ	0.539

(e) Steerable filters [26]

Measure	Score	Measure	Score	Measure	Score
Φ^*	0.625	$SFoM$	0.468	$\theta_{\delta_{TH}=5}$	0.996
χ^{2*}	0.907	$MFoM$	0.715	$\Omega_{\delta_{TH}=1}$	0.979
P^*_m	0.812	D_P	0.187	Δ^k	0.995
F^*_a	0.683	Υ	0.421	$f_2 d_6$	0.983
$SSIM$	0.219	H	0.999	$S^k_{k=1}$	0.974
FoM	0.431	$H_{5\%}$	0.999	$S^k_{k=2}$	0.992
F	0.654	$D^k_{k=2}$	0.108	Γ	0.326
d_4	0.599	$\theta_{\delta_{TH}=1}$	0.989	Ψ	0.363

(f) Half Gaussian kernels [6]

Measure	Score	Measure	Score	Measure	Score
Φ^*	0.669	$SFoM$	0.378	$\theta_{\delta_{TH}=5}$	0.995
χ^{2*}	0.903	$MFoM$	0.686	$\Omega_{\delta_{TH}=1}$	0.986
P^*_m	0.805	D_P	0.211	Δ^k	0.996
F^*_a	0.673	Υ	0.338	$f_2 d_6$	0.978
$SSIM$	0.198	H	0.999	$S^k_{k=1}$	0.970
FoM	0.371	$H_{5\%}$	0.999	$S^k_{k=2}$	0.991
F	0.622	$D^k_{k=2}$	0.120	Γ	0.203
d_4	0.604	$\theta_{\delta_{TH}=1}$	0.988	Ψ	0.260

Fig. 8. Comparison measures of different edge detections. A score close to 0 indicates a good edge map whereas a score 1 translates a poor segmentation.

Fig. 8 must be close to 1 for Sobel and a little less for Canny, but decrease with reasonable error for HK (scores involving KPI for non-normalized algorithms, Eq. 4). Thus, Γ and Ψ respect this evolution and indicate a good measurement value. FoM, F, d_4, $SFoM$, $MFoM$ and Υ evolve similarly, but the score for the HK remains too elevated. Also, Φ^*, χ^{2*}, P_m^*, F_α^* and D_p do not indicate a significant difference between all the segmentations. Further, other non normalized methods are not adapted to give a score between 0 and 1 using a KPI. Eventually, given the segmented images, Γ and Ψ indicate a good measurement value. Other results involving other edge images are available on the website: http://hkaljaf.wixsite.com/hasanabdulrahman/edge-detection-and-evaluation.

4   Conclusion and Future Works

In this paper, several referenced-based boundary detection evaluations are detailed, pointing their advantages and disadvantages through concrete examples of edge images. A new normalized supervised edge map quality measure is proposed, comparing a ground truth contour image, the candidate contour image and their associated spacial nearness. The strategy to normalize the evaluation enables to consider a score close to 0 as a good edge map, whereas a score 1 translates a poor segmentation. Eventually, compared to other edge evaluation assessments, the score of the new evaluation indicates confidently the quality of a segmentation. Next on our work program agenda is to compare different edge detectors with their different parameters and binary image matching.

Acknowledgements. The authors wish to thank the Iraqi Ministry of Higher Education and Scientific Research for funding and supporting this work.

References

1. Heath, M.D., Sarkar, S., Sanocki, T., Bowyer, K.W.: A robust visual method for assessing the relative performance of edge-detection algorithms. IEEE TPAMI **19**(12), 1338–1359 (1997)
2. Dubuisson, M.-P., Jain, A.K.: A modified hausdorff distance for object matching. In: IEEE ICPR, vol. 1, pp. 566–568 (1994)
3. Chabrier, S., Laurent, H., Rosenberger, C., Emile, B.: Comparative study of contour detection evaluation criteria based on dissimilarity measures. EURASIP J. Image Video Process. (2008). Article ID 693053, http://dx.doi.org/10.1155/2008/693053
4. Lopez-Molina, C., De Baets, B., Bustince, H.: Quantitative error measures for edge detection. Pattern Recogn. **46**(4), 1125–1139 (2013)
5. Wang, Z., Bovik, A.C., Sheikh, H.R., Simoncelli, E.P.: Image quality assessment: from error visibility to structural similarity. IEEE TIP **13**(4), 600–612 (2004)
6. Magnier, B., Montesinos, P., Diep, D.: Fast anisotropic edge detection using gamma correction in color images. In: IEEE ISPA, pp. 212–217 (2011)
7. Magnier, B., Aberkane, A., Borianne, P., Montesinos, P., Jourdan, C.: Multi-scale crest line extraction based on half Gaussian kernels. In: IEEE ICASSP, pp. 5105–5109 (2014)

8. Bowyer, K., Kranenburg, C., Dougherty, S.: Edge detector evaluation using empirical ROC curves. CVIU **84**, 77–103 (2001)
9. Martin, D.R., Fowlkes, C.C., Malik, J.: Learning to detect natural image boundaries using local brightness, color, and texture cues. IEEE TPAMI **26**(5), 530–549 (2004)
10. Canny, J.: A computational approach to edge detection. IEEE TPAMI **6**, 679–698 (1986)
11. Grigorescu, C., Petkov, N., Westenberg, M.: Contour detection based on nonclassical receptive field inhibition. IEEE TIP **12**(7), 729–739 (2003)
12. Venkatesh, S., Rosin, P.L.: Dynamic threshold determination by local and global edge evaluation. CVGIP **57**(2), 146–160 (1995)
13. Yitzhaky, Y., Peli, E.: A method for objective edge detection evaluation and detector parameter selection. IEEE TPAMI **25**(8), 1027–1033 (2003)
14. Abdou, I.E., Pratt, W.K.: Quantitative design and evaluation of enhancement/thresholding edge detectors. Proc. IEEE **67**, 753–763 (1979)
15. Pinho, A.J., Almeida, L.B.: Edge detection filters based on artificial neural networks. In: Braccini, C., DeFloriani, L., Vernazza, G. (eds.) ICIAP 1995. LNCS, vol. 974, pp. 159–164. Springer, Heidelberg (1995). doi:10.1007/3-540-60298-4_252
16. Boaventura, A.G., Gonzaga, A.: Method to evaluate the performance of edge detector (2009)
17. Yasnoff, W.A., Galbraith, W., Bacus, J.W.: Error measures for objective assessment of scene segmentation algorithms. Anal. Quant. Cytol. **1**(2), 107–121 (1978)
18. Huttenlocher, D.P., Rucklidge, W.J.: A multi-resolution technique for comparing images using the hausdorff distance. In: IEEE CVPR, pp. 705–706 (1993)
19. Peli, T., Malah, D.: A study of edge detection algorithms. CGIP **20**(1), 1–21 (1982)
20. Haralick, R.M.: Digital step edges from zero crossing of second directional derivatives. IEEE TPAMI **6**(1), 58–68 (1984)
21. Odet, C., Belaroussi, B., Benoit-Cattin, H.: Scalable discrepancy measures for segmentation evaluation. In: IEEE ICIP, vol. 1, pp. 785–788 (2002)
22. Baddeley, A.J.: An error metric for binary images. In: Förstner, W. (ed.) Robust Computer Vision: Quality of Vision Algorithms, pp. 59–78. Wichmann, Karlsruhe (1992)
23. Panetta, K., Gao, C., Agaian, S., Nercessian, S.: A new reference-based edge map quality measure. IEEE Trans. Syst. Man Cybern. Syst. **46**(11), 1505–1517 (2016)
24. Magnier, B., Le, A., Zogo, A.: A quantitative error measure for the evaluation of roof edge detectors. In: IEEE IST, pp. 429–434 (2016)
25. Freeman, W.T., Adelson, E.H.: The design and use of steerable filters. IEEE TPAMI **13**, 891–906 (1991)
26. Jacob, M., Unser, M.: Design of steerable filters for feature detection using canny-like criteria. IEEE TPAMI **26**(8), 1007–1019 (2004)
27. Hou, X., Yuille, A., Koch, C.: Boundary detection benchmarking: beyond F-measures. In: IEEE CVPR, pp. 2123–2130 (2013)

Medical Image

Similarity Metrics for Intensity-Based Registration Using Breast Density Maps

Eloy García[1]([✉]), Arnau Oliver[1], Yago Diez[2], Oliver Diaz[1], Xavier Lladó[1], Robert Martí[1], and Joan Martí[1]

[1] Institute of Computer Vision and Robotics, University of Girona, Girona, Spain
egarcia@silver.udg.edu
[2] Tokuyama Laboratory GSIS, Tohoku University, Sendai, Japan

Abstract. Intensity-based registration algorithms have been widely used in medical image applications. This type of registration algorithms uses an object function to compute a transformation and optimizes a measure of similarity between the images being registered. The most common similarity metrics used in registration are sum of squared differences, mutual information and normalized cross-correlation. This paper aims to compare these similarity metrics, using common registration algorithms applied to breast density maps registration. To evaluate the results, we use the protocols for evaluation of similarity measures proposed by Škerl et al. They consist in defining a set of random directions in the parameter space of the registration algorithm and compute statistical measures, such as the accuracy, capture range, number of maxima and risk of non-convergence, along these directions. The obtained results show a better performance corresponding to normalized cross-correlation for the rigid registration algorithm, while the sum of squared difference obtains the best result for the B-Spline method.

1 Introduction

Breast density maps is a type of image in which the intensity pixels values correspond to the glandular tissue thickness presented in the mammogram. Figure 1 shows an example of these images, obtained using the commercial software Volpara^{TM}. Establishing a correlation between two density maps, alike to mammograms, can improve the detection and follow-up of breast diseases. This is not an easy task. Due to the different patient positioning during the acquisition, image registration is needed to compensate the errors yielded [4,7].

Several registration algorithms have been proposed to establish spatial correspondence between images [3,5]. The registration problem is expressed as a minimization of an energy composed of a regularization and a similarity term. Registration algorithms can be divided into two categories: feature- and intensity-based algorithms. In particular, intensity-based registration algorithms consist in maximizing the matching criterion, usually a similarity metric between images. This kind of algorithms can be decomposed into three principal components [1]:

– the similarity metric, which specifies the agreement between the images,

© Springer International Publishing AG 2017
L.A. Alexandre et al. (Eds.): IbPRIA 2017, LNCS 10255, pp. 217–225, 2017.
DOI: 10.1007/978-3-319-58838-4_24

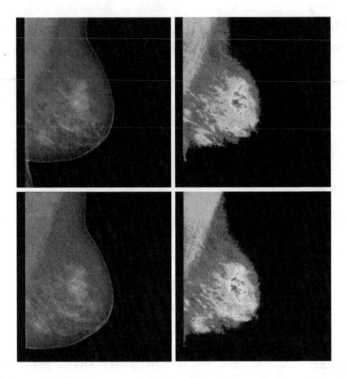

Fig. 1. Pair of repeated mammograms (left), acquired within a short time interval, and their respective density maps (right) computed by the commercial software Volpara^{TM}. Red color represents denser areas (Color figure online).

- the transformation model, which defines the transformation of the source image to match the target,
- the optimization strategy, which improves the parameters of the transformation model, based on the metric.

The definition of the similarity criterion relies on the nature of image gray-level dependencies [6] and, moreover, the most popular optimization algorithms, such as the gradient-descent algorithm, use the surface defined by the metric in the parameter space to reach the optimum. Therefore, the similarity metric is one of the factors that affect the quality of registrations [8]. Intensity-based metrics can define non-convex topologies. Defining a suitable metric reduces the likelihood of obtaining a suboptimal solution by means of locating a small number of maxima, reducing the risk of non-convergence or maximizing the capture range of the global maxima during the optimization. Figure 2 shows a cost-function surface, from a rigid registration method, using the three similarity metric analyzed in our study: sum of squared differences (SSD), mutual information (MI) and normalized cross-correlation (NCC). Notice that the optimal solution does not change widely its position in the search space. However, sub-optimal solutions (i.e. local maxima) are found using some metrics but not others.

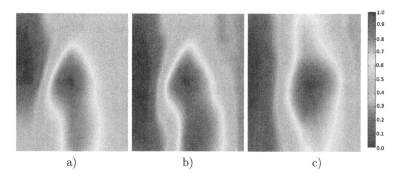

Fig. 2. (a) Sum of squared difference, (b) Mutual information and (c) Normalized cross-correlation applied to measure similarity between two density maps within the search space of a rigid registration process. The higher the values, the higher the agreement between images. The global optimal value is localized in the center of the images, while a local optimum value (red area below the global value) is visible in (b) (Color figure online).

The aim of this paper is to evaluate these three similarity metrics to lead the temporal registration of Volpara^{TM} Density Maps. We perform the registration using two widely used algorithms: affine and B-Spline registration methods. To evaluate the suitability of the metric, we test the protocol for evaluation of similarity measures proposed by Škerl et al. for rigid [8] and non-rigid [9] registration.

The rest of this document is organized as follows: Sect. 2 presents a brief review of the employed methodology, such as the registration algorithms, similarity metrics and evaluation, Sect. 3 describes the results obtained. The paper ends with the discussions and conclusions.

2   Methodology

2.1   Registration Methods

Affine Registration Algorithm. Affine registration carries out the rotation, translation, and scaling over the whole image. It is frequently used as an initialization step for a posterior non-rigid registration, although in some contexts it could also be used as a stand-alone registration tool given that it is less affected by registration artefacts [2].

B-Spline Free-Form (BSFF) Deformation Algorithm. This method uses a mesh of control points that are deformed using B-Spline interpolation looking for the maximization of a similarity measure. The degree of deformation of the mesh can be modeled with the resolution of the mesh. This produces deformation that, although local in nature, maintains coherence between neighboring points [2].

During this work, we use 5×5 nodes on the grid, considering just those within the images and not those corresponding to the boundary conditions.

2.2 Similarity Metrics

Sum of Squared Difference Metric. The SSD metric computes the squared differences between gray intensity values corresponding at each pixel. SSD is defined as:

$$SSD = \frac{1}{N \cdot M} \sum_{(x,y)} (I_1(x,y) - I_2(x,y))^2 \tag{1}$$

where $I_1(x,y)$ and $I_2(x,y)$ represent the intensity gray value -i.e. the breast density thickness- at pixel (x,y) for each image, I_1 and I_2, and $N \cdot M$ is the number of pixels of the images. When both images are identical, the sum of square difference is equal to zero.

Mutual Information Metric. MI is a measure of the mutual dependence between both images, related with Shannon entropy, and defined by the following equation:

$$MI = \sum_{i,j} p_{i,j} log \frac{p_{i,j}}{p_i \cdot p_j} \tag{2}$$

where p_i, p_j are the probability distributions of the individual images and $p_{i,j}$ is the joint probability distribution. During this work, the probabilities are obtained by using a histogram divided into 64 bins. Thus, MI allows to consider non-linear differences in intensity gray values. Regarding the evaluation of similarity, higher mutual information values imply higher agreement between images.

Normalized Cross-Correlation Metric. NCC is a standard statistical measure used to calculate whether two datasets are linearly related. It represents the 2D version of the Pearson's correlation coefficient and it is defined as follows:

$$NCC = \frac{\sum_{(x,y)} (I_1(x,y) - \bar{I}_1)(I_2(x,y) - \bar{I}_2)}{\sqrt{\sum_{(x,y)} (I_1(x,y) - \bar{I}_1)^2} \sqrt{\sum_{(x,y)} (I_2(x,y) - \bar{I}_2)^2}} \tag{3}$$

where $\bar{I}_1$ and $\bar{I}_2$ represent the mean of the intensity pixel values in the images I_1 and I_2 respectively.

2.3 Metric Evaluation

The evaluation protocols, for rigid and non-rigid registration algorithms, proposed by Škerl et al. are based on systematic simulations of the transformation state along random directions in the parameters space of the registration method. The following sections briefly expose these methods. For further references see [8,9].

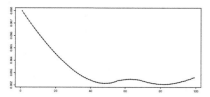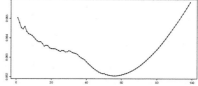

Fig. 3. Normalized SSD along two lines in the parameter space, composed of 100 points. The solution obtained during the registration corresponds to the middle (point number 50). Notice that the maximum similarity is obtained when SSD is the minimum.

Affine Registration Evaluation. Once the affine registration has reached an optimal solution, we can define a hypersphere in the parameter space. Within the hypersphere, we can define a random direction crossing from one side to the other, and traversing the center of the sphere -i.e. the optimal solution- like the radius of a wheel. Finally, we compute the similarity metric using the parameters defined along this direction. Figure 3 shows two of these lines, once the results have been normalized.

During this work, we use 50 random directions, using 100 points per line. The parameter space was defined considering the degrees of freedom of the whole image. Hence, the source image was allowed to slide in the interval $[-L_X, L_X]$ in the X direction, being L_X the length of the target image in the X direction, and $[-L_Y, L_Y]$ in the Y direction, being L_Y the length of the target image in the Y direction. The rotation parameter is defined between $-\pi$ and $+\pi$ radians. Finally, the scale factor vary from 0.5 and 1.5 due to the mammographic acquisition does not allow big changes in the breast shape.

BSFF Deformation Evaluation. In this case, localizing a hypersphere in the parameter space is a more challenging problem. Therefore, to define the direction to obtain the sample point, first, all nodes composing the mesh are initialized using a random displacement from that obtained during the registration. Then each node, consecutively, is taken as a control point. Around the control point, a circle with radius R is defined. Similarly to the previous method, we use this circle to vary the control point position, sampling along one defined direction.

For each node, 20 lines composed of 100 points were defined. In this case, the parameter space was defined in a node-wise way. Nodes are initialized considering the neighborhood, to avoid the overlap or inversion of position between two nodes. Thus, the search space of the node N_i is within the interval $[X_E, X_W]$ in the X direction, being X_W the x position of the node at left and X_E of the node at right, and $[Y_N, Y_S]$ in the Y direction, being Y_N the y position of the node above and Y_S of the node at below.

Statistics. First, during the evaluation, parametric space features and similarity values are normalized to avoid preferred variables. For instance, the translation parameters in millimeters are much larger than the rotation parameters in radians. This fact can induce to an error during the conclusions. To evaluate the similarity metrics, we use the following features:

– Accuracy (ACC), defined as the Euclidean distance between the initial optimal position X_0 and the global maxima $X_{n,max}$ in the line n. If the initial position is the actual global maxima, $ACC = 0$.

$$ACC = ||X_{n,max} - X_0|| \qquad (4)$$

– Distinctiveness of optimum (DO) is the average change of the similarity metric SM within distance r, close to the global maxima. DO shows the sharpening of the similarity metric around the global maxima.

$$DO(r) = \frac{2 * SM(X_{n,max}) - SM(X_{n,max-r/\sigma}) - SM(X_{n,max+r/\sigma})}{2r} \qquad (5)$$

where σ represents the distance between two consecutive points along a probing line.
– Capture range (CR) is the distance between the global maxima and the closest minima along the line.

$$CR = min(||X_{n,max} - X_{n,min}||) \qquad (6)$$

– Number of maxima (NOM) is the number of maxima -i.e. suboptimal solution- in each line. We have changed this feature (originally number of minima) considering that, in our case, the maxima represents a suboptimal solution.
– Risk of Non-convergence (RON) is the average of positive gradients $d_{n,m}$ within distance r from the global maxima in each line.

$$RON(r) = \frac{\sum_{n,m} d_{n,m}}{2r} \qquad (7)$$

Therefore, the better a similarity measure, the smaller the accuracy, number of maxima and risk of non-convergence and the larger the values of capture range and distinctiveness of optimum.

3   Results

The dataset was composed of 21 pairs of mammographic images (42 FFDMs in total) from 21 women, including 14 pairs of CC and 7 pairs of MLO projections. Each image pair corresponds to mammograms acquired within a very short time interval, few minutes. We used the commercial software Volpara^{TM} (Volpara Solutions[1], Wellington, New Zealand) to extract the density map of the mammogram. Both images were registered using affine registration and BSFF deformations. All registration methods were implemented using the InsightToolkit (ITK v.4.8.0) libraries. The optimization followed a gradient

---

[1] http://volparasolutions.com/.

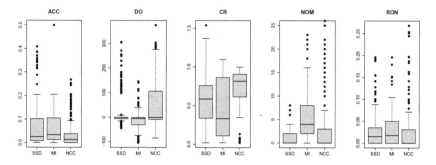

Fig. 4. Statistical measures for affine registration. The better a similarity measure, the smaller the ACC, NOM and RON and the larger the values of DO and CR.

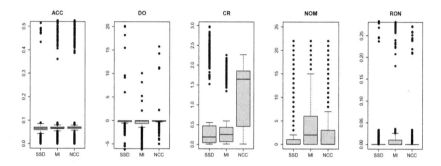

Fig. 5. Statistical measures for B-Spline registration. The better a similarity measure, the smaller the ACC, NOM and RON and the larger the values of DO and CR.

descent approach, while linear interpolation was performed for pixel interpolation. Data analysis and statistical tests were carried out using the statistical software R (v.3.0.3).

Figure 4 shows the results obtained for affine registration. The median and quartile deviation of the boxplot represent the accuracy and robustness for each metric. For instance, in this case, NCC shows a better performance in all of cases. The median of the NCC distributions for ACC, NOM and RON are smaller than those corresponding to the other metrics and, similarly, they are bigger for CR and DO. However, the same distribution shows a higher quartile deviation for NOM and a large number of outliers for NOM and RON.

On the other hand, Fig. 5 shows the results corresponding to the B-Spline registration. In this case, the results obtained with SSD shows a better performance in ACC, NOM and RON; NCC obtains the best results of CR.

4   Discussion and Conclusion

In this work, we have evaluated the three most common image similarity metrics used for intensity-based registration of density maps. To achieve this goal, we have used the protocols proposed by Škerl et al. [8,9]. In our experience, these protocols show a different performance with respect to the registration algorithm. During the evaluation of the affine registration, the protocol shows a good performance. Modifying the registration parameters allows a sampling of all the features in the hyperspace and an accurate interpretation of the parameter space around the localized optimal solution. Furthermore, ACC, CR and NOM show NCC as a robust and stable metric to lead the affine registration. The risk of non-convergence is smaller while the capture range and the accuracy of this metric is high, defining NCC as the preferred metric.

During the B-Spline registration, the number of nodes has a big impact in the likelihood of localizing a suboptimal solution. The more nodes, the smaller the local deformation and, therefore, the higher the number of maxima at each line. Furthermore, the nodes situated in the black background of the mammogram have a small impact over the metric but high in the statistics exposed. For instance, a large number of points in the black background could produce a high ACC because the movement of these points have a small impact over the final result of the similarity metric. However, these points are considered similarly to those with a high impact over the metric in the statistics. We consider that the proposed protocol is not suitable in this case. Establishing the impact of each node is mandatory to avoid wrong results or misinterpretations.

Finally, the metrics used show different behavior with respect to the registration algorithms. While NCC shows a clearly better performance during the affine registration, SSD may be the best option for B-Spline registration, due to the better performance obtained for ACC, NOM and RON. However, there is not a significant difference with respect to those obtained using NCC, which obtains a clearly better value for CR.

Acknowledgement. This research has been partially supported from the University of Girona (MPC UdG 2016/022 grant) and the Ministry of Economy and Competitiveness of Spain, under project SMARTER (DPI2015-68442-R) and the FPI grant BES-2013-065314.

References

1. Crum, W.R., Hartkens, T., Hill, D.: Non-rigid image registration: theory and practice. Br. J. Radiol. **77**, 140–153 (2004)
2. Diez, Y., Oliver, A., Lladó, X., Freixenet, J., Martí, J., Vilanova, J.C., Martí, R.: Revisiting intensity-based image registration appplied to mammography. IEEE Trans. Inf. Technol. Biomed. **15**(5), 716–725 (2011)
3. Guo, Y., Sivaramakrishna, R., Lu, C.C., Suri, J.S., Laxminarayan, S.: Breast image registration techniques: a survey. Med. Biol. Eng. Comput. **44**(1–2), 15–26 (2006)
4. Hill, D.L., Batchelor, P.G., Holden, M., Hawkes, D.J.: Medical image registration. Phys. Med. Biol. **46**(3), R1 (2001)
5. Maintz, J.A., Viergever, M.A.: A survey of medical image registration. Med. Image Anal. **2**(1), 1–36 (1998)
6. Roche, A., Malandain, G., Ayache, N.: Unifying maximum likelihood approaches in medical image registration. Ph.D. thesis, Inria (1999)

7. Rueckert, D., Schnabel, J.A.: Medical image registration. In: Deserno, T.M. (ed.) Biomedical Image Processing. Biological and Medical Physics, Biomedical Engineering, pp. 131–154. Springer, Heidelberg (2010)
8. Škerl, D., Likar, B., Pernus, F.: A protocol for evaluation of similarity measures for rigid registration. IEEE Trans. Med. Imaging **25**(6), 779–791 (2006)
9. Škerl, D., Likar, B., Pernus, F.: A protocol for evaluation of similarity measures for non-rigid registration. Med. Image Anal. **12**, 42–54 (2008)

Registration of Breast Surface Data Before and After Surgical Intervention

Sílvia Bessa[(✉)] and Hélder P. Oliveira

INESC TEC, Faculdade de Engenharia, Universidade do Porto, Porto, Portugal
{snbessa,helder.f.oliveira}@inesctec.pt

Abstract. Surgery planing of breast cancer interventions is gaining importance among physicians, who recognize value in discussing the possible aesthetic outcomes of surgery with patients. Research is been propelled to create patient-specific breast models, but breast image registration algorithms are still limited, particularly for the purpose of matching pre- and post-surgical data of patient's breast surfaces. Yet, this is a fundamental task to learn prediction models of breast healing process after surgery. In this paper, a coarse-to-fine registration strategy is proposed to match breast surface data acquired before and after surgery. Methods are evaluated in their ability to register surfaces in an anatomical reliable way, and results suggest proper alignment adequated to be used as input to train deformable models.

Keywords: Data registration · Surface fitting · Surgical planing

1 Introduction

Medical data analysis often requires fusing information from more than two images: images can be acquired at different times, from distinct viewpoints or by different modalities, which requires proper image registration methods to combine their complementary information into a single model. Several methods have been proposed to solve the problem of image registration, but this task is particularly challenging for breast data, due to the inhomogeneous, anisotropic nature of the soft-tissue within the breast, and its inherent non-rigidity characteristics [1].

In recent years, the usefulness of decision support systems is being acknowledged by physicians, which rely on them for more educated decisions, especially when the communication between doctors and patients has to be considered. In particular, the planning of breast cancer surgery, and prediction of breast deformations arising from breast cancer treatments, is gaining relevance in the medical field. The treatment of breast cancer no longer aims solely on eliminating the tumour, but also considers the impact of the aesthetic results of surgery on the quality of life (QoL) of the patient. In fact, the involvement of women in the treatment decision process has been proven benefit to accept the resulting outcomes. This highlights the necessity of creating tools to predict the outcomes

© Springer International Publishing AG 2017
L.A. Alexandre et al. (Eds.): IbPRIA 2017, LNCS 10255, pp. 226–234, 2017.
DOI: 10.1007/978-3-319-58838-4_25

of each possible option, and provide patients with visual clues of the expected results for more conscientious decisions [2]. To develop a breast surgery planning tool, it is necessary to create 3D models of the patient's breasts. However, breast image registration techniques have been primarily focused on combining multimodal radiological images for screening and diagnosis. Few works have been focused on registring surface information of pre- and post-surgical, although it is an important task when creating surgical planing applications.

The success of registration methodologies depends on the choice of the geometric transformation, which highly depends on the nature of the data to be registered. Registration techniques can use rigid or nonrigid transformations, but most medical image registration approaches are based on the latter, given the deformable nature of most of the anatomical parts of the human body. Among rigid registration techniques, Principal Component Analysis (PCA) and Singular Value Decomposition (SVD) have been used to compute an initial geometric alignment of data, but a fine registration is commonly accomplished with the Iterative Closest Point (ICP) or its variants [3]. One of the few works that address the registration of breast surfaces is the work of Schuller et al. [4], which describes a multi-step procedure to find correspondences between point clouds of pendant and compressed breasts. Point clouds were obtained from CT data, and a Finite Element Model was applied to simulate the compression of breasts. The initial correspondences between pendant and compressed data was found using ICP, but only applied to nipple regions and breast regions near the torso. Then, the symmetric nearest neighbour procedure proposed by Papademetris et al. [5] was used to identify point correspondences between the remain volume of the breast, and propagate the initial registration.

The choice of a registration algorithm generally depends on characteristics such as accuracy, computational cost, but most of all, it heavily depends on the data used. For instance, when aligning surfaces to learn breast deformation models from real data, non-rigid methods should be used with care. Pre and post-surgical data can actually differ in volume and shape, and these differences should remain intact after registration because models have capture that transformations. Moreover, nipple should not be used to match surfaces, because sometimes nipple is lost during surgery. In this work, the problem of registering the 3D surface data of pre- and post-operated breasts is adressed, using rigid registration methods. Results suggest that proper alignment of surfaces is accomplished, enabling the use of real data to learn breast deformations models useful for surgical planing.

2 Proposed Methodology

To register pre- and post-surgical surfaces of breasts, a coarse-to-fine registration strategy is proposed. In the coarse registration stage, breast surfaces are geometrically aligned only by translating their centers of mass to the origin of the coordinate center. A strategy based on fitting a plane to surface is also explored to determine the orientation between the two point clouds, and compared with PCA alignment. The fine registration of data is accomplished with ICP.

(a) Pre-Surgery Torso   (b) Post-Surgery Torso (c) Pre-Surgery   (d) Post-Surgery

Fig. 1. Point clouds of the torso and **operated** breast (patient's left) before and after surgery. Breast data was centered for visualization purposes.

Figure 1 shows an example of pre- and post-surgical data that has to be registered before learning healing process models, evidencing the differences in breast volumes and shapes. During surgery, the tumour and a margin of healthy tissue are removed, which reduces the volume of the breast. Then, healing process occurs which lasts about one year before the breast stabilizes in its new shape. The tissues usually retract to adapt to the new internal structure, causing the breast to go up. This translates to deformations that have impact less upper than lower profiles of the breast [6] Therefore, for modelling the breast shape changes after the healing process, some constraints have to be imposed on the alignment of pre- and post-surgical data. Instead of using all volume of the breast, one can argue that top profiles are more reliable to compute the transformation between that two point clouds, while preserving the expected anatomical behaviour. In fact, this was the followed strategy: both coarse and fine registration techniques were applied using different top profiles of the breast, and results were compared with the registrations using all volume of the breasts.

(a) Pre-Surgery Torso (b) Post-Surgery Torso (c) Pre-Surgery   (d) Post-Surgery

Fig. 2. Differences in the segmentation of a **non-operated** breast point cloud before and after surgery. Breast data was centered for visualization purposes.

Another challenge arises from limitations of the breast segmentation strategy [7]. Although registration is being computed using only the top areas of the breast, there is no guarantee that the segmentation algorithm outputs exactly the same surface from data acquired at different instants of times. Figure 2 shows an example of pre- and post-breast segmentations of a non-operated breast. Despite the natural shape of the breast did not change, a different segmentation resulted

Table 1. Scenarios explored in the proposed methodology. Note that all combinations of pre- and post-breast top areas were considered.

Registration srategies		Breast top area (%)	
Coarse	Fine	Pre-surgical	Post-surgical
Centroids	ICP	{20, 30, ... ,100 }	{20, 30, ... ,100}
Plane Fitting			
PCA			

from data acquired before and one year after surgery. To overcome this limitation, and for each breast, different areas of the top profile are used to register pre- and post-data. In detail, percentages between 20% up to 100% were considered to define the top profile of the breasts, with increments of 10%.

Table 1 summarizes the different scenarios considered in the proposed methodology.

3   Experimental Results

The proposed methodology was evaluated on a real database containing breast point clouds of 30 patients, using euclidean and Hausdorff distances (Eq. 1, calculated in both directions (Pre → Post, and Post → Pre).

$$h(A, B) = \max_{a \in A} \min_{b \in B} ||a - b|| \tag{1}$$

where A and B are point clouds, and $||.||$ is the euclidean distance.

Point clouds were obtained by scanning patients with Microsoft Kinect, followed by 3D reconstruction algorithm proposed in [8], and the breast segmentation strategy described in [7]. Pre- and post-surgery data is available for all patients. Data is acquired with one year interval, but no ground truth is available for assessing the quality of the registration procedure. As consequence, an exploratory analysis of the results is conducted instead, in which different percentages of the breasts are used to evaluate the registration procedure. For instance, after registration, the distances between the two point clouds are computed using equal percentages of pre- and post-breast data, between 20% and 100% of the breast points, with increments of 20%. Average and Standard Deviation of these distances are then used to search for the extents of pre- and post-data that should be used to compute the transformation between the two point clouds. The idea is that the best registration strategy is the one that aligns data with small (low average) and similar errors (low standard deviation) in all portions of the breast. Visual inspection of the results is also performed to confirm that the alignment is anatomically reliable.

In the proposed methodology, registration is constrained to top profiles of breasts. The top profile of the breast is defined in the coronal plane, and different

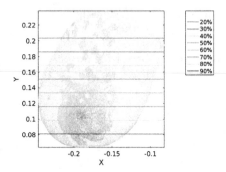

Fig. 3. The top profile of the breast is defined in the y-plane of the point cloud. Different percentage of points are considered.

percentage of points can be selected. The percentage of points that constitute the top profile of pre- and post-surgery breasts can be different (Fig. 3).

The top profiles of breasts are brought close in a coarse registration stage that considers three strategies: (i) simply center point clouds based on the centroids of the top profile of the breast, or (ii) find the rotation angle between pre- and post-data using either (iia) PCA axes or (iib) the fitting planes. Results show that despite being commonly used, PCA can produce unacceptable results when the main variance axes do not share the same direction in both point clouds (Fig. 4a), and PCA results were discarded from subsequent analysis. On the other hand, no significant differences ($p - value = 0.9364$, $IC = 5\%$) are found between the initial alignment based on centroids or fitted planes, when combined fine registration step with ICP. Figure 4b and c show the registration results of aligning pre- and post- top profile of operated breast of Fig. 1, with strategies (ii) and (iii), respectively. Note that registration results are better when using fitted planes, but the differences between centroid and plane alignment decrease when higher percentages of top breast profile are used. Yet, one can argue that a coarse fitting based on the fitting of planes to surfaces is more robust to data variability, and such strategy is advised instead of simply centering data.

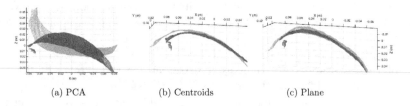

(a) PCA   (b) Centroids   (c) Plane

Fig. 4. Coarse-registration results with pre- (green) and post- (purple) top profiles (30%) of the breasts from Fig. 1. (Color figure online)

Different combinations of pre- and post-top breast areas were also considered to tickle the problem of possible different breast segmentations. However, results showed that pre- and post-top areas of breasts that differed more than 30% lead to poor results, and such combinations were no longer considered.

Regarding the overall performance of the proposed methodology, the values of distances computed in both directions were compared to infer if pre- and post-surgical breasts had different sizes. Although no significant differences were found between average euclidean distances ($p-value = 0.0889\%$, $IC = 5\%$), Hausdorff distances differed according to direction ($p - value = 0.0255\%$, $IC = 5\%$). An additional one-sided t-test additionally further revealed that Hausdorff distances computed in $Post \rightarrow Pre$ direction have higher values than in the opposite direction ($p - value = 0.0128\%$, $IC = 5\%$), which confirms the expected, that pre-surgical breasts are usually bigger than post-surgical ones.

Analysing the average euclidean distances for all combinations of pre- and post-top breast areas, computed in $Post \rightarrow Pre$ direction, it is trend that the combination of equal profiles of pre- and post-breasts have lower distances (Fig. 5a), in series using up to 60% post-breast areas. For the remaining series, though, the optimal value is found when post-top areas are combined with pre-top areas with less 10%. Note that when a higher area of post-surgery breast is used, one increases the probability of calculating registration with surfaces of different size: breast healing process usually affects more the lower profiles of the breast. As consequence, increasing the amount of breast for registration increases the chances of getting high distances between pre- and post- surgery breasts after transformation.

Figure 5b shows the results when equal portions of pre- and post-top breasts are used. The lower average euclidean distance is found when 60% of pre- and post-surgery breasts are considered in the registration, also having the low standard deviation value. The highest distances, both average and standard deviation values, are found when full breasts are used. In comparison, the average distance decreases when using low portions of breasts, but high values of standard deviation are found. This was the expected behaviour and what motivated the search for the best combination of pre- and post- top breasts areas in the first place. When using small portions of the breast, the top profiles of the breast can be very well aligned, but there is no restrain on how the remaining portions of the breasts are aligned, which causes high standard deviations. On the other hand, when full breasts are used, breasts are aligned by their lower profiles, and distances between the top areas increase. Please refer to Fig. 6 for visual support of these results.

Table 2 also provides additional metrics for evaluating the proposed registration methodology. The best average euclidean distances are found when intermediate portions of the breasts are used (bold values), regardless of the direction. As expected, due to the differences in breast sizes, Hausdorff distances are high in both directions. Yet, the analysis of Hausdorff distances evidences two interesting aspects: (i) their lowest small standard deviation values are found when full breasts although the corespondent average values are maximum and (ii) the best combination of breasts portions differed with direction ($Pre \rightarrow Post$ direction the best is 20/20%, while on the opposite direction is 60/60%). The first

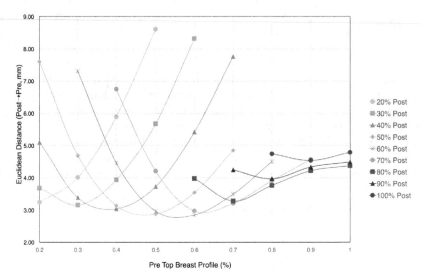

(a) All combinations of pre/post percentages.

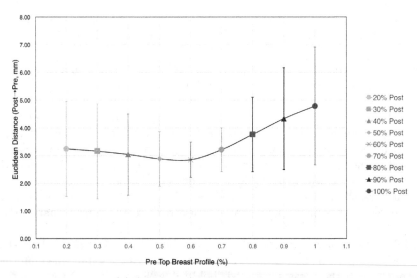

(b) Equal pre/post percentages only

Fig. 5. Average euclidean distances ($Post \rightarrow Pre$) for different combinations of pre- and post-top profile percentages.

Table 2. Euclidean and Hausdorff distances of several pairs of top profile breasts. Bold highlights the best average and standard deviation values of euclidean distances.

Top profile (%)		Pre → Post (mm)				Post → Pre (mm)			
		Euclidean		Hausdorff		Euclidean		Hausdorff	
Pre	Post	μ	σ	μ	σ	μ	σ	μ	σ
20	20	2.84	1.39	15.27	4.83	3.24	1.71	19.83	8.12
30	30	2.87	1.20	16.72	3.66	3.16	1.71	19.64	9.25
40	40	2.82	0.95	17.16	3.23	3.04	1.46	19.20	8.98
50	50	**2.61**	0.65	15.99	2.63	2.88	0.98	18.75	7.71
60	60	2.66	**0.53**	15.85	1.78	**2.85**	**0.63**	18.30	5.94
70	70	2.96	0.83	17.01	1.32	3.21	0.79	18.94	4.44
80	80	3.55	1.34	18.98	1.11	3.76	1.34	20.01	3.20
90	90	4.10	1.80	20.32	0.81	4.33	1.84	21.46	2.51
100	100	4.53	2.13	21.24	0.73	4.79	2.13	22.41	2.49

aspect emphasize the need to compare both average and standard deviations to select the best registration strategy, while the second might be a consequence of pre-surgery breasts being systematically bigger than post-surgery ones. Nevertheless, results are in line with the stated above and suggest that in average, the best strategy to register breasts after surgery and healing process, would comprise the selection of top-breast profiles with extents of 60%.

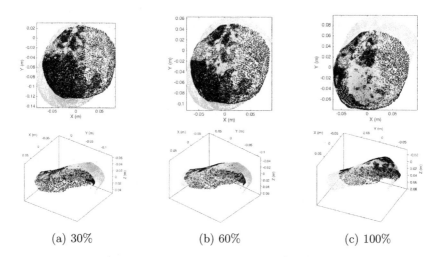

(a) 30%   (b) 60%   (c) 100%

Fig. 6. Results of pre- (skin color) and post- (black) breast registration using different extents of top profiles. (Color figure online)

4   Conclusions

The registration of pre- and post-surgery data of breasts is an essential task to develop breast healing process models useful fro surgery planing. However, this task poses some challenges, namely the lack of landmarks before and after surgery, in addition to differences in size and segmentation. To overcome this limitations, a registration strategy that uses only top profiles of breasts is proposed, and different combinations of top breast areas were explored. Results suggest that such strategy outputs good pre- and post- surgery alignments, with the better results obtained when similar and intermediate portions of pre- and post-top breasts are used. To best of knowledge, this is the first work addressing the problem of registering data of breast before and after surgery.

Acknowledgements. This work was funded by the Project "NanoSTIMA: Macro–to–Nano Human Sensing: Towards Integrated Multimodal Health Monitoring and Analytics/NORTE-01-0145-FEDER-000016" financed by the North Portugal Regional Operational Programme (NORTE 2020), under the PORTUGAL 2020 Partnership Agreement, and through the European Regional Development Fund (ERDF), and also by Fundação para a Ciência e a Tecnologia (FCT) within PhD grant number SFRH/BD/115616/2016.

References

1. Guo, Y., Suri, J., Sivaramakrishna, R.: Image registration for breast imaging: a review. In: 2005 IEEE Engineering in Medicine and Biology 27th Annual Conference, pp. 3379–3382. IEEE (2006)
2. Tőkés, T., Torgyík, L., Szentmártoni, G., Somlai, K., Tóth, A., Kulka, J., Dank, M.: Primary systemic therapy for breast cancer: does the patient's involvement in decision-making create a new future? Patient Educ. Couns. **98**(6), 695–703 (2015)
3. Bellekens, B., Spruyt, V., Berkvens, R., Penne, R., Weyn, M.: A benchmark survey of rigid 3D point cloud registration algorithm. Int. J. Adv. Intell. Syst. **8**, 118–127 (2015)
4. Schuler III., D.R., Ou, J.J., Barnes, S.L., Miga, M.I.: Automatic surface correspondence methods for a deformed breast. In: Medical Imaging. International Society for Optics and Photonics, p. 614125 (2006)
5. Papademetris, X., Sinusas, A.J., Dione, D.P., Constable, R.T., Duncan, J.S.: Estimation of 3D left ventricular deformation from medical images using biomechanical models. IEEE Trans. Med. Imaging **21**(7), 786–800 (2002)
6. Cardoso, M.J., Oliveira, H., Cardoso, J.: Assessing cosmetic results after breast conserving surgery. J. Surg. Oncol. **110**(1), 37–44 (2014)
7. Oliveira, H.P., Cardoso, J.S., Magalhães, A.T., Cardoso, M.J.: A 3D low-cost solution for the aesthetic evaluation of breast cancer conservative treatment. Comput. Methods Biomech. Biomed. Eng.: Imag. Vis. **2**(2), 90–106 (2014)
8. Costa, P., Monteiro, J.P., Zolfagharnasab, H., Oliveira, H.P.: Tessellation-based coarse registration method for 3D reconstruction of the female torso. In: 2014 IEEE International Conference on Bioinformatics and Biomedicine (BIBM), pp. 301–306. IEEE (2014)

Visualization of Distinct DNA Regions of the Modern Human Relatively to a Neanderthal Genome

Diogo Pratas$^{(\boxtimes)}$, Morteza Hosseini, Raquel M. Silva, Armando J. Pinho, and Paulo J.S.G. Ferreira

IEETA/DETI/iBiMED, University of Aveiro, Aveiro, Portugal
{pratas,seyedmorteza,raquelsilva,ap,pjf}@ua.pt

Abstract. Species-specific DNA regions are segments that are unique or share high dissimilarity relatively to close species. Their discovery is important, because they allow the localization of evolutionary traits that are often related to novel functionalities and, sometimes, diseases.

We have detected distinct DNA regions specific in the modern human, when compared to a Neanderthal high-quality genome sequence obtained from a bone of a Siberian woman. The bone is around 50,000 years old and the DNA raw data totalizes more than 418 GB. Since the data size required for localizing efficiently such events is very high, it is not practical to store the model on a table or hash table. Thus, we propose a probabilistic method to map and visualize those regions. The time complexity of the method is linear. The computational tool is available at http://pratas.github.io/chester.

The results, computed in approximately two days using a single CPU core, show several regions with documented neanderthal absent regions, namely genes associated with the brain (neurotransmiters and synapses), hearing, blood, fertility and the immune system. However, it also shows several undocumented regions, that may express new functions linked with the evolution of the modern human.

Keywords: DNA patterns · Bloom filters · Ancient DNA · Paleogenomics

1 Introduction

Given a set of books and a text, the question "Is this text unique, i.e., absent from each and every book?" poses no fundamental difficulties. The problem becomes much more difficult when we are given a very large collection of text *fragments*, in random order, and containing a large number of changes (substitutions, editions and deletions). The question now is: "Identify and locate in these books all the unique segments, not present in any of these *fragments*". We have shown a way to proceed when the fragments can be assembled in reasonably large texts [1]. Others have even proposed a distance [2]. However, if the volume of the data

© Springer International Publishing AG 2017
L.A. Alexandre et al. (Eds.): IbPRIA 2017, LNCS 10255, pp. 235–242, 2017.
DOI: 10.1007/978-3-319-58838-4_26

is very large, with fragments very small, typically from 30 to 300 symbols, and in random order, new challenges arise. This paper proposes solutions to these challenges, in the context of the recent field of computational paleogenomics, using ancient DNA.

Until a few years ago, it was only possible to obtain DNA sequences from present-day species. Mostly due to the works of Pääbo's group on methods and techniques for retrieving DNA sequences from archaeological and paleontological remains, the first *time travels* to ancient DNA hominins became possible [3–5].

One of the closest and most interesting extinct hominid groups, relative to modern humans, is the Neanderthal. Neanderthals populated Eurasia from 350,000 ± 50,000 to 35,000 ± 5,000 years ago. The availablility of Neanderthal sequences emerged as pieces [3–5], complete mitochondrial [6] and genome draft sequences [7].

The first public *complete* Neanderthal genome was released on 2010 [8], although sequenced with a low coverage. It was acquired from a woman toe phalanx bone with approximately 50,000 years, found in the Denisova Cave, in the Altai mountains of Siberia. This finding made it possible to analyze the *complete* Neanderthal whole genome at a computational level. The high coverage version (∼30-fold) of the Neanderthal genome was released in 2014 [9].

We use the high coverage whole Neanderthal genome (raw data) to localize and visualize distinct regions of the modern human DNA, using a modern human reference assembly, GRC37 (https://www.ncbi.nlm.nih.gov/grc). Recent reports have suggested that modern humans interbred with Neanderthals when they arrived to Europe [10]. This and the similarity between the Neanderthal and human genomes means that any specific, unique regions in the DNA of modern humans may be of very limited extent.

The detection of these regions, using ancient DNA, is a very complex challenge, for the following main four reasons:

1. The large volume of data involved in the analysis (>418 GB);
2. The need to deal with raw data: ancient DNA is not assembled (random order);
3. Contamination of ancient DNA samples [11];
4. High degree of substitutions in the ancient DNA data, mostly caused by PCR amplifications [12] and postmortem degradation [13].

Aware of these problems, we propose in the next section an unsupervised, probabilistic method that is alignment-free with respect to the ancient DNA. The method uses a model that is able to trade off precision and space/time resources, maintaining reasonable precision values. After describing the method, we show its results: an exhaustive identification of DNA regions that are found in the DNA of modern humans but not on Neanderthal DNA. Finally, we present some conclusions.

2   Method

The straighforward approach to solve this problem is the following: lookup each word of size k (k-mer) found in modern human DNA sequence in the Neanderthal whole data. Clearly, this approach is totally unfeasible, because, for each word, we would have to perform a search on the entire ancient data (>418 GB). For this reason, we need to invert the problem [14].

The fundamental idea of our method is the following: imagine that there is a model able to capture all the possible existing words found in the Neanderthal data. This would enable us to determine if words from the modern human DNA sequences are unique or not: we would only have to find out whether they exist in the model or not. Furthermore, we would be able to localize the unique words with precision, because—unlike the ancient DNA data—the modern DNA is assembled.

The crucial task here is of course the design of the model. That is the problem to which we now turn.

2.1   Choosing the Model

Given the large volume of the non-assembled data, a good model is crucial for an efficient computation. If one uses a binary vector to store all the possible entries indicating if a certain k-mer exists or not in the sequence, we would need 4^k bits. For $k = 30$, it would require 128 petabytes of memory, which is impracticable on current computers. Basing the model on a data structure such as a hash table would certainly be more reasonable, but the memory usage becomes dependent on the number of inserted elements. In this case, we could need over 284 billion entries. This is still unfeasible in computers with 256 GB of memory. Note that although there is redundancy with a coverage of ∼30, the high degree of substitutions in the ancient DNA data creates a new range of additional words that need to be stored in the hash table.

A third option is a probabilistic data structure, namely a Bloom filter [15], which trades space resources by precision. We have determined that a suitably large Bloom filter, with the optimum number of hash functions, can provide precisions very close to the deterministic approach at a fraction of the memory cost.

The number of elements that need to be presented to the Bloom filter, g, in this case $g = 284,388,216,658$, will be handled by a Bloom filter based on a vector of dimension m. For proper working, the condition $m \geq g$ must be respected. The number of hash functions, h, that minimizes the probability of false positives, is approximately given by

$$h = \frac{m}{g} \ln 2. \tag{1}$$

Asymptotically, for a given false positive probability p, the length m of a Bloom filter is proportional to the number of elements being filtered, g. For finite values, we have

$$p \leq \left(1 - e^{-h(g+0.5)/(m-1)}\right)^h. \qquad (2)$$

For the case of multiple hash functions, the method uses universal hashing, given by $f_i(x) = (ax+b) \mod q$, where a and b are two large pseudo-random numbers, different for each i, and q is a prime number such that $q \geq m$.

2.2 Algorithm

After setting the parameters of the size of the Bloom filter (m), the threshold (t) and the k-mer size (k), the method works as follows:

– For each ancient DNA sequence (sN_i):
  • Given m, calculate the number of optimal hash functions (h), using Eq. 1;
  • The probability p is calculated using Eq. 2 and the rounded value of h;
  • Using a slidding window, the model updates each possible k-mer in the Bloom filter;
  • Freeze the model (stop updating).
  • For each human reference chromosomal sequence (sH_i):
    * On the frozen model, search for each k-mer and also for the inverted complemented k-mer, storing the result as a boolean in a file (bH_i);
  • Do an exclusive OR on each index element of each boolean file (bH_i) and store the result in a global boolean file (bH);
  • Filter the global boolean file array (bH), given a certain window, and store it in a file containing reals for each element (fH).
  • Segment the filtered results (fH), according to a threshold t, and store them in a file (pH), along with their relative positions;
– Read the relative positions of the regions from each file stored (pH_i) and paint these in an image.

The disk writes are required mainly because of the volume of data. Thus, computers with disks having a fast access time will provide better performance.

Note that the time complexity of the method is linear in the number of ancient DNA sequences (sN) times n. Therefore, if we concatenate all the sN_i sequences in a single one, the time complexity looses the constant and becomes n. However, for a very large volume of data, setting a Bloom filter without increasing its size increases the probability of false positives. As such, this is a trade-off game.

2.3 Implementation

We have implemented the method in a fully automatic command line tool (CHESTER), written in the C language, so that it can be portable across multiple operating systems. The tool is divided into three programs: CHESTER-map (for mapping the regions), CHESTER-filter (for filtering and segmenting the regions) and CHESTER-visual (for visualizing the regions). The method can be applied to any genomic sequence, in FASTA, FASTQ or SEQ (ACGTN) format. Filtering and visual parameter setting is also available in the program. It can be accessed, under GPLv3 license (free for research studies), at http://pratas.github.io/chester.

3   Results

For the results reported in this paper, we have included one script, available at https://raw.githubusercontent.com/pratas/chester/master/ancient/runNeanderthalGRC37.sh, that allows replicating the entire results under a Linux OS.

For the analysis in this paper, we have used a Bloom filter with size of 64 GB ($m = 549, 755, 813, 888$). The maximum probability of a false positive, p, was 0.008205. We have split the Neanderthal whole genome into 5 parts, where $sN = 5$ and, hence, using a complexity time of $5n$. In our server (Intel Xeon CPU E7320 at 2.1 GHz), it took approximately 51 h to run the full experiment (without parallelization).

The full map is shown in Fig. 1. As it can be seen, there are multiple regions of singularity/divergence. Comparison with the supplementary information 19b of [9] shows that we have found more regions. This results from the deeper filter used here, namely with 0.95, and while Prufer *et al.* have focused on the regions that had 20-fold excess over randomized rank assignments, we used the whole regions. Moreover, times are much higher for their analysis.

We have found, for thresholds of 0.85, 0.90 and 0.95, respectively, 125, 170 and 2169 regions. From the 170 regions (threshold = 0.90), we have searched for genes present in at least half of the region. From those, we have detected: spermatogenesis associated 45 (149643, C1, protein coding), metastasis associated 1 family member 3 (57504, C2, protein coding), major facilitator superfamily domain containing 6 (54842, C2, protein coding), cell adhesion molecule 2 (253559, C3, protein coding), calsyntenin 2 (64084, C3, protein coding), LOC100287290 (100287290, C3, protein coding), sperm tail PG-rich repeat containing 2 (285555, C4, protein coding), TBC1 domain containing kinase (93627, C4, protein coding), pyroglutamylated RFamide peptide receptor (84109, C4, protein coding), KIAA0825 (285600, C5, protein coding), complement C4B (Chido blood group) (721, C6, protein coding), contact in associated protein-like 2 (26047, C7, protein coding), CUB and Sushi multiple domains 1 (64478, C8, protein coding), POTE ankyrin domain family member A (340441, C8, protein coding), leucine rich repeat and Ig domain containing 2 (158038, C9, protein coding), MAM and LDL receptor class A domain containing 1 (340895, C10, protein coding), myosin IIIA (53904, C10, protein coding), chromosome 10 open reading frame 11 (83938, C10, protein coding), MRGPRG antisense RNA 1 (283303, C11, ncRNA), phosphodiesterase 3B (5140, C11, protein coding), ELKS/RAB6-interacting/CAST family member 1 (23085, C12, protein coding), OVOS (408186, C12, protein coding), single-pass membrane protein with coiled-coil domains 2 (341346, C12, protein coding), synaptotagmin 1 (6857, C12, protein coding), HEAT repeat containing 4 (399671, C14, protein coding), neurexin 3 (9369, C14, protein coding), immunoglobulin heavy locus (3492, C14, protein coding), methyltransferase like 22 (79091, C16, protein coding), sorting nexin 29 (92017, C16, protein coding), envoplakin like (645027, C17, protein coding), BCAS3, microtubule associated cell migration factor (54828, C17, protein coding), BCL2, apoptosis regulator (596, C18, protein coding), coiled-coil domain containing 102B (79839, C18, protein coding), trans-2,3-enoyl-CoA reductase (9524, C19, protein coding), breast

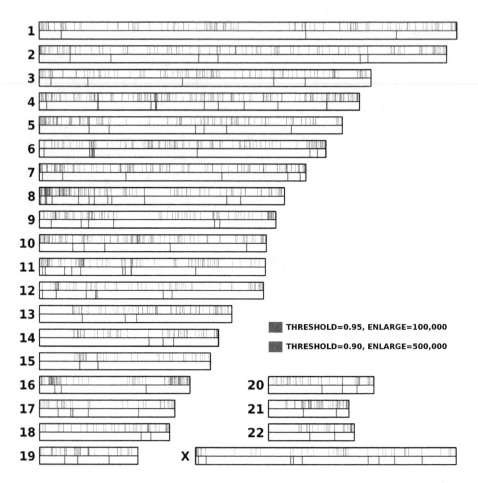

Fig. 1. Modern human chromosomal singular regions relatively to a Neanderthal. CHESTER-map ran with $k = 30$, while CHESTER-filter with "-u 100 -w 20000". Different colors represent specific running parameters, described in the figure. The "ENLARGE" represents a region that is increased with a certain number of bases only for visualization purposes.

carcinoma amplified sequence 1 (8537, C20, protein coding), ASMTL antisense RNA 1 (80161, CX, ncRNA), neuroligin 4, X-linked (57502, CX, protein coding), acyl-CoA synthetase long-chain family member 4 (2182, CX, protein coding), sarcoma antigen 2 and pseudogene (644717, CX, pseudo).

The majority are protein coding regions, while a lower part is distributed on pseudo-genes and ncRNA. From the coding regions, we highlight the following: spermatogenesis associated 45 (149643), myosin IIIA (53904), ELKS/RAB6-interacting/CAST family member 1 (23085) and synaptotagmin 1 (6857). The gene spermatogenesis associated 45 (149643) has been described recently as having an important role in reproductive efficacy and success [16]. The gene myosin

IIIA (53904) encodes a protein that plays an important role in hearing in humans. Three different recessive, loss of function mutations in the encoded protein have been shown to cause nonsyndromic progressive hearing loss [17]. The protein that is encoded by ELKS/RAB6-interacting/CAST family member 1 (23085) is a member of a family of RIM-binding proteins. RIMs are active zone proteins that regulate neurotransmitter release. Changes in the gene have been associated with autism [18]. The gene synaptotagmin 1 (6857) encodes a protein that participates in triggering neurotransmitter release at the synapses [19].

Although these results look very interesting, we need to be aware that the amplification of the sequencing process might be creating several substitutional mutations, namely C→T and G→A [20]. Therefore, future work on these results are needed to study if the differences between these regions may or not be given by these characteristics, and, if yes, to assess its impact.

4   Conclusions

We have proposed a method (and tool) to detect distinct regions of the modern human DNA, when compared to a Neanderthal high-quality genome with more than 418 GB of raw data. The method uses a fully automatic probabilistic approach to map and visualize these regions. The time complexity of the method is linear, being able to compute the results using only two days in a single core CPU.

The results show several regions that are associated with the brain, namely neurotransmiters and synapses, hearing, blood, fertility, immune system, among others. These regions may now be studied according to their expression and meaning in the evolution path. Other regions have also been detected that, although undocumented, may reveal unique functions in the Neanderthal or in the modern human.

Acknowledgments. We thank Martin Kircher, for very helpful comments and explanations, and Cláudio Teixeira, for computational infrastructures. This work was funded by FEDER (Programa Operacional Factores de Competitividade - COMPETE) and by National Funds through the FCT - Foundation for Science and Technology, in the context of the projects UID/CEC/00127/2013, UID/BIM/04501/2013, PTCD/EEI-SII/6608/2014 and the grant SFRH/BPD/111148/2015 to RMS.

References

1. Pratas, D., Silva, R.M., Pinho, A.J., Ferreira, P.J.S.G: Detection and visualisation of regions of human DNA not present in other primates. In: Proceedings of the 21st RecPad 2015, Faro, Portugal, October 2015
2. Rahman, M.S., Alatabbi, A., Athar, T., Crochemore, M., et al.: Absent words and the (dis)similarity analysis of DNA sequences: an experimental study. BMC Res. Notes **9**(1), 186 (2016)
3. Krings, M., Stone, A., Schmitz, R.W., Krainitzki, H., et al.: Neandertal DNA sequences and the origin of modern humans. Cell **90**(1), 19–30 (1997)

4. Green, R.E., Krause, J., Ptak, S.E., Briggs, A.W., et al.: Analysis of one million base pairs of Neanderthal DNA. Nature **444**(7117), 330–336 (2006)
5. Noonan, J.P., Coop, G., Kudaravalli, S., Smith, D., et al.: Sequencing and analysis of Neanderthal genomic DNA. Science **314**(5802), 1113–1118 (2006)
6. Green, R.E., Malaspinas, A.S., Krause, J., Briggs, A.W., et al.: A complete Neandertal mitochondrial genome sequence determined by high-throughput sequencing. Cell **134**(3), 416–426 (2008)
7. Green, R.E., Krause, J., Briggs, A.W., Maricic, T., et al.: A draft sequence of the Neandertal genome. Science **328**(5979), 710–722 (2010)
8. Reich, D., Green, R.E., Kircher, M., Krause, J., et al.: Genetic history of an archaic hominin group from Denisova Cave in Siberia. Nature **468**(7327), 1053–1060 (2010)
9. Prüfer, K., Racimo, F., Patterson, N., Jay, F., et al.: The complete genome sequence of a Neanderthal from the Altai Mountains. Nature **505**(7481), 43–49 (2014)
10. Fu, Q., Hajdinjak, M., Moldovan, O.T., Constantin, S., et al.: An early modern human from Romania with a recent Neanderthal ancestor. Nature **524**(7564), 216–219 (2015)
11. Skoglund, P., Northoff, B.H., Shunkov, M.V., Derevianko, A.P., et al.: Separating endogenous ancient DNA from modern day contamination in a Siberian Neandertal. PNAS **111**(6), 2229–2234 (2014)
12. Hofreiter, M., Jaenicke, V., Serre, D., von Haeseler, A., et al.: DNA sequences from multiple amplifications reveal artifacts induced by cytosine deamination in ancient DNA. Nucl. Acids Res. **29**(23), 4793–4799 (2001)
13. Briggs, A.W., Stenzel, U., Johnson, P.L., Green, R.E., et al.: Patterns of damage in genomic DNA sequences from a Neandertal. PNAS **104**(37), 14616–14621 (2007)
14. Silva, R.M., Pratas, D., Castro, L., Pinho, A.J., Ferreira, P.J.S.G.: Three minimal sequences found in Ebola virus genomes and absent from human DNA. Bioinformatics **31**(15), 2421–2425 (2015)
15. Bloom, B.H.: Space/time trade-offs in hash coding with allowable errors. Commun. ACM **13**(7), 422–426 (1970)
16. Lin, Y.L., Pavlidis, P., Karakoc, E., Ajay, J., Gokcumen, O.: The evolution and functional impact of human deletion variants shared with archaic hominin genomes. Mol. Biol. Evol. (2015). https://doi.org/10.1093/molbev/msu405
17. Qu, R., Sang, Q., Xu, Y., Feng, R., et al.: Identification of a novel homozygous mutation in MYO3A in a chinese family with DFNB30 non-syndromic hearing impairment. Int. J. Pediatr. Otorhinolaryngol. **84**, 43–47 (2016)
18. Silva, I.M., Rosenfeld, J., Antoniuk, S.A., Raskin, S., Sotomaior, V.S.: A 1.5 Mb terminal deletion of 12p associated with autism spectrum disorder. Gene **542**(1), 83–86 (2014)
19. Baker, K., Gordon, S.L., Grozeva, D., van Kogelenberg, M., et al.: Identification of a human synaptotagmin-1 mutation that perturbs synaptic vesicle cycling. J. Clin. Invest. **125**(4), 1670 (2015)
20. Meyer, M., Kircher, M., Gansauge, M.T., Li, H., et al.: A high-coverage genome sequence from an archaic Denisovan individual. Science **338**(6104), 222–226 (2012)

Transfer Learning with Partial Observability Applied to Cervical Cancer Screening

Kelwin Fernandes[1,2]([✉]), Jaime S. Cardoso[1,2], and Jessica Fernandes[3]

[1] INESC TEC, Porto, Portugal
{kafc,jaime.cardoso}@inesctec.pt
[2] Universidade do Porto, Porto, Portugal
[3] Universidad Central de Venezuela, Caracas, Venezuela

Abstract. Cervical cancer remains a significant cause of mortality in low-income countries. As in many other diseases, the existence of several screening/diagnosis methods and subjective physician preferences creates a complex ecosystem for automated methods. In order to diminish the amount of labeled data from each modality/expert we propose a regularization-based transfer learning strategy that encourages source and target models to share the same coefficient signs. We instantiated the proposed framework to predict cross-modality individual risk and cross-expert subjective quality assessment of colposcopic images for different modalities. Thus, we are able to transfer knowledge gained from one expert/modality to another.

Keywords: Transfer learning · Regularization · Cervical cancer · Digital colposcopy

1 Introduction

Despite the possibility of prevention with regular cytological screening, cervical cancer remains a significant cause of mortality in low-income countries. This being the cause of more than half a million cases per year, and killing more than a quarter of a million in the same period [1]. As in many other diseases, the existence of several screening and diagnosis methods creates a complex ecosystem from a Computed Aided Diagnosis (CAD) system point of view. For instance, in the detection of pre-cancerous cervical lesions, screening strategies include cytology, colposcopy (covering its several modalities [1]) and the gold-standard biopsy. In developing countries resources are very limited and patients usually have poor adherence to routine screening due to low problem awareness. Consequently, the prediction of the individual patient's risk and the best screening strategy during her diagnosis becomes a fundamental problem. Most of these screening methods highly depend on the physician expertise and subjective comfort on the decision process, being a key aspect to improve data acquisition using the physician preferences.

Thereby, from a technical point of view, all these predictive tasks are immersed in a multi-modal and multi-expert setting. Traditionally, supervised

© Springer International Publishing AG 2017
L.A. Alexandre et al. (Eds.): IbPRIA 2017, LNCS 10255, pp. 243–250, 2017.
DOI: 10.1007/978-3-319-58838-4_27

learning techniques would require to collect a vast amount of data from each source (i.e. modalities and experts) and to build predictive models separately for each task. Transfer learning (TL) aims to extract knowledge from at least one source task and use it when learning a predictive model for a new target task [2]. The intuition behind this idea is that learning a new task from related tasks should be easier (faster, with better solutions or with less amount of labeled data) than learning the target task in isolation. In this work, we focus on inductive TL, where both domains are represented by the same feature space and where the source and target tasks are different but related [2]. A main trend in inductive transfer consists on transferring data, namely, strategically including data from the source task in the target dataset [3]. Another approach consists on finding a shared source-target low-dimensional feature representation that is suitable for learning the target task [4]. We group these two approaches under the umbrella of data-driven transfer, where source data is re-used to train the target task. Although these approaches may seem appealing, the vast amount of training data in the source task turns the process prohibitively expensive.

TL techniques (and its community) should be focused on adapting knowledge instead of data. This idea is handled by parameter transfer approaches, which rely on the idea that individual models for related tasks should share some structure (parameters or hyper-parameters) [2]. In this sense, the knowledge generated from a source task is understood as the parameters (and hyperparameters) that define a given model: the coefficients of a regression, the weights of a neural network, the feature hierarchy of a decision tree. Previous works [5–8] explored transferring knowledge from/to linear models by means of regularizing the coefficient difference between different tasks. In this work, we extend this idea by including the notion of partial transfer where high-level properties of the source model are transferred instead of the whole model structure. Partial transfer can be understood as improving the model performance on the target task by using a partially observable source model. This capability is specially important in some scenarios, where unlimited access to the model parameters is not possible due to privacy and security concerns (e.g. health and biometrics applications). In these cases just high-level properties of the model are available. Also, regularizing high-level properties of the models allows transfer between less similar tasks. Therefore, even when the source model is fully observable, it can be interesting to study partial transfer mechanisms.

In this work we focus on transferring the coefficient sign by proposing a new regularization scheme that encourages coefficients to share the same contribution type (i.e. positive, negative) instead of the coefficient impact (i.e. actual value). In order to prove its adequacy to different problems, we instantiated this idea to two different problems: cross-modal individual risk prediction and cross-modal and cross-expert quality assessment of digital colposcopies.

2   Proposed Method

We consider the following scenario in this work. We have two learning tasks (source and target) denoted by *src* and *tgt*. We assume that both tasks share the same feature space $X \subset \mathbb{R}^d$ and output type $Y \subset \mathbb{T}$ (e.g. regression, classification). For a given task $T \in \{src, tgt\}$, we have labelled training data $D^T = X^T \times Y^T$. In order to induce similar models, a TL objective can be understood as finding the best model that balances the tradeoff between model performance on the target data and its similarity with the source model:

$$\arg \min_{M} \left(dataLoss(M, X^{tgt}) + \lambda \, dissimilarity(M, M^{src}) \right), \, \lambda \geq 0 \qquad (1)$$

Since a predictive model is a succinct representation of the data, this framework is an efficient way to introduce knowledge obtained from the source task without resorting to the source data. Therefore, it is also useful in scenarios where source data is unavailable at transfer time or in online learning settings.

2.1   Partial Model Transfer: Sign Regularization

Using the proposed framework we can selectively transfer knowledge. This can be done by considering regularization schemes that explore high-level properties of the model instead of its actual state (i.e. assumed values). This can be understood as having partial observability of the model structure.

In this work we focus on linear predictive models for regression (e.g. Linear Regression) and classification (e.g. Logistic Regression, Support Vector Machines). Thereby, we assume that our model can be defined by a vector of coefficients $\omega \in \mathbb{R}^{d+1}$, which includes the bias term ω_0. Here, we are interested in transferring the contribution direction of each feature (i.e. coefficient sign) instead of its importance in the source task (i.e. coefficient magnitude). Equation (2) defines a dissimilarity regularizer that encourages sign relatedness, where ω^{src} and ω^{tgt} denote the source and target coefficients respectively.

$$\delta_p(\omega^{tgt}, \omega^{src}) = \sum_{i=1}^{d} \max(0, -\omega_i^{tgt} \cdot \operatorname{sign}(\omega_i^{src}))^p, \, p > 0 \qquad (2)$$

Although this regularizer is able to control the sign change between source and target task, it does not establish any type of control on models with large coefficients with the same sign. Thereby, we introduce the classical L_p-norm regularizer (see Eq. (3)). Figure 1 illustrates the behavior of two particular instances of the proposed regularizer with $p = 1$ and $p = 2$.

$$\Delta_{p,\alpha}(\omega_i^{tgt}, \omega_i^{src}) = \alpha \delta_p(\omega_i^{tgt}, \omega_i^{src}) + (1 - \alpha) \parallel \omega^{tgt} \parallel_p^p, \, 0 \leq \alpha \leq 1 \qquad (3)$$

The proposed regularizer is based on the Hinge loss traditionally used in the optimization of Support Vector Machines. In this sense, the particular case when $p = 2$ is a smooth version that allows gradient computation on its entire domain (see Eq. (4)). Thereby, it can be easily included in gradient descent optimization strategies.

$$\frac{\partial}{\partial \omega_i^{tgt}} \Delta_{2,\alpha} = (1 - \alpha)\omega_i^{tgt} + \alpha \begin{cases} 0, & \operatorname{sign}(\omega_i^{src}) = \operatorname{sign}(\omega_i^{tgt}) \\ -|\omega_i^{tgt}|\operatorname{sign}(\omega_i^{src}), & \text{otherwise} \end{cases} \qquad (4)$$

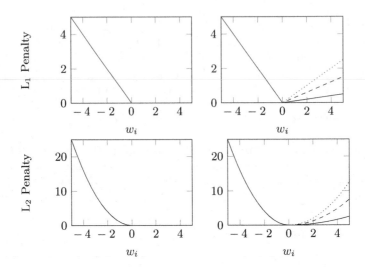

Fig. 1. Regularization factors assuming $w_i^{src} > 0$. First row illustrates the penalization using L_1 regularizers ($p = 1$) with same-sign uncontrolled penalty on the left and with different α values on the right (0.9 - solid, 0.7 - dashed, 0.5 - dotted). Second row is analogous to the first row but using L_2 penalty ($p = 2$).

On the other hand, when $p = 1$, the derivative at $\omega_i = 0$ is non-deterministic. However, the subgradient at $\omega_i = 0$ can be computed, inducing a subgradient descent optimization strategy. Due to space limitations we only present results for the smooth version of the proposed regularizer.

3   Experiments

Data was split using a stratified training-test partition (80–20). Then, in order to validate the model performance on different stages of the data acquisition process, the training set was randomly subsampled in 10 nested subsets with several sizes (10%, 20%, 30%, ..., 100%). Each experiment was repeated 30 times varying the test partition. The regularization factor (λ) and all the remaining intrinsic hyper-parameters were learned using Stratified K-fold cross-validation (K = 3) over the training set. For reproducibility purposes, the datasets are made available[1].

For each method, the normalized signed Area Under the gain Curve (sAUC) is measured when compared with training the model using target data only, where gain is measured in terms of percentage relative gain. Thus, positive gain reflects positive transfer and, analogously, negative gain reflects negative transfer.

We instantiate the proposed sign-transfer method to two linear models: linear regression for the risk prediction task and Support Vector Machines for the quality assessment task. In each case, we validate the proposed method with fixed

---

[1] http://vcmi.inescporto.pt/reproducible_research/ibpria2017/CervicalCancer/.

sign importance ($\alpha = 1$) - denoted as Sign - and with varying tradeoff between sign agreement and coefficient magnitude ($0 \leq \alpha \leq 1$) - denoted as α-Sign. The proposed regularizers are compared to the state-of-the-art approach, hereafter referred as Diff, where the model is learned using full-observability transfer by regularizing coefficients to be similar to the source-model coefficients [5–8].

3.1 Risk Factors

In this section we instantiate the proposed partial transfer technique to predict the individual patient's risk when multiple screening strategies are available (i.e. colposcopy using acetic acid - Hinselmann, colposcopy using Lugol iodine - Schiller, cytology and biopsy). For this purpose a database with 858 patients including demographic information, habits and historic medical records was collected (see Table 1). Several patients decided not to answer some of the questions due to privacy concerns. Hence, the features denoted by bool $\times$ T, T $\in$ {bool, int}, were encoded as two independent values: whether or not the patient answered the question and the reported value. Missing values were filled using the sample mean. Categorical features were encoded using the one-of-K scheme.

Table 1. Features acquired in the risk factors dataset.

Feature	Type	Feature	Type
Age	int	IUD (years)	int
# sexual partners	bool $\times$ int	STDs	bool $\times$ bool
Age of 1st sexual intercourse	bool $\times$ int	STDs (how many?)	int
# of pregnancies	bool $\times$ int	Diagnosed STDs	categorical
Smokes?	bool $\times$ bool	STDs (years since first diag.)	int
Smokes? (years & packs)	int $\times$ int	STDs (years last diag.)	int
Hormonal Contraceptives?	bool	Has previous cervical diag.?	bool
Horm. Contr.? (years)	int	Prev. cervical diag. (years)	int
Intrauterine device? (IUD)	bool	Prev. cervical diagnosis	categorical

Table 2 shows the results for this task using a regularized linear regression. It was validated that gains achieved by the proposed partial transfer framework were higher than the obtained by the fully observable transfer recently used in the literature. In most cases, the best results were obtained by the α-controlled sign regularization approach.

3.2 Quality Assessment

Choosing frames with good quality to perform the screening is an important step on improving physician's effectiveness. However, several challenges arise when

Table 2. sAUC obtained by the TL approaches on the risk prediction task with multiple screening strategies: Hinselmann (H), Schiller (S), Cytology (C) and Biopsy (B). Performance is measured in terms of Rooted Mean Squared Error (RMSE).

Source	Target	Diff	Sign	α-Sign	Source	Target	Diff	Sign	α-Sign
H	S	66.09	66.02	**68.96**	C	H	35.05	34.51	**35.11**
H	C	19.51	24.67	**37.12**	C	S	55.45	53.97	**55.81**
H	B	54.70	52.39	**54.96**	C	B	47.37	47.40	**47.54**
S	H	38.72	36.44	**38.74**	B	H	47.99	47.39	**48.80**
S	C	33.55	34.21	**39.90**	B	S	64.10	61.89	**66.66**
S	B	**45.48**	42.19	45.34	B	C	28.18	34.14	**43.69**

defining the quality in this context. Thus, quality becomes a subjective concept subject to human preferences. In this work we consider a binary annotation scheme (e.g. good and bad quality) to simplify the presentation of the proposed framework. However, in the future we will consider ordinal scales (e.g. poor, fair, good, excellent) and pairwise relative preferences (e.g. the image A is better than the image B). The following semantic medical features were considered:

– Image area occupied by each anatomical body part (cervix, external os and vaginal walls) and occluding objects (speculum and other artifacts).
– The area of each region occluded by artifacts or by specular reflections.
– The maximum area difference between the four cervix quadrants.
– Fitness goodness of the cervix to a given geometric model: convex hull, bounding box, circle and ellipse.
– Distance between the image center and the cervix centroid/external os.
– Mean and standard deviation of each RGB and HSV channel in the cervix area and in the entire image.

In a joint collaboration with *Hospital Universitario de Caracas*, a dataset with annotations from 6 experts on about 100 cervigrams per modality (see Fig. 2) was collected [1]. In the experimental evaluation, each region of interest was manually segmented by an expert to simplify the comparison of the transfer learning approaches.

Fig. 2. Colposcopy modalities. From left to right: Hinselmann, Green light and Schiller. (Color figure online)

Table 3. sAUC obtained by the TL approaches on the quality prediction task with several colposcopic modalities: Hinselmann (H), Green (G) and Schiller (S). Performance is measured in terms of accuracy.

Source	Target	Diff	Sign	α-Sign	Source	Target	Diff	Sign	α-Sign
H	G	53.31	**54.14**	53.83	H	S	**47.82**	46.58	45.73
G	H	64.13	68.05	**68.30**	G	S	47.07	47.98	**48.15**
S	H	**63.73**	62.67	61.02	S	G	47.16	**49.28**	48.54

Table 3 shows the results for the binary classification of the subjective image quality using SVM. The target labels are assigned using the mode of the annotations given by the physicians. Contrary to the linear regression case, the version with $\alpha = 1$ obtained better results than the α-Sign approach. This can be explained by the fact that each modality has a few annotated instances per expert (about 100), turning it difficult to correctly estimate the α parameter.

Figure 3 shows the gains obtained by the α-Sign version of the regularizer when compared with the state-of-the-art approach on a multi-expert setting. Here, source and target tasks represent different annotators' preferences (i.e. transferring from the i-th expert in the row to the j-th expert in the column). Analogously to previous experiments, the proposed transfer with partial observability obtained the best results in most cases. Schiller was the modality with highest gains. However, it was also the most unstable, being also the one with lowest gains in some cases. Using partial transfer schemes, some experts reflected poor performance as source in some modalities (e.g. expert 2 in Hinselmann) while behave as good sources in other modalities (e.g. expert 2 in Green). Moreover, since the partial model observability is a weak prior over the model space, the set of models that achieves an optimal regularization value is infinite, inducing a non-symmetric gain matrix.

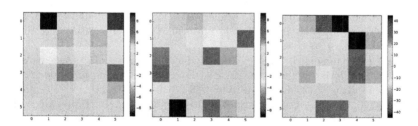

Fig. 3. Heatmap of the transfer gain obtained by the α-Sign regularizer when compared to the state-of-the-art regularizer. Transfer is done from a given expert's preferences (row) to another expert's preferences (column) between the same modality. The modalities are, from left to right: Hinselmann, Green light and Schiller. (Color figure online)

4 Conclusions

In this work we presented a regularization-based TL approach to transfer the contribution type for each feature on linear models. In order to show its adequacy to different contexts, the proposed model-relatedness regularizer was instantiated to several learning tasks related to cervical cancer screening. Positive results were obtained in most experiments, being competitive with other methods in the literature. This work suggests that the analysis of how models encode high-level properties of the domain may improve transfer performance. Future research lines will tackle this type of transfer in multi-class and ordinal classification settings. Also, we will study how to synthesize high-level transferable knowledge in other non-linear models.

Acknowledgements. This work was funded by the Project "NanoSTIMA: Macro-to-Nano Human Sensing: Towards Integrated Multimodal Health Monitoring and Analytics/NORTE-01-0145-FEDER-000016" financed by the North Portugal Regional Operational Programme (NORTE 2020), under the PORTUGAL 2020 Partnership Agreement, and through the European Regional Development Fund (ERDF), and also by Fundação para a Ciência e a Tecnologia (FCT) within PhD grant number SFRH/BD/93012/2013. The authors would like to thank the Gynecology Service of the *Hospital Universitario de Caracas*. In particular, we would like to recognize the efforts of Drs. Geramel Montero, Dulce Almeida, Jose Valentin, Leonardo Amado and Leticia Parpacen.

References

1. Fernandes, K., Cardoso, J.S., Fernandes, J.: Temporal segmentation of digital colposcopies. In: Paredes, R., Cardoso, J.S., Pardo, X.M. (eds.) IbPRIA 2015. LNCS, vol. 9117, pp. 262–271. Springer, Cham (2015). doi:10.1007/978-3-319-19390-8_30
2. Pan, S.J., Yang, Q.: A survey on transfer learning. IEEE Trans. Knowl. Data Eng. **22**(10), 1345–1359 (2010)
3. Garcke, J., Vanck, T.: Importance weighted inductive transfer learning for regression. In: Calders, T., Esposito, F., Hüllermeier, E., Meo, R. (eds.) ECML PKDD 2014. LNCS, vol. 8724, pp. 466–481. Springer, Heidelberg (2014). doi:10.1007/978-3-662-44848-9_30
4. Rückert, U., Kramer, S.: Kernel-based inductive transfer. In: Daelemans, W., Goethals, B., Morik, K. (eds.) ECML PKDD 2008. LNCS, vol. 5212, pp. 220–233. Springer, Heidelberg (2008). doi:10.1007/978-3-540-87481-2_15
5. Evgeniou, T., Pontil, M.: Regularized multi-task learning. In: Proceedings of the Tenth ACM SIGKDD International Conference on Knowledge Discovery and Data Mining, pp. 109–117. ACM (2004)
6. Lee, C., Jang, M.G.: A prior model of structural SVMs for domain adaptation. ETRI J. **33**(5), 712–719 (2011)
7. Kuzborskij, I., Orabona, F.: Stability and hypothesis transfer learning. In: ICML, pp. III-942–III-950 (2013)
8. Perrot, M., Habrard, A.: A theoretical analysis of metric hypothesis transfer learning. In: Proceedings of the 32nd International Conference on Machine Learning (ICML-15), pp. 1708–1717 (2015)

Automated Detection and Categorization of Genital Injuries Using Digital Colposcopy

Kelwin Fernandes[1,2(✉)], Jaime S. Cardoso[1,2], and Birgitte Schmidt Astrup[3]

[1] INESC TEC, Porto, Portugal
{kafc,jaime.cardoso}@inesctec.pt
[2] Universidade do Porto, Porto, Portugal
[3] Institute of Forensic Medicine, University of Southern Denmark, Odense, Denmark

Abstract. Despite the existence of patterns able to discriminate between consensual and non-consensual intercourse, the relevance of genital lesions in the corroboration of a legal rape complaint is currently under debate in many countries. The testimony of the physicians when assessing these lesions has been questioned in court due to several factors (e.g. a lack of comprehensive knowledge of lesions, wide spectrum of background area, among others). Thereby, it is relevant to provide automated tools to support the decision process in an objective manner. In this work, we compare traditional handcrafted features and deep learning techniques in the automated processing of colposcopic images for genital injury detection. Positive results where achieved by both paradigms in segmentation and classification subtasks, being traditional and deep models the best strategy for each subtask type respectively.

Keywords: Genital injury · Digital colposcopy · Deep learning · Handcrafted features · Image processing

1 Introduction

The relevance of genital lesions in the corroboration of a legal rape complaint is currently under debate in many countries [1–3]. Since genital lesions are frequent in both, consensual and non-consensual intercourse [1,4], the existence of a pattern of genital injury able to discriminate trauma seen in rape cases and trauma seen following consensual sexual intercourse has been a matter of study in the past [3]. Typical different patterns were analyzed by several authors [3,5]. Slaughter et al. [5] suggested that multiple genital lesions at multiple locations are frequent in rape victims, while single lesions in the posterior forchette are predominant in consensual sexual intercourse. Astrup et al. [3] suggested a higher frequency of abrasions, haematomas and multiple lesions in rape cases. Also, Astrup et al. [3] confirmed a higher frequency of lesions in locations other than the 6 o'clock position and the presence of larger and more complex lesions in non-consensual cases.

Although the existence of such pattern has been validated by several studies, the debate continues. Legal experts suggest the lack of comprehensive knowledge

© Springer International Publishing AG 2017
L.A. Alexandre et al. (Eds.): IbPRIA 2017, LNCS 10255, pp. 251–258, 2017.
DOI: 10.1007/978-3-319-58838-4_28

of lesions sustained during consensual sexual intercourse as a key problem [1]. Moreover, the expert responsible for conducting such evaluations as well as the physical analysis in sexual assault victims itself differ around the world [2]. For instance, in the US most examinations are done by specially trained nurses, while in many European countries the examinations are performed by gynecologists [6]. Other countries like Denmark delegate this responsibility to forensic pathologists [2]. Given the wide spectrum of background knowledge of experts and the low inter-evaluator agreement [4], the expert testimony given by these professionals in cases of genital lesions in sexual assaults has been questioned in court in several countries [2].

In this work we propose a preliminary framework for the automated detection and categorization of genital injuries on digital colposcopies using image processing and machine learning techniques. Although these techniques have been successfully used in other medical applications in order to improve and support the medical decision process (e.g. [7]), even on digital colposcopy analysis [8,9], this is the first attempt to address the detection of genital injuries from a computational perspective. Building an objective data-driven system, able to provide a unified framework for the analysis of genital lesions in digital colposcopy may increase the reliability of genital trauma findings in legal rape complaints from both, medical teams and legal experts. From a technical point of view, we study the impact of handcrafted and deep-features in the automation of several tasks of the proposed system.

2   Preliminary Definitions

In this section, we describe common concepts that are fundamental in this work. Specifically, the type of lesions of interest and the investigative techniques used in their detection. Further details about these concepts can be found in the medical literature [10].

2.1   Investigative Techniques

The usual methodologies for the detection of genital injuries cover the naked eye inspection, the colposcope and inspection after application of toluidine blue dye (see Fig. 1) [10]. In this work we merely include the two latter which allow automation.

- **Colposcope:** The investigator inspects the external genitalia and afterwards the vagina and cervix using digital colposcope. A colposcope is a binocular instrument that magnifies and illuminates a given inspected area.
- **Toluidine Blue Dye:** After inspection, a blue dye is applied to the genital mucous membranes and then wiped off. Toluidine blue stains exposed cellular nuclei but not intact mucosa, thus enhancing areas of surface disruption.

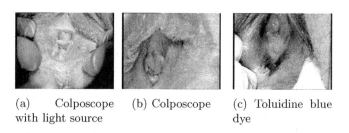

(a)   Colposcope   (b) Colposcope   (c) Toluidine blue
with light source   dye

Fig. 1. Examples of images from several acquisition techniques

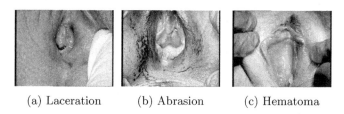

(a) Laceration   (b) Abrasion   (c) Hematoma

Fig. 2. Examples of genital injury on digital colposcopy

2.2   Injuries

The European and Australian categorization of genital injuries is used in this
work, which comprises laceration, abrasion and hematoma (see Fig. 2) [10].

- **Laceration:** Discontinuity of epidermis and dermis. Caused by blunt force
  such as tearing, crushing, or overstretching.
- **Abrasion:** Traumatic exposure of lower epidermis or upper dermis. Most often
  caused by lateral rubbing or sliding against the skin in a tangential manner.
  The outermost layer of skin is scraped away from the deeper layers.
- **Contusion/Hematoma/Bruise:** Traumatic extravasation of blood in tissues below an intact epidermis. Caused by blunt force.

3   Proposed Methodology

We subdivide the whole framework into a set of five predictive tasks: light
source detection, segmentation of gloves, detection of the investigative technique (colposcope and toluidine blue dye), segmentation of the toluidine blue
dye stained regions, classification of lesions and discrimination of consensual
and non-consensual intercourse.

3.1   Deep Learning Strategies

Two deep learning paradigms were used in this work: domain-specific neural
networks and pre-trained architectures with additional fine-tuning.

Domain-Specific Neural Networks. In this case, networks are trained from scratch using our domain specific dataset. The architecture used in this case was common for all the subtasks. We used a standard convolutional neural network (CNN) [11] with an alternating sequence of Convolutional and Max Pooling layers, followed by a Dropout layer and ending with a sequence of dense layers. We validated several activation functions for dense layers obtaining the best trade-off between convergence speed and performance with leaky rectifier units [12]. The shape and activation function of the final output layer depends on the task type. For classification tasks with global output (i.e. one output per image), we used a layer with N output values and soft-max activation function, being N the number of categories. On the other hand, for segmentation tasks, the last layer has size $rows \times cols$, returning an activation value for each output pixel. This approach has been used as an efficient alternative to encoder-decoder networks [13] traditionally used for segmentation [14]. The final parametrization for each task was fine-tuned using an independent validation set.

Pre-trained Neural Networks. Here, we used pre-trained architectures (i.e. VGG16, VGG19, ResNet50, Inception V3) on the ImageNet dataset. Then, the last dense layer of each network is fine-tuned using our own data. This approach was only applied to the classification sub-tasks. The best network was chosen using the validation data.

3.2   Strategy Based on Hand-Crafted Features

In this section we describe the methodology used in the corresponding subtasks using hand-crafted features.

Light Source Detection. Since the presence of artificial light is spatially located in approximately the same round area (see Fig. 1a), we simplified the task of segmenting the lighted-unlighted areas to a global binary classification task. The traditional pipeline designed for this task works as follows. First, the specular reflections (SR) are removed and the images are quantized using an index of K colors obtained with the K-means algorithm [15]. Then, the image is segmented into a group of nested circles. The feature vector used to fit the binary classification model is the concatenation of the relative frequency difference for each color inside and outside the circles. Also, we include the average intensity difference inside and outside each circle. The binary classifier is chosen using K-fold cross-validation from a set of estimators, namely, Random Forest, AdaBoost, Support Vector Machine, Gradient Boosting and Logistic Regression.

Gloves and Toluidine Blue Dye Segmentation. For the segmentation of gloves and regions stained with toluidine blue dye we used a common framework based on superpixels classification. Images are segmented into a fixed number of regions using SLIC Superpixels (i.e. clustering on the color-distance space).

Table 1. Features used in the segmentation of gloves and toluidine blue dye.

Category	Description
Texture	Local Binary Patterns histogram. Number of edged pixels (using Canny edge detector)
Color	Relative frequency of each quantized color (color index built using K-means). μ and σ of each channel in the RGB and HSV color spaces
SR	Number of blobs and relative size
Shape	Basic statistics (i.e. min, max, μ, σ) of the pixel locations to the image center, borders and ROI mask. Size

Then, for each segment we extract a broad set of features (see Table 1) and train a binary classifier to label each cluster. The best classifier is chosen in the same way than in the previous section. Finally, images are post-processed to remove small blobs. For the toluidine blue dye, we also include an additional binary classification task regarding the presence or not of the staining substance in the image. For this subtask, we used the features from the categories texture, color and SR (see Table 1) on the whole image.

Lesion Classification and Consensual vs Non-consensual Classification.
Manually computing high-level hand-crafted features for the classification of these two tasks is a extremely challenging and time consuming labor. Thereby, we decided to apply standard pipelines for the classification of images using state-of-the-art image descriptors (e.g. SIFT, SURF). In this sense, after computing the keypoints and their corresponding descriptors, a Bag-of-Visual-Words using the K-Means algorithm on the descriptor space is trained. Then, each image is encoded by the normalized histogram of vocabulary words found on it. Finally, a binary classifier is trained using the image's encoding. The best binary classifier is chosen using K-fold cross validation in a similar way than in the previous sub-tasks. We concatenated the features obtained with the SIFT and SURF algorithms to build the binary classification model.

4 Experiments

In the experimental assessment of the proposed methods a dataset with 394 images collected by the *Southern Denmark Sexual Assault Referral Centre* was used (78 images from non-consensual intercourse and 316 from consensual intercourse). For further details about the acquisition process refer to the original source [4]. We divided the database into three disjoint sets for training, validation and test using a standard 60-20-20 partition. The distribution of images with and without artificial light, with each color of gloves and from consensual and non-consensual cases was kept constant. Since the frequency of hematoma in our dataset was very limited, abrasion and hematoma cases were combined as a single class in the categorization of lesions. The performance of each classification strategy was measured using accuracy (Acc) and macro-averaged area under the ROC curve (AUC). In counterpart, since the proposed deep architectures generate fuzzy segmentations, the fuzzy Dice coefficient is used. The fuzzy Dice coefficient (f-Dice) can be defined in a straightforward manner using the fuzzy definitions of set intersection and set cardinality.

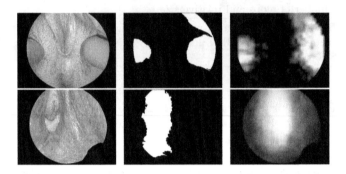

Fig. 3. Results obtained by the gloves (**top**) and toluidine blue dye (**bottom**) segmentation strategies. **Left:** original image. **Middle:** Handcrafted features. **Right:** Deep Learning. (Color figure online)

Table 2a and b show the results for the classification and segmentation subtasks respectively. The results are overall satisfactory, being able to provide positive predictive results for all the proposed subtask. As observed in related areas, deep learning strategies performed better than traditional pipelines in most classification tasks in term of AUC. However, models based on hand-crafted features

Table 2. Performance of the traditional and deep strategies on each subtask.

(a) Classification subtasks

Sub-task	Hand-crafted		Deep		Pre-Trained	
	Acc	AUC	Acc	AUC	Acc	AUC
Light source	**100.00**	**100.00**	98.73	**100.00**	97.47	99.75
Toluidine blue dye	93.67	97.44	**96.20**	**99.16**	89.87	98.51
Lesion detection (binary)	**68.35**	62.71	25.32	56.10	67.09	**71.44**
Lesion categorization	72.15	**63.47**	**74.68**	61.67	65.82	63.34
Consensual/Non-consensual	**84.81**	79.46	81.01	77.68	**84.81**	**88.10**

(b) Regression subtasks

Sub-task	Hand-crafted	Deep
Gloves	**84.99**	63.40
Toluidine blue dye	**84.30**	70.66

achieved better performance than deep architectures trained from scratch in general. Regarding accuracy, traditional models surpassed deep learning strategies in several cases, even when achieving low AUC values. These behaviors are probably due to the high complexity of deep models whose parameters cannot be properly estimated using small datasets. The low performance of the lesion detection and categorization tasks when compared to the consensual/non-consensual problem suggests that the models might be overfitting to features unrelated with the genital injuries. Thereby, further validation is required to ensure that both groups where handled indistinguishably.

The landscape is different for the segmentation subtasks, where traditional techniques outperformed deep strategies by a large margin. As can be observed in Fig. 3, the boundaries obtained by the traditional strategies are clearly defined, while the ones obtained by the deep learning methods are very smooth. This may be due to the subsampling effect generated by the convolutional/max-pooling layers or due to the high number of parameters involved in these models, turning the fitting of sound models a challenging task with small datasets. Since our segmentation subtasks are used as pre-processing steps to remove undesired regions from the input image, sharp boundaries are preferred. However, smooth behaviors are desirable in plenty medical applications and might be useful in the spatial location of genital injuries.

5   Conclusions

Despite the existence of patterns able to discriminate between consensual and non-consensual intercourse have been proved, the relevance of genital lesions in the corroboration of a legal rape complaint is currently under debate in many countries. Being the lack of comprehensive knowledge of lesions a driving factor in the acceptance of this type of evidence in courts, it is fundamental to provide objective methods to support the expert's decision. In this work, we proposed a framework that covers the preliminary steps in the automated detection of genital injuries on digital colposcopies using computer vision and machine learning. We compared the performance of traditional pipelines with handcrafted features and deep learning approaches in several subtasks.

We validated that, for our problem, both strategies are complementary being the former more suitable for segmentation tasks and problems with easily transmitted high-level discriminative information (e.g. light detection) and the later more suitable for complex tasks, where building high-level informative features is challenging (e.g. lesion classification). However, deep learning strategies require a lot of data to be trained, achieving low performance in some tasks when trained from scratch. In the future, we will work in the spatial detection of lesions in order to suggest areas of interest in the image to the physicians. Also, we will explore hybrid architectures, able to combine the best features from each paradigm.

Acknowledgements. This work was funded by the Project "NanoSTIMA: Macro-to-Nano Human Sensing: Towards Integrated Multimodal Health Monitoring and Analytics/NORTE-01-0145-FEDER-000016" financed by the North Portugal Regional Operational Programme (NORTE 2020), under the PORTUGAL 2020 Partnership Agreement, and through the European Regional Development Fund (ERDF), and also by Fundação para a Ciência e a Tecnologia (FCT) within PhD grant number SFRH/BD/93012/2013.

References

1. Astrup, B.S., Lauritsen, J., Ravn, P., Thomsen, J.L.: Genital lesions after consensual sexual intercourse: they are frequent and they last for several days. In: 19th World Meeting of the International Association of Forensic Sciences (2011)
2. Astrup, B.S., Ravn, P., Lauritsen, J., Thomsen, J.L.: Nature, frequency and duration of genital lesions after consensual sexual intercourse–implications for legal proceedings. Forensic Sci. Int. **219**(1), 50–56 (2012)
3. Astrup, B.S., Ravn, P., Thomsen, J.L., Lauritsen, J.: Patterned genital injury in cases of rape–a case–control study. J. Forensic Legal Med. **20**(5), 525–529 (2013)
4. Astrup, B.S., Lauritsen, J., Thomsen, J.L., Ravn, P.: Colposcopic photography of genital injury following sexual intercourse in adults. Forensic Sci. Med. Pathol. **9**(1), 24–30 (2013)
5. Slaughter, L., Brown, C.R., Crowley, S., Peck, R.: Patterns of genital injury in female sexual assault victims. Am. J. Obstet. Gynecol. **176**(3), 609–616 (1997)
6. Payne-James, J., Busuttil, A., Smock, W.: Forensic Medicine: Clinical and Pathological Aspects. Cambridge University Press, Cambridge (2003)
7. Doi, K.: Computer-aided diagnosis in medical imaging: historical review, current status and future potential. Comput. Med. Imaging Graph. **31**(4), 198–211 (2007)
8. Fernandes, K., Cardoso, J.S., Fernandes, J.: Temporal segmentation of digital colposcopies. In: Paredes, R., Cardoso, J.S., Pardo, X.M. (eds.) IbPRIA 2015. LNCS, vol. 9117, pp. 262–271. Springer, Cham (2015). doi:10.1007/978-3-319-19390-8_30
9. Huang, X., Wang, W., Xue, Z., Antani, S., Long, L.R., Jeronimo, J.: Tissue classification using cluster features for lesion detection in digital cervigrams. In: Medical Imaging, International Society for Optics and Photonics, p. 69141Z (2008)
10. Astrup, B.S., Lykkebo, A.W.: Post-coital genital injury in healthy women: a review. Clin. Anat. **28**(3), 331–338 (2015)
11. Krizhevsky, A., Sutskever, I., Hinton, G.E.: Imagenet classification with deep convolutional neural networks. In: Advances in Neural Information Processing Systems, pp. 1097–1105 (2012)
12. Xu, B., Wang, N., Chen, T., Li, M.: Empirical evaluation of rectified activations in convolutional network. arXiv preprint. arXiv:1505.00853 (2015)
13. Badrinarayanan, V., Kendall, A., Cipolla, R.: Segnet: A deep convolutional encoder-decoder architecture for image segmentation. arXiv preprint. arXiv:1511.00561 (2015)
14. Pan, J., McGuinness, K., Sayrol, E., O'Connor, N., Giro-i Nieto, X.: Shallow and deep convolutional networks for saliency prediction. arXiv preprint. arXiv:1603.00845 (2016)
15. Kasuga, H., Yamamoto, H., Okamoto, M.: Color quantization using the fast k-means algorithm. Syst. Comput. Jpn. **31**(8), 33–40 (2000)

On the Approximation of the Kolmogorov Complexity for DNA Sequences

Diogo Pratas$^{(\boxtimes)}$ and Armando J. Pinho

IEETA, University of Aveiro, 3810-193 Aveiro, Portugal
{pratas,ap}@ua.pt

Abstract. The Kolmogorov complexity furnishes several ways for studying different natural processes that can be expressed using sequences of symbols from a finite alphabet, such as the case of DNA sequences. Although the Kolmogorov complexity is not algorithmically computable, it can be approximated by lossless normal compressors. In this paper, we use a specific DNA compressor to approximate the Kolmogorov complexity and we assess it regarding its normality. Then, we use it on several datasets, that are constituted by different DNA sequences, representing complete genomes of different species and domains. We show several evolution-related insights associated with the complexity, namely that, globally, archaea have higher relative complexity than bacteria and eukaryotes.

Keywords: Kolmogorov complexity · Compression · DNA sequences

1 Introduction

A DNA sequence is a succession of letters, with four possible outcomes (A,C,G,T), that indicate the order and nature of nucleotides within a DNA chemical chain. The process of unveilling the chain is known as DNA sequencing. This process can be seen as a capture of small pieces from a huge puzzle with lots of repeated, changed and missing pieces. Therefore, in order to obtain a *complete* species sequence, several stages must first be accomplished, such as the assembly, causing the insertion of several errors in the final sequences. Nevertheless, for quantitative studies on global sequences, these errors are usually negligible.

In this paper, we consider the challenge of estimating the average information in (*complete*) individual and groups of DNA sequences, with the aim of extracting relevant patterns that may characterize different groups. For this purpose, we rely on the notion of algorithmic entropy to estimate the amount of information contained in the sequences.

This notion dates back to 1965, when Andrey Kolmogorov defined three approaches for quantifying the amount of information that a sequence x has, namely the combinatorial approach, the probabilistic approach and the algorithmic approach [1]. The latter became the most used nowadays and is known as the Kolmogorov complexity or algorithmic entropy [1–8].

© Springer International Publishing AG 2017
L.A. Alexandre et al. (Eds.): IbPRIA 2017, LNCS 10255, pp. 259–266, 2017.
DOI: 10.1007/978-3-319-58838-4_29

The Kolmogorov complexity of a sequence, x, represented by $K(x)$, is the size of a shortest program, which running on a universal computer (or Turing machine [9]), prints x and halts. Fixing the machine, we can write

$$K(x) = \min_{p=x} l(p),\qquad(1)$$

reading $p = x$ as "p prints x and halts".

However, the Kolmogorov complexity is non-computable in the Turing sense [4]. An admissible approximation can be made using a (lossless) normal compression algorithm, denoted by C, where

$$C(x) = \sum_{i=1}^{|x|} C(x_i|x_1^{i-1}),\qquad(2)$$

with $|x|$ denoting the size of the sequence, $x_1^n = x_1 x_2 \ldots x_n$, $x_i \in \{A, C, G, T\}$ and where (note that, since for DNA the size of the alphabet is four, then a DNA sequence x has a nominal size of $2|x|$ bits)

$$2|x| \geq C(x) \geq K(x).\qquad(3)$$

In order to attain an accurate and admissible measure, the compressor, besides the need of having the best possible model to represent the nature of the data, needs to be normal. A compressor is normal if it satisfies the following conditions:

1. Idempotency: $C(xx) = C(x)$ and $C(\lambda) = 0$, where λ is the empty sequence;
2. Monotonicity: $C(xy) \geq C(x)$;
3. Symmetry: $C(xy) = C(yx)$;
4. Distributivity: $C(xz) + C(yz) \geq C(xy) + C(z)$;

up to an additive $O(\log m)$ term, where m is the maximal length of the elements involved in the (in)equality [10, 11]. For common pitfalls in compressor settings, see [12].

Recently, we have proposed a DNA compressor that provides state-of-the-art results [13, 14]. This compressor exploits a combination of context models and extended context models (which are tolerant to substitution errors) of several orders. Furthermore, cache-hashes are employed in high order models to make the implementation more flexible. For a survey on DNA compressors see [15], while for other applications regarding the usage of Kolmogorov complexity in DNA sequences see [16, 17].

The remainder of the paper is organized as follows. In Sect. 2, we describe the methods used in the reported experiment, namely how to assess the compressor normality and how the final study was designed. In Sect. 3, we use this compressor to compute an approximation of the algorithmic complexity of the sequences. Finally, in Sect. 4 we draw some conclusions.

2   Methods

2.1   Assessment of Normality

We have used synthetic data in order to show that the compressor is asymptotically normal. Using a DNA simulator [18], we have created sequences with different sizes, using a uniform distribution. Then, we evaluated the idempotency property, as Table 1 shows. For replication of the results, the interested reader may use the script https://raw.githubusercontent.com/pratas/ANT/master/run/Idemp.sh.

Table 1. Idempotency assessment for several sizes of DNA synthetic sequences generated with a uniform distribution. Compression values given by C are in bytes, whereas $|x|$ is the number of bases. Precision is given by $C(x)$ / $C(xx)$ × 100.

$|x|$	$C(x)$	$C(xx)$	Precision (%)
10^3	289	295	97.92
10^4	2,539	2,555	99.37
10^5	25,039	25,153	99.54
10^6	250,039	251,132	99.56
10^7	2,500,080	2,510,978	99.56
10^8	25,004,102	25,114,522	99.56
10^9	250,397,375	378,312,187	66.18

As it can be seen in Table 1, with the exception of 1 GBase, for all the sizes of the sequences the precision is very high, showing the preservation of the idempotency property. For the last case (1 GBase), the precision is ∼66% because the size of the maximum number of collisions of the cache-hash was limited to 30 [13] and, hence, its value is too low to retain a complete model of x. Nevertheless, in the results, we used sequences below 100 MBases.

Regarding the monotonicity property, it is obvious that when we add an extra sequence to the compression of x, the number of bits will always be greater or equal to $C(x)$.

For assessing the symmetry, we have simulated, using the same simulator, sequences with different sizes using a uniform distribution. Then, for each sequence (each x), we have copied it and mutated it (with 10% of random substitutions), creating the other sequence (each y). Afterwards, for each pair, we have computed $C(xy)$ and $C(yx)$, resulting in the values displayed in Table 2. For replication of these results use the script https://raw.githubusercontent.com/pratas/ANT/master/run/Sym.sh.

As it can be seen in Table 2, for all the sizes of the sequences, the precision is very high, showing the preservation of the symmetry property.

For assessing the distributivity, we have created seven synthetic sequences. Then, we have tested all combinations of groups of three sequences (x, y and z),

Table 2. Symmetry assessment for several sizes of DNA synthetic sequences generated with a uniform distribution. Compression values for C are in bytes, whereas $|x|$ is the number of bases. Precision is given by $\min\{C(xy), C(yx)\}$ / $\max\{C(xy), C(yx)\} \times 100$.

$|x|$	$C(xy)$	$C(yx)$	Precision (%)
10^3	410	411	99.76
10^4	3,540	3,540	100.00
10^5	34,636	34,632	99.99
10^6	347,648	347,647	100.00
10^7	3,490,208	3,490,155	100.00
10^8	35,278,700	35,284,748	99.98
10^9	500,890,857	500,890,737	100.00

drawn from the seven sequences, totalizing 7^3 combinations. For all these the distributivity property holds. For replication or to see the settings, use the script https://raw.githubusercontent.com/pratas/ANT/master/run/Dist.sh.

2.2   Complexity of Genomes

We have downloaded the entire NCBI database for viruses, bacteria, archaea, fungi and plants, resulting in five datasets with ~216 GB. For each dataset, we have extracted only the sequences labeled as "complete genomes". The reason is that incomplete sequences may introduce errors or misleading values. Table 3 shows the filtered datasets.

Table 3. Properties of the five filtered datasets, reported by the GOOSE framework (http://pratas.github.io/goose/), including all files with the label "complete genome" on the headers of the FASTA files. Average, minimum and maximum values report the number of bases in each species.

Dataset	No. sequences	Size (MB)	Average	Minimum	Maximum
Viruses	5,522	277	51,761	220	8,212,805
Bacteria	2,257	8,471	3,879,314	1,717	14,782,125
Archaea	217	481	2,282,257	6,056	5,751,492
Fungi	62	4	55,346	22,376	191,189
Plants	1,358	222	168,201	11,348	1,999,602
Total	9,314	7,455			

Then, we have compressed each sequence from each dataset, and computed two scores. The first, was obtained from the individual normalized compression, given by Eq. 2 and normalized by the $2|x|$ term. The second, was the normalized cumulative compression, which, for all files in each dataset, is the sum of the values provided by Eq. 2, normalized by twice the total number of bases.

The experiments reported can all be replicated using the script https://raw. githubusercontent.com/pratas/ANT/master/run/OAE.sh. This includes the automatic download, extraction, filtering, compression and plotting of the results.

3   Results

For the biological results, we have computed the two mentioned scores. The first one is represented in Fig. 1. The second one, is ploted in Fig. 2.

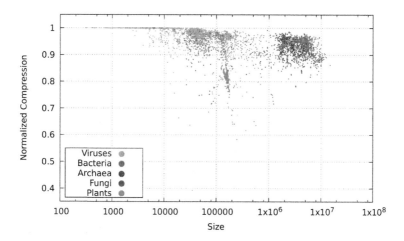

Fig. 1. Normalized compression for each sequence of the corresponding dataset, as a function of its logarithmic size.

In agreement with several proposed phylogenetic trees [19,20], the separation of bacteria, archaea, and eukaryotes domains (fungi, plants, animals) is well evident [21,22]. Despite the visual similarity to bacteria, archaea possess genes and several metabolic pathways that are more similar to those of eukaryotes, namely the enzymes involved, in transcription and translation, and their reliance on ether lipids in their cell membranes. Moreover, they are known for using more energy sources than eukaryotes do and by living in extreme environments.

According to Figs. 1 and 2, their differences in global complexity is evident, showing that after the separation with bacteria, at a DNA level, archaeas became more complex (relatively to its size) than bacteria, while eukaryotes went in the inverse direction. Perhaps, a certain level of low complexity, namely given by redundancy, is necessary to communicate and interpret efficiently a message when the communication channel introduces errors in the message.

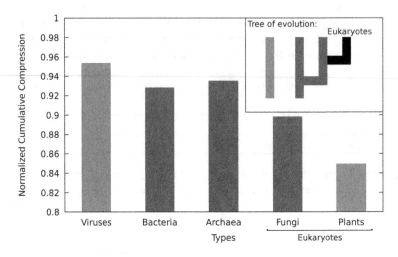

Fig. 2. Normalized cumulative compression for the viruses, bacteria, archaea, fungi and plants datasets. At the right top corner, there is the tree of evolution, according to the current literature.

Besides the three separated domains, there are the viruses. These have been defined as small infectious agents that apparently replicate inside the living cells of other organisms [23]. In fact, viruses can infect all types of life forms and, in some cases, integrate the hostage genomes [24, 25]. Their classification is currently a controversial subject, mainly because many believe that the recent discovery of the giant DNA viruses, also known as megavirus [26], should represent a separated fourth domain of life in addition to the Bacteria, Archaea and Eukarya domains [27, 28]. Despite their association with other organisms death, they are considered one of the major factors of increasing the genetic diversity of organisms [29].

According to Figs. 1 and 2, on average, viruses are short, whereas its complexity is high. However, they also have extremes, namely a few large organisms (megavirus) and a bracovirus virus with the lowest complexity from the datasets ($\sim$0.4). This bracovirus is *Microplitis demolitor* (MdBV) (gi:66527857), associated with parasitoid wasps and characterized by containing a single nucleocapsid that encapsidates one circular DNA of variable size [30].

The complexity of sequences is generally related with the length of the sequences, namely because, after communicating several messages, some patterns start to appear (unless is pure uniformly distributed), which in only one message they probably wouldn't appear [31]. However, looking for the average size (Table 3), bacteria and archaea are among the ones with larger average size, showing that archaea complexity is probably not only the consequence of its size.

4   Conclusions

The Kolmogorov complexity enables the quantification of the algorithmic complexity in DNA sequences. Because it is incomputable, we have used a normal lossless DNA compressor to obtain approximations of its value. We have assessed the compressor, showing that it is asymptotically normal. Then, we have applied it to different species and domains.

The biological results show distinct patterns of evolution on different groups of species, given their cumulative normalized compression. Namely, archaeas are more complex than bacteria, whereas eukaryotes seem to be less complex, of course regarding the average information content found in the DNA sequences. We recall that the common ancestral of archaeas and eukaryotes is generally believed to be bacteria.

However, normal compressors only show an approximation to the Kolmogorov complexity, defining an upper bound and, therefore, saying that the Kolmogorov complexity can not be higher. Therefore, it might exist a much shorter representation for a certain sequence and, hence, changing the relative results and modifying the biological conclusions.

Acknowledgments. This work was partially funded by FEDER (Programa Operacional Factores de Competitividade - COMPETE) and by National Funds through the FCT - Foundation for Science and Technology, in the context of the projects UID/CEC/00127/2013, PTCD/EEI-SII/6608/2014.

References

1. Kolmogorov, A.N.: Three approaches to the quantittative definition of information. Probl. Inf. Transm. **1**(1), 1–7 (1965)
2. Solomonoff, R.J.: A formal theory of inductive inference: Part I. Inf. Control **7**(1), 1–22 (1964)
3. Solomonoff, R.J.: A formal theory of inductive inference: Part II. Inf. Control **7**(2), 224–254 (1964)
4. Chaitin, G.J.: On the length of programs for computing finite binary sequences. J. ACM **13**, 547–569 (1966)
5. Wallace, C.S., Boulton, D.M.: An information measure for classification. Comput. J. **11**(2), 185–194 (1968)
6. Rissanen, J.: Modeling by shortest data description. Automatica **14**, 465–471 (1978)
7. Hutter, M.: Algorithmic information theory: a brief non-technical guide to the field. Scholarpedia 9620, March 2007
8. Li, M., Vitányi, P.: An Introduction to Kolmogorov Complexity and Its Applications, 3rd edn. Springer, Heidelberg (2008)
9. Turing, A.: On computable numbers, with an application to the Entscheidungs problem. Proc. Lond. Math. Soc. **42**(2), 230–265 (1936)
10. Cilibrasi, R., Vitányi, P.M.B.: Clustering by compression. IEEE Trans. Inf. Theor. **51**(4), 1523–1545 (2005)
11. Hammer, D., Romashchenko, A., Shen, A., Vereshchagin, N.: Inequalities for Shannon entropy and Kolmogorov complexity. J. Comput. Syst. Sci. **60**(2), 442–464 (2000)
12. Cebrián, M., Alfonseca, M., Ortega, A.: Common pitfalls using the normalized compression distance: what to watch out for in a compressor. Commun. Inf. Syst. **5**(4), 367–384 (2005)

13. Pratas, D., Pinho, A.J., Ferreira, P.: Efficient compression of genomic sequences. In: Proceedings of the Data Compression Conference, DCC-2016, Snowbird, UT, pp. 231–240, March 2016

14. Pratas, D.: Compression and analysis of genomic data. Ph.D. thesis, University of Aveiro (2016)

15. Hosseini, M., Pratas, D., Pinho, A.J.: A survey on data compression methods for biological sequences. Information **7**(4), 56 (2016)

16. Bywater, R.P.: Prediction of protein structural features from sequence data based on Shannon entropy and Kolmogorov complexity. PLoS ONE **10**(4), e0119306 (2015)

17. Ferreira, P.J.S.G., Pinho, A.J.: Compression-based normal similarity measures for DNA sequences. In: Proceedings of the IEEE International Conference on Acoustics, Speech, and Signal Processing, ICASSP-2014, Florence, Italy, pp. 419–423, May 2014

18. Pratas, D., Pinho, A.J., Rodrigues, J.M.O.S.: XS: a FASTQ read simulator. BMC Res. Notes **7**(1), 40 (2014)

19. Hedges, S.B.: The origin and evolution of model organisms. Nat. Rev. Genet. **3**(11), 838–849 (2002)

20. Parfrey, L.W., Grant, J., Tekle, Y.I., Lasek-Nesselquist, E., Morrison, H.G., Sogin, M.L., Patterson, D.J., Katz, L.A.: Broadly sampled multigene analyses yield a well-resolved eukaryotic tree of life. Syst. Biol. **59**(5), 518–533 (2010)

21. Podani, J., Oltvai, Z.N., Jeong, H., Tombor, B., Barabási, A.L., Szathmary, E.: Comparable system-level organization of archaea and eukaryotes. Nat. Genet. **29**(1), 54–56 (2001)

22. Wu, D., Hugenholtz, P., Mavromatis, K., Pukall, R., Dalin, E., Ivanova, N.N., Kunin, V., Goodwin, L., Wu, M., Tindall, B.J., et al.: A phylogeny-driven genomic encyclopaedia of bacteria and archaea. Nature **462**(7276), 1056–1060 (2009)

23. Koonin, E.V., Senkevich, T.G., Dolja, V.V.: The ancient virus world and evolution of cells. Biol. Direct **1**(1), 29 (2006)

24. Maumus, F., Epert, A., Nogué, F., Blanc, G.: Plant genomes enclose footprints of past infections by giant virus relatives. Nat. Commun. **5**, 4268 (2014)

25. Filée, J.: Multiple occurrences of giant virus core genes acquired by eukaryotic genomes: the visible part of the iceberg? Virology **466**, 53–59 (2014)

26. Colson, P., De Lamballerie, X., Yutin, N., Asgari, S., Bigot, Y., Bideshi, D.K., Cheng, X.W., Federici, B.A., Van Etten, J.L., Koonin, E.V., et al.: "Megavirales", a proposed new order for eukaryotic nucleocytoplasmic large DNA viruses. Arch. Virol. **158**(12), 2517–2521 (2013)

27. Forterre, P., Krupovic, M., Prangishvili, D.: Cellular domains and viral lineages. Trends Microbiol. **22**(10), 554–558 (2014)

28. Pennisi, E.: Ever-bigger viruses shake tree of life. Science **341**(6143), 226–227 (2013)

29. Canchaya, C., Fournous, G., Chibani-Chennoufi, S., Dillmann, M.L., Brüssow, H.: Phage as agents of lateral gene transfer. Curr. Opin. Microbiol. **6**(4), 417–424 (2003)

30. Bitra, K., Burke, G.R., Strand, M.R.: Permissiveness of lepidopteran hosts is linked to differential expression of bracovirus genes. Virology **492**, 259–272 (2016)

31. Pratas, D., Pinho, A.J.: Compressing the human genome using exclusively Markov models. In: Rocha, M.P., Rodríguez, J.M.C., Fdez-Riverola, F., Valencia, A. (eds.) PACBB 2011. AISC, vol. 93, pp. 213–220. Springer, Heidelberg (2011)

Prediction of Breast Deformities: A Step Forward for Planning Aesthetic Results After Breast Surgery

Sílvia Bessa$^{(\boxtimes)}$, Hooshiar Zolfagharnasab, Eduardo Pereira, and Hélder P. Oliveira

INESC TEC, Faculdade de Engenharia, Universidade do Porto, Porto, Portugal
{snbessa,hooshiar.zolfagharnasab,ejmp,helder.f.oliveira}@inesctec.pt

Abstract. The development of a three-dimensional (3D) planing tool for breast cancer surgery requires the existence of proper deformable models of the breast, with parameters that can be manipulated to obtain the desired shape. However, modelling breast is a challenging task due to the lack of physical landmarks that remain unchanged after deformation. In this paper, the fitting of a 3D point cloud of the breast to a parametric model suitable for surgery planning is investigated. Regression techniques were used to learn breast deformation functions from exemplar data, resulting in comprehensive models easy to manipulate by surgeons. New breast shapes are modelled by varying the type and degree of deformation of three common deformations: ptosis, turn and top-shape.

Keywords: Breast deformations · 3D modelling · Regression models

1 Introduction

In a world where perception of body image takes an important role in the self-esteem of most women, the high incidence rates of breast cancer have been jeopardizing the sense of femininity and quality-of-life. After being diagnosed with breast cancer, women not only face the fear of death, but also the fear of breast disfigurement, especially because surgery is still the primary treatment for this type of cancer. With the improvements in surgical procedures and oncological treatments, the aesthetic outcomes have become less dramatic. Even so, the multitude of surgical options allied with heterogeneous practices still contribute to different aesthetic results. The involvement of women in the treatment decision process has been proven benefit to accept the resulting outcomes [1]; however, the discussion of the different surgical options and the predicted cosmetic outcomes, still relies on 2D visualization of drawings, images or the use of simple morphing capabilities. Some breast surgery planing tools are already available, but modelers for surgery other than breast augmentation are less common.

Alternative 3D approaches have been addressed in later years, but they usually demand expensive 3D scanners, landmarks positioned in women torso

L.A. Alexandre et al. (Eds.): IbPRIA 2017, LNCS 10255, pp. 267–276, 2017.
DOI: 10.1007/978-3-319-58838-4_30

or complicated procedures to obtain 3D data of the patient. Moreover, most approaches are not patient-specific: they require the mapping of 3D data to a fixed model, which is posteriorly modified to describe breast deformities. This is the case of the breast modeler proposed by Seo et al. [2]. In this work, breasts are modelled with user-intuitive attributes, but 3D breast scans obtained with landmarks are mapped to a template mesh. The template mesh has a fixed number of points and triangle patches, that constitute shape vectors. Breast shapes are then generated by varying user-supplied parameters, that are translated to shape vector displacements with a linear model. Kim et al. [3] developed a 3D virtual simulator for breast plastic surgery. The subject's 3D torso data is obtained from 2D orthogonal photographs and a 3D model template is fitted to the breast, using several feature points manually marked on images. The simulation of the surgery outcome is based on the idea that each subject can be expressed as a linear combination of exemplar data. Each new breast is described as a combination of breast models in a database. The displacements between the pre and post models is known and they are used to deform the new breast.

As seen before, to develop a breast surgery planning tool, compact representations of breasts, characterized by a reduced number of parameters, are needed. A common approach to obtain such models is to fit surfaces to 3D data. Bardinet et al. [4], exploited the fitting of a deformable parametric model to 3D data. Initially, a superquadric is fitted to data, followed by a Free Form Deformation (FFD) to refine the fitting to unstructured 3D data. Chen et al. [5] also explored the use of superquadrics to model 3D data, but the parametric model of the breast is obtained by applying global deformation functions of known breast deformities, to the primitive superquadric shape. Langrarian mechanics is used to define the deformation parameters that optimizes the fitting of the model to 3D data. In alternative, Pernes et al. [6], proposed a strategy in which the fitting of the same model is accomplished by minimizing a modified version of the least squares cost function, using geometric interpretations instead of the minimum distance between data and model. It presents better fitting results in comparison with the physic-based approach of [5]. Other works [7,8] propose a parametrization of the breast by applying Principal Component Analysis (PCA) to datasets of Nuclear Magnetic Resonances. Breast models are generated by manipulating principal components to obtain the desired breast shape.

In summary, attempts to model breast deformities, usually require the positioning of landmarks on the patients' body during image acquisition. They depend on a limited number of mathematical equations, that describe particular breast deformities, or fail to be patient-specific and use adjustable parameters easy to manipulate by the common user. In this paper, it is proposed to model breast deformities by using machine-learning strategies to learn deformation parameters of known functions defined by Chen et al. [5].

2   Proposed Methodology

In an attempt to model breast surgery results, it was explored the use of machine learning techniques to learn the parameters associated with each major breast

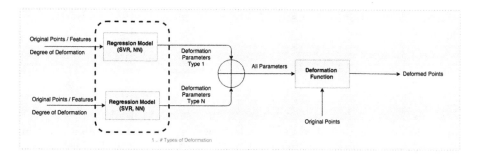

Fig. 1. Block diagram of the proposed methodology.

deformation from exemplar data. Simple adjustment parameters, such as the type and degree of deformation, are proposed to adapt the model to the desirable shape. The proposed methodology is described in the block diagram of Fig. 1. In brief, breasts are modelled by defining the types of deformations that will result from surgery, as well as the respective degrees of deformation. The user-defined parameters are combined with features automatically extracted from data and a set of regression models predict the deformation parameters, that applied to the original point cloud result in the desired shape. Considering that each deformation has to be described by a specific parametric model, there will be as many regression models as types of deformations. The final shape is the result of the combined effect of several deformations applied to the original breast.

2.1   Database

In the absence of public databases of breast deformities, the proposed methodology was developed using synthetic databases (ptosis, turn and top-shape deformations), created using the equations from [5]. In detail, first, the size of the primitive superellipsoid is defined by generating random axis values. Second, variable sets of deformation parameters are selected from a range of values, previously defined for each type of deformation: ptosis, turn, top-shape, flatten-side and top/turn deformations. These parameters are then applied to the primitive to create breasts with different appearances.

In order to train regression models for specific breast deformations, examples with varying degrees of deformation were obtained by applying the respective deformation function, with different parameters values, to the synthetic breasts. The resultant degree of deformation was subsequently quantified using a distance metric, D_{ij}, that compared the original, P_{i0}, and deformed, P_{ij}, points clouds of the breasts, as defined by Eq. 1:

$$D_{ij} = \|P_{i0} - P_{00}\| + \|P_{ij} - P_{0j}\|, \tag{1}$$

where i is a synthetic breast, to which a j set of deformation parameters was applied, and the subscript 0 refers to a reference point cloud used to align original, O and deformed breasts, M. $\|.\|$ is the normalized euclidean distance defined in:

$$\|o - m\| = \frac{\sqrt{(o_x - m_x)^2 + (o_y - m_y)^2 + (o_z - m_z)^2}}{\sqrt{o_x^2 + o_y^2 + o_z^2}}. \tag{2}$$

In this paper, regression models were trained to model ptosis, turn and top-shape deformations, described in [5]. Note, however, that the coordinate system associated to our breasts is different than the one proposed in [5]: here, z axis protrudes from the chest wall outward through the nipple (anterior-posterior), y axis goes up (inferior-superior), and x axis goes from right to left (lateral-medial). All deformations functions were adapted for this system of coordinates.

2.2   Regression Models

In pursuit of a proper regression model to predict the parameters associated with each deformation, a preliminary optimization stage was carried for ptosis. Note that ptosis describes the sagging effect of the breast, which mathematically translates to a shift in the y coordinates, defined as a quadratic function of the z coordinates of points, with b_0 and b_1 parameters: $S_y = b_0 z + b_1 z^2$ (adapted from [5]). For this study, five feature sets were designed (Table 1), and a reference feature set (REF) was defined containing the displacement in y points coordinates (S_y). By using S_y as input feature, the model is biased because this is exactly what we want to measure. However, it will serve as ground truth to validate the models. All features were normalized to the range of 0 and 1. The benefit of using PCA for feature selection was also considered.

Table 1. Feature sets of the ptosis study: DD - degree of deformation, uppercase refer to vectors of all coordinates, lowercase are average coordinates values and 0 referrers to original coordinates.

Acronym	Features						
	DD	v_0	Z_0	Y_0	z_0	y_0	S_y
REF	X	X	X				X
FS1	X	X	X				
FS2	X	X	X	X			
FS3	X	X		X			
FS4	X	X					
FS5	X	X			X	X	

For each feature set, Linear Regression (LR), Support Vector Machine (SVM) and Neural Network (NN) regression models were explored and their relative performances were compared. The simple LR was considered and polynomial basis functions up to the 4th degree were tested, either with or without intercept term. SVM regressions were trained with linear, polynomial and RBF kernels, and a grid-search optimization strategy was used to select the best parametrization. In particular, exponentially growing sequences of C and γ (only for RBF kernel) were tested: $C = 2^{-5}, 2^{-3}, ..., 2^7$, and $\gamma = 2^{-5}, 2^{-3}, ..., 2^3$. Feedforward NNs with one hidden layer were trained with a varying number of neurons, $\{5, 10, 25, 50, 75\}$, using the Scaled Conjugate Gradient Backpropagation. All regression models were optimized using 4-fold cross validation in the train datasets and the Relative Mean Squared Error as evaluation metric. Where $f(x_i)$ are the predicted values from regressions applied to testing data x_i, whose true target values of testing data are y_i. The performance of the best parametrization was evaluated on test datasets using distances between original (O) and modelled (M) breasts as indirect performance metrics. Here, both Hausdorff (Eq. 3) and mean Euclidean (Eq. 2) distances were used.

$$h(O, M) = \max_{o \in O} \min_{m \in M} ||o - m|| \qquad (3)$$

where O and M are the matrix of points (N points $\times$ 3 dimensions X, Y and Z), and $||.||$ is the normalized euclidean distance defined in Eq. 2. To provide a fairly comparison between breasts with different sizes and resolutions within the same dataset, distances are normalized by the distance of the original point cloud to the origin of the coordinate system. Distances are computed between original and modelled breasts, and in both directions; the Hausdorff distance is used because it describes the worst case scenario. Finally, the best combination of feature set, were adapted for turn and top shape deformations.

3   Experimental Results

3.1   Optimization of Regression Models

Regression models were optimized on datasets containing ptosis examples. All examples shared the same original appearance, but had different sizes. In this stage, the influence of several scenarios (Table 2) were considered when analysing the performance of models to predict single ptosis parameters at time (b_0 or b_1). Hypothesis tests with a significance level of 5% were conducted to compare and decide upon the best scenario. Statistical tests were conducted with the RMSE results of four conditions: single parameters predicted at time (b_0 or b_1) and multiple output predictions: $b_0 > b_1$ or $b_1 \geq b_0$.

To consider the effect of the number of degrees of deformation, models were trained and tested with 200/60 or 400/120 (train/test) examples, depending if 4 or 8° of deformation were used, respectively. Results of the one-sided t-test suggest that results of models trained with 8° of deformation had significantly lower RMSE ($p = 0.0027$). This was expected because, despite the use of categorical values as inputs, regression models are modelled with continuous variables. So, a higher number of degrees should lead to better fittings. LR models always performed worst than SVM or NN, but no significant differences were found

Table 2. Optimization Scenarios Explored.

Scenario	Hypothesis	Statistical test	p-value
Degrees of deformation	{4,**8**}	One-sided t-test	0.0027*
Feature selection	{**none**, PCA}	Paired t-test	0.1725
Regression model	{SVM, **NN**}	Paired t-test	0.2300

*highlights significant differences with a significance level of 5%.
Bold hypothesis were selected for subsequent stages.

between SVM and NN models. NN regression models were introduced envision-ing the task of predicting multiple parameters of the same deformation function because, contrarily to SVM, NN take in consideration the correlation of the out-puts in the learning process. So thorough analysis of the models was carried considering only multiple outputs conditions and it revealed that NN regres-sions trained with the optimal feature set had slightly better results than SVM models. Regarding feature selection, results suggest no benefit in using PCA, although the optimal feature set varied whether PCA was applied or not: when PCA was used, the best feature set was $FS2$, while without PCA, the optimal feature was $FS5$. This was not unexpected, because both $FS2$ and $FS5$ con-tain z and y coordinates produced, varying only on the number of points used. So, the similar results only corroborate the high correlation between the same coordinates of all points. Therefore, preference was given to NN models trained without PCA and using feature set $FS5$. The use of $FS5$ avoids interpolations to apply the regression models to breast point clouds with varying number of features, because only the coordinates of the average point are used.

3.2   Prediction of Ptosis, Turn and Top-Shape Deformations

Next, the optimal scenarios used to generate regression models for ptosis, turn and top-shape deformations are presented. Models were trained and tested with 384 and 64 examples, respectively, and breasts with varying sizes and shapes were used. To predict ptosis, regression models were obtained using $FS5$. An adapted version of this feature set was used to predict turn, in which x coordinates are used instead of y coordinates. This is because in turn deformation, points are changed as a quadratic function of their z coordinates, but the displacement occurs along the x axis instead: $S_x = b_0 z + b_1 z^2$ (adapted from [5]). In top-shape deformations, points change along the z axis, as function of their angular position $\mathbf{u}$ in relation to the nipple [5], where 4 parameters can be adjusted to model the top-half profile of the breast. However, only the influence of s_0 and s_1 parameters was modelled, which respectively control the slope of breast points near the chest wall and the nipple. For modelling top-shape deformations, the y coordinate in $FS5$ could have been replaced by spherical coordinates but, instead, it was included all Cartesian coordinates and relied on the NN capacity of modelling the angles by itself. Besides, the degree of deformation of top-shape deformations was quantified with a modified version of Eq. 1, in which the normalized Euclidean distance was replaced by the Hausdorff distance:

$$D_{ij} = \|P_{i0} - P_{00}\| + \max_{p_{ij} \in P_{ij}} \min_{p_{0j} \in P_{0j}} \|p_{ij} - p_{0j}\|. \qquad (4)$$

This was a necessary modification because the effect of varying the top shape slope parameters is specially notorious on the center area of the top breast profile, which makes Hausdorff distance more appropriate to quantify this effect.

Table 3 presents the indirect performances of all deformation models. Results suggest that models learned properly and no significant difference is found when measuring the distances in different directions (*Modelled* ⇒ *Original* and *Original* ⇒ *Modelled*). For all outputs, the average Euclidean and Hausdorff distances are lower than 3% and 10%, respectively. The worst case scenario is

Table 3. Indirect performance metrics of NN regression models predicting breast deformations. Relative distances (percentages) are shown.

Deformation	Outputs	Statistics	Modelled ⇒ Original		Original ⇒ Modelled	
			Euclidean	Hausdorff	Euclidean	Hausdorff
Ptosis	$b_0 > b_1$	μ	1.66	5.69	2.10	6.52
		σ	1.38	4.60	2.51	6.66
		Min	0.10	0.18	0.10	0.18
		Max	6.71	22.22	11.76	30.97
	$b_1 \geq b_0$	μ	2.98	9.64	2.08	7.25
		σ	5.56	14.44	1.95	5.10
		Min	0.16	0.46	0.16	0.46
		Max	37.94	95.87	11.90	25.79
Turn	$c_0 > c_1$	μ	2.21	6.77	2.12	6.53
		σ	2.22	6.30	1.86	5.69
		Min	0.19	0.41	0.18	0.41
		Max	11.09	29.62	8.36	26.63
	$c_1 > c_0$	μ	1.67	6.04	1.86	6.54
		σ	1.31	4.24	1.60	4.90
		Min	0.16	0.38	0.16	0.38
		Max	7.16	21.81	6.72	20.22
Top-Shape	$\|s_0\| > \|s_1^+\|$	μ	0.56	4.66	0.56	4.65
		σ	0.37	3.36	0.37	3.34
		Min	0.00	0.02	0.00	0.02
		Max	1.48	15.07	1.46	14.95
	$\|s_1\| > \|s_0\|$	μ	0.77	6.21	0.76	6.22
		σ	0.39	3.60	0.37	3.60
		Min	0.10	0.71	0.10	0.71
		Max	1.59	14.01	1.41	13.88

found in the prediction of $b_1 > b_0$, with Euclidean and Hausdorff distances going up to 38% and 96%. However, the residual analysis of this model (Fig. 2a) confirmed the existence of an outlier (signaled by a red arrow). Thorough analysis of the results showed that the outlier is an example of deformation caused by a high value, whose degree of deformation was badly assigned when converting the distance in Eq. 1 to a categorical value. In spite of the existence of an outlier, residual analysis of the model still suggests goodness of fitting for ptosis' regression model: residuals are slightly randomly dispersed in scatter plots of target, or predicted values, versus residuals; no structure is clearly identifiable in Lag plots and residuals distributions are approximately normal, as implied by residuals' histogram and normal plots. Similar analysis could be made for turn deformation, so that was not included in the paper. The performances of the top shape deformations models suggest the suitability of the proposed modifications. However, in the residuals analysis of top-shape deformations, the distribution of target versus predicted values is not as linear as in ptosis or turn deformation models, particularly in the condition $s_1^- > s_0^+$ (Fig. 2b): scatter plots of residuals suggest some structure in the residuals, confirmed by a clear linear distribution of values in the Lag plot. This means that, although the overall differences between modeled and original top shape deformations are low, the generalization of these models as to be carefully considered, perhaps including additional features or revisiting the methodology used to define the degree of deformation. Nonetheless, examples of the average predictions of ptosis, turn and top-shape deformation parameters shown in Fig. 3 confirm the ability of the models to predict breast deformations with small errors.

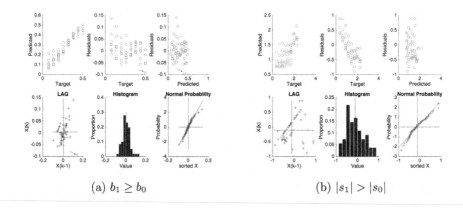

(a) $b_1 \geq b_0$ (b) $|s_1| > |s_0|$

Fig. 2. 6-plot residual analysis for ptosis (left) and top-shape (right) models. Red Arrow signals the presence of and outlier prediction. (Color figure online)

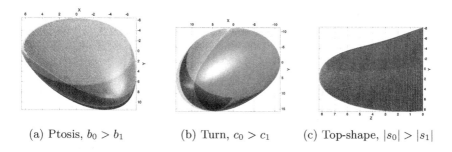

(a) Ptosis, $b_0 > b_1$ (b) Turn, $c_0 > c_1$ (c) Top-shape, $|s_0| > |s_1|$

Fig. 3. Examples of modelled breasts from average predictions (skin color), superimposed on the target shape (black) ((a) and (b) front views, (c) side-view).

4   Conclusions

In the proposed methodology, breast deformations are modelled using regression models learnt from exemplar data. At first, a complete study was carried on ptosis, to prove the usefulness of regression models, to predict parameters of know deformation functions, and the type and degree of deformation were suggested as adaptable parameters to create the desired breast shape. Next, the best type of regression model and set of features were tested in the prediction of other types of deformation, namely turn and top shape deformations. The parametric models were able to predict deformation parameters with good performances, using only the degree of deformation as simple and comprehensible parameter to adjust the shape of breast.

Acknowledgements. This work was funded by the Project NanoSTIMA: Macro to Nano Human Sensing: Towards Integrated Multimodal Health Monitoring and Analytics/NORTE-01-0145-FEDER-000016 financed by the North Portugal Regional Operational Programme (NORTE 2020), under the PORTUGAL 2020 Partnership Agreement, and through the European Regional Development Fund (ERDF), and also by Fundao para a Cincia e a Tecnologia (FCT) within PhD grant number SFRH/BD/115616/2016.

References

1. Kim, M., Kim, T., Moon, H.-G., Jin, U.S., Kim, K., Kim, J., Lee, J., Lee, E., Yoo, T.-K., Noh, D.-Y., et al.: Effect of cosmetic outcome on quality of life after breast cancer surgery. Eur. J. Surg. Oncol. (EJSO) **41**(3), 426–432 (2015)
2. Seo, H., Cordier, F., Hong, K.: A breast modeler based on analysis of breast scans. Comput. Animation Virtual Worlds **18**(2), 141–151 (2007)
3. Kim, Y., Lee, K., Kim, W.: 3D virtual simulator for breast plastic surgery. Comput. Animation Virtual Worlds **19**(3–4), 515–526 (2008)
4. Bardinet, E., Cohen, L.D., Ayache, N.: A parametric deformable model to fit unstructured 3D data. Comput. Vis. Image Underst. **71**(1), 39–54 (1998)

5. Chen, D.T., Kakadiaris, I.A., Miller, M.J., Loftin, R.B., Patrick, C.: Modeling for plastic and reconstructive breast surgery. In: Delp, S.L., DiGoia, A.M., Jaramaz, B. (eds.) MICCAI 2000. LNCS, vol. 1935, pp. 1040–1050. Springer, Heidelberg (2000). doi:10.1007/978-3-540-40899-4_108
6. Pernes, D., Cardoso, J.S., Oliveira, H.P.: Fitting of superquadrics for breast modelling by geometric distance minimization. In: 2014 IEEE International Conference on Bioinformatics and Biomedicine (BIBM), pp. 293–296. IEEE (2014)
7. Gallo, G., Guarnera, G.C., Milanese, F., Modica, D., Catanuto, G., Pane, F.: Parametric representation of human breast shapes (2009)
8. Gallo, G., Guarnera, G.C., Catanuto, G.: Human breast shape analysis using PCA.' In: BIOSIGNALS, pp. 163–167. Citeseer (2010)

Applications

Staff-Line Detection on Grayscale Images with Pixel Classification

Jorge Calvo-Zaragoza[1]([✉]), Gabriel Vigliensoni[2], and Ichiro Fujinaga[2]

[1] Pattern Recognition and Artificial Intelligence Group,
University of Alicante, Alicante, Spain
jcalvo@dlsi.ua.es

[2] Schulich School of Music, CIRMMT, McGill University, Montréal, Canada
{gabriel,ich}@music.mcgill.ca

Abstract. Staff-line detection and removal are important processing steps in most Optical Music Recognition systems. Traditional methods make use of heuristic strategies based on image processing techniques with binary images. However, binarization is a complex process for which it is difficult to achieve perfect results. In this paper we describe a novel staff-line detection and removal method that deals with grayscale images directly. Our approach uses supervised learning to classify each pixel of the image as *symbol*, *staff*, or *background*. This classification is achieved by means of Convolutional Neural Networks. The features of each pixel consist of a square window from the input image centered at the pixel to be classified. As a case of study, we performed experiments with the CVC-Muscima dataset. Our approach showed promising performance, outperforming state-of-the-art algorithms for staff-line removal.

Keywords: Music recognition · Staff-line removal · Grayscale domain

1 Introduction

A large amount of music documents scattered across cathedrals, museums, and historical archives have been carefully preserved over centuries. However, their massive digitization is an essential step for enabling access to these documents and improving their preservation. Large-scale digitization of music documents requires new Music Information Retrieval (MIR) algorithms and systems for extracting and encoding symbolic information within them [1]. The outcome of large-scale digitization initiatives is of interest for the musicological community because it will allow the study of large amounts of musical information, going beyond what a human can achieve after years of manual, tedious, and expensive transcription. As a consequence, Optical Music Recognition (OMR) systems have gained relevance since they allow the extraction of the musical information contained in the image of a music score and export its musical content into a machine-readable format.

OMR tasks are somewhat similar to Optical Character Recognition. However, the different organization and layout of music notation, in comparison to

© Springer International Publishing AG 2017
L.A. Alexandre et al. (Eds.): IbPRIA 2017, LNCS 10255, pp. 279–286, 2017.
DOI: 10.1007/978-3-319-58838-4_31

text, has led to the development of specialized techniques [2]. Although previous research has been conducted on the recognition of isolated music symbols [3,4], OMR systems have to deal with further aspects of music notation. Staff lines are necessary for human readability but they represent one of the most challenging obstacles for the automatic isolation of music symbols. Although a few previous OMR approaches took advantage of specific and unique features of the documents to process them without removing the staff lines [5,6], the most common OMR workflow include the detection and removal of staff lines [7] (see Fig. 1).

(a) Piece of score image   (b) Image after staff-line removal

Fig. 1. Example of a perfect staff-line removal process.

Even though staff-line detection and removal may seems like a simple task, it is often difficult to get accurate results. This is mainly due to sheet deformations such as discontinuities, skewing, or paper degradation (especially in ancient documents). In addition, musical documents are very heterogeneous and so it is difficult to develop methods that work on different types of scores.

Dalitz et al. [8] reviewed the first attempts in the detection and removal of staff lines, with a number of other approaches which have been proposed recently. Cardoso et al. [9] proposed a method that considers the staff lines as connecting paths between the two margins of the score. The score was modeled as a graph so that staff detection was solved as a maximization problem. They also extended the solution to deal with grayscale images [10]. Dutta et al. [11] developed a method that considered the staff line segment as a horizontal connection of vertical black runs with uniform height. Piatkowska et al. [12] designed a method that used a Swarm Intelligence algorithm. Their approach can apparently deal with any type of image, but only results on binary images were reported. Su et al. [13] fitted an approximate staff considering properties such as height and space. Geraud [14] developed a method based on a series of morphological operators to remove staff lines. Montagner et al. [15] proposed to learn image operators whose combination remove staff lines.

Traditional formulations for the staff-line detection task consider a binary image as input because it helps to reduce the complexity of the problem. In addition, binarization is mandatory for applying processes based on morphological operators, histogram analysis, or connected components. The binary nature of modern music scores (i.e., black ink over white paper) has justified somewhat this workflow. However, binarization processes are highly prone to conditions of the documents such as irregular lighting, image skewing, ink blots, and paper degradation. As a consequence, perfect performance can not be guaranteed. Since staff-line detection and removal processes are very sensitive to the accuracy of the binarization, they are limited by this preprocessing step. In this paper we present an approach that can be used for the detection and removal of staff lines on the grayscale domain. We extend the method proposed by Calvo-Zaragoza et al. [16], in which a classifier was trained to discriminate if a *foreground* pixel of a binary image belongs to a *symbol* or to a *staff line*. In our case, however, there are three potential categories for labeling a pixel: *background, staff,* or *symbol.*

The rest of this article is structured as follows: the proposed method is described in Sect. 2; results obtained are presented and discussed in Sect. 3; finally, our work is concluded in Sect. 4, in which a few paths for future work and research are presented.

2 Staff-Line Detection on Grayscale Images with Pixel Classification

Our approach considers staff-line detection and removal as a classification task at pixel level. We use a Convolutional Neural Network (CNN) trained to distinguish among the three potential categories for each pixel: *symbols, staff,* and *background.*

We assume that the region surrounding each pixel of interest contains enough information to discriminate the label of each pixel. Hence, the input to the network is a portion of the input image centered at the pixel of interest. The size of this portion is a parameter to be tuned. In this work, 28×28 feature windows were finally selected after preliminary experimentation. Figure 2 shows examples of feature windows for the categories considered from a grayscale musical score. No further feature extraction is performed on this portion of the image because this task is expected to be assumed by the CNN itself [17].

Fig. 2. Example of feature extraction with a square window size of 28×28. The pixel to be classified is located at the center of the extracted patch of image.

There are diverse topologies of CNNs but, the 3-layer topology described in Table 1 showed a fair trade-off between effectiveness and efficiency in the aforementioned preliminary experimentation. Note that the CNN used hyperbolic tangents (tanh) as activation functions because they exhibited a better generalization behavior than other functions—such as Rectified Linear Units—for our task. At the end of these layers, a softmax operator with 3 units is added to compute the probability given to each considered category.

Table 1. Description of the three convolutional-pooling layers considered for the staff-line removal task.

Convolution				Pooling	
Layer	Filters	Kernel	Activation	Kernel	Type
1	50	10×10	tanh	2×2	max
2	30	5×5	tanh	2×2	max
3	10	2×2	tanh	2×2	max

The learning of the network weights is performed by means of stochastic gradient descent with a batch size of 32, considering the adaptive learning rate proposed in [18] (default parameterization) and the *cross-entropy* loss function. Once the CNN is trained, every single pixel of a given image can be classified among the three categories considered.

3   Experimentation

In order to test the performance of our approach, we carried out an experiment with images of the dataset considered for the *ICDAR/GREC 2013 Competition on Music Scores* [19]. This corpus contains 6 000 pairs of scores with and without staff lines, divided into train and test partition of 4 000 and 2 000 pairs, respectively. Also, the scores come in binary and grayscale format. Therefore, this dataset provided us with readily available data: using the binary format and the images without the staff lines, black pixels were considered *symbol*; using the binary format and the images with staff lines, white pixels were considered *background*; finally, the XOR operation on each pixel of the two versions of the binary format, the one with the staff and the one without, produced images with black pixels of *staff* category.

Table 2. Confusion matrix depicting the percentage of pixels whose actual label is indicated in the column, classified with the label depicted in the row.

Classified as	Actual label		
	Symbol	Staff	Background
Symbol	85.63	4.62	0.59
Staff	0.68	73.36	0.63
Background	13.70	22.01	98.78

In Table 2 we show the resultant confusion matrix depicting the percentage of pixels whose actual label is indicated by the column names, classified with the label depicted in the rows, obtained after applying our approach on the test partition. In this case, the training set has not been used in its totality but

100 000 pixels from each category were selected at random. We also considered 30% of this set as validation to adjust the number of training epochs and prevent overfitting.

It can be seen that the main classification problems happened when detecting staff-line pixels, which were often mislabeled as background. As we will see later, this problem is innocuous if running a music symbol isolation task. Moreover, a noticeable percentage of symbol pixel were classified as background as well. As we will see below, this is probably caused by *symbol* pixels that are very close to the boundary, so they are often confused by those *background* pixels that are attached to a symbol. In this case, the network finds it difficult to discern between the two categories since the feature window is very similar in both cases.

In order to facilitate the assessment of these results, in Fig. 3 we show an example of the classification process for both staff-line detection and removal. As a visual, illustrative example of the performance numbers shown in Table 2, we highlighted in the resultant image each category by using a different color. While most symbols were classified correctly, the main misclassification happened in staff lines detected in background regions. On the other hand, we can observe that for task of staff-line removal, whose main objective is to isolate the music symbols of the image, the result is quite successful.

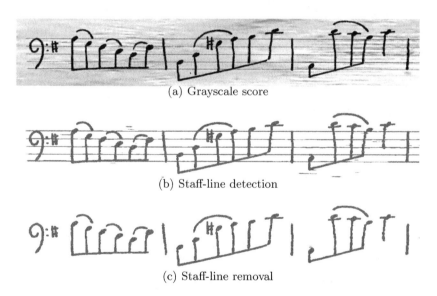

(a) Grayscale score

(b) Staff-line detection

(c) Staff-line removal

Fig. 3. Staff-line detection and removal on grayscale images. Pixels are coloured according to their predicted category: *symbol* pixels are red, *staff* pixels are blue, and *background* pixels are white. (Color figure online)

Although these preliminary results are encouraging, the biggest value of this approach is its adaptability and generalizability since the only parameters to be changed are the training data as well as the window size for the region of interest.

Therefore, it can be easily extended to other types of musical documents such as printed scores or hand-written manuscripts, in binary, grayscale, or colored images, as long as appropriate training examples are available.

3.1 Comparison with Staff-Line Removal Methods

Although the staff-line detection and removal contest from which our data was taken provided both binary and grayscale images, only two participants in the contest submitted a method to deal with grayscale images: LRDE [14] and INESC [10]. Their methods were based on published approaches (see Sect. 1). However, the actual submissions were slightly changed for the contest and so the reader is referred to the contest report to obtain a detailed description of these strategies [20].

Since the underlying objective of the contest was to detect the staff lines for their subsequent removal, it is important to emphasize that the results of our experiment are not directly comparable to the results from the contest. The contest evaluation only took into account the pixels that belonged either to staff lines or to music symbols, discarding the labels assigned to background pixels. Nevertheless, we took advantage of the contest to verify the goodness of our approach, and we merged *background* and *staff* labels since both pixel types would be eventually be removed.

The test set in the *ICDAR/GREC 2013* contest was divided into three subsets (TS1, TS2, and TS3) in order to measure the robustness of the participants' submissions with respect to deformations applied to the scores: 3D distortions in TS1 (500 scores), local noise in TS2 (500 scores), and both 3D distortion and local noise in TS3 (1000 scores). Table 3 shows the results obtained by each participant and the ones obtained by our approach. As in the contest, the performance evaluation metric is the well-known F_1 score (or F-measure).

Table 3. F_1 (%) for symbol element comparison between LRDE, INESC, and our method using grayscale images. Only actual staff lines and symbol pixels were considered. Values in bold represent the best average accuracy in each set.

Method	TS1	TS2	TS3	Global
LRDE	**92.1**	79.5	81.5	83.7
INESC	38.5	52.1	38.9	42.1
Our approach	**92.1**	**90.7**	**90.2**	**90.58**

Globally, our approach outperformed the other submissions, in particular with respect to the INESC method. LRDE had a competitive accuracy with the test set with 3D deformations, but its performance decreased noticeably when local noise was applied to the images. Our method also suffered some accuracy loss with added noise, but the results show that it was able to handle deformations and noise in a more robust way.

4   Conclusions

In this work we studied and evaluated the detection and removal of staff lines in music scores following a classification approach at pixel level. In order to avoid errors produced by non-reliable binarization methods, our method works with grayscale images directly. We compared our approach in a standard dataset for staff line detection and removal, and demonstrated to be competitive in comparison with state-of-the-art algorithms, showing a robust performance against deformations and noise added to the images.

As future work, it would be interesting to perform a thorough comparison between our approach and combinations of binarization algorithms followed by conventional staff-line removal algorithms. In addition, we are interested in checking the performance in old musical documents, for which the conditions of the sheets are more complex to learn and training data is not available easily. For this case, the use of fine-tuning strategies and data augmentation techniques are to be considered.

Acknowledgements. This work has been supported by the Social Sciences and Humanities Research Council of Canada and the Spanish Ministerio de Educación, Cultura y Deporte through a FPU Fellowship (Ref. AP2012–0939).

References

1. Typke, R., Wiering, F., Veltkamp, R.C.: A survey of music information retrieval systems. In: Proceedings of the 6th International Conference on Music Information Retrieval, London, UK, pp. 153–160 (2005)
2. Bainbridge, D., Bell, T.: The challenge of optical music recognition. Comput. Humanit. **35**(2), 95–121 (2001)
3. Rebelo, A., Capela, G., Cardoso, J.S.: Optical recognition of music symbols. Int. J. Doc. Anal. Recogn. (IJDAR) **13**(1), 19–31 (2010)
4. Calvo-Zaragoza, J., Oncina, J.: Recognition of pen-based music notation: the HOMUS dataset. In: 22nd International Conference on Pattern Recognition (ICPR), Stockholm, Sweden, pp. 3038–3043 (2014)
5. Pugin, L.: Optical music recognition of early typographic prints using hidden Markov models. In: Proceedings of the 7th International Conference on Music Information Retrieval, pp. 53–56 (2006)
6. Calvo-Zaragoza, J., Barbancho, I., Tardón, L.J., Barbancho, A.M.: Avoiding staff removal stage in optical music recognition: application to scores written in white mensural notation. Pattern Anal. Appl. **18**(4), 933–943 (2015)
7. Rebelo, A., Fujinaga, I., Paszkiewicz, F., Marçal, A.R.S., Guedes, C., Cardoso, J.S.: Optical music recognition: state-of-the-art and open issues. Int. J. Multimedia Inf. Retr. (IJMIR) **1**(3), 173–190 (2012)
8. Dalitz, C., Droettboom, M., Pranzas, B., Fujinaga, I.: A comparative study of staff removal algorithms. IEEE Trans. Pattern Anal. Mach. Intell. **30**(5), 753–766 (2008)
9. Dos Santos Cardoso, J., Capela, A., Rebelo, A., Guedes, C., Pinto da Costa, J.: Staff detection with stable paths. IEEE Trans. Pattern Anal. Mach. Intell. **31**(6), 1134–1139 (2009)

10. Rebelo, A., Cardoso, J.: Staff line detection and removal in the grayscale domain. In: Proceedings of the 12th International Conference on Document Analysis and Recognition (ICDAR), pp. 57–61, August 2013
11. Dutta, A., Pal, U., Fornés, A., Llados, J.: An efficient staff removal approach from printed musical documents. In: Proceedings of the 20th International Conference on Pattern Recognition (ICPR), pp. 1965–1968, August 2010
12. Piątkowska, W., Nowak, L., Pawłowski, M., Ogorzałek, M.: Stafflines pattern detection using the swarm intelligence algorithm. In: Bolc, L., Tadeusiewicz, R., Chmielewski, L.J., Wojciechowski, K. (eds.) ICCVG 2012. LNCS, vol. 7594, pp. 557–564. Springer, Heidelberg (2012). doi:10.1007/978-3-642-33564-8_67
13. Su, B., Lu, S., Pal, U., Tan, C.: An effective staff detection and removal technique for musical documents. In: Proceedings of the 10th IAPR International Workshop on Document Analysis Systems (DAS), pp. 160–164 (2012)
14. Géraud, T.: A morphological method for music score staff removal. In: Proceedings of the 21st International Conference on Image Processing (ICIP), Paris, France, pp. 2599–2603 (2014)
15. dos Santos Montagner, I., Hirata, R., Hirata, N.S.: A machine learning based method for staff removal. In: Proceedings of the 22nd International Conference on Pattern Recognition (ICPR), pp. 3162–3167 (2014)
16. Calvo-Zaragoza, J., Micó, L., Oncina, J.: Music staff removal with supervised pixel classification. IJDAR 19(3), 211–219 (2016)
17. LeCun, Y., Bengio, Y., Hinton, G.: Deep learning. Nature 521(7553), 436–444 (2015)
18. Zeiler, M.D.: ADADELTA: an adaptive learning rate method. CoRR abs/1212.5701 (2012)
19. Fornés, A., Kieu, V.C., Visani, M., Journet, N., Dutta, A.: The ICDAR/GREC 2013 music scores competition: staff removal. In: Proceedings of the 10th International Workshop on Graphics Recognition, Current Trends and Challenges GREC, Revised Selected Papers, Bethlehem, PA, USA, pp. 207–220 (2013)
20. Visaniy, M., Kieu, V., Fornés, A., Journet, N.: ICDAR/GREC 2013 music scores competition: staff removal. In: Proceedings of the 12th International Conference on Document Analysis and Recognition (ICDAR), pp. 1407–1411 (2013)

Information Extraction in Handwritten Marriage Licenses Books Using the MGGI Methodology

Verónica Romero[1(✉)], Alicia Fornés[2], Enrique Vidal[1],
and Joan Andreu Sánchez[1]

[1] PRHLT Research Center, Universitat Politécnica de Valéncia, Valencia, Spain
{vromero,evidal,jandreu}@prhlt.upv.es
[2] Department of Computer Science, Computer Vision Center,
Universitat Autónoma de Barcelona, Bellaterra, Spain
afornes@cvc.uab.es

Abstract. Historical records of daily activities provide intriguing insights into the life of our ancestors, useful for demographic and genealogical research. For example, marriage license books have been used for centuries by ecclesiastical and secular institutions to register marriages. These books follow a simple structure of the text in the records with a evolutionary vocabulary, mainly composed of proper names that change along the time. This distinct vocabulary makes automatic transcription and semantic information extraction difficult tasks. In previous works we studied the use of category-based language models and how a Grammatical Inference technique known as MGGI could improve the accuracy of these tasks. In this work we analyze the main causes of the semantic errors observed in previous results and apply a better implementation of the MGGI technique to solve these problems. Using the resulting language model, transcription and information extraction experiments have been carried out, and the results support our proposed approach.

Keywords: Handwritten Text Recognition · Information extraction · Language modeling · MGGI · Categories-based language model

1 Introduction

Handwritten marriage licenses books [7] have been used for centuries by ecclesiastical and secular institutions to register marriages. The information contained in these historical documents is very interesting for demography studies and genealogical research. Therefore, one of the goals of this kind of documents, rather than to transcribe them perfectly, is to extract their relevant information to allow the users to make use of it through semantic searches.

The automatic transcription of historical documents is currently based on techniques that have been used in Automatic Speech Recognition, such as Hidden Markov Models (HMM) [9] or Artificial Neural Networks (ANN) [3] for representing optical models, and n-gram models for language modeling.

© Springer International Publishing AG 2017
L.A. Alexandre et al. (Eds.): IbPRIA 2017, LNCS 10255, pp. 287–294, 2017.
DOI: 10.1007/978-3-319-58838-4_32

This is due, in part, to the problems found by traditional Optical Character Recognition (OCR) techniques to segment the linguistic components of these images like characters, words or sentences automatically. Therefore, holistic approaches, that do not need prior segmentation, are needed [5].

The language model plays a fundamental role in the Handwritten Text Recognition (HTR) process by restricting significantly the search space. Although the training of the optical models is still an incipient research field, significant improvements can be obtained by using better language models. For example, in [8], given the regular structure of marriage licenses documents, the use of a category-based language model [6] to both better representing the regularities in marriage license books and for obtaining the relevant semantic information of each record was presented with encouraging results. In [10], a Grammatical Inference technique known as MGGI [11] was studied to improve the semantic accuracy of the category-based language model obtained in [8].

In MGGI, a-priory knowledge is used to label the words of the training strings in such a way that a simple bigram can be trained from the transformed strings. The knowledge used allows the MGGI to produce a language model which captures important dependencies of the language underlying in the handwritten records considered.

In this paper we analyze the main semantic errors with the category-based language model presented in [10] and relabel the words of the training strings, before applying the MGGI methodology. Our objective is to capture important dependencies of the licenses structure that were not captured in the previous version, such as the relative position of the information within the record.

2   Task Description

In this work we have used a handwritten marriage license book from a collection conserved at the Archives of the Cathedral of Barcelona and described in [7]. It is the same book used in previous works such as [8,10].

Each marriage license typically contains information about the marriage day, groom's and bride's names, the groom's occupation, the groom's and bride's former marital status, and the socio-economic position given by the amount of the fee. This information is not written randomly but the opposite. The groom's information is written first and then the bride's information. Inside the groom's information, the given name and surnames are written first, then the birth town and then the occupation. Then the groom's father information is in a similar order, and then the bride's information. In some cases, additional information is given as well as information about a deceased parent. This structure suggests that the vocabulary changes along the license: the first part is related to the groom, with names related to men and occupations, whereas, the last part is the bride's part. Figure 1 shows an example of an isolated marriage license.

As discussed in [10], a problem when transcribing handwritten marriage license books by means of HTR methods is that the classical n-gram language models can be very inaccurate due to the restrictions of the underlying language.

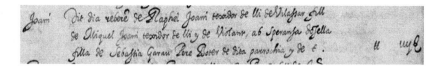

Fig. 1. Example of a marriage license.

Contrary to popular languages such as English or Spanish, these documents are written in old Catalan, and the amount of available datasets for training in this language are very scarce.

Another problem is due to the special vocabulary of this collection, since it is mainly composed of proper names. For example, consider the license of the Fig. 1 that starts with the following sentence referred to the groom:

`Dit dia rebere$ de Raphel Joani texidor de lli de Vilassar ...`

The translation of this sentence is:

`That day we received from Raphel Joani linen weaver from Vilassar ...`

Note that is quite difficult to predict the word `Raphel` from the previous words since any (groom's) given name can appear in this position. Something similar occurs for other words, like `Joani`, (groom's surname) `linen` or `Vilassar` (groom's town). However, if the groom's given name is categorized, the number of contexts in the n-gram model is reduced and, therefore, is easy to predict the correct word. This is the idea described in the following section.

3 Category-Based HTR

As shown in [8], the use of a category language model in the handwritten text recognition process can benefit both, the handwritten accuracy and the semantic information extraction process. This improvement is due to two main reason. Firstly, given that the category-based language models shares statistics between words of the same category, category-based models are able to generalize to word patterns never encountered in the training corpus. Secondly, grouping words into categories can reduce the number of contexts in an n-gram model, and thereby reduce the training set sparseness problem.

In this paper, the same semantic categories defined in [8] have been used: groom's (Gr) given name and surname, bride's (Br) given name and surname, parents' (Fa and Mo) given names and surnames, occupations (Oc), place of residence ($Resi$), geographical origin, etc. Then, a category-based language model has been generated and integrated into the handwritten text recognition process. Next, the annotated license corresponding to the image in Fig. 1 is shown. Each semantic label (marked into brackets) is immediately after the relevant word:

```
Dit dia rebere$ de Raphel[GrName] Joani[GrSurname] texidor_de_lli[GrOc]
de Vilassar[GrResi] fill de Miquel[GrFaName] Joani[GrFaSurname]
texidor_de_lli[GrFaOc] y de Violant[GrMoName], ab Sperensa[BrName]
do$sella filla de Sebastia_Garau[BrFaName]   Pere[BrFaSurname]
Boter[BrFaOc] de dita_parrochia[BrFaResi] y de t.[BrMoName]
```

As shown in the example, only some words had relevant semantic information. Our categorization focuses on these relevant words, and a partially categorized corpus was obtained. Words that do not have a category could be viewed as categories that contain a single word. For instance, we can introduce the category "DIA" containing only the word "dia". On the other hand, a word may belong to several categories. For example, the word *Ferrer* (that could be translated as Smith) could belong to the categories *husband surname, husband profession, father husband surname, father husband profession, bride surname,* etc.

Formally speaking, let $\mathbf{x}$ be a handwritten sentence image, let $\mathbf{w}$ be a word sequence, and let $\mathbf{c}$ be the sequence of categories associated to the word sequence. Following the discussion presented in [8,10], from the decoding process, we can obtain not only the best word sequence hypothesis, $\hat{\mathbf{w}}$, but also the best sequence of semantic categories $\hat{\mathbf{c}}$ used in the most probable sentence:

$$(\hat{\mathbf{c}}, \hat{\mathbf{w}}) \approx \arg \max_{\mathbf{c}, \mathbf{w}} p(\mathbf{x} \mid \mathbf{w}) \cdot p(\mathbf{w} \mid \mathbf{c}) \cdot p(\mathbf{c}) \tag{1}$$

$P(\mathbf{x} \mid \mathbf{w})$ represents the optical-lexical knowledge and is typically approximated by concatenated character models, usually HMMs [4]. $P(\mathbf{w} \mid \mathbf{c})$ is the word-category distribution, approximated by an 1-gram for each category. $p(\mathbf{c})$ is the probability of the categories sequence and is approximated by an n-gram.

4   Language Modeling Using Morphic Generator Grammatical Inference (MGGI)

As discussed in [10], it is well known that n-gram models are just a subclass of probabilistic finite-state machines (PFSM) [12,13]. Therefore the capabilities of n-grams to model relevant language contexts or restrictions is limited, not only with respect to more powerful syntactic models such as context-free grammars, but also even with respect to the general class of PFSMs. In fact, no n-gram can approach (word) string distributions involving the kind of long-span dependencies which are common in natural language.

While learning PFSMs from training strings is in general hard, there is a not-very-well-known framework which allows to learn PFSMs which can model *given*, albeit arbitrarily complex (finite-state) restrictions. This framework, known as "Morphic Generator Grammatical Inference" (MGGI), provides a methodology for using prior knowledge about the restrictions which are intesresting for the task in hand, to ensure that the trained finite-state models will comply with these restrictions. MGGI was introduced in 1987 [2], within the framework of *Grammatical Inference* for Syntactic Pattern Recognition. It is based on the well known "morphism theorem of regular languages [1], which states that every regular language" (generated or accepted by a finite-state machine) can be obtained by applying an appropriate word-by-word morphism to the strings of a *local language* over some suitable vocabulary. A probabilistic extension of this theorem is given in [13], where it is also shown that a probabilistic local language is exactly the same language described by a bigram language model.

In MGGI, a-priory knowledge is used to label the words of the training strings in such a way that a simple bigram can be trained from the transformed strings. Then an inverse transformation (the *morphism*) is applied to this bigram to obtain a PFSM which deals with the restrictions conveyed by the initial string transformation [2,13]. A direct applications of these ideas to build accurate PFSM language models for automatic speech recognition can be seen in [11].

In [10], the MGGI was applied to the recognition task of a handwritten marriage license book. In that work, the labelling used in the MGGI intend to solve the mis-categorization of the bride's family information as groom's information, due to a wrong bigram generalization.

In this work, we checked the most frequent errors committed by the language model obtained after the MGGI application in the same way than in [10] and relabel the training samples in such a way that allow to solve the detected errors. One of the most common errors was the mis-categorization of the groom's father information as groom's information. The following example shows an example of this kind of errors, where the groom's father name has been wrongly labeled as the groom's name and the same occurred with the surname and the profession:

```
... fill de Miguel[GrName] Joani[GrSurname] teixidor_de_lli[GrProf] y ...
```

This clearly happened because the bigram *"de [GrName]"* had higher probability than the bigram *"de [GrFaName]"*, since groom's information appears more often than the groom's father information. The same occurs with the bride's mother information and with the bride's information. This suggests that a better generalization of the training text could be achieved by just tagging all the text tokens (categories and words) with labels that help distinguishing their relative position in the record.

In the vast majority of the records that we considered, the information of the groom and his parents is separated by the word *"fill"* (*"son"* in English). Similarly, the information of the bride and her parents is separated by the word *"filla"* (*"daughter"* in English). Therefore, it is straightforward to label all the tokens which precede the word *"fill"* with the suffix *"G"*, those appearing between *"fill"* and *"ab"* as *"F"*, those between *"ab"* and *"filla"* as *"B"* and the rest as *"A"*. By applying this labeling scheme to the categorized training transcripts of the license of the Fig. 1, the following training text is obtained:

```
DitG diaG rebere$G deG [GrName]G [GrSurname]G [GrProf]G deG [GrResi]G
fillF deF [GrFaName]F [GrFaSurname]F [GrFaProf]F yF deF [GrMoName]F
,F ab [BrName]B do$sellaB fillaA deA [BrFaName]A [BrFaSurname]A
[BrFaProf]A deA [BrFaResi]A yA deA [BrMoName]A
```

Given that the words *"fill"*, *"filla"* and *"ab"* only appear once in each record, the relabeling can be automatically done, so there is no extra manual work by the expert user. After training the category-based bigram, the inverse transformation required by MGGI (the word-by-word morphism) consists in removing these suffixes. The resulting PFSM adequately models the dependencies conveyed by the adopted labeling.

5   Experimental Framework

We have used the ESPOSALLES[1] database [7], a marriage license book from the Cathedral of Barcelona. The corpus, written by one single writer in old Catalan in the 17th century, is composed of 173 pages, 5,447 lines grouped in 1,747 licenses. It contains around 60,000 running words from a lexicon of 3,500 different words. A paleographer transcribed and annotated the 40 categories defined by demographers, as described in [8].

Seven partitions of 25 pages were used for cross-validation. The pages were divided into line images, and normalized as explained in [7]. For each line image, we extracted a sequence of feature vectors [9] based on the gray level of the image. Since we carried out experiments at license level, the feature sequences of the lines have been concatenated into licenses.

The characters were modeled by continuous density left-to-right HMMs with 6 states and 64 Gaussian mixture components per state. These parameters worked well in previous experiments. These models were estimated by training text images represented as feature vector sequences using the Baum-Welch algorithm. For decoding we used the Viterbi algorithm [4]. A category-based bi-gram was estimated using the MGGI methodology from the training set. The words in the test partition that do not appear in the training set, named Out of Vocabulary (OOV) words, were added as singletons to the corresponding word category distribution. The word category distributions were modeled by uni-grams.

To assess the quality of the transcription, we use the *Word Error Rate* (WER), defined as the minimum number of words that need to be substituted, deleted or inserted to convert the sentences recognized by the system into the reference transcriptions, divided by the total number of words in these transcriptions. To asses the quality of the information extraction, we use the precision and recall measures, defined in terms of the number of relevant words. Relevant words are the ones that belong to any of the 40 defined categories. Formally, let R be the number of relevant words contained in the document, D the number of relevant words that the system has detected, and C the number of relevant words correctly detected by the system. Precision (π) and recall (ρ) are computed as:

$$\pi = \frac{C}{D} \qquad \rho = \frac{C}{R}$$

---

[1] It is publicly available at: http://dag.cvc.uab.es/the-esposalles-database/.

6   Results

The proposed model has been compared to our initial work on MGGI [10] and our baseline system [8], consisting in a HMM-based HTR system using a category-based 2-gram language model (CB-HTR).

Table 1 presents the results in terms of WER, Precision and Recall. The WER remains the same because the MGGI technique is focused on the semantic labeling. However, the increase in the performance in information extraction is significant. In the first case, the mean Precision and Recall are computed for the absolute number of instances. In the second case, the mean Precision and Recall are computed by averaging the Precision and Recall for each one of the categories. As it can be observed, the absolute values are higher because there are some categories that appear in few cases, and consequence, the ability of the model to learn is lower. Also, when analyzing the Precision and Recall of the individual categories, we have observed that, when a category is very frequent (e.g. Groom's surname or occupation), the performance is higher, probably due to the higher amount of training data. In low populated categories (e.g. Bride's Residence), the behavior is just the opposite. For example, there are 1736 instances of the Groom's surname, and the MGGI obtains a Recall of 84'3%. Contrary, there are 46 instances of the Bride's surname, and the performance of the MGGI decreases, obtaining a Recall of 69'7%.

Table 1. Word Error Rate (WER), precision (π) and recall (ρ) obtained with the category-based HTR system (CB) and with the MGGI HTR systems (MGGI). The mean is computed for the absolute number of instances (I) and for categories (C). All results are percentages.

	WER	I-π	I-ρ	C-π	C-ρ
CB [8]	10.1	79.2	66.6	73.5	65.2
MGGI [10]	10.1	85.3	76.2	78.3	72.2
MGGI (our approach)	10.1	87.8	82.3	80.7	76.2

Finally, it must be noted that we consider an error whenever the semantic category or the transcription are incorrect. Therefore, if a word transcription is incorrect, we will also consider it as a semantic labeling error, no matter if the category is correct. Consequently, the computation of the semantic labeling error is pessimistic, which means that it will never be lower than WER.

7   Conclusions

In this paper, we have improved the MGGI methodology for information extraction and for automatically transcribing a marriage license book. Given the fixed structure of the information included in the license, we have used it to label the words of the training strings. The labels are chosen in such a way that a bigram trained with the labeled strings deals with restrictions that a simple category-based language model can not. We can see that the MGGI methodology can be useful to automatically extract the relevant information, helping the user in this hard task. As a future work, we would like to investigate how to discover the structure in an automatic way.

Acknowledgment. This work has been partially supported through the European Union's H2020 grant READ (Recognition and Enrichment of Archival Documents) (Ref: 674943), the European project ERC-2010-AdG-20100407-269796, the MINECO/FEDER, UE projects TIN2015-70924-C2-1-R and TIN2015-70924-C2-2-R, and the Ramon y Cajal Fellowship RYC-2014-16831.

References

1. Eilenberg, S.: Automata, Languages, and Machines, vol. 1. Academic Press, Orlando (1974)
2. Garcia, P., Vidal, E., Casacuberta, F.: Local languages, the succesor method, and a step towards a general methodology for the inference of regular grammars. IEEE Trans. PAMI **6**, 841–845 (1987)
3. Graves, A., Schmidhuber, J.: Offline handwriting recognition with multidimensional recurrent neural networks. In: NIPS, pp. 545–552 (2008)
4. Jelinek, F.: Statistical Methods for Speech Recognition. MIT Press, Cambridge (1998)
5. Marti, U.-V., Bunke, H.: Using a statistical language model to improve the preformance of an HMM-based cursive handwriting recognition system. IJPRAI **15**(1), 65–90 (2001)
6. Niesler, T., Woodland, P.: A variable-length category-based n-gram language model. In: Proceedings of ICASSP 1996, vol. 1, pp. 164 –167, May 1996
7. Romero, V., Fornés, A., Serrano, N., Sánchez, J.A., Toselli, A., Frinken, V., Vidal, E., Lladós, J.: The ESPOSALLES database: an ancient marriage license corpus for off-line handwriting recognition. Pattern Recogn. **46**, 1658–1669 (2013)
8. Romero, V., Sánchez, J.A.: Category-based language models for handwriting recognition of marriage license books. In: Proceedings of ICDAR 2013, pp. 788–792 (2013)
9. Toselli, A.H., Juan, A., Keysers, D., González, J., Salvador, I., Ney, H., Vidal, E., Casacuberta, F.: Integrated handwriting recognition and interpretation using finite-state models. IJPRAI **18**(4), 519–539 (2004)
10. Romero, E.V.V., Fornés, A., Sánchez, J.A.: Using the MGGI methodology for category-based language modeling in handwritten marriage licenses books. In: ICFHR, Shenzhen, China (2016)
11. Vidal, E., Llorens, D.: Using knowledge to improve N-gram language modelling through the MGGI methodology. In: Miclet, L., Higuera, C. (eds.) ICGI 1996. LNCS, vol. 1147, pp. 179–190. Springer, Heidelberg (1996). doi:10.1007/BFb0033353
12. Vidal, E., Thollard, F., De La Higuera, C., Casacuberta, F., Carrasco, R.C.: Probabilistic finite-state machines-part I. IEEE Trans. PAMI **27**(7), 1013–1025 (2005)
13. Vidal, E., Thollard, F., De La Higuera, C., Casacuberta, F., Carrasco, R.C.: Probabilistic finite-state machines-part II. IEEE Trans. PAMI **27**(7), 1026–1039 (2005)

Leveraging Activity Indexing for Egocentric Image Retrieval

Gabriel Oliveira-Barra[1(✉)], Mariella Dimiccoli[1,2], and Petia Radeva[1,2]

[1] Department of Mathematics and Computer Science,
University of Barcelona, Barcelona, Spain
{gabriel.deoliveira,mariella.dimiccoli,petia.ivanova}@ub.edu
[2] Computer Vision Center, Cerdanyola del Vallès, Barcelona, Spain

Abstract. Wearable cameras can daily gather large amounts of image data that require powerful image indexing and retrieval techniques in order to find the information of interest. In this work, we address the indexing problem of egocentric data by exploring the relevance of different information sources provided by Convolutional Neural Networks (CNN) combined with image metadata. The proposed method was tested on a public egocentric dataset of 45.000 images and gave encouraging results.

Keywords: Image retrieval · Image indexing · Egocentric vision · First-person vision · Activity recognition · Convolutional neural networks

1 Introduction

Recent advances in wearable technology, accompanied by the decreasing cost of data storage and increase of data availability have made possible to take pictures everywhere at every time. Wearable cameras are nowadays among the most popular wearable devices; millions of people have purchased them to record their travels and daily life, often sharing the recorded data with others through internet. Besides leisure, wearable cameras are attracting a lot of attention in the field of Preventive Medicine, since the collected data can be potentially used for memory training and extracting lifestyle patterns useful to prevent noncommunicable diseases as obesity [3]. Wearable cameras are being used also for improvement of working conditions, productivity and safety monitoring [1,2].

However, the huge amount of data captured every day makes the management of lifelog data tedious and time consuming, hence preventing to exploit the full potential of wearable cameras. For instance, a wearable time-lapse oriented camera such as the Narrative Clip captures up to 3 images per minute, which means it can take more than 2.000 pictures per day, i.e. more than 70.000 per month. Hence, retrieving images related to a particular moment of a month spent traveling with friends would require to manually inspect thousands of images. An image retrieval system able to narrow the gap between raw pixels and the semantics of the images can support such tasks efficiently and in a matter of

© Springer International Publishing AG 2017
L.A. Alexandre et al. (Eds.): IbPRIA 2017, LNCS 10255, pp. 295–303, 2017.
DOI: 10.1007/978-3-319-58838-4_33

seconds. Image retrieval from egocentric images is a more difficult problem than from classical images; being the images non-intentional, the objects appearing in them are often partially occluded that decreases the reliability of automatic annotations. On the other side, given the huge amount of images, manual annotation and search are slow and cumbersome, therefore, not feasible.

Given the urge of developing efficient egocentric image retrieval systems [7], egocentric image indexing and retrieval are still open problems [4,9–12,14]. Doherty et al. [4] addressed the problem of finding *events* similar to a given event in images collected by a SenseCam. To this goal, they proposed a fusion approach of the MPEG-7 descriptors, mostly provided by the sensor, and SURF descriptors. Reyes et al. [14] focused on the problem of retrieving the last appearance of personal objects in a large egocentric dataset. This is achieved by re-ranking objects similar to the query by using their time-stamp to obtain the last location, where they were seen. Lee et al. [10] presented a summarization method for egocentric images. Kameda et al. [9] proposed an egocentric image retrieval system for pedestrian navigation in urban areas as a localization method for visually impaired people. An interactive egocentric image retrieval system was proposed by Oliveira-Barra et al. called LEMORE [11], where the system searches for a particular moment of a person's life. However, up to our knowledge, no work has been published in the literature to automatically index and retrieve activities of people wearing an egocentric camera. This problem is of special difficulty, since wearer activity is not visible in the images, but should be implied by their context: car wheel and outdoor would imply driving, dishes and table would imply eating, etc. (see Fig. 1). We need powerful Computer Vision and Machine learning techniques able to describe the context and extract the relevant objects appearance that implies a specific wearer activity.

| Biking | Driving | Talking | Plane | Shopping |

Fig. 1. Overview of the activity annotated NTCIR images used for classification with their corresponding ground-truth.

Recently, CNNs are showing great capacity to describe image context and thus, a few works in the literature claim to exploit them for retrieval in conventional and egocentric images. A first attempt was made by Razavian et al. [13], where off-the-shelf CNN features are used for content-based image retrieval. The only work that aims to support efficient content-based retrieval using CNNs on large egocentric image databases, is the method proposed in [12] that performs image-based retrieval by converting CNN features into a string form and indexing them into an inverted index. However, since activities are not directly visible, but induced by the objects and scene of the image, content-based retrieval is not giving plausible results; we need a text-based retrieval capable to learn the relation between objects and activities and thus to index and retrieve activities from images, helped by other available egocentric metadata.

In this work, we propose a fully automatic method for semantic indexing and retrieval of wearer's activities in egocentric images, based on integrating heterogeneous information from images and metadata. Our method exploits a variety of data about activity estimation, time, users and object probabilities obtained from CNNs to train classification model based on Gradient Boosting Machines [5]. Our method uses the trained model to classify new egocentric images and automatically index them to be used in a text-based retrieval engine, ranked by the class probability (certainty) reported by the classifier for each activity. Hence, the main contributions are as follows:

(a) a new text-based retrieval method to train a supervised machine learning model to index and retrieve the activities being performed by the wearer;

(b) the algorithm is capable to learn to imply the activities from objects appearance in the images and to explain the retrieval results in terms of the set of relevant objects that have been detected with the highest score in the images.

We validate our approach on a wide public egocentric dataset of 45.000 images covering 90 days of 3 users and test it by retrieving 21 basic activity categories. A visual overview of the proposed methods is given in Fig. 2.

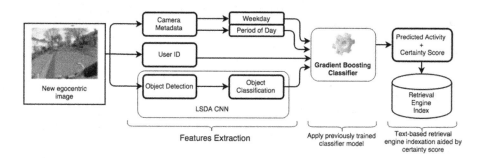

Fig. 2. A visual overview of the proposed method for indexing activities from egocentric image features.

The rest of the paper is organized as follows. In Sect. 2, we introduce the proposed approach, where we detail how we learn to predict activities from image features, rank and index them. Experimental results are discussed in Sect. 3. Finally, some concluding remarks are given in Sect. 4.

2   Feature Enhanced Egocentric Image Retrieval

Our egocentric image retrieval system obtains different features from egocentric images and indexes them in a text-based, semantically rich form in order to allow a given user to intuitively perform queries over it and present the results ranked according to different criteria.

2.1 Features Extraction

Image Features Based on Object Detection. Recently, CNNs have emerged as clear winners on object classification benchmarks, in part due to their training on 1.2M+ labeled classification images. Unfortunately, only a small fraction of those labels are available for the detection task. It has been proved to be much cheaper and easier to collect large quantities of image-level labels from search engines than collecting detection data and labelling them with precise bounding boxes. LSDA [8] is a framework that combines adaptation techniques with deep convolutional models to create a fast and effective large scale detection network. The LSDA algorithm learns the difference between the two tasks and transfers this knowledge to classifiers for categories without bounding box annotated data, turning them into detectors. This method has the potential to enable detection for the tens of thousands of categories that lack bounding box annotations, yet have plenty of classification data. In our work, we use the LSDA algorithm to detect object candidates among egocentric images and then classify them into their respective categories. We then use the category probabilities to train a GBM-based activity classifier. The problem we face with LSDA, is the large amount of categories at the raw output (7,604), since most of them can be considered noise, if used to train a classification model. To solve it, we filter out all categories that have no instance in the whole dataset with more than 10% probability. This way, after filtering, from the 7,604 categories that are very unlikely to be present on any image of the dataset, we end up with as few as 645, making the GBM much lighter, faster to train and eventually more precise.

Metadata Features. Just like most digital cameras, pictures taken by wearable cameras provide valuable metadata such as date and time embedded at each picture. In order to understand how time and weekdays can help build a model to classify what activity is taking place at a given picture, we use date as a feature, where pictures are classified into the day of the week when it was taken, and time as another feature. Pictures are classified into a continuous range of time given in minutes covering the whole day. Since daily habits, activities and objects alter, depending on the user wearing the camera, we also added the user ID as another feature to train the GBM classifier.

2.2 Egocentric Indexing Based on Gradient Boosted Machines

The GBM is based on a constructive strategy of ensemble formation. The boosting procedure adds new tree models to the ensemble sequentially. At each particular iteration, a new weak, base-learner model is trained with respect to the error of the whole ensemble learned so far. GBMs builds the additive model in a forward stage-wise fashion, where in each stage N regression trees are fit on the negative gradient of the multinomial deviance loss function.

2.3   Retrieval Engine Indexation Based on a Certainty Score

Our egocentric image retrieval system collects all the features extracted from each egocentric image, together with the activity class predicted by the GBM model and its certainty score for each image to subsequently index them on a text-based, inverted index retrieval engine. In order to use a text-based, inverted index search engine with its TF-IDF ranking, we use the approach proposed by [12], which runs over a Lucene core[1], where the authors propose a method to convert numerical certainty scores for each image and each class into a text-like document that the Lucene core is able to parse.

The resulting retrieval system is then able to perform semantically rich queries, providing a TF-IDF criteria to present ranked results to the user based on the class probabilities provided by the model.

3   Validation and Results

In the following section, we validate our method and present the results obtained by classifying activities and indexing them on the text-based retrieval engine.

3.1   Dataset

Our dataset consists of a subset of 45.000 labeled images from the NTCIR-12 dataset, that was originally presented for the Lifelog Semantic Access Task image retrieval competition [6]. This dataset consists of 89.593 egocentric pictures belonging to three different persons. We manually labeled 15,000 images per person with 21 different activity categories. We used 70% of the data for training and 30% for test that is, the dataset was split randomly in 31,500 training images and 13,500 testing images. Figures 1 and 3 show an overview of the dataset and sample egocentric images with labeled activities, respectively.

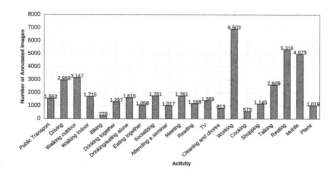

Fig. 3. Summary of the 21 annotated activities from the NTCIR-12 dataset.

---

[1] https://lucene.apache.org/.

3.2   Results and Discussion

Our system has been trained to predict activities given the detected objects with their confidence score provided by LSDA, the user ID, and information about time such as period of the day and day of the week. Since, up to our knowledge, there are no other activity indexing methods in the literature, it is not possible to compare our results to state of the art methods. Instead, we contrasted the performance of the Gradient Boosting Machines, to several other classifiers as Logistic Regression, Decision Trees, Random Forest, Support Vector Machines, Extra Trees and Gaussian Naive Bayes. Table 1 shows a comparison between them not only regarding score, but also training time and memory required to store the model. Although SVM and GBM had similar scores, SVM is not parameters-free (in our case, $\gamma = 1$ and $C = 1000$ gave the optimal results on a grid-search with 25 different configurations).

GBMs provided very similar performance to SVMs, but with much lower computational cost. Hence, GBMs proved to be an accurate and effective off-the-shelf procedure that can be used for both regression and classification problems. The advantages of GBMs are a natural handling of data of mixed type (=heterogeneous features). In our case, this heterogeneity of data is the variety of features from lifelogging data in general and egocentric images, in particular. GBMs also proved high predictive power robustness to outliers in the output space. The main disadvantage of GBMs is its lack of scalability, since the sequential nature of boosting makes it hard to be parallelized.

Table 1. Comparison between scores of different classification models.

Classifier	Precision	Recall	F1-Score	Model size (MB)	Training time
Logistic	0.62	0.61	0.59	0.129	<1 min
Decision tree	0.66	0.66	0.66	2.41	2 min
Gaussian naive bayes	0.61	0.58	0.57	0.24	<1 min
Extra trees	0.80	0.80	0.80	44.5	2 min
Random forest	0.82	0.82	0.81	2403	7 min
Support vector machine	0.83	0.83	0.83	95.2	15 min
Gradient boosting machine	0.83	0.83	0.83	25.3	22 min

Figure 4 shows the performance of the GBM on the 21 activities. The best performance is obtained for the driving, working and TV mirroring since the objects related to these activities are very successfully detected by the LSDA algorithm, while biking, cooking and cleaning are more difficult due to the fact that these activities used to be characterized by a wide set of objects (cooking, or cleaning) or the objects are hardly visible in the images (biking).

Feature Importance. When interpreting a model, a question arises: what are those important features and how do they contribute in predicting the target

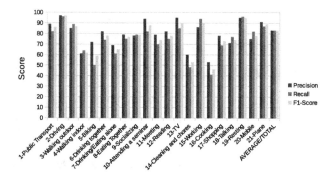

Fig. 4. Precision, recall and F-1 score of the 21 indexed activities.

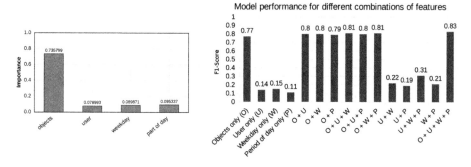

Fig. 5. Feature importance used for classifying using GBM when all available features are used for training (left). Scores obtained after training for different combinations of each available feature (right).

response? For calculating the importance of each feature, the basic idea is: the more often a feature is used in the split points, the more important that feature is [5]. The feature importance is computed as the total reduction of the criterion brought by that feature. Figure 5 presents the calculated importance of each features used for training our GBM model for activity classification, as well as the scores obtained by training the GBM classifier with different combinations of features. As can be seen, the most important are the detected objects which importance sums up to 73,58%, while the temporal features importance are: 9,53% for part of the day, 8,99% for the weekday and 7,9% for the user ID.

Figure 6 shows some retrieval results for the "Working" and "Driving" activity query over the inverted index. Note that in the first case, we obtained two erroneously retrieved images, but still they look very much as a working environment i.e. they are quite similar to the rest of the correctly retrieved images. The objects detected with the highest probability in the first case were: "monitor" and "laptop", and in the second case were: "car wheel".

(a) Retrieved results with rank 1, 5, 10, 15, and 20 for the query "Working".

(b) Retrieved results with rank 1, 5, 10, 15, and 20 for the query "Driving".

Fig. 6. Ranked textual query results for "Working" and "Driving". Green and red backgrounds represent true and false positives, respectively. (Color figure online)

4   Conclusions

In this work, we presented a complete retrieval engine based on an automatic method for classifying and indexing activities. We integrated different features provided by CNNs and metadata on large sets of egocentric images. We tested several different classifiers and achieved 83% of performance using GBM on a subset of the NTCIR-12 egocentric dataset. Next steps will be to explore the temporal image coherence to further improve the retrieval process.

References

1. Bolaños, M., Dimiccoli, M., Radeva, P.: Towards storytelling from visual lifelogging: an overview. IEEE Trans. Hum.-Mach. Syst. (2016) (in press)
2. Czerwinski, M., Gage, D.W., Gemmell, J., Marshall, C.C., Pérez-Quiñones, M.A., Skeels, M.M., Catarci, T.: Digital memories in an era of ubiquitous computing and abundant storage. Commun. ACM **49**(1), 44–50 (2006)
3. Doherty, A., Hodges, S., King, A.C., Smeaton, A., Berry, E., Moulin, C.J., Lindley, S., Kelly, P., Foster, C.: Wearable cameras in health: the state of the art and future possibilities. Am. J. Prev. Med. **44**(3), 320–323 (2013)
4. Doherty, A.R., Conaire, C., Blighe, M., Smeaton, A.F., O'Connor, N.E.: Combining image descriptors to effectively retrieve events from visual lifelogs. In: Proceedings of International Conference on Multimedia Information Retrieval, pp. 10–17. ACM (2008)
5. Friedman, J.H.: Greedy function approximation: a gradient boosting machine. Ann. Stat. **29**(5), 1189–1232 (2001)
6. Gurrin, C., Joho, H., Hopfgartner, F., Zhou, L., Albatal, R.: NTCIR lifelog: the first test collection for lifelog research. In: Proceedings of 39th International SIGIR Conference on Research and Development in Information Retrieval, Pisa, Italy, ACM, July 2016

7. Gurrin, C., Smeaton, A.F., Doherty, A.R.: Lifelogging: personal big data. Found. Trends Inf. Retr. **8**(1), 1–125 (2014)
8. Hoffman, J., Guadarrama, S., Tzeng, E., Hu, R., Donahue, J., Girshick, R., Darrell, T., Saenko, K.: LSDA: large scale detection through adaptation. In: Neural Information Processing Systems (NIPS) (2014)
9. Kameda, Y., Ohta, Y.: Image retrieval of first-person vision for pedestrian navigation in urban area. In: ICPR Conference, pp. 364–367. IEEE (2010)
10. Lee, Y.J., Ghosh, J., Grauman, K.: Discovering important people and objects for egocentric video summarization. In: CVPR, vol. 2, p. 7 (2012)
11. Oliveira-Barra, G., Ayala, A.C., Bolaños, M., Dimiccoli, M., Giro-i Nieto, X., Radeva, P.: Lemore: a lifelog engine for moments retrieval at the NTCIR-lifelog LSAT task. Age **40**(33), 48 (2016)
12. Oliveira-Barra, G., Dimiccoli, M., Radeva, P.: Egocentric image retrieval with convolutional neural network. Front. Artif. Intell. Appl. **288**, 71–76 (2016)
13. Razavian, A.S., Azizpour, H., Sullivan, J., Carlsson, S.: CNN features off-the-shelf: an astounding baseline for recognition (2014). CoRR abs/1403.6382
14. Reyes, C., Mohedano, E., McGuinness, K., O'Connor, N.E., Giro-i Nieto, X.: Where is my phone?: personal object retrieval from egocentric images. In: Proceedings of the First Workshop, LTA 2016, pp. 55–62. ACM, New York (2016)

Pupil Light Reflex Mitigation
Using Non-linear Image Warping

Tudor Nedelcu[1]([✉]), Shejin Thavalengal[2], Claudia Costache[1],
and Peter Corcoran[1,2]

[1] National University of Ireland, Galway, Ireland
`T.Nedelcu1@nuigalway.ie`
[2] Fotonation Ltd., Galway, Ireland

Abstract. The human iris is one of the most reliable biometric features.
Since it is a live organ, variations caused by pupil contraction/dilation
will degrade the performance of a biometric system based on iris. This
paper presents a method for generating images of irises with a specific
dilation coefficient. The approach presented here uses a mathematical
model that aims to emulate the dynamic of the iris with respect to the
pupil dilation/contraction. The estimated images are generated using
image an image warping technique. The iris image is approximated by re-
mapping the radius of the polar coordinates using a nonlinear function.
The proposed method benefits of low complexity and provides better
results with respect to the photorealistic aspect and to the performance of
iris biometric systems. The performance of the proposed model applied to
the iris as a biometric system is tested using a commercial iris recognition
system.

1 Introduction

The iris recognition system is one of the most reliable ones in biometry [1]. The
main challenge of a biometric systems is to recognize a pattern in spite of its intra
class variation while rejecting patterns from other classes. The pattern recognition systems based on iris can achieve great performance due to the uniqueness,
stability of the iris texture over time and the difficulty to spoof compared with
other biometric systems [1]. The complex structure of the iris has a high degree
of randomness for the inter class [2,3] and the internal structure is relatively
stable over the years [4,5]. A detailed description of the structure of the iris and
his properties that make the eye suitable for integration into a biometric system
is provided by Wildes [2].

For an iris recognition system, the intra-class variation generated by the pupil
dilation will decrease the performance [6]. The radius of the pupil constantly
changes because of the involuntary physiological mechanism to adapt to light or
as a response to strong emotions or different substances (drugs, alcohol). The
pupil is constantly compressing or expanding the biological tissue. For strong
dilation small parts of the tissue will disappear underneath the anterior layer,
and for contraction new structures will become visible. Therefore, some features

© Springer International Publishing AG 2017
L.A. Alexandre et al. (Eds.): IbPRIA 2017, LNCS 10255, pp. 304–312, 2017.
DOI: 10.1007/978-3-319-58838-4_34

of the iris pattern will disappear for dilation, and new features will arise for contraction. The PLR effect is more significant for biometric systems, when irises with a large differences of pupil size are compared.

This paper is organized as follows: in Sect. 2 are presented the method used for the mitigation the effect of pupil light reflex (PLR), the proposed method for generating images with a specific dilation coefficient (Fig. 1) is described in Sect. 3, the description dataset used is presented in Sect. 4, and the results and conclusions are presented in Sects. 5 and 6.

2   Related Work

For a photorealistic appearance, the dynamic of iris texture can be approximated by a linear function [7].

To reduce the effect of the pupil dilation for pattern recognition systems based on iris, researchers propose to use enrolment of multiple iris templates [8]. To control the pupil dilation, Costa and Gonzaga [9] propose special goggles that apply light stimuli for one of the eye, to increase the dilation coefficient. More consumer electronics devices (e.g. smartphones) will be able to acquire images from the NIR spectrum also, which make them suitable for iris recognition [10,11]. The constrained environment is not desirable for applications like consumer electronics, where the enrolment and authentication process should be fast and not too complex.

To reduce the negative effect of pupil dilation without a constrained environment, it is desirable to estimate the iris texture for different dilation coefficients [12–17] or to use new descriptor to extract features robust to dilation [18–20]. A review regarding iris surface deformation and the normalization process was performed by Thainimit, Alexandre, and Almeida [21].

Wyatt [14] proposed a meshwork for pupil dilation under PLR. The meshwork was computed considering a minimal stretch when the pupil changes its size over the natural dilation coefficient. The function used is based on a linear deformation and a non-uniform function described with a 6th order polynomial is added. The 6th order polynomial form is used to provide enough flexibility to the model.

Based on the Wyatts [14] model, Yuan and Shi [15] had developed a non-linear normalization model for iris recognition. The initial stage is to non-linearly stretch/relax the iris to a pre-defined pupil dilation coefficient by using a method similar to Wyatt, and then linearly unwrap the annular region to the polar coordinates image (similar to the rubber sheet model proposed by Daugman [22]).

Similar to the work of Wyatt [14], Wei et al. [16] propose a non-linear function used based on a Gaussian model.

Hasegawa et al. [17] have developed a methodology for generating several synthetic images with different dilation coefficients. As suggested in [8], the enrolment of multiple images (with different dilation coefficients) will enhance the performance of the iris recognition systems. To generate the synthetic images, Blender software (an open source software under GNU General Public Licence designed for animation) was used. To constrict or dilate the iris, a planar mesh which consists of 32 quadrilateral faces was used. As a result of the UV mapping and the rendering process, a modified iris texture is generated with the desired dilation coefficient.

To improve the iris recognition performance of the images of eyes with considerable different dilation coefficients, Thornton, and Savvides [12] have used a probabilistic method. For a pair of images, a maximum a posteriori map (MAP) is generated to estimate the parameters of the relative distortion. The method proposed in [12] allows some degrees of noise or distortion tolerance and the synthetic image will have a realistic aspect.

In [13] the normalized texture of the iris is approximated with respect to the dilation coefficient by using a biochemical model. The authors aim for a better estimation of the dynamic of the collagen fibbers by using a model for muscle activity and elastic properties of the iris. To enhance the computation time, several templates are generated with different dilation coefficient. The proposed method is very efficient when images with a large dilation coefficient are compared.

Zhang et al. [18] propose a robust iris feature matching for deformed irises. They make use of the dense DAISY descriptors [23] to extract features from the normalized iris area. After the key points are extracted from the enrolment and authentication images, they are matched. Geometric and photometric features are proposed later by the same authors [20]. The normalised iris images are decomposed into lowpass and bandpass component by using nonsubsampled contourlet transform (NCST). The NCST was used due to the shift invariant, multi-scale and multi-direction properties.

Fathima and Gloash [19] have also used the properties of the NCST. They enhance the iris recognition of the deformed irises by using hybrid features and they classified the deformed iris images by using KNN.

3   Pupil Light Reflex Mitigation

The pupil light reflex mitigation (PLRM) algorithm rely on the dynamic of the pupil. The contraction and dilation of the iris is more significant closer to the pupillary area due to the anatomy of the iris fibers. To generate images that simulate the iris dynamics on digital images, a new set of images is generated by up sampling or down sampling using a non-linear function (similar to the natural pupil dilation). These synthetic images can be used for enrollment and authentication for iris recognition based biometric systems.

Other methods improve the photorealistic appearance and the biometric performances with a cost of high complexity and dependency of using dedicated softwares, which is an important drawback. We proposed a low complexity method which can be integrated into an iris recognition biometric system. This is achieved by generating synthetic image (Fig. 1).

In this paper, we test the fidelity of the synthesised images using a commercial software for iris recognition [28]. Various scenarios are considering regarding the images used for enrollment and authentication as explained in Sect. 5.

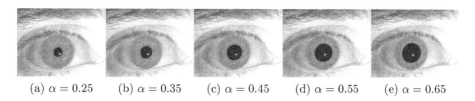

(a) $\alpha = 0.25$ (b) $\alpha = 0.35$ (c) $\alpha = 0.45$ (d) $\alpha = 0.55$ (e) $\alpha = 0.65$

Fig. 1. Synthetic images generated with a dilation coefficient from 0.25 to 0.65. The initial image dilation coefficient is 0.4567

3.1 Proposed Method

The iris recognition systems are using two iris codes for user authentication. One of the iris code is stored on the system memory and the second one is generated when an authentication is performed. For accurate results, the image used for authentication I_A should have the ratio α_A (the ratio of the pupil radius over iris radius) similar with the ratio α_E of the enrolled image I_E:

$$\frac{R_A^{(p)}}{R_A^{(i)}} = \alpha_E \tag{1}$$

where $R_A^{(p)}$ and $R_A^{(i)}$ represents the radius of the pupil and iris from the authentication image I_A. The synthetic image I_S will have the same radius of the iris as the image I_A. The pupil radius is estimated as:

$$R_S^{(p)} = R_A^{(p)} \alpha_E \tag{2}$$

Another aspect of the PLR is that the deformation is not uniform [24]. The circular muscles near the pupil will deform the iris structure more than the radial ones, which are usually between the collarette and sclera. Therefore, the radius coordinates of the synthetic image r_s can be computed as the initial values r_A where a dilation/contraction $F(i, j)$ coefficient is added:

$$r_S(i, j) = r_A(i, j) \pm F(i, j) \tag{3}$$

The gain/loss function is a uniform function with values from 0 to 1, which is converted to a non-uniform function by applying the squared function. The quadratic function is scaled with δR to obtain the desired dilation coefficients α_E:

$$F(i, j) = \left| \frac{r_A(i, j) - R_A^{(p)}}{R_A^{(i)} - R_A^{(p)}} \right|^2 |\delta R_p| \tag{4}$$

$$\delta R_p = R_A^{(p)} - R_E^{(p)} \tag{5}$$

where the δR is the difference between the radius of the pupil from the I_A and I_E. For $r_A(i, j) \rightarrow R_A^{(i)}$ the $r_S(i, j) \rightarrow R_A^{(i)}$, which mean that the iris structure will change slightly for the region closer to the sclera, and the region closer to the pupil will be synthesized by interpolation using more samples.

The synthetic image is generated by image warping using the new radius coordinates computed previously:

$$I_S(i, j) = I_E(r_S(i, j))$$ (6)

The generated image I_S is computed using interpolation of non-integer locations [25], since the mapping function $r_S \in \mathbb{Q}$.

3.2   Iris Segmentation

The difference between the centre of the pupil and iris should be addressed along with the better shape descriptor for the pupil. For large dilation, strong artifacts will be generated. For the shape of the pupil and the iris, with the known centre of each of them, a vector $d(\theta)$ is computed. In $d(\theta)$ are stored the distances between the centre of the pupil and the pupil boundary for each angle θ:

$$d(\theta) = \sum_{n=0}^{N} a_n \cos(n\theta) + b_n \sin(n\theta)$$ (7)

where a_0 is the pupil radius, and a_1, a_2, b_1, b_2 are the other parameters that provide a better approximation. We used a non-circular pupil shape descriptor proposed by Rakshit and Monro [26], Rakshit [27]. If the points that have to fit the model, $\{r_i, \theta_i; i = \dots M\}$ are irregular in θ_i, the error E is:

$$E(\theta_i) = \sum_{i=1}^{M} d(\theta_i - r_i)$$ (8)

and the squared error is:

$$E^2 = \sum_{i=1}^{M} \left\{ \left[\sum_{n=0}^{N} a_n \cos\theta_i + b_n \sin\theta_i \right] - r_i \right\}^2$$ (9)

For a better approximation of the pupil shape, the parameters (a_n, b_n) should be set to minimize the sum of the squared error. This is achieved by differentiate the above equation and set the value to zero [26, 27].

The new mapping function for the radius component is computed as:

$$F(i, j) = \left| \frac{r_A(i, j) - d(\theta)_A^p}{d(\theta)_A^i - d(\theta)_A^p} \right|^2 |\delta R_p|$$ (10)

where $d(\theta)_A^i$ represents the distance from the pupil centre to the pupil border, and $d(\theta)_A^p$ the distance to the iris.

For the images were the iris is partially occluded, the eyelids should also be segmented because the dilation/contraction should be performed only on the iris region. For the computation of the mapping function the values that are occluded by the eyelids will not be updated. We denote by M the region occluded by eyelids, and the r_S is computed as:

$$r_S(i,j) = \begin{cases} r_S(i,j), & M(i,j) = 1 \\ r_S(i,j) + F(i,j), & M(i,j) = 0 \end{cases}. \tag{11}$$

3.3 Pupil Iris Center Difference

Since the pupil centre is shifted, the distance from the centre of the pupil to the iris boundary $d(\theta)^p_A$ should be computed.

The displacement of the centres and the direction angle is computed as:

$$r' = \sqrt{\Delta x^2 + \Delta y^2} \tag{12}$$

$$\alpha = \arctan\left(\frac{\Delta x}{\Delta y}\right) \tag{13}$$

where Δx and Δy represents the variance on the vertical and horizontal directions.

The intersection of the two circles with respect to the pupil centre, can be computed as:

$$t = \arcsin\left(\frac{r'}{2d(\theta)^i}\right) \tag{14}$$

The distance between the centre of the pupil and the iris boundary will increase/decrease as:

$$d(\theta) = d(\theta) \pm r' \sin(\theta + s_{1,2}). \tag{15}$$

4   Image Database

For the testing of the proposed method we used the dataset of high quality images [27]. The images were acquired under infrared lighting with a spectrum peak of around 820 nm. A Pentax C-3516 M with 35 mm lens was deployed to capture the iris at a resolution with at least 400 pixels across the diameter of the iris. The distance between the camera and the eye was 20 cm. The NIR light source was kept close to the lens to restrict its reflections to the region within the pupil without obscuring the iris texture. The dataset used for the experiments contain 520 images (52 persons, 5 images for every eye). The minimum dilation coefficient is 0.174 and the maximum is 0.647 (Fig. 2).

5   Results

We have tested the fidelity of the estimated images using a commercial software for iris recognition (MIRLIN v2.33 [28]). The software used requires two images of an eye as input (one for enrolment and one for authentication). After

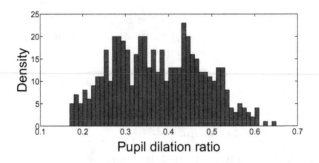

Fig. 2. Dilation coefficient of the pupils from the dataset.

the segmentation, normalization, filtering and encoding step, the Hamming distance is computed. We used the iris recognition system providing original and synthetic images (Fig. 1) for enrolment and for authentication. For the scenario where original images were used as enrolment and synthetic images were used as authentication, we artificially generated images with respect to the dilation coefficient of the image used for enrolment. The ROC curves (Fig. 3 (left)) show that the performance decrease for this scenario. We assume the performance decrease because of the false features generated or some feature were not available when a strong dilation/contraction was performed.

We have also tested the scenario where synthetic images are used for enrolment and authentication. For this scenario the results (ROC curves) show an improvement over the original images (Fig. 3 (left)). Regarding the enrolment and authentication with synthetic images, five datasets were generated with a fixed dilation coefficient form 0.25 to 0.65 and tests were performed. Each dataset was generated using the initial dataset, and each image was modified using the method described in this paper to have the specified dilation coefficient. The results (Fig. 3 (right)) shows that a dilation coefficient of 0.55 achieve the best results. This is in concordance with the results from [8], where by applying an artificial pupil dilation an overall improvement is observed.

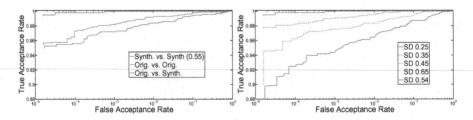

Fig. 3. ROC curves computed using raw and synthetic images for enrolment and authentication (left). ROC curves generated using only synthetic images for enrolment and authentication with a dilation coefficient form 0.25 to 0.65 (right)

6   Conclusion

We have proposed a method to estimate the iris appearance using non-linear image warping. The radius component of the image represented in polar coordinates is re-mapped with a non-linear function (quadratic function) which is used to generate a synthetic image with the desired dilation coefficient. The proposed method show a significant improvement over the images which are not processed for PLRM. Another aspect of this work is that there are no requirements of another software to generate the synthetic images and the proposed method is less complex than the other dilation models. To test the fidelity of the synthetic images, we have used a commercial software for iris recognition. A significant improvement is achieved by using synthetic images for enrolment and authentication with a fixed dilation coefficient (0.55 for the tested database).

Acknowledgments. This research is funded by the Enterprise Based Programme (EBP) of the Irish Research Council (www.research.ie).

References

1. Burge, M.J., Bowyer, K.W. (eds.): Handbook of Iris Recognition. Springer, New York (2013)
2. Wildes, R.P.: Iris recognition: an emerging biometric technology. Proc. IEEE **85**(9), 1348–1363 (1997)
3. Daugman, J.: The importance of being random: statistical principles of iris recognition. Pattern Recogn. **36**, 279–291 (2003)
4. Matey, J.R., Tabassi, E., Quinn, G.W., Chumakov, M.: IREX VI temporal stability of iris recognition accuracy NIST interagency report 7948. Technical report, NIST (2013)
5. Bowyer, K.W., Ortiz, E.: Iris recognition: does template ageing really exist? Biometric Technol. Today **2015**(10), 5–8 (2015)
6. Hollingsworth, K.P., Bowyer, K.W., Flynn, P.J.: The importance of small pupils: a study of how pupil dilation affects iris biometrics. In: IEEE 2nd International Conference on Biometrics Theory, Applications and Systems, pp. 1–6 (2008)
7. Pamplona, V.F., Oliveira, M.M.: Photorealistic models for pupil light reflex and iridal pattern deformation. ACM Trans. Graph. **28**(4), 1–12 (2009)
8. Ortiz, E., Bowyer, K.W., Flynn, P.J.: Dilation-aware enrolment for iris recognition. IET Biometrics **5**, 92–99 (2016)
9. Martins, R., Gonzaga, A.: Dynamic features for iris recognition. IEEE Trans. Syst. Man Cybern. B Cybern. **42**(4), 1072–1082 (2012)
10. Thavalengal, S., Andorko, I., Drimbarean, A., Bigioi, P., Corcoran, P.: Proof-of-concept and evaluation of a dual function visible/NIR camera for iris authentication in smartphones. IEEE Trans. Commun. El. **61**(2), 137–143 (2015)
11. Thavalengal, S., Corcoran, P.: User authentication on smartphones: focusing on iris biometrics. IEEE Consum. Electr. Mag. **5**(2), 87–93 (2016)
12. Thornton, J., Savvides, M.: A bayesian approach to deformed pattern matching of iris images. IEEE Trans. Pattern Anal. Mach. Intell. **29**(4), 596–606 (2007)
13. Tomeo-Reyes, V., Ross, A., Clark, A.D., Chandran, V.: A biomechanical approach to iris normalization. In: Proceedings of 2015 International Conference on Biometrics, pp. 9–16 (2015)

14. Wyatt, H.J.: A 'minimum-wear-and-tear' meshwork for the iris. Vis. Res. **40**, 2167–2176 (2000)
15. Yuan, X., Shi, P.: A non-linear normalization model for iris recognition. In: Li, S.Z., Sun, Z., Tan, T., Pankanti, S., Chollet, G., Zhang, D. (eds.) IWBRS 2005. LNCS, vol. 3781, pp. 135–141. Springer, Heidelberg (2005). doi:10.1007/11569947_17
16. Wei, Z., Tan, T., Sun, Z.: Nonlinear iris deformation correction based on gaussian model. In: Lee, S.-W., Li, S.Z. (eds.) ICB 2007. LNCS, vol. 4642, pp. 780–789. Springer, Heidelberg (2007). doi:10.1007/978-3-540-74549-5_82
17. Hasegawa, R., Ortiz, E., Bowyer, K.W., Stark, L., Flynn, P.J., Hughes, K.: Synthetic eye images for pupil dilation mitigation. In: Fifth IEEE International Conference on Biometrics: Theory, Applications, and Systems (BTAS), pp. 339–345 (2012)
18. Zhang, M., Sun, Z., Tan, T.: Deformable DAISY matcher for robust iris recognition. In: 18th IEEE International Conference on Image Processing, pp. 3250–3253 (2011)
19. Fathima, S., Golash, R.: An efficient method for deformed iris recognition by extracting hybrid features. In: AIT Tumkur, India, vol. 3, no. 4, pp. 741–746 (2014)
20. Zhang, M., Sun, Z., Tan, T.: Deformed iris recognition using bandpass geometric features and lowpass ordinal features. In: International Conference on Biometrics (ICB), pp. 1–6 (2013)
21. Thainimit, S., Alexandre, L.A., De Almeida, V.M.N.: Iris surface deformation and normalization. In: 13th International Symposium on Communications and Information Technologies: Communication and Information Technology for New Life Style Beyond Cloud, ISCIT 2013, pp. 501–506 (2013)
22. Daugman, J.: How iris recognition works. IEEE Trans. Circuits Syst. Video Technol. **14**(1), 21–30 (2004)
23. Tola, E., Lepetit, V., Fua, P.: DAISY: an efficient dense descriptor applied to wide-baseline stereo. IEEE Trans. Pattern Anal. Mach. Intell. (PAMI) **32**(5), 815–830 (2010)
24. Phang, S.S.: Investigating and developing a model for iris changes under varied lighting conditions. In: IEEE Transactions on Pattern Analysis and Machine Intelligence Master Thesis, Queensland University of Technology (2007)
25. OpenCV documentation. http://docs.opencv.org/2.4/doc
26. Rakshit, S., Monro, D.M.: Pupil shape description using fourier series. In: IEEE Workshop on Signal Processing Applications for Public Security and Forensics, pp. 1–4 (2007)
27. Rakshit, S.: Novel methods for accurate human iris recognition. Ph.D. thesis, University of Bath (2007)
28. Smart Sensors Ltd., MIRLIN SDK, version 2.23 (2013)

Multimodal Learning for Sign Language Recognition

Pedro M. Ferreira[(✉)], Jaime S. Cardoso, and Ana Rebelo

INESC TEC, Porto, Portugal
{pmmf,jaime.cardoso,arebelo}@inesctec.pt

Abstract. Sign Language Recognition (SLR) has becoming one of the most important research areas in the field of human computer interaction. SLR systems are meant to automatically translate sign language into text or speech, in order to reduce the communicational gap between deaf and hearing people. The aim of this paper is to exploit multimodal learning techniques for an accurate SLR, making use of data provided by Kinect and Leap Motion. In this regard, single-modality approaches as well as different multimodal methods, mainly based on convolutional neural networks, are proposed. Experimental results demonstrate that multimodal learning yields an overall improvement in the sign recognition performance.

Keywords: Sign Language Recognition · Multimodal learning · Convolutional neural networks · Kinect · Leap Motion

1 Introduction

Sign language (SL) is an integral form of communication especially used by hearing impaired people within deaf communities worldwide. It is a visual means of communication, with its own lexicon and grammar, that combines articulated hand gestures along with facial expressions to convey meaning. As most of hearing people are unfamiliar with SL, deaf people find it difficult to interact with the hearing majority. In this regard, Sign Language Recognition (SLR) has becoming an appealing topic in modern societies. Its main purpose is to automatically translate the signs from video or images into the corresponding text or speech. This is important not only to bridge the communicational gap between deaf and hearing people but also to increase the amount of contents to which the deaf can access (e.g., educational tools or games for deaf and visual dictionaries of SL).

The SLR task can be addressed by using wearable devices or vision-based approaches. Vision-based SLR is less invasive since there is no need to wear cumbersome devices that might affect the natural signing movement. A vision-based SLR system is typically composed by three main building blocks: (i) hand segmentation and/or tracking, (ii) feature extraction, and (iii) sign recognition. The SLR problem was first addressed by the computer vision community by means of just using the colour information of images and videos [1,2].

© Springer International Publishing AG 2017
L.A. Alexandre et al. (Eds.): IbPRIA 2017, LNCS 10255, pp. 313–321, 2017.
DOI: 10.1007/978-3-319-58838-4_35

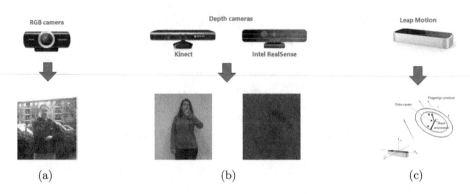

Fig. 1. Vision-based SLR systems: (a) colour information provided by RGB cameras, (b) colour and depth information provided by depth cameras, and (c) hand position and orientation provided by Leap Motion.

More recently, the emergence of low-cost consumer depth cameras (e.g., Microsoft's Kinect) has promoted the development of several approaches that try to combine colour and depth information (see Fig. 1). Bergh and Gool [3] demonstrated that depth information can be used together with colour information to increase the recognition accuracy, especially when there is superposition between hands and face. In [4], multiple depth-based descriptors are fed into a SVM classifier for gesture recognition.

The recent introduction of the Leap Motion has launched new research lines for gesture recognition. Instead of a complete depth map, the Leap Motion sensor directly provides the 3D spatial positions of the fingertips and the hand orientation with quite accuracy ($\approx 200\,\mu m$) (see Fig. 1). One of the first studies referring to the utilization of Leap Motion for SLR has been presented in [5]. The authors stated that, although Leap Motion may have a great potential for sign recognition, it is not always able to recognize all fingers in some hand configurations. In order to overcome that limitation, Marin *et al.* [6,7] combined the input data from Leap Motion with Kinect.

In this work, we extent the ideas proposed in [6,7], improving their results. In particular, our main contributions are:

- We explore the concept of convolutional neural networks (CNNs) for recognizing SL, in two different ways. First, CNNs are used to directly classify the sign. Second, CNNs are used as feature extractor, avoiding the hand-craft feature extraction process and the inherent difficulty of designing reliable features to the large variations of hand gestures.
- We develop a multimodal learning framework for the SLR problem, making use of data provided by both Kinect (colour + depth) and Leap Motion.
- We performed a comparative study between single-modality and multimodal learning techniques, in order to demonstrate the effectiveness of multimodal learning in the overall sign recognition performance.

The paper is organized in four sections including the Introduction (Sect. 1). In Sect. 2, the proposed SLR methods are fully described. Section 3 reports the experimental results. Finally, conclusions and some topics for future work are presented in Sect. 4.

2 Methodology

The aim of this paper is to explore the potential of multimodal learning for SLR. To accomplish this purpose, single-modality approaches as well as different multimodal methods, to fuse them at different levels, are proposed. Multimodal techniques include data-level, feature-level and decision-level fusion methods.

2.1 Single-Modality Sign Recognition

2.1.1 Kinect Modalities (Colour and Depth)

In this work, convolutional neural networks (CNN) were explored in two different ways. In the first approach, a CNN is used to directly classify the sign. In the second approach, the CNN is used as a feature extractor.

Both Kinect modalities, colour and depth, require a pre-processing step in order to segment the hands, from the noisy background of the image, before feature extraction and sign recognition. In the first step, a skin colour model is used to distinguish skin pixels from background pixels. This skin colour binarization is used to filter the depth map. Then, the hand segmentation is performed on the filtered depth map by just using depth information.

CNN Model as Classifier. The implemented neural network follows the traditional CNN architecture for classification, typically starting from several sequences of convolution-pooling layers to fully connected layers [8]. Hence, the implemented CNN is composed by two convolution layers and one fully connected layer (or dense layer), in which each convolution layer is followed by a 2×2 max-pooling layer. Both convolution layers have the same filters' number and size. Finally, the last layer of the CNN is a softmax output layer. The output layer contains the output probabilities for each class label. The output node that produces the largest probability is chosen as the overall classification. The architecture of implemented CNN is illustrated in Fig. 2a. During the training stage, several regularization techniques, such as the L2 norm, data augmentation and dropout [9], were applied to prevent overfitting.

CNN Model as Feature Descriptor. The later layers of a CNN seem to learn visually semantic attributes of the input [8]. Hence, these intermediate representations can be used as a generic feature descriptor. Many research works [8] stated that these CNN features are better than hand-crafted features, such as SIFT or HoG, for several computer vision tasks. In here, the CNN is used as feature extractor instead of being used as a classifier. More concretely, the

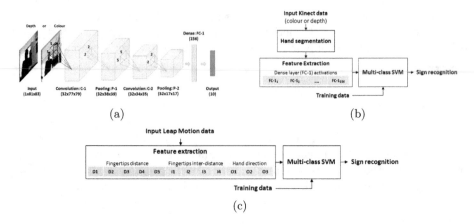

Fig. 2. Single-modality sign recognition: (a) CNN model as classifier; (b) CNN model as feature descriptor (methodologies applied to both Kinect modalities); and (c) Leap Motion sign recognition methodology.

activations of the last dense layer (FC-1) are extracted to be used as a feature descriptor (see Fig. 2a). For sign recognition, this CNN feature descriptor is fed into a multi-class SVM classifier (see Fig. 2b).

2.1.2 Leap Motion

Unlike Kinect, Leap Motion does not provide a complete depth map, instead it directly provides a set of relevant features of hand and fingertips. In this paper, 3 different types of features computed from the Leap Motion data are used:

1. **Fingertip distances** $D_i = \|F_i - C\|, i = 1, ..., N$; where N denotes the number of detected fingers and D_i represents the 3D distances between each fingertip F_i and the hand centre C.
2. **Fingertip inter-distances** $I_i = \|F_i - F_{i+1}\|, i = 1, ..., N-1$; represent the 3D distances between consecutive fingertips.
3. **Hand direction** O: represents the direction from the palm position toward the fingers. The direction is expressed as a unit vector pointing in the same direction as the directed line from the palm position to the fingers.

Both distance features are normalized by signer (user), according to the maximum fingertip distance and fingertip inter-distance of each user. This normalization is performed to make those features robust to people with different hand's size. Then, these 3 features are used as input into a multi-class SVM classifier for sign recognition. The block diagram of the implemented Leap Motion-based sign recognition approach is illustrated in Fig. 2c.

2.2   Multimodal Sign Recognition

The data provided by Kinect and Leap Motion have quite complementary characteristics, since while Leap Motion provides few accurate and relevant keypoints,

Kinect produces both a colour image and a complete depth map with a large number of less accurate 3D points. Therefore, we intend to exploit them together for SLR purposes.

According to the level of fusion, multimodal fusion techniques can be roughly grouped into three main categories: (i) data-level, (ii) feature-level, and (iii) decision-level fusion techniques [10]. As described in the following, we propose multimodal approaches of each fusion category for the SLR task, making use of 3 modalities (i.e. colour, depth and Leap Motion data).

2.2.1 Data-Level Fusion

The purpose of data-level fusion is to merge data from different modalities at an early stage. As illustrated in Fig. 3a, this methodology simply consists in the concatenation of the RGB colour image with the depth map, which results in a 4-dimensional matrix. In this approach, just both Kinect modalities (i.e. colour and depth) are considered for fusion, since the data dimensions of Leap Motion are incompatible.

2.2.2 Feature-Level Fusion

In general, feature-level fusion is characterized by three phases: (i) learning a representation, (ii) supervised training, and (iii) testing [10]. According to the order in which phases (i) and (ii) are made, feature-level fusion techniques can be roughly divided into two main groups: (1) End-to-end fusion, where the representation and the classifier are learned in parallel - see Fig. 3b; and (2) Multi-step fusion, where the representation is first learned and then the classifier is learned from it - see Fig. 3c.

End-to-End Fusion. The underlying idea of this approach is to learn an end-to-end deep neural network. In our scenario, the neural network has multiple input-specific pipes (one for each data type: colour, depth and Leap Motion), in which each input type is processed by its specific neural net. While colour and depth are both processed by a CNN, the Leap Motion data is processed by a classical neural net with one hidden layer. Then, the last hidden layers of each pipe are concatenated followed by one additional fully connected layer. All the layers are trained together end-to-end. The architecture of the implemented neural network is represented in Fig. 3b.

Multi-step Fusion. As in the end-to-end approach, a shared (multimodal) representation vector is created, by concatenating the last hidden layers of each model previous trained individually. Then, for sign recognition, the multimodal representation vector is fed into an additional classifier (i.e. a multi-class SVM). The multi-step feature-level fusion scheme is depicted in Fig. 3c.

2.2.3 Decision-Level Fusion

The purpose of decision-level fusion is to learn a specific classifier for each modality and, then, to find a decision rule between them. In this paper, we apply this

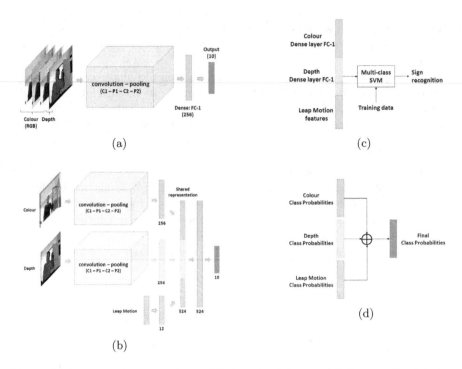

Fig. 3. Multimodal sign recognition: (a) Data-level fusion; (b) Decision-level fusion, where $\oplus$ is an aggregate operator representing the decision rule for fusion; (c) End-to-end feature-level fusion; and (d) Multi-step feature-level fusion.

concept making use of the output class probabilities of the models designed individually for each modality under analysis. Then, two main kinds of decision rules, to combine these class probabilities, were implemented: (1) pre-defined decisions rules, and (2) decision rules learned from the data (see Fig. 3d).

Pre-defined Decision Rules. Herein, two different pre-defined decision rules were implemented. In the first approach, the final prediction is given by the argument that maximizes the averaged class probabilities. In the second approach, the final prediction is given by the model with the maximum confidence. The confidence of a model in making a prediction is measured by its highest class probability.

Learned Decision Rule. The underlying idea of this approach is to learn a decision rule from the data. Therefore, a descriptor that concatenates the class probabilities, extracted from the individual models of each modality, is created and, then, used as input into a multiclass SVM classifier for sign recognition.

3   Experimental Results

The experimental evaluation of the proposed methodologies was performed in a public Microsoft Kinect and Leap Motion hand gesture recognition database [6,7]. The database is composed by 10 static gestures from the ASL. Each sign was performed by 14 different people, and repeated 10 times, which results in a total of 1400 gestures. In order to ensure signer independence, the dataset is divided into a training set of 1000 images from 10 people, and a test set of 400 images from the other 4 people. The training set is further divided in half, resulting in two subsets: one for training all single-modality methods and another for training the multimodal techniques that require input from single-modality methods, such as the feature-level and decision-level fusion approaches.

The implementation of the deep neural networks is based on Theano. The Nesterov's Accelerated Gradient Descent with momentum is used for optimization, and the categorical cross-entropy is used as the loss function. The adopted SVM classifier consists in a multi-class SVM classifier based on the one-against-one approach, in which a nonlinear Gaussian Radial Basis Function (RBF) kernel is used. The parameters (C, γ) of the RBF kernel are estimated by means of a grid search approach and cross-validation on the training set.

3.1   The Potential of Multimodal Learning

In order to access the potential of multimodal learning in the SLR context, we computed the rate of test signs for which each single-modality method made a correct prediction while the others were wrong. As presented in Table 1a, these results clearly demonstrate that there is a relative big potential to tackle the SLR problem via multi-modality. In particular, there is a higher complementarity between each Kinect modality (i.e. colour or depth) with the Leap Motion rather than between both Kinect modalities. For instance, there are 4.25% and 5.75% of test instances for which Leap Motion made correct predictions while colour and depth made incorrect ones, respectively.

3.2   Discussion

The experimental results of the proposed single-modality and multimodal sign recognition methodologies are presented in Table 1b and c, respectively. The results are reported in terms of classification accuracy (Acc), which is given by the ratio between the number of correctly classified signs t and the total number of test signs n: $Acc\% = \frac{t}{n} \times 100$. A first observation, regarding single-modality approaches, is that both colour and depth outperform Leap Motion, with accuracies of 94.75%, 91.75% and 82.00%, respectively. However, it should be noticed that Leap Motion sign recognition does not require any kind of preprocessing in order to segment the hand from the background for feature extraction. The most interesting observation is that multimodal fusion often promotes an overall improvement in the sign recognition accuracy. These results clearly demonstrate the complementarity between the three modalities. Typically, the classification

Table 1. Experimental assessment of the proposed recognition methods. (a) The potential of multimodal learning, expressed by the rate of test instances for which modality B made correct predictions while modality A made incorrect ones. (b) and (c) Experimental results of the proposed single-modality and multimodal recognition approaches, respectively. The results are presented in terms of classification accuracy (%).

(a)

Modality A	Modality B	Multi-modality potential (%)
Colour	Depth	3.00
Colour	Leap Motion	4.25
Depth	Colour	4.75
Depth	Leap Motion	5.75
Leap Motion	Colour	18.5
Leap Motion	Depth	18.25

(b)

Modality	Method	Acc (%)
Colour	CNN C[†]	93.50
	CNN FEAT[‡]	94.75
Depth	CNN C	91.75
	CNN FEAT	90.75
Leap Motion	-	82.00

[†] CNN as classifier.

[‡] CNN as feature extractor.

(c)

	Proposed multimodal learning methodologies		
Fusion-level	Method	Involved Modalities	Acc (%)
Data	-	C + D	89.75
Feature	End-to-end	C + D	93.00
		C + D + L	94.25
	Multi-step	C + D	96.25
		C + D + L	96.75
Decision	Average rule	C + D	96.00
		C + D + L	**97.00**
	Highest confidence	C + D	96.00
		C + D + L	96.50
	Learned decision rule	C + D	96.25
		C + D + L	96.75
	State-of-the-art methodologies		
Marin *et al.* 2014 [6]			91.28
Marin *et al.* 2015 [7]			96.50

accuracy increases as each modality is added to the recognition scheme. In particular, the decision-level fusion scheme, with the average decision rule, provides the best overall classification accuracy ($Acc = 97.00\%$). Still, regarding multimodal fusion techniques, it is possible to observe that, in general, decision-level fusion performs better than data-level and feature-level fusion. In fact, data-level fusion resulted in a worst model than the best single-modality method, with an Acc of 89.75%. These worst results are probably due to the curse of dimensionality, as the dimension of the input features in this model is considerable higher than in the others. Likewise, the end-to-end feature-level fusion approach also performed worst than the best single-modality method. This result might seem quite unexpected; however, a multimodal neural net architecture with multiple input-specific pipes has potentially more local minima which may explain the unsatisfying results. The initialization of the input specific weights from pre-trained single-modality networks might improve the results. Finally, it is important to stress that the best implemented multimodal fusion approach outperformed both state-of-art methods [6,7], with an Acc of 97.00% against 91.28% and 96.50%, respectively.

4 Conclusions

This paper addresses the topic of static SLR, by exploring multimodal learning techniques, making use of data from 3 distinct modalities: (i) colour; (ii) depth, both from Kinect; and (iii) Leap Motion data. In this regard, single-modality approaches as well as different multimodal methods, to fuse them at different levels, are proposed. Multimodal techniques include data-level, feature-level and decision-level fusion techniques. Experimental results suggest that both Kinect modalities are more discriminative than the Leap Motion data. However, the most interesting observation is that, in general, multimodal learning techniques outperform single-modality methods. In particular, the proposed decision-level fusion scheme, with the average decision rule, achieved the best results (*Acc* = 97.00%) and outperforms the current state-of-the-art methods. As future work, it is expected to extend the proposed methodologies for dynamic signs.

Acknowledgements. This work was funded by the Project "NanoSTIMA: Macro-to-Nano Human Sensing: Towards Integrated Multimodal Health Monitoring and Analytics/NORTE-01-0145-FEDER-000016" financed by the North Portugal Regional Operational Programme (NORTE 2020), under the PORTUGAL 2020 Partnership Agreement, and through the European Regional Development Fund (ERDF), and also by Fundação para a Ciência e a Tecnologia (FCT) within PhD and BPD grants with numbers SFRH/BD/102177/2014 and SFRH/BPD/101439/2014.

References

1. Cooper, H., Bowden, R.: Large lexicon detection of sign language. In: Lew, M., Sebe, N., Huang, T.S., Bakker, E.M. (eds.) HCI 2007. LNCS, vol. 4796, pp. 88–97. Springer, Heidelberg (2007). doi:10.1007/978-3-540-75773-3_10
2. Adithya, V., Vinod, P.R., Gopalakrishnan, U.: Artificial neural network based method for Indian sign language recognition. In: 2013 IEEE Conference on Information Communication Technologies (ICT), pp. 1080–1085 (2013)
3. den Bergh, M.V., Gool, L.V.: Combining RGB and ToF cameras for real-time 3D hand gesture interaction. In: 2011 IEEE Workshop on Applications of Computer Vision (WACV), pp. 66–72, January 2011
4. Dominio, F., Donadeo, M., Zanuttigh, P.: Combining multiple depth-based descriptors for hand gesture recognition. Pattern Recog. Lett. **50**, 101–111 (2014). Depth Image Analysis
5. Potter, L.E., Araullo, J., Carter, L.: The leap motion controller: a view on sign language. In: Proceedings of the 25th Australian Computer-Human Interaction Conference: Augmentation, Application, Innovation, Collaboration, OzCHI 2013, pp. 175–178. ACM, New York (2013)
6. Marin, G., Dominio, F., Zanuttigh, P.: Hand gesture recognition with leap motion and kinect devices. In: 2014 IEEE International Conference on Image Processing (ICIP), pp. 1565–1569, October 2014
7. Marin, G., et al.: Hand gesture recognition with jointly calibrated leap motion and depth sensor. Multimedia Tools Appl. **75**(22), 14991–15015 (2015)
8. Srinivas, S., Sarvadevabhatla, R.K., Mopuri, K.R., Prabhu, N., Kruthiventi, S., Radhakrishnan, V.B.: A taxonomy of deep convolutional neural nets for computer vision. Front. Robot. AI **2**(36), 1–13 (2016)
9. Srivastava, N., Hinton, G., Krizhevsky, A., Sutskever, I., Salakhutdinov, R.: Dropout: a simple way to prevent neural networks from overfitting. J. Mach. Learn. Res. **15**, 1929–1958 (2014)
10. Ngiam, J., Khosla, A., Kim, M., Nam, J., Lee, H., Ng, A.Y.: Multimodal deep learning. In: International Conference on Machine Learning, vol. 6 (2011)

Bayesian Approach in Kendall Shape Space for Plant Species Classification

Hibat'Allah Rouahi[1,2]([✉]), Riadh Mtibaa[1,2], and Ezzeddine Zagrouba[1,2]

[1] Institut Supérieur d'Informatique, Université de Tunis El Manar, Ariana, Tunisia
hiba_rouahi@yahoo.fr, rmtibaa@gmail.com, ezzeddine.zagrouba@fsm.rnu.tn
[2] LIMTIC Laboratory, Research Team on Intelligent Systems in Imaging and Artificial Vision (SIIVA), Ariana, Tunisia

Abstract. Modelling computer vision problems with Riemannian manifolds yields excellent results given that the visual features of these maniflods have special structures that Euclidean space doesn't capture. In this paper we propose an approach based on the Kendall manifold formalism and the Bayesian approach applied to a plant species classification problem. Kendall space is a quotient space that is provided with a Riemannian metric, which is more convenient when shapes differ only in translation, rotation and scale. However, an appropriate metric for shape classification task should not only suit certain invariance properties but also satisfy the different input properties. The non-linearity of Kendall space makes it difficult to apply common algorithms for classification. Thus, we propose to adapt the Bayes classifier to Kendalls representation using landmarks. Our main contribution consists in computing the parameters of the likelihood density functions through tangent spaces. Experimental results show that our approach is more accurate and effective.

Keywords: Kendall space · Plant species classification · Bayesian classifier · Tangent space · Landmarks

1 Introduction

The huge number and wide variety of existing plant species in the world makes human identification a tedious and time-consuming task, not only for non-experts but also for botanists who may sometimes fail in the identification of new or rare species. An automatic plant identification process has become an urgent challenge, not just to improve this process but also to preserve biodiversity which is vital to maintain the world ecosystem's health. Much research works focused on this challenge and proposed several identification tools that vary in terms of selected organs, extracted features, type of the description approach, and representation techniques. An interesting review of the existing approaches developed for plant species identification can be found in [1].

Usually, plant identification is based on the analysis of its different organs: leaves, fruits, flowers, stems, buds, etc. Among these, leaves are the most popular and basic features since they contain significant permanent information about the taxonomic identity of plants, unlike more transient organs. Consequently,

© Springer International Publishing AG 2017
L.A. Alexandre et al. (Eds.): IbPRIA 2017, LNCS 10255, pp. 322–331, 2017.
DOI: 10.1007/978-3-319-58838-4_36

plants classification based upon leaves represents the fastest and as well as the simplest way to identify a plant. There are many features that may help to describe leaves shapes: texture, margin, vein and color. Despite the transformations that leaves undergo during their development cycles, leaf shape is a relevant feature to guide the identification process as opposed to color and texture, which can vary according to the seasons and climatic conditions.

Regarding the approach used for shape description, this may be a specific or a generic approach, adapted to the context of leave shapes. Specific approaches are based on the botanical characterization extracted from the morphological features of leaves. The most commonly used features are: aspect ratio, rectangularity, convex area ratio, convex perimeter ratio, sphericity, circularity, eccentricity and form factor. Generic approaches can be subdivided into two classes: contour-based, that only exploit object boundary information, and region-based, where all the similar pixels within a surface region are taken into account to obtain the shape representation. The contour-based approaches can be classified as either global or local. Global approaches, represent the leaf shape by a single global descriptor, and local approaches compute a set of local descriptors at certain interesting points on the leaf. When global features are extracted, a global measure is used to compute the similarity between shapes. The advantages of global descriptors generally include moderate robustness to noise and the efficiency of shape matching. However, these approaches face major difficulties in capturing the finer details of shape boundaries. The Curvature Scale Space [2], the Fourier-based descriptors [3], and Zernike moments [4] are some global and contour based shape description techniques which have been tested on leaves. Local approaches represent a shape by a set of local shape descriptors, each corresponding to a certain part of the shape or simply to a sample landmark point along its contour. The advantages of local shape descriptors include superiority in describing the fine details of a shape with a higher accuracy than global ones. The main local descriptors tested in the context of leaf identification are the Multiscale Triangular approaches [5], the SIFT [6], the Harris detector [7].

Riemannian Computing in Computer Vision (RCCV) is the research field that combines tools from Riemannian geometry, for the study of structures, and statistics, for modeling variability, to develop practical computer vision solutions [8]. This combination has demonstrated superior performance in various applications. In this paper we focus on the automatic classification of plant leaves based on their shapes. The purpose of this research is to explore the Kendalls Riemannian theory using landmarks to capture the leafs shape. The landmark selection was carried out using the generic polygonal approximation approach. The classification was realised through adapting the Bayes classifier to the Riemannian context using tangent spaces which realise a good local linearisation of Kendall space. The reminder of the paper is organized as follows: in Sect. 2 we expose an overview of existing approaches related to Kendall space. Then, we present our method in Sect. 3, and the experiments in Sect. 3.5. Finally, we conclude the paper and highlight some perspectives in Sect. 4.

2   Related Works on Kendall Shape Space

The classification of objects according to shape is of capital importance in many scientific research studies. The study of shapes dates back to the biomathematician D'Arcy Thompson, however the modern algorithmic treatment of shape representations was started by David George Kendall. These representations are a process that helps attribute a mathematical structuring of information to shapes in order to ease the implementation of different algorithms. In his work, Kendall identified a shape with the geometrical information that remains after filtering out the location, scale and rotation effects from the initial representation. This standpoint led to the foundation of the Kendall shape theory [9] which is the most widely used discrete shape representation. A number of works by shape theory experts such as Bookstein [10], Dryden [11], and Kent [12], have adopted the Kendall definition to get a finite dimensional shape space from landmark coordinates.

It is well known that Kendall space has a finite-dimensional Riemannian manifold structure which makes it difficult to deal with. A significant amount of effort was deployed to resolve the problem of non-conformation between Kendall space and the classical linear classification algorithm. The solution proposed by Jayasumana et al. in [13] is to perform a shape analysis after a mapping operation from the manifold to the Hilbert space using a kernel function. Since the mapping is done from a low dimensional space to a high dimensional one, it produces a richer representation of the data, and hence typically makes tasks such as classification and clustering easier. However, only positive definite kernels yield a mapping to a Hilbert space and a poor choice of kernel can often result in a reduced classification performance. Another idea is to adapt an unsupervised learning algorithm, k-means, to the shape analysis context by integrating the Procrustes type distances with the Procrustes mean [14]. As far as we are concerned, our focus is on the adaptation of the Bayesian classifier to the Kendall space context through a linear space with finite and reduced dimensions, that is the tangent space.

3   Gaussian Bayes Classifier on Kendall Shape Space Σ_2^k

This work tries to devise a robust classifier through the combination of an efficient shape representation within the framework of the Kendall shape theory, with the Bayesian approach, renowned for its rigorous theoretical foundation and optimal classification results. We based our choice of the Kendall representation because its adequate implementation improves computational effectiveness. Indeed, this representation is actually an easy to calculate matrix from the set of infinite configurations of the same shape. In addition, the classification algorithms based on matrix-like-structures should be computationally much less time consuming compared to those using more complex structures. Concerning the Bayesian approach, the Gaussian distribution was adopted as a model.

3.1   Landmark Selection

Given that we are working within a supervised context, the number N_c of the targeted shape classes ω_i with $1 \leq i \leq N_c$ is prefixed. The selection procedure therefore generates a set $\left\{X_j^{i\star}\right\}_{1 \leq j \leq N_{ps}}$ comprising N_{ps} initial configurations of learning samples, where each learning matrix $X_j^{i\star}$ represents the k labelled selected landmarks of the jth sample, for each one of the N_c classes. More precisely, the selection consists to picking out a fixed number of landmarks from the contours of the objects' images. The procedure may exploit geometric features like curvature. In our case, we adopted a polygonal reduction procedure. In order to do so, we proceeded to the binarization of the leaves' images, then we detected the leaves' contours and reduced the contours' vertices to a specific number. We performed this by calculating the importance of each vertex according to angle and segment length and removing the least important. The process was repeated until the desired number of vertices is reached (see Algorithm 1 below).

Algorithm 1. Polygonal approximation pseudo code

Input: $P = \{p_1, p_2, \ldots, p_N\}$: Original contour (2 rows, N columns)
       Num: Desired number of selected landmarks
Output: $P = \{p_1, p_2, \ldots, p_{Num}\}$: Final contour (2 rows, Num columns)
 1: **for** $i = 1$ to N **do**
 2:    Calculate importance value of each point p_i of the original contour P.
 3:    $imp[i] \leftarrow$ **Vertex_Importance**(p_i, P, N)
 4: **end for**
 5: **repeat**
 6:    Find the index of the least important point.
 7:    Eliminate this point from the contour P and its importance value from imp.
 8:    Recalculate importance for vertices before and after the point removed.
 9: **until** $(N > Num)$
10: **return**$(P = \{p_1, p_2, \ldots, p_{Num}\})$

11: **function** **Vertex_Importance**(p_i, P, N)
12: Find adjacent vertices to p_i.
13: Obtain the two adjacent line segments to p_i and their lengths.
14: Calculate the angle between the two adjacent line segments.
15: $vImp \leftarrow$ Multiply the angle by the length of the two segments.
16: **return**$(vImp)$
17: **End function**

3.2   Shape Learning Processing

Let $X_j^{i\star} = \left(x_0^\star\ x_1^\star\ \ldots\ x_{k-1}^\star \right)$ be one of the learning samples in $\{X_j^{i\star}\}_{1 \leq j \leq N_{ps}}$ for the class ω_i. We started by calculating the center of $X_j^{i\star}$ to remove the translation effect from $X_j^{i\star}$, by moving $x_c^\star$ to the origin of the coordinates system, when each $x_\ell^\star$ is substituted with $x_\ell^\star - x_c^\star$, for all $0 \leq \ell \leq k - 1$, respectively.

$$x_c^\star = \frac{1}{k} \sum_{\ell=0}^{k-1} x_\ell^\star \qquad (1)$$

Next, we performed a dimension reduction via a right multiplication of the last version of $X_j^{i\star}$ by the recentering orthogonal matrix Q,

$$
Q = \begin{cases}
Q_{\ell 1} = \frac{1}{\sqrt{k}}, & 1 \leq \ell \leq k \; ; \\
Q_{\ell\ell} = \frac{\ell-1}{\sqrt{\ell(\ell-1)}}, & 2 \leq \ell \leq k; \\
Q_{\ell h} = -\frac{1}{\sqrt{\ell(\ell-1)}}, & 1 \leq \ell \leq h-1, 2 \leq h \leq k; \\
Q_{\ell h} = 0, & \text{otherwise.}
\end{cases}
\tag{2}
$$

to get an intermediate representation matrix $\tilde{X}_j^i$ with general form $\left(0 \; \tilde{x}_1 \; \tilde{x}_2 \ldots \tilde{x}_{k-1}\right)$ which we reduced naturally to

$$
\tilde{X}_j^i = \left(\tilde{x}_1 \; \tilde{x}_2 \ldots \tilde{x}_{k-1}\right)
\tag{3}
$$

After that, we eliminated the scaling effect through normalization to get

$$
X_j^i = \frac{1}{\sqrt{tr(\tilde{X}_j^i(\tilde{X}_j^i)^t)}}
\tag{4}
$$

The set $\left\{X_j^i\right\}_{1 \leq j \leq N_{ps}}$ coincides with points on the $2(k-1)-1$ dimensional unit sphere, denoted by S_2^k. We notice that any matrix TX_j^i has the same shape as X_j^i for $T \in \mathbf{SO}(2)$, the rotation group. So, from now on, X_j^i is treated as a pre-shape representation and the sought shape $\pi\left(X_j^i\right)$ identifies an equivalence class modulo the left action of rotations T in $\mathbf{SO}(2)$ on the pre-shape X_j^i; the space of all possible shapes is the $2(k-1)-2$ dimensional Kendall space, which is the quotient space.

$$
\Sigma_2^k = S_2^k/\mathbf{SO}(2)
\tag{5}
$$

The pseudo-singular values decomposition helps to write any pre-shape X_j^i as a three-factors product,

$$
X_j^i = U(\Lambda \; 0)V
\tag{6}
$$

where $U \in \mathbf{SO}(2)$, $V \in \mathbf{SO}(k-1)$, 0 is the null matrix of dimensions $2 \times (k-3)$, and Λ is the 2×2 diagonal matrix $diag\{\lambda_1, \lambda_2\}$ such that $\lambda_1 \geq |\lambda_2|$, $\lambda_1^2 + \lambda_2^2 = 1$, and $\lambda_2 \geq 0$ unless $k = 3$. This decomposition provides a systematic way to decide whether or not any couple of learning pre-shapes belong to the same equivalence class. In order to obtain the learning shapes in Σ_2^k (5), we calculated $U_{X_{j_1}^i}(\Lambda_{X_{j_1}^i} \; 0)V_{X_{j_1}^i}$ and $U_{X_{j_2}^i}(\Lambda_{X_{j_2}^i} \; 0)V_{X_{j_2}^i}$ of each couple of pre-shapes $X_{j_1}^i$ and $X_{j_2}^i$ in $\{X_j^i\}_{1 \leq j \leq N_{ps}}$ (6). Then, we decided that $\pi(X_{j_1}^i)$ and $\pi(X_{j_2}^i)$ are identical if and only if $\Lambda_{X_{j_1}^i} = \Lambda_{X_{j_2}^i}$ and both first rows of $V_{X_{j_1}^i}$ and $V_{X_{j_2}^i}$ are exactly the same, the remaining $k-3$ rows of $V_{X_{j_1}^i}$ and $V_{X_{j_2}^i}$ do not matter since they are multiplied by the null matrix of dimensions $2 \times (k-3)$ appearing in $(\Lambda_{X_{j_1}^i} \; 0)$ and $(\Lambda_{X_{j_2}^i} \; 0)$, respectively. Naturally, we did not care about the left acting orthogonal matrices $U_{X_{j_1}^i}$ and $U_{X_{j_2}^i}$ because they do not affect shapes. This way, we succeeded in regrouping the N_{ps} learning pre-shapes of $\{X_j^i\}_{1 \leq j \leq N_{ps}}$ into N_s^i

learning equivalence classes. Concretely, for all $1 \leq p \leq N_s^i$, the pth equivalence class is represented by any candidate denoted by $\pi(X_p^i)$, and qualified as the learning shape.

3.3   Estimation of the Likelihood Density Function Parameters

To estimate the expectation vector μ_i as well as the covariance matrix Σ_i of the Gaussian likelihood, we assume that the learning samples in each set $\left\{ \pi \left(X_p^i \right) \right\}_{1 \leq p \leq N_s^i}$ are independent and identically distributed. In a first step, we calculated the mean shape $\pi \left(\hat{\nu}_i \right)$ of the set of learning shapes $\left\{ \pi \left(X_p^i \right) \right\}_{1 \leq p \leq N_s^i}$ which we used later as a reference shape where we approximated Σ_2^k locally by its tangent space [15]. Specifically, we looked for $\pi \left(\hat{\nu}_i \right)$ as a solution of the minimization problem

$$\arg \inf_{\pi(\nu) \in \Sigma_2^k} \sum_{p=1}^{N_s^i} d_F^2 \left(\pi \left(X_p^i \right), \pi \left(\nu \right) \right) \tag{7}$$

which involves the procrustes distance between $\pi \left(X_p^i \right)$ and $\pi \left(\nu \right)$

$$d_F^2 \left(\pi \left(X_p^i \right), \pi \left(\nu \right) \right) = \sin \left(\rho \left(\pi \left(X_p^i \right), \pi \left(\nu \right) \right) \right) \tag{8}$$

Here, ρ is the distance function defined for Σ_2^k as

$$\rho \left(\pi \left(X_p^i \right), \pi \left(\nu \right) \right) = \arccos \left(\lambda_1 + \lambda_2 \right) \tag{9}$$

with the pseudo-singular values λ_1 and λ_2 of $X_p^i \nu^t$ for arbitrary pre-shapes X_p^i and ν of $\pi \left(X_p^i \right)$ and $\pi \left(\nu \right)$, respectively. In a second step, we mapped each learning shape $\pi \left(X_p^i \right)$ in $\left\{ \pi \left(X_p^i \right) \right\}_{1 \leq p \leq N_s^i}$ onto its projection $\bar{\pi}_i \left(X_p^i \right)$ computed as

$$\bar{\pi}_i \left(X_p^i \right) = \left(I_m - \pi \left(\hat{\nu}_i \right) \pi \left(\hat{\nu}_i \right)^t \right) \pi \left(X_p^i \right), \tag{10}$$

In practice, we computed $\pi \left(\hat{\nu}_i \right)$ and $\bar{\pi}_i \left(X_p^i \right)$ for all $1 \leq i \leq N_c$ and $1 \leq p \leq N_s^i$ using the generalised procrustes analysis [15]. In a last step, we reshaped each one of the matrices $\bar{\pi}_i \left(X_p^i \right)$ onto a row vector $\bar{\pi}_i^v \left(X_p^i \right)$. Then, we used the maximum likelihood method to obtain the likelihood parameters with dimensions: $1 \times 2 \left(k - 1 \right)$ and $2 \left(k - 1 \right) \times 2 \left(k - 1 \right)$, respectively.

$$\mu_i = \frac{1}{N_s^i} \sum_{p=1}^{N_s^i} \bar{\pi}_i^v \left(X_p^i \right), \tag{11}$$

$$\Sigma_i = \frac{1}{N_s^i} \sum_{p=1}^{N_s^i} \left(\bar{\pi}_i^v \left(X_p^i \right) - \mu_i \right)^t \left(\bar{\pi}_i^v \left(X_p^i \right) - \mu_i \right). \tag{12}$$

3.4   Generalization

This subsection details how the classification task of general shapes was conducted. The values of the Gaussian likelihood μ_i and Σ_i of each class ω_i were used to compute the posteriori probabilities

$$p\left(\omega_i|\pi\left(X\right)\right) = \frac{p\left(\bar{\pi}_i^v\left(X\right)|\omega_i\right)P\left(\omega_i\right)}{p\left(\bar{\pi}_i^v\left(X\right)\right)} \tag{13}$$

where

$$p\left(\bar{\pi}_i^v\left(X\right)|\omega_i\right) = \frac{1}{(2\pi)^{(k-1)}\sqrt{\det\left(\Sigma_i\right)}}\exp\left(-\frac{1}{2}\left(\bar{\pi}_i^v\left(X\right)-\mu_i\right)\Sigma_i^{-1}\left(\bar{\pi}_i^v\left(X\right)-\mu_i\right)^t\right), \tag{14}$$

$P\left(\omega_i\right)$ is an a priori probability of ω_i, and $p\left(\bar{\pi}_i^v\left(X\right)\right)$ is the evidence term. Finally, the maximum amongst the values of $p\left(\omega_i|\pi\left(X\right)\right)$ indicates the class of $\pi\left(X\right)$.

3.5   Experiment and Result Analysis

To evaluate the behaviour of our Gaussian Bayes classifier on Σ_2^k for plant species classification, the Swedish leaf dataset [16], which contains 1125 images of leaves uniformly distributed into 15 species, has been used. Each species is therefore represented by 75 images. The Swedish leaf dataset is very challenging because of its high inter-species similarity between the first, third and ninth species. The experiments essentially consisted in examining the different stages of our method. The first preprocessing stage, the landmark selection (Sect. 3.1), eliminated the least important points on the leave boundaries and kept only the k points, where the geometric information was more important. Of course, the k selected points, which are the same for all sample classes, were arranged in $X_j^{i^\star}$ configuration matrices. Figure 1 illustrates the results of the selection procedure, where the number of the selected landmarks is 27. This number is related to the number of training samples, 35, used in our case during the shape learning stage to estimate the likelihood parameters of each class. It is also related to the shape description derived from these selected landmarks. Although, adding more points brings us closer to the original shape, not much more useful detail was obtained when using more than 27 points. The second processing stage, the shape learning (Sect. 3.2), analyzes the training data derived from the selection procedure to estimate the parameters of the likelihood density functions relative to each shape class w_i (Sect. 3.3). These parameters were used during the generalization stage (Sect. 3.4) in order to classify the test samples. It should be noted here that 35 samples were used during the learning stage. The remaining 40 samples were used for the test.

The experimental results of our method are summarized, both in the presence and the absence of data corrupted by Gaussian random noise, in Table 1. These results reflected the robustness of our method and were then superposed with two other methods using the same landmarks that were already used and the same training and testing samples (Fig. 2). The first method is the same Gaussian Bayes classifier but expressed in Euclidean space. The second one is Kendall's

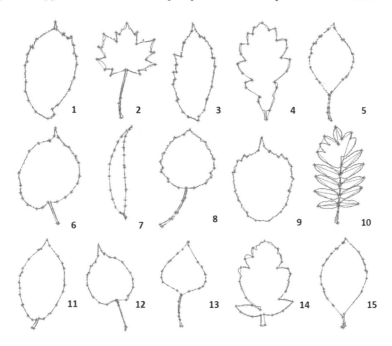

Fig. 1. The blue lines indicate the initial contours detected. The red dots indicate the selected landmarks using the polygonal approximation. (Color figure online)

Riemannian distance between the different test samples and the mean shape of each class. Equation 9 was used to calculate the mean shape from the training set. Then, the distance between the mean shape and the different test samples was measured using Eq. 7. Figure 2 proves that our method is outstanding and confirms on one hand, that the reformulation of the classical computer vision problem with Riemannian maniflods gives excellent results, and on the other makes up for the insufficiency of Kendall's Riemannian distance.

The expected improvement of the classification results comes from the lack of redundancy within the learning sets $\left\{\pi\left(X_p^i\right)\right\}_{1\leq p\leq N_s^i}$ used by our classifier in Kendall space, compared to the sets $\left\{X_j^{i\star}\right\}_{1\leq j\leq N_{ps}}$ used by the classical classifier. This lack of redundancy comes from the systematic elimination of translation, scale, and rotation effects during the construction of the learning

Table 1. Computer simulations summary

Training data	Test data	Availability
Not corrupted	Not corrupted	98%
Not corrupted	Corrupted	96.67%
Corrupted	Not corrupted	94%

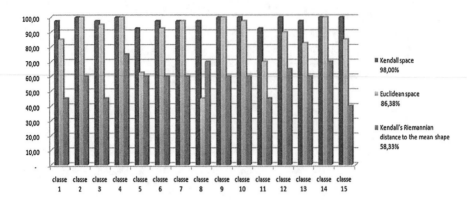

Fig. 2. Results per class for the Swedish leaf dataset

shapes. Besides, the complexity of our classifier in Kendall space amounts to an order determined mainly by the $2(k-1)\sum_{i=1}^{N_c} N_s^i$ coordinate values involved in the learning phase, which should be much smaller than the $2kN_cN_{ps}$ coordinate values involved in the learning phase of the classical classifier since $N_s^i \ll N_{ps}$, for all $1 \leq i \leq N_c$, when the initial learning data sets get larger.

4   Conclusion

In the present paper we propose a reformulation of the Gaussian Bayes classifier in Kendall shape space Σ_2^k for plant species classification. We detail the procedure that helps construct a shape learning set from initial configurations corresponding to selected landmarks from object boundaries using an automatic procedure. We then used the Riemannian structure to define the mean shape where Σ_2^k is approximated by its tangent space. This approximation turned out to be the key to resolve the problem of non-linearity of the Kendall space. Consequently, we succeed in establishing a likelihood density function on Σ_2^k which remains invariant to Euclidean similarity transformations. The experimental results performed on Swedish leaf dataset confirm the robustness of our model where the success rates are outstanding. As future work we propose validating our method in some well-known large benchmark dataset with problems such as corruption, noise, defects, distortion and occultation and try to adapt other unsupervised methods in Kendall shape space.

References

1. Sharama, S., Gupta, C.: A review of plant recognition methods and algorithms. Int. J. Innov. Res. Adv. Eng. (IJIRAE) **6**(2) (2015). ISSN 2349-2163
2. Cerutti, G., Tougne, L., Coquin, D., Vacavant, A.: Curvature-scale-based contour understanding for leaf margin shape recognition and species identification. In: International Conference on Computer Vision Theory and Applications (VISAPP), vol. 1, pp. 277–284 (2013)

3. Neto, J.C., Meyer, G.E., Jones, D.D., Samal, A.K.: Plant species identification using Elliptic Fourier leaf shape analysis. Comput. Electr. Agric. **50**(2), 121–134 (2006)
4. Kadir, A., Nugroho, L.E., Santosa, P.I.: Experiments of zernike moments for leaf identification. J. Theor. Appl. Inf. Technol. (JATIT) **41**(1), 82–93 (2012)
5. Mouine, S., Yahiaoui, I., Verroust-Blondet, A.: A shape-based approach for leaf classification using multiscaletriangular representation. In: Proceedings of the 3rd ACM Conference on International Conference on Multimedia Retrieval, pp. 127–134. ACM (2013)
6. Villena Romn, J., Lana Serrano, S., Gonzlez Cristbal, J.C.: Daedalus at Image-CLEF 2011 plant identification task: using SIFT keypoints for object detection. In: CLEF (Notebook Papers/Labs/Workshop) (2011)
7. Dimitrovski, I., Madjarov, G., Kocev, D., Lameski, P.: Maestra at LifeCLEF: plant task: plant identification using visual data. In: CLEF (Working Notes), pp. 705–714 (2014)
8. Srivastava, A., Turaga, P.K.: Welcome to Riemannian computing in computer vision. In: Turaga, P.K., Srivastava, A. (eds.) Riemannian Computing in Computer Vision, pp. 1–18. Springer, Cham (2016). doi:10.1007/978-3-319-22957-7_1
9. Kendall, D.G., Barden, D., Carne, T.K., Le, H.: Shape and Shape Theory. Wiley, New York (1999)
10. Bookstein, F.L.: Landmark methods for forms without landmarks: morphometrics of group differences in outline shape. Med. Image Anal. **1**(3), 225–243 (1997)
11. Dryden, I.L., Mardia, K.V.: Statistical Shape Analysis. Wiley, Chichester (1998)
12. Kent, J.T., Mardia, K.V.: Shape, procrustes tangent projections and bilateral symmetry. Biometrika **88**(2), 469–485 (2001)
13. Jayasumana, S., Salzmann, M., Li, H., Harandi, M.: A framework for shape analysis via Hilbert space embedding. In: Proceedings of the IEEE International Conference on Computer Vision, pp. 1249–1256 (2013)
14. Vinu, G., Sim, A., Alemany, S.: The k-means algorithm for 3D shapes with an application to apparel design. Adv. Data Anal. Classif. **10**(1), 103–132 (2014)
15. Dryden, I.L.: Shapes package. In: R Foundation for Statistical Computing, Vienna, Austria. Contributed Package (2015). https://www.maths.nottingham.ac.uk/personal/ild/shapes
16. Sderkvist, O.: Computer vision classification of leaves from swedish trees. M.S. thesis, Linkoping University, SE-581 83 Linkoping, Sweden (2001)

Pattern Recognition and Machine Learning

A Study of Prototype Selection Algorithms for Nearest Neighbour in Class-Imbalanced Problems

Jose J. Valero-Mas[(✉)], Jorge Calvo-Zaragoza, Juan R. Rico-Juan,
and José M. Iñesta

Pattern Recognition and Artificial Intelligence Group, University of Alicante,
Alicante, Spain
{jjvalero,jcalvo,juanra,inesta}@dlsi.ua.es

Abstract. Prototype Selection methods aim at improving the efficiency of the Nearest Neighbour classifier by selecting a set of representative examples of the training set. These techniques have been studied in situations in which the classes at issue are balanced, which is not representative of real-world data. Since class imbalance affects the classification performance, data-level balancing approaches that artificially create or remove data from the set have been proposed. In this work, we study the performance of a set of prototype selection algorithms in imbalanced and algorithmically-balanced contexts using data-driven approaches. Results show that the initial class balance remarkably influences the overall performance of prototype selection, being generally the best performances found when data is algorithmically balanced before the selection stage.

Keywords: kNN · Imbalanced data · Prototype selection

1 Introduction

The k-Nearest Neighbour (kNN) classifier constitutes one of the most well-known techniques for supervised non-parametric classification, mainly because of its conceptual simplicity and its bounded error rates [1]. Basically, kNN classifies a given input element by assigning the most common label among its k-nearest prototypes of the training set. Such exhaustive search for each element to be classified entails low efficiency figures in both classification time and memory usage, which constitutes the main drawback for this classifier.

Data Reduction (DR) methods are typically considered for tackling this disadvantage [2]. These strategies reduce the training set while trying to keep the classification accuracy of the original data –or even improving it– if noisy elements are removed. Among the different existing possibilities, a relatively straightforward and largely studied methodology known as prototype selection (PS) performs this reduction by selecting a representative subset of the initial training set following a particular heuristic [3].

A large number of works in the classification field assume that the classes of the elements at issue are equally represented. However, this assumption turns

© Springer International Publishing AG 2017
L.A. Alexandre et al. (Eds.): IbPRIA 2017, LNCS 10255, pp. 335–343, 2017.
DOI: 10.1007/978-3-319-58838-4_37

out not to be realistic since most data sources do not necessarily exhibit such equilibrium among the different classes, leading to *class imbalance* problems [4]. In general, the use of such imbalanced data leads to situations in which the performance of the classifier is biased towards the class representing the majority of the elements [5]. In this regard, different strategies have been considered to palliate this issue, being a rather common one the use of data sampling methodologies to artificially equilibrate the class distribution.

In this paper, we aim at studying the behaviour of PS algorithms when dealing with large-scale imbalance datasets in the context of kNN classification. More precisely, the idea is to assess the performance of PS algorithms in class-imbalance situations and compare them to the case in which a sampling-based balancing algorithm is considered as a preprocessing stage before PS.

The rest of the work is structured as follows: Sect. 2 contextualizes the problem of imbalanced classification; Sect. 3 presents the experiment proposed as well as the sampling-based balancing and PS techniques considered; Sect. 4 presents and discusses the results obtained; finally, Sect. 5 concludes the work and proposes future lines to develop.

2   Classification with Imbalanced Data

Formally, imbalanced classification tasks refer to the cases in which prior probabilities of the classes at issue significantly differ among them. This particularity generally results in a tendency of the classifier to bias towards the majority class, thus decreasing the overall performance of the system.

Different proposals may be found in the literature to palliate this issue, being typically grouped into three categories [6]: (a) data-level methods that either create artificial data for the minority classes and/or remove elements from the majority one to equilibrate the class representation; (b) algorithmic-level approaches that internally bias the classifier to compensate the skewness in the data; (c) cost-sensitive training methodologies that consider higher penalties for the misclassification of the minority class than for the majority one.

Not all classifiers show this bias towards the majority class. Instance-based algorithms such as kNN report a superior tolerance as they consider all instances during the classification stage. Nevertheless, when this imbalance effect is combined with class overlapping, performance is severely affected [7].

In this work, we study the use of PS algorithms in imbalanced and overlapped scenarios. As aforementioned, PS methods tackle the issues found in kNN related to large and noisy (overlapped) datasets. However, as these processes have not been devised for class-imbalanced sets, it seems necessary to explore their behaviour in such cases and compare the results with the ones obtained if a data-level balancing method is considered as a preprocessing stage.

3   Experimentation

Figure 1 shows the scheme implemented for the experiments. As it can be checked, the *train set* may undergo a class-balancing process and/or a PS method

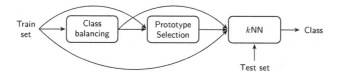

Fig. 1. Scheme proposed for the experiments.

before getting to the kNN classifier, which are the situations to be compared. For our experiments, we fixed $k = 1$ for the classifier as well as considering Euclidean distance for the dissimilarity measure.

The following sections introduce both the class-balancing techniques considered as well as the PS strategies tested. Also, one last section introducing the evaluation methodology is included.

3.1 Prototype Selection Techniques

In terms of PS methods, we have contemplated a comprehensive set of techniques from the ones in the literature.

As examples of the most classic approaches for PS, we have considered the Edited NN (ENN), the Condensed NN (CNN), and the Fast CNN (FCNN). Additionally, we considered EFCNN, which consists of an FCNN process with a previous ENN stage to remove noisy elements.

In terms of more recent approaches, we have considered the use of the Decremental Reduction Optimization Procedure (DROP3) as an example of hybrid approach between the ENN and CNN families. Also, we have tested the performance of the Cross-generational elitist selection, Heterogeneous recombination and Cataclysmic mutation search (CHC), which constitutes a very successful example of genetic algorithm applied to PS.

Finally, we also studied the use of the Farthest Neighbour (FN) and Nearest to Enemy (NE) algorithms as they constitute representative examples of the so-called *rank methods*. These methods give each prototype a score indicating its relevance with respect to classification accuracy, so that they can be ranked to eventually select a subset of them.

For a comprehensive explanation of the methods the reader is referred to [3] except for the rank ones for which reader is addressed to [8]. For our experiments we set a value of $k = 5$ for all PS schemes.

3.2 Data Sampling Class Balancing

As commented, data-level class balancing techniques equilibrate the classes in the training set by *oversampling* the minority class and/or *undersampling* the majority one. To assess their relevance in the context of this experiment, we considered a set of examples of each family as well as combinations of them.

Regarding oversampling, we considered the Synthetic Minority Oversampling Technique (SMOTE, SMT in this work) [9] as well as two existing extensions (B1 and B2 for SMOTE Borderline 1 and 2, respectively) that focus on detecting and remarking transition zones between classes [10].

So as to undersampling, we included Condensing-based undersampling (CNN), Neighborhood cleaning rule (NCL), and Tomek links (TL). Due to space issues, the reader is referred to [11] for a thorough explanation of these methods.

Finally, the combinations of techniques considered comprise all undersampling methods followed by oversampling. We set a value of $k = 5$ for all cases.

3.3   Evaluation

For the experimentation we have considered five datasets from the UJI[1] and the KEEL[2] collections. Additionally, we have considered the music dataset Prosemus[3] that is meant for *onset detection*, i.e. the detection of the beginnings of music note events in audio streams, and whose features have been extracted with the methodology in [12]. All these datasets only contain two classes as it constitutes a common practice in studies about imbalanced classification. Also, these sets contain more than 1500 instances so that PS can be reasonably applied. A 5-fold cross-validation scheme has been considered for the experimentation. Table 1 describes these datasets.

Table 1. Description of the datasets considered in terms of the amount of instances of the majority (Maj.) and minority (Min.) classes. Symbols † and ‡ depict sets obtained from the UJI or the KEEL collections, respectively.

Dataset	Min.	Maj.	Dataset	Min.	Maj.	Dataset	Min.	Maj.
Prosemus	1041	4045	Phoneme†	3673	5170	Spam†	1813	2788
Scrapie†	531	2582	Segment0‡	329	1979	Yeast3‡	163	1321

Regarding figures of merit, we considered the F-measure (F_1) as it constitutes a typical measure in the context of imbalanced classification. Focusing on the minority class, this metric summarizes the correctly classified elements (True Positives, TP), the misclassified elements from the majority class as minority ones (False Positives, FP), and the misclassified elements from the minority class as majority class (False Negative, FN) in a single value as follows:

$$F_1 = \frac{2 \cdot TP}{2 \cdot TP + FP + FN} \tag{1}$$

Note that for the case of the Prosemus set, a tolerance window of 50 ms is given, following the common evaluation procedure for onset detection [12].

Additionally, as pointed out in [13], PS evaluation may be seen as a multi-objective problem with two opposed objectives to be optimized, accuracy and set

---

[1] http://www.vision.uji.es/~sanchez/Databases/.

[2] http://sci2s.ugr.es/keel/datasets.php.

[3] http://grfia.dlsi.ua.es/cm/projects/prosemus/database.php.

size. Thus, we shall analyse the results in terms of the non-dominance concept: one solution is said to dominate another when it is better or equal in each of the two objectives considered and, at least, strictly better in one of them; the best solutions, as there may be more than one, are those that are non-dominated.

4   Results

The results obtained are shown in Table 2. These figures depict the average F_1 score and reduction rate (in percentage) obtained for the considered datasets in terms of the balancing techniques and PS strategy used.

According to the results, the use of PS on the initial imbalance situation implies a decrease in the F_1 measure for all cases. For instance, CHC lowers performance in more than 0.15 points in the F_1 measure. However, in this context, the results achieved by FCNN are particularly interesting since, although there is a decrease in performance as in the other cases, F_1 is just slightly lower than the original case (0.2 points) but with less than a third of its set size.

When an oversampling technique is considered, the results show a slight improvement but also implies an increase in the set size. Nevertheless, given that some cases retrieve competitive F_1 results but still with a large reduction rate (for instance, FCNN and EFCNN when considering SMT), this balancing scheme seems appropriate as a preprocessing stage.

Regarding the undersampling schemes, it can be checked that, in general, this balancing process results in slightly worse scores than when oversampling the set. Particularly, the use of the CNN balancing method implies a general decrease in the F_1 results when PS is applied. However, when this CNN method is used without any PS, results are remarkably good as it achieves the same F_1 as in the initial set but with roughly half of its set size. NCL and TL schemes show better performance when coupled with PS as F_1 results get to improve when compared to their corresponding PS schemes in the initial imbalanced situation.

In terms of the combined balancing strategies, it can be checked that, in general, they obtain intermediate figures between the solely use of oversampling or undersampling. For instance, for the ENN selection method scheme, CNN-B1 achieves an $F_1 = 0.49$ with a 49.1 % of set size while the oversampling B1 retrieves an $F_1 = 0.68$ with a set size of 132.2 % and undersampling CNN gets to an $F_1 = 0.60$ with 34.2 % of the initial prototypes. Thus, these solutions may suit cases with medium reduction requirements, being undersampling techniques the ones indicated for drastic size reductions.

Figure 2 graphically shows these results and allows their analysis in terms of the non-dominance criterion. As a first point, most of the non-dominance set comprises cases in which balancing is considered before PS. While all these solutions entail a (sometimes slight) decrease in the F_1 score when compared to the initial case, the resulting set is remarkably more compact than the original situation. For instance, the NCL-B1 balancing method coupled with FCNN achieves an $F_1 = 0.68$ with less than a fifth of the total number of prototypes.

Table 2. Results obtained in terms of the F_1 and reduction rate (in percentage referred to the initial case without PS) figures of merit for each combination of PS and balancing method. Bold results remark the elements that belong to the non-dominated set.

Balancing	Metric	PS method								
		ALL	CNN	FCNN	ENN	EFCNN	DROP3	CHC	$EN_{0.1}$	$FN_{0.1}$
Original	F_1	0.69	0.64	0.67	0.64	0.63	0.58	**0.52**	0.52	0.58
	Size (%)	100.0	30.6	28.2	85.6	7.2	8.0	**0.7**	1.6	3.3
SMT	F_1	0.70	0.64	0.68	0.68	0.67	0.60	**0.62**	0.53	0.59
	Size (%)	150.3	40.4	34.0	132.0	13.3	14.7	**2.1**	2.3	4.9
B1	F_1	**0.70**	0.64	0.68	0.68	**0.67**	0.60	0.59	0.48	0.55
	Size (%)	**150.3**	37.9	32.8	132.2	**12.5**	13.9	2.5	2.8	4.9
B2	F_1	0.69	0.64	0.67	0.67	0.66	0.60	0.58	0.49	0.54
	Size (%)	150.3	40.7	35.9	129.5	12.7	14.9	2.2	3.1	5.0
CNN	F_1	**0.69**	0.62	0.66	0.60	0.60	0.56	**0.47**	0.52	0.54
	Size (%)	**49.2**	27.1	26.4	34.2	4.8	5.3	**0.4**	2.5	2.7
NCL	F_1	0.69	0.64	0.67	0.66	0.65	0.56	**0.59**	0.53	0.59
	Size (%)	78.2	18.6	16.7	71.6	5.9	6.2	**0.8**	1.0	2.5
TL	F_1	0.69	0.63	0.67	0.66	**0.66**	0.58	**0.54**	0.52	0.59
	Size (%)	92.3	25.6	23.2	80.8	**7.1**	7.3	**0.7**	1.4	3.0
CNN-SMT	F_1	0.69	0.63	0.66	0.66	0.64	0.60	0.56	0.49	0.52
	Size (%)	65.8	32.4	30.0	49.1	8.4	9.4	1.0	2.9	3.2
CNN-B1	F_1	**0.69**	0.63	0.67	0.66	0.64	0.57	0.54	0.47	0.53
	Size (%)	**65.9**	31.3	29.3	49.1	8.5	9.4	1.1	3.0	3.2
CNN-B2	F_1	0.69	0.62	0.66	0.65	0.63	0.56	0.55	0.47	0.50
	Size (%)	65.9	32.3	31.1	47.9	8.9	9.3	1.0	3.1	3.3
NCL-SMT	F_1	0.69	0.65	0.67	0.67	0.67	0.61	0.59	0.52	0.58
	Size (%)	109.7	22.6	18.3	101.6	9.6	10.5	1.7	1.2	3.5
NCL-B1	F_1	0.69	0.65	**0.68**	0.68	**0.67**	0.59	0.58	0.49	0.54
	Size (%)	109.5	21.9	**18.4**	101.7	**9.4**	10.3	2.0	1.7	3.4
NCL-B2	F_1	0.69	0.64	0.67	0.67	0.66	0.60	0.58	0.49	0.53
	Size (%)	109.7	23.5	20.1	100.3	9.8	11.7	1.9	1.8	3.5
TL-SMT	F_1	0.69	0.65	0.67	0.68	0.67	0.59	**0.61**	0.52	0.59
	Size (%)	134.9	32.9	27.8	120.6	11.5	11.3	**1.7**	1.9	4.3
TL-B1	F_1	0.69	0.64	**0.68**	0.67	0.66	0.59	0.59	0.48	0.54
	Size (%)	134.9	31.2	**26.7**	120.3	10.9	11.4	2.3	2.3	4.3
TL-B2	F_1	0.69	0.64	0.67	0.67	0.65	0.59	0.58	0.48	0.53
	Size (%)	134.9	33.6	29.5	117.9	11.2	12.6	2.1	2.6	4.4

Regarding PS without balancing, CHC algorithm is the only case among the non-dominated solutions. Thus, according to this criterion, solutions involving PS without a balancing stage may not be considered as optimal, in general.

Finally, the cases that only consider the balancing scheme and avoid the PS stage are also present among the non-dominant solutions. Particularly, the

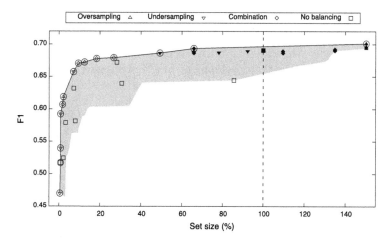

Fig. 2. Graphical representation of the results obtained. Balancing paradigms are represented by the symbols in the legend. The use or not of PS is shown by being these symbols either empty or filled, respectively. Circled symbols remark the elements belonging to the non-dominance set whereas the vertical dashed line refers to the original set size. To avoid graph overload, the grey region depicts the space occupied by all results obtained in this work from the combinations of balancing techniques (oversampling, undersampling, and combination) and PS strategies studied.

non-dominated solutions by the CNN and CNN-B1 balancing cases achieve the same F_1 scores than the original case with a remarkable set reduction. Also in this regard, it must pointed out the B1 oversampling algorithm that, despite achieving the best F_1 score, the set size is remarkably higher than the initial one, being thus an option to discard as our premise is to reduce our initial set.

5   Conclusions and Future Work

Imbalance in class distributions typically affects the performance in classification schemes as it biases the response of the system towards the majority class. To tackle it, data-level approaches that artificially equilibrate the class distribution have been proposed and studied. As a particular process found in instance-based classification schemes, prototype selection (PS) schemes are typically designed for balanced data distributions, but this is not realistic as real-life data sources do not exhibit such ideal distribution.

In this context, we performed a study comparing the performance of PS schemes on imbalanced collections and the same sets after being balanced with data-driven approaches for Nearest Neighbour classification. Results obtained considering six datasets and a comprehensive collection of PS schemes and balancing techniques suggest that general PS techniques achieve better performances when data is balanced and that some balancing techniques based on undersampling the majority class do not require of a PS stage as by themselves achieve good reduction rates while keeping fairly accurate classification figures.

Future work considers the development of PS strategies at an algorithmic level, that is, biasing their internal figure of merit so that the selection additionally considers the class imbalance present in the data.

Acknowledgements. Work partially supported by the Spanish Ministerio de Economía y Competitividad through Project TIMuL (No. TIN2013-48152-C2-1-R supported by EU FEDER funds), the Spanish Ministerio de Educación, Cultura y Deporte through FPU program (AP2012–0939) and the Vicerrectorado de Investigación, Desarrollo e Innovación de la Universidad de Alicante through FPU program (UAFPU2014–5883).

References

1. Duda, R.O., Hart, P.E., Stork, D.G.: Pattern Classification, 2nd edn. Wiley, New York (2001)
2. García, S., Luengo, J., Herrera, F.: Data Preprocessing in Data Mining. Intelligent Systems Reference Library, vol. 72. Springer, Heidelberg (2015)
3. García, S., Derrac, J., Cano, J., Herrera, F.: Prototype selection for nearest neighbor classification: taxonomy and empirical study. IEEE Trans. Pattern Anal. Mach. Intell. **34**(3), 417–435 (2012)
4. García, V., Sánchez, J., Mollineda, R.: An empirical study of the behavior of classifiers on imbalanced and overlapped data sets. In: Rueda, L., Mery, D., Kittler, J. (eds.) CIARP 2007. LNCS, vol. 4756, pp. 397–406. Springer, Heidelberg (2007). doi:10.1007/978-3-540-76725-1_42
5. López, V., Fernández, A., García, S., Palade, V., Herrera, F.: An insight into classification with imbalanced data: empirical results and current trends on using data intrinsic characteristics. Inf. Sci. **250**, 113–141 (2013)
6. García, V., Salvador, J.S., Mollineda, R.A.: On the effectiveness of preprocessing methods when dealing with different levels of class imbalance. Knowl. Based Syst. **25**(1), 13–21 (2012)
7. Fernández, A., García, S., Herrera, F.: Addressing the classification with imbalanced data: open problems and new challenges on class distribution. In: Corchado, E., Kurzyński, M., Woźniak, M. (eds.) HAIS 2011. LNCS, vol. 6678, pp. 1–10. Springer, Heidelberg (2011). doi:10.1007/978-3-642-21219-2_1
8. Rico-Juan, J.R., Iñesta, J.M.: New rank methods for reducing the size of the training set using the nearest neighbor rule. Pattern Recogn. Lett. **33**(5), 654–660 (2012)
9. Chawla, N.V., Bowyer, K.W., Hall, L.O., Kegelmeyer, W.P.: SMOTE: synthetic minority over-sampling technique. J. Artif. Intell. Res. **16**, 321–357 (2002)
10. Han, H., Wang, W.-Y., Mao, B.-H.: Borderline-SMOTE: a new over-sampling method in imbalanced data sets learning. In: Huang, D.-S., Zhang, X.-P., Huang, G.-B. (eds.) ICIC 2005. LNCS, vol. 3644, pp. 878–887. Springer, Heidelberg (2005). doi:10.1007/11538059_91
11. Prati, R.C., Batista, G.E., Monard, M.C.: Data mining with imbalanced class distributions: concepts and methods. In: Proceedings of the 4th Indian International Conference on Artificial Intelligence, India, pp. 359–376 (2009)

12. Valero-Mas, J.J., Iñesta, J.M., Pérez-Sancho, C.: Onset detection with the user in the learning loop. In: Proceedings of the 7th International Workshop on Music and Machine Learning (MML), Barcelona, Spain (2014)
13. Calvo-Zaragoza, J., Valero-Mas, J.J., Rico-Juan, J.R.: Improving kNN multi-label classification in prototype selection scenarios using class proposals. Pattern Recogn. **48**(5), 1608–1622 (2015)

Classification of Fiducial Markers in Challenging Conditions with SVM

Víctor Manuel Mondéjar-Guerra, Sergio Garrido-Jurado,
Rafael Muñoz-Salinas[✉], Manuel J. Marín-Jiménez,
and Rafael Medina-Carnicer

Department of Computing and Numerical Analysis, University of Cordoba,
Córdoba, Spain
{ava,rmsalinas}@uco.es
http://www.uco.es/grupos/ava/

Abstract. Square fiducial markers are a popular tool for camera pose estimation because of their high robustness and performance. However, state-of-the-art methods perform poorly under difficult image conditions, such as camera defocus, motion blur, small scale or non-uniform lighting. This paper tackles the marker identification problem as a classification one, proposing a methodology to train such classifiers by creating a synthetic dataset of markers affected by several transformations. Our approach employs a SVM for marker identification. Statistical analyses have been performed in order to determine the best SVM configuration for our problem, and the best one is compared to the ArUco fiducial marker systems in challenging video sequences. The results obtained show that the proposed method performs significantly better.

Keywords: ARUCO · Fiducial markers · Augmented reality · Machine learning · Support Vector Machines

1 Introduction

Camera pose estimation is an important requirement in many computer vision applications. Despite the growing interest in natural features (such as keypoints or textures) for that purpose [1], fiducial markers are still one of the preferred alternatives since their detection is faster and more robust, providing camera pose at the only expense of placing some markers in the scene. They are actively used in many applications such as augmented reality [10], robot navigation [11] or structure from motion [14].

Square fiducial markers, composed by an external wide black border and an inner code (most often binary), are the most popular ones. Their main advantage is that a single marker provides four correspondence points (its four corners), which are enough to estimate the camera pose. Detection of such markers is normally composed by two steps. The first one consists in looking for square borders, which produces a set of candidates comprised by markers and background elements (see Fig. 1). In the second step, each candidate is analysed to extract

© Springer International Publishing AG 2017
L.A. Alexandre et al. (Eds.): IbPRIA 2017, LNCS 10255, pp. 344–352, 2017.
DOI: 10.1007/978-3-319-58838-4_38

its binary code and decide whether it is a marker or part of the background. Two main approaches have been applied for extracting the binary code. The first one consists in obtaining the canonical view of the candidate which is then thresholded [7,15]. The second one uses the inverse homography to determine image locations where to perform the analysis [3,12]. Finally, if the binary code does not belong to the set of valid markers (marker dictionary), the candidate is rejected. Nonetheless, in many real-life applications, images undergo circumstances where a correct identification using the previously explained methods is not reliable, such as motion blur, non-uniform lighting conditions or reduced visibility.

Fig. 1. Example of square candidates detection in a real scene. Green candidates refer to real markers while red ones are elements of the background. (Color figure online)

Fig. 2. Random transformations generated for training. Top-left image: original image, the rest are synthetic transformations.

This work addresses the marker identification problem as a classification one. Instead of binarizing the image and then applying bit detection/correction techniques, we propose to train a classifier for the identification process. Since obtaining a large dataset of markers from real images representing a wide variety of conditions is not practical, we propose the creation of a synthetic training dataset by applying different transformations that emulate those happening in real situations. For classification, we employ a multiclass Support Vector Machine (SVM) [2] and the best configuration is found using statistical tests. The trained classifier is validated in real scenes and compared to the state-of-the-art fiducial marker systems ArUco [7].

The remainder of this paper is structured as follows. Section 2 formulates the problem and how the training set has been designed. Section 3 presents the experimentation carried out, and Sect. 4 draws some conclusions.

2   Problem Formulation and Dataset Generation

Let us denote by $\mathbb{D}$ the dictionary of n markers to be employed in a particular application. Also, let us assume that a method for detecting marker candidates in images is available. For each candidate, the homography of the projected square is calculated and its canonical view is obtained as shown in Fig. 1. Then, instead of extracting the marker bits, we directly feed a classifier with the canonical image in order to identify the markers.

Please notice that four different canonical views of a marker are possible, namely, these corresponding to rotations of 0, 90, 180 and 270 degrees. For a correct camera pose estimation, it is required to know the rotation so as to identify each marker corner correctly. Thus, apart from determining if the candidate belongs to any of the markers in $\mathbb{D}$, we need to determine the rotation of the canonical marker view.

Formulated as a classification problem, our input consists in the pixels of the grey-level canonical image, and a total $4 \times n + 1$ classes are defined: one for each possible marker rotation, and an additional one representing the negative case, i.e., indicating that the input is not a marker but part of the background.

2.1 Training Dataset Generation

In order to apply classification techniques, a labeled dataset including samples from all the considered classes is required. In our problem, it consists of a collection of canonical images of all the dictionary markers (considering the four possible rotations) and also non-marker images for the negative class. For the latter, a large amount of patches from the MIRFLICKR-25000 image dataset [9] was collected. However, since obtaining a large dataset of markers representing a wide variety of conditions from real images is not practical, we propose the creation of a synthetic training dataset by applying different transformations to the original marker images. These transformations aim at emulating those happening in real situations.

Let us denote by I the original marker image of size $s \times s$ and $I(p)$ the intensity value of pixel p. Let us also denote I' the synthetic image generated with the proposed transformations. In total, five different transformations are considered. For a given input image I, we first randomly select which transformations are applied and their order, since they are not commutative. The chance of selecting each transform varies with the possibility of finding it in real scenes, as will be explained later. Below are the transformations employed, which depends on a set of parameters $\eta_1, \ldots, \eta_5$, whose values are indicated at the end of this section.

- Blur: simulates the motion blur and defocus. A box blur kernel was used with width and height randomly selected following a bidimensional uniform distribution $\mathbf{U_2}((1, \eta_1 s)^2)$.
- Dynamic range compression: since the original input image has only the values $\{0, 255\}$, which are usually not found in real images, we randomly perform a reduction of this range by applying the following transformation to the pixels intensities, $I'(p) = min(255, aI(p) + b)$, where a and b are sampled from the following uniform probability distributions $a \backsim \mathbf{U}(\eta_2, 1)$ and $b \backsim \mathbf{U}(0, \eta_3)$. The min function ensures that the resulting values are not greater than 255.

- Affine transformation: a projective transformation simulating the errors in the corner estimation of the marker candidates is applied. To do so, the image corners of I are randomly translated adding an offset following the uniform distribution $\mathbf{U_2}((-\eta_4 s, \eta_4 s)^2)$.
- Non-uniform light: it is simulated by adding a radial gradient light modelled as a bidimensional Gaussian distribution $\mathbf{N}(c, \Sigma)$. The transformation is then defined as: $I'(p) = min\left(255, I(p) + 50 \cdot e^{-\frac{1}{2}(p-c)^t \Sigma^{-1}(p-c)}\right)$. It is assumed that the distribution is symmetric, i.e., $\Sigma = \sigma^2 \mathbf{I}$, where $\mathbf{I}$ stands for the identity matrix, and that $\sigma \backsim \mathbf{U}(s/4, s/2)$ and $c \backsim \mathbf{U_2}(\Omega^2)$, where: $\Omega = [-s, 0] \cup [s, 2s]$, so that the light origin c is out of the image.
- Dilate: simulates the effect produced by overexposure, which increases the inner white borders of the markers. The size of the structuring element used for dilation is randomly selected following the distribution $\mathbf{U_2}((1, \eta_5 s)^2)$.

Based on our experience, we have considered each transformation to be selected with a predefined probability. The first three transformations have a 0.75 chance of being applied, while the fourth and fifth have a 0.25 and 0.15 chance respectively. The lower probabilities of the last two are because, when applied, they produce stronger effects. Also, they correspond to cases not as frequently observed in real scenes as the rest of transformations. Likewise, the parameters employed for the different distributions have been empirically determined as $\eta_1 = 0.2$, $\eta_2 = 0.4$, $\eta_3 = 25$, $\eta_4 = 0.025$ and $\eta_5 = 0.08$. Figure 2 shows the original image of a marker and some of the synthetic images automatically generated.

3   Experimentation

This section describes the experimentation carried out to validate our proposal. In order to do a rigorous evaluation of the results, statistical analyses of the different alternatives have been done. First, it is explained how the dataset for training, validation and test has been elaborated. Then, the methodology employed to compare the different methods tested is described. The approach is compared to the state-of-the-art marker system ArUco. Finally, we analyze the computing times of each method so as to determine their suitability for real-time applications.

3.1   Dataset Elaboration and Comparison Methodology

For our tests, a dictionary $\mathbb{D}$ composed by 50 markers of 6×6 bits has been generated with the method proposed in [8], which guarantees the best error correction capabilities for ArUco. In total, there are $4 \times n + 1 = 201$ different marker classes.

Our dataset is divided in three parts: training, validation and test. The two first are synthetically generated as explained in Sect. 2.1, while the third one (i.e. test) is comprised by candidates extracted from real-world videos. Training and validation sets are comprised by 250 synthetic images of each class (200 for training and the rest for validation), making a total of 50 000 positive examples. Additionally, there are 210 000 images for the negative class, extracted from the MIRFLICKR-25000 image collection [9] (out of which 200 000 are for training). In order to compare the performance of the different methods, we use the precision, recall and F-measure. *Precision* reflects the capacity of correctly classifying a marker, while *Recall* indicates how many correct markers our method is able to find. As these two measures are opposite, we focus our analysis on the *F-measure*, which is a unique indicator to determine the overall performance of a method.

The test dataset consists of seven sequences recorded both in outdoor and indoor scenarios, covering challenging situations in real-life applications. The first one (Fig. 3a) shows significant motion blur due to fast camera movement. In the second one (Fig. 3b), the camera is forced to see the markers out of focus. In the third one (Fig. 3c), the environment is highly illuminated and camera over-exposure is frequent. In the fourth one (Fig. 3d), some markers are illuminated by non-uniform lighting. The fifth sequence (Fig. 3e) focuses on the identification capability at large distances, i.e. identifying small markers. The sixth sequence (Fig. 3f) shows a large outdoor scenario labeled with a high number of markers. The same is reproduced in the seventh sequence (Fig. 3g) for an indoor scenario.

The method proposed in [7] has been used to extract the candidates from the test sequences (see Fig. 1). The original size of the candidates is 40 × 40 pixels, and they have been manually labelled. In total, there are 3924 frames from which 102 829 candidates have been extracted, out of which 81% belong to background. Please notice that while training is done exclusively on synthetic images, testing is performed exclusively on real ones.

Fig. 3. Sequences for testing: (a) blur, (b) defocus, (c) overexposure, (d) non-uniform lighting, (e) scale, (f) outdoor, (g) indoor

In order to obtain a formal comparison of the considered classification methods, non-parametric tests have been employed [6] for the results obtained on the test dataset. First, the Friedman omnibus statistical test [5] has been applied to rank the methods and to figure out whether the results of the methods are statistically different or not. In case of finding statistically significant differences (the null hypothesis of equality of means is rejected) the Finner post-hoc test [4] is employed to compare the best ranked method (control method) against the others, so as to find the concrete pairwise comparisons producing the differences. For pairwise comparison the adjusted p values of Finner test have been computed. The significance level has been set to 0.05. The F-measure, which is defined as the harmonic mean of precision and recall, has been employed to analyze the performance of the tested methods.

3.2   Obtaining the Best Support Vector Machines (SVM) Classifier

This section aims at determining the best SVM configuration for the given problem. To that end, we have tested the original images of 40×40 pixels and their reduced versions of 20×20 and 10×10 pixels. Also, both linear and Radial Basis Function (RBF) kernels have been employed.

Additionally, Principal Component Analysis (PCA) [13] has been applied to further reduce the data dimensionality to the 25, 50 or 100 principal components when possible.

For each possible combination of these parameters a five-fold cross-validation have been performed by varying C in the range $[3 \cdot 10^{-2}, 2^{15}]$ and γ in the range $[3 \cdot 10^{-5}, 8]$. After the cross-validation stage, the values C, γ that achieved the best results under the validation set were selected individually to evaluate each classifier on the test data. Table 1 summarizes the results on the test data of the 15 best classifiers, sorted by their Friedman's ranking.

Table 1. Average rankings of the SVM configurations by Friedman test. In bold, configurations that are rejected by the Finner's procedure.

Ranking	Configuration	p_{Finner}	Ranking	Configuration	p_{Finner}
4.28	**10-RBF**	–	9.78	10-RBF-50	$1.64 \cdot 10^{-1}$
5.07	20-LIN	$8.20 \cdot 10^{-1}$	11.42	40-LIN-100	$6.31 \cdot 10^{-2}$
5.50	20-LIN-100	$7.43 \cdot 10^{-1}$	11.85	20-LIN-50	$5.04 \cdot 10^{-2}$
6.21	10-LIN-50	$6.15 \cdot 10^{-1}$	12.00*	*40-RBF*	$4.95 \cdot 10^{-2}$
7.64	20-RBF	$3.77 \cdot 10^{-1}$	13.00*	*40-LIN-50*	$2.51 \cdot 10^{-2}$
8.07	20-RBF-100	$3.28 \cdot 10^{-1}$	13.92*	*20-RBF-50*	$1.27 \cdot 10^{-2}$
8.28	10-LIN	$3.20 \cdot 10^{-1}$	14.35*	*20-LIN-25*	$9.71 \cdot 10^{-3}$
8.35	40-LIN	$3.20 \cdot 10^{-1}$			

The naming convention employed in the *Configuration* column is $XX - KER(-PCA)$, where XX indicates the size of the image patches, KER stands for the kernel employed (linear or RBF) and, optionally, PCA indicates the number of PCA components employed. For instance, the first line (10-RBF) is a SVM classifier using input images of 10×10 pixels, a RBF kernel, and no PCA reduction.

The *Ranking* column indicates the ranking values of each combination, an indication of how good a SVM performs compared to the others. A value of 1 would indicate that a configuration obtains the best F-measure in the seven sequences tested.

Finally, the p_{Finner} column shows the adjusted p values used for the Finner test. The methods with p value ≤ 0.05 are rejected by the Finner procedure and are highlighted in bold to ease their localization. In other words, the elements in bold are those for which the Finner test finds statistically relevant differences compared to the best ranked method, i.e., they are clearly worse than the best method. Whereas for the methods not in bold font, the differences found cannot be considered statistically relevant.

It can be observed that, although the best classifier is 10-RBF, the Finner test has not found strong statistical differences compared to the combinations that are not marked with an asterisk. However, it can be assured that the elements marked with the asterisk are worse than the best one.

From this analysis we can assert that the results are significantly worse when PCA is employed for a reduction of only 25 components. The kernel choice does not seem to affect, although the linear one ranks slightly better. It is also evident that images of only 10×10 pixels are enough to obtain the best ranking results.

3.3   Comparison with the State of the Art

In this section, we evaluate the best classifier previously obtained against the fiducial marker system ArUco [7] in the test sequences. The F-measures of each method for each sequence are shown in Table 2, while Table 3 shows the average values of precision, recall and F-measure in the test set.

It can be observed that ArUco is highly restrictive during the marker identification process, leading to a high precision at the expense of a low recall. However, when the F-measure is analyzed, the trained SVM perform significantly better than ArUco.

Table 2. F-measure of each method in each of the test sequences

	SVM	ArUco
Blur	**0.999**	0.894
Defocus	**0.942**	0.306
Overexposure	**0.988**	0.946
n. u. l	**0.922**	0.900
Zoom out	**0.871**	0.492
Room	**0.997**	0.816
Outdoor	**0.952**	0.856

Table 3. Average precision, recall and F-measure for all the test sequences.

	SVM	ArUco
Precision	0.986	**0.996**
Recall	**0.924**	0.639
F-measure	**0.953**	0.744

Finally, we present a comparison of the computational times required by each method to process a single candidate. While our SVM method requires 1.47 ms, ArUco is orders of magnitude faster requiring only $9.56 \cdot 10^{-2}$ ms. However, the computing times of the proposed approach is also valid for real-time applications.

4 Conclusions

This work has proposed to handle the fiducial marker identification problem as a classification one in order to increase the performance under difficult image conditions, such as camera defocus, motion blur, small scale or non-uniform lighting. Since obtaining a large training dataset, from real images, covering realistic and challenging situations is not practical, we propose a method to create a synthetic one by applying a set of transformations that emulates those happening in real situations.

We have evaluated SVM model using a wide variety of configurations, and the best configuration of each type has been then evaluated against the state-of-the-art fiducial marker system ArUco. The results show that, in all cases, the proposed classifiers obtain results significantly better than ArUco.

Acknowledgments. This project has been funded under projects TIN2016-75279-P, RTC-2016-5661-1 and by the "Programa propio XXI de Investigacion" of the University of Cordoba.

References

1. Chen, P., Peng, Z., Li, D., Yang, L.: An improved augmented reality system based on AndAR. J. Vis. Commun. Image Represent. **37**, 63–69 (2016)
2. Cortes, C., Vapnik, V.: Support-vector networks. Mach. Learn. **20**(3), 273–297 (1995)
3. Fiala, M.: Designing highly reliable fiducial markers. IEEE Trans. Pattern Anal. Mach. Intell. **32**(7), 1317–1324 (2010)
4. Finner, H.: On a monotonicity problem in step-down multiple test procedures. J. Am. Stat. Assoc. **88**(423), 920–923 (1993)
5. Friedman, M.: The use of ranks to avoid the assumption of normality implicit in the analysis of variance. J. Am. Stat. Assoc. **32**(200), 675–701 (1937)
6. García, S., Fernández, A., Luengo, J., Herrera, F.: Advanced nonparametric tests for multiple comparisons in the design of experiments in computational intelligence and data mining: experimental analysis of power. Inf. Sci. **180**(10), 2044–2064 (2010)
7. Garrido-Jurado, S., Muñoz Salinas, R., Madrid-Cuevas, F.J., Marín-Jiménez, M.J.: Automatic generation and detection of highly reliable fiducial markers under occlusion. Pattern Recogn. **47**(6), 2280–2292 (2014)
8. Garrido-Jurado, S., Muñoz-Salinas, R., Madrid-Cuevas, F.J., Medina-Carnicer, R.: Generation of fiducial marker dictionaries using mixed integer linear programming. Pattern Recogn. **51**, 481–491 (2016)
9. Huiskes, M.J., Lew, M.S.: The MIR flickr retrieval evaluation. In: Proceedings of the 1st ACM International Conference on Multimedia Information Retrieval, MIR 2008, pp. 39–43. ACM, New York (2008)

10. Khattak, S., Cowan, B., Chepurna, I., Hogue, A.: A real-time reconstructed 3D environment augmented with virtual objects rendered with correct occlusion. In: IEEE Games Media Entertainment (GEM), pp. 1–8. IEEE (2014)
11. Olivares-Mendez, M.A., Kannan, S., Voos, H.: Vision based fuzzy control autonomous landing with uavs: from V-rep to real experiments. In: 23th Mediterranean Conference on Control and Automation (MED), pp. 14–21, June 2015
12. Olson, E.: AprilTag: a robust and flexible visual fiducial system. In: IEEE International Conference on Robotics and Automation (ICRA), pp. 3400–3407 (2011)
13. Pearson, K.: On lines and planes of closest fit to systems of points in space. Philos. Mag. **2**(6), 559–572 (1901)
14. Rumpler, M., Daftry, S., Tscharf, A., Prettenthaler, R., Hoppe, C., Mayer, G., Bischof, H.: Automated end-to-end workflow for precise and geo-accurate reconstructions using fiducial markers. ISPRS Ann. Photogrammetry Remote Sens. Spat. Inf. Sci. **3**, 135–142 (2014)
15. Wagner, D., Schmalstieg, D.: ARToolKitPlus for pose tracking on mobile devices. In: Computer Vision Winter, Workshop, pp. 139–146 (2007)

Detecting Changes
with the Robust Competitive Detector

Leszek J. Chmielewski$^{(\boxtimes)}$ and Arkadiusz Orłowski

Faculty of Applied Informatics and Mathematics – WZIM,
Warsaw University of Life Sciences – SGGW,
ul. Nowoursynowska 159, 02-775 Warsaw, Poland
{leszek_chmielewski,arkadiusz_orlowski}@sggw.pl
http://www.wzim.sggw.pl

Abstract. The concept of the competitive filter is reminded and its ability to find changes in 1D data is extended by adding the robustness feature. The use of two affine approximators, one at the left and one at the right side of the considered data point, makes it possible to detect the points in which the function and its derivative changes, by subtracting the outputs from the approximators and analyzing their errors. The features of the detector are demonstrated on artificial as well as real-life data, with promising results.

Keywords: Competitive detector · Function change · Derivative change · Robust

1 Introduction

The changes in the observable environment are for us the main source of information. Our senses quickly get used to stable signals and tend to ignore them after some time, while the change in light intensity, a new sound or smell attracts our attention. A good indication that the changing signals are important is that even when we observe static objects our eyes are constantly making saccadic movements, which support the perception of interesting details of the scene.

The detector presented in this paper originated within the domain of image processing, where the problem of change detection is primarily related to edge detection [1], motion detection [11] and the detection of changes [10].

In 1991 Niedźwiecki, Sethares and Suchomski proposed a filter denoted as the *competitive filter* [8,9]. As a method to overcome the phenomenon of blurring the edges during image filtering, present in the methods based on averaging, they proposed to use two competing filters working simultaneously from the two sides of an edge in an image. As the output, the result from that filter was used in which the approximation error was smaller.

In 1996 one of the authors of this paper proposed to use the competitive filtering to detect edges [2]. The concept was successfully developed for one-dimensional data, but the extension to two dimensions failed [3] and was abandoned. The reason for the failure was the variety and complexity of shapes of

© Springer International Publishing AG 2017
L.A. Alexandre et al. (Eds.): IbPRIA 2017, LNCS 10255, pp. 353–362, 2017.
DOI: 10.1007/978-3-319-58838-4_39

the image intensity function near the junctions of various kinds of edges. These shapes made it difficult to define the notion of the *two sides* of an edge which was basic in competitive filtering.

It can seem unexpected but to our best knowledge there were no other publications on the idea of the competitive filter or edge detector, similar to ours, than the ones just cited. In 2003 Liang and Looney [7] proposed to use the competition in edge detection. Pixels competed towards becoming edge pixels to reduce the edge thickness. This approach was different from the ours.

At present we have decided to revive the concept of competitive edge detection, solely in the application to one-dimensional data. The detector behaved well for such data; nevertheless, to improve its stability, it has been extended by including a robust analysis mechanism to the fitting of the two filters. This paper can be treated as the proof of concept of the robust version of the detector. The concept of the detector comes from the domain of image processing, so some image processing terminology will appear in this paper, although the relation of the detector to images is only historical. In particular, we shall use the terms *change*, *edge* and *jump* interchangeably.

The method proposed is well suited to be augmented by incorporating statistical methods of verifying the significance of the detected changes (see eg. [4,5]). The work in this direction is in progress. Moreover, the presented method does not need any model of the phenomenon described by the analyzed function. No assumptions are made on the form of the function. The function given as a series of points is locally approximated, with polynomials of a chosen degree, without the assumption of continuity in the point analyzed, which is a minimalistic approach as far as assumptions are considered. Therefore, we do believe that this method could provide a valuable alternative tool for detecting changes in various kinds of time series and other one-dimensional data.

This paper is organized as follows. In the next Sect. 2.1 the detector in its introductory form is described and its operation is illustrated with the result for a synthetic test image. The new feature of robustness is explained in Sect. 2.2. Then, in Sect. 3 the results of the detection of changes in some real-life data are presented. The question of efficiency is answered in Sect. 3.1. The discussion is in Sect. 4 and the proposed directions of development close the paper in Sect. 5.

2   The Method

2.1   General Concept

According to [9] let us take a sequence of measurements $z(x) = y(x) + n(x)$, where $n(x)$ is noise. The independent variable x is discrete. If x is understood as time, the measurements are known starting from the past, up to the point x_0 and further, to $x_0 + D$. The point x_0 is the point in which the filtering is performed and can be called the *central point*. Two approximators, referred to as the *Left* and the *Right* one, are used to find $y(x_0)$, the first one working at the left side of x_0, using $z(x), x \in [x_0 - s - \Delta, x_0 - \Delta]$ to find $\hat{y}_L(x_0)$, and the second one working at the right side of x_0, using $z(x), x \in [x_0 + \Delta, x_0 + s + \Delta]$ to find $\hat{y}_R(x_0)$. The parameter s is the scale of the filter, and Δ is the gap between the central point x_0 and the estimators.

For each approximator its error is estimated: $e_L(x_0)$ and $e_R(x_0)$, respectively. As the estimate of the result at the point of interest, $\hat{y}(x_0)$, the output of the filter which performs better, that is, gives a smaller error is used. This is the competitiveness feature of the filter. In the literature, the extrapolations at x_0 from the two filters were used. In the present implementation, the output at $x_0 - \Delta$ from the left approximator, and for $x_0 + \Delta$ for the right one, is used, to avoid using extrapolated values. This stabilizes the results, especially when robust approximators are used, which will be described further.

In [2], the linear least square approximators were used as filters, and their mean square errors were used as their approximation errors. The concept of using the difference of outputs from the two filters $\hat{y}_L(x_0)$, $\hat{y}_R(x_0)$, and their derivatives, as the estimates of the step and roof edge at point x_0 was introduced. The conditions for the existence of the step was that the graphs of the approximation errors crossed in such a way that for increasing x the error from the past increased and for decreasing x the error for the future increased. In the present paper it is assumed that at least one of the errors increases in this case. These conditions were expressed in [2] in a complicated way but they can be simply written down, respectively, as

$$e_R(x_0 - \delta) > e_L(x_0 - \delta) \ \wedge \ e_R(x_0 + \delta) < e_L(x_0 + \delta),$$
$$e_R(x_0 - \delta) > e_R(x_0 + \delta) \ \vee \ e_L(x_0 - \delta) < e_L(x_0 + \delta). \tag{1}$$

Because the past error should be known for $x_0 + \delta$ then the measurements for $x_0 + D = x_0 + \Delta + s + 2\delta$ should be known. The parameter δ can be called the neighborhood parameter. In [2] it was $\Delta = \delta = 1$ and so it will be assumed in this paper. Therefore, $D = s + 3$.

The process of error graphs crossing is illustrated in Fig. 1[1].

Let us describe it in a figurative rather than in a rigorous way. Let us imagine that both approximators together with the central point are moved along the data from left to right. When a step is encountered, first the right approximator moves over it so the step enters the right approximator's support. Therefore, the error of the right approximator goes up. As the analyzed point is moved forward, the step leaves the support of the right approximator, so its error goes down, and enters that of the left one (this particular moment is shown in the figure). Now, the error of the left approximator increases.

At the crossing point, the edge intensity values E_0 for the jump of the function, and E_1 for the jump of its first derivative, respectively, are calculated as

$$E_0(x_0) = \hat{y}_R(x_0 + \Delta) - \hat{y}_L(x_0 - \Delta),$$
$$E_1(x_0) = \hat{y}'_R(x_0 + \Delta) - \hat{y}'_L(x_0 - \Delta), \tag{2}$$

where $\hat{y}'(\cdot)$ can be found from the approximators due to that they are linear. In the present application, not the filtered value but the values of the steps will be of the primary interest.

---

[1] The software and the graphs were developed in Matlab®.

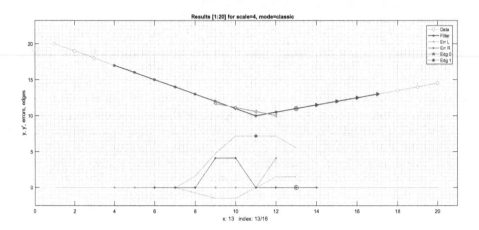

Fig. 1. Intermediate results for the two approximators up to $x_0 = 13$: Graphs of errors (thin magenta and cyan lines) cross between points 10 and 12. The meaning of types and colors of lines and marks partly explained in the legend: **Err L**: left error, **Err R**: right error; **Edg 0**: jump of the function, **Edg 1**: jump of its first derivative – this type of edge is marked at $x = 11$ with a blue star. The current central point x_0 marked with a red circle on the axis as well as on the graph of the function. The left and right approximators around the central point shown with thicker cyan and magenta lines. The approximator with zero error has full marks, the other one has marks filled with white. Angles shown in tens of degrees. Errors multiplied by 10 for better visibility. (Color figure online)

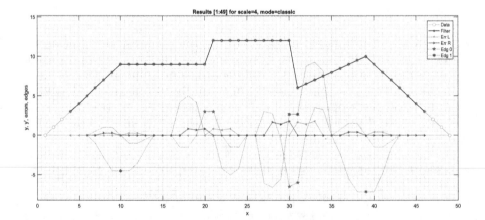

Fig. 2. Results for the classic version of the detector for synthetic data with all the detectable changes represented: function jump at $x = 20, 21$, derivative jump at $x = 10$ and 39 and combined jumps at $x = 30, 31$. Angles shown in tens of degrees.

In Fig. 2 the result is shown for data in which all the detectable changes are present: a roof edge, a step edge and a combined step and roof edge. The data are synthetic and clean. What is apparent is that the roof edge is detected in a single point, like this at $x = 1$, while the step edge, like this at $x = 20, 21$ is found at two points. This is correct due to that the jump of a discrete function appears between two points and can be assigned to both of them. It should also be stressed that there are no separate conditions for the two edge types detected. If one of the edge types is missing, then its intensity is zero.

2.2   Robustness

In [2] the use of the least median of squares [12] was mentioned as the possible approximation criterion, but in that paper it was not developed. Here we propose

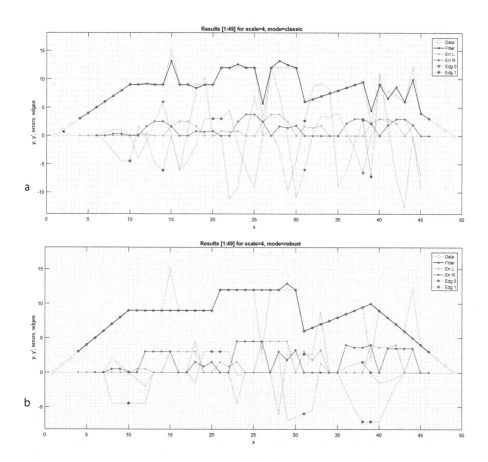

Fig. 3. Results for the data of Fig. 2 with some outlying data added. Versions of the detector:(**a**) classic; (**b**) robust. In (b) the influence of some outliers was eliminated but some interfere in the detection – see text. Angles shown in tens of degrees.

to use this criterion. We have used the algorithm from [6] with the correction pointed out in the discussion on this algorithm in its web site (given in [6]), entry of 06 Oct 2004. The issue of high time requirements of the algorithm does not constitute an important problem here because the scale of the approximators is not expected to be higher than 10 to 20.

In Fig. 3 the results for data containing all the detectable changes can be seen. Some outlying vales, or point noise-type artefacts, are added to illustrate the functioning of the robust detector. With the robust version of the detector, the influence of the outliers which are far from the edges, relatively to the scale, was eliminated. However, the outlier at $x = 26$ which is close to the step at 30 interfered with the detection of this step and prevented from finding one of its points (at $x = 30$). Also, the value of the function was slightly changed at $x = 29$. The outlier inside the roof edge at $x = 39$ gave rise to a spurious step at $x = 38$. The interferences would be greater if the scale were larger.

It is clear that the robust detector can not extinguish the influence of the outliers located in the vicinity of the edges to be detected. It should also be pointed out that it can be doubtful whether the extraneous value is an outlier or constitutes a valid part of the signal. The data point can be considered an outlier if it does not follow the trend, which is not an univocal statement. We shall come back to this problem in the next section.

3 Real-Life Example

As an example let us consider the graph of free memory of some web server in 100 intervals of one minute each, starting from 04 July 2016, 10:43:01 GMT. The memory was averaged in each minute. The graph in Fig. 4 displays an uneven load so the used memory requirement jumps are significant.

The general question which should be asked is which data should be treated as valid and which should be dismissed as outliers or noise. The extraneous values of such values as memory requirement are all measured precisely, but it is probable that some of them do not follow the current trend. So, some of them may be considered as untypical, but such values are significant. The question on the significance of single data items most probably can not be answered without looking at other measures of the state of the observed object.

The observation of approximators reveals their disadvantageous behavior, which could be expected solely on the basis of the design of the approximators.

It consists in that the intensity of the tendency to minimize the approximation errors does not depend on which end of the support of the approximator is considered: the one closer to or farther from the central point x_0. However, it is more important to minimize the error at points closer to x_0. The adverse case is shown and explained in Fig. 6. Therefore, the weighting of the minimized errors would be a preferable feature of the algorithm. This is more important in the robust approximators than in the classic ones, because in the robust approximators some data points are postponed. It is vital that the points close to the central point were postponed more rarely than the other ones.

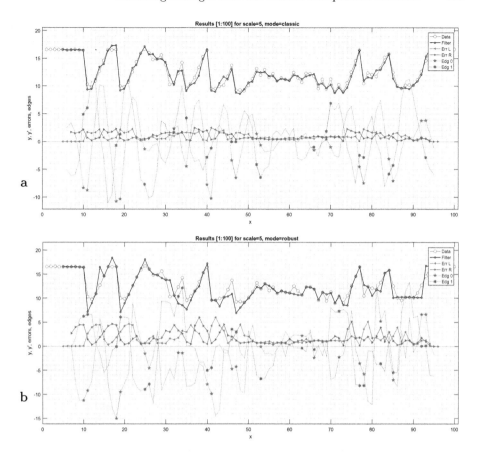

Fig. 4. Analysis of free memory of a web server averaged for 1 min intervals in 100 min (starting at 04 July 2016, 10:43:01 GMT) in GB, at scale $s = 5$ (angles shown in tens of degrees). Detectors:**(a)** classic;**(b)** robust. Some parts of the signal are deformed, for example, the vertices at the jumps are protruded in the classic as well as robust versions. The scale seems to be too large for the signal variability.

3.1 Efficiency

It can be safely stated that the time complexity of the algorithm is linear with respect to the number n of data points to be processed: $O(n)$, because the same analyzes are repeated for every part of the data (data for two approximators), and the size of this part does not depend on the data size. The complexity depends on the scale s in the same way as the approximation algorithm does. It would not be practical to set the scale to large values so the algorithm can be considered efficient. In the case of the least squares algorithm this is also linear: $O(s)$. With the least median of squares used at present it is $O(s^3 \log(s))$, but s is small and constant. Also, faster least median of square algorithms are available

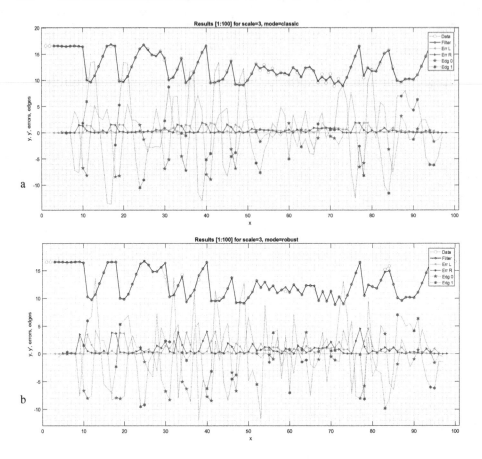

Fig. 5. Analysis of data of Fig. 4 at scale $s = 3$. The important effects – step and above all roof jumps positively detected in the majority of cases. The robust detector seems to better stick to small jumps at $x = 55 - 57$ but treats some peak points as noise at $x = 84, 85$. Detectors: (**a**) classic; (**b**) robust.

now. At the level of the proof of concept, and for linear complexity with respect to the data size, the time requirements are not the crucial factor.

In the case of least squares methods, the approximators could be implemented incrementally, so the dependence on the scale would be reduced. Moreover, in the basic implementation, one approximator performs the same operations as the other one, at the different locations of the central point, so the repeated calculations could be avoided.

4   Discussion

The proposed algorithm has a number of positive and negative features. In each of these groups of features some improvements are possible. The advantages, drawbacks and possible improvements will be summarized separately.

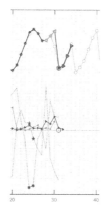

Fig. 6. Detail of Fig. 5 at $x = 31$. The left robust approximator omits the point $x = 30$ located at its end close to the central point $x_0 = 31$. This will cause the filtered value to be located far from the point $x = 30, y = 14$ and the edge value to be overestimated. This could be avoided if the approximator minimizes the error at its end close to the central point rather than at the other end.

Advantages

– Detection is performed together with the filtering process.
– Higher order approximators can be developed to fit the data more accurately.
– Higher order derivatives can be estimated according to the order of the approximating functions.
– The complexity of the algorithm with respect to the size of the data is linear.

Drawbacks

– A considerable part of data on the future must be known before the detection can be made.
– Besides the scale s of the detector, which is a meaningful and useful parameter, there are other parameters to be tuned: gap Δ and neighborhood δ.

Possible Improvements

– The algorithm should minimize the errors at those ends of the supports of the approximators, which are closer to the central point, to a larger extent than at the opposite ones. Weighting of the errors would be a desirable solution.
– The gap Δ and neighborhood δ are the parameters which could be optimized. At present they are both assumed to be equal to 1.
– The design of the error function can be improved, especially in the case of robust approximators. One of the possible measures of error could be the prediction accuracy of the approximators, for example estimated by the difference $|y(\cdot) - \hat{y}.(\cdot)|$.
– The existence of edges can be verified with statistical methods.
– Efficiency can be improved by incremental calculations and data reuse.

5   Summary and Prospects

The concept of the competitive filter was recapitulated and developed further by adding the robustness feature to the existing algorithm. This feature requires some care but can be profitable in the presence of impulsive noise. The filter was used as a detector of changes in the value and first derivative of the signal analyzed. The changes were detected with the set of conditions for the measures of errors made by the approximators, while the intensity of the jumps were found as differences of the values at the output of the approximators. Some positive results were obtained for data representing a strongly changing signal. The detector has a potential of being further developed and improved. It seems reasonable to work on higher degrees of approximating functions, on weighted error minimization and on statistical verification of changes.

References

1. Bhardwaj, S., Mittal, A.: A survey on various edge detector techniques. Procedia Technol. **4**, 220–226 (2012). doi:10.1016/j.protcy.2012.05.033
2. Chmielewski, L.: The concept of a competitive step and roof edge detector. Mach. Graph. Vis. **5**(1–2), 147–156 (1996)
3. Chmielewski, L.: Failure of the 2D version of the step and roof edge detector derived from a competitive filter, Report of the Division of Optical and Computer Methods in Mechanics, IFTR PAS, December 1997
4. Furmańczyk, K., Jaworski, S.: Large parametric change-point detection by a v-box control chart. Sequential Anal. **35**(2), 254–264 (2016). doi:10.1080/07474946.2016.1165548
5. Jaworski, S., Furmańczyk, K.: On the choice of parameters of change-point detection with application to stock exchange data. Quant. Meth. Econ. XI **I**(1), 87–96 (2011)
6. Leontitsis, A.: LMS toolbox (from MathWorks® Comunity File Exchange) (2001). www.mathworks.com/matlabcentral/fileexchange/801-lms-toolbox. Accessed 15 Nov 2016 (Online; updated 05-January-2004)
7. Liang, L.R., Looney, C.G.: Competitive fuzzy edge detection. Appl. Soft Comput. **3**(2), 123–137 (2003). doi:10.1016/S1568-4946(03)00008-5
8. Niedźwiecki, M., Sethares, W.: New filtering algorithms based on the concept of competitive smoothing. In: Proceedings 23rd International Symposium on Stochastic Systems and their Applications, Osaka, pp. 129–132 (1991)
9. Niedźwiecki, M., Suchomski, P.: On a new class of edge-preserving filters for noise rejection from images. Mach. Graph. Vis. **1–2**(3), 385–392 (1994)
10. Radke, R.J., Andra, S., Al-Kofahi, O., Roysam, B.: Image change detection algorithms: a systematic survey. IEEE Trans. Image Process. **14**(3), 294–307 (2005). doi:10.1109/TIP.2004.838698
11. Räty, T.D.: Survey on contemporary remote surveillance systems for public safety. IEEE Trans. Syst. Man Cybern. Part C (Applications and Reviews) **40**(5), 493–515 (2010). doi:10.1109/TSMCC.2010.2042446
12. Rousseeuw, P., Leroy, A.: Robust Regression and Outlier Detection. Wiley, Hoboken (1987)

Improved Compression-Based Pattern Recognition Exploiting New Useful Features

Taichi Uchino, Hisashi Koga[✉], and Takahisa Toda

Graduate School of Information Systems, University of Electro-Communications,
Tokyo 182-8585, Japan
koga@is.uec.ac.jp

Abstract. Compression-based pattern recognition measures the similarity between objects with relying on data compression techniques. This paper improves the current compression-based pattern recognition by exploiting new useful features which are easy to obtain. In particular, we study the two known methods called PRDC (Pattern Representation on Data Compression) and NMD (Normalized Compression Distance). PRDC represents an object x with a feature vector that lines up the compression ratios derived by compressing x with multiple dictionaries. We smartly enhance PRDC by extracting new novel features from the compressed files. NMD measures the similarity between two objects by comparing their compression dictionaries. We extend NMD by incorporating the length of words in the dictionaries into the similarity measure.

1 Introduction

With the prevalence of various new types of multimedia data in the big-data err, it has become more significant to classify, retrieve and recognize them in a universal way without human intervention. Traditional statistical pattern recognition involves the statistical modeling of data which accompanies the complicated configuration of parameters. Therefore, it does not necessarily meet this demand. By contrast, compression-based pattern recognition is a basically parameter-free approach toward automatic data analysis and can deal with any data types such as music, genome and images universally, once they are represented as one-dimensional strings. In principle, this approach measures the similarity between two objects by relying on data compression techniques.

The current techniques in compression-based pattern recognition are categorized into two types. The first type estimates the similarity between two objects from the compressed file size. NCD (Normalized Compression Distance) [1] is the most well-known and calculates the distance between two objects x and y from the file size acquired by compressing the concatenation of x and y. PRDC (Pattern Representation on Data Compression) [2] is another famous example. PRDC expresses an object x as a multi-dimensional vector by lining up the compression ratios at the time when x is compressed with various dictionaries.

The second type computes the distance between x and y by comparing their compression dictionaries built in the middle of data encoding by a compressor

© Springer International Publishing AG 2017
L.A. Alexandre et al. (Eds.): IbPRIA 2017, LNCS 10255, pp. 363–371, 2017.
DOI: 10.1007/978-3-319-58838-4_40

like LZW (Lempel–Ziv–Welch) [3]. This type views the dictionary of an object as its short summary. NDD (Normalized Dictionary Distance) [4] and FCD [5] (Fast Compression Distance) belong to this type. NMD (Normalized Multiset Distance) [6] which considers the word frequency in the distance computation is the state-of-the-art of this type.

Our research purposes to improve the compression-based pattern recognition by exploiting new features which have not been used so far. In particular, this paper investigates the two previous methods PRDC and NMD and devises new features for them. As for PRDC, we smartly enhance it by extracting new novel features from the compressed files. With respect to NMD, we take not only the word frequency but also the word length into account for the distance computation.

This paper is organized as follows. Section 2 reviews the related works on compression-based pattern recognition. Sections 3 and 4 describe our proposed method. Section 3 presents how to improve PRDC and Sect. 4 discusses the extension of NMD. Section 5 reports the experimental evaluation. Section 6 concludes this paper.

2   Compression-Based Pattern Recognition

Originally, compression-based pattern recognition was developed to measure the dissimilarity between two objects without examining their minute structures. It realizes general-purpose pattern recognition and, therefore, has been applied to various data types such as music [7], image analysis [8] and bioinfomatics [9]. Throughout this section, we assume that objects are represented as one-dimensional strings.

2.1   PRDC

PRDC is a kind of data representation method proposed by Watanabe *et al.* [2]. It describes an object with an N-dimensional compression-ratio vector abbreviated as CV hereafter, so that the vector-based pattern recognition techniques like the k-means and SVM may be utilized. First, PRDC prepares N base dictionaries $\{D_1, D_2 \cdots, D_N\}$ each of which is produced when the LZW compressor compresses some reference object. Then, the CV for an object x denoted by $CV(x)$ is defined as

$$CV(x) = \left(\frac{C_1(x)}{l_x}, \frac{C_2(x)}{l_x}, \ldots, \frac{C_N(x)}{l_x} \right).$$

Here, l_x means the length of x, while $C_i(x)$ presents the size of x after being compressed by D_i for $1 \leq i \leq N$. Thus, $\frac{C_i(x)}{l_x}$ becomes the compression ratio of x via D_i. This quantity is interpreted as the dissimilarity between x and the i-th reference object, because x is well compressed with D_i, if x shares many common words with the i-th reference object. In a word, PRDC tries to describe x with the relative closeness to multiple viewpoints (reference objects).

N, the number of base dictionaries is the only hyper-parameter in PRDC. Although the choice of base dictionaries is an important issue affecting the recognition performance, we do not discuss about it here, because this is not related to our research topic. See [2] and [10] for details. Since each dimension is desired to exhibit different properties, Koga *et al.* [11] proposed to modify the chosen base dictionaries to raise the independence among them.

2.2 Dictionary Distance

Given an object x, let $D(x)$ be the compression dictionary for x made by the data compressor. $D(x)$ is a set of x's substrings called words which are discovered when the compressor scans x. The dictionary distance regards $D(x)$ as a short summary of x and estimates the similarity between x and y from the distance between $D(x)$ and $D(y)$. One merit of the dictionary distance is that the distance between x and y can be computed without performing the data compression, if $D(x)$ and $D(y)$ are prepared in advance. This property is in contrast to NCD which always needs to compress the concatenation of x and y.

NDD [4] views a dictionary as a set of words and defines the distance between x and y as $\mathrm{NDD}(x,y) = \dfrac{|D(x) \cup D(y)| - \min\{|D(x)|, |D(y)|\}}{\max\{|D(x)|, |D(y)|\}}$. Here, $|D(x)|$ is the cardinality of $D(x)$, i.e., the number of distinct elements in $D(x)$. As $D(x)$ and $D(y)$ share more common words, $\mathrm{NDD}(x,y)$ decreases, since the size of $D(x) \cup D(y)$ becomes smaller.

Obviously however, the dictionary $D(x)$ cannot keep all the information held in the original object x and discards it partially. To reduce the amount of discarded information, NMD (Normalized Multiset Distance) represents the dictionary of an object x as a multiset in order to record how many times the words in $D(x)$ occurs at x. Suppose $D(x)$ consists of n words $\{w_1, w_2, ..., w_n\}$ and w_i appears m_i^x times in x for $1 \le i \le n$. Then, NMD handles the multiset $MS(x) = \{(w_1, m_1^x), (w_2, m_2^x), ..., (w_n, m_n^x)\}$. We define $|MS(x)|$, the cardinality of $MS(x)$ as $\sum_{i=1}^{n} m_i^x$. Then, Eq. (1) defines the NMD between x and y.

$$\frac{|MS(x) \cup MS(y)| - \min(|MS(x)|, |MS(y)|)}{\max(|MS(x)|, |MS(y)|)}, \tag{1}$$

In (1), the frequency of w_i in $MS(x) \cup MS(y)$ is defined as $\max(m_x(w_i), m_y(w_i))$.

3 High-Order PRDC

This section introduces our method which enhances PRDC. In PRDC, $C_i(x)$, the numerator of a compression ratio is determined according to how many times each word w in D_i appears in x and is replaced with the corresponding code shorter than w. In other words, $C_i(x)$ solely depends on the frequency of D_i's words in x. Thus, PRDC completely ignores the relations among words that happen in x. For example, the compression ratio does not mention anything about the word order in x. Motivated by this observation, we complement PRDC

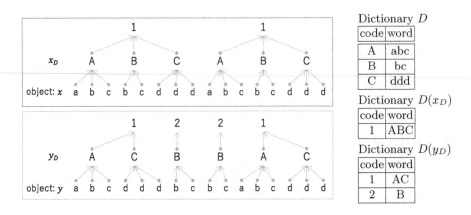

Fig. 1. Data compression and re-compression

by acquiring new features related to the word order in x from the compressed files generated after compressing x with the base dictionaries. Our method is named HOPRDC (High-Order PRDC), since it pays attention to the relation among words.

Let the compressed file obtained by compressing x with D_i be x_{D_i}. HOPRDC compresses x_{D_i} again with the LZW method and adopts the compression ratio as a new feature. Here, x_{D_i} is not compressed with D_i, but with the own dictionary of x_{D_i}, i.e., $D(x_{D_i})$. We name the compression ratio therein as the re-compression ratio. Formally, the re-compression ratio of x about D_i is defined as $\frac{R(x_{D_i})}{C_i(x)}$, where $R(x_{D_i})$ presents the compressed file size of x_{D_i}. Note that the re-compression operation is simply identical with the standard usage of LZW which compresses a text t with t's dictionary.

We illustrate that the word order in x surely affects the re-compression ratio with an example in Fig. 1. There, the two objects x and y in the bottom rows are compressed with one base dictionary D and converted to the compressed codes x_D ='ABCABC' and y_D ='ACBBAC' shown in the middle rows. At this point, the compression ratio becomes $\frac{6}{16}$ both for x and y. Thus, it does not help to distinguish x from y. This situation is caused, because all of the three words 'abc' 'ddd' and 'bc' appear in x and y the same number of times. This example demonstrates the limitations of compression ratio which counts only on the word frequency. Next, the compressed codes in the middle rows are compressed to the codes in the top rows via re-compression. Note that x_D and y_D are compressed with different dictionaries, i.e. $D(x_D)$ and $D(y_D)$. Therefore, the same code '1' represents different strings for x_D and y_D. Interestingly, the re-compression ratio can tell x from y, since it becomes $\frac{2}{6}$ for x and $\frac{4}{6}$ for y. The re-compression ratio takes different values for x and y because of the different word orders. For instance, the re-compression ratio for x reflects the fact that the word sequence 'ABC' which does not exist in y occurs at x twice.

Finally, given N base dictionaries from D_1 to D_N, HOPRDC expresses an object x with a $2N$-dimensional extended compression-ratio vector $ECV(x)$ which alternately lists the N compression ratios and the N re-compression ratios as shown below. One base dictionary is responsible for two dimensions.

$$ECV(x) = \left(\frac{C_1(x)}{l_x}, \frac{R(x_{D_1})}{C_1(x)}, \frac{C_2(x)}{l_x}, \frac{R(x_{D_2})}{C_2(x)}, \ldots, \frac{C_N(x)}{l_x}, \frac{R(x_{D_N})}{C_N(x)} \right). \quad (2)$$

$ECV(x)$ considers not only the word frequency through the compression ratios but also the word order via the re-compression ratios. Hence, HOPRDC realizes pattern recognition which considers both of word frequency and word order.

Significantly, HOPRDC does not use any additional hyper-parameter as compared with PRDC.

4   Extension of NMD

This section explains our method which improves the NMD, the state-of-the-art dictionary distance by obtaining new features from the compression dictionaries.

To recover the information in an object x which has not been inherited to the dictionary $D(x)$, NMD represents the dictionary as a multiset $MS(x)$ and memorizes the word frequency in x. However, NMD assumes that any word is evenly important without regard to its length. Namely, short words and long words are equally valued. Though this assumption is reasonable in the context of natural language processing, it is not proper for processing strings which originate from multimedia objects such as images and time series data. Since a long word occupies a wider area than a short word in the original object, it is strange to assign the same value to both of them. Let us explain the harmful effect brought about by ignoring the word length. See Fig. 2 which models an image consisting of the upper half simple region and the lower half complex region. An image of harbor city is a real instance of this image, if the simple sea locates on the upper half and the complex urban area lies on the lower half. Usually, the LZW compressor discovers a few long words from the simple region and many short words from the complex region and puts all of them into the dictionary, as in the right half of Fig. 2. Under this condition, by weighing all the words evenly irrespective of their length, the simple region shrinks more than the complex region in the dictionary. As for the image of harbor city, the sea is made lighter of than the urban area, despite the half of semantics is the sea, which opposes to the human intuition.

Thus, treating all the words uniformly causes a fault that unfairly suppresses the values of long words in the dictionary relatively to in the original object.

4.1   Weighed NMD

To mitigate the above shortcoming, we develop a new dictionary distance named WNMD (Weighed NMD) which uses the word length as a new feature in such a way that a word w in the dictionary may have a different weight $g(w)$ which

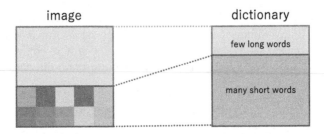

Fig. 2. Volume of words in object and in dictionary

depends on the length of w. $g(w)$ should increase, as w becomes longer. WNMD between x and y is defined as Eq. (3). $F(MS(x))$ symbolizes the modified cardinality of $MS(x) = \{(w_1, m_1^x), (w_2, m_2^x), ..., (w_n, m_n^x)\}$ and is defined as $\sum_{i=1}^{n} g(w) \times m_i^x$. Note that the modified cardinality considers the word length.

$$\frac{F(MS(x) \cup MS(y)) - \min(F(MS(x)), F(MS(y)))}{\max(F(MS(x)), F(MS(y)))}. \tag{3}$$

What should be $g(w)$? Ideally, $g(w)$ shall equal the amount of information in w. However, computing the amount of information kept in w is very difficult in general. For the sake of simplicity, we choose as $g(w)$ the minimum description length (DL) of the simplest string of $|w|$ characters that only contain characters of a single kind. That is, $T = \underbrace{aa \cdots a}_{|w|}$. The DL of T is defined as

(DL of T described by a model word A) + (DL of A)

and takes the minimum value of $O(\sqrt{|w|})$, when $A = \underbrace{aa \cdots a}_{\sqrt{|w|}}$ and $T = \underbrace{AA \cdots A}_{\sqrt{|w|}}$.

Thus, we decided that $g(w) = \sqrt{|w|}$.

5   Experimental Evaluation

We evaluate our two algorithms by applying them to image classification and image retrieval. To compare fairly with the previous work [6] on NMD, we use the same image dataset as [6] called the Wang database [12]. This image dataset is a subset of 1000 images of the Corel photo stock database which contains 100 instances of 10 object classes {Africa, beach, buildings, dinosaurs, elephants, flowers, horses, mountains, food}.

To treat images in the compression-based pattern recognition, an image has to be converted to a one-dimensional string. Again, we convert the images exactly in the same way as [6]. First, we quantize a color of each pixel to one of $5^3 = 125$ characters by segmenting the RGB color axes into 5 pieces. Then, the image is converted to a string by concatenating the characters in the scanning of the image row by row.

Let us remark that, through these experiments, we do not intend to argue that our method is comparable to the latest methods in the research community on image recognition based on deep learning and so on. In principle, compression-based pattern recognition is suitable for new applications about which the way to handle data efficiently has not been yet established rather than for image processing. We use the known image datasets simply in order to get the ground truth easily and to evaluate the algorithms objectively. Thus, it is important for us to show that our method works better than the previous algorithms categorized into compression-based pattern recognition.

5.1 Evaluation of HOPRDC

First, we compare HOPRDC with PRDC by applying them to the image classification. We first choose 10 images by randomly picking up 1 image per class and adopt them as the 10 base dictionaries. Then, we randomly separate the remaining 990 images into 100 test images and 890 training images such that there exist 10 test images and 89 training images per class. The 100 test images are classified into one of the 10 classes with the K-NN classifier with $K = 5$. The algorithms are evaluated with the accuracy rate defined as $\frac{\#correct}{100}$, where $\#correct$ is the number of test images categorized correctly. Since this experimental procedure is randomized, we report the average accuracy rate over 100 trials.

As the result, the average accuracy rate becomes 0.691 for HOPRDC and 0.652 for PRDC. Thus, the relative gain of HOPRDC over PRDC grows 5.9%. Figure 4 shows the accuracy rate per class. HOPRDC excels to PRDC greatly for the two classes "flower" and "bus". These classes have a feature that the instances have similar structures and shapes. HOPRDC behaves well for these classes, since it retains the structural information richer in the feature vectors by considering the word order than PRDC which simply counts the word frequency. Figure 3 supports this claim. This figure shows the top-10 most similar images answered by HOPRDC and PRDC, when the leftmost flower image is given as the query. PRDC tends to return more false positives whose colors are similar but whose structures are dissimilar to the query than HOPRDC.

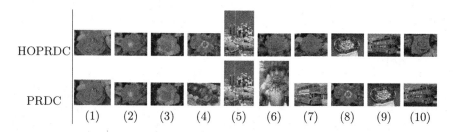

Fig. 3. The top 10 most similar images to query flower image

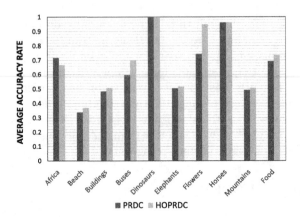

Fig. 4. Average Accuracy Rates

Table 1. Precision values

	WNMD	NMD (Ours)	NMD in [6]
precision@10	0.816	0.808	0.795
precision@100	0.530	0.509	0.513

5.2   Evaluation of WNMD

We compare our WNMD with NMD by conducting completely the same experiment as the paper that proposed NMD [6]: We perform the similar image retrieval based on the dictionary distance, where the query Q is one image from the Wang database and the similar images to Q are searched from the whole 1000 images. The retrieval result is evaluated with precision@10 and precision@100, that is, the ratio of images belonging to the same class as Q out of the top 10/100 most similar images to Q. Table 1 shows the average precision values of WNMD and NMD, where the average is taken by changing the query so that every image may serve as the query exactly once. Regarding to NMD, we show the precision values achieved by our implementation and those reported in [6]. This table concludes that our WNMD outperforms the state-of-the-art dictionary distance NMD.

6   Conclusion

This paper improves the current compression-based pattern recognition by incorporating new features which are easily derived. We study the two previous methods PRDC and the state-of-the-art NMD. As for PRDC, our HOPRDC method succeeds in embedding the information on word order into the feature vectors, while they depend only on the word frequency in the original PRDC. Specifically, HOPRDC extracts the information on word order via the re-compression ratio that is the compression ratio to compress the file compressed with the base dictionary once more. Significantly, HOPRDC does not use any additional hyper-parameter. Regarding to NMD, we develop a new dictionary distance WNMD in which each word has a different weight according to its length. Since this strategy mitigates the problem that long words are less valued in the dictionary than in the actual object, WNMD enables the dictionary to serve as a more faithful sketch of the original object.

Experimentally, HOPRDC and WNMD achieves a better performance than PRDC and NMD respectively.

Acknowledgments. This work was supported by JSPS KAKENHI Grant Number JP15K00148, 2016.

References

1. Li, M., Chen, X., Li, X., Ma, B., Vitanyi, P.: The similarity metric. IEEE Trans. Inf. Theor. **50**(12), 3250–3264 (2004)
2. Watanabe, T., Sugawara, K., Sugihara, H.: A new pattern representation scheme using data compression. IEEE Trans. Pattern Anal. Mach. Intell. **24**(5), 579–590 (2002)
3. Welch, T.A.: A technique for high-performance data compression. Computer **17**(6), 8–19 (1984)
4. Macedonas, A., Besiris, D., Economou, G., Fotopoulos, S.: Dictionary based color image retrieval. J. Vis. Commun. Image Represent. **19**(7), 464–470 (2008)
5. Cerra, D., Datcu, M.: A fast compression-based similarity measure with applications to content-based image retrieval. J. Vis. Commun. Image Represent. **23**(2), 293–302 (2012)
6. Besiris, D., Zigouris, E.: Dictionary-based color image retrieval using multiset theory. J. Vis. Commun. Image Represent. **24**(7), 1155–1167 (2013)
7. Cilibrasi, R., Vitányi, P., De Wolf, R.: Algorithmic clustering of music based on string compression. Comput. Music J. **28**(4), 49–67 (2004)
8. Cerra, D., Datcu, M.: Expanding the algorithmic information theory frame for applications to earth observation. Entropy **15**(1), 407–415 (2013)
9. Hagenauer, J., Mueller, J.: Genomic analysis using methods from information theory. In: Proceedings of IEEE Information Theory Workshop, pp. 55–59 (2004)
10. Cilibrasi, R.: Statistical inference through data compression. Ph.D. thesis, Institute for Logic, language and Computation, Universiteit van Amsterdam (2007)
11. Koga, H., Nakajina, Y., Toda, T.: Effective construction of compression-based feature space. In: Proceedings of International Symposium on Information Theory and Its Applications (ISITA 2016), pp. 116–120 (2016)
12. Wang, J., Li, J., Wiederhold, G.: Simplicity: semantics-sensitive integrated matching for picture libraries. IEEE Trans. Pattern Anal. Mach. Intell. **23**, 947–963 (2001)

VIBIKNet: Visual Bidirectional Kernelized Network for Visual Question Answering

Marc Bolaños[1,2]([⊠]), Álvaro Peris[3], Francisco Casacuberta[3],
and Petia Radeva[1,2]

[1] Universitat de Barcelona, Barcelona, Spain
{marc.bolanos,petia.ivanova}@ub.edu
[2] Computer Vision Center, Bellaterra, Spain
[3] PRHLT Research Center, Universitat Politècnica de València,
Valencia, Spain
{lvapeab,fcn}@prhlt.upv.es

Abstract. In this paper, we address the problem of visual question answering by proposing a novel model, called VIBIKNet. Our model is based on integrating Kernelized Convolutional Neural Networks and Long-Short Term Memory units to generate an answer given a question about an image. We prove that VIBIKNet is an optimal trade-off between accuracy and computational load, in terms of memory and time consumption. We validate our method on the VQA challenge dataset and compare it to the top performing methods in order to illustrate its performance and speed.

Keywords: Visual Qestion Aswering · Convolutional Neural Networks · Long short-term memory networks

1 Introduction

Deep learning has proven to be applicable to several problems and data modalities (e.g. object detection, speech recognition, machine translation, etc.). Furthermore, it has been able to set new records, beating the state of the art in several artificial intelligence areas. Now, new machine learning problems may be tackled, taking profit from the capabilities of deep learning methods for combining multiple data modalities and be end-to-end trainable, thus, having potential to enable new research and application areas. Some multimodal problems are image captioning [18], video captioning [12] or multimodal machine translation and crosslingual image captioning [15]. In this work, we address the challenging Visual Question Answering (VQA) [1] problem.

From the visual modality perspective, a clear proposal for processing images are Convolutional Neural Networks (CNNs) [17]. CNNs are a powerful tool, not only for image classification, but also for feature extraction. Nevertheless, they are not fully scale and rotation invariant, unless they have been specifically trained with enough varied examples [3]. Furthermore, this invariance problem

© Springer International Publishing AG 2017
L.A. Alexandre et al. (Eds.): IbPRIA 2017, LNCS 10255, pp. 372–380, 2017.
DOI: 10.1007/978-3-319-58838-4_41

gets more acute in scene images, which are composed of multiple elements at possibly different rotations and scales. In order to tackle this problem, Liu proposed in [9] a Kernelized approach for learning a rich representation for images composed of multiple objects in any possible rotation and scale.

From the textual modality perspective, Recurrent Neural Networks (RNNs) have shown to be effective sequence modelers. The use of gated units, such as Long Short-Term Memory (LSTM) [6], allows to properly process long sequences. In the last years, LSTM networks have been used in a wide variety of tasks, such as machine translation [16] or image and video captioning [12,18].

After the appearance of the VQA dataset [1] and the organization of the VQA Challenge, several models appeared addressing this problem. Some notable examples are the ones by Kim et al. [7], where image and question was separately described by a CNN and by a RNN, and then a Multimodal Residual Network (MRN) was used for combining both modalities. Fukui et al. [4] used a CNN for describing the image and a two-layered LSTM for the question; followed by a Multimodal Compact Bilinear Pooling (MCB) for fusion. Nam et al. [10], after describing the input image and question, applied a powerful Dual Attention Network (DAN) for fusing both modalities.

In this work, we propose a model for open-ended VQA which uses the most powerful state-of-the-art methods for image and text characterization. More precisely, we use a Kernelized CNN (KCNN) for image characterization, which takes profit from detecting and characterizing all objects in the image for generating a combined feature descriptor. For question modeling, we apply pre-trained word embeddings from Glove [11], taking advantage from the transfer learning capabilities of neural networks; and a Bidirectional LSTM (BLSTM), able to learn rich question information by taking into account temporal relationships both in past-to-future and future-to-past manner. Next, we fuse both modalities and finish by applying a classification model for obtaining the resulting answer.

This paper is organized as follows: in Sect. 2, we present the proposed method, VIBIKNet. In Sect. 3, we describe the dataset and the evaluation metrics. We evaluate our model and compare it with the state of the art. Finally, in Sect. 4, we give some concluding remarks and future work directions.

2   VIBIKNet

In this section, we describe our VQA system, named Visual Bidirectional Kernelized Network (VIBIKNet), whose general scheme can be seen in Fig. 1. We also make public the complete source code[1] for reproducing the results obtained.

The VQA problem consists in computing a function f which, having as input an image X and a related question Q, produces a textual answer A:

$$f(X, Q) = A \tag{1}$$

where Q and A are two variable-sized sequences of words, which can be formalized as $Q = q_1, q_2, ..., q_N$ and $A = a_1, a_2, ..., a_M$, respectively.

---

[1] https://github.com/MarcBS/VIBIKNet.

We formulate the problem under a probabilistic framework. Given the clear multimodality of it, first, we propose to extract independent representations for image and question. For obtaining a rich representation of the image, we apply a KCNN [9] (Sect. 2.1). We process the question with a BLSTM network (Sect. 2.2), which considers the full question context. Next, we need to combine modalities into a single representation. To this purpose we propose using a simple, yet effective, element-wise summation (see Sect. 2.3) after embedding the visual information into the textual one. Finally, we predict the output answer, which can be estimated with a simple classifier for the dataset at hand.

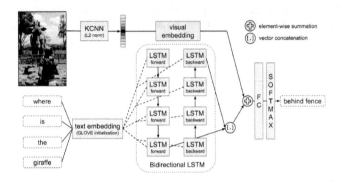

Fig. 1. General scheme of the proposed VIBIKNet model.

2.1   KCNN for Image Representation

A key factor that makes humans able to understand what happens on a picture is the ability to distinguish each of the present elements in it, regarding any possible scale or orientation, together with the relationships and actions that are taking place between them. When we talk about elements we refer to any object, person or animal appearing in the images.

Following this idea, the so-called Kernelized Deep Convolutional Neural Network method [9] has the ability to capture all these aspects. In Fig. 2 we show the general pipeline of steps for extracting KCNN features from images.

More formally, given two images, X and Y, and a set of variable-sized regions for each of them $X = \{x_1, x_2, ..., x_n\}$, and $Y = \{y_1, y_2, ..., y_m\}$, we can define their similarity given by a kernel K as:

$$K(X,Y) = \; < \sum_{x_i \in X} \psi(x_i), \sum_{y_j \in Y} \psi(y_j) > \; = \; < \Psi(X), \Psi(Y) > \tag{2}$$

where the similarity between two regions is computed by their inner product, ψ denotes a linear/non-linear transformation and Ψ denotes the final vectorial image representation composed by the set of initial regions.

Going back to the general scheme applied, initially, an object detector is used for extracting object candidate bounding boxes from each image, x_i. After that,

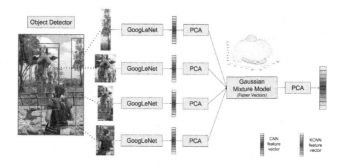

Fig. 2. Steps for the extraction of Kernelized CNN features.

and in order to provide robustness to the point of view, a set of rotations are applied separately to each of the extracted image regions before extracting their image features through a CNN, ψ in Eq. (2). Next, a PCA transformation is applied to the vectors from all image regions. In order to aggregate all vectors from a single image, we learn a Fisher kernel [13] which, similarly to a Bag-of-Words approach [14], jointly models the features distribution by learning a Gaussian Mixture Model (GMM), namely Ψ in Eq. (2). In order to have manageable vector sizes, an additional PCA is applied to the resulting aggregated vectors. This produces an l-size representation of the image, which is finally normalized in order to obtain the final representation of the image ($\Phi(X)$).

2.2 Bidirectional LSTM for Question Representation

As stated above, a question $Q = q_1, q_2, ..., q_N$ is a variable-sized sequence of words. We use a powerful sequence modeler such a RNN for characterizing Q: each word is inputted to the system following a 1-hot codification. Next, we project each word to a continuous space by means of a learnable word embedding matrix. In order to effectively train our word embedding model, we start from pre-trained word vectors provided by Glove [11] and we fine-tune them with the questions corpus. Words not included in Glove are randomly initialized.

The sequence of word embeddings is then inputted to a bidirectional RNN. Bidirectional RNNs are made up of two independent recurrent layers, each of them analyzing the input sequence in one direction. Hence, the forward layer processes the sequence from the left to the right while the backward layer process it from the right to the left. In our case, each recurrent layer is an LSTM layer.

LSTM networks allow to deal with the vanishing gradient problem. These layers maintain two internal states, namely the hidden state (**h**) and the memory state (**c**). The amount of information that flows through the network is modulated by the input (**i**), output (**o**) and forget (**f**) gates. Refer to [5] for a more in-depth review of the LSTM networks.

For obtaining a representation of the complete question, we concatenate the last hidden state from the forward and backward layers:

$$\mathbb{Q} = [\mathbf{h}_N^f, \mathbf{h}_N^b] \tag{3}$$

where $\mathbf{h}_N^f \in \mathbb{R}^m$ and $\mathbf{h}_N^b \in \mathbb{R}^m$ are the last forward and backward hidden states, of size m. $[\cdot , \cdot]$ denotes vectorial concatenation and $\mathbb{Q}$ is the final representation of Q. Since each LSTM layer processes the complete input sequence in one direction, $\mathbb{Q}$ contains both left-to-right and right-to-left dependencies.

2.3   Multimodal Fusion and Prediction

Multimodal Fusion. Hence, we must combine both image and text representations, given that image X is the KCNN feature vector $\Phi(X)$ of size l, and question Q is represented as $\mathbb{Q}$, of size $2m$.

In order to properly combine both modalities, we first linearly project the image representation to the same space as the question representation, by means of a *visual embedding* matrix:

$$\mathbb{X} = \mathbf{W}_m \Phi(X) \tag{4}$$

where $\mathbf{W}_m$ is a $2m \times l$ matrix, jointly estimated with the rest of the model.

Then, a fusion operation is applied on both modalities, $\mathbb{X}$ and $\mathbb{Q}$:

$$\mathbb{M} = \mathbb{X} \oplus \mathbb{Q} \tag{5}$$

where $\oplus$ is the fusion operator and $\mathbb{M}$ is the joint, multimodal representation of the image and question.

Prediction. Given the nature of the task at hand, a typical answer has few words. More precisely, in the VQA dataset (Sect. 3.1), the 89.3% of the answers are single-worded; and the 99.0% of the answers have three or less words [1].

Therefore, we treat our problem as a classification task over the K most repeated answers. The obtained fusion of vision and text ($\mathbb{M}$) is inputted to a fully-connected layer with the set of answers as output. Applying a softmax activation, we define a probability over the possible answers. At test time, we choose the answer $\hat{a}$ with the highest probability:

$$\hat{a} = \underset{a \in K}{\arg \max} \; p(a|Q, X) \tag{6}$$

3   Experiments and Results

In this section we set up the experimentation and evaluation procedure. Moreover, we study and discuss the obtained results in the VQA Challenge[2].

---

[2] The VQA Challenge leaderboard is available at http://visualqa.org/roe.html.

3.1 Dataset and Evaluation

We evaluate our model on the VQA dataset [1], on the real open-ended task. The dataset consists of approximately 200,000 images from the MSCOCO dataset [2]. Each image has three questions associated and each question has ten answers, which were provided by human annotators. We used the default splits for the task: *Train* (80,000 images) for training, *Test-Dev* (40,000 images) for validating the model and *Test-Standard* (80,000 images) for testing it. An additional partition, *Test-Challenge*, was used for evaluating the model at the VQA Challenge.

We followed the VQA evaluation protocol [1], which computes an accuracy between the system output ($\hat{a}$) and the answers provided by the humans:

$$Acc(\hat{a}) = \min\left\{\frac{\#\,\text{humans that said}\,\hat{a}}{3}, 1\right\} \tag{7}$$

3.2 Experimental Setup

We set the model hyperparameters according to empirical results. For extracting the KCNN features, we used: EdgeBoxes [19] for proposing 100 object regions, a set of 8 different object rotations of $R = \{0, 45, 90, 135, 180, 225, 270, 315\}$ degrees, the last FC layer of GoogLeNet [17] (1024-dimensional) for extracting features on each object, applied a PCA of dimensions 128 before, and $l = 1024$ after the GMM, respectively, and learned 128 gaussians during GMM training.

Since we used Glove vectors, the word embedding size was fixed to 300. The BLSTM network had $m = 250$ units in each layer. The visual embedding had a size of $2m = 500$. We applied a classification over the 2,000 most frequent answers, covering a 86.8% of the whole dataset. As fusion operator ($\oplus$ in Eq. (5)) we tested element-wise summation, concatenation and MCB pooling [4].

We used the Adam [8] optimizer with an initial learning rate of 10^{-3}. As regularization strategy, we only applied dropout before the classification layer.

3.3 Experimental Results

Table 1 shows the accuracies of variations of our model (top) and of other works (bottom) for the *Test-Dev* and *Test-Standard* splits, together with the average μs needed for each of the most relevant methods to perform a forward and backward pass on a Titan X with a batch size of 128. Results are separated according to the type of answer, namely yes/no (Y/N), numerical (Num.) and other (Other) answers. We also report the overall accuracy of the task (All).

It can be seen that both summation and concatenation fusion strategies performed similarly. In terms of performance, MCB was also similar to them. Nevertheless, MCB was much more resource-demanding: while the average time per iteration of summation was 10.25 μs, MCB required 244.14 μs. Such differences come from two different sources. First, the MCB operation is not completely GPU-friendly, which makes it expensive. Second, the MCB network involves the estimation of 22 million parameters, while the number of parameters that

Table 1. Proposed models compared to the state of the art. G stands for GoogLeNet, R for ResNet-152, K for KCNN, L for LSTM, BL for BLSTM, FC for fully-connected layer on text before fusing, sum and cat for fusion by summation and concatenation, respectively, +val for training using train+val. VIBIKNet is "G-K BL sum".

	Test-Dev [%]				Test-Standard [%]				μs/iter
	Y/N	Num.	Other	All	Y/N	Num.	Other	All	
G-K L sum	79.0	33.7	38.2	52.9	–	–	–	–	8.4
G-K BL FC sum	78.6	33.6	36.9	52.1	–	–	–	–	12.7
G-K BL FC cat	79.0	33.6	38.3	53.0	–	–	–	–	16.3
R BL sum	77.8	30.6	38.6	52.3	–	–	–	–	15.2
G-K BL cat	79.0	33.4	38.5	53.0	–	–	–	–	16.3
G-K BL MCB	79.2	33.2	37.5	52.5	–	–	–	–	244.1
VIBIKNet	79.1	33.5	38.3	53.1	78.3	38.9	39.0	54.9	10.2
VIBIKNet +val	–	–	–	–	78.9	36.3	40.3	55.8	–
MRN [7]	–	–	–	–	82.4	38.2	49.4	61.8	–
DAN [10]	83.0	39.1	53.9	64.3	82.8	38.1	54.0	64.2	–
MCB [4]	82.3	37.2	57.4	65.4	–	–	–	–	–
Human [1]	–	–	–	–	95.8	83.4	72.7	83.3	–

Fig. 3. Examples of the predictions provided by VIBIKNet; in green correctly predicted and in red wrongly predicted answers. (Color figure online)

VIBIKNet needs to estimate is below 8 million. For comparison, the MCB architecture proposed in [4] requires the estimation of 48 million parameters, which make us hypothesize that such architecture is notoriously slower than our proposal. Thus, although MCB has the potential to provide a better modalities' fusion, simpler methods like summation are more efficient when dealing with low computationally demanding methods, which have the capacity to learn a question-image embedding representation for applying the summation strategy. Moreover, adding a fully-connected layer after text characterization and before fusion did not help, meaning that the visual embedding mechanism suffices for providing a robust visual-text embedding. Regarding image characterization, if we compare the results using ResNet-152 vs GoogLeNet-KCNN, we can see that even using a less powerful CNN architecture, the adoption of the KCNN representation provided better results than simply using the ResNet output. Finally, it is worth noting that we used a single model for prediction. The use of network ensembles typically offer a performance boost [4]. In Fig. 3 we can see some qualitative examples of our methodology.

4   Conclusions and Future Work

We proposed a method for VQA which offers a trade-off between the accuracy and the computational cost of the model. We have proven that kernelized methods for image representation based on CNNs are very powerful for the problem at hand. Additionally, we have shown that using simple fusion methods like summation or concatenation can produce similar results to more elaborate methods at the same time that provide a very efficient computation. Nevertheless, we are aware that performing the multimodal fusion at deeper levels may be beneficial.

As future directions, we aim to delve into better fusion strategies but keeping a low computational cost. We extracted KCNN features based on local representations (objects appearance), but using them together with end-to-end trainable attention mechanisms may lead to higher performances [4].

Acknowledgments. This work was partially funded by TIN2015-66951-C2-1-R, SGR 1219, CERCA Programme/Generalitat de Catalunya, CoMUN-HaT - TIN2015-70924-C2-1-R (MINECO/FEDER), PrometeoII/2014/030 and R-MIPRCV. P. Radeva is partially supported by ICREA Academia2014. We acknowledge NVIDIA Corporation for the donation of a GPU used in this work.

References

1. Antol, S., Agrawal, A., Lu, J., Mitchell, M., Batra, D., Zitnick, C.L., Parikh., D.: VQA: visual question answering. In: ICCV, pp. 2425–2433 (2015)
2. Chen, X., Fang, H., Lin, T.-Y., Vedantam, R., Gupta, S., Dollár, P., Zitnick, C.L.: Microsoft COCO captions: data collection and evaluation server. arXiv:1504.00325 (2015)
3. Cheng, G., Zhou, P., Han, J.: RIFD-CNN: rotation-invariant and fisher discriminative convolutional neural networks for object detection. In: CVPR, pp. 2884–2893 (2016)
4. Fukui, A., Park, D.H., Yang, D., Rohrbach, A., Darrell, T., Rohrbach, M.: Multimodal compact bilinear pooling for visual question answering and visual grounding. arXiv:1606.01847 (2016)
5. Gers, F.A., Schmidhuber, J., Cummins, F.: Learning to forget: continual prediction with LSTM. Neural Comput. **12**(10), 2451–2471 (2000)
6. Hochreiter, S., Schmidhuber, J.: Long short-term memory. Neural Comput. **9**(8), 1735–1780 (1997)
7. Kim, J.-H., Lee, S.-W., Kwak, D.-H., Heo, M.-O., Kim, J., Ha, J.-W., Zhang, B.-T.: Multimodal residual learning for visual QA. arXiv:1606.01455 (2016)

8. Kingma, D.P., Ba, J.: Adam: A method for stochastic optimization. arXiv:1412.6980 (2014)

9. Liu, Z.: Kernelized deep convolutional neural network for describing complex images. arXiv:1509.04581 (2015)

10. Nam, H., Ha, J.-W., Kim, J.: Dual attention networks for multimodal reasoning and matching. arXiv:1611.00471 (2016)

11. Pennington, J., Socher, R., Manning, C.D.: Glove: global vectors for word representation. In: EMNLP, pp. 1532–1543 (2014)

12. Peris, Á., Bolaños, M., Radeva, P., Casacuberta, F.: Video description using bidirectional recurrent neural networks. In: Villa, A.E.P., Masulli, P., Pons Rivero, A.J. (eds.) ICANN 2016. LNCS, vol. 9887, pp. 3–11. Springer, Cham (2016). doi:10.1007/978-3-319-44781-0_1

13. Perronnin, F., Sánchez, J., Mensink, T.: Improving the fisher kernel for large-scale image classification. In: Daniilidis, K., Maragos, P., Paragios, N. (eds.) ECCV 2010. LNCS, vol. 6314, pp. 143–156. Springer, Heidelberg (2010). doi:10.1007/978-3-642-15561-1_11

14. Sivic, J., Zisserman, A.: Efficient visual search of videos cast as text retrieval. PAMI 31(4), 591–606 (2009)

15. Specia, L., Frank, S., Sima'an, K., Elliott, D.: A shared task on multimodal machine translation and crosslingual image description. In: Proceedings of the First Conference on Machine Translation, pp. 543–553. ACL (2016)

16. Sutskever, I., Vinyals, O., Le, Q.V.: Sequence to sequence learning with neural networks. In: NIPS, vol. 27, pp. 3104–3112 (2014)

17. Szegedy, C., Liu, W., Jia, Y., Sermanet, P., Reed, S., Anguelov, D., Erhan, D., Vanhoucke, V., Rabinovich, A.: Going deeper with convolutions. In: CVPR, pp. 1–9 (2015)

18. Xu, K., Ba, J., Kiros, R., Courville, A., Salakhutdinov, R., Zemel, R., Bengio, Y.: Show, attend and tell: neural image caption generation with visual attention. arXiv:1502.03044 (2015)

19. Zitnick, C.L., Dollár, P.: Edge boxes: locating object proposals from edges. In: Fleet, D., Pajdla, T., Schiele, B., Tuytelaars, T. (eds.) ECCV 2014. LNCS, vol. 8693, pp. 391–405. Springer, Cham (2014). doi:10.1007/978-3-319-10602-1_26

On the Use of Spearman's Rho to Measure the Stability of Feature Rankings

Sarah Nogueira$^{(\boxtimes)}$, Konstantinos Sechidis, and Gavin Brown

School of Computer Science, University of Manchester,
Manchester M13 9PL, UK
sarah.nogueira@manchester.ac.uk
http://www.cs.man.ac.uk/~nogueirs/

Abstract. Producing stable feature rankings is critical in many areas, such as in bioinformatics where the robustness of a list of ranked genes is crucial to interpretation by a domain expert. In this paper, we study Spearman's rho as a measure of stability to training data perturbations - not just as a heuristic, but here *proving* that it is the natural measure of stability when using mean rank aggregation. We provide insights on the properties of this stability measure, allowing a useful interpretation of stability values - e.g. how close a stability value is to that of a purely random feature ranking process, and concepts such as the *expected value* of a stability estimator.

Keywords: Stability · Robustness · Feature rankings · Ensembles · Spearman's rho · Mean rank aggregation

1 Introduction

Feature selection is a broad topic that consists in identifying the relevant features for future use in a predictive model or for interpretation by domain experts. The output of a feature selection algorithm might be one of 3 types: a scoring on the features (e.g. the coefficients of a regression model), a ranking on the features (e.g. with any sequential forward selection) or a feature set (e.g. when using hypothesis testing procedures). In this paper we focus on feature rankings.

Stability (or robustness) of a feature ranker (FR) is its *sensitivity to small perturbations in the training set* [12]. In information retrieval, ranking systems on search engines are expected to be robust to spam [8]. In bioinformatics, where by nature the training samples are usually small, the removal of only one example on the training set can cause substantially different rankings making the feature rankings non-interpretable and not reliable for clinical use. For this reason, robust FRs have become a major requirement in the field of gene selection, biomarker identification or molecular profiling [1,3,7,10,20].

Many measures of stability have been proposed in the literature. Some measures focus on the stability of *partial* feature rankings or in giving more weight to features with higher rankings [11]. In this paper, we focus on a popular measure

© Springer International Publishing AG 2017
L.A. Alexandre et al. (Eds.): IbPRIA 2017, LNCS 10255, pp. 381–391, 2017.
DOI: 10.1007/978-3-319-58838-4_42

used to measure the stability of full feature rankings: the Spearman rank-order correlation coefficient, also commonly called Spearman's ρ. The main contributions of this paper include an understanding of the properties of this measure for useful interpretation of stability values; a proof that unstable FRs yield *better* rankings than individual rankings do on average when aggregated by their mean and an *explanation* of why mean rank aggregation produces more stable FRs.

The paper is structured as follows. Section 2 provides background material to the quantification of stability of FRs. Section 3 provides a statistical interpretation and derives the properties of this measure. Section 4 focuses on the topic of mean rank aggregation and Sect. 5 illustrates some of our theoretical results on mean rank aggregation.

2   Background

Let us assume there are d features in total. A ranking $\mathbf{r}$ can be modelled as a vector of d **distinct** natural numbers taken from 1 to d (i.e. as a permutation of the numbers from 1 to d). To quantify stability, we measure the variability of the rankings obtained when *small* perturbations are applied to the dataset. In most literature, the general procedure to evaluate the stability of a FR consists in taking M bootstrap samples of the dataset and then to apply the FR to each one of the M samples hence giving M rankings [9,12].

Let us take an example: assume that we have a dataset with $d = 5$ features and that we apply a FR to $M = 3$ bootstrap samples. Then we can represent the output of the FR as follows:

$$\mathcal{R} = \begin{bmatrix} \mathbf{r}_1 \\ \mathbf{r}_2 \\ \mathbf{r}_3 \end{bmatrix} = \begin{bmatrix} 5\ 3\ 1\ 4\ 2 \\ 4\ 3\ 1\ 5\ 2 \\ 5\ 3\ 2\ 4\ 1 \end{bmatrix} \Bigg\} M = 3 \text{ feature rankings}$$

where $\mathbf{r}_i$ is the ranking obtained on the ith dataset. In the first ranking $\mathbf{r}_1$, the first feature is ranked 5th, the second feature is ranked 3rd and so on. We can see that there are some variations in between the three rankings $\mathbf{r}_1$, $\mathbf{r}_2$ and $\mathbf{r}_3$. Even though the 2nd feature is always ranked in the 3rd position, the other features present some variations in their ranks. A fully stable FR would have produced identical rankings (i.e. $\mathbf{r}_1 = \mathbf{r}_2 = \mathbf{r}_3$) on the different data samples. In general, the M rankings can be represented by a matrix $\mathcal{R}$ as follows:

$$\mathcal{R} = \begin{bmatrix} \mathbf{r}_1 \\ \vdots \\ \mathbf{r}_M \end{bmatrix} = \begin{bmatrix} r_{1,1} & r_{1,2} & \cdots & r_{1,d} \\ r_{2,1} & r_{2,2} & \cdots & r_{2,d} \\ \vdots & \vdots & \ddots & \vdots \\ r_{M,1} & r_{M,2} & \cdots & r_{M,d} \end{bmatrix}$$

where $\mathbf{r}_i$ is the feature ranking on the ith bootstrap sample. Quantifying the stability of a FR consists in defining a measure $\hat{\Phi}$ taking as an input such a matrix $\mathcal{R}$ to quantify these variations. We can wonder what would be a sensible definition for $\hat{\Phi}$ and which properties should a stability measure have so that the stability values are interpretable and comparable in different contexts.

Let ϕ be a function that takes as an input two feature rankings $\mathbf{r}_i$ and $\mathbf{r}_j$ and returns a *similarity* value between the two rankings. A common approach to measure the stability of a FR is to define the stability as the average pairwise similarities between all possible *unique* pairs of rankings in $\mathcal{R}$ [12], that is:

$$\hat{\Phi}(\mathcal{R}) = \frac{1}{M(M-1)} \sum_{i=1}^{M} \sum_{\substack{j=1 \\ j \neq i}}^{M} \phi(\mathbf{r}_i, \mathbf{r}_j). \tag{1}$$

Several proposals have been made in the literature for the similarity measure ϕ. Such measures include the Kendall Tau [19], the Canberra Distance [10], the scaled Spearman footrule [17] or the Spearman's ρ [12,15]. In this paper, we focus on the use of Spearman's ρ which is formally defined as:.

$$\rho(\mathbf{r}_i, \mathbf{r}_j) = 1 - \frac{6 \sum_{f=1}^{d} (r_{i,f} - r_{j,f})^2}{d(d^2-1)}. \tag{2}$$

Hereafter, $\hat{\Phi}$ will denote the stability measure using Spearman's ρ. In the next section, we study the properties of this stability measure and show that $\hat{\Phi}$ should be interpreted as a *random variable*.

3 Pairwise Spearman's Rho as a Stability Measure

3.1 Statistical Interpretation

An important point is that Eq. (1) is an *estimator*, based on a random process (bootstrapping) – therefore $\hat{\Phi}$ is a *random variable*, and we can discuss concepts such as the expectation and the convergence of that random variable. Surprisingly, these concepts – the expectation/convergence of stability estimates have not been considered in the literature before. We proceed below by characterising this random variable for the case of Spearman's Rho.

We can see each ranking $\mathbf{r}$ as a draw from a an unknown distribution and therefore $\hat{\Phi}$ is an estimator of a population parameter Φ that depends on the parameters of that distribution. Let X_f be the random variable corresponding to the rank of the fth feature. We can therefore see f^{th} column of $\mathcal{R}$ as a realisation of X_f. The *maximum likelihood estimate* σ_f^2 of the variance of X_f and the unbiased sample variance s_f^2 are by definition:

$$\sigma_f^2 = \left[\left(\frac{1}{M} \sum_{i=1}^{M} r_{i,f}^2 \right) - \left(\frac{1}{M} \sum_{i=1}^{M} r_{i,f} \right)^2 \right] \quad \text{and} \quad s_f^2 = \frac{M}{M-1} \sigma_f^2. \tag{3}$$

We build upon this with a novel theorem, our first contribution, Theorem 1.

Theorem 1. *The stability $\hat{\Phi}$ using Spearman's ρ can be re-written as follows:*

$$\hat{\Phi}(\mathcal{R}) = 1 - \frac{\frac{1}{d}\sum_{f=1}^{d} s_f^2}{V_r}, \tag{4}$$

where $V_r = \frac{d^2-1}{12}$ is a constant only depending on d.

Proof. All proofs of theorems/corollaries are in the Supplementary Material[1].

One interpretation of the stability of $\hat{\Phi}$, from the form of Eq. (1), is the average correlation between the rankings in $\mathcal{R}$. Theorem 1 gives another interpretation. In fact, we can see the value of $\hat{\Phi}$ as an *estimator* of the average variance of X_f over the d features rescaled by a constant depending only on d. First of all, this gives us a natural and novel multivariate extension of Spearman's ρ for a set of M rankings since it reduces to Spearman's ρ for $M = 2$ (which has been a topic of interest in the statistical literature [16]). When the FR is *fully stable*, i.e. when all the rankings in $\mathcal{R}$ are identical, the sample variance of X_f will be equal to 0 and therefore $\hat{\Phi}(\mathcal{R})$ will be equal to 1. Computing the stability using Eqs. (4) instead of (1) reduces the computational complexity from $\mathcal{O}(M^2 d)$ to $\mathcal{O}(Md)$. Since s_f^2 is an unbiased and consistent estimator of the true variance $\mathrm{Var}(X_f)$, we can derive the result given in Corollary 1. This corollary shows that the estimated stability $\hat{\Phi}$ will converge in probability to the population stability Φ.

Corollary 1. *$\hat{\Phi}(\mathcal{R})$ is an unbiased and consistent estimator of:*

$$\Phi = 1 - \frac{\frac{1}{d}\sum_{f=1}^{d}\mathrm{Var}(X_f)}{V_r}. \tag{5}$$

We can wonder what happens if we use the maximum likelihood estimate of the variance σ_f^2 instead of the unbiased estimator s_f^2 to estimate the true variance of X_f in Eq. (4). It turns out that quantity corresponds to the average pairwise Spearman's ρ between all M^2 pairs of rankings (i.e. the $M(M-1)$ pairs we already had plus the M correlations of each ranking with itself). Let us call that latter quantity $\hat{\Phi}^{all}$. We have that:

$$\hat{\Phi}^{all}(\mathcal{R}) = \frac{1}{M^2}\left(M(M-1)\hat{\Phi}(\mathcal{R}) + \sum_{i=1}^{M}\rho(\mathbf{r}_i, \mathbf{r}_i)\right) = 1 - \frac{\frac{1}{d}\sum_{f=1}^{d}\mathrm{Var}(X_f)}{V_r}. \tag{6}$$

The only difference between $\hat{\Phi}$ and $\hat{\Phi}^{all}$ lies in the way the true variance of X_f is estimated. Even though the maximum likelihood estimator σ_f^2 is biased, it converges to the population parameter $\mathrm{Var}(X_f)$ as M goes to infinity. In other words, when M is large enough, these two quantities can be used interchangeably. This will be critical in introducing the concepts discussed in Sect. 4.

---

[1] Available online at
http://www.cs.man.ac.uk/~nogueirs/files/IbPRIA2017-supplementary-material.pdf.

3.2 Properties

We know from the statistical literature the Spearman's ρ is a *chance-corrected* measure of correlation and that $-1 \leq \rho \leq 1$ [2]. But we can wonder what are the properties of the average pairwise Spearman's ρ? In this section, we prove two properties for $\hat{\Phi}$ that we argue to be useful for interpretation and comparison of stability values in different settings.

Theorem 2 (Bounds). *$\hat{\Phi}$ is asymptotically bounded ($M \to \infty$) by 0 and 1.*

Even though ρ can take negative values, Theorem 2 shows that the resulting stability estimate $\hat{\Phi}$ is asymptotically non-negative. We expect this result since the population parameter Φ we are estimating –Eq. (5)– is in the interval $[0, 1]$.

Theorem 3 (Correction for Chance). *The stability estimate $\hat{\Phi}$ is corrected by chance which means that its expected value is constant and equal to 0 when the FR is random (i.e. when all rankings/permutations have equal probability).*

Theorem 3 shows that no matter what is the total number of features d, the stability estimate $\hat{\Phi}$ of a random FR will be 0 in expectation. As pointed out by [2], "chance-corrected measures yield values that are interpreted as a proportion above that expected by chance alone". We can therefore interpret the stability estimate $\hat{\Phi}$ as the proportion of agreement above chance between the rankings in $\mathcal{R}$. Some popular measures of stability used in the literature do not have this property. For instance, the stability of a random FR using the Canberra distance [10] will systematically increase with the number of features d, which means it cannot be used to compare the stability of ranked gene lists of different sizes.

3.3 Relationship to Other Stability Measures

Finally, we can point out that the use of Spearman's ρ is in line with the stability measures used for different types of feature selection outputs. Since the sample Pearson correlation coefficient reduces to Spearman's ρ in the cases of untied ranks, it is strongly related to the literature that makes use of the average pairwise sample Pearson's correlation coefficient in the case of feature weights [12] and in the case of feature sets [14], which suggests that the use of Spearman's ρ goes towards a unification of the stability literature. We can also point out that the use of the average pairwise Pearson's correlation has been shown to hold a set of desirable properties and to reduce to the very popular Kuncheva's measure [13] in the case of feature sets [14].

4 Ensemble Feature Ranking

In the ensemble learning literature, it is known that a set of *diverse* regression models can be aggregated together to form a more robust model [5]. Inspired by that field, *ensemble feature selection* [15] aims at building more robust feature selectors by using a set of unstable individual FRs and aggregating them together to increase the stability. Nevertheless, there has been no theoretical work that guarantees that the error and the stability of a FR will be improved by the ensemble. Moreover, some works question the use of ensembles since it has empirically been shown not to always increase the stability [6]. We focus on the case of mean rank aggregation. We first show that the *error* of the aggregated ranking will be guaranteed to be lower than the one of an individual ranking on average. Then, we give a theoretical argument showing why the stability of the aggregated rank should improve as the number of ensemble members increases.

4.1 Mean Rank Aggregation

The general procedure to build feature ranking ensembles is to take K bootstrap samples of the data, to apply the FR to each one of the samples and then to combine the K resulting feature rankings using a given *rank aggregation technique*. The reason why we denote by K the number of FRs in ensemble (and not by M) is because we want to distinguish it from the number of bootstrap samples M used to *estimate* $\hat{\Phi}$. In this paper, we focus on the popular mean rank aggregation that consists in taking the mean ranking $\bar{\mathbf{r}} = (\bar{r}_1, ..., \bar{r}_d)$ of each feature over the K rankings (i.e. $\bar{r}_f = \frac{1}{K} \sum_{i=1}^{K} r_{i,f}$). For full rankings, the mean rank aggregation has been proved to be equivalent to the Borda Count aggregation technique [20].

4.2 The "Ambiguity" Decomposition

Let us assume there exists a *true* ranking $\mathbf{r}^* = (r_1^*, ..., r_d^*)$, where r_f^* is the true rank of the fth feature, and that the FR is trying to estimate that true ranking $\mathbf{r}^*$ when producing a ranking $\mathbf{r}_i$. One way to measure the quality of the rank of the fth feature is to measure the *squared error* (SE) of $r_{i,f}$ compared to the true ranking r_f^* as follows: $(r_{i,f} - r_f^*)^2$. Now, assuming we have K ranks $(r_{1,f}, .., r_{K,f})$ for the fth feature, we can define the mean squared error (MSE) as the mean of the squared errors of each one of the K rankings: $\frac{1}{K} \sum_{i=1}^{K} (r_{i,f} - r_f^*)^2$. Similarly to the *ambiguity decomposition* that exists for ensembles of regression predictors [4], we provide an ambiguity decomposition for mean rank aggregation.

Theorem 4. *The average squared error of the mean rank over the d features can be decomposed into two **positive** terms as follows:*

$$\underbrace{\frac{1}{d} \sum_{f=1}^{d} (\bar{r}_f - r_f^*)^2}_{av.\ SE\ of\ the\ mean\ ranker} = \underbrace{\frac{1}{d} \sum_{f=1}^{d} \left(\frac{1}{K} \sum_{i=1}^{K} (r_{i,f} - r_f^*)^2 \right)}_{av.\ MSE\ of\ the\ K\ rankers} - \underbrace{(1 - \hat{\Phi}^{all}) V_r}_{ambiguity\ term}, \quad (7)$$

where the ambiguity term is also equal to $\frac{1}{d} \sum_{f=1}^{d} \sigma_f^2$ and where $V_r = \frac{d^2 - 1}{12}$. Therefore, the error of the ensemble ranker is guaranteed to be less or equal than the one of the individual rankers on average.

Theorem 4 provides a decomposition of the squared error of the mean ranking $\bar{\mathbf{r}}$ into two *positive* terms: the average MSE of the K rankers (which is the average of the MSE over the d features of the K rankings) and the ambiguity term, which is a linear function of the stability estimate $\hat{\Phi}^{all}$. Since these two terms are positive, we can see that for a given MSE, having a higher ambiguity term (which corresponds to having a less stable set of rankers) will result in a lower average SE for the mean ranking $\bar{\mathbf{r}}$. This decomposition shows two things:

1. The mean rank $\bar{\mathbf{r}}$ is guaranteed to be *closer* to the true ranking than would be an individual ranker on average.
2. The use of Spearman's ρ to estimate stability is a sensible choice since it can be interpreted as the ambiguity term of this decomposition.

Naturally, this decomposition does not show that the aggregated ranker will be more stable then the individual ranker, which is the topic of the next section.

4.3   Does Mean Rank Aggregation Always Increase Stability?

We aim at giving an explanation of why we should expect a higher stability when performing mean rank aggregation. The mean ranking is not a permutation of the integers 1 to d any more: since $\bar{r}_f = \frac{1}{K}\sum_{f=1}^{d} r_{i,f}$, the mean rank of the fth feature can be any real number in the interval $[1, d]$. Similarly to Eq. (5) where the true stability Φ of a FR is a linear function of the average variance of X_f, we can define the stability of the mean ranking $\bar{\mathbf{r}}$ as a linear function of the average variance of mean rankings $\bar{r}_f$ over the d features as follows:

$$\Psi(\bar{\mathbf{r}}) = 1 - \frac{\frac{1}{d}\sum_{f=1}^{d} \text{Var}(\bar{r}_f)}{V_r}. \tag{8}$$

Theorem 5 derives the stability Ψ of the mean ranking $\bar{\mathbf{r}}$ as a linear function of the true stability Φ of the individual FR. This theorem shows that Ψ increases with the number of FRs in the ensemble and that eventually, as we keep adding FRs to the ensemble, the ensemble will be fully stable (as Ψ converges to 1 when K goes to infinity). Figure 1 illustrates the value of Φ against the number of FRs in the ensemble K for different values of Φ. We can see that this value converges to 1 as K increases.

Theorem 5. *Assuming the K rankings in the ensemble are independent and identically distributed (i.i.d), the stability of the mean ranking is reduced by $\frac{1}{K}$ compared to the stability of the individual FR:*

$$\Psi = \frac{K-1}{K} + \frac{\Phi}{K}. \tag{9}$$

One could question the choice of Ψ as a stability measure for the aggregated *mean* ranking. As we can see in Eq. (8), Ψ is a linear function of the variance of the mean rank of each feature. In the literature, a threshold τ is often applied to the mean ranking to obtain a feature set. For example, we could decide to select

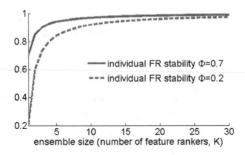

Fig. 1. Stability of the mean rank aggregation against the number of ensemble members K when the individual ranker has a stability $\Phi = 0.7$ and $\Phi = 0.4$.

all the features for which the mean rank $\bar{r}_f < \tau$ and discard the other features. Therefore, if the mean rank $\bar{r}_f$ of each feature has a low variance (which corresponds to a high value of Ψ), it is more likely that the same features would be selected when small perturbations are applied to the training set, hence producing a stable feature set.

5   Experiments

In this section, we aim at illustrating the results of Sect. 4. To be able to illustrate the result of Theorem 4, we need to know the *true* ranking $\mathbf{r}^*$. For this reason, we generate an artificial dataset consisting of $d = 20$ binary features with different degrees of dependency with the target class Y [18]. To create the data, firstly we generate the values of Y, by taking n samples from a Bernoulli distribution with $p(y = 1) = 0.50$. Then, for each feature X, we randomly choose the parameters $p(x|y)$ that guarantee the desired degree of dependency expressed in terms of $I(X;Y)$ and we use these parameters to sample the values of X. The mutual information $I(X;Y)$ population values for each features are:

$$[9\ 9.5\ 8.5\ 8\ 7.5\ 7\ 6.5\ 6\ 5.5\ 5\ 4.5\ 4\ 3.5\ 3\ 2.5\ 2\ 1.5\ 1\ 0.5\ 0.1] \times 10^{-2},$$

where a high mutual information translates into a high rank of the feature. We repeat the experiment taking different sample sizes n as given in Table 1. Then, we take $M = 100$ bootstrap samples of each one of these datasets and estimate the mutual information on each bootstrap, thus getting M rankings.

We can see in Table 1 that as we increase the sample size n, the stability of the FR increases and therefore, the ambiguity term decreases. This is expected since the mutual information estimates become better as we increase the sample size and thus, the ranking become more accurate. We can observe that for lower stability values, the improvement in terms of error (which corresponds to the difference between the average SE of the mean ranking and the average MSE of the M rankings and therefore to the ambiguity term) is larger; as we expected from Theorem 4. This follows the idea that an unstable set of FRs will yield better results once aggregated.

Table 1. Demonstration that unstable FRs (in the sense of pairwise Spearman's ρ) provide a better ranking when aggregated together by their mean. The difference between the error of the mean rank and the mean error of the individual rankings is larger for lower stability values.

n	Error of the mean rank $\bar{r}$	Mean error of the K rankers	Ambiguity	Stability $\hat{\phi}^{all}$
30	29.5	46.0	16.5	0.505
50	36.9	49.4	12.6	0.622
500	2.91	7.77	4.85	0.854
1000	2.05	4.23	2.19	0.934
10000	0.149	0.52	0.366	0.989

We now aim at illustrating the result of Sect. 4.3. Since we are considering small sample sizes, we use the jackknife resampling technique (which corresponds to a leave-one-out resampling) to get several ensembles of FRs and we estimate the value of Ψ. Table 2 shows the evolution of the stability of the aggregated ranking as we increase K. As expected, the estimated stability of the aggregated mean rank $\hat{\Psi}$ increases with K and converges to 1.

Table 2. The estimated stability $\hat{\Psi}$ of the mean rank increases with the number of FRs K aggregated. This illustrates the result of Theorem 5.

n	K	Stability of the individual ranker $\hat{\phi}^{all}$	Stability of the mean ranker $\hat{\Psi}$
30	2	0.505	0.738
	5		0.887
	10		0.931
	50		0.975
500	2	0.854	0.926
	5		0.971
	10		0.985
	50		0.997

6   Conclusions

In this work, we showed that the stability of feature rankings using Spearman's ρ is in fact a random variable. Therefore, when we "calculate" stability, we are only estimating the *true* stability of a FR for a specific dataset. Our work also derives a set of properties deemed useful for interpretation and comparison of stability estimates. To the best of our knowledge, this is the first work proposing a statistical perspective on the stability values obtained when using Spearman's rho. We further provide an theoretical guarantees on the *error* and the true stability of the mean rank aggregation. Future work could include the derivation of asymptotic distribution for the stability estimate, which would allow to derive such tools as hypothesis testing for stability values and/or confidence intervals.

Acknowledgements. The authors gratefully acknowledge the support of the EPSRC for the Manchester Centre for Doctoral Training in Computer Science (EP/I028099/1) and the LAMBDA project (EP/N035127/1).

References

1. Abeel, T., Helleputte, T., Van de Peer, Y., Dupont, P., Saeys, Y.: Robust biomarker identification for cancer diagnosis with ensemble feature selection methods. Bioinformatics **26**, 392–398 (2010)
2. Berry, K.J., Mielke Jr., P.W., Johnston, J.E.: Permutation Statistical Methods: An Integrated Approach. Springer, Heidelberg (2016)
3. Boulesteix, A.L., Slawski, M.: Stability and aggregation of ranked gene lists. Brief. Bioinform. **10**, 556–568 (2009)
4. Brown, G., Wyatt, J.L.: The use of the ambiguity decomposition in neural network ensemble learning methods. In: Fawcett, T., Mishra, N. (eds.) ICML (2003)
5. Brown, G., Wyatt, J.L., Tiňo, P.: Managing diversity in regression ensembles. J. Mach. Learn. Res. **6**, 1621–1650 (2005)
6. Dessì, N., Pes, B.: Stability in biomarker discovery: does ensemble feature selection really help? In: Proceedings IEA/AIE 2015 (2015)
7. Dittman, D.J., Khoshgoftaar, T.M., Wald, R., Napolitano, A.: Classification performance of rank aggregation techniques for ensemble gene selection. In: FLAIRS Conference. AAAI Press (2013)
8. Dwork, C., Kumar, R., Naor, M., Sivakumar, D.: Rank aggregation methods for the web. In: Proceedings International Conference on World Wide Web (2001)
9. He, Z., Yu, W.: Stable feature selection for biomarker discovery. Comput. Biol. Chem. **34**, 215–225 (2010)
10. Jurman, G., Merler, S., Barla, A., Paoli, S., Galea, A., Furlanello, C.: Algebraic stability indicators for ranked lists in molecular profiling. Bioinformatics **24**, 258–264 (2008)
11. Jurman, G., Riccadonna, S., Visintainer, R., Furlanello, C.: Algebraic comparison of partial lists in bioinformatics. PLoS one **7**, e36540 (2012)
12. Kalousis, A., Prados, J., Hilario, M.: Stability of feature selection algorithms: a study on high-dimensional spaces. Knowl. Inf. Syst. **12**, 95–116 (2007)
13. Kuncheva, L.I.: A stability index for feature selection. In: Proceedings of Artificial Intelligence and Applications (2007)
14. Nogueira, S., Brown, G.: Measuring the stability of feature selection. In: Frasconi, P., Landwehr, N., Manco, G., Vreeken, J. (eds.) ECML PKDD 2016. LNCS, vol. 9852, pp. 442–457. Springer, Cham (2016). doi:10.1007/978-3-319-46227-1_28
15. Saeys, Y., Abeel, T., Peer, Y.: Robust feature selection using ensemble feature selection techniques. In: Daelemans, W., Goethals, B., Morik, K. (eds.) ECML PKDD 2008. LNCS, vol. 5212, pp. 313–325. Springer, Heidelberg (2008). doi:10.1007/978-3-540-87481-2_21

16. Schmid, F., Schmidt, R.: Multivariate extensions of Spearman's rho and related statistics. Stat. Probab. Lett. **77**, 407–416 (2007)
17. Sculley, D.: Rank aggregation for similar items. In: Proceedings of the Seventh SIAM International Conference on Data Mining (2007)
18. Sechidis, K.: Hypothesis testing and feature selection in semi-supervised data. Ph.D. thesis, School of Computer Science, University of Manchester, UK (2015)
19. Voorhees, E.M.: Evaluation by highly relevant documents. In: Proceedings of the 24th Annual International ACM SIGIR Conference on Research and Development in Information Retrieval, SIGIR 2001. ACM (2001)
20. Wald, R., Khoshgoftaar, T.M., Dittman, D.J., Awada, W., Napolitano, A.: An extensive comparison of feature ranking aggregation techniques in bioinformatics. In: IRI. IEEE (2012)

Graph Embedding Through Probabilistic Graphical Model Applied to Symbolic Graphs

Hana Jarraya[✉], Oriol Ramos Terrades, and Josep Lladós

Computer Vision Center, Universitat Autònoma de Barcelona, CVC Campus UAB, Edifici O, s/n, Cerdanyola del Vallès, 08193 Barcelona, Spain
{hanajarraya,oriolrt,josep}@cvc.uab.es

Abstract. We propose a new Graph Embedding (GEM) method that takes advantages of structural pattern representation. It models an Attributed Graph (AG) as a Probabilistic Graphical Model (PGM). Then, it learns the parameters of this PGM presented by a vector. This vector is a signature of AG in a lower dimensional vectorial space. We apply Structured Support Vector Machines (SSVM) to process classification task. As first tentative, results on the GREC dataset are encouraging enough to go further on this direction.

Keywords: Attributed Graph · Probabilistic Graphical Model · Graph Embedding · Structured Support Vector Machines

1 Introduction

The use of structural information such as graphs is defined within Structural PR (SPR) field. Graphs are powerful because they model two important aspects: hierarchical composition of sub-patterns from complex pattern; and relations between these sub-patterns. The SPR problems are the capacity of finding sub-structures, sub-graph matching, and the high computational complexity of matching algorithms and benefits from rich Statistical PR algorithms. Here, the GEM is used to moderate the high complexity [1]. It is defined to encode graphs into vectors, then applies Statistical PR techniques on them. It allows to define approximate polynomial solution for hard combinatorial problems, reduce noise sensitivity and preserve structure [2]. The noise is defined by variant distortions. The structure is defined by edges relating different nodes. PGM is suitable framework to satisfy these two properties. It learns distortions as probabilities over complex structure. The output is a parameter vector learned taking into account the attributes, nodes and edges of one graph. Structured classifier is applied on AG signature, called SSVM [3,4].

Our proposition is to define a new general GEM method. It uses PGM for learning a parameter vector representing an AG. First choosing the different nodes, edges and attributes is a modeling problem solved by the experimentation. Second, using the chosen PGM, we learn parameter vector using SSVM algorithm. We validate our proposition by embedding GREC graphs [5]. The first

© Springer International Publishing AG 2017
L.A. Alexandre et al. (Eds.): IbPRIA 2017, LNCS 10255, pp. 392–399, 2017.
DOI: 10.1007/978-3-319-58838-4_43

obtained results are good enough to guideline our research. The literature demonstrates other important GEM methods applied on symbol recognition [1,6], we will only consider the latest. Section 2 illustrates related works on Explicit GEM methods applied on Symbol Recognition. We define the main concepts, in Sect. 3. In Sect. 4, we detail the proposed GEM. In Sect. 5, we discuss the tests applied on the learning parameters and interpret misclassification. Section 6 presents the conclusion and future work.

2   Related Works

GEM approaches encode either explicitly or implicitly graphs into high dimensional spaces as we can perform the statistical PR algorithms. In one hand, implicit GEM methods are based on graph kernel, defined as a dot product evaluated in graph space. But it does not permit all operations that could be defined on vector spaces [2]. In other hand, explicit GEM methods explicitly embed an input graph into a feature vector and thus enable the use of mature Statistical PR. This vector is of fixed size no matter is the size and order of graph. It requires to contain relevant representative attributes, at the same time fairly well generic to describe any input graph. The most important challenges are loss of structural information, different encoded attributes types and noise impact [2].

Topological Embedding method has important properties that are the topology preservation and attributes encoding [2]. It uses a generic lexicon of topological structures as a non isomorphic graphs network composed of n edges up to N.

The Attributes Statistic based Embedding method maps an AG into a naive feature vector [2]. It computes the frequencies of simple sub-graph. It is limited to node coordinates space attributes and no consideration for edge attributes.

The Fuzzy Multilevel Graph Embedding (FMGE) method [2] defines a vector based on learning of histogram fuzzy intervals. It uses fuzzy logic to reduce noise, substructures homogeneity and topology information to reserve the structure and encoding edges and nodes attributes to be generic.

Compared to the state-of-the-art, our proposition is general since it encodes different types of graph attributes and robust to noise and structure preserved based on learning PGM [4].

3   Definitions and Notations

Our general GEM method is based on encoding an AG enriched by a topological attribute called Morgan Index (MI) into a vector. We will define the concepts: AG, explicit GEM and MI [1,7,8].

Definition 1. *AG: Let A_V and A_E denote the domains of possible values including null value for attributed vertices and edges respectively. An AG over (A_V, A_E) is undirected defined by a four-tuple: $AG = (V, E, \mu^V, \mu^E)$, where V is a set of vertices, $E \subseteq V \times V$ is a set of edges, $\mu^V : V \mapsto A_V^k$, V is function assigning*

k attributes to vertices and, $\mu^E : E \mapsto A^l_E$ is a function assigning l attributes to edges. AG order is given by $|V|$. AG size is given by $|E|$. The degree of a vertex v_i in AG is the number of edges connected to v_i.

Definition 2. *Explicit GEM: Given an AG, explicit GEM is a function ϕ, which maps graph AG from graph space G to a point $(f_1, f_2, \ldots, f_n)$ in n dimensional vector space $\mathbb{R}^n$. It is given as:*

$$\phi : G \mapsto R^n$$
$$AG \mapsto \phi(AG) = (f_1, f_2, \ldots, f_n)$$

Definition 3. *MI: Given an AG and a node $v \in AG$, MI of v as [8]:*

$$MI_i(v) = \begin{cases} MI_0(v) = node\_degree(v), & if\ i = 0 \\ \sum_u MI_{i-1}(u), & Otherwise \end{cases}$$

where u is a node adjacent to v, the MI of level 0 is the node degree, i is the level of Morgan Index and $MI_{i-1}(u)$ is the summation of the adjacent nodes degree of v in previous iteration $i - 1$ of the propagation MI technique.

Definition 4. *PGM: It is defined by observed and hidden variables X and Y as nodes of PGM and unary and pairwise feature functions Φ and Ψ as edges. The parametrized conditional probability distribution is:*

$$P(Y|X, \omega^c) = \frac{1}{Z(X,\omega)} \exp\left(\sum_{i \in V} \omega^c_i \Phi(x_i, y_i) + \sum_{(i,j) \in E} \omega^c_{i,j} \Psi(x_{i,j}, y_i, y_j) \right) \quad (1)$$

where the partition function is:

$$Z(X, \omega^c) = \sum_{x \in V} \exp\left(\sum_{i \in V} \omega^c_i \Phi(x_i, y_i) + \sum_{(i,j) \in E} \omega^c_{i,j} \Psi(x_{i,j}, y_i, y_j) \right) \quad (2)$$

where $\omega = \{(\omega^c_i, \omega^c_{i,j}), c \in classes\}$ is the set of unary and pairwise parameters.

4   Graph EMbedding by Probabilistic Graphical Model

Our general GEM method defines a learned parameter vector characterizing complex structure presented in PGM. It aims to find the best parameter vector ω^* that makes the probability distribution $P(y|x, \omega)$ close to $P(y|x)$. The structured learning problem is formulated in two steps: first, supervised learning of PGM parameters; second, this parameter vector should maximize to approximate the computation of predicted probabilities over the random variables in PGM. We use SSVM for learning [3]. Challenging questions on learning are (a) are we using the best learning algorithm for our problem? (b) do we have enough data for training? Is there other feature function that better models the AG?

4.1   Graph Attributes and Structure

As application framework in this paper, we have defined AGs or graphical symbols from the GREC database. The graph nodes represent x, y and *type* and graph edges *frequency*, *type* and *angle*. Here, we explain the different types of encoded attributes associated to the graph and the different types of used graph structures. First, we consider the symbolic/numeric attributes as the following:

- Geometrical attributes: associated to the nodes and edges of the AG, extracted from symbol drawing such as length and orientation of line and coordinates x and y of intersection points;
- Structural attributes: node degree and sub-graph homogeneity [1];
- Topological attributes: MI, with fixed level.

Different graph structures have been studied. (1) Full graph: it has attributes associated to nodes and edges; (2) Void graph: it has attributes associated only to nodes; (3) Connected graph: it has edges relating different nodes without attributes; (4) Unconnected graph: it has only attributed nodes.

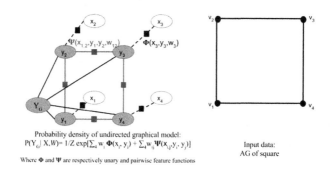

Probability density of undirected graphical model:
$P(Y_G| X,W)= 1/Z \exp[\sum_4 w_i \Phi(x_i, y_i) + \sum_4 w_{ij} \Psi(x_{ij}, y_i, y_j)]$

Where Φ and Ψ are respectively unary and pairwise feature functions

Input data:
AG of square

Fig. 1. AG of square symbol with four nodes connected with four edges where x_i is the one node attributes and $x_{i,j}$ is the one edge attributes represented by PGM.

4.2   Model the AG as PGM

We built the PGM based on an AG. We are given an $AG = (V, E, \mu^V, \mu^E)$ and a *PGM* defined by X that are observed variables and Y that are hidden variables and dependencies between these variables. x_i defines the label for the node v_i based on its attributes μ^{v_i} and y_i is hidden variable associated to it. The variables are connected according to AG structure of the input data, defined as the conditional independence structure of PGM. Thus, $x_{i,j}$ defines the attributes of the edge (i,j). The distribution probability defined over the PGM previously is based on the Definition 4 and the notation defined here based on the AG as input data. The output of our proposed general GEM is the n dimensional parameters vector defined by $\omega = \{(\omega_i^c, \omega_{i,j}^c), c \in classes\}$. $\mathcal{Y}^n$ is the n dimensional space that represents all the possible class configurations. The classification problem y' is defined as maximization problem: $y' = \mathrm{argmax}_{y \in \mathcal{Y}^n} P(y/x)$. We use a majority vote strategy to assign a class to AG. The most occurring over nodes' classes of AG chosen as the class for AG. Figure 1 is an example of modeling a symbol of shape square as undirected PGM where the class of the graph is Y_G.

5   Experimentation

We use GREC dataset [5] build as below. Images occur at five different distortion levels. For each distortion level one example of a drawing is given. Depending on the distortion level, either erosion, dilation, or other morphological operations are applied. Graphs are extracted from the resulting denoised images by tracing the lines from end to end and detecting intersections as well as corners. Nodes are ending points, corners, intersections and circles with their coordinates as attributes. Undirected edges links them and attributed by line or arc and angle with respect to the horizontal direction or the diameter in case of arcs. All graphs are distorted 9 times to obtain a data set containing 1,100 graphs uniformly distributed over the 22 classes. The maximum number of nodes and edges is respectively 25 and 30. They are balanced between training (286) and validation (286) and test (528). We computed some attributes as explained in Sect. 4.1. The level is equal to 2 for MI. We used Structured training library pystruct [9], particularly SSVM on its N-Slack formulation. Several experiments are done to study our proposition performance. First, we study N-Slack algorithm stability based on 3 parameters: the number of iterations, the regularization parameter C and the inference algorithm. Second, we evaluate the impact of different attributes on the Accuracy Rate (AR). Then, we analyze misclassification.

5.1   Training Algorithm Parameters Impact

We study the strength of the training algorithm SSVM based on its three parameters. The first is the iteration that is the maximum number of steps over

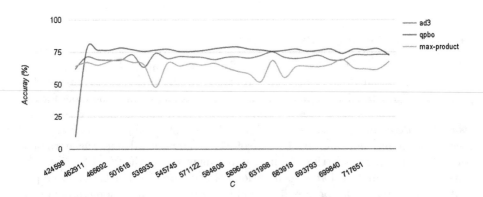

Fig. 2. Impact of inference methods.

dataset to find the constraints of SSVM algorithm. Secondly, C is the penalization parameter of the SSVM as defined in [3]. The third is the inference algorithm used on training, by the N-Slack algorithm and also on when building the GEM. First, while varying the iteration parameter, we get the same results of ER for the three inference algorithms. So, this parameter has no influence on SSVM.

Inference methods varies depending on the parameter C. They are Quadratic Pseudo-Boolean Optimization QPBO, approximate maximum a posteriori AD3 and belief propagation as an iterative, local, message-passing algorithm for finding the maximum a posteriori max-product. We vary C from $4 \cdot 10^5$ to $8 \cdot 10^5$ uniformly. AR varies from 9% to 77%. It increases respectively with the increase of C, from appreciatively 9% to 73% for QPBO, from 61% to 73% for AD3 and from 63% to 67%. We conclude that QPBO is the best compared to the others over the interval of C values in a way it always offers higher AR, see Fig. 2.

5.2 Impact of Structural and Topological Attributes

We evaluate the impact of attributes and structure on the performance of our approach. The graph structure is varying within the different structures defined in Sect. 4.1: unconnected graph, Void connected graph and Full connected graph. The used attributes can be: geometrical attributes, structural attributes and topological attributes. We use the inference unary for the case of unconnected graph and QPBO for the rest cases.

Table 1. SVM classification GREC dataset.

Input	Accuracy rate(AR %)		
Graph str./enriched	Geometrical att.	Structural att.	Topological att.
Full connected	59.1	71.4	76.22
Void connected	25.95	72.35	79.55
unconnected	16.66	15.34	32

Table 1 presents AR while learning more information, with best configuration of its parameters for each case of GREC graph. While varying the combination of parameters, we get flat ARs curves graphics. That's why, we addressed the problem to choose the best configuration by quadratic polynomial regression function corresponding to a list of a fixed random combinations values. The ARs have been obtained by employing SSVM classifier. Table 1 shows that the structural attributes added to the graph structure offer better ARs than geometrical attributes. Topological attributes provide better ARs than the structural attributes. This is first because the number of attributes for each graph is increasing while adding the structural and topological attributes. This is thanks to the fact that they provide severely discerning information about the graph. The embedded graph development clearly shows that our general GEM method gets a discriminatory power from structural and topological attributes.

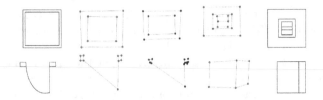

Fig. 3. 3 misclassified graphs. 1st row: ground truth of class 10, graph from class 10 labeled as 1, ground truth of class 1. 2nd row: ground truth of class 5, graph from class 5 labeled as 18, ground truth of class 18.

We compare our model with the FMGE [1] based on classification task. FMGE solves the problem of noise sensitivity and topology reservation by Fuzzy Logic and homogeneity information but our model solves it by learning structured dependencies in a probabilistic model. Our method provides 79% as AR. And FMGE presents 99.4%. Our current results are smaller than FMGE results. However, our proposed GEM guaranties the properties of noise robustness and structure preservation. Future work will focus on improving them by adapting more the used learning algorithm to AG.

5.3 Why Do We Have Such Classification Errors?

We will analyze misclassified Full connected graphs with topological attributes for $C \simeq 536$. Table 2 gives statistic about these mis-classifications. Each ground truth class is confused with a wrong predicted class with a percentage. This percentage is the number of assigned graphs to this wrong predicted class. For the first example, the class 10 is confused with class 1 (Fig. 3). Graph includes inside it unconnected small parts are negligible. Other examples of misclassified graphs, have the same problem. The GEM is neglecting small parts outside connected to big parts. For the second example, the edge in class 5 is of type arc. So, our GEM considers it as similar to an edge of type line. The 2nd example presents structure loss. For other examples, the model shows invariance to rotation. We categorize, somehow, the kind of errors as the following (see Fig. 3):

- negligence of: first, small parts that are: inside connected, outside connected, inside unconnected, second, small length edges. The edge relating two nodes very closely is negligible compared to the longest edge.
- confusion between geometrical attributes: arc and line of edges, the coordinates of nodes. It considers 2 nodes or 2 edges as 1.

Table 2. SVM classification GREC dataset with $C \simeq 536$.

Ground truth class	10	5	0	1	4	2	10	16	7	15	18	1	3	17	18	1	4	8	11	15	21
Predicted class	1	18	4	15	0	8	6	0,21	1	0	2	6	7	2	8	7	20	6,9,16	2	6	0,6
AR(%)	41	33	29	25		20.8			16.6			12.5				8.3					

6   Conclusion

Our general explicit GEM is demonstrated by learning PGM parameters vector of AG. This vector is the AG proposed signature in lower vectorial space. Classification results are encouraging. To improve, a suitable learning algorithm for AG and trying other learning methods are required.

Acknowledgment. This work has been partially supported by the Spanish project TIN2015-70924-C2-2-R and the CERCA Programme/Generalitat de Catalunya.

References

1. Luqman, M.M., Ramel, J.Y., Lladós, J., Brouard, T.: Fuzzy multilevel graph embedding. Pattern Recogn. **46**(2), 551–565 (2013)
2. Conte, D., Ramel, J.-Y., Sidère, N., Luqman, M.M., Gaüzère, B., Gibert, J., Brun, L., Vento, M.: A comparison of explicit and implicit graph embedding methods for pattern recognition. In: Kropatsch, W.G., Artner, N.M., Haxhimusa, Y., Jiang, X. (eds.) GbRPR 2013. LNCS, vol. 7877, pp. 81–90. Springer, Heidelberg (2013). doi:10.1007/978-3-642-38221-5_9
3. Joachims, T., Finley, T., Yu, C.N.J.: Cutting-plane training of structural SVMS. Mach. Learn. **77**(1), 27–59 (2009)
4. Nowozin, S., Lampert, C.H.: Structured learning and prediction in computer vision. Found. Trends Comput. Graph. Vis. **6**(3–4), 185–365 (2011)
5. Riesen, K., Bunke, H.: IAM graph database repository for graph based pattern recognition and machine learning. In: da Vitoria Lobo, N., et al. (eds.) SSPR/SPR 2008. LNCS, vol. 5342, pp. 287–297. Springer, Heidelberg (2008). doi:10.1007/978-3-540-89689-0_33
6. Santosh, K., Wendling, L.: Graphical symbol recognition. In: Wiley Encyclopedia of Electrical and Electronics Engineering (2015)
7. Fankhauser, S., Riesen, K., Bunke, H., Dickinson, P.: Suboptimal graph isomorphism using bipartite matching. Int. J. Pattern Recogn. Artif. Intell. **26**(06), 1250013 (2012)
8. Morgan, H.: The generation of a unique machine description for chemical structures-a technique developed at chemical abstracts service. J. Chem. Doc. **5**(2), 107–113 (1965)
9. Müller, A.C., Behnke, S.: Pystruct: learning structured prediction in python. J. Mach. Learn. Res. **15**(1), 2055–2060 (2014)

Automatic Documents Counterfeit Classification Using Image Processing and Analysis

Rafael Vieira[1], Mário Antunes[1,3(✉)], Catarina Silva[1,2], and Ana Assis[4]

[1] School of Technology and Management,
Polytechnic Institute of Leiria, Leiria, Portugal
2141500@my.ipleiria.pt, {mario.antunes,catarina}@ipleiria.pt
[2] Department of Informatics Engineering, Center for Informatics and Systems
of the University of Coimbra (CISUC), Coimbra, Portugal
catarina@dei.uc.pt
[3] Center for Research in Advanced Computing Systems (CRACS), INESC-TEC,
University of Porto, Porto, Portugal
mantunes@dcc.fc.up.pt
[4] Scientific Police Laboratory Judiciary Police, Lisbon, Portugal
ana.assis@pj.pt

Abstract. Counterfeit detection in official documents has challenged forensic experts on trying to correlate them to improve the identification of forgery authors by criminal investigators. Past counterfeit investigation on the Portuguese Police Forensic Laboratory allowed the construction of an organized set of digital images related to counterfeited documents, helping manual identification of new counterfeiters *modus operandi*. However, these images are usually stored in distinct resolutions, may have different sizes and could have been captured under different types of illumination.

In this paper we present a methodology to automate a counterfeit identification *modus operandi*, by comparing a given document image with a database of previously catalogued counterfeited documents images. The proposed method ranks the identified counterfeited documents and allows the forensic experts to drive their attention to the most similar documents. It takes advantage of scalable algorithms under the OpenCV framework that compare images, match patterns and analyse textures and colours. We present a set of tests with distinct datasets with promising results.

1 Introduction

Manipulation of digital documents images is gaining increasing interest by criminals that use forged documents on illegal activities. Among the most common forged documents, we may find citizen cards, driving licenses and passports. However, forgery activities may also be found in trademark symbols, currency notes, and official writting documents. The quality of image manipulation, reproduction, and printing is increasing and such activities are usually carried on by organized criminal groups with high level of technical and technological skills.

© Springer International Publishing AG 2017
L.A. Alexandre et al. (Eds.): IbPRIA 2017, LNCS 10255, pp. 400–407, 2017.
DOI: 10.1007/978-3-319-58838-4_44

Such forged documents and symbols can be produced by various digital techniques like resampling, copy-paste and splicing. After digital production, most of these documents are printed in high quality systems that could deceive even experienced professionals.

Forensic laboratories apply a wide set of illumination techniques to identify the printing processes that were used in a questioned document, and to analyze other security features (holograms, watermarks and others).

Verification of old cases, similar to the current one being analyzed, is carried out and if a match is found, the counterfeit is identified and a correlation with all the identical cases already detected in the past will be successfully achieved. Otherwise, a new counterfeit identification will be created for the case, for future new and unseen correlations. The whole process is mostly manual in Portuguese Police Forensic Laboratory. Assuming a reasonable number of documents stored in an organized set of previously identified counterfeit documents, which will involve several interactions between the input document and the examples stored in the documents database, the time involved in the manual analysis may the prohibitive and hamper ongoing investigations.

Image detection algorithms aim to distinguish different types of features and printing techniques in specific regions of an image. That is, to identify the area of the document to be processed and the type of tests and comparisons that should be applied. The algorithm should also be able to deal with the content of the data source, like the type of document and illumination that was used, and to identify if it is the front or back of the document. Having such a heterogeneous set of examples, it is expected that the performance of the algorithm could be affected by both the lack of documents normalization and the number related stored images. Some issues that may delude the algorithm include images with ultraviolet filters, the existence of zoomed zones and the existence of a scale rule. A way to deal with these issues is to consider only the documents that match the overall criteria related with the country, type of document and main printing technique. For example, if the input example is a Portuguese identity card, only these examples, regardless of the printing technique that was used, will be processed.

After collecting the stored images that share the same type of document and country with the input example, the next step is to rank them by a level of similitude. This methodology does not intend to replace the human intervention. Instead, aims to drive forensic experts attentions to the most relevant documents, that is those that have closer affinity and higher similitude with the input document being analysed.

The rest of the paper is organized as follows. Section 2 presents the fundamentals regarding image processing algorithms and fraud techniques applied to documents. Section 3 details the proposed methodology and the experimental setup adopted. Section 4 depicts the results obtained and further analyses them. Section 5 presents the conclusions and delineates future lines of research.

2   Background

In this section we present the main background topics that are needed to understand this work, namely the meaning of counterfeit in security documents and an introduction to OpenCV and its most relevant algorithms for this work digital image processing.

2.1   Types of Counterfeiting

Counterfeit documents are usually reproductions or imitations of the originals ones. Counterfeiters start by producing a digital version, or a "copy", of the original document. Next, they produce the physical document by printing the digital image in a material similar to the original. For this purpose, there is a wide set of innovative and high quality materials and printing techniques that sometimes makes the fake document almost indistinguishable from the original [1].

A set of physical and chemical techniques and methodologies are used to analyze all the materials and security features of a document (e.g. watermarks, fluorescent fibers and planchettes, guilloche pattern, fluorescent and magnetic inks, optically variable inks, rainbow printing, microprinting, latent images, scrambled indicia, laser printing, photos, signatures, embossing, stamps, optically variable devices, protective films, perforations, machine readable security and retro-reflective pattern), and thus to identify it as false or genuine. The use of these techniques aims to conduct to the discovery of the counterfeiting characteristics.

2.2   Algorithms for Image Processing

OpenCV (www.opencv.org) is a well-known and very popular open source library for computer vision that has a wide set of tools for digital image processing.

The Harris Corner Detection algorithm [2] uses a mathematic model to detect corners and edges using a function that calculates a correlation. This function considers window in the image and determines the average changes of image intensity that result from shifting the window by a small amount of pixels in various directions. It is used to detect corners in digital images, by comparing the same area in both fake and genuine documents.

Lowe proposed the Scale-Invariant Feature Transform (SIFT) algorithm [3]. SIFT was created with the purpose to be invariant to image scale and rotation, that is not to affect the corner detection by image zoom.

Bay et al. presented a new variation of SIFT, named Speeded-Up Robust Features (SURF) [4], which obtains an optimized version to computer vision processing. Rosten and Drummond developed the Fast Algorithm for Corner Detection (FAST) [5], aiming to have better performance in real time applications.

Rublee et al. developed Oriented fast and Rotated Brief (ORB) algorithm [6], that can be seen as a mix of SIFT and FAST algorithms. OpenCV framework includes an implementation of ORB free implementation along with other functionalities to deal with patterns detection in digital images.

3   Proposed Methodology to Automate Couterfeited Document Analysis

In [7] we have described a deployed methodology to automate the analysis process of a counterfeit document. The overall process is depicted in Fig. 1. Firstly, the input document is compared with the stored documents that match the criteria. Keypoint descriptors algorithms, like SURF, SIFT and ORB present in the OpenCV framework, are applied, to analyse texture, compare image areas and detect similar imperfections between both documents. For each comparison an array of pixel characteristics is produced and finally, based on all the arrays obtained, a rank of images more similar to the input document is presented [7].

For testing purposes we deployed a client/server web based application. The image processing application was built in $C++$ with OpenCV version 2.4.9. Past counterfeit images are stored in a PostgreSQL version 9.5 database accessed through an Apache version 2.4.7 web server with PHP version 5.5.9.

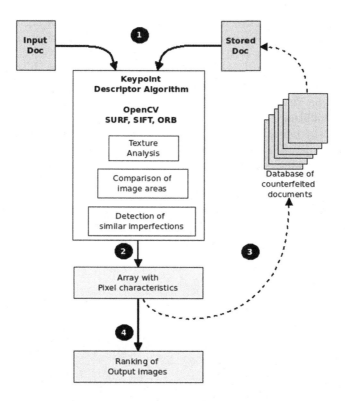

Fig. 1. Automation method for counterfeit classification

4   Tests Setup and Experimental Results

Our tests covered three distinct types of images: a trademark symbol (Subsect. 4.1), an *old* Portuguese Identity Card (Subsect. 4.2) and a Portuguese passport card (Subsect. 4.3). Using SURF algorithm, we have computed the closeness between the input document and the selected images that match the initial criteria (e.g. country, type of document and printing process), by identifying for each image the most important keypoints.

The final score denotes a percentage of similitude that was calculated by the arithmetic average of all the similar keypoints between the input document and all the stored images.

4.1   Test 1 - Trademark Symbol

Trademark symbols are appealing images that, for criminals, are worth counterfeiting. These fake symbols may be printed and further attached to counterfeited goods like clothing parts. In this example we've used a trade symbol of a Portuguese football team that sells a wide variety of merchandising clothes, like caps, scarfs, shirts and sports shorts. The trade symbol is printed in a fabric label and attached to fake clothes, being sold as genuine and "official" products.

We have compared an input image, which represents a counterfeit symbol, against a dataset of 109 stored images of similar counterfeits. Figure 2 illustrates the input image (Fig. 2(a)) and the "top 4" images with which there is a higher similitude, respectively 90.65%, 85.36%, 81.57% and 70.32%. Even though Fig. 2(b) belongs to the same case, and thus is supposed to have the highest similitude, the others images are related to different ones and the calculated similitude value is above 85%. The execution time for this test was 18 s.

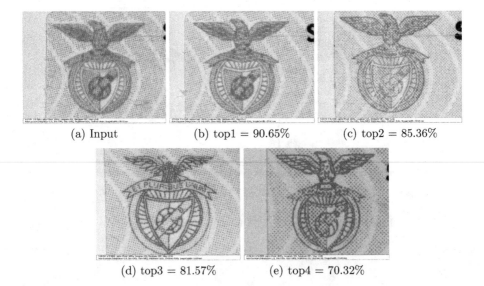

(a) Input   (b) top1 = 90.65%   (c) top2 = 85.36%

(d) top3 = 81.57%   (e) top4 = 70.32%

Fig. 2. Water mark of a counterfeit trade symbol

4.2   Test 2 - Portuguese Identity Card

The second test involves the old version of the Portuguese Identity Card, that was replaced by a new and more secure version in January 2008. Although no new *old* identification cards had been delivered since then, there exists a vast number of citizens that still hold it, which provides forgery opportunity and consequently used in illicit activities.

In this test the input image is the area of the Coat-of-Arms of the Portuguese Republic, a part of the Portuguese Identity Card that is frequently counterfeited. We have compared the input image against a dataset of 1368 images, that include forged images of both the whole identity cards and also part of the card with the Coat-of-Arms. The results are shown in Fig. 3. The input image (Fig. 3(a)) has the higher levels of similitude with the illustrated top four images, with the following values: 94.64%, 86.23%, 84.45% and 83.70%. The execution time for this test was 5 min and 32 s.

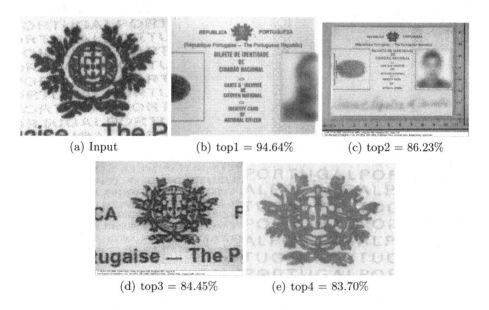

(a) Input   (b) top1 = 94.64%   (c) top2 = 86.23%

(d) top3 = 84.45%   (e) top4 = 83.70%

Fig. 3. Portuguese Identity Card counterfeit

4.3   Test 3 - Portuguese Passport

The third test was made with the Portuguese passport and follows the aim of the test described in Sect. 3. Passports are appealing documents to forge and to use in illicit activities, namely those related with illegal immigration and false identity issues.

We have compared an input image of the Portuguese Coat-of-Arms, that is stamped in the passport front cover, against a dataset of 628 stored images. The results are shown in Fig. 4, which depicts the input image (Fig. 4(a)) followed

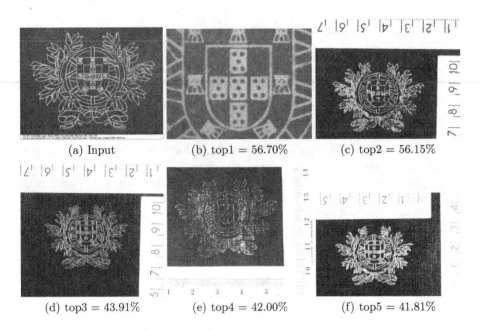

(a) Input   (b) top1 = 56.70%   (c) top2 = 56.15%

(d) top3 = 43.91%   (e) top4 = 42.00%   (f) top5 = 41.81%

Fig. 4. Portuguese passport counterfeit

by the top five documents with which it has higher similitude. In this case, the level of similitude is respectively 56.70%, 56.15%, 43.91%, 42.00% and 41.81%. The execution time for this test was 4 min and 34 s.

In this test the levels of similitude are around 50%, which gives lower confidence to the experts when comparing with the previous tests. With this kind of results forensics experts should have to pay more attention into the details when manually examining the documents.

5   Conclusion

The purpose of this paper was to deal with the correlation of images of forged documents, in order to identify similar *modus operandi*. For a criminal investigation, this correlation is essential to retrieve information about the counterfeited documents manufacturer source.

Nowadays, this process of obtaining a similitude correlation between previous cases and the new ones is carried out mostly manually with a related human resources time consuming. To fulfill this gap, we developed a system that uses visual computing algorithms that computes a degree of similitude for each image in the dataset, by giving a source image. Results obtained and presented in this paper reinforce the robustness of the overall architecture, the algorithm we have developed to rank the images and the image processing framework and algorithms we have used.

The algorithm was designed to avoid false-negatives, which results in a possibility of having entries in the top candidates with a low similitude degree, that is somewhere between 50% and 60%. These situations were observed in the tests with the Portuguese passport and emphasizes the importance of having the validation by the forensics expert. The methodology we have developed is a decision support system in a way that, at the end, forensic experts will always have the last work and decide about the forged document classification.

It is worth noting that images have different values in some important features, like resolution, the use of filters, the size and the region being analysed. That is, in some cases the algorithm has to compare a small portion of the input image against a region (or regions) of the stored images that have that kind of pattern. This architecture is now being under evaluation at Portuguese judiciary police. According to the results obtained thus far, a manual observation that could take from 15 min (in the most obvious cases) to hours, can now be reduced with this system to less than 7 min in complex cases. Our further developments go towards the following two main directions: to implement a GPU parallel computing version; to evaluate the effectiveness of using this system with other kind of official documents or images, like stamps and banknotes.

Acknowledgments. This work is financed by the ERDF - European Regional Development Fund through the Operational Programme for Competitiveness and Internationalisation - COMPETE 2020 Programme within project POCI-01-0145-FEDER-006961, and by National Funds through the FCT - Fundacão para a Ciência e a Tecnologia (Portuguese Foundation for Science and Technology) as part of project UID/EEA/50014/2013.

References

1. Bertrand, R., Gomez-Krmer, P., Ramos Terrades, O., Franco, P., Ogier, J.-M.: A system based on intrinsic features for fraudulent document detection. In: 2013 12th International Conference on Document Analysis and Recognition, pp. 106–110. IEEE (2013)
2. Harris, C., Stephens, M.: A combined corner and edge detector. In: Alvey Vision Conference, vol. 15, No. 50 (1988)
3. Lowe, D.G.: Distinctive image features from scale-invariant keypoints. Int. J. Comput. Vis. **60**(2), 91–110 (2004)
4. Bay, H., Ess, A., Tuytelaars, T., Van Gool, L.: Speeded-up robust features (SURF). Comput. Vis. Image Underst. **110**(3), 346–359 (2008)
5. Rosten, E., Drummond, T.: Machine learning for high-speed corner detection. In: Leonardis, A., Bischof, H., Pinz, A. (eds.) ECCV 2006. LNCS, vol. 3951, pp. 430–443. Springer, Heidelberg (2006). doi:10.1007/11744023_34
6. Rublee, E., Rabaud, V., Konolige, K., Bradski, G.: ORB: an efficient alternative to SIFT or SURF. In: 2011 International conference on computer vision, pp. 2564–2571. IEEE (2011)
7. Vieira, R., Silva, C., Antunes, M., Assis, A.: Information system for automation of counterfeited documents images correlation. Procedia Comput. Sci. **100**, 421–428 (2016)

Computer Vision

Feature-Based Scaffolding for Object Tracking

Carlos Orrite$^{(\boxtimes)}$ and Elena Pollo

Instituto de Investigacion en Ingenieria de Aragon,
University of Zaragoza, Zaragoza, Spain
corrite@unizar.es
http://i3a.unizar.es/

Abstract. This paper aims at the development of a video-based object tracking algorithm capable to achieve stable and reliable results in a complex situation, facing illumination variation, shape and scale change, background clutter, appearance change caused by camera moving, partial occlusions, etc. The proposal is based on modelling the target object at multiple resolutions by an attributed graph at every scale. Barycentric coordinates are an elegant way to transfer the structure information of a triangle in a particular scale to the neighbouring vertices in the graph to a different scale. The tracking is based on two steps: On the one hand a hill climbing approach is followed to track keypoints. On the other hand the structure of the graph is taken into account to filter out false assignments. The tracking process starts in a rough scale and further it is refined in lower scales to finally localize the keypoints.

Keywords: Tracking · Feature descriptors · Attribute graph · Mean-shift

1 Introduction

Video-based object tracking has become one of the hottest topics in computer vision due to its relevant application in different fields. In spite of the large literature dealing with this hot issue, it remains a challenging topic for achieving stable and reliable tracking results in a complex situation, facing illumination variation, shape and scale change, background clutter, appearance change caused by camera moving, partial occlusions, etc.

A large number of vision applications, such as visual correspondence, object matching, 3D reconstruction and motion tracking, rely on matching keypoints across images. Effective and efficient generation of keypoints from an image is a well-studied problem in the literature and constitutes the basis of many Computer Vision applications. In a recent paper, authors evaluate state-of-the-art (SIFT, SURF, BRIEF, BRISK, ORB and FREAK) detectors and descriptors in object class matching [1]. Their experiments provided interesting findings in regard to object matching, proposing new research on optimization of the detector joined to specialized descriptors for visual class parts and regions and dense scaling and rotation invariant interest points.

© Springer International Publishing AG 2017
L.A. Alexandre et al. (Eds.): IbPRIA 2017, LNCS 10255, pp. 411–418, 2017.
DOI: 10.1007/978-3-319-58838-4_45

In general all the applications using these descriptors suffer from two main drawbacks. On the one hand, these features were devised for a general purpose. So that it can be seen as a benefit, they can be used for 3D reconstruction or motion tracking, may be considered as a limitation, because they do not take into account the intrinsic nature of the problem to tackle. On the other hand, they are local representations of the image, decomposing and image into local regions of interest or features. In this sense, only a few work has been developed to join this set of local features to global structure. In [2] the authors propose an attribute graph to represent the structure of a target object in the problem of tracking it along time. The structure of the model yields in the change of shape when the object moves, adapting continuously the edge ratio in each triangle of the graph. As in many other computer vision problems when adapting the model according to the appearance of the object it can easily degenerate to loose the target when the model no longer fit to the object.

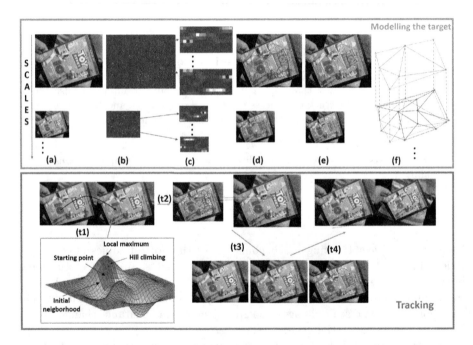

Fig. 1. Overview of our approach. Top: Modelling the target. Bottom: Tracking.

1.1   Overview of the Paper

Inspired by [2], in this work the target object is represented by an attribute graph, where its vertices represent salient features (keypoints) and its edges encode their spatial relationships. The edges are inserted following the rules of the Delaunay triangulation. Moreover, as the target may suffer from changes in scale we propose to model it by several graphs each of them capturing the most representative features at each scale. Barycentric coordinates are an elegant way to transfer the information of a triangle to the previous scale neighbouring vertices in the graph structure. This scaffolding structure allows holding the relationship between keypoints at different scales.

Figure 1 shows graphically the two main contributions of this paper, i.e., the modelling of the target and the tracking process. Figure 1(a) shows the original image sub-sampled at different scales; (b) feature detectors; (c) feature descriptors; (d) attributed graph for these feature keypoints; (e) refined attributed graph; (f) relationship between attributed graphs at different scales. Tracking: (t1) keypoint tracker based on mean-shift; (t2) structure refinement and keypoint projection to the next scale; (t3) mean-shift in the new scale and correction by structure model; (t4) corner detection by keypoint homography.

In order to compare our results with previous works, we have chosen the standard approach followed so far for feature matching, see for example [3]. It relies on several steps. The first one is to find feature points in each image. Next, keypoint descriptors are matched for each pair of images using the approximate nearest neighbour (ANN). After matching features for an image pair the fundamental matrix is robustly estimated for the pair using RANSAC [4] in order to determinate inliers. Although RANSAC works well in many cases, there is no guarantee that it will obtain a reasonable solution even if there exists one.

2   Keypoint Detection for Tracking

In this paper we start defining the feature descriptor best suitable for tracking taking into account changes in orientation. Later, we propose some rules to detect keypoints at different scales.

2.1   Feature Descriptor: Matrix of Oriented Gradients

As mentioned before there exits many algorithms to find local image features. According to [5] the most accurate and robust techniques are based on Histograms of Oriented Gradientes (HOG) such as SIFT and SURF descriptors which are statistics from the HOG. However, in each of these cases, the gradients must be oriented for the descriptor to be rotation-invariant. Some authors [5] simplify this approach by computing gradients which are intrinsically rotation-invariant by computing radial gradients. This approach is computationally costly as it involves the change from Cartesian gradients to Radial gradients. Moreover, it does not take into account the intrinsic nature of the problem we are tackling, i.e., tracking. In this sense, we propose a feature descriptor which organizes gradients in a radial way, as graphically depicted in Fig. 2. This Matrix of oriented gradients exhibits an interesting property when the image suffers from a rotation, as graphically shown in Fig. 2 (right), where the target is rotated by $\pi/2$, the same rotation experimented by the gradients. So, when tracking a target it is just necessary to track only an angle in the matrix (for example θ) as the other

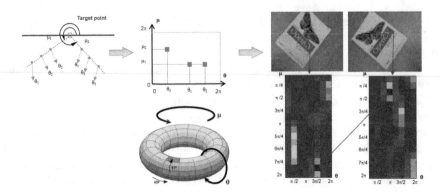

Fig. 2. Feature descriptor: (Left) Matrix of oriented gradients around the target; (left bottom) toroidal representation; (right) how this matrix changes with target rotation.

(μ) will be the same. It allows to reorganize the matrix into a vector in an easy way without any complex matrix correlation to obtain the maximum between the target and the object in the image.

2.2   Feature Detector for Tracking

Once the feature descriptor has been introduced and taking into account the nature of the tracking algorithm, we establish a set of criteria in order to determinate the most relevant keypoints in an image. It is well known that features have to be discriminant, reliable and the lowest number of them.

Discriminant means to determinate those keypoints in the target model which can suffer a greatest displacement in the image and the hill climbing procedure will be able to localize the maximum. In a naive approach we can consider that the point at time t yields in the same position and orientation in time $t + 1$. The hill climbing algorithm is in charge to find the new position. The more displacement has suffered the point, the more iterations the algorithm needs to converge and it will only converge to the right point if it first does not find a local maximum outlier. Therefore, we have analysed all points in the image and considering how far it could be from the initial position.

The other property to take into account is the reliability, i.e., how reliable is any point in presence of noise? We have identified two kinds of situations. Firstly, those points belonging to flat regions. For this particular picture we can find some good discriminant points belonging to this area. However, in incoming pictures this situation can be reversed due to noise. Noise will be more dangerous for keypoints with low values in its HoG. So, in order to determinate keypoints we reject those points exhibiting low HoG, i.e. flatness regardless how discriminant is that point taking for hill climbing. The second situation under analysis faces high HoG points corresponding to borders, what we consider as uniqueness. Noise can affect in the same way as before and what was the highest point in the hill climbing procedure may be assigned a neighbour in the next frame due to noise. Therefore, those points belonging to a contour are rejected.

3   Appearance and Structural Based Tracker

The tracking is based on two steps: On the one hand a hill climbing approach is followed to track keypoints. On the other hand the structure of the graph is taken into account to filter out false assignments. The tracking process starts in a rough scale and further it is refined in lower scales to finally localize the keypoints. Figure 1 (traking) shows our proposal for the appearance-structure tracker, where (t1) represents the keypoint tracker based on mean-shift; (t2) structure refinement between scales and keypoint projection to the next scale; (t3) mean-shift in the new scale and correction by structure model; (t4) corner detection by keypoint homography.

Hill climbing is employed as appearance-based tracker, where appearance is the matrix of oriented gradients used as feature descriptor for every keypoint. This procedure constitutes the core of some well-known tracking algorithms such as Mean-shift or Cam-shift. In each frame, it finds the locally optimal position p for each keypoint. This takes place in an iterative process, starting from the previous frame position. Hill climbing searches, in a local neighbourhood, for a position which maximizes the similarity to the feature descriptor of the model, as graphically depicted in Fig. 1 (tracking).

To estimate the 2D position (x, y) of the keypoint as well as its orientation μ, hill climbing is accomplished in three dimensions. A matrix of oriented gradients around the estimated new state $s = \{x, y, \mu\}$ is calculated as descriptor $M_{\mu, \theta}(I(s, t))$. In order to calculate the similarity of the new matrix with the original k-ies keypoint descriptor, a similarity measurement is determined by the Bhattacharyya coefficient $BC(p, q) = \sum_{b=1}^{128} \sqrt{p(b)q(b)}$, being p y q the 128 bin histograms obtained by reordering the respective matrix seen in Sect. 2.

4   Experimental Results

Next, we describe a set of experiments used to verify our theoretical results. We use the Stanford Streaming Mobile Augmented Reality Data Set for testing [6]. In this work we use 4 videos for moving objects recorded with a moving camera where the ground-through is provided: Barry White Moving, Chris Brown Moving, Titanic Moving, and Toy Story Moving. These videos help to study the effect of background clutter when there is a relative motion between the object and the background. Each video is 100 frames long, recorded at 30 fps with resolution 640 × 480 with different amounts of camera motion, glare, blur, zoom, rotation and perspective changes. In order to test the robustness of our approach in relation to partial occlusions, we occlude one corner in every frame of the video-sequence with a square generated by the background clutter. We repeat the experiment for the four corners. The degree of occlusion for some frames is up to 70% of the target region, as shown in Fig. 3. All experiments have been implemented in Matlab. For all datasets we use the SIFT descriptor, running the code provided by [7]. The algorithm provides a feature vector of salient keypoints. For every keypoint the x and y coordinates, the scale and

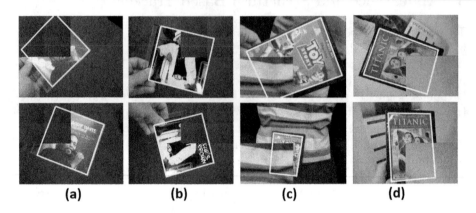

Fig. 3. The four moving objects under several partial occlusions. (a) Barry White Moving; (b) Chris Brown Moving; (c) ToyStory Moving; (d) Titanic Moving. Top row shows the starting frame and the bottom one the last frame in the sequence.

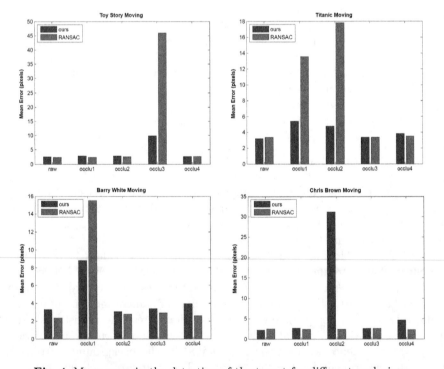

Fig. 4. Mean error in the detection of the target for different occlusions.

the orientation are given. Additionally, the code provides a 128-d histogram as feature descriptor for every keypoint. It is well known that Hellinger measures outperform Euclidean distance when comparing histograms. So, in our experiments we follow the so called RootSIFT approach proposed by [8] to improve the matching. As the Hellinger distance goes from 0 to 1, we use a 0.95 value as a threshold to valid the feature descriptor matching. approximated nearest neighbour (ARR) is computed by k-d tree. In these experiments we compared the performance of the proposed algorithm with that of RANSAC provided by [9]. For all these methods, the number of iterations was set to 100, and in each iteration the fundamental matrix was calculated using the eight-point algorithm, the Chi squared probability threshold for inliers is set to 0.99.

Figure 4 shows the mean error for the four corners along the whole sequence for the four datasets. We consider the case of no occlusion and the four kind of occlusions shown in Fig. 3. In general both methods under study, structural based tracker and RANSAC behave in a similar way. However, under occlusions and for some frames, the corners are not properly localized giving as a result a peak in the mean error. More precisely, there are four cases when RANSAC approach is not able to localize the corners by only two in our approach.

To highlight our approach we have run a new experiment where the occlusion patch is very similar to the target. Figure 5 shows an example where the RANSAC approach fails to match points between the target and the image. The mismatch assignment is represented in broader line, showing that both points have identical feature descriptor provided by SIFT but structurally they cannot be matched. When all the sequence is considered, we obtain a mean error of $8.5 pixels$ for our approach and $15.9 pixels$ following RANSAC filtering.

Fig. 5. RANSAC fails to filter out a mismatching for two similar descriptors.

5   Conclusions and Future Work

In education, scaffolding refers to a variety of instructional techniques used to move students progressively toward stronger understanding. In addition, scaffolding is often used to bridge learning gaps. In this paper we have extended this idea to object tracking by modelling the target at different scales by an attributed graph. When tracking we start at a rough scales, in which the target may have suffered a great change in pose and it is further localized at lower scales. The occlusion problem is solved by the structure graph, assigning keypoints equally spread over the target roi. Preliminary results using the Stanford Streaming Mobile Augmented Reality Dataset have confirmed the better performance of our approach in relation to traditional methods based on RANSAC.

Acknowledgements. This work was partially supported by Spanish Grant TIN2013-45312-R (MINECO), Gobierno de Aragon and the European Social Found.

References

1. Hietanen, A., Lankinen, J., Buch, A.G., Kämäräinen, J.-K., Küger, N.: A comparison of feature detectors and descriptors for object class matching. Neurocomputing **184**, 3–12 (2016)
2. Artner, N.M., Kropatsch, W.G.: Structural cues in 2D tracking: edge lengths vs. Barycentric coordinates. In: Ruiz-Shulcloper, J., Sanniti di Baja, G. (eds.) CIARP 2013. LNCS, vol. 8259, pp. 503–511. Springer, Heidelberg (2013). doi:10.1007/978-3-642-41827-3_63
3. Snavely, N., Seitz, S.M., Szeliski, R.: Modeling the world from internet photo collections. Int. J. Comput. Vis. **80**(2), 189–210 (2008)
4. Fischler, M.A., Bolles, R.C.: Random sample consensus: a paradigm for model fitting with applications to image analysis and automated cartography. Commun. ACM **24**(6), 381–395 (1981)
5. Takacs, G., Chandrasekhar, V., Tsai, S.S., Chen, D.M., Grzeszczuk, R., Girod, B.: Fast computation of rotation-invariant image features by an approximate radial gradient transform. IEEE Trans. Image Process. **22**(8), 2970–2982 (2013)
6. Chandrasekhar, V.R., Chen, D.M., Tsai, S.S., Cheung, N.-M., Chen, H., Takacs, G., Reznik, Y., Vedantham, R., Grzeszczuk, R., Bach, J., Girod, B.: The Stanford mobile visual search data set. In: Proceedings of the Second Annual ACM Conference on Multimedia Systems, pp. 117–122 (2011)
7. Vedaldi, A., Fulkerson, B.: VLFeat: an open and portable library of computer vision algorithms (2008). http://www.vlfeat.org/
8. Arandjelović, R., Zisserman, A.: Three things everyone should know to improve object retrieval. In: IEEE Conference on Computer Vision and Pattern Recognition (2012)
9. Kovesi, P.: RANSACFITFUNDMATRIX fits fundamental matrix using RANSAC (2005). http://www.vlfeat.org/

Sign Language Gesture Recognition Using HMM

Zuzanna Parcheta[1(⊠)] and Carlos-D. Martínez-Hinarejos[2]

[1] Sciling S.L., Carrer del Riu 321, Pinedo, 46012 Valencia, Spain
zparcheta@sciling.com
[2] Pattern Recognition and Human Language Technology Research Center,
Universitat Politècnica de València,
Camino de Vera, s/n, 46022 Valencia, Spain

Abstract. Gesture recognition is very useful in everyday life for tasks related to computer-human interaction. Gesture recognition systems are usually tested with a very large, complete, standardised and intuitive database of gesture: sign language. Unfortunately, such data is typically very large and contains very similar data which makes difficult to create a low cost system that can differentiate a large enough number of signs. This makes difficult to create a useful tool for allowing deaf people to communicate with the hearing people. The present work presents a sign recognition system for the Spanish sign language. The experiments conducted include separated gesture recognition and sequences of gestures. This work extends previous work by augmenting the size of data set (91 signs), higher than most of the state of the art systems (around 20 gestures). Apart from that, the proposed recognition system performs recognition of dynamic gestures, in contrast to most studies that use static gestures, which are easier to recognise. Finally, the work studies the recognition of sequences of gestures corresponding to grammatically correct phrases in Spanish sign language. For both tasks, Hidden Markov Models are used as recognition models. Results presented for classification of separated gestures are compared with other usual classification techniques, showing a better recognition performance. The current data set, which has been captured using the *Leap Motion* sensor, will be publicly available to the research community in gesture recognition.

Keywords: Gesture classification · Sign language translator · HTK · Leap Motion · HMM · K-NN · DTW

1 Introduction

In the world there are 70 million deaf people who use sign language as their first language [1]. In case of Spain, there are over 100,000 people native users of Spanish sign language (LSE). To communicate with non-users, interpreter service is required. However, this service is available only in special situations, such as interactions with police, help with administrative matters, etc. At the moment there is no tool that facilitates communication between deaf and hearing

© Springer International Publishing AG 2017
L.A. Alexandre et al. (Eds.): IbPRIA 2017, LNCS 10255, pp. 419–426, 2017.
DOI: 10.1007/978-3-319-58838-4_46

people in everyday life. From a long time ago, researchers have been struggling to create a tool that can automatically translate sign language into oral language. Therefore, the main motivation of this work is to explore tools and models that, in the future, can become an aid in the daily life of the deaf people.

More formally, this work deals mainly with gesture recognition of Spanish sign language by means of Hidden Markov Models (HMM) and their comparison with other techniques such as K-Nearest Neighbour (K-NN) and Dynamic Time Warping (DTW). The gesture acquisition tool is from the *Leap Motion* sensor[1]. Paper is organised as follows: Sect. 2 presents previous related work, Sect. 3 describes the followed methodology, Sect. 4 provides the experimental framework and the results, and Sect. 5 summarises conclusions and future work lines.

2   Related Work

Current state of the art in the area of gesture recognition covers different approximations. There are many studies on sign gesture recognition but most of them are related gestures corresponding to alphabetical signs. In such case, the set of data is very reduced (about 25 gestures) and signs are typically static. Hence, the gestures can be captured with a digital image camera. For example, in [2], they recognised 23 gestures from the Colombian sign language alphabet in which they obtained a 98.15% of accuracy. In [3] similar techniques were used, but in addition to a digital camera to capture data, they also used the *Kinect* sensor. From 30 gestures they could recognise 20 signs using a digital camera and 25 using the *Kinect* sensor. The work presented in [4] also used *Kinect* combined with Dynamic Time Warping (DTW) to obtain a 96.7% of accuracy using a data set consisting of 8 different gestures with 28 samples per gesture class.

Other studies only used three dimensional data captured with different sensors. For example, in [5], experiments of classification of 18 dynamics signs were conducted by using *Leap Motion* for data capture. The gesture data was separated into 2 parts: *(1)* the static part, which was the initial shape of the hand before conducting a gesture, which was recognised using K-NN; and *(2)* the trajectory followed by the hand during the gesture, which was recognised by DTW. The accuracy in case *(1)* was 95.8% and in case *(2)* was 86.1%. However, the gesture was only considered to be correctly recognised if both parts match, giving a final accuracy of 44.4%. In [6], phrases from American sign language formed by 40 different signs were recognised. This data set comprised 395 of 5 words each one. 99 phrases were dedicated to evaluation purposes and the rest to training. The training and the recognition was done using Hidden Markov Models. The gestures were captured using a digital camera. The accuracy of this experiment was a 95%. Surprisingly, very few works are found in the literature (apart from this one) that employ HMM for sign language recognition.

The current work provides a study about recognition of phrases of sign language with a larger size (when compared to previous work) data set. Also,

---

[1] https://www.leapmotion.com/product/desktop.

the novelty of this work is about providing a study about the gestures recognition using HMM and a sensor which provides 3D data.

3   Methodology

3.1   The *Leap Motion* Sensor

Leap Motion is an optimised sensor in order to obtain three-dimensional information from hands gestures. The gesture device emits infrared light with which illuminates its effective range. Objects in the effective range reflect infrared light, and depending on the amount of light incident on the two-camera lenses incorporated in the sensor, it is possible to determine how far a given object is from the sensor. Of all the gestural interfaces available in the market, this one was chosen because it is optimised to obtain three-dimensional information from the hands. In addition, it is very small and discreet, it has a suitable effective range for gestures of sign language, it has a very complete application programming interface (API), it is very precise, and it has a good quality/price ratio. Apart from all these advantages it has certain limitations. For instance, it has many problems with gestures where hands overlap or touch one another. Therefore, the gestures used in this work are approximations to the real gestures of sign language. Also, sunlight interferes with the sensor, producing noise, because its operating principles are based on the reflection of infrared light.

3.2   Hidden Markov Models

For years, HMMs have had special success in speech recognition [7]. Nowadays they constitute a popular technique applied for modelling time sequence data, like gesture recognition [8], recognition of handwritten text [9], etc. The HMM represents probability distributions over sequences of hidden states and observations. Two types of HMMs exist according to the kind of symbols observed: discrete HMMs, where the symbols correspond to discrete magnitudes, and continuous, if the symbols correspond to continuous magnitudes [10]. In this work, HMMs are used for gesture recognition. In this case, the emitted symbols are feature vectors in a real space (i.e., continuous HMM were used) obtained from the gestures corresponding to signs from LSE.

3.3   Hidden Markov Model Toolkit

The Hidden Markov Model Toolkit (*HTK*) [11] is a set of tools created to manipulate HMMs. *HTK* was primarily created to manipulate data for speech recognition, but it can also be used to solve other problems by using stochastic analysis techniques, such as image recognition, determination of valid sequences of human DNA, or gesture recognition. The architecture of *HTK* for HMM management is very flexible and allows to adjust multiple parameters depending on the type and the complexity of the problem to solve. For all these reasons, this tool was used for the experiments commented in this article.

4 Experimental Framework

4.1 3D Data Set

For the experiments, an own data set was created with the idea of making it public[2]. The gestures that compose our database approach the LSE gestures due to the limitations of the sensor. Sampling has been carried out with the software described in [5], where only one-hand signs were performed. For this work, gestures were made with one and both hands. This program segments different gestures when the movement amount threshold[3] is exceeded. The program starts capturing the data, and ends the capture when the variable that describes the amount of movement produced goes below the threshold. The sampling rate is fixed at 30 frames per second. The sensor provides the data in numerical format. Finally, a gesture is a matrix where the number of rows is the number of captured images and the number of columns is the number of observed variables.

The variables involved were the directions on the X, Y and Z axes of each hand and each finger, where each of them describe the direction in one of the axes (i.e., the hand/finger points) and the inclination of the hand according to the X, Y and Z axes (which expresses the hand angle with respect to the horizontal plane). In total, 21 variables are available for each hand, that is, 42 variables in total. In order to avoid training problems with *HTK*, when single-hand gestures appeared, the data of the other hand were replicated from the data of the moving hand. In the case of very short samples, which might cause training problems, the number of frames was incremented by using interpolation.

The data set for the classification task of separated gestures consisted of 91 isolated words with 40 samples per word (a total of 3640 samples). Data were acquired from 4 different people, because each person performs the gestures in a different way. The words that have been chosen come from an on-line course [12] and a LSE dictionary [13]. The words were chosen in order to give the possibility of forming different sentences that have a correct grammatical structure and semantics in sign language. Attending to that, the chosen words pertained to the followings groups: colours, numbers, personal pronouns, possessive adjectives, adverbs, greetings, courtesy phrases, verbs, names, confirmation, quantities, prepositions, and interrogative pronouns.

For the task of consecutive gesture recognition, 274 sentences were captured. The vocabulary is the same than that appears in first task. These data have the same format than the isolated gestures. In both tasks the evaluation was conducted with cross validation using 4 partitions.

4.2 Gesture Classification

This section provides results on the recognition of the 91 separated gestures. Data were generated using the aforementioned *Leap Motion* sensor. Training

---

[2] The data is available in https://github.com/Sasanita/spanish-sign-language-db.git.
[3] The value of the movement is the weighted sum of several variables, such as the speed of each hand between two consecutive images [5].

and evaluation were performed using the *HTK* toolkit. For this experiment, the data were divided were into 4 partitions to use cross validation technique. For training different HMM topologies were tried by employing initially models of 4, 5, 6, 7 and 8 states (including artificial initial and final states). In speech recognition the transcription file used to train the model contains the phonemes transcribed from the audio sample, but in the case of this work, the transcription file contains whole words as basic units. A standard training approximation with common initialisation for all words and Forward-Backward estimation was employed. Effects of the number of Forward-Backward iterations were explored. Finally, the results shown in Fig. 1 were obtained. Models with 7 and 8 states obtained the same results. The best accuracy was obtained with the model of 7/8 states and 7 training iterations. This model obtained 84.6% word accuracy.

To improve this result, increment of the number of Gaussians within the emission probability mixture model was conducted. The model with the highest accuracy was used in the increment. In Fig. 2 the comparison of models of 8 states with 1 Gaussian and 2 Gaussians is shown. The accuracy increased to 87.4%. A mixture model with 4 Gaussians was tried but the number of samples by Gaussian was insufficient to train the model and caused training errors. Apart from accuracy, training and test speed were measured. The time required to obtain the best topology was 8:32 min. The second training with 2 Gaussian Mixtures lasted 1:45 min. In total, the time consumed by the complete experiment was about 10:17 min. In addition, the experiment using the methodology described in [5] with the data from the current work was conducted. The purpose was to achieve an objective comparison of results of both works. First, the classification using K-NN and DTW algorithms was done. For K-NN we took the first frame (42 values) of each sample, which represents the initial shape of hands. The next step was calculating the Euclidean distance between each vectors of test samples and all vectors of training samples. The smallest distance determines the class which belongs to. In order to recognise the trajectory with DTW, we took the complete data matrix of each sample. We calculated the sum of the distances between each column (vector of each variable).

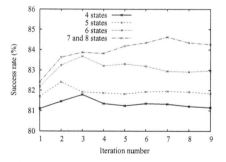

Fig. 1. Topologies comparison.

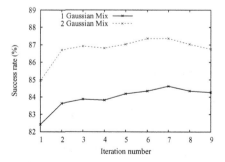

Fig. 2. Model of 8 states trained with 1 and 2 Gaussian Mixtures.

Table 1. Results using the methodology of [5] and comparission with actual metodology. Times in seconds.

	HMM	KNN + DTW
Accuracy	87.4%	88.4%
Elapsed time	519	9383

Table 2. Confusion matrix of most confused signs (40 samples for each sign). Original words in Spanish.

Sign	Confused sign and corresponding frequency				
She	You(female)-8	We(female)-7			
Not	One-10	You(female)-6	He-2	Eleven-2	Forget-1
How are you	Well-13	Grey-2			
So-so	Please-7	Good night-4	How are you-3	Born-2	
Red	Spain-6	Eyes-4	Me-4	Shirt-1	

   When the recognition of the static part (initial configuration of hands) using K-NN and the trajectory using DTW, which both belong to the correct class, the final recognition result for each sample is considered as correctly recognised. Apart from accuracy, elapsed time was also measured. Table 1 shows classification accuracy obtained by using HMM and by using K-NN + DTW. The accuracy of the previous work is about 1% better, but the time required is much higher. Our method is 18 times faster, since DTW has to perform the sum of differences of each variable and of classification it is necessary to calculate the difference between each pair of samples. Table 2 provides the confusion matrix of most confused signs. Different groups of confused signs have similar initial or final shape of hands, similar trajectory or some part of gesture are exactly the same. For example, to indicate male or female gender, only an additional movement is required, which makes it prone to confusion.

4.3   Consecutive Gesture Recognition

This task performed recognition of consecutive gestures. In Sect. 1 it has been mentioned that context may help in determining the meaning of a sign, which is the focus of this task. The experiment consists in using the consecutive signs contained within the data set in order to build logical sentences. These sentences were automatically generated using a grammar file created in collaboration with the *Fesord*[4] association. Only 68 words were used in this grammar file, since data acquisition was very costly. Listing 1.1 shows part of this grammar. In order for training to be statistically significant, at least 3 examples of use of each word

---
[4] http://www.fesord.org.

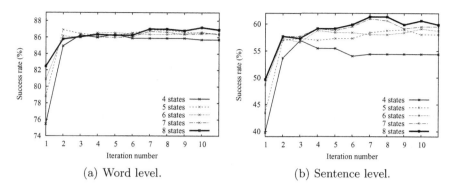

(a) Word level.   (b) Sentence level.

Fig. 3. Topologies comparison for consecutive gesture recognition.

in each partition are needed. That is the reason why the number of used words was reduced in this task. In total, 274 sentences were implemented and cross validation with 4 partitions was used.

Listing 1.1. Part of the grammar file used to generate logical LSE sentences.

```
1   $colour = black | yellow | blue | red | green | brown;
2   $number = one | two | three | ... | eight | nine | ten;
3   $person = father | mother | child | brother;
4   $personalpronoun = I | you | we | she | he | them;
5   $family = $personalpronoun ( brother | child ) $number (
        to_have | not_to_have );
6   $like = ( $personalpronoun | $personalpronoun $person ) (
        $activity | $colour ) ( to_like | not_to_like);
7   ( $like | $understand | ... | $give | $know | $family )
```

Figure 3 shows the word accuracy and Fig. 3b the sentence accuracy for different topologies and training iterations. The best result was obtained with the model with 8 states after 7 training iterations, which led to 61.3% sentence accuracy and 87.0% word accuracy. In the case of consecutive gesture recognition it was impossible to increase the number of Gaussians due to lack of data.

4.4 Discussion

The results of the isolated gestures recognition provided 87.4% gesture accuracy. In the consecutive gesture recognition part, accuracies were 87.0% at the word level and 61.3% at the sentence level. We consider these results satisfactory as a first step towards creating a useful tool for deaf people. Regarding previous work, several improvements have been introduced: more complex models (such as HMMs) have been used, the speed of training and recognition was improved, and the use of a parametric classifier leads to lower storage space requirements in the device where the gesture recognition system will be used.

5 Conclusions and Future Work

In this work we presented a first approximation to gesture classification and recognition for LSE. Results are promising and allow us to think of a future implementation that may aid deaf people in their daily communication.

In future work, we would like to expand the data set and investigate the use of more Gaussians, as well as deep learning, in the consecutive gesture recognition task. Different techniques of surrogate data, described in [14], will be tested to avoid the expensive manual generation of data.

As mentioned earlier, this work is only a small step for the creation of a tool that could enhance the quality of people's life who use LSE. It is expected that with the continuation of this work, a system could be achieved that could effectively break down communicative barriers between many people.

Acknowledgements. Work partially supported by MINECO under grant DI-15-08169, by Sciling under its R+D programme, by MINECO/FEDER under project CoMUN-HaT (TIN2015-70924-C2-1-R), and by Generalitat Valenciana (GVA) under reference PROMETEOII/2014/030.

References

1. World federation of the deaf. wfdeaf.org/human-rights/crpd/sign-language/
2. Guerrero-Balaguera, J.D., Pérez-Holguín, W.J.: FPGA-based translation system from colombian sign language to text. DYNA **82**, 172–181 (2015)
3. Priego Pérez, F.P.: Reconocimiento de imágenes del lenguaje de señal Mexicano. TFG, Instituto Politécnico Nacional (2012)
4. Celebi, S., Aydin, A.S., Temiz, T.T., Arici, T.: Gesture recognition using skeleton data with weighted dynamic time warping. In: VISAPP, pp. 620–625 (2013)
5. Parcheta, Z.: Estudio para la selección de descriptores de gestos a partir de la biblioteca "LeapMotion". TFG, EPSG, UPV (2015)
6. Starner, T.E.: Visual recognition of American sign language using hidden Markov models. MIT, DTIC Document (1995)
7. Huang, X., Ariki, Y., Jack, M.: Hidden Markov Models for Speech Recognition. Columbia University Press, New York (1990)
8. Liu, K., Chen, C., Jafari, R., Kehtarnavaz, N.: Multi-HMM classification for hand gesture recognition using two differing modality sensors. In: Circuits and Systems Conference (DCAS), pp. 1–4. IEEE, Dallas (2014)
9. Patil, P., Ansari, S.: Online handwritten devnagari word recognition using HMM based technique. Int. J. Comput. Appl. **95**(17), 17–21 (2014)
10. Salcedo Campos, F.J.: Modelos Ocultos de Markov. Del reconocimiento de voz a la música. LuLu (2007)
11. Young, S., et al.: The HTK Book. Entropic Cambridge Research Laboratory, Cambridge (2006)
12. Curso online de LSE. http://xurl.es/zjuqm
13. Diccionario online de LSE. https://www.spreadthesign.com/es/
14. Schreiber, T., Schmitz, A.: Surrogate time series. Physica D **142**(3–4), 346–382 (2000)

RGB-D Computer Vision Techniques
for Simulated Prosthetic Vision

Jesus Bermudez-Cameo$^{(\boxtimes)}$, Alberto Badias-Herbera, Manuel Guerrero-Viu,
Gonzalo Lopez-Nicolas, and Jose J. Guerrero

Instituto de Investigación en Ingeniería de Aragón, I3A,
Universidad de Zaragoza, Zaragoza, Spain
bermudez@unizar.es

Abstract. Recent research on visual prosthesis demonstrates the possibility of providing visual perception to people with certain blindness. Bypassing the damaged part of the visual path, electrical stimulation provokes spot percepts known as phosphenes. Due to physiological and technological limitations the information received by patients has very low resolution and reduced dynamic range. In this context, the inclusion of new computer vision techniques to improve the semantic content in this information channel is an active and open key topic. In this paper, we present a system for Simulated Prosthetic Vision based on a head-mounted display with an RGB-D camera, and two tools, one focused on human interaction and the other oriented to navigation, exploring different proposals of phosphenic representations.

Keywords: Simulated prosthetic vision · Head-mounted displays · RGB-D vision

1 Introduction

A novel approach for treating blindness caused by retinal degenerative disorders is implanting retinal prosthesis. Cell degeneration of photoreceptors caused by retinitis pigmentosa and macular degeneration can be bypassed by artificially stimulating non-damaged cells like retinal ganglion cells and sometimes bipolar cells [36]. This effect is achieved with an implanted electrode array that provokes a set of electrical stimuli which is perceived by the blind patient as a pattern of visual spots, usually known as phosphenes [10].

The research in last years reports significant advances in the development of visual prostheses. There exist different types of visual prostheses according to the problem causing blindness: retinal prostheses, optic nerve prostheses or direct stimulation of the cortex. If the patient suffers from damaged retina receptors (cones and rods) any of the three classes is adequate. But if the damage is caused in an advanced part of the optic pathway, the visual cortex may be the most appropriate place. In particular, retinal prostheses are based in retinal ganglion cells stimulation. This may be achieved via placement of epiretinal,

© Springer International Publishing AG 2017
L.A. Alexandre et al. (Eds.): IbPRIA 2017, LNCS 10255, pp. 427–436, 2017.
DOI: 10.1007/978-3-319-58838-4_47

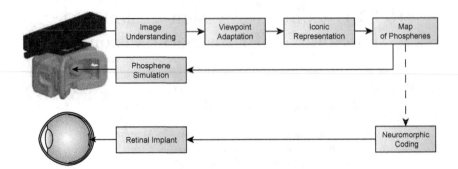

Fig. 1. Flowchart for simulated prosthetic vision (top). SPV facilitates research on new methods to generate maps of phosphenes. Next step, would be to transfer the research results to final patients (bottom).

subretinal or suprachoroidal stimulating electrode arrays. Five representative models are Argus II, Boston Retinal Implant Project, Epi-Ret 3, Intelligent Medical Implants (IMI) and Alpha-IMS (Retina Implant AG). Currently, two of them have regulatory approval (America and Europe) for the treatment of retinitis pigmentosa: the Argus II (epiretinal) and Alpha IMS (subretinal), the Boston Retinal Implant is in animal studies and all others are in clinical trials. The perception system used by most of current visual prostheses, with some exceptions, is based on the acquisition of images with an external camera. The acquired images are generally processed using basic image processing techniques to generate a phosphenes-based image which is sent to the prosthesis.

Table 1. Examples of works using basic image processing techniques performed in visual prostheses.

Institute	Image processing
Stanford University [3]	Geometric/Spatio-temporal
Dobelle Institute (University of Utah) [11]	Contour detection
Intelligent Medical Implants [16]	Spatio-temporal filtration
Second Sight (Argus II) [28]	Contrast improvement/Contour detection
University of New South Wales, Sydney [32]	Mean/Gaussian filter, zoom

A simulated prosthetic vision (SPV) generally consists of a vision-based system and a head-mounted display on a normal sighted subject (see Fig. 1). This system allows representing the descriptions of phosphene perception reported by visual prosthesis patients. The advantages of using SPV in prosthetic vision research have been acknowledged [1]. In particular, this approach avoids the implications derived of treating with final patients allowing an early non-invasive evaluation of advanced computer vision techniques and different representations. Most of the current approaches used in prosthetic vision and SPV are based on basic image processing techniques (see Table 1) like in [4,5]. However this configuration (camera+prosthesis) allows exploring more advanced computer vision techniques to enhance the semantics and the relevance of the information displayed to the patient. For example, visual recognition can be used for enhancing the saliency of meaningful objects [15,17], face detection can be used for human interaction [21] and going further, the recent advances in 3D visual odometry [13,25] could be used for assisting navigation with prosthetic vision.

In this paper we present a prototype consisting of a device for simulated prosthetic vision based on RGB-D vision (Sect. 2), a human interaction tool (Sect. 3) and a navigation tool (Sect. 4) where different representations displaying maps of phosphenes are discussed. A key issue in our proposal is to consider depth information to enhance basic image processing with advanced computer vision techniques in the context of SPVs. Note that with current technology, depth perception is transmitted by stereo displays to non-blinded people, however, since intrinsic technical limitations of prosthetic vision prevents from transmitting the stereo effect, it requires alternative strategies to be represented such as using an iconic way.

1.1 Related Work

Simulated prosthetic vision has already disclosed useful for reflecting clinical findings [1], being used for studying performance in tasks such as reading [12], finding text [9], hand-eye coordination, and mobility [29]. Most of these insights are related with the number of electrodes needed for achieving a given task. For example, according to Cha et al. [6] a pattern of 25×25 phosphenes allows to recognize text in a reading speed of 100 words per minute for stationary text and 170 words per minute for text moving automatically, however harder tasks like face recognition requires hundreds of phosphenes [31,33]. Despite the advances in prostheses development increase the available resolution there exist physical restrictions when miniaturizing the electrode array. In [24] the limits when increasing the number of electrodes by current spread and new strategies for improving the stimuli are discussed.

First addressed task in navigation for SPV is obstacle avoidance [2,27]. Parikh et al. [26] presented a computationally model for detecting salient regions in an image frame to avoid obstacles. Another visual processing system for bionic eye with a focus on obstacle avoidance was implemented by [30]. Obstacle detection and simultaneous localization and mapping were applied to guide a user on a safe path using a stereo camera as input of the implanted prosthetic vision, and vibration motors on the shoulders [34]. In [22] a technique to find a ground-plane and the boundary with objects is presented. Objects and boundaries can be then augmented to ensure object boundary visibility [19]. More recently, [35] uses VR-based environments for evaluating the visual response for obstacle avoidance in SPVs with a simpler set-up.

Representing depth in SPV is a key concept for achieving assisted navigation, but its implementation is particularly challenging. Systems displaying depth and contrast edges in a phosphene-based display are described in [18,21] and more recently in [23]. In [14], a semantic labelling of the image provides a representation for obstacle avoidance.

2   RGB-D Based Prototype for Simulated Prosthetic Vision

A device for Simulated Prosthetic Vision (SPV) allows simulating the performance of a given vision algorithm without intervention of a blinded person. Our first prototype combines a head-mounted display (HMD)[1] with an RGB-D camera[2]. The use of a depth sensor allows representing images from the point of view of the user despite the camera is not exactly placed on the view-point of the user. The localization of the display with respect to the camera is indirectly estimated by using the external camera provided by Oculus. For calibrating the system this camera has to simultaneously perceive a led-pattern carried by the HMD and a chess pattern which is also viewed by the RGB-D sensor. The external camera is used only once to calibrate the system, since HMD and RGB-D sensor are coupled. The resulting Euclidean transformations are the transformation of the HMD from the external camera T_{ED}, the transformation of the external camera from the chess pattern T_{PE} and the transformation of the RGB-D sensor from the chess pattern T_{PC} (see Fig. 2). These transformations are linearly related by

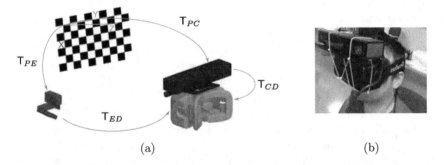

(a)   (b)

Fig. 2. (a) Scheme for extrinsic calibration of the head-mounted display with respect to the RGB-D sensor. (b) Our prototype for simulating prosthetic vision.

$$\mathsf{T}_{CD} = \mathsf{T}_{PC}^{-1}\mathsf{T}_{PE}\mathsf{T}_{ED} \tag{1}$$

The map of phosphenes is represented using Gaussian spots with a modular configuration (e.g. [8]). This is certainly not a precise representation of the appearance of most phosphenes, but it is a standard representation used in the literature [7,31]. We also assume a circular field of view. Given a resultant processed image point, we use a look-up table for computing the corresponding

---

[1] Oculus Rift www.oculus.com/rift/.
[2] Microsoft Kinect V2.

phosphene. This look-up table is initialized by computing the nearest phosphene defined by the Euclidean distance. For addressing the focusing problem in very close displays and provide wider field of view, the HMD combines aspheric lenses with a correcting barrel distortion. However, we can avoid computing the intrinsic calibration of the RGB-D sensor and the HMD since they are internally provided by the corresponding SDKs (we have separately calibrated both systems and checked that the internal calibrations provided by SDKs are correct). Finally we have performed a perceptual validation of the whole system representing the coloured point cloud captured by the RGB-D camera in the reference of the HMD. With this configuration, different subjects have tested the prototype by performing different tasks such as executing grasping tasks in short distances and launching tasks in medium distances. In the first evaluation we measure the time invested by a subject for grasping a bottle and return it to its original location without blowing out the others. The evaluation considers two cases: first (see Fig. 3(a)) considers separated bottles and second considers the grasping of a bottle surrounded by other bottles (see Fig. 3(b)). This evaluation is performed 8 times by 6 different subjects in three different series to study the human adaptation to the device (see Fig. 4). In the second evaluation we measure the success rate of introducing a small bottle in a basket located 2 m far away

$$\text{(a)} \qquad\qquad\qquad \text{(b)} \qquad\qquad\qquad \text{(c)}$$

Fig. 3. Perceptual validation of calibration. (a–b) The subject must grasp a bottle and return it to its original location without blowing out the others. (c) The subject must introduce a small bottle in a basket.

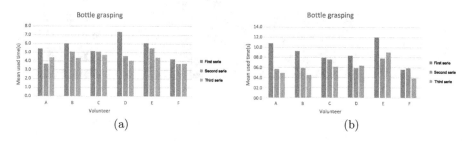

$$\text{(a)} \qquad\qquad\qquad\qquad\qquad\qquad \text{(b)}$$

Fig. 4. Mean time used for each subject to grasp the bottle (8 executions per subject).

from the subject (see Fig. 3(c)). The obtained success rate is 57% in comparison with a success rate equal to 67% for the same evaluation with natural vision. Conclusions from these evaluations are that the prototype permits to correctly estimate 3D location and object dimensions once it has been calibrated. There is also a fast human adaptation to the given virtual reality prototype.

3   Iconic Representation of Humans for Prosthetic Vision

Human interaction is very important for patients with impaired vision where identifying the presence of a person, its identity, knowing if the person is approaching or understanding their expressions is a very valuable information. A retinal prosthesis can be used to enhance the human interaction experience. However, the low resolution and reduced dynamic range of the phosphenic video stream can impede an adequate understanding of the scene. In fact, human detection and recognition are difficult tasks when having any kind of impaired vision. An interesting approach here is using computer vision techniques to perform this recognition on the original images and to present an iconic representation to the

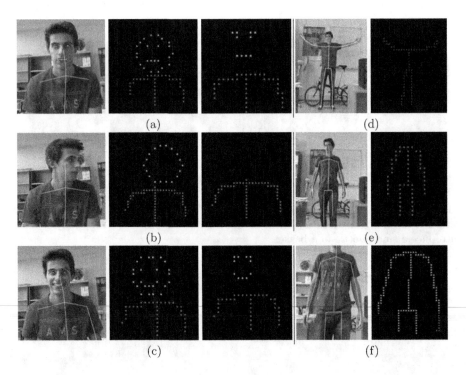

Fig. 5. Iconic representation of humans using map of phosphenes. Faces: (a) Representation for a neutral expression. (b) Representation for a face not looking at the user. (c) Representation for a happy expression. Human skeleton representation: (d) Far. (e) Middle. (f) Near.

patient [18,21]. In this work, we exploit that the RGB-D camera provides human detection describing skeletons and face parameters and we use this information for an iconic representation of the person and its face. In particular, Kinect v2 API provides 3D position of human joints, eyes and mouth location, face orientation in 3D and detects other binary features like expressions. In Fig. 5 we show iconic representations of a subject using a map of phosphenes. The RGB-D sensor allows estimating the location of the person and the expression which is represented with a variation in the iconic representation. We also detect and represent the gaze direction. We have evaluated different representations taking into account the available resolution of the simulated prosthesis. In particular, we have evaluated two representations in three different resolutions. One representation involves eyes and mouth (Fig. 5(a–c) right) and the other also includes a circle for representing the face (Fig. 5(a–c) middle). In Fig. 5(d–f) we show a detail of the iconic representation of the skeleton of a person. Depending on the depth we codify the range of the phosphenes. We also attach an example in the available video.[3]

4   Depth for Navigation Using Prosthetic Vision

Assisted navigation for prosthetic vision can take advantage of the last advances in 3D localization using computer vision and RGB-D sensors [13,25]. The location of the patient in combination with a map which can be simultaneously estimated or previously stored is valuable information that can guide the patient in day to day tasks but also in emergency evacuations.

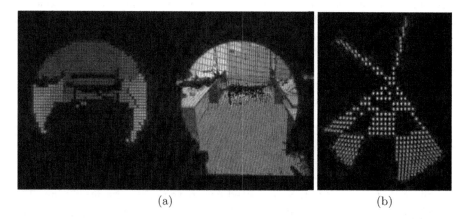

(a)   (b)

Fig. 6. (a) Ground removal from depth information for a better saliency on 3D scenario with SPV. (b) Iconic representation of a corridor using chess floor and vanishing points for showing a direction.

---

[3] http://webdiis.unizar.es/%7Ebermudez/phosphenicRepresentation.wmv.

Even when the complete environment is known, transmitting depth sensation is hard due to low resolution and low dynamic range of prosthetic visual devices. Notice that stereo vision is not possible since only monocular prostheses are possible. A straight-forward approach is encoding the depth, which can be estimated with the RGB-D sensor, in a gray low-resolution image using the dynamic range of the phosphene representation [20]. However, the available gray-level is considerably low making difficult the environment understanding. A first improvement of this representation is removing the background of the image (for example the ground [22]) in order to emphasize objects which are candidates to be obstacles. In Fig. 6(a) we show an example of ground removal using a RANSAC based estimation of the ground plane.

Another of our proposals for describing depth is using an iconic description of perspective projection. Inspired by old low-resolution 3D games and exploiting the localization and mapping obtained from modern visual odometry systems, the displacement with respect the ground can be evoked by using chess patterns. Indoor scenes described by a high level map, can be represented using iconic layouts representing main directions using pairs of parallel lines. This description allows easily representing walls and corridors. In Fig. 6(b) and in the attached video (see Footnote 3) we show an example of the proposed representation of a corridor using our map of phosphenes.

5   Discussion

In this paper we present a prototype for Simulated Prosthetic Vision based on a head-mounted display and a RGB-D camera. This system is the framework used to present two tools for human interaction and navigation. We have explored different alternatives for depth and human representation in SPV. We observe that there exist a tradeoff between the available resolution and the amount of information being possible to represent. Iconic representations require more performance in computer vision but they provide more understanding of the environment. As future work we consider integrating a robust visual odometry for fully exploiting the iconic representation of layouts.

Simulated prosthetic vision open new possibilities for understanding the performance of computer vision algorithms for prosthetic vision. On the one hand we have flexibility for testing different algorithms in simulations of different prostheses. On the other hand using SVPs allows validating the proposals in testing groups crowded enough for obtaining design parameters with statistical meaning. We believe that these first steps presented here pave the way for improving SPV state-of-the-art techniques by including depth information inside the perception loop. The main challenging issue here is to encapsulate depth information in the constrained representation of the prosthetic vision system, and our proposals aim towards these goals.

Acknowledgements. This work was supported by Spanish Government/European Union projects DPI2014-61792-EXP and DPI2015-65962-R (MINECO/FEDER).

References

1. Ahuja, A.K., Behrend, M.R.: The Argus^{TM} II retinal prosthesis: factors affecting patient selection for implantation. Progr. Retinal Eye Res. **36**, 1–23 (2013)
2. Aladren, A., Lopez-Nicolas, G., Puig, L., Guerrero, J.J.: Navigation assistance for the visually impaired using RGB-D sensor with range expansion. IEEE Syst. J. **10**(3), 922–932 (2016)
3. Asher, A., Segal, W.A., Baccus, S.A., Yaroslavsky, L.P., Palanker, D.V.: Image processing for a high-resolution optoelectronic retinal prosthesis. IEEE Trans. Biomed. Eng. **54**(6), 993–1004 (2007)
4. Ayton, L.N., Luu, C.D., Bentley, S.A., Allen, P.J., Guymer, R.H.: Image processing for visual prostheses: a clinical perspective. In: IEEE International Conference on Image Processing, pp. 1540–1544 (2013)
5. Barnes, N.: An overview of vision processing in implantable prosthetic vision. In: IEEE International Conference on Image Processing, pp. 1532–1535 (2013)
6. Cha, K., Boman, D.K., Horch, K.W., Normann, R.A.: Reading speed with a pixelized vision system. JOSA A **9**(5), 673–677 (1992)
7. Chang, M., Kim, H., Shin, J., Park, K.: Facial identification in very low-resolution images simulating prosthetic vision. J. Neural Eng. **9**(4), 046012 (2012)
8. Chen, S.C., Suaning, G.J., Morley, J.W., Lovell, N.H.: Simulating prosthetic vision: visual models of phosphenes. Vis. Res. **49**(12), 1493–1506 (2009)
9. Denis, G., Jouffrais, C., Mailhes, C., Macé, M.J.: Simulated prosthetic vision: improving text accessibility with retinal prostheses. In: Annual International Conference of the IEEE Engineering in Medicine and Biology Society, pp. 1719–1722 (2014)
10. Dobelle, W.H., Mladejovsky, M., Girvin, J.: Artificial vision for the blind: electrical stimulation of visual cortex offers hope for a functional prosthesis. Science **183**(4123), 440–444 (1974)
11. Dobelle, W.H.: Artificial vision for the blind by connecting a television camera to the visual cortex. ASAIO J. **46**(1), 3–9 (2000)
12. Fornos, A.P., Sommerhalder, J., Pelizzone, M.: Reading with a simulated 60-channel implant. Front. Neurosci. **5**, 57 (2011)
13. Gutiérrez-Gómez, D., Mayol-Cuevas, W., Guerrero, J.J.: Inverse depth for accurate photometric and geometric error minimisation in RGB-D dense visual odometry. In: IEEE International Conference on Robotics and Automation, pp. 83–89 (2015)
14. Horne, L., Alvarez, J., McCarthy, C., Salzmann, M., Barnes, N.: Semantic labeling for prosthetic vision. Comput. Vis. Image Underst. **149**, 113–125 (2016)
15. Horne, L., Barnes, N., McCarthy, C., He, X.: Image segmentation for enhancing symbol recognition in prosthetic vision. In: Annual International Conference of the IEEE Engineering in Medicine and Biology Society, pp. 2792–2795 (2012)
16. Hornig, R., Zehnder, T., Velikay-Parel, M., Laube, T., Feucht, M., Richard, G.: The IMI retinal implant system. In: Humayun, M.S., Weiland, J.D., Chader, G., Greenbaum, E. (eds.) Artificial Sight, pp. 111–128. Springer, New York (2007)
17. Jung, J.H., Aloni, D., Yitzhaky, Y., Peli, E.: Active confocal imaging for visual prostheses. Vis. Res. **111**, 182–196 (2015)
18. Li, W.: Wearable computer vision systems for a cortical visual prosthesis. In: Proceedings of the IEEE International Conference on Computer Vision Workshops, pp. 428–435 (2013)
19. Li, Y., McCarthy, C., Barnes, N.: On just noticeable difference for bionic eye. In: Annual International Conference of the IEEE Engineering in Medicine and Biology Society, pp. 2961–2964 (2012)

20. Lieby, P., Barnes, N., McCarthy, C., Liu, N., Dennett, H., Walker, J.G., Botea, V., Scott, A.F.: Substituting depth for intensity and real-time phosphene rendering: visual navigation under low vision conditions. In: Annual International Conference of the IEEE Engineering in Medicine and Biology Society, pp. 8017–8020 (2011)

21. Lui, W.L.D., Browne, D., Kleeman, L., Drummond, T., Li, W.H.: Transformative reality: improving bionic vision with robotic sensing. In: Annual International Conference of the IEEE Engineering in Medicine and Biology Society, pp. 304–307 (2012)

22. McCarthy, C., Barnes, N., Lieby, P.: Ground surface segmentation for navigation with a low resolution visual prosthesis. In: Annual International Conference of the IEEE Engineering in Medicine and Biology Society, pp. 4457–4460 (2011)

23. McCarthy, C., Walker, J.G., Lieby, P., Scott, A., Barnes, N.: Mobility and low contrast trip hazard avoidance using augmented depth. J. Neural Eng. 12(1), 016003 (2014)

24. Meffin, H.: What limits spatial perception with retinal implants?. In: IEEE International Conference on Image Processing, pp. 1545–1549 (2013)

25. Mur-Artal, R., Montiel, J., Tardós, J.D.: ORB-SLAM: a versatile and accurate monocular slam system. IEEE Trans. Robot. 31(5), 1147–1163 (2015)

26. Parikh, N., Itti, L., Weiland, J.: Saliency-based image processing for retinal prostheses. J. Neural Eng. 7(1), 016006 (2010)

27. Perez-Yus, A., Gutierrez-Gomez, D., Lopez-Nicolas, G., Guerrero, J.J.: Stairs detection with odometry-aided traversal from a wearable RGB-D camera. Comput. Vis. Image Underst. 154, 192–205 (2017)

28. Products, S.S.M.: Argus II retinal prosthesis system surgeon manual (2013)

29. Srivastava, N.R., Troyk, P.R., Dagnelie, G.: Detection, eye-hand coordination and virtual mobility performance in simulated vision for a cortical visual prosthesis device. J. Neural Eng. 6(3), 035008 (2009)

30. Stacey, A., Li, Y., Barnes, N.: A salient information processing system for bionic eye with application to obstacle avoidance. In: Annual International Conference of the IEEE Engineering in Medicine and Biology Society, pp. 5116–5119 (2011)

31. Thompson, R.W., Barnett, G.D., Humayun, M.S., Dagnelie, G.: Facial recognition using simulated prosthetic pixelized vision. Invest. Ophthalmol. Vis. Sci. 44(11), 5035–5042 (2003)

32. Tsai, D., Morley, J., Suaning, G.J., Lovell, N.H.: A wearable real-time image processor for a vision prosthesis. Comput. Methods Programs Biomed. 95(3), 258–269 (2009)

33. Wang, J., Wu, X., Lu, Y., Wu, H., Kan, H., Chai, X.: Face recognition in simulated prosthetic vision: face detection-based image processing strategies. J. Neural Eng. 11(4), 046009 (2014)

34. Weiland, J.D., Parikh, N., Pradeep, V., Medioni, G.: Smart image processing system for retinal prosthesis. In: Annual International Conference of the IEEE Engineering in Medicine and Biology Society, pp. 300–303 (2012)

35. Zapf, M.P.H., Boon, M.Y., Lovell, N.H., Suaning, G.J.: Assistive peripheral phosphene arrays deliver advantages in obstacle avoidance in simulated end-stage retinitis pigmentosa: a virtual-reality study. J. Neural Eng. 13(2), 026022 (2016)

36. Zrenner, E.: Will retinal implants restore vision? Science 295(5557), 1022–1025 (2002)

A Study on the Cardinality of Ordered Average Pooling in Visual Recognition

Miguel Pagola$^{(\boxtimes)}$, Juan I. Forcen, Edurne Barrenechea, Javier Fernández, and Humberto Bustince

Universidad Pública de Navarra, 31006 Pamplona, Spain
miguel.pagola@unavarra.es

Abstract. Bag-of-Words methods can be robust to image scaling, translation, and occlusion. An important step in this methodology, and other visual recognition systems like Convolutional Neural Networks, is spatial pooling, where the descriptors of neighbouring elements are combined into a local or a global feature vector. The combined vector must contain relevant information, while removing irrelevant and confusing details. Maximum and average are the most common aggregation functions used in the pooling step. In this work we present a study about the cardinality of ordered average pooling, i.e. the number of ordered elements to be aggregated such that after the pooling process the relevant information is maintained without degrading their discriminative power for classification. We provide an extensive evaluation that shows that for different values of cardinalities we can obtain results better than simple average pooling and than maximum pooling when dealing with small dictionary sizes.

Keywords: Pooling · Cardinality · Image classification · Bag-of-Words · Mid-level features · Coding

1 Introduction

A critical aspect in image classification is to find descriptive image features. Bag-of-Words (BoW) is a popular approach which transforms, previously computed image descriptors into an image representation that is used in matching and classification. Basically the BoW model for image classification can be summarised in the following steps:

1. First, local image descriptors, such as SIFT [1], HOG [2] or Gabor are extracted from images at interest points or in a dense grid.
2. An unsupervised learning algorithm is used to discover a set of prototype descriptors that is called a dictionary. This operation is usually done with k-means clustering, Gaussian mixtures or Sparse coding. Each of the descriptors found in the dictionary is called a visual word.

© Springer International Publishing AG 2017
L.A. Alexandre et al. (Eds.): IbPRIA 2017, LNCS 10255, pp. 437–444, 2017.
DOI: 10.1007/978-3-319-58838-4_48

3. In the feature coding step, image descriptors are locally transformed in a new vector decomposing the initial feature on the dictionary. It can be understood as an activation function for the dictionary, activating each of the visual words according to the local descriptor. In the classical BoW representation, the coding function activates only the visual word closest to the descriptor, assigning zero weight to all others.
4. In the pooling step the codes associated with local image features are combined over some image neighbourhood. The codes within each cell are aggregated to create a single feature vector. Average and maximum pooling are widely used.
5. Training and classification can be performed on the final feature vectors (usually the concatenation of the signature feature vectors of different cells) by a classifier, e.g. SVM [3].

Pooling is a crucial step in image classification in BoW model and in other visual recognition methodologies as Convolutional Neural Networks (CNN). There are two key factors for a pooling operation: one is the region whose local features will be selected for pooling, and the other is the aggregation operator g which defines the way to merge the local features. The most popular aggregation operator is average pooling, in which the obtained vector is the average over the activations of each visual word.

After the pooling step, descriptors which occur frequently will be more influential in the final representation than the ones occurring rarely. However, such frequent descriptors are not necessarily the most informative ones. On the other hand, the most discriminative descriptors might be highly localized and therefore correspond to only a set of locations. Therefore, it is very important to ensure that even those rare descriptors contribute significantly to the final representation. Taking into account these considerations and the idea of Koniusz et al. in [4] we propose a new pooling scheme called ordered average pooling (OAP). Such a way that the pooling operation is to average over the set of $\mathcal{N}$ largest elements.

This work is divide in the following sections: first, in notation and related work, basic concepts of the BoW, i.e. coding and pooling methods are recalled. In Sect. 3 we give a detailed explanation of our proposal and in the next section we show the experimental results. Finally the conclusions and future work are presented.

2   Notation and Related Work

In this section we introduce some notation used throughout the work. Let an image I be represented by a set of low-level descriptors or local features (e.g. SIFT) $\boldsymbol{x}_i$ at N locations identified with their indices $i = 1, \ldots, N$. (Eq. 1). Based in Spatial Pyramid [5] representation, let M regions of interest be defined on the image, with $\mathcal{N}_m$ denoting the set of indices within the region m (Eq. 2). We will denote as f and g coding and pooling operators, respectively. The signature vector z representing the whole image is obtained by sequentially coding and pooling over all regions and concatenating the pooled vectors:

$$\boldsymbol{\alpha}_i = f(\boldsymbol{x}_i), \quad i = 1, \ldots, N \tag{1}$$

$$\boldsymbol{h}_m = g(\{\boldsymbol{\alpha}_i\}_{i \in \mathcal{N}_m}), \quad m = 1, \ldots, M \tag{2}$$

$$\boldsymbol{z}^T = [\boldsymbol{h}_1^T \ldots \boldsymbol{h}_M^T] \tag{3}$$

The classification performance using $\boldsymbol{z}$ as the input of a classifier (e.g. SVM [3]) depends on the properties and the combination of f and g.

2.1 Coding

In the BoW framework, we have a set of prototypes or visual dictionary $\boldsymbol{D} = \{\boldsymbol{d}_k\}_{k=1}^K$, usually learned by an unsupervised algorithm like K-means. The goal of f is embedding the local descriptors into the visual dictionary space. Next, we describe four coding methods that are used in the experimental evaluation.

Hard Quantization. Hard quantization is the simplest form of coding, in particular, every local feature $\boldsymbol{x}_i$ is assigned to its nearest visual word in the dictionary $\boldsymbol{D}$ with activation equal to 1. Let $\boldsymbol{\alpha}_i \in \{0, 1\}^K$ the coded vector:

$$\boldsymbol{\alpha}_{i,j} = \begin{cases} 1 & \text{iff } j = \underset{1 \le j \le K}{\operatorname{argmin}} ||\boldsymbol{x}_i - \boldsymbol{d}_j||_2^2 \\ 0 & \text{otherwise.} \end{cases} \tag{4}$$

Soft Quantization. Due to the high quantization error of Hard quantization Van Gemert et al. [6] propose a soft method where a parameter β controls the softness of the assignment. Soft quantization describes each local feature by applying a Gaussian kernel on the euclidean distance between the local feature and the visual word of the dictionary.

$$\boldsymbol{\alpha}_{i,j} = \frac{exp(-\beta||\boldsymbol{x}_i - \boldsymbol{d}_j||_2^2)}{\sum_{k=1}^K exp(-\beta||\boldsymbol{x}_i - \boldsymbol{d}_k||_2^2)} \tag{5}$$

Triangle Assignment. In Coates et al. [7] propose a simple but effective non-linear mapping that attempts to softer the Hard quantization, while also keeping some sparsity:

$$\boldsymbol{\alpha}_{i,j} = \max\{0, \mu(\boldsymbol{x}_i) - ||\boldsymbol{x}_i - \boldsymbol{d}_j||_2^2\} \tag{6}$$

where $\mu(\boldsymbol{x}_i) = \frac{1}{K}\sum_{k=1}^K ||\boldsymbol{x}_i - \boldsymbol{d}_k||_2^2$ is the mean of distances between the local feature and all the visual words of the dictionary. This method outputs 0 for any feature where the distance to the visual word $\boldsymbol{d}_k$ is above average.

Sparse Coding. The goal of sparse coding is to express each local feature as a sparse linear combination of the visual words given in the dictionary $\boldsymbol{D}$.

$$\boldsymbol{\alpha}_i = \underset{\alpha}{\operatorname{argmin}} ||\boldsymbol{x}_i - \boldsymbol{D}\boldsymbol{\alpha}||_2^2 + \lambda||\boldsymbol{\alpha}||_1 \tag{7}$$

where $||\boldsymbol{\alpha}||_1$ denotes de l_1 norm of vector $\boldsymbol{\alpha}$ and λ is the sparsity parameter. The dictionary $\boldsymbol{D}$ is trained by minimizing the average of Eq. (7) over all samples, alternatively over $\boldsymbol{D}$ and over $\boldsymbol{\alpha}_i$.

In addition to the above methods (that will be used in our experimental study), other feature coding methods have been proposed, in [8] it can be found a useful overview.

2.2   Pooling

Pooling is an operation which aggregates coded features into a new and more usable vector. It is used to achieve more compact representation and better robustness to noise, clutter and invariance to image transformations. Pooling is performed in each cell $\mathcal{N}_m$ defined on the image.

Average Pooling. This method is widely accepted in CNN and the BoW model. Basically, the obtained vector $\boldsymbol{h}_m$ is the average over the activations of the elements of the cell for each component of the coded vector.

$$h_m = \frac{1}{|\mathcal{N}_m|} \sum_{i \in \mathcal{N}_m} \alpha_i \tag{8}$$

In [8] for small vocabulary sizes the performance of average was better than maximum pooling in several databases and with different coding schemes.

Maximum Pooling. This method selects the largest value between the activations of the elements of the cell for each component of the coded vector.

$$h_{m,j} = \max_{i \in \mathcal{N}_m} \{\alpha_{i,j}\}, \quad \text{for } j = 1, \ldots, K \tag{9}$$

In Boureau et al. [9,10] provide a theoretical study and an empirical comparison between maximum and average pooling. Furthermore in [4,8] maximum pooling was better than average pooling with large dictionary sizes, i.e. when the features have low probability of activation and high discriminative power.

Expected Maximum Pooling. In the case of binary codes (Hard quantization), using the Bernoulli distribution under the i.i.d. assumption [10], the maximum can be expected using the mean computed using all samples of the cell.

$$h_m = 1 - \left(1 - \frac{1}{|\mathcal{N}_m|} \sum_{i \in \mathcal{N}_m} \alpha_i\right)^{|\mathcal{N}_m|} \tag{10}$$

which is called the maximum expectation. In all cases tested in [10] the maximum expectation outperforms both average and maximum.

3   Ordered Average Pooling

Due to the i.i.d. assumption the value of the expected maximum usually is a smoothed maximum. The idea of smoothing the maximum comes from the fact that a negative factor of the pooling operation is the activation of a visual word given a descriptor, that should not occur but it does, due to features not representing it but having visual appearances similar to it, i.e. visual words with high activation but low representativeness of the object of the image. Based on this idea Koniusz et al. [4] proposed to use any pooling operator on a fixed number n of the largest values of the region to be pooled.

Taking into account the facts described previously we propose a new pooling operator called ordered average pooling (OAP).

$$h_m = \sum_{i \in \mathcal{N}_m} w_i(\alpha_i \searrow) \tag{11}$$

Where $(\alpha_i \searrow)$ is the ordered vector of activations and w_i are the weights. Taking the weights vector as $w = (1/\mathcal{N}, \dots, 1/\mathcal{N}, 0, \dots, 0)$, i.e. $w_i = 1/\mathcal{N}$ for the first $\mathcal{N}$ elements results in averaging the $\mathcal{N}$ largest activations.

Our hypothesis is that pooling over the $\mathcal{N}$ larger values smooths the maximum so avoids the problem of using the maximum in small pooling cardinalities. Moreover, it should outperform the average pooling, because OAP aggregates the most significant elements of the region to be pooled. Therefore with OAP visual words with high activation but low representativeness of the object of the image should be filtered.

4   Experimental Evaluation

In this section we provide an extensive comparison on the effect of OAP. We use the Caltech-101 [11] (102 classes and from 31 to 800 images per class) and Scenes [5] (15 classes and from 200 to 400 images per class) datasets as benchmarks.

Low-level descriptors x_i are 128-dimensional SIFT descriptors [1] of 16×16 patches. The descriptors are extracted on a dense grid every 8 pixels. The dictionary D is calculated from 200.000 random descriptors. The vocabulary sizes tested are $[2^4, 2^5, .., 2^{11}]$. Coding step is carried out by hard quantization, soft quantization (parameter $\beta = 2$), triangle assignment and sparse coding. The same dictionary was used with all the coding methods. The pooling regions m are the cells of 4×4, 2×2 and 1×1 grids (forming a three-level pyramid). Although having several cells of different size provides some smoothing in the results, we think that these results should be more useful for practical applications.

Following the usual procedure, we use 30 training images and the rest for testing (with a maximum of 50 test images) on the Caltech-101 dataset, and 100 training images and the rest for testing on the Scenes dataset. Experiments are conducted over 10 random splits of the data, and we report the mean accuracy. Multi-class classification is done with a linear kernel support vector machine L2-SVM trained using the one-versus-all rule: a classifier is learned to separate each class from the rest, and a test image is assigned the label of the classifier with the highest response. L2-SVM uses the square sum of the slack variables (the regularization term) in the objective function instead of the linear sum. The value of the regularization parameter C is selected by cross-validation within the training set.

Experiment. We compare average pooling, maximum pooling and maximum expectation[1] with four different relative cardinalities. The OAP is done over the 1%, 10%, 20% and 50% of the largest activations of each region.

In the Figs. 1 and 2 is depicted the classification accuracy of Scenes dataset and Caltech-101 respectively. In both benchmarks and with the four different coding methods the performance of the pooling methods is quite similar. For small sizes of the dictionary (≤ 256) the average and, especially OAP outperforms the maximum and the expected maximum. Therefore, when the visual words are not very discriminative in the pooling step the aggregation of important information

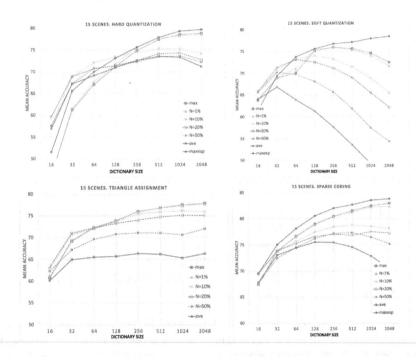

Fig. 1. Mean accuracy at 15 Scenes dataset with four different types of coding: hard, soft, mean and sparse coding from top left to down right. In each one are depicted 7 different types of pooling: *maximum (max), maximum expectation (maxexp), average (ave) and four OAP with* $\mathcal{N} = 1\%$, $\mathcal{N} = 10\%$, $\mathcal{N} = 20\%$ and $\mathcal{N} = 50\%$. (Color figure online)

---

[1] Maximum expectation is not used with triangle assignment coding due to its values are bigger than 1.

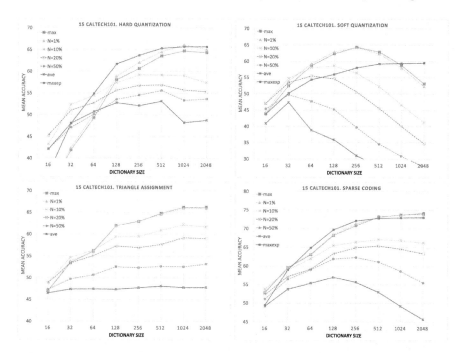

Fig. 2. Classification accuracy at Caltech 101 dataset with four different types of coding: hard, soft, mean and sparse coding from top left to down right. In each one are depicted 7 different types of pooling: *maximum (max), maximum expectation (maxexp), average (ave)* and four *OAP* with $\mathcal{N} = 1\%$, $\mathcal{N} = 10\%$, $\mathcal{N} = 20\%$ and $\mathcal{N} = 50\%$. (Color figure online)

is very useful. Best results are obtained pooling over the 10% of the most activated elements works well. For larger sizes of the dictionary, when the visual words are more discriminative, maximum, expected maximum and averaging over the 1% greater values are the best performers. In our experiment, we validate the results of [4, 10] about smoothing the maximum with the expected maximum. The expected maximum outperforms the maximum in both benchmarks specially with sparse coding.

5   Conclusions

In this work we propose a pooling method based on averaging over the ordered values. In the framework of BOW for image classification we empirically study the performance of OAP compared to average, maximum and expectation of maximum. We consider four typical coding methods, different vocabulary sizes and two well known image data sets. Based on the experimental results we can draw three main conclusions: (1) for small dictionary sizes OAP with is the best method, (2) cardinality is important in the performance of the OAP methods, such that if the cardinality is 1% for every region, the results are similar to the maximum and (3) smoothing the maximum improves the results for large dictionary sizes, specially the maximum expectation obtains the highest accuracy values. We consider that these results are helpful in the choice of the pooling function for a better design of recognition architectures.

Further directions of research are adapting pooling parameters separately for each feature and spatial ordered pooling in which the vector of x_i is sorted by their value and taking into account their location in the image. We also plan to apply OAP in CNN and other architectures in which average or the sum performs better than the maximum.

References

1. Lowe, D.G.: Distinctive image features from scale invariant keypoints. Int. J. Comput. Vis. **60**, 91–110 (2004)
2. Dalal, N., Triggs, B.: Histograms of oriented gradients for human detection. In: IEEE Conference on Computer Vision and Pattern Recognition (CVPR) (2005)
3. Cortes, C., Vapnik, V.: Support-vector networks. Mach. Learn. **20**(3), 273–297 (1995)
4. Koniusz, P., Yan, F., Mikolajczyk, K.: Comparison of mid-level feature coding approaches and pooling strategies in visual concept detection. Comput. Vis. Image Underst. **117**(5), 479–492 (2013)
5. Lazebnik, S., Schmid, C., Ponce, J.: Beyond bags of features: spatial pyramid matching for recognizing natural scene categories. In: Proceedings of the IEEE Computer Society Conference on Computer Vision and Pattern Recognition, vol. 2, pp. 2169–2178 (2006)
6. Van Gemert, J.C., Veenman, C.J., Smeulders, A.W.M., Geusebroek, J.M.: Visual word ambiguity. IEEE Trans. Pattern Anal. Mach. Intell. **32**(7), 1271–1283 (2010)
7. Coates, A., Arbor, A., Ng, A.Y.: An analysis of single-layer networks in unsupervised feature learning. Aistats **2011**, 215–223 (2011)
8. Wang, C., Huang, K.: How to use Bag-of-Words model better for image classification. Image Vis. Comput. **38**, 65–74 (2015)
9. Boureau, Y.L., Bach, F., LeCun, Y., Ponce, J.: Learning mid-level features for recognition. In: Proceedings of the IEEE Computer Society Conference on Computer Vision and Pattern Recognition, pp. 2559–2566 (2010)
10. Boureau, Y.L., Ponce, J., LeCun, Y.: A theoretical analysis of feature pooling in visual recognition. In: ICML, pp. 111–118 (2010)
11. Fei-Fei, L., Fergus, R., Perona, P.: Learning generative visual models from few training examples: an incremental bayesian approach tested on 101 object categories. In: Conference on Computer Vision and Pattern Recognition Workshop (CVPR 2004), p. 178 (2004)

VFH-Color and Deep Belief Network for 3D Point Cloud Recognition

Nabila Zrira$^{(\boxtimes)}$, Mohamed Hannat, and El Houssine Bouyakhf

LIMIARF Laboratory, Faculty of Sciences Rabat,
Mohammed V University, Rabat, Morocco
nabilazrira@gmail.com, mohamedhannat@gmail.com, bouyakhf@mtds.com

Abstract. With the invention of Microsoft Kinect sensor, 3D object recognition has become an important task in computer vision research in recent years. The Viewpoint Feature Histogram (VFH) is a Point Cloud Library (PCL) descriptor that encodes only geometry and viewpoint of 3D point cloud data. In this paper, we propose a new approach to representing and learning 3D point cloud classes. First, we develop a new descriptor called VFH-Color that combines the original version of VFH descriptor with the color quantization histogram, thus adding the appearance information that would improve the recognition rate. Then, we use those features for training deep learning algorithm called Deep Belief Network (DBN). We have also tested our approach on Washington RGBD dataset and have obtained highly promising results.

Keywords: 3D object recognition · Viewpoint Feature Histogram (VFH) · Point Cloud Library (PCL) · VFH-Color · Deep Belief Network

1 Introduction

The development of 3D perception sensors like Microsoft Kinect has triggered a wide availability and use of 3D point clouds. It creates suitable data representations that facilitate object detection, recognition, and categorization. The Point Cloud Library (PCL) was developed by Rusu et al. [8] in 2010 and was officially published in 2011. This open source library, licensed under Berkeley Software Distribution (BSD) terms, represents a collection of state-of-the-art algorithms and tools that operate with 3D point clouds. PCL integrates several 3D detectors as well as 3D local and global descriptors. In 3D local descriptors, each point is described by its local geometry. They are developed for specific applications such as object recognition, and local surface categorization. On the other hand, the 3D global descriptors describe object geometry. They are not computed for individual points, but for a whole cluster instead. The global descriptors are high-dimensional representations of object geometry. They are more efficient in object recognition, geometric categorization, and shape retrieval. They are usually calculated for subsets of the point clouds that are likely to be objects.

In general, 3D object recognition methods that use the Kinect camera attain different perspectives. Approaches based on local descriptors are used thanks to

© Springer International Publishing AG 2017
L.A. Alexandre et al. (Eds.): IbPRIA 2017, LNCS 10255, pp. 445–452, 2017.
DOI: 10.1007/978-3-319-58838-4_49

the color information, unlike approaches based on global appearance which are more practical thanks to the use of depth information. In this paper, we present a new 3D object recognition method, which is based on the new VFH-Color descriptor that combines both the color information and the geometric features extracted from the previous version of VFH descriptor. We extract the color information for point cloud data, then we use the color quantization technique to obtain the color histogram which is combined with VFH histogram. Our new features are then learned with Deep Belief Network (DBN) architecture. In summary, we make the following contributions in this paper:

- we develop a new descriptor called VFH-Color that combines geometric and color features;
- we learn the extracted VFH-Color features using Deep Belief Network (DBN).

After the introduction of our work, the subsequent sections will be laid out as follows. Section 2 covers previous works. Section 3 gives a brief description of VFH descriptor as well as our new VFH-Color descriptor. Section 4 illustrates DBN architecture. Section 5 presents our proposed approach for 3D object recognition. Section 6 evaluates VFH-Color descriptor in comparison with the previous version of VFH and SHOTCOLOR descriptor on Washington RGBD dataset. And the last section includes the main conclusions.

2   Previous Works

Most of the 3D categorization algorithms are based on features, shapes, and Bag of Words extracted from certain projections of the 3D objects. Schwarz et al. [9] developed a meaningful feature set that results from the pre-trained stage of Convolutional Neural Network (CNN). The depth and RGB images are processed independently by CNN and the resulting features are then concatenated to determine the category, instance, and pose of the object. Eitel et al. [2] presented two separate CNN processing streams for RGBD object recognition. RGB and colorized depth images consist of five convolutional layers and two fully connected layers. Both streams are processed separately through several layers and converge into one fully connected layer and a softmax layer for the classification task. Alex [1] proposed a new approach for RGBD object classification. The author trains four independent Convolutional Neural Networks (CNNs), one for depth data and three for RGB data, then trains these CNNs in a sequence. The decisions of each network are combined to obtain the final classification result. Madai et al. [5] reinvestigated Deep Convolutional Neural Networks (DCNNs) for RGBD object recognition. They proposed a new method for depth colorization based on surface normals, which colorized the surface normals for every pixel and computed the gradients in a horizontal direction (x-axis) and vertical direction (y-axis) using the Sobel operator. The authors defined two 3D vectors a and b in direction of the z-axis in order to calculate the surface normal n. As n has 3 dimensions, the authors map each of the three values of the surface normal to a corresponding RGB channels.

3   VFH-Color Descriptor

3.1   VFH Descriptor

The Viewpoint Feature Histogram (VFH) [7] computes a global descriptor of the point cloud and consists of two components: a surface shape component and a viewpoint direction component. VFH aims to combine the viewpoint direction directly into the relative normal angle calculation in the FPFH descriptor [6]. The viewpoint-dependent component of the descriptor is a histogram of the angles between the vector $(p_c - p_v)$ and each point's normal. This component is binned into a 128-bin histogram. The other component is a simplified point feature histogram (SPFH) estimated for the centroid of the point cloud, and an additional histogram of distances of all points in the cloud to the cloud's centroid. The three angles (α, ϕ, θ) with the distance d between each point and the centroid are binned into a 45-bin histogram. The total length of VFH descriptor is the combination of these two histograms and is equal to 308 bins.

3.2   Color Quantization Histogram

Color quantization is a vector quantization that aims to select K vectors in N dimensional space in order to represent N vectors from that space ($K << N$). In general, color quantization is applied to reduce the number of colors in a given image while maintaining the visual appearance of the original image.

Color quantization is applied in a 3-dimensional space RGB and follows the following steps:

1. Extract RGB features for each point from the point cloud data;
2. Obtain the matrix of RGB features (number of points $\times$ 3);

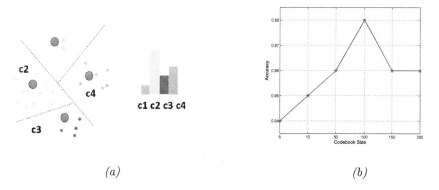

(a)   (b)

Fig. 1. (a) Color quantization process. The codebook (C1, C2, C3, and C4) denote cluster centers. The RGB features are clustered in order to optimize the space. The histogram counts the occurrence of each codebook in the point cloud. (b) The classification performance with respect to the codebook size.

3. Compute K-means algorithm for the RGB matrix in order to generate the codebook (cluster centers);
4. Count the occurrence of each codebook in the point cloud.

The codebook size represents the bins of color quantization histogram. As shown in Fig. 1(b), the highest value of accuracy is achieved with codebook equal to 100. Therefore, VFH-Color histogram concatenates 308 values of original VFH descriptor and 100 values of color quantization histogram, thus giving the total size of 408 values.

4   Deep Belief Network (DBN)

4.1   Restricted Boltzmann Machines (RBMs)

Restricted Boltzmann Machines (RBMs) [10] are a specific category of energy based model which include hidden variables. RBMs are restricted in the sense so that no hidden-hidden or variable-variable connections exist. RBMs are a parameterized generative model that represents a probability distribution. They involve two types of units:

1. The first layer (visible units): it contains visible units (x) that correspond to the components of an observation (i.e. VFH-Color descriptors);
2. The second layer (hidden units): it contains hidden units (h) that model dependencies between the components of observations.

The energy function of an RBM is defined as:

$$E(x, h) = -b^{'}x - c^{'}h - h^{'}Wx \tag{1}$$

where:

- W: represents the symmetric interaction term between visible units (x) and hidden units (h);
- b and c: are vectors that store the visible (input) and hidden biases (respectively).

RBMs are proposed as building blocks of multi-layer learning deep architectures called deep belief networks. The idea behind is that the hidden neurons extract pertinent features from the visible neurons. These features can work as the input to another RBM. By stacking RBMs in this way, the model can learn features from features in the aim of attending a high-level representation.

4.2   DBN Architecture

Deep Belief Network (DBN) is the probabilistic generative model with many layers of stochastic and hidden variables. Hinton et al. [3] introduced the motivation for using a deep network versus a single hidden layer (i.e. a DBN vs. an

RBM). The power of deep networks is achieved by having more hidden layers. However, one of the major problems for training deep network is how to initialize the weights W between the units of two consecutive layers ($j-1$ and j), and the biases b of layer j. Random initializations of these parameters can cause poor local minima of the error function resulting in low generalization. For this reason, Hinton et al. [3] have introduced a DBN architecture based on training sequence of RBMs. DBN train sequentially as many RBMs as the number of hidden layers that constitute its architecture, i.e. for a DBN architecture with l hidden layers, the model has to train l RBMs. For the first RBM, the inputs consist of the DBN's input layer (visible units) and the first hidden layer. For the second RBM, the inputs consist of the hidden unit activations of the previous RBM and the second hidden layer. The same holds for the remaining RBMs to browse through the l layers. After the model performs this layer-wise algorithm, it obtains a good initialization of the biases and the hidden weights of the DBN. At this stage, the model should determine the weights from the last hidden layer for the outputs. To obtain a successfully supervised learning, the model "fine-tunes" the resulting weights of all layers together.

5   3D Object Recognition Approach

In this work, we propose a new 3D recognition pipeline for point cloud data. As shown in Fig. 2, for each point cloud we extract two types of features: (1) geometric features extracted from Viewpoint Feature Histogram (VFH) (308 bins), and (2) color features extracted from color quantization (100 bins). These features are then combined into a single vector, being $308 + 100 = 408$ dimensional. These features are considered as the input layer x of DBN architecture that contains one visible layer x and three hidden layers h_1, h_2 and h_3. The input layer has a number N of input node for each of the entries in the feature vector. In our case, our feature vector would be of length 408, thus there would be 408 nodes in the input layer x. These nodes are connected to a series of hidden layers when each hidden layer is an unsupervised RBM. The output of each RBM in the hidden layer sequence is considered as input to the next. The last hidden

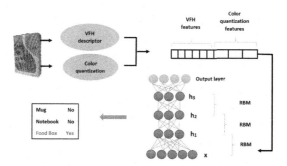

Fig. 2. Overview of our approach.

layer h_3 is connected to the output layer. Finally, the output layer contains the probabilities for each class label. The output node that produces the highest probability is chosen as the overall classification.

6   Experimental Results

In this section, we tested our recognition approach on Washington RGBD dataset which collects 300 common household objects which are organized into 51 categories. Each object is placed on a turntable and is captured for one whole rotation in order to obtain all object views using Kinect camera that records synchronized and aligned 640×480 RGB and depth images at 30 Hz [4]. In our experiments, we use only 10 classes: apple, ball, bowl, cereal_box, food_box, food_jar, notebook, onion, orange, and tomato which have similar shape. The goal of this choice is to make sure of the efficiency of our new descriptor VFH-Color that recognize these objects despite the similarity of their shape.

6.1   3D Object Recognition Analysis

DBN aims to allow each RBM model in the sequence to receive a different representation of the data. In other words, after RBM has been learned, the activity values of its hidden units are used as the training data for learning a higher-level RBM. The input layer has a number N of units, equal to the size of sample data x (size of VFH-Color descriptor). The number of units for hidden layers, currently, are pre-defined according to the experiment. We fixed DBN with three hidden layers $h1$, $h2$ and $h3$. The general DBN characteristics are shown in Table 1.

Figure 3 represents the confusion matrix across all 10 classes. Most model's results are very reasonable showing that VFH-Color can provide high-quality features. The classes that are consistently misclassified are onion, orange, ball (basketball), tomato and apple which are very similar in appearance and shape.

6.2   Comparison to Other Methods

In this subsection, we compare our approach to related state-of-the-art approaches. Table 3 shows the main accuracy values and compares our 3D recognition pipeline to the published results [2,5,9]. The previous approaches used the

Table 1. DBN characteristics that are used in our experiment.

Characteristics	Values
Hidden layer units	600-600-600
Learn rates	0.01
Learn rate decays	0.9
Epochs	200
Input layer units	Size of descriptor (408)

Table 2. The performance of our 3D recognition model.

Classes	Metrics			
	Wrong class	f1-score	Recall	Precision
(1)	(2), (8), (10)	96%	92%	99%
(2)	(8)	96%	98%	94%
(3)	–	100%	100%	100%
(4)	–	100%	100%	100%
(5)	–	100%	100%	100%
(6)	–	99%	99%	100%
(7)	–	100%	100%	100%
(8)	(2), (9), (10)	94%	94%	94%
(9)	(8), (10)	98%	98%	98%
(10)	(8)	98%	99%	97%
Average	–	98.1%	98.2%	98.2%

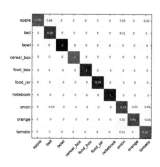

Fig. 3. Confusion matrix of our 3D recognition model.

color-coding depth maps and RGB images for training separately CNN architecture. In our work, we learn our features (VFH-Color features) using DBN with three hidden layers that model a deep network architecture. The results show also that our recognition pipeline works perfectly with the accuracy rate of 98.14% and outperforms all methods that are mentioned in the state-of-the-art.

Moreover, we evaluate the performance of VFH-Color against the previous version of VFH and SHOTCOLOR. The accuracy using VFH-Color performs 4% better than VFH that models only the geometric features. This result shows the effectiveness of the approach after adding the color information. We also notice that SHOTCOLOR presents the best accuracy (98.99%), although this descriptor encounters a problem when it is not able to compute the local reference frame for some point clouds. In this set of experiments, 10% of point clouds from the dataset are not computed with SHOTCOLOR. This problem becomes significant when 3D object recognition is in real time. Indeed, VFH-Color descriptor can be used in the real-time applications thanks to its estimation for every point cloud as well as its good recognition rates as shown in Table 2.

Table 3. The comparison of 3D object recognition accuracies and PCL descriptors on the Washington RGBD dataset.

Approaches	Accuracy rates
Eitel et al. [2]	91%
Madai et al. [5]	94%
Schwarz et al. [9]	94.1%
VFH and DBN	94%
SHOTCOLOR and DBN	98.99%
VFH-Color and DBN	**98.14%**

7   Conclusion

In this paper, we focused on 3D object recognition of point cloud data. We proposed the VFH-Color descriptor which combined geometric features extracted from Viewpoint Feature Histogram (VFH) descriptor and color information extracted from color quantization method. Then, we learned the resulting features with Deep Belief Network (DBN) classifier. The experimental results are encouraging, especially that our approach performed the state-of-the-art methods in recognizing 3D objects under different views. Also, our approach improved the recognition rates thanks to the use of color information.

References

1. Alexandre, L.A.: 3D object recognition using convolutional neural networks with transfer learning between input channels. In: Menegatti, E., Michael, N., Berns, K., Yamaguchi, H. (eds.) Intelligent Autonomous Systems 13. AISC, vol. 302, pp. 889–898. Springer, Cham (2016). doi:10.1007/978-3-319-08338-4_64
2. Eitel, A., Springenberg, J.T., Spinello, L., Riedmiller, M., Burgard, W.: Multimodal deep learning for robust RGB-D object recognition. In: 2015 IEEE/RSJ International Conference on Intelligent Robots and Systems (IROS), pp. 681–687. IEEE (2015)
3. Hinton, G.E., Osindero, S., Teh, Y.-W.: A fast learning algorithm for deep belief nets. Neural Comput. 18(7), 1527–1554 (2006)
4. Lai, K., Bo, L., Ren, X., Fox, D.: A large-scale hierarchical multi-view RGB-D object dataset. In: 2011 IEEE International Conference on Robotics and Automation (ICRA), pp. 1817–1824. IEEE (2011)
5. Madai-Tahy, L., Otte, S., Hanten, R., Zell, A.: Revisiting deep convolutional neural networks for RGB-D based object recognition. In: Villa, A.E.P., Masulli, P., Pons Rivero, A.J. (eds.) ICANN 2016. LNCS, vol. 9887, pp. 29–37. Springer, Cham (2016). doi:10.1007/978-3-319-44781-0_4
6. Rusu, R., Blodow, N., Beetz, M.: Fast point feature histograms (FPFH) for 3D registration. In: IEEE International Conference on Robotics and Automation, ICRA 2009, pp. 3212–3217. IEEE (2009)
7. Rusu, R., Bradski, G., Thibaux, R., Hsu, J.: Fast 3D recognition and pose using the viewpoint feature histogram. In: 2010 IEEE/RSJ International Conference on Intelligent Robots and Systems (IROS), pp. 2155–2162. IEEE (2010)
8. Rusu, R., Cousins, S.: 3D is here: point cloud library (PCL). In: IEEE International Conference on Robotics and Automation (ICRA), Shanghai, China, 9–13 May 2011
9. Schwarz, M., Schulz, H., Behnke, S.: RGB-D object recognition and pose estimation based on pre-trained convolutional neural network features. In: 2015 IEEE International Conference on Robotics and Automation (ICRA), pp. 1329–1335. IEEE (2015)
10. Smolensky, P.: Information processing in dynamical systems: foundations of harmony theory (1986)

Body Shape-Based Biometric Person Recognition from mmW Images

Ruben Vera-Rodriguez, Ester Gonzalez-Sosa$^{(\boxtimes)}$, Javier Hernandez-Ortega, and Julian Fierrez

Biometric and Data Pattern Analytics Lab (BiDA) Lab-ATVS,
Universidad Autonoma de Madrid,
Avda. Francisco Tomas y Valiente, 11 - Cantoblanco, 28049 Madrid, Spain
{ruben.vera,ester.gonzalezs,javier.hernandezo,julian.fierrez}@uam.es

Abstract. A growing interest has arisen in the security community for the use of millimeter waves in order to detect weapons and concealed objects. Also, the use of millimetre wave images has been proposed recently for biometric person recognition to overcome certain limitations of images acquired at visible frequencies. This paper proposes a biometric person recognition system based on shape information extracted from millimetre wave images. To this aim, we report experimental results using millimeter wave images with different body shape-based feature approaches: contour coordinates, shape contexts, Fourier descriptors and row and column profiles, using Dynamic Time Warping for matching. Results suggest the potential of performing person recognition through millimetre waves using only shape information, a functionality that could be easily integrated in the security scanners deployed in airports.

Keywords: mmW imaging · Body shape information · Biometrics · Border control security · Dynamic Time Warping

1 Introduction

Millimeter waves are high-frequency electromagnetic waves in the range of 30–300 GHz with wavelengths between 10 to 1 mm, recently found to have interesting properties for various pattern recognition applications. Concretely, imaging using millimetre waves (mmW) has gained the interest of the security community [1–3], mainly due to its low intrusiveness and the ability to pass through clothing and other occlusions.

Traditional applications of this technology include the detection of concealed weapons, explosive and dangerous objects [4]. Millimeter wave scanners have been deployed in several airports such as Los Angeles International Airport or Schiphol Airport, replacing the former X-rays scanners, among other reasons because mmW are not ionizing and therefore less harmful to the health of human beings. The suitability of these frequencies for concealed weapon detection relies on the different signature (due to difference of temperatures) between metallic objects and the human body skin. Automatic detection of dangerous objects

© Springer International Publishing AG 2017
L.A. Alexandre et al. (Eds.): IbPRIA 2017, LNCS 10255, pp. 453–461, 2017.
DOI: 10.1007/978-3-319-58838-4_50

Table 1. Existing mmW databases for person recognition purposes

Database	Nature	Mode	Scenarios	Subjects
BIOGIGA [16]	Synthetic simulation	Active and passive	Outdoors and indoors	25 male and 25 women
mmW TNO [9]	Real scanner	Passive	Outdoors	50 male

and weapons through mmW is still an active research line. Several works have Quiniti MMW sensor [4,5].

In the area of biometric person recognition, researchers have commonly proposed the use of images acquired at other spectral ranges: X-ray [6], infrared [7], with the aim of overcoming limitations such as illumination variations and body occlusions due to clothing, make up, hair, etc. However, only few works have used mmW images with recognition purposes. This shortage of biometric recognition research based on mmW images is mainly due to the lack of databases of images of people acquired at this band, as a consequence of the privacy concerns of these images [8].

Alefs *et al.* were the first to propose a holistic recognition approach based on the texture information using real mmW images [9]. They exploited the texture information contained in the torso region of the image through multilinear eigenspaces techniques. On the other hand, the works by Moreno-Moreno *et al.* [10] and by Gonzalez-Sosa *et al.* [11] proposed and analyzed a biometric person recognition system based on shape information extracted from synthetic mmW images, exploiting geometrical measures between different silhouette landmarks and features based on contour coordinates, respectively. In all cases, images were extracted in the range of 94 GHz.

Taking into account the interest of the security community in these frequencies and the promising results obtained in the past few works of recognition through mmW [10,12], one may consider the possibility of using mmW images acquired from the screening scanners simultaneously for detecting hidden objects and performing human recognition. With this approach, the security and recognition control procedures, indispensable for a society threaded constantly, would be enhanced. Body shape mmW information may not substitute primary biometrics such as face, iris or fingerprint, but it may be useful for narrowing the search of possible suspects with very little effort, as a soft biometric [13–15].

Previous works exploiting shape information have been carried out using synthetic images from the BioGiga database [16]. In the present work, we will analyse the discrimination capability of shape-based features using real mmW images from the mmW TNO Database [9]. Table 1 summarizes the key information of the two mmW databases.

This paper is structured as follows. The real mmW database used in the experiments is explained in Sect. 2. Section 3 describes the different features and classifier used in the biometric system. The experimental protocol and evaluation of these methods is performed in Sects. 4 and 5 respectively, and conclusions are finally drawn in Sect. 6.

2   The mmW TNO Database

The mmW TNO database (created by the Dutch Research Institute TNO in The Hague) is the only database available for research purposes that contains images of subjects extracted in the range of millimeter waves specifically designed for person recognition purposes [9]. Images are recorded using a passive stereo radiometer scanner in an outdoor scenario. The passive millimeter-wave radiation reflected by the subject arrives to a mirror that provides the millimetre-wave passive radiation to two hyperbolic antennas. Figure 1 shows the result of a full scanning, which is a set of two images with slightly different points of view of size 696 × 499 (width × height).

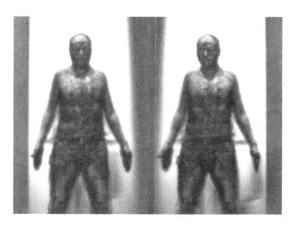

Fig. 1. Pair of millimetre-wave images from the mmW TNO Database. This full scanning image is set in *frontal viewpoint* and *no disguise*.

The database is comprised of images belonging to 50 different male subjects in 4 different scenarios. These 4 different scenarios derive from the combination of 2 different viewpoints and 2 different facial configurations. In the first viewpoint configuration, the subject is first asked to stand in front of the scanner with head and arms position at a fixed rack (*frontal viewpoint*). In the second viewpoint configuration (*lateral head viewpoint*), the subject is asked to turned his head leftward while the torso is asked to remain fixed (it may suffer some small changes due to the head movement).

In order to prove the benefits of millimetre-wave imaging above visual imaging, images with different facial configurations were also extracted. In this case, a second round of images with the first and second viewpoint configurations were extracted but now a large part of the facial region was occluded using an artificial beard or balaclava. We will refer to these two different facial clutter configurations as *disguise* and *non disguise*, respectively.

As mentioned before, each scanning is a set of two images. By dividing this set of images into single images o 348 × 499, the TNO database is comprised of

50 subjects × 2 viewpoint configurations × 2 facial clutter configurations × 2 images per set, making a total of 400 images in the whole TNO database.

3   System Description

The biometric recognition module of this work aims to perform person recognition through body shape-based information. In this section, details about the different shape features and classifier employed in this work are given. As all the features are shape-based, a segmentation stage is needed. The mmW images of this work have been manually segmented. All the shape features used in this work are extracted from mmW binarized images.

3.1   Shape-Based Body Features

Contour Coordinates are used as the baseline feature approach. By coordinate we mean the 2-dimensional vector which specifies the x and y position

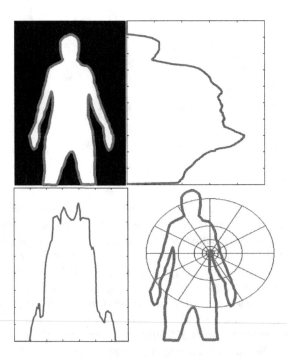

Fig. 2. Body shape features proposed in this work to perform person recognition through millimetre wave images. From the binarized image in the upper left corner we compute the sum of foreground pixels at row level (right side), while the sum of foreground pixels at column level is computed from left to right (below). The contour coordinates (lower right corner) is also extracted from the binarized image. The shape context descriptor (log polar histogram) of all contour points is also obtained.

of every single point within the silhouette of the body. The resolution of the contour is defined by the number of coordinates, being the resolution of the contours extracted from the mmW binarized images of around 2000 points. The starting point of the sequence is the middle point of the head. Figure 2, on its right lower corner shows an example of the contour coordinates that describe a subject silhouette.

Shape Contexts were first introduced by Belongie *et al.* [17]. This technique describes a specific point considering the relative distance and angle of the rest of the points within a shape. This method considers the set of vectors originating from a point to all other sample points on a shape. The number of radial bins (r_bins) and theta bins (θ_bins) are the main parameters of this descriptor. As a result, the shape contexts of a shape with N points forms a vector of size ($N * r\_bins * \theta\_bins$). Note that the log-polar histogram used in this case has a dimension of 12×5 (we decide to use the same configuration of parameters the author originally proposed), where 12 accounts for the number of theta bins and 5 accounts for the number of radial bins (see Fig. 2 bottom right). In order to compute the similarity between two shape contexts, different distance methods may be applied.

Row and Column Profiles. Give the binarized mmW image, we compute the sum of foreground pixels at row level from top to bottom (row profile), resulting a 499-vector and the sum of foreground pixels at column level from left to right (column profile), resulting a 398-vector (see Fig. 2).

Fourier Descriptors. Fourier descriptors [18] are simple to compute and robust against translations and rotations since the effect these transformations cause on the descriptors is completely known. To compute them, first we need to represent the contour coordinates as complex numbers ($u = x + jy$). Secondly, we apply the Fourier transform to these complex numbers to obtain the Fourier descriptor.

3.2   Matching

We have decided to use the Dynamic Time Warping (DTW) distance, which turned out to be better than other distances and classifiers like SVM in previous works [12]. The goal of DTW is to find an elastic match among samples of a pair of sequences that minimize a given distance measure [19]. In this work, DTW is used to obtain a cumulative distance between two sequences of coordinates, which is known to be minimal. Distances are converted into scores through exponential operations, previously normalizing the distance by the number of aligned points between two sequences (k). One of the main advantages of this algorithm is the possibility of dealing with sequences of points that do not have the same dimensionality. In our case, contours from different images do not have the same amount of points.

In the specific case of Fourier descriptors, individual distances are computed independently between row profiles (d_row) and column profiles (d_col). Then, those distances are averaged.

4   Experimental Protocol

The experimental protocol followed in the previous work using the mmW TNO database [9] was very optimistic. It assumed 4 images as input (test images) and 4 images as training. Individual distances were computed comparing pair of images under the same viewpoint conditions. Then, the final distance was the minimum over the 4 former individual distances.

The experimental protocol proposed in this work aims to simulate the situation in which a traveller would enter in the mmW scanner deployed in the security area of an airport, hence, using only 1 test image as input. At the same time the subject is being scanned to target concealed weapons or dangerous objects, he is also compared with a previously enrolled image to verify his identity. To simulate that scenario, we use in our experiments the subset of *frontal viewpoint* images of the TNO Database. This subset comprises a total of 200 images (50 subjects × 1 viewpoint configurations × 2 facial clutter configurations × 2 images per set), which are compared one to one.

5   Results

This section describes the experimental work carried out to analyse the performance of the difference body shape approaches described in Sect. 3. The aforementioned methods are tested with the mmW TNO database in verification mode following the experimental protocol from Sect. 4.

Figure 3 presents the DET curves obtained using different body shape-based features approaches. It is clear the superiority of the contour coordinates approach over the other approaches. In terms of EER, the row and column profiles slightly surpass the shape contexts approach. However, at False Acceptance Rate=1%, we have True Positive Rates of 85, 69, 62 and 59% for contour coordinates, shape contexts, row and column profile and Fourier descriptors, respectively. The dimensionality and computational cost of the different approaches vary significantly, being the dimensionality maximum for shape contexts ($N * r\_bins * \theta\_bins = 2000 \times 12 \times 5$) and the minimum for row and column profiles ($348 + 499$).

Fourier descriptors result in the worst performance reaching an EER of 11.00%, which may be due to the unappropriated use of DTW to match this type of features.

It is worth noting that the performance obtained with contour coordinates is improved in the mmW TNO database (7.00%) compared to the 10.00% obtained with BioGiga database using a similar experimental protocol. Subjects in the BioGiga database were simulated with the arms outstretched in the vertical line between shoulders, whereas the arms position from TNO database is unconstrained. This fact suggest the robustness of contour coordinates over the arm

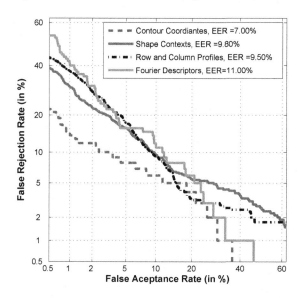

Fig. 3. DET curves for the biometric recognition system using different shape features extracted from mmW images

position. However, performance using shape contexts and Fourier descriptors is worsened considerably (from 6.00% and 7.00% in the BioGiga database to 9.85% and 11% in the mmW TNO database respectively), which indicates that those descriptors are less suitable for real mmW images.

An additional factor to bear in mind apart from the real/synthetic difference between the TNO and BioGiga databases, is the gender difference. The mmW TNO database only contains images from male subjects, while BIOGIGA contains a gender-balanced number of images. This difference in gender may be also affecting the performance of shape features used in this work.

6   Conclusions

The use of millimetre waves radiation has been recently introduced in computer vision applications such as weapons detection or even biometric person recognition applications.

This is the first work addressing the problem of person recognition through body-shape information using real mmW images. The experiments carried out show that person recognition through shape information contained in mmW images is feasible. For future work, texture information will be also considered and analysed, to study the discrimination capability of the whole body mmW signature (shape and texture).

Performing person recognition through mmW images while scanning subjects seeking for hidden objects would provide additional security to border control applications. One may notice however, that the real mmW images used in this work have been extracted using a passive mmW scanner, which obtained good results in outdoor applications where thermal radiation contrast is significant. However, if person recognition is operated inside airports, passive mmW images may not be enough to reach reasonable person recognition rates. Screening scanners actually deployed in airports operate in active mode, that is, artificial illumination is used to produce images with enough resolution to detect weapons and dangerous objects. Hence, more experiments using active mmW images will be needed to gain more insight in this new technology.

Acknowledgment. This work has been partially supported by project CogniMetrics TEC2015-70627-R (MINECO/FEDER), and the SPATEK network (TEC2015-68766-REDC). E. Gonzalez-Sosa is supported by a PhD scholarship from Universidad Autonoma de Madrid. Authors wish to thank also TNO for providing access to the database.

References

1. Appleby, R., Anderton, R.N.: Millimeter-wave and submillimeter-wave imaging for security and surveillance. Proc. IEEE **95**(8), 1683–1690 (2007)
2. Yujiri, L.: Passive millimeter wave imaging. In: IEEE MTT-S International Microwave Symposium Digest, pp. 98–101 (2006)
3. Patel, V.M., Mait, J.N.: Passive millimeter-wave imaging with extended depth of field and sparse data. In: Proceedings IEEE International Conference Acoustics, Speech and Signal Processing (ICASSP), pp. 2521–2524 (2012)
4. Haworth, C.D., Petillot, Y.R., Trucco, E.: Image processing techniques for metallic object detection with millimetre-wave images. Pattern Recogn. Lett. **27**(15), 1843–1851 (2006)
5. Murphy, K.S.J., Appleby, R., Sinclair, G., McClumpha, A., Tatlock, K., Doney, R., Hutcheson, I.: Millimetre wave aviation security scanner. In: Proceedings IEEE 36th International Carnahan Conference on Security Technology, pp. 162–166 (2002)
6. Jain, A.K., Chen, H.: Matching of dental x-ray images for human identification. Pattern Recogn. **37**(7), 1519–1532 (2004)
7. Morales, A., González, E., Ferrer, M.A.: On the feasibility of interoperable schemes in hand biometrics. Sensors **12**(2), 1352–1382 (2012)
8. Tugas, J.F.: Privacy and body scanners at eu airports. In: International Federation for Information Processing, p. 49 (2013)
9. Alefs, B., den Hollander, R., Nennie, F., van der Houwen, E., Bruijn, M., van der Mark, W., Noordam, J.: Thorax biometrics from millimetre-wave images. Pattern Recogn. Lett. **31**(15), 2357–2363 (2010)
10. Moreno-Moreno, M., Fierrez, J., Vera-Rodriguez, R., Parron, J.: Distance-based feature extraction for biometric recognition of millimeter wave body images. In: Proceedings IEEE International Carnahan Conference on Security Technology, ICCST, pp. 1–6 (2011)
11. Gonzalez-Sosa, E., Vera-Rodriguez, R., Fierrez, J., Ortega-Garcia, J.: Body shape-based biometric recognition using millimeter wave images. In: Proceedings IEEE Intlernational Carnahan Conference on Security Technology, ICCST (2013)

12. Gonzalez-Sosa, E., Vera-Rodriguez, R., Fierrez, J., Moreno-Moreno, M., Ortega-Garcia, J.: Feature exploration for biometric recognition using millimetre wave body images. EURASIP J. Image and Video Process. **30**(1), 1–13 (2015)

13. Tome, P., Fierrez, J., Vera-Rodriguez, R., Nixon, M.S.: Soft biometrics and their application in person recognition at a distance. IEEE Trans. Inf. Forensics Secur. **9**(3), 464–475 (2014)

14. Gonzalez-Sosa, E., Dantcheva, A., Vera-Rodriguez, R., Dugelay, J., Bremond, F., Fierrez, J.: Image-based gender estimation from body and face across distances. In: Proceedings ICPR (2016)

15. Dantcheva, A., Elia, P., Ross, A.: What else does your biometric data reveal? a survey on soft biometrics. IEEE Trans. Inf. Forensics Secur. **11**(3), 441–467 (2016)

16. Moreno-Moreno, M., Fierrez, J., Vera-Rodriguez, R., Parron, J.: Simulation of millimeter wave body images and its application to biometric recognition. In: Proceedings of SPIE, vol. 8362 (2012)

17. Belongie, S., Malik, J., Puzicha, J.: Shape matching and object recognition using shape contexts. IEEE Trans. Pattern Anal. Mach. Intell. **24**(4), 509–522 (2002)

18. Yang, M., Kpalma, K., Ronsin, J., et al.: A survey of shape feature extraction techniques. Pattern Recognition, pp. 43–90 (2008)

19. Martinez-Diaz, M., Fierrez, J., Hangai, S.: Signature matching. In: Li, S.Z., Jain, A.K. (eds.) Encyclopedia of Biometrics, pp. 1382–1387. Springer, New york (2015)

Spacial Aliasing Artefact Detection on T1-Weighted MRI Images

João F. Teixeira[(✉)] and Hélder P. Oliveira

INESC TEC, Faculdade de Engenharia, Universidade do Porto, Porto, Portugal
jpfteixeira.eng@gmail.com, helder.f.oliveira@inesctec.pt

Abstract. Magnetic Resonance Imaging (MRI) exams suffer from unde-sirable structure replicating and overlapping effects on certain acquisi-tion settings. These are called Spatial Aliasing Artefacts (SAA) and their presence interferes with the segmentation of other anatomical structures. This paper addresses the segmentation of the SAA in T1-weighted MRI image sets, in order to effectively remove their influence over the legiti-mately positioned body structures. The proposed method comprises an initial thresholding, employing the Triangle method, an aggregation of neighboring voxels through Region Growing. Further refinement of the objects contour is obtained with Convex Hull and a Minimum Path algo-rithm applied to two orthogonal planes (Sagittal and Axial).

Some experiments concerning the extension of the pipeline used are reported and the results seem promising. The average contour distance concerning the Ground Truth (GT) rounds $2.5\,mm$ and area metrics point out average overlaps above 64% with the GT. Some issues concern-ing the fusion between the output from the two planes are to be perfected. Nevertheless, the results seems sufficient to neutralize the influence of SAA and expedite the downstream anatomical segmentation tasks.

Keywords: Segmentation · Aliasing · Minimum Path · MRI · T1-weighted

1 Introduction

Medical imaging processing and analysis has been a thriving research field for some decades, and has proven to provide valuable assistance in the identification and diagnosis processes of illnesses. Part of the interest on this field is only indirectly related with diagnosis and may be more focused on human metrics and production of generic or individualized atlases. The authors' main research focus is on medical imaging anatomical segmentation, with particular interest in Breast Cancer related MRI images and detection relevant anatomical key points.

The work developed concerns the identification of undesirable markings on MRI sets (Fig. 1). The purpose of such delineation is to remove them, or mit-igate their effects, preventing from interfering with the segmentation of other structures. These specific marking can be found on the centre of patient's body, and do not correspond to any expected anatomical structure for that position.

ⓒ Springer International Publishing AG 2017
L.A. Alexandre et al. (Eds.): IbPRIA 2017, LNCS 10255, pp. 462–470, 2017.
DOI: 10.1007/978-3-319-58838-4_51

These Spatial Aliasing Artefacts (SAA), are a known consequence of having body regions outside the machine's field of view (FOV), during a Magnetic Resonance Imaging (MRI) exam [1]. The portions out of the FOV are spatially shifted and overlapped onto the signal, interfering with the expected structures' signal.

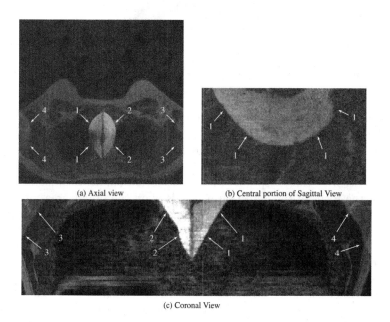

(a) Axial view   (b) Central portion of Sagittal View

(c) Coronal View

Fig. 1. Spatial aliasing artefact: the left shoulder copies are arrows 1 & 3 while the right shoulder copies are arrows 2 & 4

In this work, this effect concerns the shifting of cropped shoulders to both centre and opposing side of the body (Fig. 2). The images used belong to the radiologic image database for breast cancer research from the PICTURE project[1].

During their daily practice, the radiology and breast cancer professionals' findings are not affected by this issue, since the shoulders' anterior-posterior position does not coincide with the breasts (main subject of their study). However, for medical image analysis researchers directed at producing a body atlas, for instance segmenting the Sternum bones or the *Latissimus Dorsi* muscle, this interference presents a challenge to conventional segmentation algorithms. Thus, we propose a method to segment this interference, in order to remove it's influence for downstream tasks. The method proposed comprises a first focus on the overall unique features of the SAA (its intensity) and progressively aggregates similar regions. A final object surface refinement is performed by path optimization. Overall results are very promising, although some path optimization step issues must be revised to remove error propagation.

---

[1] http://www.vph-picture.eu/.

Fig. 2. Reconstitution of cropped portion of image based on the central SAA

2   Applicable Image Segmentation Approaches

Structure segmentation is a prevalent goal for medical image processing tasks. Similar works on MRI images, in particular concerning breast cancer, are not that frequent, with the exception of lesion detection aiming for diagnosis. Consequently, the focus of the detection methods is on the breast area rather than the whole body. To the best of our knowledge there has been no published work trying to identify or remove the kind of interference that is tackled on this work. Thus, this experiments had to rely on general purpose methods for segmentation.

Due to the images' settings, the obvious first segmentation choice could be a combination of adaptive thresholding, such as *Otsu's method* [2], and connected components selection based on their properties, such as shape and location. However, as Fig. 1a suggests, a unique thresholding approach would be insufficient since some cases' shape include an outward portion with uneven intensity.

Region Growing [3] has the potential to iteratively aggregate regions that may not follow the majority of a distribution, provided they comply to some other inclusive criteria. This however, also has the potential to include a considerable amount of inaccurate regions if the inclusive criteria are not strict enough. Thus, the balance of the method's configuration is delicate. Additional options can be included when the input map is previously processed, resulting in different, perhaps more trivial to define, inclusion criteria.

Another promising method for the segmentation of roughly regular shapes is *Active Contours* [4], also known as Snakes. These require an energy map, normally gradients, in order to enhance edges of objects, to which the contour progresses iteratively. Similarly to *Region Growing*, the *Snakes'* results may vary significantly depending on the input map provided. In the case depicted in Fig. 1, the gradient may induce inward dents to the contour, due to the intensity pattern disparity of the region. On the other hand, *Active Contours* also needs to configure elasticity and curvature of the contours, which may not be trivial concerning the great deal of anatomical variability.

As with many works on segmentation, the results of a method, downstream in the pipeline, may be significantly changed by a pre-processing of the original images. Image enhancement has a broad array of available techniques that could be applied. One of the simplest concerns intensity expansion/compression through manipulation of the images' gamma value. This non-linearity alters the influence of certain intensity ranges. Provided the objects' dynamic range includes other structures, this approach would most likely provide minimal upturn. Denoising through Wavelets decomposition, thresholding the high frequency components and reversing the decomposition [3] is also a quite common enhancement approach. Regional denoising methods such as average and median filters [3] have been largely used to remove background noise. Shannon Entropy [5] and Homogeneity [6] measures have also been successfully used for segmentation tasks.

Despite not having found any particular methodology to apply to this particular problem, several generic approaches seem likely to produce satisfactory results. In this work, some of the most promising and least subject to parameter fine-tuning were combined. The focus of the method concerns restricted path optimization to obtain the most accurate contour on objects with fairly consistent shape in spite of sometimes having uneven intensity distributions.

3 Methodology

The images, due to the nature of the artefact, present a brighter intensity on the central portion of the body and are less bright on the portions nearer the opposing shoulder (Fig. 1). This last position presents another bright anatomical structure on the original signal, leading to a harder segmentation challenge. Thus, this work focuses on delineating the SAA's central copies. The outcome could then be shifted and fitted to the remaining lateral copies of the SAA.

3.1 Proposed Pipeline

The proposed solution is composed by four modules, which were combined to solve certain issues on the accurate detection of the artefact. First, thresholding is performed and the resulting objects are selected based on their attributes. Second, a region growing algorithm is applied, over an entropy map. Then, to approximate the contours to their correct shape (for objects with gradual intensity decay), a convex hull is calculated. To obtain the precise SAA contours, a *Minimum Path* algorithm is used across the slices. Due to some misalignment of the left and right shoulder copies, each half was processed independently.

Coarse Object Selection. The base segmentation, which is reshaped by later modules of the pipeline, uses a thresholding approach due to the overall voxel intensity of the region. On a histogram, the desired intensity region generally presents a much broader and lower peak than the background image. The *Triangle method* [7] was designed to solve similar cases and thus, was used to find the first estimate of the objects. Whenever the segmented objects included a portion of the breast region, the *Triangle thresholding* is calculated again over the objects, narrowing further the selection range. Afterwards, the objects outside the sagittal and coronal profiles (x and y axis, respectively) are removed, on the basis that the artefacts occupy a large enough number of voxels.

Entropy Map and Region Growing. To extend the previous segmentation, the *Region Growing* [3] method was applied to the volume. This method requires three inputs: a 3D map (β), seed points and inclusion criteria. Inspired by Top *et al.* [5], the adaptation of *Shannon Entropy* (Eq. 1) measure was observed to produce interesting results, concerning the diminishing of the effect of noise.

$$\beta(x) = -p(x) \log_2 p(x) - (1 - p(x)) \log_2(1 - p(x)) \tag{1}$$

$p(x)$ refers to the probability of the intensity of voxel at position x in the volume being classified as object rather than background (based on histogram frequencies). Another input consists of seed points based on the previous segmentation. Each axial object was lightly eroded and thinned, generating new contours, that were then sampled by a factor of $1/4$. This sampled version of the 3D contour was used as seed points, preserving most of the shape of the previous segmentation. Lastly, it used an 8-neighborhood connectivity and included points within a range of 2.5σ of the μ intensity at the seeds' positions.

Convex Hull. In cases similar to the one in Fig. 1, the *Region Growing* was insufficient to complete the apparently degraded part of the SAA. As artefacts refer to shoulder anatomy, they are mostly convex, both in axial slices, as it has a rather monotonic growth from the bottom to top, across the sagittal axis. Thus, it stands to reason trying to compensate the gaps from the previous algorithm using a *Convex Hull* algorithm. In this work, the *QHull* [8] approach was used.

Bi-perspective Polar Minimum Path. This last module draws much of it's concept from the work of Oliveira *et al.* [9], having suffered some adaptations for this particular problem. That work consisted in obtaining the accurate contour using a *Minimum Path* algorithm that is restricted in the sense that it only moves forward or in the forward diagonal (8-connected), from margin to margin, turning the image into a graph. Similarly here, each half (left and right), axial and sagittal slice-wise, consists of quasi-elliptic shapes. Hence, the Cartesian to Polar conversion was restricted to half the angle span. A transformation of a sagittal slice is depicted in Fig. 3a, with the *Minimum Path* result in Fig. 3b.

The *Polar Minimum Path* behaves poorly in the presence of small objects. Conversely, the shape of the SAA is uneven, since the bottom region appears larger on the sagittal plane and, similarly, the top region on the axial plane. This setting favors a bi-parted application of the *Polar Minimum Path*, starting on the sagittal plane and then moving to the axial plane for processing the remaining top slices. The centre positions for the *Polar Minimum Path* are found using the centroid of the previous segmentation. The Sagittal/Axial processing vertical limit is the middle slice containing object from the previous segmentation.

The two perspectives also present undesirable objects in a slightly different fashion, hence the *Minimum Path* cost maps were calculated differently. For the bottom part a Sobel vertical gradient sufficed. The map for the top part was enhanced by a 75% Top-hap operation of the normalized image, and 25% of the

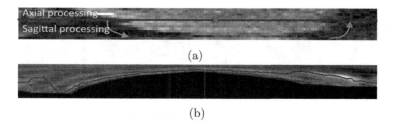

(a)

(b)

Fig. 3. (a) Sagittal slice with Polar centre as dark blue cross and light blue arrows as Polar transformation direction for the bottom part; (b) Polar transformed, Sobel of (a) with *Minimum Path* result in red (Color figure online)

complementary of the result of Laplacian of Gaussian filter on the original image. The values were empirically tuned to reduce noise and enhance high gradients.

Moreover, the image input of the *Minimum Path* is further processed prior to being used. To prevent misinterpretation of undesired high gradient regions over desired low gradient ones, regions are blocked by a mask calculated from the previous module's segmentation. The mask is produced by eroding and dilating the existing objects and subtracting them to produce a curved strip with a shape similar to the desired path. The masked region is shown as black in Fig. 3b.

4   Results

4.1   Database and Annotations

The database used is comprised by a subset from the PICTURE project (see Footnote 1) data-base. In particular, it was used 21 T1-weighted MRI image sets, containing approximately 60 axial slices each, with an average voxel resolution of $0.59 \times 0.59 \times 3$ mm. The total number of artefacts (shoulder copies) present in the database is 36. Naturally, the shape and size of the SAA vary among patients due to anatomical variability, patient size and acquisition pose. However the objects are generally smaller than half the axial slices dimension. The database was annotated by an expert and contains the delineation of each separate shoulder.

4.2   Results

The proposed pipeline (P1234) is comprised of the modules: (1) *Coarse selection*, (2) *Region Growing*, (3) Convex Hull and (4) *Minimum Path*. As explained in Sect. 3 the methods were subsequently introduced to solve specific issues with the base pipeline (P14-first and last modules). To verify the usefulness of each step, experiments concerning the alternating removal of the middle modules were conducted. The sequential improvement can be seen in Fig. 4 and Table 1.

The evaluation of the results, present in Table 1, was performed using Pixel-Area and Contour-wise metrics: Area Overlap Measure (AOM), the Combined

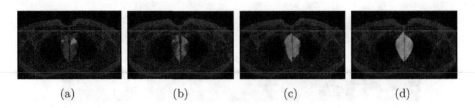

| (a) | (b) | (c) | (d) |

Fig. 4. Segmentation results along the modules: (a) Coarse selection, (b) Region growing, (c) Convex hull and (d) Bi-perspective minimum path

Table 1. Average and standard deviation results of the segmentation pipelines.

Pipelines	AOM		CM		AD		AMED		HAUSD	
P1	50	(28)	66	(19)	6.03	(7.03)	6.94	(6.94)	29.23	(17.90)
P12	56	(29)	70	(20)	4.89	(6.04)	5.62	(6.07)	25.76	(17.49)
P123	62	(24)	71	(21)	3.11	(4.59)	3.82	(5.09)	20.59	(14.43)
P1234	**64**	**(26)**	**72**	**(24)**	**2.52**	**(3.55)**	**3.15**	**(4.25)**	**18.75**	**(13.57)**
P124	62	(28)	71	(25)	3.68	(4.79)	4.39	(5.11)	22.82	(17.11)
P13	60	(26)	70	(22)	4.01	(5.53)	4.93	(5.70)	27.41	(16.12)
P134	63	(28)	71	(25)	3.17	(4.92)	3.94	(5.67)	22.80	(16.64)
P14	62	(28)	71	(25)	4.23	(5.97)	5.05	(6.56)	23.04	(17.57)

P_{xx} relate to the module steps, (1) Coarse detection, (2) EntropyRG, (3) Convex Hull, (4) Min. Path.
Metrics units: AOM and CM-% (max is best); AD, AMED and HAUSD-mm (min is best)

Measure (CM) of AOM, under-segmentation and over-segmentation [10]; the Average Minimum Euclidean Distance (AMED) and Hausdorff distance (HD) [11].

The overall results seem to indicate a contour rather close to the Ground Truth (GT), on the best case averaging (*Avg*) 2.52 mm over the AD and 3.15 mm on the AMED. The AOM implies a missing third of the overlapped area that is either of GT, segmentation or crossed mismatch. The growth of this measure correlates with the CM measure, which tries to balance the AOM, under and over-segmentation metrics. It is noteworthy that CM also slightly increases in the standard deviation (*Std dev*) along the inclusion of modules on the pipeline, which seems to model two trends according to visual inspection. The first corresponds to the inclusion of real object's missing portions and the second relates to the inclusion of non-object regions on segmented area. The first module (P1) often has smaller objects whenever the images present contour diffusion. With the introduction of spatially unconstrained *Region Growing* (P12), the segmentation tends to have both under-segmented regions and over-segmented regions, due to the closeness to the breast and other bright structures. This leads to an increase of CM and AOM's *Std dev*. On step 3 (P123), the under-segmentation decreases significantly due to the external restrictions of the *Convex Hull* (smaller AOM *Std dev*), but the over-segmentation stays the same or slightly worse (CM's *Std dev* small increase). Step 4 (P1234) perfects the contour in most of the cases but creates some over-segmentation issues (Fig. 5), worsening the overall *Std dev* (AOM and CM), with slightly better *Avg* and the best contour metrics for all tested. The concordant larger values of AOM and CM's *Std dev*, and HAUSD (*Avg* and *Std dev*) suggest that the cases are generally good, with a few cases where the results fail considerably, leaving AD and AMED mostly unscathed.

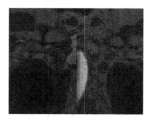

Fig. 5. Undesirable result. Propagation of error

5   Conclusion

The work presented concerns the identification of a troublesome superimposition of cropped anatomy over other structures of interest. The images available presented objects of the highest intensity over all the database, despite in several cases having uneven areas near the object's borders. The proposed method comprised of modules that progressively narrowed down the contour to the correct position, finalizing the delineation with a path optimization method.

According to the metrics employed, the complete pipeline seems to have been improved over the tested module combinations. However, there were only 36 SAAs in the database, which is not be sufficient for a strong validation. Furthermore, only a small set of methods was employed, thus requiring further experimentation for a consistent validation. Some experiments involving removing the intermediate modules were performed. Even if lightly, the results suggested against their removal and reinforce the reasons for their initial setup.

The influence of small missing portions or inclusion of random objects would rarely be felt after module 4, since the mask was the only persistence from earlier steps. Only if the mask was too narrow or far from the desired contour, those problems would sufficiently misguide the *Minimum Path* to produce poor results. Yet, when inclusion issues occurs, their effect was propagated, resulting on substantial over-segmentation. The algorithm at times ran over isolated incorrect earlier segmentation. This was mainly caused by a mismatch of the *Minimum Path* positioning due to the bi-parted processing slice interface.

This work tackled an issue that arose from the task of segmenting anatomical structures from MRI data. Despite the contours' average error of around 3 mm (mostly due to some over-detection portions), this may be more than sufficient to have accurate results on the pipeline's next step, i.e. detection of other structures.

Future work will explore *Wavelet Decomposition* filtering to reduce the effect of smaller structures, and the tuning of the path finding methods. Also, this work will be used to clean the SAA from the images, revealing the real structures.

Acknowledgements. This work was funded by the Project "NanoSTIMA: Macro-to-Nano Human Sensing: Towards Integrated Multimodal Health Monitoring and Analytics/NORTE-01-0145-FEDER-000016" financed by the North Portugal Regional Operational Programme (NORTE 2020), under the PORTUGAL 2020 Partnership Agreement, and through the European Regional Development Fund (ERDF).

References

1. Fiaschetti, V., Pistolese, C., Funel, V., Rascioni, M., Claroni, G., Gatta, F.D., Cossu, E., Perretta, T., Simonetti, G.: Breast MRI artefacts: evaluation and solutions in 630 consecutive patients. Clin. Radiol. **68**(11), e601–e608 (2013). doi:10.1016/j.crad.2013.05.103
2. Otsu, N.: A threshold selection method from gray-level histograms. IEEE Trans. Syst. Man Cybern. **9**, 62–66 (1979)
3. Gonzalez, R.C., Woods, R.E.: Digital Image Processing, 3rd edn. Prentice-Hall Inc., Upper Saddle River (2006)
4. Caselles, V., Kimmel, R., Sapiro, G.: Geodesic active contours. Int. J. Comput. Vis. **22**(1), 61–79 (1997). doi:10.1023/A:1007979827043
5. Top, A., Hamarneh, G., Abugharbieh, R.: Active learning for interactive 3D image segmentation. In: Fichtinger, G., Martel, A., Peters, T. (eds.) MICCAI 2011. LNCS, vol. 6893, pp. 603–610. Springer, Heidelberg (2011). doi:10.1007/978-3-642-23626-6_74
6. Pal, S., Pal, N.: Segmentation using contrast and homogeneity measures. Pattern Recogn. Lett. **5**(4), 293–304 (1987). doi:10.1016/0167-8655(87)90061-4
7. Zack, G.W., Rogers, W.E., Latt, S.A.: Automatic measurement of sister chromatid exchange frequency. J. Histochem. Cytochem. **25**, 741–753 (1977)
8. Barber, C.B., Dobkin, D.P., Huhdanpaa, H.: The quickhull algorithm for convex hulls. ACM Trans. Math. Softw. **22**(4), 469–483 (1996). doi:10.1145/235815.235821
9. Oliveira, H.P., Cardoso, J.S., Magalhães, A.T., Cardoso, M.J.: A 3D low-cost solution for the aesthetic evaluation of breast cancer conservative treatment. Comput. Methods Biomech. Biomed. Eng. Imaging Vis. **2**(2), 90–106 (2013). doi:10.1080/21681163.2013.858403
10. Elter, M., Held, C., Wittenberg, T.: Contour tracing for segmentation of mammographic masses. Phys. Med. Biol. **55**(18), 5299–5315 (2010). doi:10.1088/0031-9155/55/18/004
11. Song, E., Xu, S., Xu, X., Zeng, J., Lan, Y., Zhang, S., Hung, C.-C.: Hybrid segmentation of mass in mammograms using template matching and dynamic programming. Acad. Radiol. **17**(11), 1414–1424 (2010). doi:10.1016/j.acra.2010.07.008

Sentiment Recognition in Egocentric Photostreams

Estefania Talavera[1,2]([⊠]), Nicola Strisciuglio[1], Nicolai Petkov[1],
and Petia Radeva[2,3]

[1] Intelligent Systems Group, University of Groningen, Groningen, The Netherlands
`e.talavera.martinez@rug.nl`
[2] Department of Mathematics and Computer Science, University of Barcelona,
Barcelona, Spain
[3] Computer Vision Center, Barcelona, Spain

Abstract. Lifelogging is a process of collecting rich source of information about daily life of people. In this paper, we introduce the problem of sentiment analysis in egocentric events focusing on the moments that compose the images recalling positive, neutral or negative feelings to the observer. We propose a method for the classification of the sentiments in egocentric pictures based on global and semantic image features extracted by Convolutional Neural Networks. We carried out experiments on an egocentric dataset, which we organized in 3 classes on the basis of the sentiment that is recalled to the user (positive, negative or neutral).

Keywords: Egocentric photos · Lifelogging · Sentiment image analysis

1 Introduction

Mental imagery is the process in which the feeling of an experience is imagined by a person in the absence of external stimuli. It has been assumed by therapists to be directly related with emotions [7], opening some questions when images describing past moments of our lives are available: *Can an image make the process of mental imagery easier?* or *Can specific images help us to retrieve or imply feelings and moods?*

Lifelogging is a recent trend consisting in constructing a digital collection from an egocentric point of view of the events of a person that wears a recording device. It is a tool for the analysis of the lifestyle of users, since it provides objective information of what happened during different moments of the day, and a powerful tool for memory enhancement [11]. Using wearable cameras, each day up to 2000 egocentric photostreams are usually recorded, i.e. up to 70000 per month. A lot of these images are redundant, non-informative or routine and thus without special value for the wearer to be preserved. Usually, users are interested in keeping special moments, images with sentiments that will allow them in the future to re-live the personal moments captured by the camera. An automatic tool for sentiment analysis of egocentric images is of high interest to

© Springer International Publishing AG 2017
L.A. Alexandre et al. (Eds.): IbPRIA 2017, LNCS 10255, pp. 471–479, 2017.
DOI: 10.1007/978-3-319-58838-4_52

Fig. 1. Examples of positive (green), negative (red) and neutral (yellow) images. (Color figure online)

make possible the processing of the big collection of lifelogging data and keeping out just the images of interest i.e. of high charge of positive sentiments.

However, the automatic sentiment image analysis is a complicated task first of all, because of the lack of clear definition of it. There is no consensus between the different sentiment ontologies in the literature. Table 1 illustrates the ambiguity of the problem, reporting several sentiments ontology in images. The first group [13,18,21] assigns 8 main sentiments as excitement, awe or sadness to the images with assigned discrete positive (1) and negative (−1) sentiment value. The second group [4,10] defines a different set of sentiments as valence or arousal and discrete positive (1), neutral (0) or negative (−1) values assigned to the images according to the sentiments. In contrast, the third group [14] assigns up to 17 sentiments (6 basics and 9 complex) and each image of the dataset is assigned a continuous value in a scale from 1 to 4. Given the ambiguity of the semantic sentiment assignment, with labels difficult to classify into positive or negative sentiments, the last group [1] defines up to 3244 Adjective Noun Pairs (ANP) (e.g. 'beautiful_girl') and assigns a continuous sentiment value in a range of [−2,2] to them. The main idea is that the same object according to its appearance has positive or negative sentiment value like 'angry_dog' (−1.55) and 'adorable_dog' (+1.45). A natural question is until which extent the 3244 ANPs represent a scene captured by the image, taking into account the difficulty to detect them automatically (Mean average accuracy ∼25%).

Given the difficulty of image sentiment determination, ambiguity and lack of consensus in the bibliography, added by the difficulty of the egocentric images, we focus on the image sentiment as a discrete value expressing a ternary sentiment value (positive (1), negative (−1) or neutral (0) value) similar to [20]. Egocentric data is of special difficulty, since we do not observe the wearer and his/her, i.e. from facial or corporal expressions, but rather from the perspective of what the user sees. Moreover, in real life fortunately, negative emotions have much less prevalence than neutral and positive, that makes very difficult to have enough examples of negative egocentric images and events. Thus, the problem we address in this article is what effect an egocentric image or event has on an observer (positive, neutral or negative) (see Fig. 1), instead of attempting to specify an explicit semantic image sentiment like sadness; and how to develop automatic tool for sentiment value detection (positive, vs. neutral vs. negative) and egocentric dataset in order to validate its results. Going further, in contrast

Table 1. Different image sentiment ontologies.

DataSets	Source	Images	Semantic sentiment labels	Sentiment values
Abstract & Artphoto [13]		280 & 806	positive: contentment, amusement, excitement, awe, negative: sadness, fear, disgust, and anger	$\{1,-1\}$
You's Dataset [21]	Flickr Instagram	23000	positive: contentment, amusement, excitement, awe, negative: sadness, fear, disgust, and anger	$\{1,-1\}$
CASIA-WebFace [18]		494k	anger, disgust, fear happy, neutral, sad, surprise	$[1,0,-1]$
IAPS [10]		1182	valence, arousal, and dominance	$[1,7]$
GAPED [4]		732	valence, arousal, and normative significance	$\{1,0,-1\}$
EmoReact [14]	Youtube	1102 clips	17 sentiments: 6 basic emotions (positive: happiness, surprise, negative: sadness, fear, disgust, and anger), and 9 complex emotions: (curiosity, uncertainty, excitement, attentiveness, exploration, confusion, anxiety, embarrassment, frustration)	$[1,4]$
VSO + TwitterIm [1]	Flickr Twitter	0.5M	Not, but adjective noun pairs (3244)	Flickr$[-2,2]$ Twitter$[-1,1]$
You_ RobustSet [20]	Twitter	1269	Non-semantic labels: positive and Negative	$\{1,-1\}$
UBRUG-EgoSenti*	Wearable camera	12088	Non-semantic labels: positive, neutral and negative	$\{1,0,-1\}$

to the published work, we claim to automatically analyse the sentiment value of egocentric events i.e. a group of sequential images that represents the same scene. In the case of egocentric images, the probability that a single image describes an event is low; there are a lot of images that just capture wall, sky, ground or partially objects. For this reason, we are interested to automatically discover how the event captured by the camera influences the observer, that is to automatically determine the ternary sentiment values of the events, which are richer in information and involve the whole moment's experience. For example, an event being in a dark and narrow, grey space would influence negatively, a routine scene like working in the wearer's office could influence the observer neutrally and an event where the wearer has spent some time with friends in a nice outdoor space could influence positively to the observer.

Automatic sentiment analysis from images is a recent research field. In the literature, sentiment recognition in conventional images has been approached by computing and combining visual, textual, or audio features [14,15,17,19]. Other characteristics, such as facial expressions have also been used for sentiment prediction [23]. The combination of visual and textual features extracted from images is possible due to the wide use of online social media and microblogs, where images are posted accompanied by short comments. Therefore, multi-modal approaches were proposed, where both sources of information are merged [17,19] for automatic sentiment value detection.

Recently, with the outstanding performance of Convolutional Neural Networks (CNN), several approaches to sentiment analysis relied on deep learning techniques for classification and/or features extraction combined with other networks or methods [2,12,21,22]. The work in [21] applies fine-tuning on the AlexNet to classify the 8 emotions: sadness, angry, content, etc. In contrast, in [2] they propose to fine-tuned CaffeNet with oversampling to classify into Positive or Negative sentiments. In [12] a novel transformations of image intensities to 3D spaces is proposed to reduce the amount of data required to effectively train deep CNN models. In [22] the authors use logistic regression to classify into 3 sentiments using CNN features. In [3], the authors perform a fine-tuning on a CNN model and modify the last layer to classify 2089 ANPs. However, no work has addressed the sentiment image and event analysis in egocentric datasets.

To address the egocentric data sentiment analysis, we propose to combine semantic concepts in terms of ANPs, given that they have sentiment values associated [1], with general visual features extracted from a CNN [9]. ANPs represent a finite subset of concepts present in the image, so they bring strong sentiment value, but can not ensure to cover the whole image content. Visual features extracted by CNNs can help to summarize the whole image content in an intermediate level. We test our method on a new egocentric dataset of 12088 pictures with ternary sentiment values acquired from 3 users and 20 days. A very preliminary stage of this work has been presented in [16].

Therefore, our contributions here are three-fold: (a) a model for ternary sentiment value analysis in egocentric images, (b) extension of the approach to egocentric events, and (c) the first egocentric sentiment value dataset from 12088 images covering 20 days of 3 persons.

The paper is organized as follows. We describe the proposed approach and the dataset in Sects. 2 and 3, respectively. In Sect. 4, we describe the experimental setup, the quantitative and qualitative evaluation, and discuss our findings. Finally, Sect. 5 draws conclusions and outlines future works.

2   Proposed Method

In this section, we describe the proposed method for sentiment recognition from egocentric photostreams, which is based on visual (extracted by CNN) and semantic (in terms of ANPs) features extracted from the images. An architectural overview of the proposed system is depicted in Fig. 2.

(a) **Temporal Segmentation:** Given that egocentric images have smaller field of view and thus do not capture entirely the context of the event, we need to detect the events of the days. To this aim, we apply the SR-Clustering algorithm for temporal segmentation of photostreams [5]. The clustering procedure is performed on an image representation that combines visual features extracted by a CNN with semantic features in terms of visual concepts extracted by Imagga's auto-tagging technology (http://www.imagga.com/solutions/auto-tagging.html).

(b) **Features Extraction:** For the computation of the semantic features in terms of the ANPs, we use the DeepSentiBank Network [3]. Given an image, the DeepSentiBank network considers the 2089 best performing ANPs. Applying the DeepSentiBank on them gives a 2089-D feature vector, where the feature values correspond to the ANPs likelihood in the image. These values are multiplied by the sentiment value associated to the concepts. Note that each ANP has a positive or negative sentiment value assigned, but not 0 for a neutral sentiment.

However, the 2089 ANPs not necessarily have the power to explain the "richness" of any scene in an image. Hence, we integrate the ANPs feature vector with a feature descriptor provided by the penultimate layer if a CNN [9] that summarizes the whole context of the image. The resulting feature vector is composed by 4096 features. We combine the ANPs and the CNN feature vectors into a 6185-D feature vector, in order to construct a more reliable and rich image representation that relates image semantics expressed by the ANPs with clear sentiment value with the CNN cues as an intermediate image representation. We apply the Signed Root Normalization (SRN) to transform the CNN feature vectors to a more uniformly distributed space followed by a l_2-normalization [24].

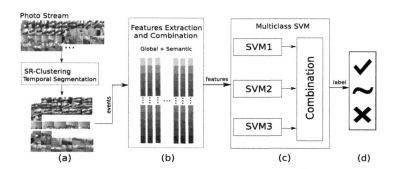

Fig. 2. Architecture of the proposed method. (a) Temporal segmentation of the photostream into events. (b) CNN and ANPs features are extracted from the images and (c) used as input to the trained multi-class SVM model. (d) The model labels the input image as positive, neutral or negative.

(c) Classification: We use the proposed feature vectors to train a multi-class SVM classifier due to its high generalization capability [8]. This is ensured by the SVM learning algorithm that finds a separation hyperplane that maximizes the separation margin between the classes. We employ a 1-vs-all design for the multi-class problem, as suggested in [6]. The cardinality of the classes in the proposed dataset is not balanced, which affects the computation of the training error cos. In order to classify an event, we use a majority vote on the image level classification output.

3   Dataset

We collected a dataset of 12471 egocentric pictures, which we call UBRUG-EgoSenti. The users were asked to wear a Narrative Clip Camera, which takes a picture every 30 s, hence each day around 1500 images are collected for processing. The images have a resolution of 5MP and JPG format.

   We organize the images into events according to the output of the SR-clustering algorithm [5]. From the originally recorded data, we discarded those events that are composed of less than 6 images, so obtaining a dataset composed of 12088 images grouped in a total of 233 events, with an average of 51.87 images per event and std of 52.19. We manually labelled the events following how the user felt while reviewing them by assigning *Positive*, *Negative* and *Neutral* values to them, some examples of which are given in Fig. 1. The dataset, for which the details are in Table 2, is publicly available and can be downloaded from: http://www.ub.edu/cvub/dataset/.

Table 2. Description of the UBRUG-EgoSenti dataset.

Class	Images	#Events	Mean Im Event	Std Im Event
Positive	4737	83	57.07	52.34
Neutral	6169	107	57.65	57.18
Negative	1182	43	27.49	26.44
Total	12088	233	51.88	52.19

4   Experiments

4.1   Evaluation and Results

We carried out 10-fold cross-validation. Events from different classes are uniformly distributed among the various folds, which are thus independent from each other. We evaluated the performance of the proposed system on single images and at event level. For the UBRUG-Senti dataset, the groundtruth labels are given at event level. All the images that compose a certain event, are considered as having the same label of such event. Given an event composed of M

Table 3. Performance results achieved at image and event level.

	Image classification					Event classification				
	Pos	Neg	Neu	All		Pos	Neg	Neu	All	
	Mean			Mean	Std	Mean			Mean	Std
Semantic features	59.2	42.4	44.4	48.67	22.87	71.2	42	47.3	53.50	30.77
CNN features	70	61.3	45.7	59.00	22.80	80.8	71	48.9	66.90	27.67
Semantic+CNN features	72	60.8	46	59.60	23.17	82.1	73.5	48.9	68.17	30.07

images, we aggregate the M classification decisions by majority vote. We measure the performance results of our method by computing the average accuracy.

In Table 3, we report the results achieved by the proposed methods at image and event level. We achieved an average image classification rate of 59.60% with a standard deviation of 23.17, when we apply the proposed method. The average event classification rate is 68%, when the proposed features are employed, which corresponds to 82%, 73.5% and 49% for positive, negative and neutral events, respectively. Up to our knowledge, unfortunately, there is no work in the literature on egocentric image sentiment recognition neither event sentiment recognition to compared with. Even the works on image sentiment analysis in conventional images [2,12,21,22] use different datasets and objectives (8 semantic sentiments vs. binary or ternary sentiment values) that make difficult their direct comparison. Figure 3 shows some example results. As can be seen, the algorithm learns to classify events with presence of routine objects into *neutral* events. Events wrongly classified as *neutral* are shown in Fig. 3(left) and Fig. 3(middle). As an example, the last row of Fig. 3(left) is classified as *neutral*, probably due to the presence of the *pc* in the image, while it was manually labelled as *positive*, because it shows social interactions. As for Fig. 3(left) and Fig. 3(right), events were mislabelled as *negative* probably due to the "homogeneity" and "greyness" of the images within the events, e.g. events were considered as *negative* when most of the information in the image corresponded to the asphalt of the road.

4.2   Discussion

Sentiments recognition from an image or a collection of images is a difficult process due to its ambiguity. A challenge in the model construction for sentiment recognition consists in taking into account the bias due to the subjective interpretation of images by different users. Furthermore, the boundaries between neutral/positive and neutral/negative sentiments are not clearly defined. A *neutral* feeling is difficult to interpret. From the results, we observe that *neutral* events are the most challenging ones to classify. Another challenging aspect concerns the grouping of image sentiments into event sentiment, since events can have non-uniform sentiments.

Fig. 3. Examples of the automatic event sentiment classification. The events are grouped based on the sentiment defined by the user: (right) Positive, (middle) Negative, and (left) Neutral. The events frame colour corresponds to the label given by the model: Positive (green), Negative (red) and Neutral (yellow). (Color figure online)

A further step towards better understanding of the image and sentiment analysis is needed, due to the subjectivity of what an image can recall to different persons. To this aim, having annotations by different persons is critical to evaluate the inter- and intra-observer variability.

From the results, the intuition that we get is that non-routine events and specially when moments are social, have a higher probability of being positive. In contrast, routine events will most probably be considered as neutral. Negative events as accidents have low prevalence to be learned. Yet, hostile and empty environments could lead to negative sentiments too. Future works will address the study of emotional events and their relation to daily routine.

5   Conclusions

In this work, we propose, for the first time, a system and a dataset for egocentric sentiment image and event recognition based on the extraction of CNN and semantic features with sentiment value associated. We introduced a new labelled dataset of egocentric images composed of 233 events, grouping 12088 images, from 20 days of 3 users grouped. We presented preliminary results, obtaining an average events and image sentiment accuracy of 68.17% and 58.60%, with std of 30.07% and 23.17%, respectively.

Acknowledgements. This work was partially founded by TIN2015-66951-C2, SGR 1219, CERCA, *ICREA Academia'14* and Grant 20141510 (MaratóTV3). The funders had no role in the study design, data collection, analysis, and preparation of the manuscript.

References

1. Borth, D., Ji, R., Chen, T., Breuel, T., Chang, S.-F.: Large-scale visual sentiment ontology and detectors using adjective noun pairs, pp. 223–232. ACM (2013)
2. Campos, V., et al.: Diving deep into sentiment: understanding fine-tuned CNNs for visual sentiment prediction. In: ASM, pp. 57–62 (2015)

3. Chen, T., Borth, D., Darrell, T., Chang, S.-F.: DeepSentiBank: visual sentiment concept classification with deep convolutional neural networks, p. 7 (2014)
4. Dan-Glauser, E.S., Scherer, K.R.: The Geneva affective picture database (GAPED): a new 730-picture database focusing on valence and normative significance. Behav. Res. Meth. **43**(2), 468–477 (2011)
5. Dimiccoli, M., Talavera, E., Nikolov, S.G., Radeva, P.: SR-clustering: semantic regularized clustering for egocentric photo streams segmentation (2015)
6. Foggia, P., Petkov, N., Saggese, A., Strisciuglio, N., Vento, M.: Reliable detection of audio events in highly noisy environments. PRL **65**(1), 22–28 (2015)
7. Holmes, E.A., et al.: Positive interpretation training: effects of mental imagery versus verbal training on positive mood. Behav. Ther. **37**(3), 237–247 (2006)
8. Joachims, T.: Estimating the generalization performance of a SVM efficiently. In: ICML, pp. 431–438 (2000)
9. Krizhevsky, A., Sulskever, I., Hinton, G.E.: ImageNet classification with deep convolutional neural networks. In: NIPS, pp. 1–9 (2012)
10. Lang, P., Bradley, M., Cuthbert, B.: International affective picture system (IAPS): technical manual and affective ratings. In: NIMH, pp. 39–58 (1997)
11. Lee, M.L., Dey, A.K.: Lifelogging memory appliance for people with episodic memory impairment. In: UbiComp (2008)
12. Levi, G., Hassner, T.: Emotion recognition in the wild via convolutional neural networks and mapped binary patterns. In: ICMI, pp. 503–510 (2015)
13. Machajdik, J., Hanbury, A.: Affecitve image classification using features inspired by psychology and art theory. In: ICM, pp. 83–92 (2010)
14. Nojavanasghar, B., et al.: EmoReact: a multimodal approach and dataset for recognizing emotional responses in children. In: ICMI 2016, pp. 137–144 (2016)
15. Poria, S., et al.: Fusing audio, visual and textual clues for sentiment analysis from multimodal content. Neurocomputing **174**, 50–59 (2014)
16. Talavera, E., Radeva, P., Petkov, N.: Towards egocentric sentiment analysis. In: 16th International Conference on Computer Aided Systems Theory (2017)
17. Wang, M., Cao, D., Li, L., Li, S., Ji, R.: Microblog sentiment analysis based on cross-media bag-of-words model. In: ICIMCS, pp. 76–80 (2014)
18. Yi, D., Lei, Z., Liao, S., Li, S.Z.: Learning face representation from scratch. arXiv (2014)
19. You, Q., et al.: Cross-modality consistent regression for joint visual-textual sentiment analysis of social multimedia. In: WSDM, pp. 13–22 (2016)
20. You, Q., et al.: Robust image sentiment analysis using progressively trained and domain transferred deep networks. In: AAAI, pp. 381–388 (2015)
21. You, Q., Luo, J., Jin, H., Yang, J.: Building a large scale dataset for image emotion recognition: the fine print and the benchmark. CoRR (2016)
22. Yu, Y., Lin, H., Meng, J., Zhao, Z.: Visual and textual sentiment analysis of a microblog using deep convolutional neural networks. Algorithms **9**(2), 41 (2016)
23. Yuan, J., et al.: Sentribute: image sentiment analysis from a mid-level perspective categories and subject descriptors. In: WISDOM, pp. 101–108 (2013)
24. Zheng, L., Wang, S., He, F., Tian, Q.: Seeing the big picture: deep embedding with contextual evidences, p. 10 (2014)

Image and Signal Processing

An Insight on the 'Large G, Small n' Problem in Gene-Expression Microarray Classification

V. García[1], J.S. Sánchez[2]([✉]) [iD], L. Cleofas-Sánchez[3], H.J. Ochoa-Domínguez[4], and F. López-Orozco[1]

[1] Multidisciplinary University Division, Universidad Autónoma de Ciudad Juárez, Ciudad Juárez, Chihuahua, Mexico
[2] Department of Computer Languages and Systems, Institute of New Imaging Technologies, Universitat Jaume I, Castelló de la Plana, Spain
sanchez@uji.es
[3] National Institute of Genomic Medicine, Ciudad de México, D.F., Mexico
[4] Department of Electrical and Computer Engineering, Universidad Autónoma de Ciudad Juárez, Ciudad Juárez, Chihuahua, Mexico

Abstract. This paper analyzes the effect of the high-dimensional, low-sample size problem in cancer classification using gene-expression microarrays. Here the two key questions addressed are: (i) What is the percentage of genes that can ensure highly accurate classification?, and (ii) Does this percentage differ from one classifier to another? Both these issues are investigated by developing a pool of experiments with two gene ranking algorithms, five classifiers and four DNA microarray databases.

Keywords: DNA microarray · Gene expression · Feature ranking · Cancer classification

1 Introduction

Conventional methods for cancer classification rely on a variety of morphological, clinical and molecular variables, but they exhibit several limitations that make difficult an accurate diagnosis. The rapid development of high-throughput biotechnologies such as DNA microarray analysis allow to record and monitor the expression levels of thousands of genes simultaneously from a few samples [8], which has attracted the attention of scientists for its application in basic and translational cancer research [5,14,15,18]. Many studies utilizing DNA microarrays have been directed to (i) distinguish between cancerous and non-cancerous tissue samples, (ii) classify different types or subtypes of tumors, and (iii) predict the response to a particular therapeutic drug and/or the risk of relapse.

Cancer classification using microarrays, which focuses on predicting the class of a new sample based on its expression profile, poses two major challenges. First, the gene-expression data are characterized by the so-called 'large G,

© Springer International Publishing AG 2017
L.A. Alexandre et al. (Eds.): IbPRIA 2017, LNCS 10255, pp. 483–490, 2017.
DOI: 10.1007/978-3-319-58838-4_53

small n' problem, that is, the number of genes (G) heavily exceeds the sample size (n). And second, most genes are irrelevant to discriminate samples of different types [6]. These issues may increase the complexity of the prediction problem, degrade the generalization ability of classifiers and hinder the understanding of the relationships between the genes and the tissue samples [4,19]. Under these circumstances, feature selection plays a very important role in cancer classification because it can alleviate (minimize) the effects of both those problems.

A particularly popular approach to feature selection using DNA microarrays is gene ranking [9,13,17,20]. Gene ranking methods are filters that encompass some scoring function to quantify how much more statistically significant each gene is than the others [7], and as a result they rank genes in decreasing order of the estimated scores under the assumption that the top-ranked genes correspond to the most informative (or differentially expressed) ones.

The question the present study intends to answer is how the 'large G, small n' problem affects the classification performance using gene-expression microarrays. In particular, this paper examines the impact of high-dimensional biological data on several standard classifiers. To this end, two feature ranking algorithms are applied to select a percentage of the top-ranked genes, which are further used to classify new tissue samples and record the performance of classifiers in terms of both overall accuracy and false-negative rate.

2   Gene Ranking Algorithms

Some well-established gene ranking strategies include t-test, information-theoretic measures, symmetric uncertainty, correlation coefficient, χ^2-statistic and ReliefF, among others. In this section, the two feature ranking methods used in the experiments are briefly described.

2.1   ReliefF

The basic idea of the ReliefF algorithm [12,16] lies on adjusting the weights of a vector $W = [w(1), w(2), \ldots, w(G)]$ to give more relevance to features that better discriminate the samples from neighbors of different class.

It randomly picks out a sample x and searches for k nearest neighbors of the same class (hits, h_i) and k nearest neighbors from each of the different classes (misses, m_i). If x and h_i have different values on feature f, then the weight $w(f)$ is decreased because it is interpreted as a bad property of this feature. In contrast, if x and m_i have different values on the feature f, then $w(f)$ is increased. This process is repeated t times, updating the values of the weight vector W as follows

$$w(f) = w(f) - \frac{\sum_{i=1}^{k} dist(f, x, h_i)}{t \cdot k} \tag{1}$$

$$+ \sum_{c \neq class(x)} \frac{P(c)}{1 - P(class(x))} \cdot \frac{\sum_{i=1}^{k} dist(f, x, m_i)}{t \cdot k}$$

where $P(c)$ is the prior probability of class c, $P(class(x))$ denotes the probability for the class of x, and $dist(f, x, m_i)$ represents the absolute distance between samples x and m_i in the feature f.

2.2   Gain Ratio

The Gain ratio is an extension of information gain in order to overcome the biased behavior of selecting the features with the largest number of values. Let X be a set of n samples that belong to C distinct classes and let n_i be the number of samples in class i. The entropy of any subset can be calculated using the following formula

$$H(X) = -\sum_{i=1}^{C}((n_i/n) \cdot \log(n_i/n)) \tag{2}$$

To find the information gain of feature f, one has to sum the entropy for each value f_j $(j = 1, \ldots, v)$ of the feature:

$$H(X|f) = \sum_{j=1}^{v}((|f_j|/n) \cdot H(X|f = f_j)) \tag{3}$$

where $H(X|f = f_j)$ is the entropy calculated relative to the subset of instances that have a value of f_j for feature f.

The information gain of a feature is measured by the reduction in entropy as $IG(f) = H(X) - H(X|f)$. The greater the decrease in entropy when considering feature f individually, the more significant this is for prediction.

In general, a feature will be most useful when maximizing the information gain while simultaneously minimizing the number of feature values. Then the intrinsic value of a feature f can be computed as:

$$IV(f) = -\sum_{i=1}^{v}((|f_i|/n) \cdot \log(|f_i|/n)) \tag{4}$$

Thus the Gain ratio of f is defined as

$$Gain\ ratio(f) = \frac{IG(f)}{IV(f)} = \frac{H(X) - H(X|f)}{H(f)} \tag{5}$$

3   Databases and Experimental Setting

We conducted a series of experiments on a collection of publicly available microarray cancer data sets taken from the Kent Ridge Biomedical Data Set Repository (http://datam.i2r.a-star.edu.sg/datasets/krbd). Table 1 summarizes the main characteristics of these data sets, including the number of genes (features), the number of tissue samples, and the size of the positive and negative classes.

Table 1. Characteristics of the gene-expression microarray data sets.

	#Genes	#Samples	Positive–Negative
Breast	24481	97	Relapse (46)–Non-relapse (51)
CNS	7129	60	Failure (39)–Survivor (21)
Colon	2000	62	Tumor (22)–Normal (40)
Prostate	12600	136	Tumor (77)–Normal (59)

The 5-fold cross-validation method was adopted for the experimental design because it appears to be the best estimator of classification performance compared to other methods, such as bootstrap with a high computational cost or re-substitution with a biased behavior [1].

We focused our study on the ReliefF and Gain ratio feature ranking algorithms and five classification models: the nearest neighbor rule (1-NN), a support vector machine (SVM) using a linear kernel function with the soft-margin constant $C = 1.0$ and a tolerance of 0.001, the C4.5 decision tree, the naive Bayes (NBayes) classifier, the radial basis function neural network (RBF) with the K-means clustering to provide the basis functions, and a hybrid associative memory (HAM) with translation of the coordinate axes.

The experiments aim to analyze the classification accuracy when varying the percentage of genes selected by ReliefF and Gain ratio from 5% to 100% with a step size of 5%. For the purpose of this paper, the key question is how many genes should be selected to perform the best with microarray gene-expression data. Besides, we are interested in investigating whether or not the optimal percentage of genes depends on the characteristics of each classifier.

Note that the classification accuracy is just the number of samples being correctly classified, but this is not the most appropriate in the case of cancer classification problems. To discriminate between normal and cancerous data, it is especially important to take care of the false-positives and the false-negatives in order to perform a thorough comparison on the performance of different methods. False-positives are tolerable since further clinical experiments will be done to confirm the initial cancer diagnosis, but false-negatives are extremely detrimental because an ill patient might be misclassified as healthy.

4   Results and Discussion

Figure 1 shows the plot between accuracy rates and the percentage of the top-ranked genes for each database. It is found that all classifiers provide the highest accuracy using less than 20% of genes, irrespective of the feature selection algorithm. Examination of this figure reveals that in general, the RBF neural network and the naive Bayes classifier are the models most affected by the use of a large number of genes. For instance, in the Breast database the accuracy of RBF with the 5% top-ranked genes selected by ReliefF is 83.51%, but it significantly drops down to 52.58% when using the whole set of genes. Similarly, in the Colon

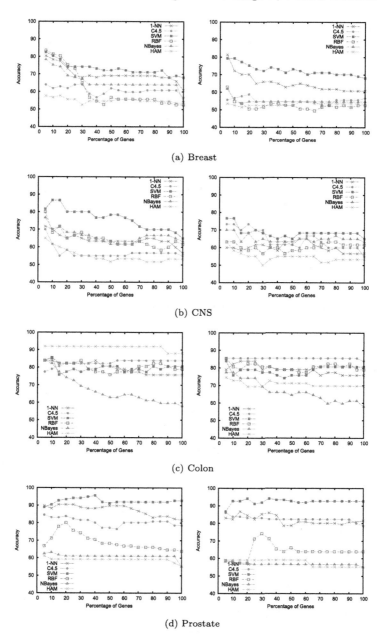

(a) Breast

(b) CNS

(c) Colon

(d) Prostate

Fig. 1. Plots of the classification accuracy rates when varying the percentage of genes selected by the ReliefF (left) and Gain ratio (right) ranking algorithms

database the NBayes accuracy goes down from 77.42% with the 5% top-ranked genes selected by the Gain ratio to 58.06% with the total number of genes. It is also interesting to remark that the SVM has shown superior performance in most cancer classification problems, probably because of its ability to deal with high-dimensional data and its robustness to noise [3,11], and also because all these data sets are linearly separable [2].

At this point, it could be especially interesting to show the relationship between the number of genes and the amount of samples in order to better understand how the 'large G, small n' problem affects the classification results of gene-expression microarrays. To this end, the average number of samples per dimension (genes) for each database has been plotted in Fig. 2. This corresponds to the T2 data complexity measure [10], which describes the density of spatial distributions of samples by comparing the number of samples in the data set to the number of genes, (n/G). As can be seen, there exists a negative correlation between the percentage of genes and the T2 measure, that is, higher values of X (% genes) are associated with lower values of Y (T2). This shows that, although the values of T2 are extremely small in all cases, the underlying difficulty of gene-expression microarray classification increases as the number of genes increases, which explains the decreasing tendency of accuracies presented in Fig. 1.

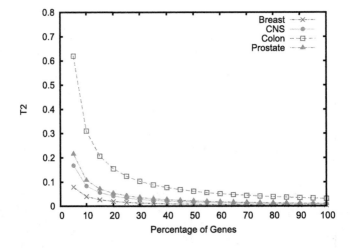

Fig. 2. Values of T2 when varying the percentage of genes

As already pointed out in Sect. 3, the false-negatives are even more relevant than the classification accuracy when assessing the performance of models for cancer classification based on gene-expression microarrays. Accordingly, Tables 2 and 3 report the false-negative rates given by each classifier both with the whole set of genes (100% of genes available) and the subset of genes that performed the best in terms of accuracy. The best result for each pair (database, classifier) is highlighted in bold. It is observed that the false-negative rate achieved with the best subset of genes is lower than that using 100% of genes in most cases: 22 out of 24 (4 data sets × 6 classifiers) with the ReliefF algorithm and 19 out of 24 with the Gain ratio feature ranking approach. These results corroborate

Table 2. False-negative rates with the ReliefF algorithm.

	1-NN		C4.5		SVM		RBF		NBayes		HAM	
	Best	100%	Best	100%	Best	100%	Best	100%	Best	100%	Best	100%
Breast	**0.196**	0.543	**0.283**	0.413	**0.217**	0.348	**0.109**	0.717	**0.196**	0.503	**0.283**	0.543
CNS	**0.077**	0.359	**0.179**	0.359	**0.077**	0.179	**0.179**	0.256	**0.231**	0.308	**0.179**	0.359
Colon	**0.318**	0.364	**0.182**	0.318	**0.227**	0.273	**0.182**	0.409	**0.182**	0.227	**0.227**	0.364
Prostate	**0.065**	0.130	**0.143**	0.156	**0.052**	0.078	0.273	**0.143**	0.571	0.675	0.256	**0.143**

Table 3. False-negative rates with the Gain ratio.

	1-NN		C4.5		SVM		RBF		NBayes		HAM	
	Best	100%	Best	100%	Best	100%	Best	100%	Best	100%	Best	100%
Breast	**0.217**	0.543	**0.348**	0.413	**0.239**	0.348	**0.413**	0.717	0.804	**0.503**	0.543	**0.503**
CNS	**0.282**	0.359	**0.154**	0.359	**0.128**	0.179	**0.231**	0.256	**0.256**	0.308	**0.256**	0.359
Colon	**0.227**	0.364	**0.273**	0.318	**0.227**	0.273	**0.182**	0.409	**0.136**	0.227	**0.273**	0.318
Prostate	**0.117**	0.130	**0.104**	0.156	**0.039**	0.078	0.299	**0.143**	0.675	0.675	0.503	**0.227**

the initial hypothesis that the removal of irrelevant (and redundant) genes leads to very significant gains in performance when the number of samples is large in comparison to the number of features, and it also produces a considerable decrease in computational requirements.

5   Concluding Remarks

The present paper has analyzed the effect of the high-dimensional, low-sample size problem for the classification of gene-expression microarrays. To this end, two feature ranking methods and six classifiers have been applied over four biomedical databases.

The experimental results have shown that the highest performance (as measured by the accuracy rate) was achieved by using a very small number of genes (in general, less than 20% of the total amount of genes), independently of both the gene ranking algorithm and the classifier. In addition, the T2 measure has shown that the complexity of classifying gene-expression microarrays increases as the amount of genes increases.

It has also been observed that RBF and naive Bayes appear to be the models most affected by (sensitive to) the 'large G, small n' problem. On the other hand, the SVM with a linear kernel has performed the best in nearly all cases, probably because the experimental data sets are linearly separable. Finally, the false-negative rates have highlighted the benefits of using a subset with the top-ranked genes instead of the whole set because the presence of irrelevant genes may distort the classification problem in hand.

Acknowledgment. This work has partially been supported by the Spanish Ministry of Economy [TIN2013-46522-P], the Mexican PRODEP [DSA/103.5/15/7004], and the Generalitat Valenciana [PROMETEOII/2014/062].

References

1. Alpaydin, E.: Introduction to Machine Learning. MIT Press, Cambridge (2010)
2. Bolón-Canedo, V., Morán-Fernández, L., Alonso-Betanzos, A.: An insight on complexity measures and classification in microarray data. In: Proceedings of International Joint Conference on Neural Networks, Killarney, Ireland, pp. 1–8 (2015)
3. Cristianini, N., Shawe-Taylor, J.: An Introduction to Support Vector Machines: And Other Kernel-based Learning Methods. Cambridge University Press, New York (2000)
4. Dougherty, E.R.: Small sample issues for microarray-based classification. Comp. Funct. Genomics 2(1), 28–34 (2001)
5. García, V., Sánchez, J.S.: Mapping microarray gene expression data into dissimilarity spaces for tumor classification. Inform. Sci. 294, 362–375 (2015)
6. Golub, T.R., Slonim, D.K., Tamayo, P., Huard, C., Gaasenbeek, M., Mesirov, J.P., Coller, H., Loh, M.L., Downing, J.R., Caligiuri, M.A., Bloomfield, C.D., Lander, E.S.: Molecular classification of cancer: class discovery and class prediction by gene expression monitoring. Science 286(5439), 531–537 (1999)
7. Guyon, I., Elisseeff, A.: An introduction to variable and feature selection. J. Mach. Learn. Res. 3, 1157–1182 (2003)
8. Heller, M.J.: DNA microarray technology: devices, systems, and applications. Annu. Rev. Biomed. Eng. 4, 129–153 (2002)
9. Hira, Z.M., Gillies, D.F.: A review of feature selection and feature extraction methods applied on microarray data. Adv. Bioinform. 2015, 1–13 (2015). ID: 198363
10. Ho, T.K., Basu, M.: Complexity measures of supervised classification problems. IEEE Trans. Pattern Anal. Mach. Intell. 24(3), 289–300 (2002)
11. Huang, L., Zhang, H.H., Zeng, Z.B., Bushel, P.R.: Improved sparse multi-class SVM and its application for gene selection in cancer classification. Cancer Inform. 12, 143–153 (2013)
12. Kononenko, I.: Estimating attributes: analysis and extensions of RELIEF. In: Bergadano, F., Raedt, L. (eds.) ECML 1994. LNCS, vol. 784, pp. 171–182. Springer, Heidelberg (1994). doi:10.1007/3-540-57868-4_57
13. Lazar, C., Taminau, J., Meganck, S., Steenhoff, D., Coletta, A., Molter, C., de Schaetzen, V., Duque, R., Bersini, H., Nowe, A.: A survey on filter techniques for feature selection in gene expression microarray analysis. IEEE-ACM Trans. Comput. Biol. Bioinform. 9(4), 1106–1119 (2012)
14. Lu, Y., Han, J.: Cancer classification using gene expression data. Inf. Syst. 28(4), 243–268 (2003)
15. Raspe, E., Decraene, C., Berx, G.: Gene expression profiling to dissect the complexity of cancer biology: pitfalls and promise. Semin. Cancer Biol. 22(3), 250–260 (2012)
16. Robnik-Šikonja, M., Kononenko, I.: Theoretical and empirical analysis of ReliefF and RReliefF. Mach. Learn. 53(1–2), 23–69 (2003)
17. Saeys, Y., Inza, I., Larrañaga, P.: A review of feature selection techniques in bioinformatics. Bioinformatics 23(19), 2507–2517 (2007)
18. Simon, R.: Analysis of DNA microarray expression data. Best Pract. Res. Clin. Haematol. 22(2), 271–282 (2009)
19. Wang, L., Chu, F., Xie, W.: Accurate cancer classification using expressions of very few genes. IEEE-ACM Trans. Comput. Biol. Bioinform. 4(1), 40–53 (2007)
20. Zhang, C., Lu, X., Zhang, X.: Significance of gene ranking for classification of microarray samples. IEEE-ACM Trans. Comput. Biol. Bioinform. 3(3), 312–320 (2006)

Neighbor Distance Ratios and Dynamic Weighting in Multi-biometric Fusion

Naser Damer[1]([✉]), Wael Alkhatib[1,2], Andreas Braun[1], and Arjan Kuijper[1,3]

[1] Fraunhofer Institute for Computer Graphics Research (IGD),
Darmstadt, Germany
{naser.damer,andreas.braun,arjan.kuijper}@igd.fraunhofer.de
[2] Multimedia Communications Lab, Technische Universitat Darmstadt,
Darmstadt, Germany
wael.alkhatib@kom.tu-darmstadt.de
[3] Mathematical and Applied Visual Computing,
Technische Universitat Darmstadt, Darmstadt, Germany

Abstract. Multi-biometrics aims at building more accurate unified biometric decisions based on the information provided by multiple biometric sources. Information fusion is used to optimize the process of creating this unified decision. In previous works dealing with score-level multi-biometric fusion, the scores of different biometric sources belonging to the comparison of interest are used to create the fused score. This is usually achieved by assigning static weights for the different biometric sources. In contrast, we focus on integrating the information imbedded in the relative relation between the comparison scores (within a 1:N comparison) in the biometric fusion process using a dynamic weighting scheme. This is performed by considering the neighbors distance ratio in the ranked comparisons to influence the dynamic weights of the fused scores. The evaluation was performed on the Biometric Scores Set BSSR1 database. The enhanced performance induced by including the neighbors distance ratio information within a dynamic weighting scheme in comparison to the baseline solution was shown by an average reduction of the equal error rate by more than 40% over the different test scenarios.

Keywords: Multi-biometrics · Score-level fusion · Biometric verification

1 Introduction

Biometrics technology aims at identifying or verifying the identity of individuals based on their physical or behavioral characteristics. Combining more than one biometric source is often performed to increase the accuracy, robustness and usability of biometrics. The different biometric sources can be based on different characteristics, captures, algorithms, sensors, or instances. Putting together the information provided by these sources and creating a unified biometric decision is referred to as multi-biometric fusion.

The fusion process can be applied on different levels such as the data, feature, score, or rank level. Higher levels such as score and rank provide a more flexible

© Springer International Publishing AG 2017
L.A. Alexandre et al. (Eds.): IbPRIA 2017, LNCS 10255, pp. 491–500, 2017.
DOI: 10.1007/978-3-319-58838-4_54

and integrable solution. Data and feature fusion levels provide more information but affect the integrability and may be hard to achieve in certain multi-biometric combinations. In this work, the score-level fusion will be considered as it provides a fair tradeoff between performance and integrability.

This work presents a scheme for *integrating the information imbedded in the relative relation between the comparison scores (within a 1:N comparison) in the biometric fusion process by utilizing dynamic weighting*. These weights are based on the individual neighbor distance ratio of each score in the fusion process. The weights are then applied within a simple combination weighted sum rule. The work also investigates the combination between the dynamic weight and a conventional static weight such as equal error rate weighting (EERW).

The proposed fusion technique is evaluated on the Biometric Scores Set BSSR1 - multimodal database [1]. The proposed technique proved to outperform the baseline solution and the results are presented as Receiver Operating Characteristics (ROC) curves and Equal Error Rate values (EER). The achieved EER was reduced by an average higher than 40% compared to the baseline solution.

The next Sect. 2 contains a short overview of related works motivating and leading to the presented approach. In Sect. 3 the proposed solution is discussed along with the evaluated baseline solution. The experiment setup and the achieved results are then presented in Sects. 4 and 5. Finally, in Sect. 6, a conclusion of the work is drawn.

2   Related Work

Score-level biometric fusion techniques can be categorized into two main groups, combination-based and classification-based fusion. Combination-based fusion consists of simple operations performed on the normalized scores of different biometric sources. These operations produce a combined score that is used to build a biometric decision. One of the most used combination rules is the weighted sum rule, where each biometric source is assigned a relative weight that optimizes the source effect on the final fused decision. The weights are related to the performance metrics of the biometric sources, a comparative study of biometric source weighting is presented by Chia et al. [2] and extended later by Damer et al. [3,4].

Classification-based fusion views the biometric scores of a certain comparison as a feature vector. A classifier is trained to classify those vectors optimally into genuine or impostor comparisons. Different types of classifiers were used to perform multi-biometric fusion, some of those are support vector machines (SVM) [5–7], neural networks [8], and the likelihood ratio methods [9].

More advanced approaches of multi-biometric fusion considered dynamic weights that adapt to the comparison set in hand. Hui et al. proposed a dynamic weighting approach for multi-biometric fuzzy-logic based fusion [10]. The dynamic weights took into account the variations during data acquisition (e.g. lighting, noise and user-device interactions). Other works applied dynamic weights based on capture quality and scenario on a feature level fusion process [11,12].

A biometric system usually operates under one of two scenarios, verification or identification. Verification is the authentication of a claimed identity based on the captured biometric characteristics. Identification is assigning an identity to an unknown individual based on their biometric characteristics. Identification can operate as a closed-set identification where the user is known to be included in the biometric references set, or as an open-set identification where the user is not definitely included in the references set. In open-set identification, a verification final step is required to verify that the top ranked identification match is certainly the same captured subject and not an unenrolled subject.

Keeping the open-set identification scenario in mind, previous works by Damer et al. [7,13] tried to use the information provided by the ranked set of comparisons to perform more accurate verification of the top rank. The assumption was that a genuine top rank comparison has a lower distance ratio to its rank neighbors than that of an impostor comparison, this distance ratio was referred to as the neighbor distance ratio (NDR). This information was integrated into a classification-based fusion approach using SVM. However, dealing with a small number of inputs using complex fusion techniques such as SVM, which is usually able to find complex separators, can only estimates separation lines optimal for the separation of overlapping classes while having small degree of liberty [14]. Simpler fusion approaches, such as weighted sum rule, proved to achieve comparable performances to more complex approaches [9,15] while maintaining simpler and easily integrable design. Therefore, this work focuses on integrating NDR information in the fusion process using a simple weighted sum approach.

3   Methodology

The fusion approach presented here is based on the weighted sum combination rule. Considering the static weighting approaches, each score value S_k is weighted by the weight w_k of its source k to produce the fused score. The weights w_k are calculated from the training data of each biometric source. The fused score F by the weighted sum rule for K score sources is given as:

$$F = \sum_{k=1}^{K} w_k S_k, k = \{1, \ldots, K\} \tag{1}$$

The proposed dynamic weighting does not only consider the properties of the biometric source, but considers properties related to the individual fused scores as well. Thus, the fused score is given by:

$$F = \sum_{k=1}^{K} w_{k,l} S_{k,l}, k = \{1, \ldots, K\}, l = \{1, \ldots, L\} \tag{2}$$

where $S_{k,l}$ is a score of the biometric source k of the comparison indexed by l within a 1:N comparison and $w_{k,l}$ is its corresponding dynamic weight. K is the number of biometric sources (modalities, algorithms, etc.) and L is the total number of comparisons done by a biometric source.

In the following, the proposed dynamic weighting solution is presented in more details. A static-weighting baseline solutions used to benchmark the performance is also discussed.

3.1 Baseline Solution

The weights used to benchmark the results are based on EER values. The EER weighting (EERW) is based on the EER value which is the common value of the false acceptance rate (FAR) and the false rejection rate (FRR) at the operational point where both FAR and FRR are equal. EER weighting was used to linearly combine biometric scores in the work of Jain et al. [16]. The EER is inverse proportional to the performance of the biometric source. Therefore, for a multi-biometric system that combines K biometric sources, the EER weight for a biometric source k is given by:

$$w_k(EER_k) = \frac{\frac{1}{EER_k}}{\sum_{k=1}^{K} \frac{1}{EER_k}} \tag{3}$$

3.2 Proposed Solution

Neighbor Distance Ratio (NDR): The main assumption that builds the bases of the proposed solution in this work is anchored on the Neighbor Distance Ratio (NDR). Given a rank set of comparison scores that represents an $1 : N$ comparison, NDR is defined as the ratio between one score in this set and a score of a higher rank (neighbor distance). A similar principle was previously used in the literature to match interest key point descriptors in images [17].

Looking into the NDR from the biometric prospective, the inverse ratio between a genuine similarity score and the next highest score (within a ranked $1 : N$ comparison) is assumed to be lower than the ratio between an impostor score and the next highest score. In different words, a genuine score of a certain subject is relatively higher and distanced from the clustered set of impostor scores produced by the same subject. This relative (to neighbor ranks) difference is not considered in conventional biometric verification where only the absolute value of the genuine or impostor comparison score is considered. A realistic genuine-impostor distributions of NDR values were presented in [7] and showed a clear discrimination between impostor and genuine comparisons. In this work, the considered NDR values were the 2nd-rank-to-1st-rank.

Dynamic weighting: The proposed solution aims at giving scores with a lower NDR values a relative higher weight. This is based on the assumption that a low NDR points out a higher probability for a score to be of a genuine comparison, and thus should point out more aggressively to a genuine decision. A score with a high NDR value points out a higher probability for a score to be of a impostor comparison, and thus should relatively point more aggressively to an impostor decision (less aggressively to a genuine decision). Therefore, the NDR weight for each score is inversely proportional to its NDR value:

$$w_{k,l}(NDR_{k,l}) = \frac{1}{NDR_{k,l}} \tag{4}$$

where the $NDR_{k,l}$ value for a score $S_{k,l}$ of the source k and the rank (index) l in a ranked score set is given by:

$$NDR_{k,l} = \frac{S_{k,l-1}}{S_{k,l}} \tag{5}$$

Combining static and dynamic weights: To capture both the general performance of each biometric source and the individual certainty represented by the NDR, a combined weight was proposed as follows:

$$w_{k,l}(NDR_{k,l}, EER_k) = \beta w_{k,l}(NDR_{k,l}) + (1 - \beta)w_k(EER_k) \tag{6}$$

Here, β is a constant between zero and one $[0, 1]$. β controls the relative effect of the dynamic and static weights. Different values of β are evaluated to optimize the tradeoff between both types of weights.

4   Experimental Setup

The overall fusion process is presented in Fig. 1. Here, after normalizing the scores, the NDR values are calculated for each score. These values are normalized and influenced on the scores by applying weighting. Finally, the fused score is produced by a hybrid dynamic/static weighted sum rule fusion.

The database used to develop and evaluate the proposed solution is the Biometric Scores Set BSSR1 - multimodal database [1]. The database contains comparison scores for left and right fingerprints (Fli and Fri) and two face matchers (Fc and Fg). BSSR1 - multimodal database contains 517 genuine and 266, 772

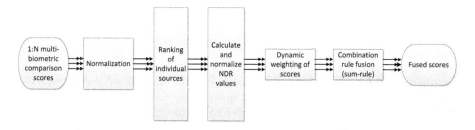

Fig. 1. An overview of our fusion process. The input scores of an 1:N comparison is ranked (per source) to calculate the NDR value for each score. Dynamic weighting is applied and the weighted scores are fused by a simple combination rule.

impostor scores. The experiments here considered all possible pairs between finger and face matchers. To evaluate the statistical performance of the proposed solutions, the database was split into three equal-sized partitions. Experiments were performed on all possible fold combinations where one partition is used as an evaluation set and the other two are used as a development set. All the reported results are the averaged results of the three evaluation/development combinations.

Score normalization: Performance anchored normalization (PAN) was used to bring comparison scores produced by different biometric sources to a comparable range and align their performance. The PAN-min-max normalization is used as described in [18]. Here, the min-max normalization is extended by anchoring the middle point of the score range at the EER operational threshold point TH_{EER} (the score decision threshold that achieves EER). The PAN-min-max normalized score S' is given by:

$$
S' = \begin{cases} \frac{S-min\{S_k\}}{2(TH_{EER}\{S_k\}-min\{S_k\})} & if\ S <= TH_{EER} \\ 0.5 + \frac{S-TH_{EER}\{S_k\}}{max\{S_k\}-TH_{EER}\{S_k\}} & if\ S > TH_{EER} \end{cases} \tag{7}
$$

where S_k here represents the whole development comparison scores set of a certain biometric source k.

NDR calculation and normalization: each comparison between two identities was assumed to resemble a comparison in an open-set identification scenario (1:N comparisons). This scenario is common in large scale application such as duplicate enrollment checks. For each score in each comparison between two identities, the NDR value was calculated by ranking the L scores of the concerned biometric source. Then calculating the NDR between the current score and the next score (2nd-rank-to-1st-rank) as in Eq. 5. The NDR values are normalized based on the properties of the development data. Min-max normalization was used to bring NDR values to a comparable range. Min-max normalized NDR for the biometric source k is given as:

$$
NDR' = \frac{NDR - min\{NDR_k\}}{max\{NDR_k\} - min\{NDR_k\}} \tag{8}
$$

where $min\{NDR_k\}$ and $max\{NDR_k\}$ are the minimum and maximum value of NDR existing in the training data of the corresponding biometric source. And NDR' is the normalized NDR value.

Dynamic weighting: weights were applied to the normalized scores under a weighted sum approach. As in Eq. 6, β determines the influence degree of the NDR weight. Different β values were evaluated (0, 0.2, 0.4, 0.6, 0.8, and 1.0). Here, a β value of zero points to a standard EERW static weighting and a β value of one points to pure NDR weighting. After calculating the weights, the fused score is calculated as in Eq. 2.

5   Results

The achieved results under different experiment settings are presented as receiver operating characteristic (ROC) curves and EER values. Those evaluation metrics were calculated for each of the bi-modal biometric combinations in the BSSR1 database. Only bi-modal biometric fusion results are reported as the fusion of all biometric sources results in a very small error and thus small margin for comparison. The EER is the common value of the false acceptance rate (FAR) and false rejection rate (FRR) at the operational point (decision threshold) where both rates are equal. The EER value provides a general and comparable measure of the evaluation performance, lower EER values corresponds to higher performance. The EER values achieved are presented in Table 1. It is clear that the lowest EER values were achieved when the proposed dynamic weighting is used. Best results were clear when β values (Eq. 6) are in the range of 0.2 – 0.6. Depending solely on the NDR weights ($\beta = 1.0$) will overlook the general quality of each biometric source, represented by the static weight, and will result in higher errors in comparison to the cases where a combined weight is used.

Table 1. The EER values achieved by the proposed solution and the discussed baseline approach on the different bi-modal biometric combinations. Here, a β value of 0 represents the baseline pure static EER weighting.

β	Fc-Fli	Fc-Flr	Fg-Fli	Fg-Flr
0	0.01331	0.01209	0.030715	0.01596
0.2	**0.01182**	**0.00598**	0.02364	0.01151
0.4	0.01370	0.00754	0.01926	0.00773
0.6	0.01565	0.00600	**0.01724**	**0.00610**
0.8	0.01740	0.00643	0.01737	0.00849
1.0	0.01981	0.01590	0.02532	0.02040

The verification performance of the proposed solution is presented in ROC curves, see Fig. 2. ROC curves plots the false acceptance rate (FAR) and the true acceptance rate (TAR) at different operational points (thresholds) and presents the tradeoff performance between the two rates. In contrast to EER values, ROC curves provides a wider insight into the verification performance at all possible operational points. This might be of interest for a user focused on a relatively low FAR or FRR rate for a specific application. The curves presented in this work are graphically averaged curves over the three testing folds of the database in a similar manner to vertical averaging discussed in [19].

From the curves in Fig. 2, it is clear that the proposed dynamic weighting outperforms the baseline static approach ($\beta = 0$) over a wide range of operational points. Best performances are achieved when the β values are in the 0.2–0.4 range.

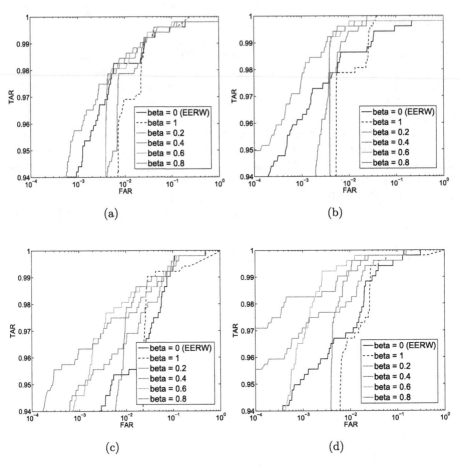

Fig. 2. ROC curves achieved on the BSSR1 database: The rates shown here are for bi-modal combinations of face matchers (Fc and Fg) and finger matchers (Fli and Flr) in the BSSR1 database. (a) Fc and Fli, (b) Fg and Fli, (c) Fc and Flr, (d) Fg and Flr. Enhanced performance introduced by integrating NDR-based dynamic weights is clearly presented.

6   Conclusion

This work presented a novel multi-biometric score-level fusion approach and evaluated it along with a baseline approach. The novelty of the work is integrating relative information between comparison scores in dynamic weights within a weighted sum score-level fusion. These weights are based on the individual neighbor distance ratios of the involved scores. This aims at including the scores relation to other comparisons within a 1:N biometric comparison in the fusion process. The evaluation was performed on the BSSR1 database and proved the superiority of the proposed solution compared to the baseline method. The results show that integrating the NDR-based dynamic weights with the conventional static weights reduced the equal error rate by more than 40% on average and improved the biometric decision performance over a wide range of operational points.

Acknowledgments. This work was partially funded by the Center for Research in Security and Privacy CRISP in Darmstadt, Germany.

References

1. National Institute of Standards and Technology: NIST Biometric Scores Set. Database (2004)
2. Chia, C., Sherkat, N., Nolle, L.: Towards a best linear combination for multimodal biometric fusion. In: 2010 20th International Conference on Pattern Recognition (ICPR), pp. 1176–1179 (2010)
3. Damer, N., Opel, A., Nouak, A.: Biometric source weighting in multi-biometric fusion: towards a generalized and robust solution. In: 22nd European Signal Processing Conference, EUSIPCO 2014, Lisbon, Portugal, pp. 1382–1386. IEEE, 1–5 September 2014
4. Damer, N., Opel, A., Nouak, A.: CMC curve properties and biometric source weighting in multi-biometric score-level fusion. In: 17th International Conference on Information Fusion, FUSION 2014, Salamanca, Spain, pp. 1–6. IEEE, 7–10 July 2014
5. Singh, R., Vatsa, M., Noore, A.: Intelligent biometric information fusion using support vector machine. In: Nachtegael, M., Van der Weken, D., Kerre, E., Philips, W. (eds.) Soft Computing in Image Processing. STUDFUZZ, vol. 210, pp. 325–349. Springer, Heidelberg (2007)
6. Gutschoven, B., Verlinde, P.: Multi-modal identity verification using support vector machines (SVM). In: Proceedings of the Third International Conference on Information Fusion, FUSION 2000, vol. 2, pp. THB3/3–THB3/8, July 2000
7. Damer, N., Opel, A.: Multi-biometric score-level fusion and the integration of the neighbors distance ratio. In: Campilho, A.J.C., Kamel, M.S. (eds.) ICIAR 2014. LNCS, vol. 8815, pp. 85–93. Springer, Cham (2014). doi:10.1007/978-3-319-11755-3_10
8. Alsaade, F.: A study of neural network and its properties of training and adaptability in enhancing accuracy in a multimodal biometrics scenario. Inf. Technol. J. **9**, 188–191 (2010)
9. Nandakumar, K., Chen, Y., Dass, S.C., Jain, A.: Likelihood ratio-based biometric score fusion. IEEE Trans. Pattern Anal. Mach. Intell. **30**(2), 342–347 (2008)
10. Hui, H., Meng, H., Mak, M.W.: Adaptive weight estimation in multi-biometric verification using fuzzy logic decision fusion. In: IEEE International Conference on Acoustics, Speech and Signal Processing, ICASSP 2007, vol. 1, pp. I-501–I-504, April 2007
11. Wu, Q., Wang, L., Geng, X., Li, M., He, X.: Dynamic biometrics fusion at feature level for video-based human recognition. In: Proceedings of Image and Vision Computing New Zealand 2007, Hamilton, New Zealand, pp. 152–157 (2007)
12. Yang, Y., Lin, K., Han, F., Zhang, Z.: Dynamic weighting for effective fusion of fingerprint and finger vein. Prog. Intell. Comput. Appl. **1**(1), 50–61 (2012)

13. Damer, N., Nouak, A.: Weighted integration of neighbors distance ratio in multi-biometric fusion. In: Brömme, A., Busch, C., Rathgeb, C., Uhl, A. (eds.) BIOSIG - Proceedings of the 14th International Conference of the Biometrics Special Interest Group. LNI, vol. 245, pp. 255–262. GI, Darmstadt (2015)
14. Raghavendra, R., Dorizzi, B., Rao, A., Kumar, G.H.: Designing efficient fusion schemes for multimodal biometric systems using face and palmprint. Pattern Recogn. **44**(5), 1076–1088 (2011)
15. Ross, A.A., Nandakumar, K., Jain, A.K.: Handbook of Multibiometrics. International Series on Biometrics. Springer, New York (2006)
16. Jain, A., Nandakumar, K., Ross, A.: Score normalization in multimodal biometric systems. Pattern Recogn. **38**(12), 2270–2285 (2005)
17. Mikolajczyk, K., Schmid, C.: A performance evaluation of local descriptors. IEEE Trans. Pattern Anal. Mach. Intell. **27**(10), 1615–1630 (2005)
18. Damer, N., Opel, A., Nouak, A.: Performance anchored score normalization for multi-biometric fusion. In: Bebis, G., Boyle, R., Parvin, B., Koracin, D., Li, B., Porikli, F., Zordan, V.B., Klosowski, J.T., Coquillart, S., Luo, X., Chen, M., Gotz, D. (eds.) ISVC 2013. LNCS, vol. 8034, pp. 68–75. Springer, Heidelberg (2013). doi:10.1007/978-3-642-41939-3_7
19. Poh, N., Martin, A., Bengio, S.: Performance generalization in biometric authentication using joint user-specific and sample bootstraps. IEEE Trans. Pattern Anal. Mach. Intell. **29**(3), 492–498 (2007)

Detecting Spatio-Temporally Interest Points Using the Shearlet Transform

Damiano Malafronte$^{(\boxtimes)}$, Francesca Odone, and Ernesto De Vito

Università degli Studi di Genova, Genoa, GE, Italy
damiano.malafronte@dibris.unige.it, francesca.odone@unige.it,
devito@dima.unige.it

Abstract. In this paper we address the problem of detecting spatio-temporal interest points in video sequences and we introduce a novel detection algorithm based on the three-dimensional shearlet transform. By evaluating our method on different application scenarios, we show we are able to extract meaningful spatio-temporal features from video sequences of human movements, including full body movements selected from benchmark datasets of human actions and human-machine interaction sequences where the goal is to segment drawing activities in smaller action primitives.

Keywords: Spatio-temporal features · Video analysis · Shearlet transform

1 Introduction

The analysis of dynamic events by space-time interest point detection has been addressed for over a decade primarily in the field of action recognition. The concept of space-time local features has been first formulated in [14], where the connections with scale-space have also been highlighted, and application to action recognition proposed [19]. Applications to action and behavior recognition can be also found in [3,22] where the authors also propose significant improvements on the computational cost and the overall descriptiveness of the procedure. An evaluation of the different approaches has been presented in [21] where the authors provide an analysis which is based on the joint evaluation of detectors and descriptors. A different approach has been taken in [10] and later in [20] with the goal of learning instead than engineering space-time features and descriptors.

In this work we discuss a work in progress where we propose the adoption of a well founded theoretical framework, the 3D shearlet transform [1], as a starting point for feature detection on a 2D+T signal. It is known that wavelets provide an optimal multi-scale representation only for 1D-signals. Shearlets are a multi-scale system of filters encoding directional informations and extending the main properties of wavelets to multivariate functions, as for example:

© Springer International Publishing AG 2017
L.A. Alexandre et al. (Eds.): IbPRIA 2017, LNCS 10255, pp. 501–510, 2017.
DOI: 10.1007/978-3-319-58838-4_55

(a) optimal sparse representation for functions with singularities along curves and surfaces;

(b) both a continuous and a discrete representation with a well established theory;

(c) shearlets with compact support either in the space domain or in the frequency domain;

(d) a large class of mother shearlets devised for specific applications (as denoising, inpainting, edge/corner detection to name a few);

(e) many discrete fast implementations with freely available codes.

We refer to the book [11] and references therein for details and updated bibliography. In the recent past shearlets have been applied with success to multi-scale feature detection in images [5,23]. The extension to the 3D case [1,6,7,12] makes it possible to address shape/volume analysis and video analysis problems. Regarding volume analysis the shearlets have been applied to the reconstruction and the analysis of medical images volumetric medical imaging [4,8]; as for video analysis it is worth mentioning an application to video denoising and inpainting [17] and to video saliency analysis [15].

Specifically, we propose a feature detection algorithm based on the Shear-lab3D implementation of three dimensional shearlets [13]. Our pipeline is very simple and the whole procedure is embedded in the computation of an interest measure derived from the good properties of the shearlet coefficients, which allows us to enhance local discontinuities in space-time. Figure 1 shows the main steps of the algorithm on an example frame.

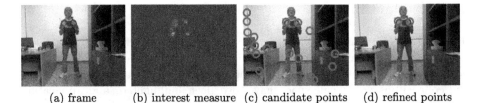

(a) frame   (b) interest measure   (c) candidate points   (d) refined points

Fig. 1. A summary of the detection pipeline we propose. (a) a frame I_t from the original video (from ChaLearn dataset); (b) interest measure IM derived from 3D shearlet coefficients enhancing interesting elements on I_t; (c) candidate local features surviving a non-maxima suppression on a space-time local neighborhood; (d) the detected meaningful points obtained by hard thresholding.

We discuss the quality of the detected points in the context of a variety of possible different applications, including action classification, salient frames extraction, and the detection of view-invariant keypoints in human gestures performed in a human-machine interaction (HMI) setting. The preliminary results speak in favor of the accuracy and meaning of the detected points.

The remainder of the paper is organized as follows. In Sect. 2 we review the theory of 2D+T shearlets, in Sect. 3 we describe our space-time interest point detection algorithm. In Sect. 4 we report an analysis of the detection results on a set of different possible scenarios. Finally, Sect. 5 is left to the conclusions.

2   Shearlets: An Overview

Following [13] we briefly review the construction of the shearlet transform of a $2D + T$ signal f, first introduced in [1]. Denoted by L^2 the Hilbert space of square-integrable functions $f : \mathbb{R}^2 \times \mathbb{R} \to \mathbb{C}$ with the usual scalar product $\langle f, f' \rangle$, the discrete shearlet transform $SH[f]$ of a signal $f \in L^2$ is the sequence of coefficients

$$SH[f](\ell, j, k, m) = \langle f, \Psi_{\ell, j, k, m} \rangle$$

where $\{\Psi_{\ell, j, k, m}\}$ is a family of filters parametrized by

(a) a label $\ell = 0, \ldots, 3$ associated with four regions in the frequency domain;
(b) the scale parameter $j \in \mathbb{N}$;
(c) the shearing vector $k = (k_1, k_2)$ where $k_1, k_2 = -\lceil 2^{j/2} \rceil, \ldots, \lceil 2^{j/2} \rceil$;
(d) the translation vector $m = (m_1, m_2, m_3) \in \mathbb{Z}^3$.

For $\ell = 0$ the filters do not depend on j and k and are given by

$$\Psi_{0,m}(x, y, t) = \varphi(x - cm_1)\varphi(y - cm_2)\varphi(t - cm_3) \tag{1}$$

where $c > 0$ is a step size, φ is a $1D$-scaling function and the system $\{\Psi_{0,m}\}_m$ takes care of the low frequency cube

$$\mathcal{P}_0 = \{(\xi_1, \xi_2, \xi_3) \in \widehat{\mathbb{R}}^3 \mid |\xi_1| \leq 1, |\xi_2| \leq 1, |\xi_3| \leq 1\}.$$

For $\ell = 1$ the filters are defined in terms of translations and two transformations,

$$A_{1,j} = \begin{pmatrix} 2^j & 0 & 0 \\ 0 & 2^{j/2} & 0 \\ 0 & 0 & 2^{j/2} \end{pmatrix} \qquad S_{1,k} = \begin{pmatrix} 1 & k_1 & k_2 \\ 0 & 1 & 0 \\ 0 & 0 & 1 \end{pmatrix},$$

namely the parabolic dilations and the shearings. Indeed

$$\Psi_{1,j,k,m}(x, y, t) = 2^j \psi_1 \left(S_{1,k} A_{1,j} \begin{pmatrix} x \\ y \\ t \end{pmatrix} - \begin{pmatrix} cm_1 \\ \hat{c}m_2 \\ \hat{c}m_3 \end{pmatrix} \right), \tag{2}$$

where c is as in (1) and $\hat{c}$ is another step size (in the rest of the paper we assume that $c = \hat{c} = 1$ for sake of simplicity), and the mother shearlet is

$$\widehat{\psi}_1(\xi_1, \xi_2, \xi_3) = \widehat{\psi}(\xi_1) \, P(\xi_1, \xi_2)\widehat{\varphi}(\xi_2) \, P(\xi_1, \xi_3)\widehat{\varphi}(\xi_3), \tag{3}$$

where P is a given polynomial 2D Fan filter [2], ψ is the 1D wavelet function associated with the scaling function φ (here $\hat{f}$ denotes the Fourier transform of a function f). Note that, according to (2), the coarsest scale corresponds to $j = 0$.

The system $\{\Psi_{1,j,k,m}\}$ takes care of the high frequencies in the pyramid along the x-axis

$$\mathcal{P}_1 = \{(\xi_1, \xi_2, \xi_3) \in \widehat{\mathbb{R}}^3 \mid |\xi_1| > 1, |\frac{\xi_2}{\xi_1}| \le 1, |\frac{\xi_3}{\xi_1}| \le 1\}.$$

For $\ell = 2, 3$ we have a similar definition by interchanging the role of x and y (for $\ell = 2$) and of x and t (for $\ell = 3$).

Our detection algorithm is based on the following nice property of the shearlet coefficients. As shown in [6,7,12] if f is locally regular in a neighborhood of m, then $SH[f](\ell, j, k, m)$ has a fast decay when j goes to infinity for any $\ell \ne 0$ and k. If f has a surface singularity at m with normal vector $(1, n_1, n_2) \in \mathcal{P}_1$, then $SH[f](\ell, j, k, m)$ has a fast decay for any $\ell \ne 1$ or $k \ne (\lceil 2^{j/2}n_1 \rceil, \lceil 2^{j/2}n_2 \rceil) =: k^*$, whereas if $\ell = 1$ and $k = k^*$ the shearlet coefficients have slow decay (a similar result holds if the normal direction of the surface singularity belongs to the other two pyramids). Based on the above result, we can uniquely associate a direction (without orientation) to any shearing vector $k = (k_1, k_2)$ and conversely. The correspondence explicitly depends on ℓ (due to the discretization the number of shearings increases with the scale, so that there is a formal dependence on j).

To compute the shearlet coefficients we use the digital implementation described in [13] based on the relation between the pair scaling function/wavelet (φ, ψ) and the quadrature mirror filter pair (h, g), which in our application is the filter pair introduced in [16].

3   Feature Detection Method

In this section we show how to detect spatio-temporally interest point only by means of the information provided by the shearlet transform $SH[f]$ where f is an image sequence $f(x, y, t)$.

As recalled at the end of the previous section, points that belong to a surface singularity are characterized by a slow decay of the corresponding shearlet coefficients, as the scale parameter j grows and the shearing parameter k (and the pyramid label ℓ) corresponds to the normal vector to the surface. A similar behavior holds true for singularities along the boundary of the surface, where two or more shearings can be meaningful [9]. Hence, we expect that the points of interest of a video are associated with high values of the shearlet coefficients and different spatial/temporal features can be extracted by looking to different pyramid labels ℓ.

These observations suggest to extend to video signals the edge detector introduced in [16] for wavelets and in [5,23] for shearlets.

To this purpose, we first define an *interest measure IM* representing a response function calculated for each point $m = (x, y, t)$ in our signal. At a fixed scale j:

$$IM_j[f](m) = \prod_{\ell=1}^{3} \sum_{k=(k_1,k_2)} |SH[f](\ell, j, k, m)|$$

Our detection algorithm is based on the use of the measure IM as a feature enhancement process. The space-time feature detection procedure is summarized in four steps, shown in an example in Fig. 1:

(a) We compute $IM_j[f]$ for $j = 1, 2$ — we control the computational cost of the procedure, by limiting the number of scales. We skip the scale $j = 0$ as it does not enhance properly the meaningful information in the signal.

(b) Then, we define an overall interest measure by multiplying the values calculated for $IM_j[f]$ when we consider only the two finest scales $j = 1, 2$ namely

$$IM[f](m) = IM_2[f](m) \cdot IM_1[f](m)$$

Since we only have three scales, the analysis across scales in [16] is not meaningful. We observed that the points of interest produce high values in both the scales $j = 1, 2$ and this remark is at the root of the above definition.

(c) We perform a non-maxima suppression in a spatio-temporal window N_m of size $w \times w \times w$ by setting to 0 non-maxima coefficients.

(d) Finally, we detect meaningful points m on the signal by means of a thresholding step $IM[f](m) > \tau$.

Notice that the IM measure is shown for a fixed t, then it includes values that appear to be high relative to all values in t (e.g. the areas corresponding to the elbows). Those points do not appear to survive the non-maxima suppression procedure (they are not highlighted in figure (c)) as they are not maxima with respect to the temporal direction (they will be marked as candidates in some neighboring time instant).

4   Evaluation

In this section we discuss the potential of our approach to feature detection on a variety of different applications. In what follows the neighbourhood size w is set to 9, and threshold τ is chosen on an appropriate validation set.

Detecting Features in Action Sequences. We start by showing examples of the extracted features in human action sequences. Figure 2 shows the results on a walking person, in two different visualization modalities: a 3D shape of the person silhouette evolving in time where the detected features are marked in blue; a map where the positions of detected points across the whole sequence are merged. It can be noticed how all meaningful points (in particular all points corresponding to a change in direction of the foot) have been nicely detected. Similarly, Fig. 3 shows an example of a different human action, a handwaving, where most features are detected on the tip of the hands.

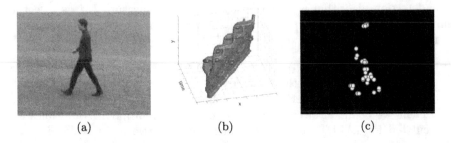

(a)   (b)   (c)

Fig. 2. A *walking* action (a) observed as (b) feature detection on a 2D+T surface (where we flipped the surface upside down to better show the points detected) and (c) summarized on a reference time instant (detected features are translated w.r.t the body centroid). (Color figure online)

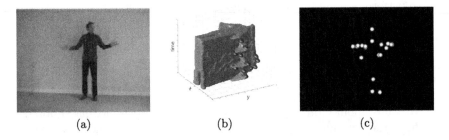

(a)   (b)   (c)

Fig. 3. A *handwaving* action (a) observed as (b) feature detection on a 2D+T surface (in this case there is a subset of features which are not visible, the ones lying within the surface and corresponding to the "claps") and (c) summarized on a reference time instant. (Color figure online)

Salient Frames Extraction. The space-time interest points we are detecting correspond to a "special" point in the scene (a corner) as it is undergoing some significant velocity change. The presence of these points is a cue of some interesting movement going on in the sequence. Their presence can be used as a guideline on the importance of a given frame in a video summarization process. We evaluate the number of space-time interest points detected in each frame and select the most meaningful frames as the one containing a large number of those points. While doing so we also apply a non maxima suppression on the temporal neighborhood to avoid the selection of frames too close in time. Figure 4 shows examples of the number of detected interest points across time in two sequences we considered, the *walking* (from KTH) and the *che vuoi* (from ChaLearn - italian lexicon) ones.

For the sake of the experiment, we select three frames in the sequences with the highest number of points detected. Figure 5 shows the most meaningful frames of a walking sequence, corresponding to the beginning of a new stride in the walk executed in the sequence. Figure 6 shows the three most meaningful

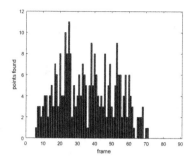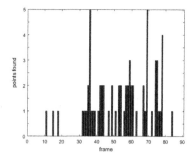

Fig. 4. Distribution of interest points found over time (a) in the *walking* and (b) in the *che vuoi* sequences.

Fig. 5. Salient frames selected for the *walking* sequence (KTH).

Fig. 6. Salient frames selected for the *che vuoi* gesture sequence (ChaLearn).

frames of the *cosa vuoi* sequence, where a male subject is executing a gesture in which he raises both his hands, shakes them, and then moves them back in the starting position. Similarly to the previous case, the three frames identified highlight very peculiar elements of the acquired action.

Detecting Gesture Primitives in HMI. We conclude with a reference to a human-machine interaction (HMI) problem. An artificial agent is observing a human performing a set of predefined planar activities (drawing different shapes). Each activity must be divided into smaller action primitives, similarly to [18]. Figures 7 and 8 show candidate frames corresponding to extrema of action primitives (where the hand features are undergoing a major velocity change): the former shows the results on a sequence of repeated line drawing actions

Fig. 7. Frames corresponding to a change in action primitive on the *drawing line* sequence.

Fig. 8. Frames corresponding to a change in action primitive on the *drawing rectangle* sequence.

performed on a frontal transparent surface (artificial agent view), the latter the crucial points of the action of drawing a rectangle on a table (human view). In both cases the points where the pen is changing direction have been detected.

5 Conclusions

In this paper we presented a space-time interest point detector based on 3D shearlets. The method is grounded on a sound mathematical theory and appears to be very promising for different video analysis applications. We are currently working on developing a complete video analysis pipeline (including noise removal, detection, and description of local features) entirely based on the same transformation, where we are aiming at exploiting at best its multiscale and multidirectional properties.

Acknowledgements. The authors would like to thank Alessia Vignolo for providing the drawing data used in the experiments.

References

1. Dahlke, S., Steidl, G., Teschke, G.: The continuous shearlet transform in arbitrary space dimensions. J. Fourier Anal. Appl. **16**(3), 340–364 (2010)
2. Do, M.N., Vetterli, M.: The contourlet transform: an efficient directional multiresolution image representation. Trans. Image Process. **14**, 2091–2106 (2005)

3. Dollár, P., Rabaud, V., Cottrell, G., Belongie, S.: Behavior recognition via sparse spatio-temporal features. In: 2005 IEEE International Workshop on Visual Surveillance and Performance Evaluation of Tracking and Surveillance, pp. 65–72. IEEE (2005)

4. Duan, C., Wang, S., Wang, X.G., Huang, Q.H.: MRI volume fusion based on 3D shearlet decompositions. J. Biomed. Imaging **2014**, 4 (2014)

5. Duval-Poo, M.A., Odone, F., De Vito, E.: Edges and corners with shearlets. IEEE Trans. Image Process. **24**(11), 3768–3780 (2015)

6. Guo, K., Labate, D.: Analysis and detection of surface discontinuities using the 3D continuous shearlet transform. Appl. Comput. Harmonic Anal. **30**(2), 231–242 (2011)

7. Guo, K., Labate, D.: Optimally sparse representations of 3D data with C^2 surface singularities using Parseval frames of shearlets. SIAM J. Math. Anal. **2**, 851–886 (2012)

8. Guo, K., Labate, D.: Optimal recovery of 3D X-ray tomographic data via shearlet decomposition. Adv. Comput. Math. **39**(2), 227–255 (2013)

9. Houska, R., Labate, D.: Detection of boundary curves on the piecewise smooth boundary surface of three dimensional solids. Appl. Comput. Harmonic Anal. **40**(1), 137–171 (2016)

10. Jhuang, H., Serre, T., Wolf, L., Poggio, T.: A biologically inspired system for action recognition. In: 2007 IEEE 11th International Conference on Computer Vision, pp. 1–8 (2007)

11. Kutyniok, G., Labate, D.: Shearlets. Applied and Numerical Harmonic Analysis. Springer, New York (2012)

12. Kutyniok, G., Lemvig, J., Lim, W.Q.: Optimally sparse approximations of 3D functions by compactly supported shearlet frames. SIAM J. Math. Anal. **44**(4), 2962–3017 (2012)

13. Kutyniok, G., Lim, W.Q., Reisenhofer, R.: Shearlab 3D: faithful digital shearlet transforms based on compactly supported shearlets. ACM Trans. Math. Softw. **42**(1), 5 (2016)

14. Laptev, I.: On space-time interest points. Int. J. Comput. Vis. **64**(2), 107–123 (2005)

15. Lei, B., Xiongwei, Z., Yunfei, Z., Yang, L.: Video saliency detection using 3D shearlet transform. Multimedia Tools Appl. **75**(13), 7761–7778 (2016)

16. Mallat, S., Zhong, S.: Characterization of signals from multiscale edges. IEEE Trans. Pattern Anal. Mach. Intell. **14**, 710–732 (1992)

17. Negi, P.S., Labate, D.: 3D discrete shearlet transform and video processing. IEEE Trans. Image Process. **21**, 2944–2954 (2012)

18. Rao, C., Yilmaz, A., Shah, M.: View-invariant representation and recognition of actions. Int. J. Comput. Vis. **50**(2), 203–226 (2002)

19. Schuldt, C., Laptev, I., Caputo, B.: Recognizing human actions: a local SVM approach. In: Proceedings of the 17th International Conference on Pattern Recognition, ICPR 2004, vol. 3, pp. 32–36. IEEE (2004)

20. Taylor, G.W., Fergus, R., LeCun, Y., Bregler, C.: Convolutional learning of spatio-temporal features. In: Daniilidis, K., Maragos, P., Paragios, N. (eds.) ECCV 2010. LNCS, vol. 6316, pp. 140–153. Springer, Heidelberg (2010). doi:10.1007/978-3-642-15567-3_11

21. Wang, H., Ullah, M.M., Klaser, A., Laptev, I., Schmid, C.: Evaluation of local spatio-temporal features for action recognition. In: BMVC 2009-British Machine Vision Conference, pp. 124.1–124.11. BMVA Press (2009)

22. Willems, G., Tuytelaars, T., Van Gool, L.: An efficient dense and scale-invariant spatio-temporal interest point detector. In: Forsyth, D., Torr, P., Zisserman, A. (eds.) ECCV 2008. LNCS, vol. 5303, pp. 650–663. Springer, Heidelberg (2008). doi:10.1007/978-3-540-88688-4_48
23. Yi, S., Labate, D., Easley, G.R., Krim, H.: A shearlet approach to edge analysis and detection. IEEE Trans. Image Process. **18**(5), 929–941 (2009)

Space-Time Flexible Kernel for Recognizing Activities from Wearable Cameras

Mario Rodriguez[1]([✉]), Carlos Orrite[1], and Carlos Medrano[2]

[1] CVLab, I3A, Zaragoza University, Zaragoza, Spain
mrodrigo@unizar.es
[2] EduQTech, IIS, Zaragoza University, Zaragoza, Spain

Abstract. Recognizing activities of daily living is useful for ambient assisted living. In this regard, the use of wearable cameras is a promising technology. In this paper, we propose a novel approach for recognizing activities of daily living using egocentric viewpoint video clips. First, in every frame the appearing objects are detected and labelled depending if they are being used or not by the subject. Later, the video clip is divided into spatio temporal bins created with an object centric cut. Finally, a support vector machine classifier is computed using a spatio-temporal flexible kernel between video clips. The validity of the proposed method has been proved by conducting experiments in the ADL dataset. Results confirm the suitability of using the space-time location of objects as information for the classification of activities using an egocentric viewpoint.

Keywords: Activities of Daily Living · Ambient Assisted Living · Wearable cameras · Activity recognition

1 Introduction

Ambient Assisted Living (AAL) is a promising and necessary research field for the near future. Thanks to medicine advances the life expectancy is increasing and so the number of dependant people, including not only elderly but also sick and disable ones. Furthermore, the total fertility rate (TFR) is low in many developed countries, as for instance in Spain [1]. The increase of dependent people and the, at least, stagnation of the TFR makes it impossible to rely on younger generations for future assistance of the dependent population, and this quite certain future makes the development in AAL even more important. The understanding of what people with special needs are doing is a key factor for a successful AAL where people are helped in their daily activities. It is here where the use of human activity recognition systems becomes handy. Video cameras provide richer sensory information than the traditional sensors used in AAL and are more useful to solve the activity recognition however, privacy concerns arise from the use of video cameras that can be used to identify users. Therefore, currently we can observe an increase in researches using egocentric vision for recognizing activities of daily living (ADL) [2] where the subject identification

© Springer International Publishing AG 2017
L.A. Alexandre et al. (Eds.): IbPRIA 2017, LNCS 10255, pp. 511–518, 2017.
DOI: 10.1007/978-3-319-58838-4_56

is prevented. There are more benefits regarding egocentric vision, for instance occlusion of manipulated objects are minimized and the workplace position is consistent. Moreover, life-logging using egocentric images can be beneficial to patients with a variety of memory impairments [3].

The information provided by the presence of different objects and the subject interaction with them may be essential for recognizing activities using egocentric viewpoints [4]. In this regard, several methods have been proposed for recognizing activities in first-person videos [5–7], while in third-person videos the use of ad-hoc local space-time descriptors are more common [8]. An advantage of using object detection as discriminant information is the dimensionality reduction in the classifier input in contrast with using dense local descriptors.

The object categorization into being manipulated (active) and present in the scene (passive) has been experimented in [5] where active objects are differentiated into a sub-category and additional object detectors are trained for them. The information obtained from the object detectors is encoded in a Bag of Words (BoW) descriptor including active and passive bins. Since BoW discards any order information and inspired in the spatial pyramid representation for images [9], in [5] they encode the activities in temporal pyramids where the activity is divided into two blocks of the same number of frames. Following this idea, in [6], they perform spatio-temporal pyramids and instead of using uniformly placed divisions they decide the bins based on Object Centric (OC) divisions. As the division can be critical because a pyramid method constrains the comparison between video clips to the selected bins, the authors propose to train several weak classifiers with Randomized Object-Centric Space-Time Pyramids (RSTP-OCC) that are later combined in with a boosting learning algorithm. In [7], they extend the categorization of objects introducing the idea of attention so an object can be active or passive and salient or non salient.

In a recent work [10] the constraint of pyramid assignment where bins are only compared with their counterparts has been avoided with the Time Flexible Kernel (TFK). In this paper, we propose to extend TFK to Space-Time Flexible Kernel (STFK) avoiding the need of training several weak classifiers as proposed by [6]. The computation of the kernel among the different video clips is used for classifying with a Support Vector Machine (SVM). This methodology has been tested in the Activities of Daily Living (ADL) dataset [5] where results show how STFK not only avoids the training of several classifiers but also obtains better results than (RSTP-OCC).

The rest of the paper is divided as follows. In Sect. 2 we review the TFK methods proposing the extension to a STFK and we describe the encoding of the video clips obtained with an OC division. In Sect. 3 we show the results obtained in the (ADL) dataset and compare them with the literature. Finally, in Sect. 4 we give some final thoughts about the proposed method.

2   Space-Time Flexible Kernel

The definition of an appropriate kernel between activity video clips allows the use of a Support Vector Machine (SVM) classifier in a space where activity classes are separable. In this regard, we have selected the TFK framework [10] and adapted it to a spatio-temporal structure, STFK.

2.1 Generalization of Time Flexible Kernel Framework

Although the original TFK was designed between sequences of different length, its formal definition can be generalized to complexer structures by modifying the domain in 1-dimensional variable t explained in [10] to a C-dimensional variable $\mathbf{s} \in \mathbb{R}^C$. Therefore, TFK is defined between two sequences $\mathbf{X} = \{\mathbf{x}_1, \ldots, \mathbf{x}_N\}$ and $\mathbf{Y} = \{\mathbf{y}_1, \ldots, \mathbf{y}_M\}$ of D-dimensional elements as follows.

Having the function space $\Gamma : \mathbb{R}^C \longrightarrow \mathbb{R}^D$, the functions $F, G \in \Gamma$ are defined using $\mathbf{X}$ and $\mathbf{Y}$:

$$F(\mathbf{s}) = \sum_{i=1}^{N} f_i(\mathbf{s})\mathbf{x}_i \tag{1}$$

$$G(\mathbf{s}) = \sum_{j=1}^{M} g_j(\mathbf{s})\mathbf{y}_j \tag{2}$$

with $\mathbf{x}_i, \mathbf{y}_j \in \mathbb{R}^D$. Each sequence vector element is linked to a specific function $f_i, g_j : \mathbb{R}^C \longrightarrow \mathbb{R}$ used to introduce the structural configuration of each element. These functions weigh each sequence element according to variable $\mathbf{s} \in \mathbb{R}^C$.

The TFK is then defined as:

$$TFK(F, G) = \int_{\mathbf{s}} F(\mathbf{s})^T G(\mathbf{s}) \, d\mathbf{s} \tag{3}$$

and may be reordered into Eq. (4) as shown in [10]:

$$TFK(F, G) = \sum_{i=1}^{N} \sum_{j=1}^{M} K_{ST}\left(f_i(\mathbf{s}), g_j(\mathbf{s})\right) K_{LIN}\left(\mathbf{x}_i, \mathbf{y}_j\right) \tag{4}$$

This equation shows how the TFK is composed by the product of two different kernels: (i) a linear kernel between sequence elements and (ii) a structural kernel between the assigned functions to each one of the sequence elements. The selected space-time functions used in the structure modelling are defined in the next subsection.

2.2 Space-Time Flexible Kernel

In [10], the TFK framework was defined between temporal sequences. In this regard, a 1-dimensional Gaussian was assigned to each one of the sequence elements in $\mathbf{X}$ and $\mathbf{Y}$, as shown in Fig. 1(i) where $\mathbf{X}$ and $\mathbf{Y}$ are sequences of two elements. In this case, TFK combines a linear kernel between the elements,

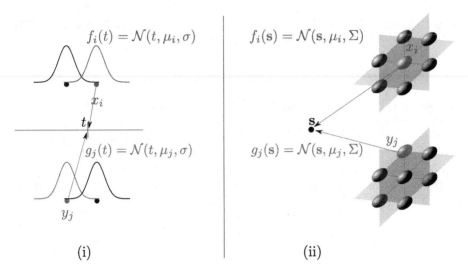

Fig. 1. (i) Kernel structure for TFK where a 1-Dimensional Gaussian is assigned to each vector. (ii) Kernel structure for STFK where a 3-Dimensional Gaussian is assigned to each vector.

$K_{LIN}\left(\mathbf{x}_i, \mathbf{y}_j\right)$, with a structural kernel, $K_{ST}\left(f_i\left(t\right), g_j\left(t\right)\right)$, defined by the Probability Product Kernel (PKK) proposed by [11] and simplified to 1-dimensional Gaussians as defined in Eq. (5).

$$K_{GAUSS_\rho}\left(f_i(t), g_j(t)\right) = \frac{(2\pi\sigma_x\sigma_y)^{(1-2\rho)/2}}{NM\sqrt{2\rho}} e^{\frac{-\|\mu_i - \mu_j\|^2}{4\sigma_x\sigma_y/\rho}} \tag{5}$$

Object positions provide discriminative information for recognizing activities, as confirmed in [6]. Therefore, we propose to extend the TFK framework from a video-clip time division to a space-time division, designing a space-time flexible kernel (STFK). As depicted in Fig. 1(ii), each video clip is cut into eight space-time bins each one represented by a 3-dimensional position vector (space and time). Moreover, the feature extraction per bin is represented by a descriptor in $\mathbb{R}^D$. The structural kernel is computed using the 3-dimensional position vector which represents the centre of a Gaussian function. We use again the PKK as structural kernel [11], but now defined for C-dimensional Gaussians (in our case $C = 3$) as shown in Eq. (6):

$$K_{GAUSS_\rho}\left(f_i(\mathbf{s}), g_j(\mathbf{s})\right) =$$
$$(2\pi)^{(1-2\rho)\frac{C}{2}} \rho^{\frac{-C}{2}} |\Sigma^\dagger|^{\frac{1}{2}} |\Sigma_x|^{\frac{-\rho}{2}} |\Sigma_y|^{\frac{-\rho}{2}} e^{(-\frac{\rho}{2}(\mu_i^T \Sigma_x^{-1}\mu_i + \mu_j^T \Sigma_y^{-1}\mu_j - \mu^{\dagger T} \Sigma^{\dagger-1}\mu^\dagger)} \tag{6}$$

where $\Sigma^\dagger = (\Sigma_x^{-1} + \Sigma_y^{-1})^{-1}$ and $\mu^\dagger = \Sigma_x^{-1}\mu_i + \Sigma_y^{-1}\mu_j$. Selecting $\rho = 1/2$ the Bhattacharyya kernel is obtained.

2.3   Space-Time Division with Object Centric Cut

Previously we have defined a kernel which keeps the spatio-temporal structure of the video clips, but to do so a spatio-temporal division is needed. As shown in [6] an Object Centric division obtains better results when the object detection is used as discriminant information.

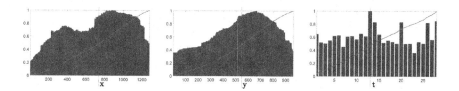

Fig. 2. Histograms of objects detection in each of the spatio-temporal dimensions. Normalized cumulative sum of the histograms and cut decision represented in red lines. (Color figure online)

Regarding an OC division we have cut each dimension (space x, y and time t) so to have sections with equal number of object detections per bin. This process is accomplished by counting the object appearance by dimension. Each detected object increase the value of the pixels in its bounding-box by $0.45/Np$ for passive objects and by $0.7/Np$ for active objects, being Np the number of pixels in the bounding-box, based on the provided code in [5]. In Fig. 2 we represent the histogram of object detections per dimension in a randomly selected video-clip. With an increasing red line we represent the normalized cumulative histogram and the vertical red line represents the selected cut per dimension.

Once the video has been divided, a BoW per division is obtained. The bounding box of the detected objects may be contained in more than one division so we assign to the corresponding word of each BoW the proportional section of the bounding box as represented in Fig. 3.

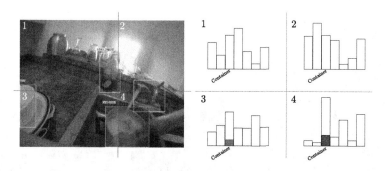

Fig. 3. Object Centric division and proportional assignment of the detected objects in one frame to the corresponding BoW.

2.4 Time Granularity Combination

So far we have defined a framework that makes the obtaining of a kernel with space-time information of a video clip possible. Moreover, we have divided the video clips into eight spatio-temporal bins, cutting each dimension into two. However, several experiments have shown how the combination of different division granularities may provide a better representation [9,10,12]. Regarding those researches we combine results of different granularities into one kernel as described in Eq. (7).

$$CombK = \sum_{k=1}^{K} STFK_k(F_k, G_k) \qquad (7)$$

3 Experiments

In order to validate the proposed method we have conducted activity recognition experiments using the ADL dataset [5] where object detections are provided.

3.1 ADLDatast

In the ADL dataset the capture of video clips has been done with a GoPro camera designed for wearable recording. The camera captures images of 1280×960 pixels at a frame rate of 30 fps with 170° of viewing angle. Attending quality and easiness, the authors of the dataset have decided to capture from a chest-mount device instead of a helmet. We can see some annotated examples of the captured frames in Fig. 4. Being one of the largest and most diverse datasets for egocentric videos, the ADL dataset is composed of roughly 10 h of video in total collected from 20 people performing 18 different activities in their own home. In addition of being large and diverse, the ADL dataset has been the most cited one as claimed by [2] so the results are comparable.

The authors of the dataset provide the label and bounding box of detected objects discriminating between active and passive objects (AP). Moreover, they provide code to test their approach with these information. They also have made a perfect annotation giving the idealized object annotations (IAP) and the segmented activity labels. Videos from the first six subjects have been used to train their object detector and therefore they should be discarded for testing.

Fig. 4. Examples of the ADL dataset

3.2 Results

We conduct the experiments following the same protocol given in [5]. Discarding the first six subjects we use the remaining 14 in a leave-one-subject-out experiment, training the activities with the other 13 persons. We have used both, AP and IAP object annotations. With this experiments we obtain the average recognition rate for the 18 activities evaluated shown in Table 1.

Table 1. Average accuracy in ADL dataset for different approaches

	BoW [5]	TempPyr [5]	RSTP-OCC [6]	TFK [10]	STFK (Ours)	CombK (Ours)
AP	34.9%	36.9%	38.7%	37.3%	39.6%	42.2%
IAP	60.9%	63.3%	-	65.7%	66.3%	67.2%

For our experiments, in TFK we have divided the video clips into two temporal windows while for STFK we have divided the video clips into eight bins, in both cases using the proposed OC cut. All the experiments use an SVM for doing the classification. Results show how both TFK and the proposed STFK improve the results obtained with a simple BoW descriptor as well as the ones obtained using the original TempPyr [5] and the improved method with the boost combination of weak classifiers RSTP-OCC [6]. Moreover, as expected, the combination of different cuts provides a better classification as the best results are obtained with the CombK kernel, where BoW, TFK and STFK are combined. All the methods evaluated in this paper use the object labellings provided by [5] with information of active or passive objects for both AP and IAP. Results confirm the usefulness of the STFK method but also suggest that a better object labelling may improve the results.

4 Conclusion

In this paper we have defined the TFK extension to a space-time flexible kernel STFK and we have used an OC cut of the dimensions. We have used this novel approach for recognizing activities of daily life recorded with wearable cameras, obtaining a significant improvement in the accuracy. Results suggest two ideas: first, STFK is a suitable method for including space-time information into a kernel computation; second, the spatial information provides discriminant data for recognizing the activity classes. Moreover, we confirm in the experiments how combining different granularities of divisions can improve the discriminative information.

Finally, the use of suitable information is important for a correct classification as shown in the results, and usually the combination of sources of information improves the method. Therefore, in future researches, the use of STFK should be combined with different feature extractors in order to improve the recognition rate. As well, a reliable object detector would boost the results as shown in the ideal example.

Acknowledgments. This work was partially supported by Spanish Grant TIN2013-45312-R (MINECO), Gobierno de Aragon and the European Social Found.

References

1. INE. Mujeres y hombres en España. Technical report, Catálogo de publicaciones de la Administración General del Estado (2014)
2. Nguyen, T.-H.-C., Nebel, J.-C., Florez-Revuelta, F.: Recognition of activities of daily living with egocentric vision: a review. Sensors **16**(1), 72 (2016)
3. Hodges, S., Berry, E., Wood, K.: Sensecam: a wearable camera that stimulates and rehabilitates autobiographical memory. Memory **19**(7), 685–696 (2011). PMID: 21995708
4. Fathi, A., Farhadi, A., Rehg, J.M.: Understanding egocentric activities. In: 2011 IEEE International Conference on Computer Vision (ICCV), pp. 407–414. IEEE, November 2011
5. Pirsiavash, H., Ramanan, D.: Detecting activities of daily living in first-person camera views. In: IEEE Conference on Computer Vision and Pattern Recognition (CVPR). IEEE (2012)
6. McCandless, T., Grauman, K.: Object-centric spatio-temporal pyramids for egocentric activity recognition. In: British Machine Vision Conference, BMVC 2013, Bristol, UK, 9–13 September 2013
7. Matsuo, K., Yamada, K., Ueno, S., Naito, S.: An attention-based activity recognition for egocentric video. In: IEEE Conference on Computer Vision and Pattern Recognition, CVPR Workshops 2014, Columbus, OH, USA, 23–28 June 2014, pp. 565–570 (2014)
8. Wang, H., Schmid, C.: Action recognition with improved trajectories. In: IEEE International Conference on Computer Vision (ICCV) (2013)
9. Lazebnik, S., Schmid, C., Ponce, J.: Beyond bags of features: spatial pyramid matching for recognizing natural scene categories. In: IEEE Conference on Computer Vision and Pattern Recognition (CVPR), vol. 2, pp. 2169–2178 (2006)
10. Rodriguez, M., Orrite, C., Medrano, C., Makris, D.: A time flexible kernel framework for video-based activity recognition. Image Vis. Comput. **48**, 26–36 (2016)
11. Jebara, T., Kondor, R., Howard, A.: Probability product kernels. J. Mach. Learn. Res. **5**, 819–844 (2004)
12. Choi, J., Wang, Z., Lee, S.-C., Jeon, W.J.: A spatio-temporal pyramid matching for video retrieval. Comput. Vis. Image Underst. **117**(6), 660–669 (2013)

Multi-modal Complete Breast Segmentation

Hooshiar Zolfagharnasab[1](✉), João P. Monteiro[1], João F. Teixeira[1],
Filipa Borlinhas[2], and Hélder P. Oliveira[1]

[1] INESC TEC, Faculdade de Engenheira, Universidade do Porto, Porto, Portugal
{hooshiar.h.z,jpsm}@ieee.org,
{jpfteixeira.eng,helder.f.oliveira}@inesctec.pt
[2] Portuguese Oncology Institute of Lisbon (IPOLFG, EPE), Lisboa, Portugal
filipaborlinhas@gmail.com

Abstract. Automatic segmentation of breast is an important step in
the context of providing a planning tool for breast cancer conservative
treatment, being important to segment completely the breast region in
an objective way; however, current methodologies need user interaction
or detect breast contour partially. In this paper, we propose a methodology to detect the complete breast contour, including the pectoral muscle,
using multi-modality data. Exterior contour is obtained from 3D reconstructed data acquired from low-cost RGB-D sensors, and the interior
contour (pectoral muscle) is obtained from Magnetic Resonance Imaging (MRI) data. Quantitative evaluation indicates that the proposed
methodology performs an acceptable detection of breast contour, which
is also confirmed by visual evaluation.

Keywords: Image analysis · Bio-medical image processing · Breast contour detection

1 Introduction

According to American Cancer Society, breast cancer is known as the second
most frequent cancer among females. However, it is becoming an increasingly
treatable disease with a 10-year survival rate for 83% of patients [1]. Two types
of surgery are mostly considered in treatment: Mastectomy, and Breast Conservative Cancer Treatment (BCCT). While survival rate is almost equal in both
treatment, BCCT is considered to have more satisfactory aesthetic outcome after
surgery [4]. Nevertheless, invasive treatments usually have an unpleasant impact
on patients Quality of Life (QoL) through imposing breast deformations [10].

H. Zolfagharnasab—This work was funded by the Project NanoSTIMA: Macro-
to-Nano Human Sensing: Towards Integrated Multimodal Health Monitoring
and Analytics/NORTE-01-0145-FEDER-000016 financed by the North Portugal
Regional Operational Programme (NORTE 2020), under the PORTUGAL 2020
Partnership Agreement, and through the European Regional Development Fund
(ERDF), and also by Fundação para a Ciência e a Tecnologia (FCT) within PhD
grant number SFRH/BD/97698/2013.

© Springer International Publishing AG 2017
L.A. Alexandre et al. (Eds.): IbPRIA 2017, LNCS 10255, pp. 519–527, 2017.
DOI: 10.1007/978-3-319-58838-4_57

Therefore, during the process of planning the treatment, the existence of a planning tool can help on the interaction between patients and physicians, allowing patients to participate in the decision process and to be more informed about the consequences of the treatment. The main requirement of such tool is a complete segmented breast in order to be used in the planning actions. Current methodologies for breast segmentation require user interaction to select contour endpoints [2], or perform an incomplete detection of breast region [7,8]. Hence, in order to meet all the requirements of current applications, it is mandatory to segment the complete breast region.

In this paper, we propose a multi-modal approach to detect the complete breast region using Three-Dimensional (3D) data. Our proposal includes the segmentation of the outer border from 3D reconstructed data, and the interior border (pectoral muscle), obtained from RGB-D sensor and MRI data, respectively (see Fig. 1).

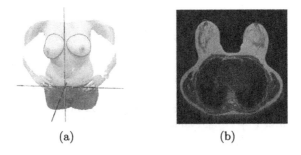

(a)   (b)

Fig. 1. Input data (a) RGB-D reconstructed data - breast region delimited by the red contour; (b) MRI slice data - pectoral muscle delimited by the red region. (Color figure online)

2 A Brief History on Breast Region Segmentation

The breast region segmentation is being studied for many years both in Two-Dimensional (2D) and 3D data. Previous studies have been widely focused on finding the inferior contour, which outlines the lower half of the breast up the sternum in one side and in the vicinity of axilla in the other side. In the research performed by Cardoso *et al.* [2] the breast contour detection was performed using frontal RGB images. This approach was formulated by computing the shortest path between the end points of the breast contour, after transforming the image as a weighted graph using gradient information. This was based on a semi-automatic approach, since some key points were manually identified: breast contour end points and nipples position. Subsequently, improvements to the methodology were performed for the complete automation and correct detection of the contour [3]. Anatomically, the contour is approximately circular and centered in the nipple. This fact inspired the authors to solve the shortest path problem in polar coordinate; thus, a cost map is generated by converting the Cartesian coordinate to polar, centered in the nipple position. However, it is generally accepted that using only RGB images is difficult to find a generalized method for breast contour delimitation, since it is characterized as too sensitive in changes of the gradient [7].

In another research, Lee *et al.* [7] studied active contours with shape constraints to detect the breast contour. They initiated the active contour with a catenary curve which has been proved not only to capture the overall shape of breast contour, but also to quantify the breast morphology. An optimized catenary curve was rotated to fit to the orientation of the breast, and then it was inflated with proper balloon force to prevent the active contour from collapsing in an unique point. Their evaluations showed that the proposed constraint for the active contour maintained the typical shape of breast; however, since their initial model was an open curve, the superior contour was ignored.

The research presented in [9] was focused on detecting inferior breast-chest contour in 3D data. Developping a curvature based algorithm, they found inferior contour candidates through points of the concave regions, where the minimum principal curvature was less than the average curvature of the model. To remove false positive candidates, a reference point was determined near to the peak point of the breast where the breast surface slopes down toward the chest wall.

Breast contour detection has also been used for segmenting breast in thermogram images. Kamath et al. [6] used both horizontal and vertical projection profile to locate lower and upper borders of the breast as Region of Interest (RoI). Then the infra-mammary fold and the axilla are detected by analyzing the horizontal gradient of RoI. Visual evaluation of their method indicated that the right and left contours of breast were well detected, but the infra-mammary and superior contours were flattened due to strict upper and lower borders.

In order to overcome the issues of the methodologies that uses RGB images, Oliveira *et al.* [8] proposed an approach using depth data acquired with a Microsoft Kinect device. In top-down view, their proposal employs two main stages; a template matching to find the fiducial points followed by a shortest path approach in polar coordinates. Whereas the nipple was not visually distinguishable in the depth image, breast peak point was selected alternatively as the centre of the associated polar coordinate space. Breast peak points were found based on gradient vector field information associated with convergence filter theory. Although this was a totally automatic approach, similar to the other methodologies described, only the lower contour was found, mostly due to the lack of discontinuities in the upper part of the breast. In this way, the upper part of the breast was defined as the horizontal line connecting the two contour end points.

In summary, from the literature review, it is possible to conclude that existing approaches lack on automation or do not detect the correct delimitation of breast shape, mainly on the upper part of the breast contour, and also they disregard the pectoral muscle limit.

3   Multi-modal Breast Segmentation

In order to obtain the complete breast region, a multi-modal scenario is proposed. For the exterior contour, the input data is based on reconstructed 3D surface information obtained with the algorithm of Costa *et al.* [5]. The pectoral muscle information is obtained from MRI volumes manually annotated by experts. The work of Oliveira *et al.* [8] was used as basis for the framework proposed in this paper. The proposed algorithm can be implemented as a sequence of a few high-level operations, as presented in Fig. 2.

3.1   Exterior Breast Contour Segmentation

Instead of using depth data (2.5D frontal view) used by the baseline method [8], the considered method uses 3D data as input. Therefore, the 3D data was projected into the coronal plane in order to convert to the 2.5D space, since it is easier to perform the segmentation in this space. In this operation, it is guaranteed that projected data (patient body) is parallel to the acquisition device.

As in the baseline method, the breast contour is modelled as a shortest path in a graph whose nodes are the pixels of the image, and the edges are the connection of neighboring pixels. The breast contour corresponds to a low-cost path through edge pixels, with the appropriate weight function. Intuitively, breast contour is characterized by a difference in the pixel's grey-level values, which originate an edge in the image. The breast contour is approximately circular; thus, the computation is more naturally performed by adopting polar coordinates. Each column in the polar image corresponds to the gradient along each radial line in the original space, computed using a 3-point numerical differentiation [8]. The centre of the polar coordinates is defined as *breast peak*, which corresponds to the point in the breast where disparity attains the lowest value. The typically round shape of breast leads to a distinctive pattern in the gradient vector field where the gradient diverge in all directions [8]. The peak is detected using a Convergence Index Filter with a divergent radial vector field template. Finally, the breast contour is found by taking the end-points as reference, that are automatically obtained by measuring the 'strength' of vertical edges in the external boundary of the breast [8]. This was always a drawback in the framework, in this sense, a new methodology is proposed based on template matching.

Although the exact location of breast contour endpoints has not been consensually defined in medical community, it can be assumed that the external, and internal end-points are in the vicinity of the axilla, and below the sternum,

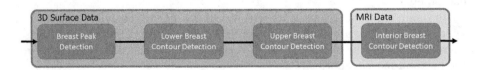

Fig. 2. Algorithm flowchart

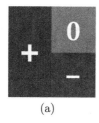 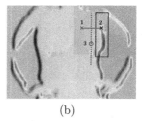

(a)   (b)

Fig. 3. (a) Suggested template for detection of left external endpoint, (b) response of the template matching on the left breast RoI is shown colorful. The external endpoint (labeled 1, or $s_{beginning}$) is used together with breast peak point (labeled 3) to locate the internal endpoint (labeled 2, or s_{ending}). (Color figure online)

respectively. In this regard, the kernel depicted in Fig. 3(a) has been designed in order to detect external end-point of the patient's left breast contour. The size of kernel has been experimentally tuned to 17 pixels. This is performed in a RoI delimited taken into account the position of *breast peak* point. The external end-point is defined as the topmost extremity of the response to the template matching, after applying a threshold defined as the average of candidates' intensity value. Finally, the internal endpoint is located in the opposite side, but at the same distance of the breast vertical median plane defined by the *breast peak* point. In Fig. 3(b), it is possible to visualize all previously mentioned details. Similarly, the detection of the external end-point in the right breast, can be performed by flipping horizontally the kernel presented in Fig. 3(a).

One of the contributions of this paper is related with the definition of the upper breast contour, which to the best of our knowledge there is no other work performing this task. After detecting the lower breast contour as explained previously [8], the procedure which is described in Algorithm 1 is performed. The region where upper breast contour exists, is characterized as an edge-less region, thus, the use of an approach similar to the one applied to the lower breast contour would lead to a wrong detection. To solve this, the values of the cost map are rectified by element-wise multiplication in $\alpha_{r,c}$.

$$\alpha_{r,c} = \begin{cases} 1 & r - w \leq a \times c + b \leq r + w \\ 0 & otherwise \end{cases} \tag{1}$$

Algorithm 1. Procedure to find the breast superior contour

1: **procedure** SUPERIOR CONTOUR DETECTION(Cost map)
2:     $s_{beginning} \leftarrow$ external endpoint of inferior contour
3:     $s_{ending} \leftarrow$ internal endpoint of breast contour
4:     $Cost\ map \leftarrow rectify(Cost\ map, s_{beginning}, s_{ending})$
5:     $C_{superior} \leftarrow shortestpath(Cost\ map, s_{beginning}, s_{ending})$
6: **end procedure**

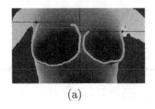 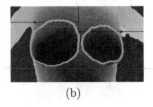

(a)   (b)

Fig. 4. Detecting breast contour, (a) lower contour, and (b) lower contour together with upper contour obtained by the described procedure

where r, c are rows and columns of cost map (in polar coordinates) respectively, and $a \times c + b$ is the line which connects the endpoints in cost map. This multiplication imposes a tunnel with initial width of $w = 1$ pixel between the end-points where the upper contour lies upon. With this approach, a more natural segmented breast shape is obtained (see Fig. 4). Once the tunnel is constructed, the upper contour is detected via finding the shortest path connecting the mentioned endpoints through the tunnel. Since the initial width of tunnel may not be sufficient for finding the shortest path, w is increased iteratively until the upper contour is discovered.

3.2   Interior Breast Contour Segmentation

The interior breast contour, a.k.a. pectoral muscle, cannot be detected from RGB-D data since it is not visible in this type of data. One option to define the pectoral muscle location is by the use of MRI data. However, in order to combine the information from the two modalities (RGB-D and MRI) a transformation must be performed, since RGB-D is acquired in upright and MRI in supine position. Besides the differences in scanning position, a slight side flatness is observed in MRI due to the stabilization padding and in some cases whenever breast is larger than the tables depth a considerable frontal deformation. The compression effect on breast during MRI acquisition is visible in Fig. 1(b).

To simplify the problem, it is assumed that unlike the breast tissue, the pectoral muscle is not deformed, or changed its shape while the MRI is taken. Also, it should be adjudged that changing in the patient position (from upright to prone) has no effect in the rigidity of breast model. Besides, the pectoral muscle keeps its relative position with respect to the skin (sternum region) in both acquisitions. The aforementioned assumptions provide a strategy to define a framework for the required transformation. In this way, two solutions are proposed, in which require the definition of 4 fiducial points, in both data, which are assumed to be in the same locations on the patient's torso.

Fitting Planes to the Corresponding Fiducial Points. In this solution, 4 planes are fitted to the regions defined by the 4 fiducial points in the RGB-D space. These planes serve as a guide for the correct positioning of the pectoral

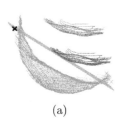 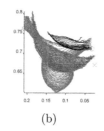 

(a)   (b)   (c)

Fig. 5. (a) First (red) and last (blue) iteration of navigating the pectoral muscle to the transformed fitting plane (cyan) of the fiducial points (black). (b) and (c) MRI data before the first iteration (b), and after final iteration (c) of semi-rigid transformation of MRI data. Fiducial points of MRI and RGB-D torso are denoted by green circle and cross, respectively. (Color figure online)

muscle, by an iterative process. Figure 5(a), depicts the first and last iteration of navigating the pectoral muscle in the suggested solution.

Semi-rigid Transformation of MRI Data. Inspiring from the Iterative Closing Points (ICP) algorithm, this solution transforms pectoral muscle obtained from MRI data to RGB-D space in an iteratively process by coarsely matching of the fiducial points. During the iterative process, the required parameters for rotation, translation and scaling are determined, which are consecutively applied to MRI data until the average distance between transfomred models in consecutive iterations becomes less than 0.1 mm (see Fig. 5(b) and (c)).

4   Results and Discussion

The proposed methodology is evaluated both in a quantitative and qualitative way. Ground-truth annotation was performed on depth data regarding the limitation of breast region (exterior breast contour).

4.1   Database

A database consisting of 32 patients was used for the evaluation. Each patient 3D reconstructed model was obtained using the framework developed by Costa et al. [5]. Besides, pectoral muscle information was obtained from MRI slices manually annotated by an expert.

4.2   Exterior Breast Contour Segmentation

Evaluation is performed using the Hausdorff and average distance between the ground-truth contour and the contour obtained from the proposed methodology (see Table 1). The Hausdorff distance between point sets A and B is defined as:

$$h(A, B) = \max_{a \in A} \ \min_{b \in B} \ \| \ a - b \ \| \tag{2}$$

Table 1. Breast contour detection error (in mm).

| | Detected → Ground-truth | | Ground-truth → Detected | |
	Average	Hausdorff	Average	Hausdorff
Mean	3.84	11.51	2.64	9.00
Std	1.41	4.77	0.95	3.92
Max	7.23	23.08	5.54	20.18
Min	1.69	5.45	1.02	3.84

where $\| \, . \, \|$ is the Euclidean distance. The motivation for using this metric is that it represents the worst case scenario. The average error of 3.84 mm from detected contour to the ground-truth indicates that the exterior contour has been found in a reasonable region. As long as the visual evaluation of inferior contour indicates a competitive detection comparing with the ground-truth, there is a small visible gap between the discovered superior contour of the manually annotated one (see Fig. 6(a)). Although the presence of this gap influences the numerical evaluation, the detected contour is still found in the consensual accepted region that is also certified by the Hausdorff metric.

4.3 Interior Breast Contour Segmentation

The lack of ground-truth for the interior contour, makes it possible to perform only a qualitative evaluation, through the visualization of pectoral muscle position against the location of the breast. It has been shown that the pectoral muscle is located in an accepted anatomical location toward both the breast tissue and sternum bone, mainly using the second approach (Semi-rigid transformation of MRI data). Figure 6(b), (c) and (d) depict the visual output for one of the patients of the database.

(a)   (b)   (c)   (d)

Fig. 6. (a) Visual evaluation of contour detection; detected contour (white), and ground-truth (green), breast peaks (triangle), infra-mammary endpoint (blue circle), internal endpoints (red cross), and external endpoints (yellow diamond) (b) perspective view, (c) top view, and (d) lateral view of pectoral muscle transforming suggestions; the suggestion powered by fitting planes is shown in blue while the output of semi-rigid transformation solution is shown in red. (Color figure online)

5   Conclusion

In this paper, an automatic methodology have been proposed for the complete segmentation of breast region using a multi-modal approach. The contributions of this paper are related with the correct delimitation of the breast region including the upper part and the inclusion of the interior breast contour (pectoral muscle). Quantitative and visual inspections of the results indicate a good performance and robustness for a wide variety of patients. Future work will focus on the use of these results incorporated in the planning tool, which will permit the improvement of the interaction between patients and physicians, allowing patients participate in the decision process and be more informed about the consequences of the treatment.

References

1. American Cancer Society: Breast cancer facts and figures 2015–2016. American Cancer Society (ACS) (2015)
2. Cardoso, J., Cardoso, M.J.: Breast contour detection for the aesthetic evaluation of breast cancer conservative treatment. Comput. Recogn. Syst. **2**, 518–525 (2007)
3. Cardoso, J.S., Sousa, R., Teixeira, L.F., Cardoso, M.J.: Breast contour detection with stable paths. Biomed. Eng. Syst. Technol. **25**, 439–452 (2009)
4. Cardoso, M.J., Oliveira, H.P., Cardoso, J.S.: Assessing cosmetic results after breast conserving surgery. J. Surg. Oncol. **110**(1), 37–44 (2014)
5. Costa, P., Monteiro, J.P., Zolfagharnasab, H., Oliveira, H.P.: Tessellation-based coarse registration method for 3d reconstruction of the female torso. In: 8th IEEE International Conference on Bioinformatics and Biomedicine, pp. 301–306 (2014)
6. Kamath, D., Kamath, S., Prasad, K., Rajagopal, K.V.: Segmentation of breast thermogram images for the detection of breast cancer - a projection profile approach. J. Image Graph. **3**(1), 47–51 (2015)
7. Lee, J., Muralidhar, G.S., Reece, G.P., Markey, M.K.: A shape constrained parametric active contour model for breast contour detection. In: 34th International Conference of the IEEE Engineering in Medicine and Biology Society, pp. 4450–4453 (2012)
8. Oliveira, H.P., Cardoso, J.S., Magalhães, A.T., Cardoso, M.J.: A 3d low-cost solution for the aesthetic evaluation of breast cancer conservative treatment. Comput. Methods Biomechan. Biomed. Eng.: Imaging Vis. **2**(2), 90–106 (2014)
9. Zhao, L., Cheong, A., Reece, G.P., Fingeret, M.C., Shah, S.K., Merchant, F.A.: Inferior breast-chest contour detection in 3-d images of the female torso. IEEE J. Transl. Eng. Health Med. **4**, 1–10 (2016)
10. Zolfagharnasab, H., Cardoso, J.S., Oliveira, H.P.: Fitting of breast data using free form deformation technique. In: Campilho, A., Karray, F. (eds.) ICIAR 2016. LNCS, vol. 9730, pp. 608–615. Springer, Cham (2016). doi:10.1007/978-3-319-41501-7_68

Local Features Applied to Dermoscopy Images: Bag-of-Features versus Sparse Coding

Catarina Barata[1,3(✉)], Mário A.T. Figueiredo[2,3], M. Emre Celebi[4],
and Jorge S. Marques[1,3]

[1] Institute for Systems and Robotics, Lisbon, Portugal
ana.c.fidalgo.barata@ist.utl.pt
[2] Instituto de Telecomunicações, Lisbon, Portugal
[3] Instituto Superior Técnico, Universidade de Lisboa, Lisbon, Portugal
[4] Department of Computer Science,
University of Central Arkansas, Conway, AR, USA

Abstract. Feature extraction is a crucial step in any computer aided diagnosis (CAD) system for melanoma diagnosis. Therefore, it is important to select features that are able to efficiently characterize the properties of the different types of lesions. Local features that separately characterize and distinguish different regions of the lesions have been shown to provide good descriptors for these skin lesions. Two powerful methods can be used to obtain local features: bag-of-features (BoF) and sparse coding (SC). Both methods have been applied to dermoscopy with promising results. However, a comparison between the two strategies is lacking. In this work, we fill this gap by developing a framework to compare the two methods in the melanoma diagnosis task. The results show that SC significantly outperforms BoF, achieving sensitivity = 85.5% and specificity = 75.1% versus sensitivity = 81.7% and specificity = 66.5%.

Keywords: Melanoma diagnosis · Computer aided diagnosis · Local features · Bag-of-features · Sparse coding

1 Introduction

Melanoma is one of the most common types of cancer in Europe, North America, and Australia. Due to its rapid growth, it is able to metastasize to other organs, such as lungs, bones, or brain [1]. The diagnosis of skin lesions follows a specific guideline: (i) inspection of the lesion using a magnification device; (ii) assessment of different criteria, such as the ABCD rule [2] or the 7-point checklist [3]; and (iii) scoring the lesion based on the identified criteria. Although the aforementioned medical rules are well established and guarantee an increase in the accuracy of the diagnosis, the evaluation still critically hinges on visual inspection and on the expertise of the dermatologist [1]. This means that the analysis of lesions is a highly subjective and difficult task.

© Springer International Publishing AG 2017
L.A. Alexandre et al. (Eds.): IbPRIA 2017, LNCS 10255, pp. 528–536, 2017.
DOI: 10.1007/978-3-319-58838-4_58

Modern inspection devices are able to acquire images of the lesions, obtained with or without special illumination, dividing the images into two types: dermoscopy and clinical. For the past two decades, research groups have been working on computer aided diagnosis (CAD) systems to diagnose the skin lesions, using either dermoscopy or clinical images [4,5]. These CAD systems can be used as a support tool by dermatologists with any level of expertise, reducing the subjectivity of the diagnosis. This work uses dermoscopy images, thus from this point on we will discuss specific aspects of its automatic analysis.

CAD systems follow three main steps: (i) lesion segmentation; (ii) feature extraction; and (iii) lesion diagnosis [4]. Aside from lesion segmentation, which by itself is a major challenge, there is a significant diversity in the type of features and classifiers used in steps (ii) and (iii). A short list of classifiers that have been applied includes K-nearest neighbor, AdaBoost, support vector machines, and neural networks [5]. The extracted features can be divided into two categories: global and local. The former consists of computing a single vector to describe the entire lesion. This vector can comprise information about the shape and symmetry of the lesion (*e.g.*, area, circularity measure, shape symmetry), color (*e.g.*, RGB or HSV histograms), and texture *e.g.*, gray level co-occurrence Matrix) [6]. Local features allow us to separately characterize different regions of the lesion. This can be seen as an approximation of the analysis performed by dermatologists, since they also assess different regions of the lesions. A simple strategy to compute local features is the bag-of-features (BoF) approach, which has been applied with success in different works (*e.g.*, [7,8]). More recently, a different method has been used to obtain local features: sparse coding (SC) [9,10]. This strategy arises from relaxing the restrictive constraints of the BoF optimization problem, as will be discussed in Sect. 2, and has been shown to be efficient in capturing salient properties of the image in different computer vision problems (*e.g.*, [11,12]).

Both BoF and SC have achieved promising classification results in dermoscopy image analysis. However, a direct comparison between the two types of features has been missing. In this paper, we fill this gap by providing a comparison between the two methods, to assess which one performs the best. The remaining sections of the paper are organized as follows. In Sect. 2, we discuss the formulations of BoF and SC and compare them. In Sect. 3 we describe the experimental framework, and in Sect. 4 we present the results.

2   Local Features - From BoF to Sparse Coding

The BoF method assumes that an image can be represented as a collection of elements of a dictionary of *visual words* (atoms). Assuming that a dictionary D of K elements is known, any image is processed as follows: (i) a set of M patches is extracted and a feature vector $x_m \in \mathbb{R}^D$ is computed for each of them; (ii) the features are matched to the closest dictionary element, as follows

$$\min_{\alpha_m} \|x_m - D\alpha_m\|_2^2$$
$$\textbf{s.t} \quad \alpha_m \in \{0,1\}^K, \|\alpha_m\|_0 = 1, \tag{1}$$

where $\|.\|_0$ denotes the ℓ_0 "norm"; (iii) this information is summarized into a histogram of occurrences that counts the number of times each atom was selected.

The constraint used in (1) is very restrictive. In order to deal with this issue one can use the SC formulation. Similarly to BoF, the first step of SC is the extraction of a set of M image patches, followed by the computation of a feature vector to characterize each patch. The following step is to match the feature vectors to atoms of a known dictionary. However, instead of assuming that each vector is only associated with one of the atoms, SC assumes that each vector is a combination of a small number of atoms. This can be formulated as an optimization problem with a regularization based on the ℓ_1 norm

$$\min_{\alpha_m} \|x_m - D\alpha_m\|_2^2 + \lambda\|\alpha_m\|_1, \tag{2}$$

where $\alpha_m \in \mathbb{R}^K$ is a vector of coefficients and λ is a non-negative parameter specified by the user, which controls the relevance of the regularization term. Using the ℓ_1 norm in the regularization term encourages sparsity of the coefficients, i.e., only a small number of them is non-zero. Additional constraints can be added to the problem, such as setting $\alpha_m \geq 0$ [12].

Aside from the patch representation, another main difference between BoF and SC is the strategy used to estimate the dictionaries. In both cases these are estimated using a training set of N feature vectors $\{x_1, ..., x_N\} \in \mathbb{R}^D$, extracted from the patches of several images. According to the BoF formulation (see (1)) D can be estimated as follows

$$\min_{\alpha_1,...,\alpha_N,D} \sum_{n=1}^{N} \|x_n - D\alpha_n\|_2^2$$
$$\text{s.t}\quad \alpha_n \in \{0,1\}^K, \ \|\alpha_n\|_0 = 1, \ \forall n. \tag{3}$$

This optimization problem can be solved using a clustering algorithm, such as k-means [13].

In the SC formulation, a dictionary of K elements is obtained by solving the following optimization problem

$$\min_{\alpha_1,...,\alpha_N,D} \sum_{n=1}^{N} \|x_n - D\alpha_n\|_2^2 + \lambda\|\alpha_n\|_1$$
$$\text{s.t}\quad \|d_k\|_2 \leq 1, \ k = 1, ..., K, \tag{4}$$

where $d_k \in \mathbb{R}^K$ is the k-th column of D. The normalization constraint $\|d_k\|_2 = 1$ is used to avoid trivial solutions for the dictionary, namely having the columns of D growing to infinity and the α coefficients approaching zero.

The estimation of α according to (2) is a convex problem, which can be solved using one of several special-purpose algorithms that have been developed of this problem [14]. On the other hand, the problem (4) is not convex and has been the focus of a considerable amount of recent research. The standard approach to solve (4) is to alternate between estimating the SC coefficients, keeping the dictionary fixed, and updating the dictionary [14]. Formally:

(i) Fix the dictionary D and solve

$$\min_{\alpha_1,...\alpha_N} ||x_n - D\alpha_n||_2^2 + \lambda ||\alpha_n||_1. \tag{5}$$

(ii) Fix $\alpha_1, ..., \alpha_N$ and solve

$$\min_D \sum_{n=1}^N ||x_n - D\alpha_n||_2^2, \quad \text{s.t. } ||d_k||_2 \leq 1, \ k = 1, ..., K. \tag{6}$$

These two steps are repeated for a predefined number of iterations or until some convergence criterion is satisfied. An extensive review on different methods to solve these optimizations can be found in [14].

A final difference between the two methods resides in how the final image representation is obtained. As stated at the beginning of this section, BoF represents the image as a histogram of occurrences of atoms. The same approach can not be directly applied to SC, since the vectors α_m select more than one atom, with different weights. Different pooling strategies have been proposed to tackle this issue: *e.g.*, max-pooling or mean of the absolute values of α [11].

3 Experimental Framework

The goal of this paper is to perform a fair comparison between the BoF and SC representations. Therefore, we must maintain common parameters of the methods constant, such as the type and size of patches extracted from the images and the features used to describe them, and adjust only what is specific of each method. In the sequel we present the experimental setting used obtain our results.

(i) **Patch extraction/image sampling:** 16×16 overlapping (step of 8 pixels) patches are extracted from all of the images. Although it is possible to extract patches from the entire image (*e.g.*, [9]), we chose to extract patches only from a bounding box around the lesion. This allows working with the images in their original size (average 560×750), without unbearable computational costs. The area of the image containing the lesion is identified using manual segmentation.

(ii) **Patch features:** Color and texture features are computed for each patch, namely color histograms for the RGB and HSV color spaces, and gradient histograms (amplitude and orientation). All these histograms have 16 bins. The aforementioned fetures are not the ones used in other sparsity-based dermoscopy works [9,10]. Those works use the vectorized patches in either gray level or RGB space, and learn dictionaries to represent that information. Nowadays, learning the dictionaries directly from image patches is a very popular approach [14]. Image patches are not suitable to be tested in the BoF framework, because the size of the resulting feature vectors lead to very high computational costs. Nonetheless, we will use image patches as features in SC, in order to establish a comparison with related works.

(iii) **Dictionary learning:** k-means was used to obtain the BoF dictionaries, while the online dictionary learning method [15] (available in the SPAMS software package[1]) was used to obtain the SC dictionaries. The size of all the dictionaries was chosen in the set $K \in \{2^7, 2^8, 2^9\}$.

(iv) **Pooling:** The final BoF descriptor was obtained using the traditional vector quantization approach (see (1)), followed by histogram building.

In the case of SC, the α vectors of the patches were obtained using the LARS algorithm [16] (available in SPAMS). Two optimization problems were applied on this phase: the traditional one (2) and one obtained by inserting a non-negativity constraint. The combination of all of the α_m vectors of a certain image is performed using two strategies: max-pooling (max) and average absolute pooling (abs), respectively defined as follows:

$$\alpha^j = \max\{|\alpha_1^j|, |\alpha_2^j|, ..., |\alpha_M^j|\}, \tag{7}$$

$$\alpha^j = \frac{1}{M} \sum_{m=1}^{M} |\alpha_m^j|, \tag{8}$$

where α^j is the j-th component of the vector α, M is the number of patches, and α_m^j is the j-th component of the m-th patch vector.

(v) **Classification:** The diagnosis was obtained using a SVM with a radial basis function (RBF) kernel (available in MATLAB 2015b®). A different classifier was trained for each of the possible feature configurations, using a set of dermoscopy images diagnosed by experts. In each of the experiments we tunned the width of the RBF kernel $\rho \in \{2^{-12}, 2^{-5}, ..., 2^{12}\}$ and the penalty term $C \in \{2^{-6}, 2^{-4}, ..., 2^6\}$ given to the soft margin.

4   Experimental Results

4.1   Dataset and Performance Metrics

All of the experiments were carried out on a heterogeneous dataset of 804 images (241 melanomas), selected from the EDRA database [1]. The ground-truth diagnosis was provided by a group of experts.

The different configurations were evaluated in terms of sensitivity (SE), specificity (SP), and a cost score (S) defined as follows

$$S = \frac{c_{10}(1 - SE) + c_{01}(1 - SP)}{c_{10} + c_{01}}, \tag{9}$$

where c_{10} is the cost of an incorrectly classified melanoma (false negative) and c_{01} is the cost of an incorrectly classified non-melanoma (false positive). Since we consider that an incorrect classification of a melanoma is a more serious error, we set $c_{10} = 1.5c_{01}$ and $c_{01} = 1$. The results were obtained using a 10-fold nested cross-validation strategy, where the images were divided into 10-folds, each with

---

[1] http://spams-devel.gforge.inria.fr/.

approximately the same proportion of benign and malignant lesions. One of the folds was kept for testing, while the remaining nine were used for training and parameter selection. This procedure was repeated ten times with a different fold for testing, and the results are the average performance.

4.2   Results

Table 1 shows the comparison between BoF and SC for the different features herein considered. Several conclusions can be drawn from these scores. The first is that *max*-pooling leads to significantly better results than *abs*-pooling. This happens in almost all the features. Moreover, the non-negativity constraint also improves the results (only showed for *max*-pooling). Interestingly, the features used in other dermoscopy works (gray level and RGB patches) achieve worse scores than the other tested color and texture features. Finally, we are able to show that SC outperforms BoF in almost all of the experiments, which suggest that this approach is more efficient.

Table 1. Results for melanoma diagnosis using BoF and SC. In **bold** we highlight the best results.

Features	BoF	SC-abs	SC-max	SC-max & $\alpha \geq 0$
Amplitude histogram	$SE = 64.2\%$	$SE = 68.0\%$	$SE = 69.7\%$	**SE =76.3%**
	$SP = 72.8\%$	$SP = 64.1\%$	$SP = 64.3\%$	**SP =60.4%**
	$S = 0.3236$	$S = 0.3356$	$S = 0.3246$	**S =0.3005**
Orientation histogram	$SE = 66.7\%$	$SE = 75.4\%$	**SE=74.2%**	$SE = 73.8\%$
	$SP = 68.6\%$	$SP = 63.4\%$	**SP =67.9%**	$SP = 67.7\%$
	$S = 0.3254$	$S = 0.2940$	**S =0.2832**	$S = 0.2834$
RGB histogram	$SE = 77.6\%$	$SE = 76.7\%$	$SE = 87.9\%$	**SE =82.9%**
	$SP = 70.3\%$	$SP = 72.3\%$	$SP = 70.0\%$	**SP = 77.3%**
	$S = 0.2532$	$S = 0.2504$	$S = 0.1953$	**S =0.1934**
HSV histogram	$SE = 81.7\%$	$SE = 79.6\%$	$SE = 82.1\%$	**SE =85.5%**
	$SP = 66.5\%$	$SP = 67.3\%$	$SP = 79.0\%$	**SP = 75.1%**
	$S = 0.2438$	$S = 0.2529$	$S = 0.1910$	**S =0.1860**
Gray level patches	-	**SE =68.0%**	$SE = 73.9\%$	$SE = 73.8\%$
		SP = 70.9%	$SP = 52.6\%$	$SP = 54.4\%$
		S =0.3084	$S = 0.3462$	$S = 0.3396$
RGB patches	-	$SE = 65.5\%$	$SE = 72.6\%$	**SE =79.2%**
		$SP = 68.4\%$	$SP = 70.0\%$	**SP = 71.8%**
		$S = 0.3334$	$S = 0.2844$	**S =0.2376**

Table 2 shows the number of images that are correctly and incorrectly classified by BoF and SC, using the best configuration (HSV histogram). These values show that 50% of the images incorrectly classified by BoF are correctly classified by SC. Although the opposite is also true (58 images), it happens in a much

Table 2. Number of images correctly and incorrectly classified by each of the methods using the HSV histograms as patch features.

		Sparse coding	
		Correct	Incorrect
BoF	Correct	513	58
	Incorrect	116	117

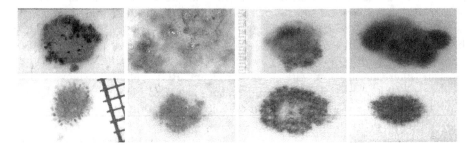

Fig. 1. Malignant (1st row) and benign (2nd row) lesions, correctly classified by both methods.

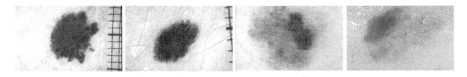

Fig. 2. Malignant (1st and 3rd columns) and benign (2nd and 4th columns) lesions, incorrectly classified by BoF (1st–2nd columns) and SC (3rd–4th columns).

smaller extent. We would like to point out that the scores obtained with SC using a single feature still outperform the best results obtained for this dataset with feature fusion ($SE = 83\%$, $SP = 76\%$) [17].

Figure 1 shows examples of lesions correctly classified by both methods, using their best configurations, while Fig. 2 shows examples of lesions incorrectly classified by one of the methods.

5   Conclusions

In this paper, we have compared bag-of-features and sparse coding in the problem of melanoma diagnosis. A simple framework was used to compare the two methods, where the idea was to keep fixed the common variables and only adjust the key aspects that are specific of each of the methods. This allowed us to perform a fair comparison and show that SC outperforms BoF, obtaining a sensitivity = 85.5% and specificity = 73.4% vs. sensitivity = 81.7% and specificity = 66.5%, for the corresponding best configurations.

Acknowledgments. This work was partially funded with grant SFRH/BD/84658/ 2012 and by the FCT projects [UID/EEA/50009/2013] and PTDC/EEIPRO/ 0426/2014.

References

1. Argenziano, G., Soyer, H.P., De Giorgi, V., Piccolo, D., Carli, P., Delfino, M., Ferrari, A., Hofmann-Wellenhog, V., Massi, D., Mazzocchetti, G., Scalvenzi, M., Wolf, I.H.: Interactive Atlas of Dermoscopy. EDRA Medical Publishing & New Media, Milan (2000)
2. Stolz, W., Riemann, A., Cognetta, A.B.: ABCD rule of dermatoscopy: a new practical method for early recognition of malignant melanoma. Eur. J. Dermatol. **4**, 521–527 (1994)
3. Argenziano, G., Fabbrocini, G., Carli, P., De Giorgi, V., Sammarco, E., Delfino, E.: Epiluminescence microscopy for the diagnosis of doubtful melanocytic skin lesions. Comparison of the ABCD rule of dermatoscopy and a new 7-point checklist based on pattern analysis. Arch. Dermatol. **134**, 1563–1570 (1998)
4. Korotkov, K., Garcia, R.: Computerized analysis of pigmented skin lesions: a review. Artif. Intell. Med. **56**(2), 69–90 (2012)
5. Oliveira, R., Papa, J., Pereira, A., Tavares, J.: Computational methods for pigmented skin lesion classification in images: review and future trends. Neural Comput. Appl., 1–24 (2016)
6. Celebi, M., Kingravi, H., Uddin, B., Iyatomi, H., Aslandogan, Y.A., Stoecker, W., Moss, R.: A methodological approach to the classification of dermoscopy images. Comput. Med. Imaging Graph. **31**(6), 362–373 (2007)
7. Barata, C., Ruela, M., Francisco, M., Mendonça, T., Marques, J.: Two systems for the detection of melanomas in dermoscopy images using texture and color features. IEEE Syst. J. **8**(3), 965–979 (2014)
8. Rastgoo, M., Garcia, R., Morel, O., Marzani, F.: Automatic differentiation of melanoma from dysplastic nevi. Comput. Med. Imaging Graph. **43**, 44–52 (2015)
9. Codella, N., Cai, J., Abedini, M., Garnavi, R., Halpern, A., Smith, J.R.: Deep learning, sparse coding, and SVM for melanoma recognition in dermoscopy images. In: Zhou, L., Wang, L., Wang, Q., Shi, Y. (eds.) MLMI 2015. LNCS, vol. 9352, pp. 118–126. Springer, Cham (2015). doi:10.1007/978-3-319-24888-2_15
10. Rastgoo, M., Lemaitre, G., Morel, O., Massich, J., Garcia, R., Meriaudeau, F., Marzani, F., Sidibé, D.: Classification of melanoma lesions using sparse coded features and random forests. In: SPIE Medical Imaging, p. 97850C. International Society for Optics and Photonics (2016)
11. Yang, J., Yu, K., Gong, Y., Huang, T.: Linear spatial pyramid matching using sparse coding for image classification. In: IEEE Conference on Computer Vision and Pattern Recognition (CVPR), pp. 1794–1801. IEEE (2009)
12. Zhang, C., Liu, J., Tian, Q., Xu, C., Lu, H., Ma, S.: Image classification by non-negative sparse coding, low-rank and sparse decomposition. In: IEEE Conference on Computer Vision and Pattern Recognition (CVPR), pp. 1673–1680. IEEE (2011)
13. Sivic, J., Zisserman, A.: Video google: a text retrieval approach to object matching in videos. In: Ninth IEEE International Conference on Computer Vision (ICCV), vol. 2, pp. 1470–1477. IEEE (2003)
14. Mairal, J., Bach, F., Ponce, J.: Sparse modeling for image and vision processing. Found. Trends Comput. Graph. Vis. **8**(2–3), 85–283 (2014)

15. Mairal, J., Bach, F., Ponce, J., Sapiro, G.: Online learning for matrix factorization and sparse coding. J. Mach. Learn. Res. **11**, 19–60 (2010)
16. Efron, B., Hastie, T., Johnstone, I., Tibshirani, R.: Least angle regression. Ann. Stat. **32**(2), 407–499 (2004)
17. Barata, C., Celebi, M., Marques, J.: Melanoma detection algorithm based on feature fusion. In: 37th Annual International Conference of the IEEE Engineering in Medicine and Biology Society (EMBC), pp. 2653–2656. IEEE (2015)

Segmentation of the Rectus Abdominis Muscle Anterior Fascia for the Analysis of Deep Inferior Epigastric Perforators

Ricardo J. Araújo$^{(\boxtimes)}$ and Hélder P. Oliveira

INESC TEC, Faculdade de Engenharia, Universidade do Porto, Porto, Portugal
{ricardo.j.araujo,helder.f.oliveira}@inesctec.pt

Abstract. The segmentation of the anterior fascia of the rectus abdominis muscle is an important step towards the analysis of abdominal vasculature. It may advance Computer Aided Detection tools that support the activity of clinicians who study vessels for breast reconstruction using the Deep Inferior Epigastric Perforator flap. In this paper, we propose a two-fold methodology to detect the anterior fascia in Computerized Tomographic Angiography volumes. First, a slice-wise thresholding is applied and followed by a post-processing phase. Finally, an interpolation framework is used to obtain a final smooth fascia detection. We evaluated our method in 20 different volumes, by calculating the mean Euclidean distance to manual annotations, achieving subvoxel error.

Keywords: Medical image · Segmentation · Abdominal anterior fascia

1 Introduction

In the United States, breast cancer is the leading cause of cancer death in women aged 20 to 59 years, being only surpassed by lung cancer in higher ages. This tendency occurs at a worldwide level. It is estimated that more than 230.000 new cases of breast cancer will affect women in the United States during 2016 [1].

The mastectomy, a surgical procedure where the whole breast is removed, is highly recurrent and has even been increasing in some institutions [2,3]. Reconstruction methods allow to recreate the breast shape, improving women's self-confidence and their image after the breast(s) removal. Among the existing options, the Deep Inferior Epigastric Perforator (DIEP) flap has become the state-of-art technique for autologous tissue based breast reconstruction [4]. In this procedure, skin, fat and vessels are moved from the abdominal region to the chest, without interfering with the rectus abdominis muscle. The harvested vessels are the DIEPs, regularly known as perforators. They have origin in bifurcations of the Deep Inferior Epigastric Arteries (DIEAs) and then perforate the rectus abdominis muscle, heading to the superficial tissues of the abdomen.

As microsurgery techniques are involved in the DIEP flap, medical imaging has been used for preoperative planning. The clinician characterizes the existing

© Springer International Publishing AG 2017
L.A. Alexandre et al. (Eds.): IbPRIA 2017, LNCS 10255, pp. 537–545, 2017.
DOI: 10.1007/978-3-319-58838-4_59

perforators, since the viability of the flap depends upon several features of the harvested perforator(s) [5]. This step requires the extraction of characteristics from the subcutaneous and intramuscular portions of the perforators. The anterior fascia of the rectus abdominis muscle separates both of these regions, hence its automatic segmentation facilitates the use of computer based routines to automatically retrieve the required measures. Furthermore, the automatic detection of the fascia would help to determine the origin of each perforator subcutaneous course, which is required to create an accurate map of the dissection locations.

To the best of our knowledge, the literature does not include a method targeting this specific problem. Even then, the segmentation of abdominal organs such as the liver, spleen, pancreas and kidneys, has been actively studied in the past years. Recent trends regarding this topic concern the simultaneous segmentation of these organs, by using manually labeled atlases to get target specific priors and, then, obtain segmentations through the graph cuts method [6,7].

In this paper, we propose a semi-automatic method for the segmentation of the anterior fascia of the rectus abdominis muscle, in the region where the perforators arise. It relies on the binarization of the intensities in the area of interest and further refinement, in order to obtain a first segmentation of the anterior fascia. Then, a local interpolation framework is proposed to remove the influence of structures in the neighborhood of the anterior fascia.

2   Rectus Abdominis Muscle Anterior Fascia Segmentation

In this section, we present a methodology that extracts the anterior fascia layer of the rectus abdominis muscle in the region that is relevant for DIEP analysis. Such region is defined as the volume that includes the end of the subcutaneous course of each perforator and the locations where DIEAs enter the posterior lamella of the rectus muscle (Fig. 1 shows these landmarks in a sagittal view representation of the local anatomy). A margin was also considered, in order to prevent discarding portions of vessels which have a tortuous path.

In terms of image intensities, the fascia cannot be distinguished from the rectus abdominis muscle. Hence, it is considered to be the boundary between this muscle and the subcutaneous region, characterized by a transition from pixels with low intensity (subcutaneous region) to pixels with higher intensity (muscle), which exists over all the columns of each axial slice of the volume of interest. Figure 2 shows example axial slices of a volume and the corresponding anterior fascia location.

2.1   Preliminary Fascia Segmentation

To obtain a preliminary segmentation of the anterior fascia, the pipeline presented in Fig. 3 was applied to each axial slice of the volume of interest. Let B_s be the binary image after step s. The involved steps are described below:

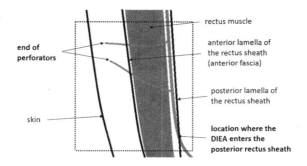

Fig. 1. Sagittal view representation of the abdominal wall anatomy. The box contains the region of interest.

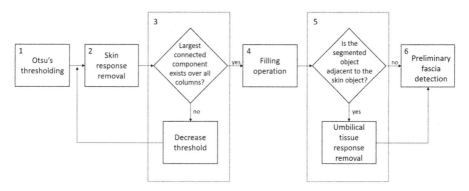

Fig. 2. Example axial slices of the volume of interest. The anterior fascia is in white.

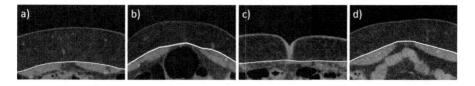

Fig. 3. Pipeline used to obtain a preliminary fascia detection for each axial slice of the volume of interest.

1. **Otsu's thresholding:** The Otsu's method [8] was used with the goal of obtaining a threshold that distinguishes the muscle from the subcutaneous region. Thresholding the original images using such threshold produces a first segmentation - B_1 (see Fig. 4). Occasionally, there are structures that also respond to the threshold and appear connected to the anterior region of the muscle, such as perforators and umbilical tissue (see images (b), (c) of Fig. 4, respectively). The last modules of the pipeline address these unwanted detections.

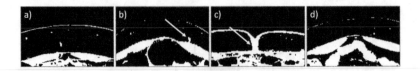

Fig. 4. B_1 segmentations of slices of Fig. 2, using the threshold given by the Otsu's method [8]. The white arrows in (b), (c) point to perforator and umbilical tissue responses, respectively.

2. **Skin removal:** The regions of the original image, where the intensities are equal to zero, are extracted (they include the region outside the body of the patient and cavities filled with air). Among those regions, the area outside the body of the patient is obtained by keeping the largest connected component. Then, we use its dilated version to remove the skin object present in B_1 (see Fig. 5).

3. **Largest connected component:** The largest connected component that exists over all the columns of B_2 is selected. If there is none, we iteratively decrease the Otsu's threshold until such requirement is satisfied. The top row of Fig. 6 presents segmentations after this step (B_3). Notice how unwanted results occur when there are bright and large connected regions below the muscle (see image (d) of Fig. 6). This is uncommon and leads to misdetections that are corrected using the method described in Subsect. 2.2.

4. **Filling operation:** Regions lying below the biggest connected component are filled, producing B_4 (see bottom row of Fig. 6).

5. **Umbilical tissue removal:** Some images have umbilical tissue connecting the skin and muscle regions. When that occurs, it is common that B_4 includes an unwanted detection of part of the umbilical tissue (see image (g) of Fig. 6). To detect slices where this happens, we analyze whether the skin object removed in step 2 is adjacent to B_4. This is true if the OR operation between them creates a single object (see bottom row of Fig. 7). If this is the case, the horizontal derivatives of the OR image are obtained through the Sobel operator, which produces high responses at the isthmus that links the skin and B_4. From those detections, a rectangular mask is created and used to remove the connection (see Fig. 8), producing B_5. If not, B_5 is equal to B_4.

6. **Preliminary fascia detection:** Vertical transitions are obtained for each column of B_5. Connected contours, considering 8-neighborhood, smaller than n pixels, where n was empirically set to 11, are discarded. We lose the influence of vertical oriented structures which might be still connected to the segmentations, such as vessels. Figure 9 shows examples of preliminary fascia segmentation results. Notice that the employed processing did not solve yet the misdetections that occasionally occur at step 3 (see image (d) of Fig. 9).

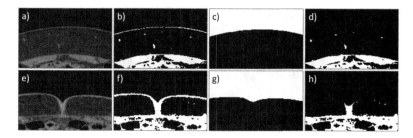

Fig. 5. B_2 segmentations of slices (a), (c) of Fig. 2, obtained after removing the skin object from B_1. (a), (e) original images; (b), (f) B_1 segmentations; (c), (g) dilated masks of the region outside the patient body; (d), (h) segmentations after removing the skin object (B_2).

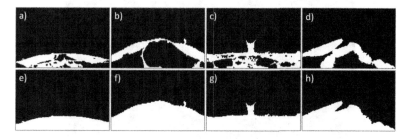

Fig. 6. B_3 (top row) and B_4 (bottom row) segmentations of the slices of Fig. 2, obtained by the procedure described in steps 3 and 4, respectively.

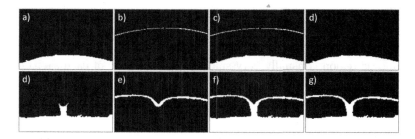

Fig. 7. Illustration of the test performed to check if the skin and B_4 were initially connected, for the images (a), (c) of Fig. 2. (a), (d) B_4 segmentations; (b), (e) skin objects removed in step 2; (c), (f) OR between both objects; (d), (g) largest connected component after the OR operation. The bottom case is eligible for umbilical tissue removal.

2.2   Final Fascia Segmentation

To obtain a complete and smooth final segmentation, fascia estimations are set as the output of local regressions using the preliminary fascia detections on the sagittal plane. In sagittal slices, the boundary between the muscle and the

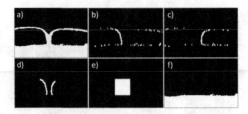

Fig. 8. B_5 segmentation, obtained by removing the isthmus. (a) OR between B_4 and the skin object; (b), (c) Sobel derivative responses; (d) OR between largest connected components of (b) and (c); (e) rectangular mask containing the objects in (d); (f) B_5 segmentation, after removing object (e) and the skin object.

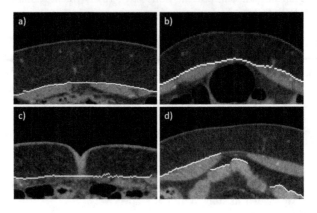

Fig. 9. Preliminary fascia segmentation (white) for the example slices shown in Fig. 2.

subcutaneous region is usually very smooth. For each row of each sagittal slice of our volume of interest, a new fascia point (p_{row}, p_{col}) is given by the equation:

$$p_{col} = P(p_{row}) \tag{1}$$

where P is a local regression model based on Tukey's bisquare objective function taking into account the sagittal neighbors contained in the range $[p_{row} - n, p_{row} + n]$, being n expressed by:

$$n = k \cdot \frac{m}{s} \tag{2}$$

where s is the distance in mm between consecutive pixels, characteristic of the volume (same in every direction of the volume after interpolation of data), m is the size of the biggest structures to be neglected, also in mm (vessel with largest caliber in the dataset), and k is a constant. This last parameter can be seen as the amount of data which has to be considered to remove the influence of a certain structure. In this work, $m = 5$ was considered, and $k = 5$ was empirically obtained. We propose this interpolation method since it is less influenced by outliers, in our case occasional misdetections, such as the one represented in

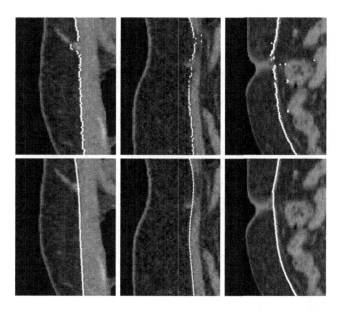

Fig. 10. Example sagittal slices of the volume of interest. Comparison between preliminary (top row) and final fascia segmentations (bottom row).

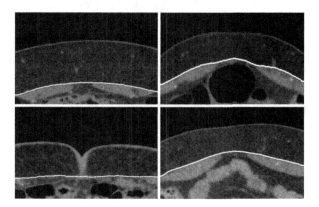

Fig. 11. Final fascia segmentation (white) for the example slices shown in Fig. 2.

image (d) of Fig. 9. A comparison between the preliminary and final fascia, in sagittal view, can be seen in Fig. 10. The results for the axial slices that have been used as example are present in Fig. 11. These figures show that this interpolation framework is able to model the smooth anterior fascia boundary, while neglecting neighbor structures and misdetections coming from step 3.

3   Results

The Breast Unit of Fundação Champalimaud provided CTA volumes from 20 different patients. The number of slices and the resolution along the long axis of the body varies across the volumes. For each volume of the database, the end of each perforator and the locations where the DIEAs perforate the posterior lamella of the rectus muscle were provided, such that we could define the volumes of interest. For each axial slice of each volume of interest, a manual annotation of the anterior fascia was performed by an expert (radiologist), in order to posteriorly evaluate the performance of the developed algorithm. Following the proposed methodology, we obtained 20 fascia segmentations and measured the Euclidean and Hausdorff distances to the corresponding manual annotations. Table 1 shows the mean, best and worst performances achieved.

Table 1. Evaluation of the proposed methodology. The Euclidean (E) and Hausdorff (H) distances were calculated between each volume final fascia segmentation and the corresponding manual annotation. Mean, best and worst performances are shown.

Case	E distance (mm)		H distance (mm)	
	GT → seg	seg → GT	GT → seg	seg → GT
Mean	0.49 ± 0.33	0.51 ± 0.40	1.52 ± 0.76	1.63 ± 1.15
Best	0.28	0.28	0.79	0.79
Worst	1.78	2.15	4.25	6.13

The voxel spacing differs from volume to volume, varying between 0.7 and 0.9 mm. This shows that the proposed method was able to provide segmentations whose mean Euclidean distance to the manual annotations was lower than the spacing between consecutive voxels. The relatively low mean Hausdorff distance shows that the detections were commonly very stable. There was a single case (worst in Table 1) where the resulting segmentation in a particular region of the volume was erroneous. This occurred because in that region, the preliminary fascia segmentation contained a high number of consecutive misdetections, and the robust regression was not able to provide an accurate result. As already mentioned, these misdetections occured due to the occasional malfunction of step 3 of the proposed pipeline, where we consider the muscle object the biggest connected component that exists over all the columns of B_2. By analyzing image (d) of Fig. 9, we can conclude that the existence of high intensity regions below the muscle might put at risk such assumption. The experiments were run in an Intel Core i7-4500U CPU 1.80@2.40 GHz using MATLAB R2014a, and took, in average, 636 s for each volume.

4   Conclusion

In this paper, we propose a method to segment the anterior fascia of the rectus abdominis muscle, which is relevant for the analysis of DIEP. Intensity thresholding and post-processing are used to obtain a preliminary fascia segmentation. Then, a robust interpolation framework is proposed to produce a smooth detection of the fascia, without interferences from neighbor structures. Our method achieved promising results since it produced segmentations whose mean Euclidean distance to the manual annotations was lower than the distance between consecutive voxels. Regarding future work, we should consider more robust methods for step 3 of the pipeline, as it was responsible for the misdetections we had.

Acknowledgments. This work was funded by the Project "NanoSTIMA: Macro–to–Nano Human Sensing: Towards Integrated Multimodal Health Monitoring and Analytics/NORTE–01–0145–FEDER–000016" financed by the North Portugal Regional Operational Programme (NORTE 2020), under the PORTUGAL 2020 Partnership Agreement, and through the European Regional Development Fund (ERDF), and also by Fundação para a Ciência e a Tecnologia (FCT) within Ph.D grant number SFRH/BD/126224/2016.

References

1. Siegel, R., Miller, K., Jemal, A.: Global cancer statistics. Cancer J. Clin. **65**, 5–29 (2015)
2. Dragun, A.E., Huang, B., Tucker, T.C., Spanos, W.J.: Increasing mastectomy rates among all age groups for early stage breast cancer: a 10-year study of surgical choice. Breast J. **18**, 318–325 (2012)
3. Mahmood, U., Hanlon, A.L., Koshy, M., Buras, R., Chumsri, S., Tkaczuk, K.H., Cheston, S.B., Regine, W.F., Feigenberg, S.J.: Increasing national mastectomy rates for the treatment of early stage breast cancer. Ann. Surg. Oncol. **20**, 1436–1443 (2013)
4. Cina, A., Salgarello, M., Barone-Adesi, L., Rinaldi, P., Bonomo, L.: Planning breast reconstruction with deep inferior epigastric artery perforating vessels: multidetector CT angiography versus Color Doppler US. Radiology **255**, 979–987 (2010)
5. Phillips, T.J., Stella, D.L., Rozen, W.M., Ashton, M., Taylor, G.I.: Abdominal wall CT angiography: a detailed account of a newly established preoperative imaging technique. Radiology **249**, 32–44 (2008)
6. Tong, T., Wolz, R., Wang, Z., Gao, Q., Misawa, K., Fujiwara, M., Mori, K., Hajnal, J.V., Rueckert, D.: Discriminative dictionary learning for abdominal multi-organ segmentation. Med. Image Anal. **23**, 92–104 (2015)
7. Wolz, R., Chu, C., Misawa, K., Fujiwara, M., Mori, K., Rueckert, D.: Automated abdominal multi-organ segmentation with subject-specific atlas generation. IEEE Trans. Med. Imaging **32**, 1723–1730 (2013)
8. Otsu, N.: A threshold selection method from gray-level histograms. IEEE Trans. Syst. Man Cybern. **9**, 62–66 (1979)

Author Index